T0215736

Lecture Notes in Computer Science   12206

Panayiotis Zaphiris · Andri Ioannou (Eds.)

Learning and Collaboration Technologies

Human and Technology Ecosystems

7th International Conference, LCT 2020
Held as Part of the 22nd HCI International Conference, HCII 2020
Copenhagen, Denmark, July 19–24, 2020
Proceedings, Part II

 Springer

Editors
Panayiotis Zaphiris
Cyprus University of Technology
Limassol, Cyprus

Andri Ioannou (iD)
Cyprus University of Technology
Limassol, Cyprus

Research Center on Interactive Media,
Smart Systems and Emerging
Technologies (RISE)
Limassol, Cyprus

ISSN 0302-9743   ISSN 1611-3349 (electronic)
Lecture Notes in Computer Science
ISBN 978-3-030-50505-9   ISBN 978-3-030-50506-6 (eBook)
https://doi.org/10.1007/978-3-030-50506-6

LNCS Sublibrary: SL3 – Information Systems and Applications, incl. Internet/Web, and HCI

This Springer imprint is published by the registered company Springer Nature Switzerland AG
The registered company address is: Gewerbestrasse 11, 6330 Cham, Switzerland

Foreword

The 22nd International Conference on Human-Computer Interaction, HCI International 2020 (HCII 2020), was planned to be held at the AC Bella Sky Hotel and Bella Center, Copenhagen, Denmark, during July 19–24, 2020. Due to the COVID-19 coronavirus pandemic and the resolution of the Danish government not to allow events larger than 500 people to be hosted until September 1, 2020, HCII 2020 had to be held virtually. It incorporated the 21 thematic areas and affiliated conferences listed on the following page.

A total of 6,326 individuals from academia, research institutes, industry, and governmental agencies from 97 countries submitted contributions, and 1,439 papers and 238 posters were included in the conference proceedings. These contributions address the latest research and development efforts and highlight the human aspects of design and use of computing systems. The contributions thoroughly cover the entire field of human-computer interaction, addressing major advances in knowledge and effective use of computers in a variety of application areas. The volumes constituting the full set of the conference proceedings are listed in the following pages.

The HCI International (HCII) conference also offers the option of "late-breaking work" which applies both for papers and posters and the corresponding volume(s) of the proceedings will be published just after the conference. Full papers will be included in the "HCII 2020 - Late Breaking Papers" volume of the proceedings to be published in the Springer LNCS series, while poster extended abstracts will be included as short papers in the "HCII 2020 - Late Breaking Posters" volume to be published in the Springer CCIS series.

I would like to thank the program board chairs and the members of the program boards of all thematic areas and affiliated conferences for their contribution to the highest scientific quality and the overall success of the HCI International 2020 conference.

This conference would not have been possible without the continuous and unwavering support and advice of the founder, Conference General Chair Emeritus and Conference Scientific Advisor Prof. Gavriel Salvendy. For his outstanding efforts, I would like to express my appreciation to the communications chair and editor of HCI International News, Dr. Abbas Moallem.

July 2020   Constantine Stephanidis

HCI International 2020 Thematic Areas and Affiliated Conferences

Thematic areas:

- HCI 2020: Human-Computer Interaction
- HIMI 2020: Human Interface and the Management of Information

Affiliated conferences:

- EPCE: 17th International Conference on Engineering Psychology and Cognitive Ergonomics
- UAHCI: 14th International Conference on Universal Access in Human-Computer Interaction
- VAMR: 12th International Conference on Virtual, Augmented and Mixed Reality
- CCD: 12th International Conference on Cross-Cultural Design
- SCSM: 12th International Conference on Social Computing and Social Media
- AC: 14th International Conference on Augmented Cognition
- DHM: 11th International Conference on Digital Human Modeling and Applications in Health, Safety, Ergonomics and Risk Management
- DUXU: 9th International Conference on Design, User Experience and Usability
- DAPI: 8th International Conference on Distributed, Ambient and Pervasive Interactions
- HCIBGO: 7th International Conference on HCI in Business, Government and Organizations
- LCT: 7th International Conference on Learning and Collaboration Technologies
- ITAP: 6th International Conference on Human Aspects of IT for the Aged Population
- HCI-CPT: Second International Conference on HCI for Cybersecurity, Privacy and Trust
- HCI-Games: Second International Conference on HCI in Games
- MobiTAS: Second International Conference on HCI in Mobility, Transport and Automotive Systems
- AIS: Second International Conference on Adaptive Instructional Systems
- C&C: 8th International Conference on Culture and Computing
- MOBILE: First International Conference on Design, Operation and Evaluation of Mobile Communications
- AI-HCI: First International Conference on Artificial Intelligence in HCI

Conference Proceedings Volumes Full List

38. CCIS 1224, HCI International 2020 Posters - Part I, edited by Constantine Stephanidis and Margherita Antona
39. CCIS 1225, HCI International 2020 Posters - Part II, edited by Constantine Stephanidis and Margherita Antona
40. CCIS 1226, HCI International 2020 Posters - Part III, edited by Constantine Stephanidis and Margherita Antona

http://2020.hci.international/proceedings

7th International Conference on Learning and Collaboration Technologies (LCT 2020)

Program Board Chairs: **Panayiotis Zaphiris, Cyprus University of Technology, Cyprus, and Andri Ioannou, Cyprus University of Technology and RISE, Cyprus**

- Ruthi Aladjem, Israel
- Kaushal Kumar Bhagat, India
- Fisnik Dalipi, Sweden
- Camille Dickson-Deane, Australia
- Daphne Economou, UK
- Maka Eradze, Italy
- David Fonseca, Spain
- Yiannis Georgiou, Cyprus
- Preben Hansen, Sweden
- Tomaž Klobučar, Slovenia
- Birgy Lorenz, Estonia
- Ana Loureiro, Portugal
- Alejandra Martínez-Monés, Spain
- Markos Mentzelopoulos, UK
- Antigoni Parmaxi, Cyprus
- Marcos Román González, Spain

The full list with the Program Board Chairs and the members of the Program Boards of all thematic areas and affiliated conferences is available online at:

http://www.hci.international/board-members-2020.php

HCI International 2021

The 23rd International Conference on Human-Computer Interaction, HCI International 2021 (HCII 2021), will be held jointly with the affiliated conferences in Washington DC, USA, at the Washington Hilton Hotel, July 24–29, 2021. It will cover a broad spectrum of themes related to Human-Computer Interaction (HCI), including theoretical issues, methods, tools, processes, and case studies in HCI design, as well as novel interaction techniques, interfaces, and applications. The proceedings will be published by Springer. More information will be available on the conference website: http://2021.hci.international/.

General Chair
Prof. Constantine Stephanidis
University of Crete and ICS-FORTH
Heraklion, Crete, Greece
Email: general_chair@hcii2021.org

http://2021.hci.international/

Contents – Part II

Communication and Conversation in Learning

Cognition, Emotions and Learning

Games and Gamification in Learning

VR, Robot and IoT in Learning

Collaboration Technology and Collaborative Learning

Contents – Part I

Learning Analytics, Dashboards and Learners Models

Language Learning and Teaching

Technology in Education: Policies and Practice

Communication and Conversation in Learning

Sign Language Interactive Learning - Measuring the User Engagement

Pietro Battistoni, Marianna Di Gregorio, Marco Romano[✉],
Monica Sebillo, Giuliana Vitiello, and Giandomenico Solimando

HCI-UsE Lab, Department of Computer Science, University of Salerno,
Fisciano, Italy
{pbattistoni,madigregorio,marromano,msebillo,
gvitiello}@unisa.it, g.solimando@studenti.unisa.it

Abstract. The knowledge of sign language by hearing people is not wide-spread and this may pose unpleasant barriers with the deaf. One of the biggest challenges is to raise the awareness about the importance of sign language while providing support for learning it. Our research aims at providing sign language learners with an advantageous interactive experience. In the paper we analyze the engagement of users learning through our intelligent interactive system and show that higher motivation is achieved.

Keywords: Sign language · User engagement · Learning experience

1 Introduction

The knowledge of sign language by hearing people is very rare and this does not allow deaf people to be adequately understood affecting also the sense of inclusiveness of the community [1, 15]. Indeed, the United Nations Convention on the Rights of Persons with Disabilities recommends States Parties to facilitate and promote the learning of sign language, stating that sign languages have the same status as spoken languages [3]. One of the biggest challenges is to raise on the one hand the awareness about the importance of learning sign language and, on the other, to provide stimulating support for learning it [16]. The accessibility to information systems by impaired users is a very timely topic. In the past, considering the community of visually impaired people, we experienced the value of on multimodal interfaces, that allow users to interact using specific gestures [19], or a combination of vibrations and sounds [20], or virtual reality [18].

Aiming at providing sign language learners with an advantageous interactive experience, we have designed a gesture recognition system that uses Convolutional Neural Networks. These are machine learning algorithms that have been incredibly successful in managing a variety of activities related to video and image processing. Our network, after being trained on a set of images, allows the recognition of gestures made by the Sign language learner. Although many works in the literature feature a sign language recognition system [5, 8, 9], none of them was designed to be used as a learning system.

© Springer Nature Switzerland AG 2020
P. Zaphiris and A. Ioannou (Eds.): HCII 2020, LNCS 12206, pp. 3–12, 2020.
https://doi.org/10.1007/978-3-030-50506-6_1

In this paper, we present a study conducted to evaluate the system potentials in engaging people and motivating them to learn the sign language.

As a result of the study, we can point out that the learning perception and the intention of use are significantly relevant and there is no noteworthy difference between people with high interest in the topic and those who do not have any special interest in learning the sign language. Therefore, we may conclude that the proposed solution can foster the learning commitment of people even without an initial interest in sign language.

The paper is structured as follows. Some related work is presented in Sect. 2. Section 3 presents the system prototype we realized to recognize the American Sign Language (ASL) alphabet. Section 4 describes the evaluation study and, Sect. 5 summarizes the results formalized in four *lessons learnt*.

2 Related Work

The ASL recognition task is formulated as two subtasks: feature extraction and subsequent classification. Researchers have been using different methods to extract discriminative features and create powerful classifiers.

In [21], Pugeault and Bowden apply Gabor filters to extract features from both color and depth images at 4 different scales to recognize the 24 static ASL alphabet signs. Half of the signs could not be recognized, showing that Gabor filters cannot capture enough discriminative information for differentiating different signs. Also, Wang et al. used color and depth images for recognition [22]. They proposed a Superpixel Earth Mover's Distance (SP- EMD) metric. In [23] Maqueda et al. used a Support Vector Machine (SVM) classifier. In [24] features were extracted from only depth images on randomly positioned line segments and a random forest was used for classification.

Some studies attempted to exploit the 3D information embedded in the depth images (3D approach) [25–29]. Such 3D approaches are promising to achieve better performance than image representations due to the extra dimension. However, the 3D point cloud obtained from the depth image is sparse at the regions with large gradients and absent at the occluded areas, which affects the overall performance.

Due to the articulated structure of hands, some studies implemented a hand part segmentation step before the gesture recognition (bottom-up approach). In [30], Keskin et al. extracted depth comparison features from depth images following the method proposed in [31] and fed them into a per-pixel random forest classifier. This classifier was trained using synthetic depth images that have the parts' ground truth of a hand.

One of the major drawbacks of those bottom-up approaches is that the sign recognition performance is highly dependent upon the result of the hand part segmentation, and it is hard to improve the performance of the hand part segmentation because of the high complexities and constant occlusions.

Recently, deep learning methods, such as Convolutional Neural Networks (CNNs), have demonstrated their extraordinary performance in various classification and recognition tasks.

For this reason, our work is based on an image recognition system that uses CNN to provide sign language learners with an advantageous interactive experience. The system was developed at the HCI-UsE laboratory of the University of Salerno and was presented for the first time in [17].

3   The System Prototype

The system prototype is designed to recognize the sign language gestures of the American alphabet performed by a user who is learning the sign language alphabet. The system is based on an application desktop able to capture photos of the gestures through a webcam. Once the gesture images are captured, they are sent to the CNN net one by one. Each time, the net classifies the image and gives feedback on the goodness of the pose.

The CNN network, after being trained, allows the recognition of gestures, through 24 static letters of the American sign language alphabet. The CNN network training was carried out on 58,944 images of various kinds. The images have been reduced in size to be consistent with the specifications of the network used. Each image was resized to 227×227 pixels.

In Fig. 1 we can see an image that represents the flow of the use of the system. The idea of our system is to offer to those who are inexperienced in this language a simple and interactive learning method based on the trial and error method.

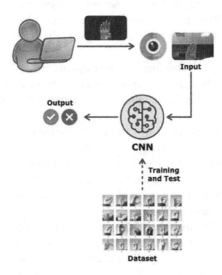

Fig. 1. The user input is a photo that is analyzed by the CNN using a preexisting dataset of signs graphic samples.

Figure 2 shows the system interface: it shows a short video of the gesture built in 3D that must be replicated by the user in front of the camera. The video of the correct gesture repeats until the user decides to be ready to check the gesture. The camera flow is reproduced on the screen to help the user to see the accuracy of the gesture. Figure 3 shows a user practicing with the software.

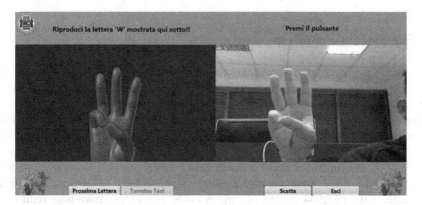

Fig. 2. This is the core page of system. In the screen a user gesturing a sign. This is the core page of system. In the screen a user gesturing a sign.

4   The Evaluation

To evaluate the effects of the system on user engagement and intention to use it, we tested the system with 30 users. Our participants were aged between 22 and 37 and we made sure that none of them had prior knowledge of sign language, in order to avoid biases.

In the ethnographic questionnaire, 15 participants defined themselves as highly interested in the topic while the remaining 15 participants declared not to have any special interest in learning the sign language. They represent the two user groups of the experiment.

After experimenting with the software, the participants were asked to fill out a questionnaire about their engagement and usefulness of the tool in learning the sign language. To calculate the level of engagement, we designed a questionnaire (based on an extended version of [7]. The original questionnaire is based on 12 items measuring the *focused attention* (FA), the *perceived usability* (PU), the *aesthetic and sensory appeal* (AE), and the *reward* (RW).

Moreover, with the objective to evaluate the perception of the learning progress and the users' intent to learn sign language through the system, we added three additional items about the *perceived learning* (PL) and two regarding the *intention of use* (IU) starting from the work of [2]. Table 1 reports the 15 items forming the questionnaire divided into the 6 scales just outlined.

Questions were answered using a 5-point Likert scale with 1 for strongly disagree, 5 for strongly agree and 3 for a neutral response. According to the literature, a 5-point Likert scale increases the response rate and quality and it also reduces respondents' "frustration level" [10, 11].

Fig. 3. A participant while experimenting the system.

Table 1. Engagement questionnaire in learning the sign language

Id	Item
FA.1	I lost myself in this learning experience
FA.2	The time I spent learning just slipped away
FA.3	I was absorbed in my learning task
PU.1	I felt frustrated while executing the gestures in front of the camera
PU.2	I found this system confusing to use
PU.3	Using this system was taxing
AE.1	The interface is attractive
AE.2	The interface was aesthetically appealing
AE.3	This interface appealed to my senses
RW.1	Learning using this system was worthwhile
RW.2	My learning experience was rewarding
RW.3	I felt interested in my learning task
PL.1	Using the system helps to understand the gestures quickly
PL.2	After using the system, I will be able to replicate the gestures again
PL.3	Overall, I find the system useful for learning
IU.1	I intend to use this system for learning the sign language
IU.2	I will recommend to others to use this system

The new questionnaire results passed a validation centered on a reliability analysis test based on the Cronbach's Alpha coefficient and were analyzed on the basis of their means and standard deviation. Moreover, we also conducted the non-parametric test of Mann–Whitney [6] to compare the two groups. The goal was to evaluate whether we could reject the null hypothesis that *there is no difference between the means of the two groups for the same item.* Such a test is appropriate when one needs to test differences between two conditions and different participants, and it is appropriate to compare Likert scale means [4].

4.1   Tasks Execution

The experiment started with an experimenter explaining the task and the system to the participants. First, participants were introduced to the purpose of the experiment that is to test and evaluate a new intelligent sign language learning system. We made sure they understood we were not evaluating their abilities. Then, they were asked to replicate the gesture reproduced by a 3D animation, trying to simulate it as precisely as possible.

The participants were positioned less than a meter from the computer on which the application was launched, comfortably seated in an armchair to create as much as possible a natural environment to be used. Figure 3 shows a user practicing with the system. After each try, they visualize the result of the execution.

After the experiment, participants were asked to complete the questionnaire explained in the previous section. The whole session lasted about 15 min.

4.2   Results

According to the questionnaire data, we can give some first considerations. As reported in Table 2, the standard deviation for each item is relatively low and in general, participants were satisfied with their experience.

Table 2. the table reports the mean and the standard deviation for each item of the questionnaire

Item	Mean	S.D.
FA1	3,9	1,2
FA2	4,4	0,9
FA3	4,2	0,8
PU1	4,1	1,3
PU2	**4,8**	1,0
PU3	**4,7**	0,6
AE1	4,2	1,0
AE2	4,1	0,9
AE3	4,3	0,9
RW1	4,4	1,0
RW2	4,5	0,8
RW3	4,2	1,1
PL1	**4,6**	0,6
PL2	4,4	0,9
PL3	4,5	0,9
IU1	4,2	1,1
IU2	**4,6**	1,0

The highest cases, with a mean larger than 4.5, are related to

1. the usability (PU2 and PU3), highlighting the simplicity of the system
2. the perception of learning progress (PL1)
3. the willingness to recommend the system to other fellows (IU2)

Participants also gave some interesting comments about the prototype. One said: *"I'd like to have richer feedback about the signs I perform. For example, the accuracy of the gesture or something like a mark, this would help me to be more motivated to improve my abilities"*. On the other hand, some of the participants felt frustrated when they did not understand negative feedback to the sign performed. Another user discussed about usability concerns: *"The interface is pretty easy, but it would be more intuitive if the system could give me information about the framing and focus, for example painting a frame indicating the right position of the user"*. Another suggested to add more importance to the meaning of the sign before showing it to raise users' awareness about the specific letter/word. Finally, many participants felt the experience as playful, one stated: *"Working with the system is funny and would be even more funny if I could compete with other users of the system"*. Indeed, researchers observed some participants after the experiment trying to communicate with each other using signs in a playful context.

In the ethnographic questionnaire 15 participants defined themselves as highly interested in the topic while the remaining 15 participants declared not to have any interest in learning the sign language. For such reason we also conducted the non-parametric test of Mann– Whitney [6] to compare the two groups. The goal was to evaluate whether we could reject the null hypothesis *there is no difference between the means of the two groups for the same item*. Such a test is appropriate when one needs to test differences between two conditions and different participants, and it is appropriate to compare Likert scale means [4]. In this test, if the Sig(2-tailed) p-value is less than .05 then the two groups are significantly different. Table 3 shows the p-value for each item and demonstrates that there is no difference between the answers of the two groups. This suggests that the user engagement and the intention of use are not affected by the initial interest in the topic of sign language.

Table 3. It shows the *p-value* for each item of the questionnaire

Item	p-value	Item	p-value
FA1	0,137	RW1	0,73
FA2	0,544	RW2	0,816
FA3	0,114	RW3	0,621
PU1	0,701	PL1	0,038
PU2	0,232	PL2	0,348
PU3	0,114	PL3	0,952
AE1	1	IU1	0,359
AE2	0,467	IU2	0,114
AE3	0,362		

Though the sample size of our pilot study is relatively small, we also ran a reliability analysis test based on the Cronbach's Alpha coefficient [12] using the IBM SPSS Statistics software. The most used rule of thumb in literature is that if such coefficient value is above 0.7 the scale reliability is acceptable [13], however, also 0.6 is often considered a valid result. Generally, the Cronbach's Alpha analysis is applied on sample bigger than 100, even though in [14] the author states that it is recommendable to run it to validate small studies with small size samples under 25, but in this case, the coefficient should be near to 0.8. In our case (Table 4), all the elements reached the threshold of 0.8 except for FA (measuring the perceived Focused Attention), which got 0.7 that even if it is still a good result can be defined as questionable. However, eliminating FA2 the coefficient reaches 0.8. Actually, during the experiment some participants felt confused and asked for clarification about FA2 statement. This means that the latter item should be properly revised and if necessary eliminated.

Table 4. The table shows the Cronbach's Alpha coefficient for each scale of the questionnaire

FA	0,7
PU	0,8
AE	0,8
RW	0,9
PL	0,8
IU	0,8

5 Lessons Learnt and Conclusions

After the experiment, we formalized 4 lessons learnt in a way that other researchers or developers can reuse them in their projects.

Lesson.1 – Using an interactive system to learn sign language is perceived by users as a valid learning tool. They consider the system as a way to learn gestures quickly and are confident to be able to replicate the signs in the future.

Lesson.2 – Interactive systems can even foster learning commitment of people without an initial interest in the topic.

Lesson.3 – Users may perceive the usage of an interactive learning system as a funny and playful activity able to enhance their motivation to learn. This suggests designing similar systems taking into account the introduction of gaming mechanisms even including a students' ranking.

Lesson.4 – For this kind of system, a timely and appropriate feedback is paramount to help the user progress. A constructive feedback may motivate users, while a poor and bad feedback may even frustrate them. More meaningful feedback can be used to explain mistakes, correct them and to evaluate the accuracy.

In this work, we learned that artificial intelligence combined with interactive interfaces have a crucial role in motivating people during sign language learning. In the future, we plan to continue this research so as to explore new forms of communication between deaf people and the rest of the world, and pursue the goal of a more inclusive community.

Acknowledgements. Funding: This research was partially funded by MIUR, PRIN 2017 grant number 2017JMHK4F_004.

References

1. Antia, S.D., Stinson, M.S., Gaustad, M.G.: Developing membership in the education (2002)
2. Balog, A., Pribeanu, C.: The role of perceived enjoyment in the students' acceptance of an augmented reality teaching platform: a structural equation modelling approach. Stud. Inf. Control **19**(3), 319–330 (2010)
3. Convention on the Rights of Persons with Disabilities (CRPD). https://www.un.org/development/desa/disabilities/convention-on-the-rights-of-persons-with-disabilities.html. Accessed Aug 2019
4. Field, A.: Discovering Statistics Using SPSS. Sage Publications, Thousand Oaks (2009)
5. Rao, G.A., Syamala, K., Kishore, P.V.V., Sastry, A.S.C.S.: Deep convolutional neural networks for sign language recognition. In: 2018 Conference on Signal Processing And Communication Engineering Systems (SPACES), Vijayawada, pp. 194–197 (2018).https://doi.org/10.1109/spaces.2018.8316344
6. Mann, H.B., Whitney, D.R.: On a test of whether one of two random variables is stochastically larger than the other. Ann. Math. Stat. **18**(1), 50–60 (1947)
7. O'brien, H.L., Cairns, P., Hall, M.: A practical approach to measuring user engagement with the refined user engagement scale (UES) and new UES short form. Int. J. Hum.–Comput. Stud. **112**, 28–39 (2018)
8. Pigou, L., Dieleman, S., Kindermans, P.-J., Schrauwen, B.: Sign language recognition using convolutional neural networks. In: Agapito, L., Bronstein, Michael, M., Rother, C. (eds.) ECCV 2014. LNCS, vol. 8925, pp. 572–578. Springer, Cham (2015). https://doi.org/10.1007/978-3-319-16178-5_40
9. Suresh, S., Mithun, H.T.P., Supriya, M.H.: 2019 5th International Conference on Sign Language Recognition System Advanced Computing & Communication Systems (ICACCS), pp. 614–618 (2019)
10. Babakus, E., Mangold, W.G.: Adapting the SERVQUAL scale to hospital services: an empirical investigation. Health Serv. Res. **26**(6), 767 (1992)
11. Buttle, F. (ed.): Relationship Marketing: Theory and Practice. Sage, Thousand Oaks (1996)
12. Cronbach, L.J.: Coefficient alpha and the internal structure of tests. Psychometrika **16**(3), 297–334 (1951)
13. Kline, P.: A Handbook of Psychological Testing, 2nd edn. Routledge, London (1999)
14. Hertzog, M.A.: Considerations in determining sample size for pilot studies. Res. Nurs. Health **31**(2), 180–191 (2008)
15. Battistoni, P., Sebillo, M., Di Gregorio, M., Vitiello, G., Romano, M.: ProSign+ a cloud-based platform supporting inclusiveness in public communication. In: 2020 IEEE 17th Annual Consumer Communications & Networking Conference (CCNC), pp. 1–5. IEEE, January 2020

16. Di Gregorio, M., Sebillo, M., Vitiello, G., Pizza, A., Vitale, F.: ProSign everywhere-addressing communication empowerment goals for deaf people. In: Proceedings of the 5th EAI International Conference on Smart Objects and Technologies for Social Good, pp. 207–212 (2019)

17. Battistoni, P., Di Gregorio, M., Sebillo, M., Vitiello, G.: AI at the edge for sign language learning support. In: 2019 IEEE International Conference on Humanized Computing and Communication (HCC), pp. 16–23. IEEE (2019)

18. Vitiello, G., et al.: Do you like my outfit? Cromnia, a mobile assistant for blind users. In: Proceedings of the 4th EAI International Conference on Smart Objects and Technologies for Social Good, pp. 249–254. ACM (2018)

19. Romano, M., Bellucci, A., Aedo, I.: Understanding touch and motion gestures for blind people on mobile devices. In: Abascal, J., Barbosa, S., Fetter, M., Gross, T., Palanque, P., Winckler, M. (eds.) INTERACT 2015. LNCS, vol. 9296, pp. 38–46. Springer, Cham (2015). https://doi.org/10.1007/978-3-319-22701-6_3

20. Di Chiara, G., et al.: The framy user interface for visually-impaired users. In: 2011 Sixth International Conference on Digital Information Management, pp. 36–41. IEEE (2011)

21. Pugeault, N., Bowden, R.R.: Spelling it out: real-time ASL fingerspelling recognition. In: IEEE International Conference on Computer Vision Workshops (ICCV Workshops), pp. 1114–1119 (2011)

22. Wang, C., Liu, Z., Chan, S.-C.: Superpixel-based hand gesture recognition with kinect depth camera. IEEE Trans. Multimed. **17**(1), 29–39 (2015)

23. Maqueda, A.I., del Blanco, C.R., Jaureguizar, F., García, N.: Human– computer interaction based on visual hand-gesture recognition using volumetric spatiograms of local binary patterns. Comput. Vis. Image Underst. **141**, 126–137 (2015)

24. Nai, W., Liu, Y., Rempel, D., Wang, Y.: Fast hand posture classification using depth features extracted from random line segments. Pattern Recognit. **65**, 1–10 (2017). https://doi.org/10.1016/j.patcog.2016.11.022. ISSN 0031-3203

25. Kuznetsova, A., Leal-Taixé, L., Rosenhahn, B.: Real-time sign language recognition using a consumer depth camera. In: IEEE International Conference on Computer Vision Workshops, pp. 83–90 (2013)

26. Wohlkinger, W., Vincze, M.: Ensemble of shape functions for 3D object classification. In: IEEE International Conference on Robotics and Biomimetics, pp. 2987–2992 (2011)

27. Zhang, C., Tian, Y.: Histogram of 3D facets: a depth descriptor for human action and hand gesture recognition. Comput. Vis. Image Underst. **139**, 29–39 (2015). https://doi.org/10.1016/j.cviu.2015.05.010. ISSN 1077-3142

28. Zhang, C., Yang, X., Tian, Y.: Histogram of 3D facets: a characteristic descriptor for hand gesture recognition. In: 10th IEEE International Conference and Workshops on Automatic Face and Gesture Recognition (FG), pp. 1–8 (2013). https://doi.org/10.1109/fg.2013.6553754

29. Rioux-Maldague, L., Giguere, P.L.: Sign language fingerspelling classification from depth and color images using a deep belief network. In: Canadian Conference on Computer and Robot Vision, Montreal, QC, pp. 92–97 (2014). https://doi.org/10.1109/crv.2014.20

30. Keskin, C., Kıraç, F., Kara, Y.E., Akarun, L.: Hand pose estimation and hand shape classification using multi-layered randomized decision forests. In: Fitzgibbon, A., Lazebnik, S., Perona, P., Sato, Y., Schmid, C. (eds.) ECCV 2012. LNCS, vol. 7577, pp. 852–863. Springer, Heidelberg (2012). https://doi.org/10.1007/978-3-642-33783-3_61

31. Shotton, J., et al.: Real-time human pose recognition in parts from single depth images. In: Proceedings of CVPR 2011, Colorado Springs, CO, USA, pp. 1297–1304 (2013). https://doi.org/10.1109/cvpr.2011.5995316

Co-design for a Competency Self-assessment Chatbot and Survey in Science Education

Eva Durall[1]([✉]) and Evangelos Kapros[2,3]

[1] Aalto University, Espoo, Finland
eva.durall@aalto.fi
[2] Science Gallery, Trinity College Dublin, Dublin, Ireland
ekapros@tcd.ie
[3] Endurae OÜ, World Trade Center Tallinn, Tallinn, Estonia
info@endurae.com

Abstract. This paper describes a co-design process for a formative assessment tool in the area of core competencies such as creativity, communication, collaboration, and critical thinking. This process has been carried out in the context of non-formal science education institutions in 19 countries in Europe and the Middle East. The results of the co-design have been influential in the design of a formative assessment chatbot and survey that supports learner competency and self-regulation. We also discuss some preliminary results from the use of the tool and introduce additional considerations with regard to inclusion, technical aspects, and ethics, towards a set of best practices in this area.

Keywords: Co-design · Chatbots · Competencies

1 Chatbots for Learning and Assessment

While chatbots are increasingly adopted in diverse fields, in education their implementation has been limited [23]. To date, main uses of chatbots have focused on supporting student well-being (see for instance services like Differ[1] or the Ash chatbot[2] at Monash University), engaging students and reducing costs (see tools like Snatchbot[3]), supporting teaching (see, e.g., Botsify[4]), and assisting students (see for instance Deakin Genie[5] at Deakin University).

Contemporary design and implementation of chatbots in educational contexts show that this technology can support different *pedagogical approaches*,

---

[1] https://www.differ.chat/.
[2] http://newmediaresearch.educ.monash.edu.au/lnm/meet-ash-the-monash-chatbot-a-youth-wellbeing-companion/.
[3] https://snatchbot.me/education.
[4] https://botsify.com/education-chatbot.
[5] https://www.deakin.edu.au/life-at-deakin/why-study-at-deakin/deakin-genie.

© Springer Nature Switzerland AG 2020
P. Zaphiris and A. Ioannou (Eds.): HCII 2020, LNCS 12206, pp. 13–24, 2020.
https://doi.org/10.1007/978-3-030-50506-6_2

whose emphasis ranges from stimulus-response and reinforcement (see, i.e., SuperMemo[6], Duolingo[7]), to students being encouraged to build a chatbot knowledgebase as a strategy to support learning (the case of Anne G. Neering [5]).

Chatbots can also work as safe environments, where students can be in control without the pressure of being judged [24]. Furthermore, from an inclusion perspective, chatbots have been considered as potentially inclusive environments accessible for people with special needs [1,16].

Chatbots in teaching and learning have not been explored to their full potential yet; a recent report [8] has identified no examples of chatbots around 'reflection and metacognitive strategies'. We believe a great opportunity exists in this area: while educational technology can be seen as unequally facilitating learners [22], iterative self-assessment of skills/competencies can level the playing field as each learner only needs to improve in comparison to their previous condition [9]. This seems to be more so with soft skills, i.e. core competencies such as creativity, collaboration, communication, or critical thinking. Considering that self-assessment skills play an important role in the self-regulation of learning [14], chatbots can be a promising tool for supporting self-regulated learning. Moreover, the lack of objectively right answers akin to hard-skill summative assessments due to the subjectivity involved in soft skills lends itself to formative assessment.

Chatbots seem to be a suitable medium for formative assessment. Our experience with teenagers tells us that filling in a formal questionnaire during or after a learning experience can be intimidating for many, and is seen mostly as non-engaging. We propose that a chatbot experience can remove this barrier, thus being more engaging, and also lower the cognitive workload for learners as they only have to answer one item at a time. In doing so, and by accommodating learners of all levels of performance, chatbots have the capacity to be an inclusive "tide that raises all boats", if designed and implemented correctly.

Challenges regarding the use of chatbots in education are diverse. From a learning perspective, they might generate learners' dependency and narrow the scope of what is valuable in learning. From a technical perspective, chatbots might neglect protecting the learners' data, prioritise algorithms that are easier to implement as opposed beneficial for the users, or leave a universe of discourse so open that a bot would fail to fulfil any concrete purpose [6,12].

2   Designing a Chatbot for Self-assessment

Cooperative Design Approaches in Technology-Enhanced Learning. The mutual influence between technology and social relations has been a central concern of Information and Communication Technology (ICT) scholars [3]. For researchers involved in ICT design, acknowledging this bidirectional relation has strong implications in the methodological approaches for designing ICT systems,

---

[6] https://www.supermemo.com/en.
[7] https://www.duolingo.com/.

as well as in the role of designers throughout the design process. For instance, the recognition that technological systems play a key role in the "cultural production of new forms of practice" [21] has been a central claim of design approaches like cooperative design.

Considering the impact that a technology design may have in people's practices, cooperative design approaches such as Participatory Design (PD) and co-design advocate for the need to involve the people who will be affected by the design in the design process. By supporting the design beneficiaries' active participation, it is expected that the design solution becomes a meaningful contribution that answers the needs and wishes of the people who will ultimately receive the design [17].

While we acknowledge the diversity of approaches to co-design, in this study we draw from the definition provided by [15]: "We define co-design as a highly facilitated, team-based process in which teachers, researchers, and developers work together in defined roles to design an educational innovation, realize the design in one or more prototypes, and evaluate each prototype's significance for addressing a concrete educational need." (p.53). As [18] suggest, co-design spaces tend to happen at early stages of the design process in order to engage designers and non-designers in creative work around complex challenges.

In technology-Enhanced Learning (TEL), scholars have advocated for the use of cooperative design approaches when designing tools for learning [2,11]. Recent initiatives in the design of tools and services for children also recognise the need to actively involve children and their communities in the design process (see the Design for Children's Rights Association recommended methods and practices[8]). In this regard, the adoption of a co-design approach has been considered as a valuable strategy to balance power relations, and create ownership of the solutions generated.

2.1 Our Design Context and Stakeholders

Co-design has been considered a useful approach to the design of learning tools due to its alignment to learner-centred design, as well as the opportunities it creates to actively involve teachers and draw from their expertise [15]. For instance, in science education co-design has been used for the design of assessment tools [15], mobile science collaboratories [20], as well as for supporting inquiry-based science learning with mobile devices [25]. Based on the positive experiences of previous studies using co-design to support innovation in technology-enhanced learning, this research followed a co-design approach to explore how to enhance assessment in non-formal science learning.

For the purpose of this study, we have taken into consideration the following science learning contexts in 19 countries from Europe and the Middle East: science and art museums and centres, makerspaces, fablabs and hacklabs, science galleries, public libraries, organisations offering after-school activities, festivals,

---

[8] https://childrensdesignguide.org/.

summer camps, science competitions and hackathons, and civil organisations involved in activism and promotion of science learning.

Defining who are the beneficiaries is a central issue in design. In co-design and in learner-centred design, practitioners have claimed for the need to define the beneficiaries in a broad sense [10]. The beneficiaries, also known as stakeholders, are the people, groups and individuals, who may be affected by the outcome of a project. Thus, in this research the stakeholders include the learners, but also non-formal science educators and facilitators, as well as other members of the educational community.

2.2   The Co-design Process

Co-design processes start with an inquiry on the context of use [15]. During this contextual inquiry we collected information about hundreds of stakeholders, ranging from learners, parents/guardians, science educators and facilitators, pedagogical coordinators, to activists and makers, people working in non-governmental organisations focused on groups at risk of social exclusion, and working in local and professional organisations focused on promoting science learning. The methods used for collecting data consisted in informal and semi-structured interviews, questionnaires, focus groups and field observations.

The data collected during the contextual inquiry helped us gain understanding on challenges in non-formal science learning related to barriers to access scientific culture, learners' self-concepts and sustaining interest in science learning. These challenges were used to inform the elaboration of design materials used in an international co-design workshop.

The co-design workshop took place at Aalto University in Espoo, Finland during two days and gathered 55 stakeholders (learners, educators and people involved in different type of organisations focused on science learning) (see Fig. 1). The goal of this meeting was to build shared understanding on the challenges and opportunities in non-formal and informal science learning, as well as to generate design concepts. The co-design workshop participants were distributed in three working groups, each of them focused on a particular issue: inclusion, engagement, assessment and recognition of learning. During the workshop sessions, participants engaged in diverse tasks that helped them develop a shared understanding and gradually move the discussions from defining the challenges to propose opportunities for action. In order to ensure that everyone had the opportunity to participate, the groups were subdivided in smaller ones. Sharing of groups' works was encouraged by scheduling specific moments for that purpose throughout the co-design workshop sessions (see Fig. 1).

At the co-design workshop, participants explored the challenges and opportunities connected to the different issues and at the end of the second day the groups generated twelve design concepts around inclusion[9], engagement, and

---

[9] Working definition adopted from: https://idrc.ocadu.ca/resources/idrc-online/49-articles-and-papers/443-whatisinclusivedesign.

Fig. 1. Image of the co-design workshop held with non-formal science education stakeholders.

assessment and recognition of learning. Interestingly, the majority of the concepts heavily draw on the following aspects: active participation, self-assessment, self-improvement, creativity, and a fluid approach to evaluation that shifts the focus away from quantitative measuring and summative evaluations.

For the purpose of this paper, we have focused on analysing the co-design outputs connected to the assessment and recognition of learning. At the co-design workshop, 18 people chose to work on this topic and at the end of the second day four design concepts had been generated. Amongst the opportunities for supporting assessment and recognition of learning in non-formal science education, participants highlighted the need to expand definitions and the set of skills, support spontaneous observation, as well as face-to-face interaction and feedback, distinguish between groups and individuals, support trans-organisation and cross-border collaboration, development of new tools and solutions that are easy to adopt and not tied to a specific domain. Interestingly, all the proposed solutions heavily draw on the following aspects: self-assessment, self-improvement, creativity and a fluid approach to evaluation that shift the focus away from quantitative measuring and summative evaluations.

The analysis of the co-design workshop outputs brought us to the definition of the following requirements:

– Support self-assessment of transversal competencies throughout the learning process.

– Adoption of tools that can be accessible in different contexts and that can be used independently (without much guidance) by users of a wide age range and different skill levels.
– Adapt to learners' current familiar technological practices, which in the stakeholders' specific contexts can be characterised by being always-connected, and assuming fast and effortless interactions.

Based on these, a chatbot solution was selected to support flexible, formative self-assessment that helps learners activate a range of soft skills, at their own level. Thus, our concept prototype uses a chatbot solution to explore the opportunities and challenges that this technology poses for learning and education. We also devised a non-digital alternative, which is beyond the scope of this paper.

2.3 Prototype Chatbot Description

The prototype under development is a rule-based conversational web application for the self-assessment of core competencies. It can be accessed from any modern desktop or mobile web browser. Its input can be text, a button selection, or voice, and its output can be any medium accessible through an HTML <form> element. It supports data binding for a single session, while data are not stored nor coupled with fields for consecutive sessions. The user interface appears as a common messaging application. The application is built upon the open source Conversational Form library[10], which allows branching: namely, the conversation can follow a rule, or rules, which lays out the future direction of the output directed to the user depending on the user's previous input.

At the moment, our prototype does not use natural language processing (NLP). Rather, user input is validated against pre-programmed rules and button selections are enforced when a deadlock is detected. When a button-selection input is required, open text does not pass the validation rules, so as to avoid a usability issue where a user could respond via text to a button selection, thus driving the chatbot to a deadlock. This decision is related to the broad age-range of the subjects of the intended trial of the prototype (9 to 20 years old), and does not consist a strong suggestion for future development. Age notwithstanding, the amount of NLP to be used is a topic to be addressed with caution when the topic is so sensitive as self-evaluating core competencies.

The conversational approach is intended to offer a lightweight, accessible, and usable solution, integrated with technology commonly used by teenagers and young adults, thus providing horizontal mobility across formal subjects or informal activities (such as STEM centres), as opposed to previous approaches [9,13] that focused on formal education.

Before the prototype's development started, the 'principles of designing for children with children's rights and ethics'[11] were used as a checklist to ensure

---

[10] https://space10-community.github.io/conversational-form/docs/0.9.90/getting-started/.

[11] https://childrensdesignguide.org/principles/.

that the prototype would follow expert-led ethical standards and best practice. Data are being stored in the European Union, and each language[12] is being served through a separate link, so as to process data from different trial locations separately. Incidentally, the use of HTML elements minimises the work required for localisation, such as the text's direction etc.

The chatbot experience starts by a) onboarding the learner to self-assessment of core competencies (4Cs: creativity, collaboration, communication, critical thinking[13]), then b) proceeds with conversation intending to raise awareness and spark curiosity to learners concerning competencies, c) continues to build a better understanding of and personal relation with core competencies, d) asks from the learners to apply their understanding of 4Cs, and e) summarises the experience aiming to build confidence to the learners around their 4Cs (see Fig. 2). Learners are allowed to engage with only some competencies at each stage. The chatbot will be piloted in 8 science centres/museums across Europe and the Middle East.

3   Preliminary Results

Two preliminary activities took place at the Science Gallery Dublin from the summer to the autumn of 2019. One at a STEAM summer programme and one at a Léargas Erasmus+ activity.

The Léargas[14] participants of the self-evaluation tool enhanced their understanding and gained confidence with regard to core competencies (communication, collaboration, creativity, critical thinking). The tool consists of a set of questionnaires, one per day, with questions that progressively focus on specific activities, according to Bloom's taxonomy and Costa's "assessment spiral" [4, 9]. The participants showed significant awareness of the competencies throughout; however, their confidence in their self-evaluation rose during the activities and using the tool. They were 18–28 years old, with an average age of 22.5. They used the survey, as opposed to the chatbot, format.

Specifically, 7 participants replied to questions about communication, 4 about collaboration, 4 about creativity, and 2 about critical thinking. At the initial steps of the questionnaires, most participants (16 out of 17) correctly identified the definition of their preferred skill according to the World Economic Forum, which shows a high level of awareness. While participation dropped to 12 participants by day 5, they still identified the definitions correctly at the end of the questionnaires (all 12 participants).

The participants self-evaluated their use of the skills as follows. The option was available after providing a question concerning the context of use of the skill, and the evaluation scale was: "I still need help", "Improving, I still need reminders", "Good, I am doing well", and "Excellent, I can explain it to others",

---

[12] Planned languages to date are Arabic, Dutch, English, Farsi, French, German, Greek, Hebrew, Irish, Italian, Serbian, and Slovenian.

[13] https://widgets.weforum.org/nve-2015/chapter1.html.

[14] https://www.leargas.ie.

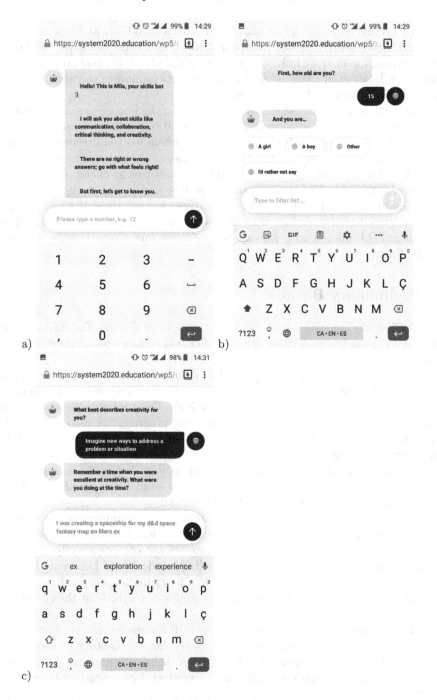

Fig. 2. Screengrabs of the chatbot prototype: a) the onboarding process, where the numerical input informs the keyboard content, b) button-like options to select the gender, and c) questions to enhance understanding. Voice input and automatic spelling correction is available where appropriate.

according to Marzano's self-assessment scale. In order to calculate the average rating, the above scale was operationalised as numbers from 1 to 4, but the numerical scale was not visible to the participants. In addition, the options were shuffled so as to avoid priming bias. Additionally, the participants were asked to provide a certainty of their response, at a scale from 1 to 3 (1 not sure, 3 very sure). Results from the initial and the last day of the self-evaluation can provide evidence for the effect of the activity in the understanding and certainty around the skills, as practised by the participants. Self-evaluation ratings for creativity rose from an average of 1.5 to 2.66, and the certainty of the evaluation from 1.75 to 2.66, for collaboration from 2.75 to 3, and from 2 to 3, for communication from 1.86 to 2.5, and from 2 to 2, and for critical thinking the average self-evaluation rating rose from 2 on the first day to 2.75 on the last day, with confidence rising from 2 to 2.5, respectively. The consistent increase in self-evaluation ratings and confidence strongly indicates that, notwithstanding the initial high awareness level around skills, participants benefited from the program activity with regard to putting their core competencies into practice.

Additionally, the participants had to qualify their responses via open-ended text questions. In various questions the participants associated empathy, challenging assumptions, thinking outside the box, and assessing arguments with the core competencies. They provided examples of how they used the above in specific activities, i.e. in creating personas or scenarios for a story or podcast. Finally, the participants mentioned the demanding workload of the program, and that despite that they enjoyed the group work and having to think about the competencies as they were progressing through the week. The usability of the tool was positive (approx. 5 out of 7 on a daily evaluation), therefore the form factor does not seem to have interfered with the content of the answers. The qualitative text answers seem to complement the quantitative analysis, in that the participants provide specific examples of putting their competencies to use, and reflect on this use by linking it to personality traits such as empathy or inquisitiveness.

Overall, the participants seem to have benefited quite consciously from the program activity with regard to putting their core competencies into practice. A quantitative and qualitative self-evaluation supports this, additionally to the demonstrated ability of the participants to reflect on this experience.

The ARTificial Intelligence Lab[15] is a summer programme for 15–18 year olds featuring art, design and robots. A collaboration between the Trinity College Dublin Robotics & Innovation Lab, and Science Gallery Dublin, this week-long summer programme is a chance to explore science, engineering, art and design and to work through the creative process of devising technology-based solutions to real-life problems. The ∼20 participants participated in an A/B test where the chatbot experience was ported to online forms, specifically on the Google Education platform[16]. Completion rate was 100% for both formats.

---

[15] https://dublin.sciencegallery.com/events/2019/09/artificialintelligencelabsummer school.

[16] https://edu.google.com/products/gsuite-for-education/.

Both the chatbot and the online form received positive feedback; however, 75% of the answers were more positive about the form than the chatbot. Several form participants appreciated being able to calculate the workload of each day, as they were able to scroll to the bottom of the form, while chatbot participants appreciated receiving one question at a time, as they claimed it helped them focus. As the prototype to date does not use NLP as stated above, some participants commented that the chatbot responded too quickly, which might convey the perception that the input of the learners does not matter, as the response does not depend on it. The use of delay in the response and the appearance of an ellipsis text [...] was recommended.

4   Discussion

This paper discussed the co-design and preliminary implementation of a rule-based dialogical tool for the self-evaluation of core competencies. While this initial implementation lacked features that would make it technically novel, it was considered positively in both a chatbot and a form appearance. The tool was not directly compared against traditional assessment questionnaires, but preliminary results suggest that the dialogical approach did actually surface evidence about the cultivation of competencies during STEM/STEAM activities. Therefore, at this stage only a claim for the validity of the dialogical approach can be made, but not a comparison with traditional methods.

From a pedagogical point of view, chatbots have the ability to trigger reflection by using questions [4]. Purposeful effort needs to go into the design of dialogues to achieve this effect. Firstly, including learners and stakeholders that understand learners and their needs in the design of the dialogue flow is of paramount importance. Secondly, NLP advances will not replace this human intervention in the near future: complete automation would leave an unsupervised universe of discourse open to misuse or abuse. Additional *ethical* considerations apply, such as who would own and initiate the use of a pedagogical chatbot, and who would own and how would they use the gathered data and metadata [6,12]. A facilitated, curated, or otherwise regulated NLP seems more suitable, and researchers and practitioners will need to find the equilibrium between enough automation to enhance the educators' and learners' experience, and a level of regulation that neither becomes a burden for the educators nor inhibits the learning experience.

Chatbot development can bring social benefits by supporting autonomy, competence, and social relatedness [7]. We consider that our chatbot design based on self-assessment may contribute to foster learners' ability to self-regulate and thus, their autonomy by helping them gain awareness and increase their competence level regarding creativity, collaboration, communication, and critical thinking. Further work requires testing and iterating the chatbot prototype based on learner and stakeholder feedback.

Acknowledgements. This research has received funding from the European Union's Horizon 2020 research and innovation programme under the Grant Agreement No. 788317.

The ARTificial Intelligence Lab programme is co-funded by the Creative Europe Programme for the European Union through the European ARTificial Intelligence Lab project.

Léargas are the National Agency for Erasmus+ in Adult Education, School Education, Vocational Education and Training, and Youth in Ireland.

References

1. Bigham, J.P., Aller, M.B., Brudvik, J.T., Leung, J.O., Yazzolino, L.A., Ladner, R.E.: Inspiring blind high school students to pursue computer science with instant messaging chatbots. In: ACM SIGCSE Bulletin, vol. 40, no. 1, pp. 449–453. ACM (2008)
2. Bonsignore, E., et al.: Embedding participatory design into designs for learning: an untapped interdisciplinary resource. In: Proceedings of CSCL, vol. 13 (2013)
3. Bruce, B.C.: Technology as social practice. Educ. Found. **10**(4), 51–58 (1996)
4. Costa, A., Kallick, B.: Assessment Strategies for Self-Directed Learning. Corwin, Thousand Oaks (2004)
5. Crown, S., Fuentes, A., Jones, R., Nambiar, R., Crown, D.: Ann G. Neering: interactive chatbot to motivate and engage engineering students. Am. Soc. Eng. Educ. **15**(1), 1–13 (2010)
6. Elsevier artificial intelligence program. In: Artificial Intelligence: How Knowledge is Created, Transferred, and Used, pp. 70–77. Elsevier (2018)
7. Følstad, A., Brandtzaeg, P.B., Feltwell, T., Law, E.L., Tscheligi, M., Luger, E.A.: Sig: chatbots for social good. In Extended Abstract, CHI Conference. ACM (2018)
8. Garcia Brustenga, G., Fuertes-Alpiste, M., Molas-Castells, N.: Briefing paper: chatbots in education. eLearn Center, Barcelona. Universitat Oberta de Catalunya (2018)
9. Kipp, K., Kapros, E., O'Keeffe, I.: A universally accessible self-assessment gamified framework and software application to capture 21st century skills. In: Kapros, E., Koutsombogera, M. (eds.) Designing for the User Experience in Learning Systems. HIS, pp. 41–64. Springer, Cham (2018). https://doi.org/10.1007/978-3-319-94794-5_3
10. Kapros, E., Koutsombogera, M.: Introduction: user experience in and for learning. In: Kapros, E., Koutsombogera, M. (eds.) Designing for the User Experience in Learning Systems. HIS, pp. 1–13. Springer, Cham (2018). https://doi.org/10.1007/978-3-319-94794-5_1
11. Leinonen, T., Toikkanen, T., Silfvast, K.: Software as hypothesis: research-based design methodology. In: Proceedings of the Tenth Anniversary Conference on Participatory Design 2008, pp. 61–70. Indiana University (2008)
12. Nadler, A., Crain, M., Donovan, J.: Weaponizing the digital influence machine: the political perils of online ad tech. Data & Society Research Institute (2018)
13. Organization for Economic Cooperation and Development (OECD): Pisa 2015 Draft Collaborative Problem Solving Framework. OECD (2013)
14. Panadero, E., Alonso-Tapia, J.: Self-assessment: theoretical and practical connotations, when it happens, how is it acquired and what to do to develop it in our students. Electron. J. Res. Educ. Psychol. **11**(2), 551–576 (2013)

15. Penuel, W.R., Roschelle, J., Shechtman, N.: Designing formative assessment software with teachers: an analysis of the co-design process. Res. Pract. Technol. Enhanc. Learn. **2**(01), 51–74 (2007)
16. Rajendran, G., Mitchell, P.: Computer mediated interaction in Asperger's syndrome: the bubble dialogue program. Comput. Educ. **35**(3), 189–207 (2000)
17. Sanders, E.B.N.: From user-centered to participatory design approaches. In: Design and the Social Sciences, pp. 18–25. CRC Press (2002)
18. Sanders, E.B.N., Westerlund, B.: Experiencing, exploring and experimenting in and with co-design spaces. Nordes (4) (2011)
19. Silvervarg, A., Kirkegaard, C., Nirme, J., Haake, M., Gulz, A.: Steps towards a challenging teachable agent. In: Intelligent Virtual Agents Conference (IVA) (2014)
20. Spikol, D., Milrad, M., Maldonado, H., Pea, R.: Integrating co-design practices into the development of mobile science collaboratories. In: 2009 Ninth IEEE International Conference on Advanced Learning Technologies, pp. 393–397. IEEE (2009)
21. Suchman, L., Blomberg, J., Orr, J.E., Trigg, R.: Reconstructing technologies as social practice. Am. Behav. Sci. **43**(3), 392–408 (1999)
22. Warschauer, M., Knobel, M., Stone, L.: Technology and equity in schooling: deconstructing the digital divide. Educ. Policy **18**(4), 562–588 (2004)
23. Winkler, R., Söllner, M.: Unleashing the potential of chatbots in education: a state-of-the-art analysis. In: Academy of Management Annual Meeting (AOM) (2018)
24. Wegerif, R.: The role of educational software as a support for teaching and learning conversations. Comput. Educ. **43**(1), 179–191 (2004)
25. Zhang, B., Looi, C.K., Seow, P., et al.: Deconstructing and reconstructing: transforming primary science learning via a mobilized curriculum. Comput. Educ. **55**(4), 1504–1523 (2010)

Use of an Emotional Chatbot for the Analysis of a Discussion Forum for the Improvement of an E-Learning Platform

Karim Elia Fraoua[1](✉), Jean-Marc Leblanc[2], and Amos David[3]

[1] Université Paris Est Marne-La-Vallée, Equipe Dispositifs d'Information et de Communication à l'Ere Numérique (DICEN IDF), Conservatoire national des arts et métiers, Paris-Est Paris-Ouest, EA 7339, Serris, France
fraoua@u-pem.fr
[2] Université Paris Est Creteil, Céditec EA 3119, Créteil, France
[3] Université Lorraine, Equipe Dispositifs d'Information et de Communication à l'Ere Numérique (DICEN IDF), Conservatoire national des arts et métiers, Paris-Est Paris-Ouest, EA 7339, Serris, France

Abstract. In this work, we try to show that the contribution of a chatbot in an e-learning platform can bring more efficiency in learning. The observation being that many learners either abandon their learning. They judge that it's not very effective, because often their questions are not answered adequately. Our emotional chatbot proposal shows that if we take into account the emotional state of the learner, we can offer him an answer adapted to his concerns that appear during their learning processes

Keywords: E-learning · Emotion · Chatbot

1 Introduction

Interactions in learning platforms remain relatively weak, although the notion of mediating artifact is an important element in the realization of an online course. This creates the obvious problem of online learning and their relative failure for this reason among others. We want to reproduce as much as possible a face-to-face course and transpose it into a virtual space, taking into account the learning methods. In a previous work, we insisted on learning methods like constructivism or socioconstructivism [1] and their implications on different online course structures like the Adaptive Learning Design (ALD), in order to adapt the pedagogical approach to the modalities of implementation of the online course [2]. It is certain that we have not integrated all the pedagogical methods, but we considered that this approach, in a first trajectory, is sufficient. In the socio-constructivist approach, the presence of a mediating artefact is essential, because in a real situation as in the school, the importance of having a trainer is fundamental.

We consider that it is necessary to insist on the establishment of a forum of exchange between the learners and that this space is also the opportunity for the learners their comments verbally freely on the course and ask any questions that they

P. Zaphiris and A. Ioannou (Eds.): HCII 2020, LNCS 12206, pp. 25–35, 2020.
https://doi.org/10.1007/978-3-030-50506-6_3

consider necessary to better assimilate notions and knowledge, allowing thus interaction between learners and the trainer [3]. We obviously see that the presence of a trainer on an exchange forum will not allow resolution of all possible situations especially if in the online course the size of the class is too large for it to handle all the requests. Therefore, we need to introduce a chatbot that will ensure the role, at least partially, of mediator artifact or trainer whose role would be the animation of this space for exchange.

For this chatbot, it must therefore be able to have behaviors quite similar to the trainer and in particular the management of the learners' emotions. This happens in the classroom when a trainer observes the attitude of the learners. So, we need to find the best approach that allows us to understand what the learner feels. For this exercise, we will consider the comments that are posted in the discussion areas. To do this, we will take as basis of our consideration the text analysis technique [4] which will allow us to step in, taking into account another aspect that face-to-face trainers encounter, namely the emotional state of the learner.

This approach will respond to one of the issues that we have considered, which is to allow to the learner to get answer to his questions as well as his concerns. First of all, textmining will make it possible to analyze which elements pose a problem to the learner [5] or to all learners and in which case, this can allow us to create clusters of learners who have common characteristics, either by level, or having the same social or cultural construction. This notion is important because we can design chatbots that allow us to respond comprehensively but also specifically to groups of learners in regard to socio-constructivism model.

The education system must always create interest in learning, avoiding negative feelings like disgust, despondency, or abandonment. The trainers know that frustration generally precedes abandonment and thanks to the trainers, we try to accompany the students at these times to maintain their motivations [6]. It is for this reason that we have raised the question of pedagogical ability. By observing the emotion expressed by a student, the trainer responds optimally by providing personalized support [7]. Indeed, if the learning task increases in difficulty, the student may feel frustration or anxiety. Learning can be abandoned because of these negative feelings. The efficient trainer detects these signals and responds appropriately. Knowing that Enthusiasm is contagious in learning, the teacher who expresses his enthusiasm can often arouse similar feelings in the student [8].

In this regard, it will therefore be necessary to establish a prior emotional profile thanks to this data that we have on the learners via their exchanges on the forum. This information then allows us to focus on the assessment of the learners by using for example known models namely for example the so-called FFM model (five factor model) which first considers the personality [9]. The elements described in this model are descriptive of the person we will try to identify, five characteristics, which are, assessed namely Extraversion, Pleasantness, Consciousness, Neuroticism and Openness. We consider that the evolution of textual analysis tools makes it possible to extract traits from the learner's personality which constitutes a starting point for our reflection. Indeed, later we will analyze other emotions and we will take as model those of Ekman who defined six emotional states: anger, disgust, fear, happiness, sadness or surprise [10].

Without considering the personality state of the person, we think that the emotional state is not structuring. The joy expressed by a person who is considered Pleasant is not the same as that which is considered to be extroverted. In fact when a person is in a good mood, he reacts better to a voice [11]. On the other hand, a stressed person would react better to a more sober voice. If the voice is happy, on the contrary, it would irritate it even more and increase the number of accidents. In the field of education, a virtual tutor who would adapt his strategy to the emotional state of a student could allow him to progress more quickly and with more pleasure (Comparative studies of two versions of a tool, one with a processing module on affective states, as basic as it is, and another without this module, the user will systematically prefer the affective version and this will often affect its performance).

To justify our approach and its implementation, we will rely on the discipline of affective computing [12]. This discipline is interested in the development of tools, methods, systems and devices to give them the ability to recognize, express, synthesize and model human emotions. It's an interdisciplinary crossroads and we'll just look at areas like computing, information and communication science and tackle the tools that allow the interaction between technology and sentiment. This is how our choice fell on the power of the content of the texts, and their ability to provide us with a certain amount of information allowing the emergence of new possibilities in order to improve several uses.

In addition, if the learner realizes that the chatbot is not human, he risks not communicating with it in an optimal way. We aim to consider the personality and the emotion of the learner. However, if the chatbot takes the learner's emotions into account, this approach will respond to one of the problems that we have considered, which is to allow the learner to answer his questions as well as his concerns. We are aware that the Turing test will allow us to assess our chatbot. It is clear that by integrating more and more human characteristics, we can hope to tend towards a better use of these tools in an educational platform. Emotions can always be perceived in the text and can still be aroused by its content [13]. According to Picard, a machine will have difficulty passing the Turing test if it is unable to perceive and express emotions [12].

1.1 Objective and Scientific Positioning

Socio-constructivism is nowadays an educational model extremely influencing the construction and the unfolding of a classroom course. It requires a number of educational skills [14]. Indeed, it is recognized mainly that the knowledge is acquired through social interactions, in which the trainer plays the role of mediator promoting these interactions and the debates between learners [15]. This is a notable difference from constructivism, where the learner builds his knowledge based on his own experiences [16].

The trainer or mediator artefact therefore has a role of facilitator and its presence is therefore fundamental and must have an educational function. In the constructivist model, the trainer accompanies the learner in the creation of knowledge by recreating with him learning situations close to his experience. These states can be observed as part of a face-to-face course, and the trainer will be able to measure all the elements that can promote interactions, in particular emotional states and by having a more or less important knowledge of the personality of the learner. As teachers, there is a general tendency to create categories indicating the personality of the student, whether he has a voluntary participatory process or whether he should be encouraged to do so. In the classroom, the learner may not appreciate what he is learning or at least the teaching method implemented. This can lead us to review the course that is offered and to be able to consider whether it is an individual or a cluster of learners. We can also reason in terms of polarity, namely the attitude of the learner versus the course, we can assess whether the polarity is positive, negative or neutral.

2   Identify Emotions in the Text

More and more trade institutions are resorting to linguistic analysis, and to put it in another way, very few fields escape it. The applications are plethora and the fields of application are widening more and more like the automatic detection of emotions in texts [17], opinion exploration [18], or natural language interfaces such as online learning environments or educational games. The sentiment analysis is no longer only an extraction of polarity, namely positive, negative or neutral, but more and more in details, indicating a very interesting level of finesse, and which allows very useful manipulations. The technical interfaces are made easier with increasingly practical APIs but also increasingly standardized data formats such as JSON format.

Human-computer interaction must improve its efficiency and above all show an increasingly natural aspect and therefore do not create a bias and consider that these two points are essential. The expression of emotions by conversational agents is considered to be a key element in improving the quality of human-machine interfaces [19]. It has long been thought that the user only needs to answer these questions and it is becoming increasingly clear that the notion of emotion is as essential as technical response. In this regard, in the communication strategy developed on the basis of the work of Goleman [20] and not starting on the concepts of emotions which today make consensus including among the editors of applications: anger, disgust, fear, joy, sadness, surprise.

3   Personality and Emotional State

As we said before, we have chosen to consider the FFM (Five Factor Model) [21] approach among others because it is fairly comprehensive and often used in general to assess someone's personality. This will have an impact on the interactions between the learners. The model in question first considers the personality; it is an important element on the constitution of the course structure that will be offered. This five-factor model is confirmed by Costa and McCrae [22].

Extraversion, Pleasantness, Consciousness, Neuroticism, and Openness are the five elements domains of traits that constitute the five-factor personality model (FFM). This vision makes it possible to classify individuals according to their personality traits which clearly show how people express their emotions when faced to an event and informs us about how people will perceive the world, whether if they are optimist or pessimist ... [21]. For example, we can detect extroverted people. These people will have more positive emotions and will have more social interactions. According to Jackson and Soto [21]:

- Extraversion: Affirmed and sociable person.
- Pleasantness: Cooperative and polite person.
- Consciousness: Task-oriented and organized person.
- Neuroticism: Negative emotions, such as anxiety.
- Openness: Open to a wide range of interests.

The FFM model was actually developed to represent the variability in the personality of individuals, using only a small set of stroke dimensions. Many psychologists show that these five areas give a fairly comprehensive idea of the most important and fundamental individual differences.

These five factors do not provide completely exhaustive explanations of personality. The five factors are not necessarily traits in themselves, but factors in which many related traits and characteristics fit. Obviously, this corresponds to the reality that we know in a class without having to go into the details of the personality, and which allows us to classify students to optimize the pedagogical approach and to create more suitable learning models. Beyond the question of personality, the trainer in the classroom can observe the polarity of feeling in the learner and this can have an impact on others, since a positive feeling will be able to encourage exchanges and that negative feeling, will produce the opposite effect.

The extent to which people express their emotions, how they express their emotions and the valence of this emotion can tell us how people experience the world. People react radically differently to traumatic or important events; the way people respond can say a lot about how they cope with the event and the extent to which the event plays a role in the future. People's emotional response is at the heart of reaction and event management.

4 Emotion Theories

The question of emotion is quite wide and several studies and research have focused on the question, for our part, we will consider that each state is described in terms of different assessments such as for example the intensity or duration as indicated by Scherer [23].

- The Emotion itself such as anger, joy, sadness, fear.
- Positions between person, or Interpersonal Stances with distance, coldness, ..
- Moods such as being happy, depressed, or in a good mood.
- Attitudes like friendship, desire.
- Affective dispositions such as being nervous or anxious.

Emotion has a major influence on the quality of our life, with our relationships with others and it will have several influences as well on our judgment, and several biases exist and are largely due to emotions. Several fields of study in neuroscience are devoted to these biases and how to correct these biases by dimensioning the notion of emotion. Since Damasio's work [24], notably with Descartes's Error, emotion has had an impact on our reasoning and decision-making. It also influences attention, motivation, memory, problem solving... To better understand this emotional issue, it is useful to understand its structure and complexity at the same time. According to several of these theories, basic emotions have evolved in order to adapt to certain difficulties characteristic of life such as competition (anger), danger (fear), loss (sadness) [25].

Paul Ekman gives nine characteristics allowing to distinguish the basic emotions and by studying the facial expressions he defined six emotions (Anger, Fear, Sadness, Disgust, Joy, Surprise) [10]. Paul Ekman considered facial expression to analyze people's emotions. Of course this approach is confronted with biases and which will depend on the culture of the people even if Ekman considers that these expressions are quite primitive. The main contribution of Ekman's work is that when the person learns to recognize their feelings, there is an improvement in their relationships with others.

However, emotions are actually more complex and considered as the association or combination of several basic emotions. For Plutchik, who evokes a mixed state of basic emotion, the two basic emotions are observable in the mixture. Plutchik explored how to represent all of the emotions. He identifies eight prototypes: fear/terror, anger/rage, sadness/sorrow, acceptance/confidence, disgust/repugnance, hope/anticipation and surprise [26]. He also considered that the emotions vary in intensity, and that some emotions are closer than others. To establish the classification of emotions, Plutchik uses a wheel with color palettes and in which he can set up the opposite emotions (Fig. 1).

5   Textual Analysis and Sentiments

The words we use in our everyday life reflect what we pay attention to, what we think about, what we try to avoid, how we feel and how we organize and analyze our worlds. Indeed, the different uses of the language differ according to age, sex, personality and socio-professional environment. The use of language, like any behavioral manifestation, can reflect individual differences. Language in its most basic function is to communicate. Words provide information on social processes by analyzing whether the exchanges are numerous and involve all the members of the group [27].

The content word categories reveal how people feel. Indeed, from a structural point of view, people use words or language structures that express human thought. If someone wishes to express a situation in which he is involved, or others who think like him will categorize this notion [28]. As an example, a tool like LIWC which has been widely used in particular by Facebook [29] makes it possible to extract The five major personality traits that we explained above [9].

We can go even further depending on the amount of textual data available in order to refine more and more the emotional nature involved. The tool TexObsever developed by J-M. Leblanc [30] will allow us to extract useful corpora to define areas in which will be inserted appropriately according to the polarity at first and then define semantic categories to better visualize the emotional states of the learners. To do this, emotion databases must be incorporated. There are several databases on word emotions

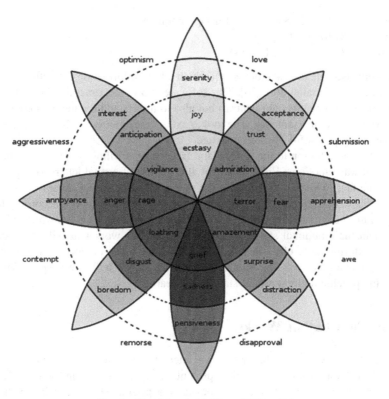

Fig. 1. Plutchik wheel (From Wikipedia)

like WordNet Affect [31] and several algorithms are considered effective for detecting emotions like Latent Semantic Analysis (LSA) [32]. We also used the Google NLP tool [33] which allows us to have also the polarities of the sentiment of learners through the collection of text gathered from the learning platform Google Classroom [34] and not yet the emotion in the sense that we have been able to analyze it before.

Of course there are other tools that we could test like the Q°Emotion [35] tool among others which allows to extract a certain amount of information on emotions and which will extract these elements with an accuracy of 85%:

- Emotional index.
- Primary emotions.
- Main sensations mentioned by the public in their comments
- Voice engagement
- Semantic automatic text analysis

Q°emotion will reveal emotions in the form of temperature

- From 31 °C to 40 °C: happiness
- From 21 °C to 30 °C: Surprise
- From 11 °C to 20 °C: Calm
- From 6 °C to 10 °C: fear

- From −5 °C to 5 °C: Sadness and disappointment
- From −14 °C to −6 °C: Anger
- From −20 °C to −15 °C: Disgust

We were also able to test another tool which allows information extraction via APIs or JSON files like Parallel dots [36]. This software allows to extract the three classes of feelings (positive, negative and neutral) but also to understand the nuances concerning the underlying tone of a sentence. The tool to extract the emotions behind a message is: happy, sad, angry, fearful, excited or bored.

In writing, in addition to the vocabulary used, many spellings express in a more or less explicit way emotions: Emoticons, but also the use of capital letters to express for example the fact of shouting or raising the voice, doubling of consonants or vowels

Once this work is done, we can configure suitable chatbots as well according to the polarity of the learners as the extracted feelings and then adopt chatbots which will take into account the emotional state of the learner. It is this work that will make online learning platforms more efficient by taking into account the preponderant role of the mediating artefact which is the trainer, in the sense that it will intervene, taking into account the psychic and emotional state of the learner.

6 How the Chatbot Works

From the above, we know that when we interact with learners, we will take into account their emotional state and this represents in a fairly important way the answer will be perceived. A good trainer is necessarily a person who is capable of having empathy and it is in this sense that we consider in the socio-constructivist model that it is a facilitator. Learners' emotions play a key role in understanding and acquiring knowledge. When we take these emotions into account, we can influence learning effectiveness [37].

In the case of an online course, this analysis carried out by the trainer disappears at the expense of an interface, regardless of the design, which remains fairly neutral or the place of exchange, be it the discussion forum or other types of interaction. We consider from our previous proposition that the text reflects both a person's personality and emotion, or at least the feelings they have at the time. In our case, if a learner has not learned a concept, he will actually ask his question online and the way he will write it can indicate if he is anxious for example or in good or bad mood or in anger.

In this case, our chatbot must interact with the learner taking this emotional aspect into account and provide him with a contextual answer that will try to bring him another way of presenting this knowledge. It can also be to offer additional readings which can be stored in a knowledge base in the form of a tutorial, whether documents to read or videos. We must not forget that students can have sometimes disparate levels and that the prerequisites are not necessarily received or acquired.

The process therefore that we propose is as follows. Once the text is collected, we analyze it with sentiment and emotion analysis tools and as the texts are collected, we will also analyze them with TextObserver in order to be able to form clusters in order to constitute groups of students in order, for example, to measure their learning preferences or the specifics of exchanges with them. Once this data is collected, it will enrich the chatbot which has been set up through the intents which make it possible to operate a chatbot.

As it stands, we're working in the ecosystem on Google Classroom with the Google NLP Sentiment Analysis Tool and the Dialogflow chatbot [38]. For the rest of this work, we aim to integrate emotional analysis tools such as ParallelDots, Aylien or Q°Emotion in order to further enrich our Chatbot.

7 Conclusion

In conclusion, we see that there is currently a great difficulty in ensuring online courses, judging by the amount of dropout that is observed and it is not a question of building a beautiful interface by playing on the quality design or set up a collection of course presentations, be it ppt, pdf, videos or any other support. We must create the learning conditions that allow us to respond to emotional situations that the learner encounters during their learning journey. In fact, emotions play a fundamental role in our learning and when the course takes place in a class, this notion is generally taken into account by the trainer. In this work, we present a perspective that we are validating with the establishment of a chatbot which for the moment only analyzes the polarity, namely a positive, negative or neutral feeling. In the future, we will further integrate the notion of grouping of learners on the basis of their attitude during the first course, in order to define specific chatbots and which will encourage interactions between learners, because the socio-constructivist model demonstrates that the better the interaction between the actors are, the better the learning is. Our ChatBot will also be in charge of considering emotion more and more in the sense defined by Plutchick to regulate emotion more within the discussion forum and thus allow the learner to have adequate answers adapted to their Questions.

References

1. Barak, M.: Science teacher education in the twenty-first century: a pedagogical framework for technology-integrated social constructivism. Res. Sci. Educ. **47**(2), 283–303 (2017). https://doi.org/10.1007/s11165-015-9501-y
2. Berlanga, A., García, F.: A proposal to define adaptive learning designs. In: Proceedings of Workshop on Applications of Semantic Web Technologies for Educational Adaptive Hypermedia (SW-EL 2004) in AH 2004, vol. 23, pp. 04–19 (2004)
3. Conole, G.: The role of mediating artefacts in learning design. In: Handbook of Research on Learning Design and Learning Objects: Issues, Applications, and Technologies, pp. 188–208. IGI Global (2009)
4. Nahl, D.: A discourse analysis technique for charting the flow of micro-information behavior. J. Doc. (2007)
5. Flowerdew, L.: Applying corpus linguistics to pedagogy: a critical evaluation. Int. J. Corpus Linguist. **14**(3), 393–417 (2009)
6. Boekaerts, M.: The crucial role of motivation and emotion in classroom learning. In: The Nature of Learning: Using Research to Inspire Practice, pp. 91–111 (2010)

7. Kort, B., Reilly, R., Picard, R.W.: An affective model of interplay between emotions and learning: Reengineering educational pedagogy-building a learning companion. In Proceedings IEEE International Conference on Advanced Learning Technologies, pp. 43–46. IEEE (2001)
8. Becker, E.S., Goetz, T., Morger, V., Ranellucci, J.: The importance of teachers' emotions and instructional behavior for their students' emotions–An experience sampling analysis. Teach. Teach. Educ. **43**, 15–26 (2014)
9. McCrae, R.R., Costa Jr, P.T.: The five-factor theory of personality (2008)
10. Ekman, P.: Basic emotions. Handb. Cognit. Emot. **98**(45–60), 16 (1999)
11. Nass, C.I., Brave, S.: Wired for Speech: How Voice Activates and Advances the Human-Computer Relationship, p. 9. MIT Press, Cambridge (2005)
12. Picard, R.W.: Affective Computing. MIT Press, Cambridge (2002)
13. Yin, D., Bond, S.D., Zhang, H.: Anxious or angry? Effects of discrete emotions on the perceived helpfulness of online reviews. MIS Q. **38**(2), 539–560 (2014)
14. Hirtle, J.S.P.: Social constructivism. Engl. J. **85**(1), 91 (1996)
15. Rovai, A.P.: Facilitating online discussions effectively. Internet High. Educ. **10**(1), 77–88 (2007)
16. Woo, Y., Reeves, T.C.: Meaningful interaction in web-based learning: a social constructivist interpretation. Internet High. Educ. **10**(1), 15–25 (2007)
17. Mohammad, S.M.: Sentiment analysis: detecting valence, emotions, and other affectual states from text. In: Emotion Measurement, pp. 201–237. Woodhead Publishing (2016)
18. Das, A., Bandyopadhyay, S.: Theme detection an exploration of opinion subjectivity. In: 2009 3rd International Conference on Affective Computing and Intelligent Interaction and Workshops, pp. 1–6. IEEE (2009)
19. Pelachaud, C.: Multimodal expressive embodied conversational agents. In: Proceedings of the 13th Annual ACM International Conference on Multimedia, pp. 683–689 (2005)
20. Cherniss, C., Goleman, D.: The emotionally intelligence workplace. How to select for measure and improve emotional intelligence in individuals, groups and organizations. Jossey-Bass, San Francisco (2001)
21. Jackson, J.J., Soto, C.J.: Five-factor model of personality. Oxford Bibliogr. Psychol. **1** (2015)
22. Costa, P.T., McCrae, R.R.: Trait theories of personality. In: Barone, D.F., Hersen, M., Van Hasselt, V.B. (eds.) Advanced Personality, pp. 103–121. Springer, Boston (1998). https://doi.org/10.1007/978-1-4419-8580-4_5
23. Scherer, K.R.: What are emotions? And how can they be measured? Soc. Sci. Inf. **44**(4), 695–729 (2005)
24. Damasio, A.R.: L'erreur de Descartes: la raison des émotions. Odile Jacob (2006)
25. Izard, C.E.: Basic emotions, natural kinds, emotion schemas, and a new paradigm. Perspect. Psychol. Sci. **2**(3), 260–280 (2007)
26. Plutchik, R., Kellerman, H. (eds.): Theories of Emotion, vol. 1. Academic Press, Cambridge (2013)
27. Tausczik, Y.R., Pennebaker, J.W.: The psychological meaning of words: LIWC and computerized text analysis methods. J. Lang. Soc. Psychol. **29**(1), 24–54 (2010)
28. Chung, C., Pennebaker, J.W.: The psychological functions of function words. Soc. Commun. **1**, 343–359 (2007)
29. Tandera, T., Suhartono, D., Wongso, R., Prasetio, Y.L.: Personality prediction system from facebook users. Procedia Comput. Sci. **116**, 604–611 (2017)
30. Leblanc, J.M.: Textobserver: une démarche textométrique expérimentale pour l'analyse de la variation. De linguistique fonctionnelle (2016)

31. Strapparava, C., Valitutti, A.: Wordnet affect: an affective extension of wordnet. In: LREC, vol. 4, no. 1083–1086, p. 40 (2004)

32. Ahmad, S.N., Laroche, M.: How do expressed emotions affect the helpfulness of a product review? Evidence from reviews using latent semantic analysis. Inte. J. Electron. Commer. **20** (1), 76–111 (2015)

33. https://cloud.google.com/natural-language/?utm_source=google&utm_medium=cpc&utm_campaign=emea-fr-all-en-dr-bkws-all-all-trial-e-gcp-1008073&utm_content=text-ad-none-any-DEV_c-CRE_253521614522-ADGP_Hybrid+%7C+AW+SEM+%7C+BKWS+~+EXA_1:1_FR_EN_Cloud_ML_NL+API_Gap+Analysis+01.11.2017-KWID_43700027737971410-kwd-324090677250-userloc_9056531&utm_term=KW_google%20nlp-ST_google+nlp&ds_rl=1242853&ds_rl=1245734&ds_rl=1245734&gclid=EAIaIQobChMIt6-jtYKu5wIVCIbVCh0JzwCIEAAYASAAEgJ0zfD_BwE

34. Iftakhar, S.: Google classroom: what works and how. J. Educ. Soc. Sci. **3**(1), 12–18 (2016)

35. https://www.qemotion.com/fr/

36. https://www.paralleldots.com/

37. Pekrun, R.: Emotions and learning. In: Educational Practices Series, p. 24 (2014)

38. Janarthanam, S.: Hands-on chatbots and conversational UI development: build chatbots and voice user interfaces with Chatfuel, Dialogflow, Microsoft Bot Framework, Twilio, and Alexa Skills. Packt Publishing Ltd. (2017)

Compare Differences of Communication and Creativity Between Different Team Composition and Using Different Conceptual Analysis Integrational Tools

Yi Chi Fu and Chao Yang Yang[✉]

Department of Industrial Design, Tatung University, Taipei, Taiwan
dillon.yang@gmail.com

Abstract. With the advancement of science and technology, it is difficult to innovate only from one domain. No matter how the media or education policy emphasizes the importance of interdisciplinary thinking and design thinking, cross-domain communication is no longer a dual-professional cooperation without rules; the value of design thinking is not limited to the innovation and entrepreneurship. And the inspiration is started from cultivation of education, many domestic schools are also establishing a systematic interdisciplinary lecture model.

This research takes the design thinking workshop as an example. Effective teaching tools can improve the communication quality between team members and the creative performance of students in different fields. In order to achieve higher level of interdisciplinary talent cultivation, and apply appropriate assessments and evaluation after teaching. This research makes the problem based team use different conceptual analysis tools and different domain composition to realize the differences of communication and creativity between different groups. The difference in performance found that cross-domain composition has a tendency to rely on common experience to combine ideas, while the same domain composition refers to common knowledge and skills; and the main teaching tool of this study, CTM, has been found to stimulate more team dialogues, clearer problem solving process, task-area communication and negative social reactions.

The research is divided into three stages. First, it is defined the connection between design thinking and mind of interdisciplinary, and visiting six experienced interdisciplinary teachers and summarizing the difficulties in the current teaching situation to formulate the teaching indicators for interdisciplinary curriculum; in the second stages, the integrated teaching tool, CTM will be brought to the real teaching site, recorded the communication behaviors and innovations of the students, and tested the control groups that use the KJ method under the same conditions. In the third stage, its evaluated the innovations with the Finke's creative cognition. The last, its compared the difference of creativity between different team composition and using different conceptual analysis tool, and then test whether the CTM tool cause the difference of the overall effect, which can be used as the basis for the innovative group to enhance the creativity and communication of the team.

© Springer Nature Switzerland AG 2020
P. Zaphiris and A. Ioannou (Eds.): HCII 2020, LNCS 12206, pp. 36–44, 2020.
https://doi.org/10.1007/978-3-030-50506-6_4

Keywords: Design thinking · Interdisciplinary · Communication behavior · Creativity

1   Introduction

In recent years, the cognitive aspect of design has received attention as the basis of design education. Schön (1985) focused on design thinking, cognition, and experimental research in design pedagogy. Because design teaching provides a complete construction method, cognitive research is an important topic in design education. The trend of people-oriented design thinking is applicable to the fields of financial technology, agricultural services, and medical systems. In real life, a single profession or even a T-type talent cannot connect with the drive of society. Society requires talents with both professional depth and expertise in multiple fields. However, school systems are often guided by the transfer of professional knowledge and the cultivation of talents in a single field. Under government control, design thinking and cross-domain thinking are gradually being promoted and cultivated. The next stage of development and how to make this thinking deep-rooted we can't help it.

To develop the concepts of interprofessional interactive application and communication skills in future students, design and thinking cross-domain talent cultivation workshops are a form of thinking that provide teaching experience. A combination of cross-domain teachers and student teams use knowledge to solve a single problem; however, with a suitable teaching framework and existing teaching tools, the communication problems caused by the combination of different professional teams are a major concern. Many educators remain unaware regarding how design thinking is used to practice value innovation and regarding the methods for evaluating and selecting the most effective design thinking model for their personal innovation practice (Tschimmel 2012). Design evaluation is another crucial aspect of a design process (Kalay 1992). Thus, the instrumentalisation of design teaching and establishment of creative value measurement standards can improve the acceptance of and provide substantial benefits for different professional interactions as well as enhance the implementation of cross-domain education. Obstacles for and important indicators in the promotion of cross-domain and design thinking.

In January 2018, the Ministry of Education introduced the design thinking cross-domain talent cultivation plan (nursery plan), which is based on the design of key industries, as the scope of the nursery plan. Through dual-teacher cross-domain cooperative teaching, students are trained to implement practical solutions to actual problems. With the cross-disciplinary teamwork experience and ability of design thinking, a concept triangulation map (CTM) cross tool mentioned in the plan is being tested in the planned second year curriculum. The tool is used to match the possibilities of different field combinations. In this study, we used a qualitative research method to test whether the CTM tool improved the willingness of students in different fields to cooperate, quality of innovation output, and efficiency of communication when it was applied to form teams with members from different fields.

2 Design Thinking

Brown (2008), the president of the IDEO design company, once stated that design thinking is a people-oriented design method that considers human requirements, human behaviours, and the feasibility of a technology or business. Design thinking is a people-oriented problem-solving methodology based on human requirements. It provides innovative solutions to various problems and creates different possibilities.

Twenty years ago, design thinking was mainly defined as the cognitive process of a designer (Cross et al. 1992). At that time, studies mainly attempted to obtain highly in-depth design creativity. In addition to finding general design methods, most studies were conducted to confirm the strategic foundation of the designer during the execution of a plan.

Oxman (2004) proposed a teaching framework and think maps for design learning and teaching. In this framework, when domain knowledge becomes clear, the structure of the learner concept is closely linked to that of other teaching concepts. These structures are populated with the content from specific design domains or tasks. Moreover, Oxman suggested that the cognitive content of design thinking must consider education as the goal and provide teachers and learners with a means for understanding the knowledge.

3 Collaborative and Cross-Domain Teaching

Under the current trend, we expect students to face problems appropriately in modern society. We encouraged students to major in various fields and actively cultivated cross-disciplinary skills and literacy. We focused on problems that societies confront and on developing their solutions.

Interdisciplinary teaching refers to teaching activities conducted by professors or students from two or more disciplines by using the knowledge or methods of each discipline to cooperate with each other and achieve the same goal, which is usually solving problems that cannot be solved by a single student or teacher. Cases of cross-field cooperation have certain things in common. The findings of these studies were not only ground-breaking but also crossed over into different fields to provide new ideas. The medici effect indicated that when people from different fields, disciplines, and cultures meet, they create numerous breakthrough ideas by combining existing ideas, which results in the formation of meeting points. Johansson (2005) proposed inter-sectional innovation.

Teachers play a vital role in an education system; however, teaching is considered as one of the most isolated fields (Cookson 2008; Heider 2005). Collaborative teaching breaks the traditional isolated teaching style. Because of limited knowledge, sharing knowledge, technology, and experience is the most crucial advantage of collaboration (Mohrman et al. 1995); thus, collaborative teaching is a cross-field learning practice. Sharplin, the father of collaborative teaching, reported collaborative teaching to be a type of a teaching organisation that includes staff and students who teach and are collectively responsible for all teaching or the main part of the same group of students (Shaplin and Olds 1964). Buckley (1999) defined collaborative teaching as teaching conducted by a group of teachers for a group of students through purposeful, routine, and cooperative work. The teachers in the team set course goals and design lesson schedules, prepare individual lesson plans, practically teach students together, and work together on assessment results. They share ideas, debate with each other, and even encourage students to do what is right.

The integration of issues without rules often leads to insufficient integration of the curriculum, scattered, contradictory, broken and missing. Moreover, students confront unknown problems with limited experience and skills. Waiting for students to explore fields by themselves is not a suitable option.

4   Creativity

Creativity is the driving force of the continually progressing human technology and civilisation. Humans must be wisely creative to lead humankind to a better future Gardner and Claxton (2007). Csikszentmihalyi (1996) stated that if humans cannot suitably select their creation, humanity will eventually be destroyed by their creation.

The significance of creativity is widely known; however, not everyone is born with this ability. No method has been developed to actively help inspire creativity. Promoting creativity through education has always been a topic of interest. Many scholars have regarded creativity and innovation as the main information processing activities (DeMeyer 1985; Moenaert et al. 2000). A core of design creativity is the generation and reweaving of knowledge (Leenders et al. 2003), which is an expression of personal thinking and an excellent method for design thinking and cross-domain communication.

5   Creativity Evaluation

Because the object of experimentation was a cross-disciplinary professional team, a concept integration tool widely used in innovative talent cultivation courses was adopted. For easy-to-understand features, a more representative KJ method was employed as the control group of the experiment. According to a discriminative model provided by Finke (1996) for creative ideas, it was conducted for two indicators: originality and practicality.

The maximum score of the two indicators was 10 points, and the score is scored at 0.5 points. For scoring, eight design scholars were invited to rate the ideas generated by different communication modes according to innovative and practical standards. All the evaluators had an experience of >3 years in the design profession.

6   Communication

The value of cross-disciplinary teams depends on the knowledge gap and experience of different members, which may lead to conflicts among them because of specialisation in different fields. Knight (1999) divided conflict into two types, namely conflict behaviours caused by interpersonal disharmony and conflict behaviours caused by team members due to interpersonal disharmony, emotional conflicts, and task conflicts (negative emotions). Task conflict is the inability of team members to reach a consensus during a task (disagreement on the content, goals, and procedures).

Eisenhardt (1997) indicated that high-performance companies exhibited more task conflicts in their management teams than low-performance companies did. Amason's (1997) research on high-level management teams revealed that task conflicts highly influenced the decision quality. According to the aforementioned literature, the evaluation method of team communication effectiveness does not determine whether the team is harmonious but whether team members understand the differences among each other and their areas of expertise through frequent constructive communication and use different perspectives for solving common problems.

7 CTM-Tools

CTM tools are mainly employed to compare design concepts through analogy. The differences between the specific definitions of distance and azimuth are illustrated. By comparing the vertical (relevant to the core theme) and horizontal (relationship with different dimensions) dimensions, the design concept is set in place for future self-assessment (see Fig. 1).

Amabile (1983) treated creativity as a sum of personal characteristics, cognitive abilities, and social environment, conceptualising them as personality traits and comprehensive cognitive abilities, and proposed domain-relevant skills, creativity-relevant processes, and task motivation. According to the knowledge, experience, and sensory correspondence, respectively. This research defined the design and thinking process of cross-domain workshop teams with problem-solving as the core literacy. The differences between professional knowledge and skills in various fields, perception and

Fig. 1. CTM-Tools

motivation of individuals in facing problems, and relevance of individual judgements regarding correctness and experience were examined in this research.

8 Research Method

For design or creativity-related fields, creativity and communication are often considered crucial parts of the design process. Fuhriman (1984) reported that the research of relevant groups should be based on a combination of qualitative and quantitative research methods to provide specific and complete group research data. In addition to innovative achievements, this study recorded the communication process of students, which provided diversity and continuity to the study.

The purpose of this study was to determine whether the implementation of the design solution and use of creativity was improved with the CTM when a student team implemented the solution, regardless of subject area. Prior to the tool operation, the students were briefed about design thinking and problem-solving processes. The CTM analysis and integration tool provided a communication and discussion platform to help students rationally structure team creative thinking within a given time. In the discussion of innovation issues, can generate and share ideas in the established structure and process, to observe the results produced by the different communication mode teams take Finke (1996)'s distinguishing model for creative ideas as the scoring criterion, invite eight design-related scholars with experience in teaching innovative courses will be scored for the two axes of innovation and practicality. The discussion processes of different types of case groups during the implementation of the textbook were also recorded in the research. The correlation between the results of group members during the discussion of innovation problems and different innovation dimensions was understood through in-depth analysis. Moreover, cross-domain workshops were implemented for acquiring comparison results to obtain appropriate communication models for reference.

9 Results and Discussion

9.1 Comparison of Creativity Results Under Different Conditions

After eight scholars with an experience of >3 years in design teaching (V1, V2,... V8 represent the evaluators who facilitate analysis and comparison) evaluated the communication process, brief descriptions were made of the concepts generated under four communication modes. The innovative and practical average scores as well as the overall comprehensive score performance of the conceptual results obtained from different groups. In the comprehensive score evaluation, G1 represents the use of cross-domain composition and CTM tools (M = 6.97), G2 represents the use of cross-domain composition and the KJ method (M = 4.94), G3 represents the use of the same field composition and CTM tools (M = 6.50), and G4 represents the use of the same field composition and the KJ method (M = 5.66). The composite scores obtained from the four groups exhibited no significant difference (R = 2.03).

However, when the creative index and practical evaluation were examined together, the two factors exhibited obvious differences due to the use of different conceptual analyses and integration tools. The result indicates that the creative performance of the group with the CTM tool was close to the opposite in terms of innovation and practical performance compared with that of the group without the tool. The practical performance of G1 and G3 was higher than the creativity performance of G1 and G3, and the innovation performance of G2 and G4 was higher than the practical performance of G2 and G4. The following section explains whether different communication modes under a fixed independent variable influence creativity and practicality.

9.2   Experimental Process and Observations

The heterogeneity of the cross-domain composition may have inspired creativity in team members and may have influenced the creativity performance. This study compared the differences in creativity between different teams. Different conceptual analysis methods and integration tools were used to determine whether the use of CTM tools benefits team creativity and communication. The problem-solving-oriented innovation team consisted of member composition, tool use, communication establishment, and discussion of innovation results. Reference for verbatim texts and observer notes of different team conversations in the workshop were made, and the results of the data were speculated.

Effect of the CTM Analysis Integration Tool on Team Creativity

The improvement of CTM tools to help creativity provides clarity to the description of team construction problems. The performance of comprehensive scores and practical average scores in creativity was G1 > G2 and G3 > G4. The practical scores exhibited significant differences, which proved that regardless of whether the team composition was cross-domain, the CTM tool helped the team more than the KJ method did in improving the practicality of creativity. This finding may be related to the operation process of the CTM tool used for guiding the students to acquire knowledge, sensory skills, and experience when they divergently contemplate over a specific topic. In addition to visualising knowledge areas with large gaps between majors, the tool can improve the efficiency of professional interaction. It emphasises the prevalence of thinkers' perception of senses and experience when they are creative and uses this perception as a team advantage to virtually establish a common language based on senses and experience.

Effect of the CTM Analysis Integration Tool on Team Communication

CTM tools May Motivate Group Conversations
Communication is a crucial parameter of teamwork (Shah et al. 2001). According to Csikszentmihalyi (1996), creativity does not occur in an individual's brain but is acquired through continuous communication and interactions, and an increased frequency of interactions enables innovation. The possibility of achieving the idea highly improves (West 1990). To achieve a goal, a team requires a commitment relationship

between members and several communication behaviours. Whether it is task-oriented or social–emotional, more opportunities for team communication were easy to stir.`

Effective Communication Behaviour

According to the aforementioned inference, we reviewed the total number of communication behaviours of the team in the limited time: G1 > G2 and G3 > G4. The use of CTM tools may stimulate more group dialogue behaviours under the same team composition. Because the consensus of this tool was based on real-life knowledge, sensory skills, and experience, everyone had a chance to mentally experience nothingness and emptiness; thus, achieving resonance in the team was easy. Moreover, in a short time, the standardism was removed in various fields. Consequently, the willingness of people to share ideas with each other increased.

10 Conclusion

This research investigated whether different team composition models and the use of different conceptual integration tools influenced the creative and practical results of creativity under different variables and tested whether CTM tools caused the teams to conduct processes by using the design of different communication models. The overall creativity and communication effectiveness of design ideas were different. From the research results, we obtained the following three conclusions:

1. In terms of creative innovation, no data trends were obtained and the analysis results did not achieve a significant level; thus, we cannot confirm whether the CTM tool is superior to the KJ method, which generally guides students to use creative thinking. In terms of practicality, the practical improvement achieved with the CTM tools was superior to that achieved with the KJ method. The practical improvement results obtained with the two methods exhibited a significant difference.
2. We could not confirm the relationship between the composition of different teams and the innovative and practical performance of the teams because statistical significance was not reached.
3. According to the results, CTM tools may stimulate team conversations, clearer problem convergence processes, task-oriented communication, and negative social–emotional communication behaviour.

References

Amabile, T.M.: The social psychology of creativity: a componential conceptualization. J. Pers. Soc. Psychol. **45**(2), 357 (1983)

Amason, A., Sapienza, H.: The effects of top management team size & interaction norms on cognitive and affective conflict. J. Manag. **23**, 496–516 (1997)

Brown, T.: Design thinking. Harvard Bus. Rev. **86**(6), 84 (2008)

Buckley, F.J.: Team Teaching-What, Why, and How?. Sage, Thousand Oaks (1999)

Cookson, Jr.: The Challenge of Isolation. http://www.teachingk-8.com/archives/your_first_year/the_challenge_of_isolation_by_peter_w__cookson_jr.html. Accessed 28 May 2008

Cross, N., Dorst, K., Roozenburg, N.: Research in Design Thinking. Delft University Press (1992)

Csikszentmibalyi, M.: Creativity: Flow and the Psychology of Discovery and Invention. HarperCollins, New York (1996)

DeMeyer, A.C.L.: The flow of technological innovation in an R&D department. Res. Policy **14** (6), 315–328 (1985)

Eisenhardt, K.M., Kahwajy, J.L., Bourgeois, L.J.: Conflict & strategic choice how top management teams disagree. Calif. Manag. Rev. **39**(2), 42–62 (1997)

Finke, R.A.: Imagery, creativity and emergent structure. Conscious. Cogn. **5**(3), 381–393 (1996)

Fuhriman, A., Drescher, S., Burlingame, G.: Conceptualizing small group process. Small Group Behav. **15**(4), 427–440 (1984)

Gardner, H.: Creating Minds. Basic Books, New York (1993)

Heider, K.L.: Teacher isolation: how mentoring programs can help. Curr. Issues Educ. **8**(14) (2005). http://cie.ed.asu.edu/volume8/number14/. Accessed 23 June 2005

Johansson, F., Tillman, M.: Medici-ilmiö: Huippuoivalluksia alojen välimaastossa. Talentum (2005)

Kalay, Y.E.: Evaluating and Predicting Design Performance. Wiley, Hoboken (1992)

Knight, D.J.: Performance measures for increasing intellectual capital. Strategy Leadersh. **27**(2), 22–27 (1999)

Leenders, R.T.A., Van Engelen, J.M., Kratzer, J.: Virtuality, communication, and new product team creativity: a social network perspective. J. Eng. Tech. Manage. **20**(1–2), 69–92 (2003)

Moenaert, R.K., Caeldries, F., Lievens, A., Wauters, E.: Communication flows in international product innovation teams. J. Prod. Innov. Manag. **17**(5), 360–377 (2000)

Mohrman, S.A., Cohen, S.G., Mohrman, A.M.: Designing Team-Based Organization: New Forms for Knowledge Work. Jossey-Bass, San Francisco (1995)

Oxman, R.: Think-maps: teaching design thinking in design education. Des. Stud. **25**(1), 63–91 (2004)

Schön, D.A.: The Design Studio: An Exploration of its Traditions and Potentials. International Specialized Book Service Incorporated, Portland (1985)

Shah, J.J., Vargas-Hernandez, N., Summers, J.D., Kulkarni, S.: Collaborative sketching (C-Sketch)– An idea generation technique for engineering design. J. Creative Behav. **35**(3), 1–31 (2001)

Shaplin, J.T., Olds, H.F.: Team Teaching. Harper & Row, New York (1964)

Tschimmel, K.: Design thinking as an effective toolkit for innovation. In: ISPIM Conference Proceedings. The International Society for Professional Innovation Management (ISPIM), p. 1 (2012)

West, S.S.: Student Perceptions of Teaching Effectiveness. Texas A&M University, Texas (1990)

Development of a Visualization System to Analyze Student-Teacher Conversations

Jun Iio[1]([⊠]) ⓘ and Ryuichi Sugiyama[2] ⓘ

[1] Chuo University, Shinjuku-ku, Tokyo 162-8478, Japan
iiojun@tamacc.chuo-u.ac.jp
[2] PADECO, Co. Ltd., Minato-ku, Tokyo 105-0004, Japan
rsugiyama@padeco.co.jp

Abstract. Rwanda is a low-income country in Africa. It is a small sized country that has experienced a rapid growth in its economic and social sectors since the genocide in 1994. The country aims to transform the society from agriculture-based to knowledge-based with middle-income status by 2035. To meet the demand of well-educated citizens required to achieve this goal, a complete curriculum reform was performed in 2016. This required teachers to employ active learning during their lessons, to prepare students for jobs that have not yet been created. From 2017 to 2019, Japan and Rwanda have conducted a joint project, which provided on-the job training for in-service teachers to equip them with the necessary active learning skills. Several conversations between students and teachers during practical lessons were transcribed through the activities of this project. Subsequently, we developed a system that visualizes the trends in these conversations from the transcribed data of each lesson to objectively verify if teachers appropriately engage students in active learning. The system generated various meaningful images. This was our first attempt to effectively guide in-service teachers to transform their mode of teaching. This paper presents the background of our study, the architecture of the prototype system, and an overview of the pre-trials on 75 lessons.

Keywords: Visualization system · Discourse analysis · Teacher education

1 Introduction

Rwanda is a small, landlocked, agrarian country located in the central part of Africa. Even though it possesses limited exploitable natural resources, its political stability following the 1994 genocide against the Tutsi has ensured its economic growth. During the period of 2002–2016, the growth rate of the annual average gross domestic product reached 7.8%, which exceeded the Sub-Saharan Africa average (World Bank 2017). Rwanda aspires to transform its economy from an agriculture-based with low-income status to a knowledge-based with a middle-income status by 2035 and to a high-income status by 2050 (Ministry of Education of Rwanda 2017). This national aspiration demands highly educated human resources and a consequent significant paradigm shift of the school education system in Rwanda. Teachers are requested to foster students for jobs that have not yet been created yet. Moreover, students are expected to address

© Springer Nature Switzerland AG 2020
P. Zaphiris and A. Ioannou (Eds.): HCII 2020, LNCS 12206, pp. 45–58, 2020.
https://doi.org/10.1007/978-3-030-50506-6_5

unpredictable problems generated in the future society. Thus, in 2016, the Government of Rwanda (GoR) completely revised the pre-primary, primary, and secondary school curriculum. Additionally, a new curriculum named as competence-based curriculum (CBC) was introduced.

CBC requires teachers to apply "learner-centered pedagogy" or "active learning" to improve the logical thinking and problem-solving skills of students rather than the conventional "rote learning." The GoR has provided a series of nationwide CBC induction trainings for all in-service teachers, to equip them with such new teaching approaches. However, Iwasaki et al. (2019) observed a negative tendency in their discourse analysis, which was conducted after the induction training in 2017; they reported that student-teacher conversations during lessons were ineffective and that students only participated passively during these lessons.

Under these circumstances, the Japan International Cooperation Agency and the GoR have conducted a joint project to change and improve the mode of teaching for the CBC in the subjects of mathematics and science for upper primary and secondary schools, from 2017 to 2019. The project provided on-the-job training for in-service teachers of selected pilot schools. Mathematics and science education advisors were sent to these schools on a weekly basis to provide guidance on improving the quality of the mathematics and science lessons.

We collected several records of student-teacher conversations in the classrooms through the intervention of this project, to monitor the improvements in the lessons conducted in the pilot schools. A total of 75 case studies were stored in our database. Thus, we required a user-friendly system to interpret the results of the discourse analysis for Rwandan teachers and educators, who were not familiar with such an analysis. To address this need, we developed a prototype system that visualizes the implicit structure of the discourse data.

This study is the first attempt to use student-teacher conversation records to visually understand the difference between effective and redundant lessons. We expect to deduce an appropriate structure for good lessons through this study, to effectively guide and enable teachers to conduct high-quality CBC lessons in Rwanda.

Following the literature survey presented in Sect. 2, we explain the need of visualization system in Sect. 3. Thereafter, an overview of the prototype system is described in Sect. 4. In Sect. 5, a few results from the visualization of 75 cases are discussed. Finally, Sect. 6 provides a summary and presents the future works.

2 Related Work

Discourse analysis has been widely used in several studies to review structures and the sequences of talks and conversations. In the field of education research, Flanders (1960) developed the famous Flanders system of interaction analysis to classify verbal behaviors of teachers and students in a classroom. It provided significant insights for the development of analytical systems and improvement of classroom instructions (Amatari 2015). Since this remarkable work, various researches have proposed an analytical system to understand the tendencies of conversations in lessons, according to the context and purpose of the research. However, introduction of educational technologies in lessons has been changing the interaction patterns. Students often communicate with computers in recent classrooms and such behaviors reduce conversation with teachers. It prevents to apply traditional discourse analysis in classrooms.

On the contrary, the conventional discourse analysis is still useful in developing countries due to the shortage of the advanced teaching and learning materials. We can find several researches applying discourse analysis to review the structure of conversations in lessons in Africa. Ikeya (2012) proposed a coding rule to classify the classroom talks of teachers and students during the analysis of mathematics lessons in Zambia. Yamashita et al. (2017) and Iwasaki et al. (2019) referred to this coding rule and conducted a discourse analysis in Rwanda. These studies attempted to extract tendencies from the distribution of classified talks.

Recent technology has provided different insights for analyzing talks. Various studies have discussed the potential and advantages of visualizing conversation analyses.

Choi (2015) created a tool named "Interactional Discourse Lab" (IDlab) to analyze discourse data, and he published it as an open-source software[1]. IDlab provides several functions for the discourse analysis, and it can be widely implemented for various purposes because it is freely downloadable and modifiable. However, it requires conversational data, which includes the name of the speakers. In our study, personal information of teachers and students were anonymized; thus, we could not adopt IDlab.

González-Howard (2016) discussed the interactional patterns in scientific arguments conducted on social networking services. He also proposed methods for visualizing the interactions during such arguments (González-Howard 2019). His study provides a network visualization similar to that provided by us; however, his network graph is a sociogram, and it basically represents the relation between individuals.

Similar network graphs have been provided by Yamada et al. (2019). They analyzed the number of students working as staff in the active learning class and cooperating with their colleagues. Their analysis was based on the postings on a bulletin board, and they confirmed that the instructor mediated the communication between student staff. In their discussion, they proposed several network graphs based on their analysis to represent the relations between participants of the discourse.

There are several aspiring challenges associated with improving the quality of education by developing measures and tools to evaluate the interactions between teachers and students. Lee and Irving (2018) proposed a novel evaluation tool named "classroom discourse analysis tool." Similar visual analyzing tools have also been proposed by Gómez-Aguilar (2009, 2011, and 2015).

3   Problems

To sort out teachers' and student's verbal behaviors in lessons, we originally followed the discourse analysis adopted by Yamashita et al. (2017). This analytical system provides a coding rule for teachers' and students' talks. Conversations in lessons were

---

[1] https://interactionaldiscourselab.net.

transcribed and classified for teachers and students separately based on the coding rule. Then the codes were aggregated to review their frequencies and distributions in lessons. The results obtained from this procedure were like the one shown in Table 3 in session 5. When Yamashita et al. applied this method, it simply and clearly revealed some negative tendencies in Rwandan lessons and thus it was easily understood by Rwandan teachers and educators.

Therefore, we decided to use the same discourse analysis during the project to monitor improvements of lessons. We elaborated their examples of each code to the ones frequently occurred in Rwandan lessons as shown in Tables 1 and 2, respectively. We observed some changes in the distribution of codes on our lesson practices given by this analysis. However, it was difficult for us to judge if the changes moved to the positive or negative direction. Particularly, the system did not provide the procedure to analyze the interactions between these teachers' and students' talks. Teachers hardly understand how they have to improve their conversations in lessons. We required a user-friendly system to interpret the results of the discourse analysis for Rwandan teachers and educators.

Table 1. Teacher code list

Code	Acronym	Examples of talks
Explanation	Xpl	We are going to…
Closed Question	CQ	What is the topic?/One times three is equal to?/Who can tell us the content of this lesson? (one correct answer)
Open Question	OQ	Why? (invite diverse answers/thinking of learners)
Rephrase teacher	Rph-T	How can we sustain the environment?/What can we do to stop deforestation? (replace teacher's question or statement with simple/easy words the learners understand)
Rephrase student	Rph-S	Student: Rain takes away soil / Teacher: Rain causes soil erosion. (Teacher gives technical terms or generalize students' statement)
Call attention	Agr	Are we together?
Point student	Po	(names of students)
Confirmation	Cmf	Is it true?/Do you understand?
Instruction	Inst	You form the groups./Write./Do the exercise
Encouragement	Enc	Clap for him./Very good./Wonderful
Justification	Jst	Okay./Not./Here is the correct
Clap	Cl	–
Inaudible	Imp	–
Others	Oth	Greeting, etc.

Table 2. Learner code list

Code	Acronym	Examples of talks
Yes/No answer to teacher	Yn-T	Yes./No
Yes/No answer to other students	Yn-S	
One term answer to teacher	Num-T	One./Integers./-1 times -1./Ten point five
One term answer to other students	Num-S	
Question to teacher	Qst-T	What is the meaning of R (Real number)?
Question to other students	Qst-S	
Opinion to teacher	Op-T	Thank you for the explanation. I think you are right
Opinion to other students	Op-S	because...
Incomplete answer	Inc	Subt...
Repeating or just reading	Rd	Just repeat or read sentences or numbers
Silent to teacher	Na-T	(No responses against what the teacher said)
Silent to another student	Na-S	(No responses against what students said)
Point student	Po	(names of students)
Presentation	Pr	(explanation on findings, solution, etc.)
Clap	Cl	–
Writing or gesture to teacher	Wri-T	(Write something on black board, Obey to instruction, Point out numbers or places)
Writing or gesture to other students	Writ-S	
Inaudible	Imp	–
Others	Oth	–

4 Prototype System

We developed a visualization system to analyze student-teacher conversations. An overview of the prototype system and its architecture are presented in this section.

4.1 System Overview

Figure 1 presents screenshots of the prototype system. The screen on the left in Fig. 1 prompts users to upload coded data in a comma-separated-values (CSV) format. In addition, it illustrates the method to prepare the CSV data from original coded data in a Microsoft Excel format.

If the uploaded data file is appropriately formatted, calculation proceeds on the server-side. The data file is divided into two parts: discourse codes of the former half of the lesson and discourse codes of the latter half of the lesson. After separating the data file in these two parts, the system draws the code-transition graphs based on each discourse data. The right part of Fig. 1 depicts an example of the results, which consists of two code-transition graphs.

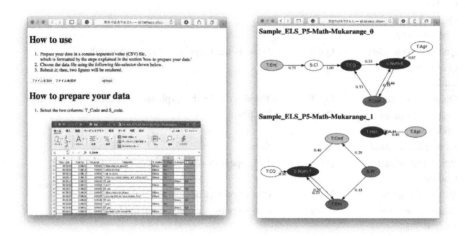

Fig. 1. Screenshots of the prototype system. Users prepare their data in CSV-format and upload the data to the system (left). On uploading correct data, code-transition graphs are displayed (right).

4.2   Data Format

All video-recorded lessons were initially transcribed by Rwandan surveyors. In Rwanda, English is used as an instructional language in schools, except for lower primary level (i.e., grades one to three). The project targeted upper primary (i.e., grades four to six) and secondary (i.e., grades seven to twelve) classes; these students are basically taught in English. Teachers occasionally used local language in cases where students appeared to misunderstand the teachers' instructions. In such cases, the surveyors translated the local language to English. The surveyors assigned initial codes according to the coding rules shown in Tables 1 and 2. Subsequently, secondary reviewers in Japan with similar coding experience checked the transcripts and codes. In cases where the code to be assigned to the transcripts was uncertain, the Japanese supervisors in the project determined the code.

As the codes were prepared for teachers as well as students, the original discourse-code data involves two columns: the first column is the code sequence of teacher's talks and the second column is that of students' talks (as shown in Fig. 2). As the visualization system only requires these two columns, users need to create the CSV formatted data of these columns from the original data.

Fig. 2. Example of original coded data that contains two key columns titled "T_Code" (teacher's code) and "S_Code" (students' code).

Note that the labels "T_Code" and "S_Code" are required in the first row. The system omits the first row of the uploaded data. Hence, the code data placed in the first row are not used in the calculation.

4.3 System Architecture

The prototype system is written in PHP. However, the PHP code is only a driver and the interface between a web server and calculation scripts. The uploaded data is passed to a shell script which divides the former and the latter parts of the discourse in the lesson (the reason of this division is explained in sub-Sect. 4.5) and transfers them to the ruby scripts.

The primary calculations are conducted by a sequence of ruby scripts. First, a ruby code extracts the paired T_Code and S_Code. The pairs are aggregated, and their probability of occurrence is calculated. According to the results, the dot scripts for drawing two code-transition graphs are created. Finally, the code-transition graphs are drawn using the dot command from GraphViz tools (see Fig. 3) as PNG image files.

After the images are created, the system returns the PNG images of code-transition graphs to the users.

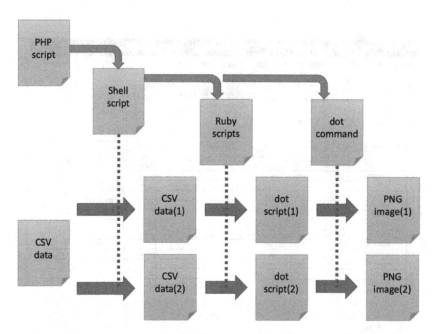

Fig. 3. Structure of data processing. The PHP script drives a shell script. Ruby scripts convert the data into dot scripts. Finally, the dot command creates PNG images according to the dot scripts.

4.4   Code-Transition Graph

Figure 4 presents an example of a code-transition graph. This graph contains eight nodes, which indicate frequently occurring codes in the discourse.

Only the codes whose probability of occurrence is more than 0.03 appear in the code-transition graph. The colors of nodes indicate their probability of occurrence; the white node indicates a value less than 0.06, light gray node indicates a value less than 0.09, gray node indicates a value less than 0.12, and navy blue one indicates a value exceeding 0.12.

The numbers drawn along with arrows represent the transition probabilities. The transition probability $P_T(A, B)$ from code A to code B is calculated using the following equation.

$$P_T(A, B) = (\# \text{ of codes } B \text{ which appears just after the code } A)/(\# \text{ of codes } A) \quad (1)$$

To simplify the code-transition graph, arrows are only drawn if their transition probability is greater than 0.25.

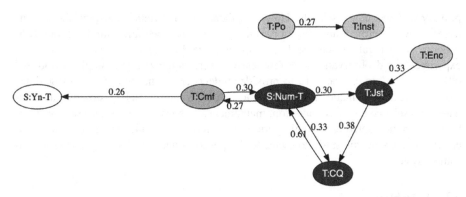

Fig. 4. Example of a code-transition graph. It contains eight codes that have relatively high probabilities of occurrence. The arrows with numbers indicate the transition frequencies.

4.5 Tuning

Throughout our experiments, we needed some tuning on the prototype system.

Eliminating Irrelevant Codes. We observed that a few codes, such as PO (point student), appear frequently, regardless of the context of the lesson. These codes significantly influence the shape of the graph. However, these talks are not directory links to teaching and learning process. Therefore, we decided to eliminate these codes from the graph to extract essential conversations that characterize the lessons.

Breakdown of the Lesson. A lesson in primary and secondary schools usually comprises three parts: "introduction," "body," and "summary and conclusion." As "body" is the main part of a lesson, we anticipated that tendencies or characteristics of each lesson appear strongly in the "body" part. To clearly extract the characteristics, we decided to divide the codes into first and second half of a lesson to analyze the tendencies in each part after several initial tests. This was done because

1) The graph of an entire lesson including all codes generalizes the tendencies. Graphs of each lesson are highly similar;
2) Separating codes into three or more parts considerably simplifies the analysis of the tendencies. Additionally, the graphs are considerably similar.

5   Overview of Results

This section presents an overview of the results of our investigation employing the prototype system. It discusses several typical examples from 75 cases.

5.1 Preliminary Analysis

First, we reviewed the generated graphs to verify the effectiveness of the visualization system. Samples were collected from the mathematics and science classes conducted in primary and secondary schools. However, there was a variation between the lessons targeted by the project and the transcribed lessons. This variation hindered our verification. In general, a science lesson involves various learning activities such as experiments and observations. A few lessons were organized as a single period and others involved double periods, to provide students additional time for investigations. Conversely, a mathematics lesson tends to involve a more standard structure as compared to a science lesson. In addition, mathematics lessons in the primary schools were basically implemented as a single period. Therefore, we decided to review the mathematics lessons in this study to evaluate the potential and effectiveness of the visualization system.

5.2 Case Study

Grade six mathematics lessons from different schools recorded in June 2019 were selected for this examination as their lesson topics were similar each other. In total, six samples were in our database, and the results of the aggregation of the discourse analysis are presented in Table 3. The project supported schools A, C, and D. School B was supported by another aid program. Thus, these schools received intensive assistance to improve their lessons. Schools E and F received common induction trainings provided by the GoR (they are referred to as 'control' in the table).

Table 3. Distribution of codes observed in six mathematics lessons in 2019.

School		School A		School B		School C		School D		School E		School F	
Type		Pilot		Other aid		Pilot		Pilot		Control		Control	
Evaluation		Excellent		Excellent		Fair		Fair		Poor		Poor	
Code		#	%	#	%	#	%	#	%	#	%	#	%
Teacher	Xpl	7	7.2	30	18.4	19	9.5	6	6.5	9	3.0	16	18.8
	CQ	23	23.7	37	22.7	71	35.5	13	14	66	21.9	11	12.9
	OQ	2	2.1	1	0.6	2	1.0	0	0.0	3	1.0	0	0.0
	Rph-T	0	0.0	1	0.6	17	8.5	0	0.0	23	7.6	2	2.4
	Rph-S	0	0.0	2	1.2	4	2.0	1	1.1	3	1.0	4	4.7
	Agr	3	3.1	10	6.1	17	8.5	5	5.4	15	5.0	1	1.2
	Po	0	0.0	12	7.4	19	9.5	20	21.5	17	5.6	13	15.3
	Cmf	36	37.1	35	21.5	12	6.0	13	14.0	46	15.2	11	12.9
	Inst	15	15.5	16	9.8	17	8.5	13	14.0	44	14.6	13	15.3
	Enc	3	3.1	6	3.7	13	6.5	13	14.0	15	5.0	0	0.0
	Jst	2	2.1	8	4.9	0	0.0	1	1.1	38	12.6	5	5.9
	Cl	0	0.0	0	0.0	0	0.0	0	0.0	0	0.0	0	0.0
	Imp	1	1.0	0	0.0	0	0.0	0	0.0	0	0.0	0	0.0
	Oth	5	5.2	5	3.1	9	4.5	8	8.6	23	7.6	9	10.6
	Total	97	100.0	163	100.0	200	100.0	93	100.0	302	100.0	85	100.0

(continued)

Table 3. (*continued*)

School		School A		School B		School C		School D		School E		School F	
Type		Pilot		Other aid		Pilot		Pilot		Control		Control	
Evaluation		Excellent		Excellent		Fair		Fair		Poor		Poor	
Code		#	%	#	%	#	%	#	%	#	%	#	%
Student	Yn-T	23	32.9	11	16.9	8	9.4	2	3.8	7	5.2	5	11.4
	Yn-S	0	0.0	0	0.0	1	1.2	0	0.0	0	0.0	0	0.0
	Num-T	21	30.0	31	47.7	48	56.5	27	51.9	73	54.5	17	38.6
	Num-S	2	2.9	0	0.0	0	0.0	0	0.0	0	0.0	0	0.0
	Qst-T	0	0.0	0	0.0	1	1.2	0	0.0	0	0.0	0	0.0
	Qst-S	0	0.0	0	0.0	0	0.0	0	0.0	0	0.0	0	0.0
	Op-T	5	7.1	21	32.3	8	9.4	1	1.9	11	8.2	1	2.3
	Op-S	0	0.0	0	0.0	0	0.0	0	0.0	0	0.0	0	0.0
	Inc	1	1.4	0	0.0	0	0.0	0	0.0	1	0.7	0	0.0
	Rd	1	1.4	1	1.5	3	3.5	0	0.0	18	13.4	8	18.2
	Na-T	0	0.0	0	0.0	0	0.0	0	0.0	0	0.0	0	0.0
	Na-S	0	0.0	0	0.0	0	0.0	0	0.0	0	0.0	0	0.0
	Po	0	0.0	0	0.0	0	0.0	0	0.0	0	0.0	0	0.0
	Pr	1	1.4	0	0.0	0	0.0	7	13.5	0	0.0	3	6.8
	Cl	1	1.4	0	0.0	1	1.2	3	5.8	0	0.0	0	0.0
	Wri-T	7	10.0	0	0.0	0	0.0	0	0.0	0	0.0	0	0.0
	Writ-S	1	1.4	0	0.0	0	0.0	0	0.0	0	0.0	0	0.0
	Imp	1	1.4	0	0.0	1	1.2	0	0.0	0	0.0	1	2.3
	Oth	6	8.6	1	1.5	14	16.5	12	23.1	24	17.9	9	20.5
	Total	70	100.0	65	100.0	85	100.0	52	100.0	134	100.0	44	100.0

These lessons were observed by Japanese education experts involved in the project either directly or through videos. They subjectively evaluated the lessons based on their experience and impression and agreed that the lessons in schools A and B were "excellent" in quality, whereas those of schools C and D were "fair" and those of schools E and F were "poor."

Figure 5 presents the graphs of the six lessons generated by the visualization system. In each lesson, the left graph represents the code-transition pattern in the first half of the lesson, and the right side depicts that of the second half. The graphs for "excellent," "fair," and "poor" lessons are arranged in the upper, middle, and lower rows, respectively.

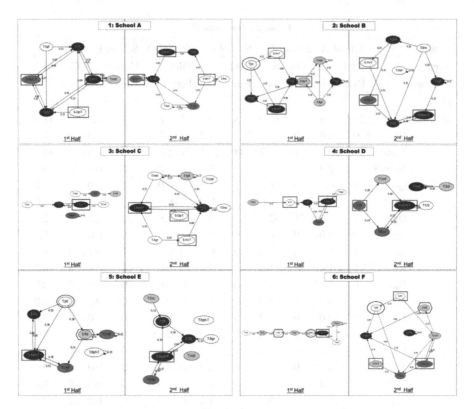

Fig. 5. Graphs of mathematics lessons generated via the visualization system. The left graph in each lesson represents the code-transition pattern in the first half of the lesson, and the right side represents the second half.

We examined if these graphs could represent meaningful conversation patterns to differentiate between good and bad lessons. We first noticed that the excellent lessons result in more complicated polygonal shape graphs in the first as well as second halves, as compared to other lessons. Conversely, the visualization system tended to create linear shape graphs for the fair and poor lessons, particularly in the first half of the lesson. This difference appeared to be caused by the appearance of "S_Code" nodes (indicated by the rectangular shape in the graphs). This implies that excellent lessons actively engaged students in learning, which corresponded to the impression of the experts.

We also observed that "S:Rd" (indicated by the hexagon) and "T:Jst" (indicated by the oval) generally appeared in the graphs for poor lessons. "S:Rd" represents the verbal behavior when students repeat what the teacher and other students have said. This is commonly referred to as a "chorus answer," which symbolizes "rote learning." "T:Jst" is assigned when a teacher justifies if the answer is correct or not. This is also related to "rote learning" as students are not given opportunities to verify the answers by themselves. Thus, these two codes are not favorably applied in CBC lessons in most cases.

Table 4 lists the scores for each lesson, based on the above discussed findings. We attributed marks if the shapes were polygonal and according to the number of S_Code, except for "S:Rd." When "S:Rd" and "T:Jst" were found, we deducted marks. The results indicate that the scores are in agreement with the evaluation of the experts.

Table 4. Scoring of six lessons.

School	School A		School B		School C		School D		School E		School F	
Part	1st	2nd	1st	2nd	1st	2nd	1st	2nd	1st	2nd	1st	2nd
Shape	1	1	1	1	0	1	0	1	1	1	0	1
S_Code	3	3	3	3	1	3	2	2	1	1	1	3
S_Rd	0	0	0	0	0	0	0	0	−1	0	−1	−1
T_Jst	0	0	−1	0	0	0	0	0	−1	1	−1	−1
Sub-total	4	4	3	4	1	4	2	3	0	1	−1	2
Total	8		7		5		5		1		1	

6   Conclusions and Future Work

This case study reveals the potential of the visualization system. The shape of the graph could differentiate between effective and ineffective lessons. The scores obtained from an observation of the graphs were in agreement with the expert's evaluation. Therefore, our visualization system effectively disclosed the information structure of the discourses between teachers and students during mathematics classes at primary schools in Rwanda. This study presents six results among 75 case studies.

Three patterns were identified in our visualization: one for excellent classes, whose information structure provides polygonal code-transition graphs, and another for poor classes, which are represented by monotonous graphs. The remaining pattern represents the intermediate class between these two types.

This study is only the first step of this research, and further investigations will be required. For instance, the problem of whether other classes can be evaluated using our system will be examined. Additionally, evaluation criteria to determine the score of polygonal features must be discussed. The automatization of the transcription and coding processes by adopting artificial intelligence technologies remains as our future work.

References

World Bank: Rwanda economic update, tenth edition: World Bank Rwanda, Kigali (2017)

Ministry of Education of Rwanda: Education sector strategic plan 2018/19-2023/24, Author, Kigali (2017)

Iwasaki, Y.K., Sugiyama, R., Matsuzuki, S., Ono, Y., Ohara, K., Bevan, G.: Quality learning for all: policy and practice of school-based continuous professional development in Rwanda. In: Huber, T., O'Meara G.J. (eds.) Teacher Education at the Edge: Expanding Access and Exploring Frontiers, pp. 179–230. Information Age Publishing, Charlotte (2019)

Flanders, N.A.: Teacher influence, pupil attitudes, and achievement: final report: University of Minnesota, Minneapolis (1960)

Amatari, O.V.: The instructional process: a review of flanders' interaction analysis in a classroom setting. Int. J. Second. Educ. **3**(5), 43–49 (2015)

Ikeya, T.: Zambia kouki kiso kyouiku ni okeru sugakuka jugyo bunseki no kenkyu: Kyoushi‧ seito no gengo katsudou wo chushin ni [Lesson analysis of mathematics at upper basic education in Zambia: focusing on verbal interaction between teacher and students]. J. Int. Dev. Coop. **15**(1/2), 125–140 (2009)

Yamashita, K., Mutsinzi, A., Abe, T., Ono, Y., Sugiyama, R., Matsuzuki, S.: Implementation of competence-based curriculum (CBC) in Rwanda: the case of mathematics. Paper prepared for annual Conference of the Distance Education and Teachers' Training in Africa, Kigali (2017)

Choi, S.: The case for open source software: the interactional discourse lab. Appl. Linguist. **37** (1), 100–120 (2015). https://doi.org/10.1093/applin/amv066

González-Howard, M., McNeill, K.L.: Using social network analysis to examine interactional patterns in scientific argumentation. Paper presented at the Annual Meeting of the American Education Research Association, Washington, D.C. (2016)

González-Howard, M.: Exploring the utility of social network analysis for visualizing interactions during argumentation discussions. Sci. Educ. **103**, 503–528 (2019). https://doi. org/10.1002/sce.21505

Yamada, M., Tohyama, S., Kondo, H., Ohsaki, A.: A case study of multidimensional analysis for student-staff collective cognitive responsibility in active learning classroom. Int. J. Educ. Media Technol. **13**(1), 115–124 (2019)

Lee, S.C., Irving, K.E.: Development of two-dimensional classroom discourse analysis tool (CDAT): scientific reasoning and dialog patterns in the secondary science classes. Int. J. STEM Educ. **5**, 5 (2018). https://doi.org/10.1186/s40594-018-0100-0

Gómez-Aguilar, D.A., Therón, R., García-Peñalvo, F.J.: Semantic spiral timelines used as support for e-learning. J. Univ. Comput. Sci. **15**(7), 1526–1545 (2009). https://doi.org/10. 3217/jucs-015-07-1526

Gomez-Aguilar, D., Conde-Gonzalez, M., Theron, R., Garcia-Peñalvo, F.: Supporting moodle-based lesson through visual analysis. In: Campos, P., Graham, N., Jorge, J., Nunes, N., Palanque, P., Winckler, M. (eds.) INTERACT 2011. LNCS, vol. 6949, pp. 604–607. Springer, Heidelberg (2011). https://doi.org/10.1007/978-3-642-23768-3_93

Gómez-Aguilar, D.A., Hernández-García, Á., García-Peñalvo, F.J., Therón, R.: Tap into visual analysis of customization of grouping of activities in eLearning. Comput. Hum. Behav. **47**, 60–67 (2015). https://doi.org/10.1016/j.chb.2014.11.001

Voice Interaction for Training: Opportunities, Challenges, and Recommendations from HCI Perspective

Irina Kondratova[1]([⊠]) [iD] and Bruno Emond[2] [iD]

[1] Digital Technologies Research Centre, National Research Council Canada, Fredericton, Canada
Irina.Kondratova@nrc-cnrc.gc.ca
[2] Digital Technologies Research Centre, National Research Council Canada, Ottawa, Canada
Bruno.Emond@nrc-cnrc.gc.ca

Abstract. This paper examines voice interaction requirements in the context of learning and training. The authors reviewed relevant publications, focusing on usability and user experience with conversational interfaces, including speech and chat interfaces. We examined technology trends and limitations, HCI research on speech interfaces, usability evaluations of conversational interfaces in training, including formal evaluation methodologies, and our research projects on voice interaction for military and law enforcement training. Examples of voice technology applications in several domains are provided, along with a set of recommendations for successful design, evaluation and use of voice interaction in training applications.

Keywords: Conversational interface · Speech interface · Evaluation · Design recommendations

1 Introduction

Voice interaction presents considerable opportunity to enhance virtual, mixed and augmented reality training, including interactions between synthetic agents and trainees [1–5]. It is projected that conversational platforms will drive the next big paradigm shift in how humans interact with the digital world and simulations [6, 7]. Currently, conversational interfaces are mostly implemented in spoken or written natural language. In time, other input/output mechanisms will be added to exploit sight, taste, smell and touch for multi-channel interaction. Expanded sensory channels will support advanced software capabilities, such as emotion detection through facial expression analysis. Emotion detection could enable delivery of better feedback during training and real-time training modifications based on trainees' responses [8]. Already, a combination of speech with other input modalities (such as gesture, gaze, etc.) offers a flexible and integrated set of interaction tools for Augmented Reality (AR), and Virtual Reality (VR) training applications [4, 9–14].

© Springer Nature Switzerland AG 2020
P. Zaphiris and A. Ioannou (Eds.): HCII 2020, LNCS 12206, pp. 59–75, 2020.
https://doi.org/10.1007/978-3-030-50506-6_6

The next section of the paper provides insights into technologies that enable conversational user interfaces and voice interaction.

2 Natural Language Interface

Natural language interfaces (NLIs), such as conversational and voice interfaces, are becoming widely used for interaction with digital systems such as Virtual Assistants (VA), and in immersive training applications [4, 6, 7, 15, 16]. In particular, natural language (or voice) interfaces have been widely applied to military training applications, including: Navy training [9], ASPO Navy training [10], tactical language and culture training for the Army [17], mixed reality training for tactical army and police training [11, 12], negotiations over tasks in hybrid human-agent teams [18], and in virtual environments for dismounted soldier simulation, training, and mission rehearsal [19].

2.1 Conversational Interface

Gartner technology report projects that conversational platforms will drive the next big paradigm shift in how humans interact with the digital world and simulations [6]. A conversational system takes a question or a command from the user in natural language (text or speech), and respond by executing a function, presenting content or asking for an additional input. Candello and Pinhanez [20] define a conversational interfaces as "computational systems which interact with humans through dialogues using spoken or written natural language." In time, other input/output mechanisms will be added to broaden the scope of channels for interaction between humans and digital technologies, to exploit sight, taste, smell and touch for multi-channel interaction. The use of expanded sensory channels could support advanced capabilities, such as emotion detection through facial expression analysis. Emotion detection will be beneficial in training applications, and could help a system to provide a proper feedback during training, and modify the training based on trainees' responses to achieve better training outcomes.

A current trend in the conversational user interface is an increase in use of chat-based (text-based) interfaces (chatbots over voice interfaces [7, 21]. In some military training simulations, chatbots are designed to act as synthetic teammates that can comprehend human language, generate synthetic language and have the ability to manage a chat dialogue [22]. By using chatbots, designers try to avoid challenges of speech processing, and use digital text as the most direct and unambiguous form of communication. These systems utilize natural language processing (NLP) for interactions between computers and human (natural) languages in order to extract commands and intentions directly from users' textual messages.

While text-based interfaces are less prone to challenges related to environmental context, such as ambient noise, and to speech recognition errors, there still remain certain challenges with language understanding for a chat text-based interface [7, 23]. For example, in many real-life scenarios, a complex text chat dialog could break down due to simple misunderstandings, because of unexpected turns of phrase, or due to the fact that the user's context cannot be fully elicited from a text conversation. Other challenges include technical design challenges, such as chatbots being too responsive, not understanding user utterances, lack of personality consistency for the bots, as well as providing too many options in the form of buttons for users, that could negatively affect user experience with text-based interfaces [20]. To improve design of the text-based conversational interfaces, researchers [20] conducted studies, including a Wizard of Oz study (a study in which participants think they interact with a computer system, but it is actually being operated by a human), that allowed them to understand some general human-machine conversation patterns, and map typical users' reactions to chatbot's answers. Researchers collected data including user questions to build the conversational system corpus, and, after thorough data analysis, derived a set of fourteen design recommendations for text-based conversational interfaces. Some of these context-free design recommendations [20] are directly applicable to speech interfaces, and will be discussed in the next sections of the paper.

Whilst research demonstrates that for training applications the text-based communication with synthetic agents tends to be more reliable than voice-based communication [24], it is not the best fit in time pressured situations or tasks, or in mobile learning applications. Ideally, in such situations, a speech interface with continuous speech recognition capability, supported by an Automatic Speech Recognition (ASR) system, would allow trainees to speak naturally to a machine teammate, or to a simulator.

2.2 Speech Interface

Speech interfaces are systems that use speech recognition and either pre-recorded or synthesized speech to communicate or interact with users [25, 26]. Speech can be used as a primary input or output, or in a two-way dialogue. Systems using speech synthesis as their primary medium for communicating information to the user [27] are similar to audio user interfaces [26]. In this type of interaction, speech is only produced by the system, as an output. Speech can also be used solely as an input modality, and is often used in "command and control" of systems or devices (e.g., in Smart House applications).

The user's voice input is recognized by automatic speech recognition (ASR) and natural language understanding (NLU) components of the system to identify user intent, or commands. Automatic speech recognition (ASR) is the use of computer hardware and software-based techniques to identify and process human voice. Despite being a focus of significant research efforts since the 1980s, current capabilities of both NLP and ASR technologies are limited. Even the most advanced modern ASR systems frequently have troubles with word classification accuracy and limited semantic understanding of continuous speech [16].

Speech interfaces include spoken dialogue systems (SDS), where the system and the user can interact through spoken natural language. The dialogue can range from structured question-answer pairs, where the system keeps the initiative and the user responds to "How may I help you?" questions, and systems where the user can formulate wider queries and the system computes the optimal next move, to systems which allow some user initiative by permitting users to interrupt and change a task.

In some instances speech interfaces are used in conjunction with other input/output modalities to facilitate interaction [26]. For example, speech can be used as either input or output along with graphical user interfaces (GUIs), which is commonly seen in speech dictation for word-processing tasks, or in a screen-reading technology to support the navigation of websites. SDS's such as personal Voice Assistants (e.g., Siri, Google Voice Assistant, Alexa, etc.) can display content and request user input through the screen, as well as through speech [28].

Research demonstrates [5] that voice input, as a natural mode of interaction, presents considerable opportunities to harness virtual, mixed and augmented reality (VR, MR and AR) based interactions. Language processing software can support two-way communications between synthetic agents in simulations and humans [22]. A rapid proliferation of high-tech microphones and speech processing systems in consumer gaming devices, including the Microsoft's Kinect, points to a growing opportunity for game designers to build novel experiences around voice interaction, and make conversational interfaces and interaction with virtual characters more enjoyable and engaging for users [29]. For example, in military training applications for serious games, a speech recognition engine and a Microsoft Kinect system were successfully incorporated into the Training in Urban Operation Skills simulator to train the communication skills in a virtual world simulation [30], and to train police officers in the police trainer [12].

In the next section of the paper we provide some examples of real-life implementation of voice user interactions and conversational interfaces in training and learning applications, highlighting technology benefits, challenges and limitations.

3 Voice Interaction for Training–Examples, Challenges and Limitations

3.1 Voice Interaction for Serious Gaming

Our expertise in developing voice interaction for serious gaming was acquired in several development projects for voice enabled military and law enforcement training. For the first project, a team of researchers and developers at NRC, in partnership with the Department of National Defense Canada, developed a mixed reality technology prototype for close-quarters combat training [11]. The IRET training platform enabled novel interaction techniques in an immersive game environment, including voice command and simulated weapons, such as laser rifles, and an electronic flashbang, incorporated into a serious gaming platform with intelligent agents, cognitive models, and a mobile control interface for instructors. The IRET platform was designed to allow infantry, law enforcement, or public safety personnel to train using a virtual environment in a manner similar to training in a real physical environment (which could be quite costly).

Adding voice interaction capabilities to the IRET system allowed more natural interaction with the game for trainees. The major challenge with speech recognition in the IRET training context is that the environment is extremely noisy by nature of the tasks - soldiers shouting commands to enemy combatants, sounds of gun fire and explosives - thus presenting significant challenges to the efficacy of voice-based interaction. Ambient noises, such as gunfire, flash bangs, and the simultaneous shouts of multiple soldiers, negatively impacted achievable speech recognition rates. Additionally, the negative impact of different speaking styles on the accuracy of speech recognition–e.g., shouting commands versus talking versus whispering - was significant. Furthermore, trainees were exposed to various stress inducing battle situations which were negatively impacting speech patterns, and resulted in lower accuracy of speech recognition. Ambient noise, speaking style, stress-induced speech variations, and accents (many trial users of the system were Francophones), were some of the challenges for speech recognition presented by the IRET simulator. To overcome these challenges, we implemented several multimodal interaction options to improve speech-based interactions by exploiting complementary to speech modalities, such as simulated electronic weapons, and touch interfaces for dynamic game interaction, and including remote input instructor interface that allowed to operate the virtual environment in case speech recognition fails.

The usability of IRET components was validated through a pilot study in a laboratory setting with volunteer participants recruited from among the course instructors at CFB Gagetown, Canada [11]. The participants conducted several simulated training scenarios in a large HCI laboratory. Results of the pilot evaluation indicate that speech-based interaction is critical in ensuring the realism of the interaction with the virtual environment. The accuracy of speech recognition can vary significantly across training conditions, but can be easily compensated for by using complementary modalities, such as the tablet-based trainer interface that enables remote-input to complement speech interactions.

Based on the successful evaluation of the IRET prototype, NRC research extended the IRET platform to include MS Kinect gesture and motion interface for the law enforcement scenario. In addition, we supplemented the speech user interface with easy to use grammar builder interface that provided instructors with the option to make changes within the system vocabulary to reflect different police usage scenarios [12]. All animations and actions that the simulator can perform could be initiated through the trainer control interface. Additionally, the simulator actions initiated by trainees through spoken commands could be overridden by instructors (e.g. when the speech recognition system did not accurately process the command), or reversed by instructors to create "on-the-fly" training situations that test the responsiveness and judgment of the trainees, as, for example, introducing non-compliant behaviour for the virtual game characters. Other research studies [4, 21, 31–35] also investigated speech as an input in a military VR and in Virtual Assistant applications and revealed the following overall challenges in using voice interaction when talking to a computer versus a human, as depicted in Table 1.

Table 1. Overall challenges in using voice interaction when talking to a computer versus a human.

People use shorter commands and fewer relative terms when they talk to a machine because they think the machine would not understand more complex commands
Since the short commands are not detailed enough, there is often a need to repeat or elaborate in order to complete the task, resulting in taking longer and using more commands to complete the task when talking to a computer
To reduce the task completion time, a more open and general task grammar needs to be developed using the most popular commands that users find the most intuitive and easy to learn
People can easily change words in the question or change commands when talking to human teammates, but machines might not understand the language or the meaning
While there are known issues with the accuracy of speech recognition for non-native speakers of the language (accents) or for native speakers under stress; some improvements in accuracy could be made by utilizing a modern speech recognition engine based on large datasets
A major research challenge is building a machine speech interface that can understand their own limitations during the course of a dialog with the human and direct the conversation back to a more familiar area
Ambient noise, speaking style, stress-induced speech variations, and accents as well as factors such as stress, fear, sickness, and pain may induce voice variability and reduce accuracy of speech recognition
One of the common challenges is low user acceptance of synthetic voices for virtual agents

These general limitations of the NLP and ASR technologies should be addressed when using voice interfaces for serious games. However, there are some additional technology limitations associated with military training environments that should be considered, when deciding on the use of voice interaction in a military training simulator. For example, in a military setting it is typical to use word commands within a constrained and specified lexicon, instead of continuous speech, thus it is more effective to program ASR systems to understand discrete military commands using a limited defined lexicon. Research demonstrates [16] that a limited ASR lexicon is likely to show better overall performance and robustness in challenging environments, since applying a lexicon tailored to a particular application domain helps to limit NLP search space, resulting in better recognition accuracy for discrete commands. Additionally, tailoring speech commands to preferences and conventions of potential users allows for better user retention for the language used for commands, resulting in fewer errors, and more efficient operations.

Another challenge in applying speech recognition in military simulators is that most people operating on military communication systems do not use a normal speech grammar. Along with some verbal commands, they often use acronyms, sometimes spelled out and sometimes said as a word, and not necessarily an English word [36]. This type of domain specific communication could significantly impair many conventional speech recognition systems. However, some modern speech recognition engines allow for creation of the specialized grammar and lexicon, making it easier to constrain a vocabulary and create special grammar rules directly applicable to the military communication [9, 10, 36]. An additional significant challenge for successful continuous speech recognition in military operations and training is noise from background sounds such as engine noise, gunfire, echoes, and reverberations. To overcome this challenge it is advisable to use a push-to-talk or a voice activated microphone, and a headset that cancels external noise [37].

In respect to the user's acceptance of synthetic voice technologies, it was demonstrated [38] that more human-sounding synthesizers evoke stronger emotional responses, than less humanlike synthesizers. Further, comparisons between less and more human-like voices showed that more human-sounding synthesizers evoke significant emotion-related facial muscle and pupil responses in humans. In addition, the lexical content of the messages has a strong effect on people, and the impression of the voice quality is affected by the content of the spoken message. Usability evaluations confirmed that while users perceive high-quality synthetic voices as nearly equal to professional voice talent, pairing a synthetic face with a natural voice was problematic for some users [38, 39].

3.2 Conversational Agents for Learning

The conversational agent system is based on a form of intelligent agent system, or on the pedagogical (or educational) agent that provides an important paradigm for use in learning environments, such as a humanlike tutor. Conversational agents can deliver formative assessment, constructive learning, and adaptive instruction. A pedagogical agent is a type of educational software, with human characteristics or appearances, that are designed to facilitate and support learning [40]. The pedagogical agent sometimes has a simulated human-like interface that facilitates interactions between the learner and the content, where the role of the agent focuses primarily on delivering instructional content [41].

Researchers [42] envision the future for learning technologies where the learner will be holding conversation in natural language via multimedia channels with conversational agents, and interact with them as they interact with teachers and tutors. As a prototype of these future technologies, the authors [42] developed the Autotutor system that simulates a human tutor by holding a conversation with the learner in the natural language, via text-based interface, with a dialogue delivered through an animated conversational agent that has text-to-speech engine, facial expressions, gestures and pointing. This agent could be augmented with sensing devices and signal processing models that classify affective state of learners, with emotions being classified based on several features, including dialogue patterns during tutoring, the content covered, facial expressions, speech parameters, body posture, haptic mouse pressure, and keyboard pressure. The system analyzes the patterns and classifies the input into basic affective states of the user such as confusion, frustration, boredom, interest, excitement, and insight. Based on the detected student's emotional state, such a system can adjust learning dialogue options to improve learning outcomes.

Others investigated the use of Embodied Pedagogical Agents (EPAs) in computer-based serious gaming learning environments to facilitate learning in the absence of live instruction [8]. EPAs are used as the communication layer within an Intelligent

Tutoring System (ITS), where human intervention is replaced by Artificial Intelligence methods. Research demonstrates that the elements of the persona affect agent's characteristics that optimize learning outcomes. This involves both physical elements of appearance (i.e., voice inflection, hairstyle, clothing, ethnicity, gender, etc.), and stereotype perceptions associated with appearance (i.e., usefulness, credibility, and intelligence). The modality of a real-time feedback from an agent can affect learning outcomes in a simulation-based training scenario. Results of the study [8] demonstrate that learners receiving feedback as an audio source showed better decision-making performance compared to learners getting feedback via printed text. These results fit well within the theory of multimedia learning [43]. The theory implies that learners can process information more efficiently when material and feedback are presented as a mix of visual and auditory stimuli. The notion is to exploit alternative modes of feedback presentation (e.g., acoustic, visual, etc.) to avoid cognitive overload due to modality effects encountered when presenting guidance information in the same format as other elements in the training environment.

Other results [8] show that EPA feedback leads to better performance than audio only feedback (Voice of God, VOG). Authors reason that the performance-based feedback given in the VOG group can be perceived as if it is directly part of the scenario, being implicitly delivered as natural component of the game environment. In the VOG scenario, participants are reacting to a feedback provided by the Intelligent Tutoring System, as if it is part of the game, due to removal of the EPA introduction that notifies the user that explicit information will be provided. This finding may help to explain why individuals in the VOG condition scored the highest during the training scenario, while producing the worst transfer and retention results on subsequent assessments.

There is additional evidence [44] that students prefer spoken to written information. This is best achieved by proving an opportunity for the trainee to verbally interact with the avatar-based system [45]. Another important aspect is users' acceptance of the Virtual Agent's voice, for example, during the user evaluation of the educational Virtual Assistant [45], the users found the avatar's tone of voice either very appealing, quite appealing or moderately appealing. This was unexpected by the authors, as they were not entirely satisfied with the quality of the avatar's voice and previous research [46–48] has found that subjects respond to artificial voices in the same way as they do with real human voices.

4 HCI Research for Speech Interface

Despite recent rapid proliferation of speech interfaces and Virtual Assistant technologies, a recent comprehensive review of HCI aspects related to voice interaction development and deployment identified some serious gaps in speech UI design approaches [49]. The authors of the review conducted a thematic analysis of a large number of recent research papers on the topic, and found that current speech HCI research mainly focuses on several key topics: system speech production, modality comparison, user speech production, assistive technology and accessibility, design insight, experiences with interactive voice response (IVR) systems, using speech technology for development, people's experiences with intelligent personal assistants (IPAs), and how user memory affects speech interface interaction.

4.1 Challenges for Design and Evaluation of Speech Interface

Researchers [49] identified some major challenges for HCI research on speech interfaces. In particular, the authors found the lack of design research for speech interfaces, and the lack of clear design considerations, or robust heuristics, for developing user centred speech interactions, while noting that some research sources do exist to support the design of voice user interfaces (VUIs) [50]. With the popularity of speech interfaces increasing, there is a real need for this type of design knowledge to guide improvements and development of future speech interfaces. The authors [49] also found that the majority of papers in their comprehensive review only investigated single user interactions. The study of situations that include multiple users and multiple speech interfaces would be highly valuable, as this is likely to become more common in the near future, especially for training applications.

Researchers [49] identified several gaps in HCI speech research, such as the need to develop theories of speech interface interaction, grow critical mass in this domain, increase design work including design guidelines, and expand research from single to multiple users interaction contexts. In addition, authors highlight the goal to improve speech interface evaluation and measures, such as reliability, validity and consistency, with a focus on deployment of speech interfaces in real-life conditions, and improving capability to build fully functional speech interfaces for research purposes.

4.2 Design Guidelines for Speech Interface

A recent paper by a team of HCI researchers [51] attempts to address the abovementioned lack of design guidelines for speech user interfaces by analyzing how existing graphical user interface (GUI) guidelines could be applicable to speech interfaces. The authors focus on hands-free speech interactions, and on design guidelines that help to solve usability and learnability issues for hands-free voice interaction. These issues are critical for training applications, as speech interfaces are now widely used in a mobile context, and in the context of AR/VR interactions. Based on an extensive review of research papers [51], the authors conducted a thorough analysis of how GUI design principles could apply to hands-free voice interfaces. Their resulting design guideline analysis, along with our suggestions on possible design solutions for speech UIs, are listed in Table 2.

The design guidelines listed in Table 2, while not exhaustive, could form a basis for a broader set of recommendations to assure successful design and implementation of speech user interfaces for training. We suggest adding to this list a set of context-free design recommendations for conversational interfaces [20] that are applicable to speech user interfaces (see Table 3).

Table 2. GUI design guidelines applicable for speech interface, based on [51].

GUI guideline	Application example
G1: maintain visibility/feedback of system status	Users need to know when to speak. Provide system feedback and transparency to users on what UI could do and if the system understood their spoken input
G2: provide mapping between system and real world	Give users an example of a familiar interaction in the world that could increase task performance and ease of use, while unfamiliarity with the interaction style can decrease usability
G3: support user control and freedom	Provide users with control over voice interaction. For example, an option to interrupt a voice dialogue by saying "help" or "home" can improve performance and user satisfaction
G4: maintain consistency throughout the interface	Use consistent familiar commands for system interaction. Users need to know what to expect from the system
G5: help to prevent user errors	Design voice interaction to prevent user errors (including NLP errors), this will increase trust in the speech interface
G6: design for recognition rather than recall	Using audio as the only output modality increases cognitive load, providing too many options to a user increases the struggle of recalling them
G7: increase flexibility and efficiency of use	Speech interaction can improve efficiency. Users are able to just say their requests, instead of searching through a GUI
G8: maintain minimalism in design and dialogue	Having five or more options could help users' ability to remember earlier options; provide feedback statements to confirm that the speech interface understood the user correctly
G9: allow users to recognize and recover from errors	Design to allow users to recognize and recover from errors, e.g. provide feedback and use "help" or "home" commands
G10: provide training, help and documentation	Provide contextual help progressively throughout interaction

Table 3. Design recommendations for speech interface, based on [20].

Design recommendation	Reasoning
DR1: The system must be prepared to be challenged by the users. Repeated user questions may have a more complete answer and new information	Sometimes users could repeatedly ask for more information because they were not satisfied with the first answer, or thought the system did not understand them
DR2: The system could help users to ask new questions	Sometimes the users do not have a basic knowledge of a particular domain that would give ideas of what to ask, the system should help them
DR3: The system must engage a user in the conversation	This could improve the flow of the conversation

(*continued*)

Table 3. (*continued*)

Design recommendation	Reasoning
DR4: The system should identify the context of the question	Users do not always include all context in the dialogue, the system should help them in identifying the context
DR5: People expect the system to respond as a person even knowing that it is not a person	Questions allocated to the system should be answered even if the system don't have enough information (e.g. "I don't have enough information" answer)
DR6: The system should introduce itself as a machine	This could make it easier for the users to cope with how the system understands utterances and punctuations and try to be extra careful with pronunciation
DR7: Dialogue and vocabulary should consider the ambiguity of words	Words with double meanings should be carefully considered not to confuse users

5 Automated and Semi-automated Dialogue Evaluation Methods

The other sections of the paper provide a set of recommendations and HCI guidelines for the successful use of voice interaction in training applications. These recommendations are based on technology trends and limitations, HCI research on speech interfaces, usability evaluations of conversational interfaces in training, and our research projects on speech for military and law enforcement training. HCI design principles are abstract user interface design guidelines based on best practices, empirical evidence, or derived from empirically validated psychological theories. If followed, these principles produce user interfaces that are easy to learn and use, help the users complete their tasks efficiently, and do not mislead the users, violate their expectations, or lead users to commit errors.

In addition, the current section examines methods and techniques for the automated and semi-automated evaluation of speech dialog management systems for training. As a complement to the HCI guidelines and recommendations, automated and semi-automated evaluation methods aim at determining quality metrics for dialog management systems based on a set of system performance measures, coupled with user and/or expert assessments. Excluding language acquisition, dialog management systems to support training and learning can be applied in two contexts: 1) as pedagogical agents, acting as tutors [52, 53], or 2) as synthetic agents simulating teammates [1, 2, 54], or opponents [9, 10].

According to Deriu et al. [55], in addition to allowing a comparison between different systems, dialog system evaluation should meet the following requirements: 1) evaluation should be automatic (cost and effort reduction), 2) it should be repeatable, 3) it should be correlated with human judgments, and 4) it should allow for the identification of specific dialog management components responsible for the good or poor quality of a system [55]. Automatized methods either focus on whole system evaluation using models of human judgments, models of user behaviours interacting with a system, or system feature-specific methods [55]. We list several commonly applied dialogue evaluation frameworks below.

The PARAdigm for Dialogue System Evaluation (PARADISE), is a prototypical automated evaluation framework. Its evaluation of a dialog management system provides a score of user satisfaction using a utility measure combining the maximization of task execution at the minimal cost. The success of task execution is calculated using a Kappa coefficient over a confusion matrix of tasks successes and failures. The cost of the dialog is normally calculated using efficiency measures such as the number of sentences required to execute the task, and qualitative measures such as response delay, repair ratio, and inappropriate response ratio. The performance of a system is modelled as a weighted function of a task-based success measure and dialogue-based cost measures, where weights are computed by correlating user satisfaction with performance [56]. The method applies to a whole dialog as the unit measure.

The interaction quality (IQ) framework [57] follows the approach of PARADISE, but the dialog performance score is applied on dialog exchange, at any time during an interaction, and not to the overall dialog. The framework also uses expert annotations on user interactions, and not user satisfaction data. The analysis shows that there is a high-correlation between the user satisfaction data and the expert judgments. This method is less costly and intrusive for the user.

However, automated and semi-automated dialog management system evaluation methods have been developed and applied almost exclusively for non-training contexts, with the exception of the Wolska et al. simulated human-machine (Wizard-of-Oz) corpus for learning to do mathematical proofs [58, 59]. This situation is well exemplified by the availability of human-machine communication dialog corpus, which covers mostly application domains such as restaurant and travel information, and open-domain knowledge retrieval interface to search engines [59].

It appears that any evaluation of dialog management systems designed for training and learning would require a different set of success evaluation criteria, than for systems designed to achieve the completion of simple transactions, like booking a flight. In particular, training applications supported by dialogue management systems need ultimately to be evaluated in terms of learning efficiency and effectiveness metrics with a scope extending over a set of learning tasks. Training applications supported by dialogue management systems are clearly feasible, given their successful deployment in the last 20 years [52]. However, the current feasibility is bound to relatively conversational context with imprecise verbal content, low-to-medium user knowledge about a topic, and literal replies from both the learner and the dialog management system [60].

6   How to Design Usable Voice Interactions for Training

To complement the fore mentioned design guidelines and recommendations for speech interface (Tables 2 and 3), and based on lessons learned from the usability evaluations for speech and conversational UIs for training, we propose the following list of

Table 4. Additional recommendations for designing usable voice interactions for training

Design recommendation	Reasoning
For closed domain training choose speech recognition software that supports customizable grammar and lexicon	In many domains it is common to use discrete word commands within a constrained lexicon instead of continuous speech
Develop the lexicon and grammar in collaboration with the intended users of the training system	This will positively impact user acceptance and usability of the system
If applicable, include gesture commands and commands for other modalities suitable for interaction with the system	This can improve the quality of speech recognition and user experience with the system
Incorporate the noise level and the acoustic conditions of a real-life environment into the training system	This improves realism of training and user satisfaction
Use voice activated or push button microphones and headsets that cancel external noise	This helps to improve the quality of speech recognition in noisy environment
Use human-sounding voice synthesizers	Pairing a synthetic face with a natural voice could be problematic for some users
Use automated and semi-automated methods in determining quality metrics for your speech interface	This testing should be incorporated in the set of system performance measures coupled with user and/or expert assessments

additional recommendations that will help to design and successfully deploy usable voice interactions for training (see Table 4).

7   Conclusions

Our paper examined design challenges, limitations, existing guidelines, and recommendations for voice interaction in the context of learning and training, with a focus on usability. We examined existing HCI research guidelines for speech and text chat interfaces, and summarized lessons learned from usability evaluations of conversational interfaces in training, including our own research projects for voice interaction in military and law enforcement training. As a result, guidelines, recommendations and evaluation methodologies were identified and proposed that hold a potential to help with practical design of usable voice interaction for learning and training. We also found that there is still a great deal of research work that needs to be done in this area, especially research related to HCI aspects of speech and conversational user interfaces for training, focussing on their effect on learning outcomes.

References

1. Ball, J., et al.: The synthetic teammate project. Comput. Math. Organ. Theory **16**, 271–299 (2010). https://doi.org/10.1007/s10588-010-9065-3
2. Demir, M., McNeese, N.J., Cooke, N.J., Ball, J.T., Myers, C., Friedman, M.: Synthetic teammate communication and coordination with humans. In: Proceedings of the Human Factors and Ergonomics Society, pp. 951–955 (2015). https://doi.org/10.1177/1541931215591275
3. Jenkins, M., Wollocko, A., Negri, A., Ficthl, T.: Augmented reality and mixed reality prototypes for enhanced mission command/battle management command and control (BMC2) execution. In: Chen, J.Y.C., Fragomeni, G. (eds.) VAMR 2018. LNCS, vol. 10910, pp. 272–288. Springer, Cham (2018). https://doi.org/10.1007/978-3-319-91584-5_22
4. Stedmon, A.W., Patel, H., Sharples, S.C., Wilson, J.R.: Developing speech input for virtual reality applications: a reality based interaction approach. Int. J. Hum. Comput. Stud. **69**, 3–8 (2011). https://doi.org/10.1016/j.ijhcs.2010.09.002
5. Weiss, B., Wechsung, I., Kühnel, C., Möller, S.: Evaluating embodied conversational agents in multimodal interfaces. Comput. Cogn. Sci. **1**, 6 (2015). https://doi.org/10.1186/s40469-015-0006-9
6. Cearley, D.W., Burke, B., Walker, M.J.: Top 10 strategic technology trends for 2018. Gart. Res. **10**, 1–9 (2017)
7. Klopfenstein, L.C., Delpriori, S., Malatini, S., Bogliolo, A.: The rise of bots: a survey of conversational interfaces, patterns, and paradigms. In: Proceedings of the 2017 Conference on Designing Interactive Systems, pp. 555–565 (2017)
8. Goldberg, B., Cannon-Bowers, J.: Feedback source modality effects on training outcomes in a serious game: pedagogical agents make a difference. Comput. Hum. Behav. **52**, 1–11 (2015). https://doi.org/10.1016/j.chb.2015.05.008
9. Emond, B., et al.: Adaptive training simulation using speech interaction for training navy officers. In: Interservice/Industry Training, Simulation, and Education Conference (I/ITSEC), pp. 2924–2934. National Training and Simulation Association, Orlando (2016)
10. Emond, B., Kondratova, I., Durand, G., Valdés, J.J.: A multi-role reconfigurable trainer for naval combat information operators. In: Interservice/Industry Training, Simulation and Education Conference (I/ITSEC), p. 14. National Training and Simulation Association, Orlando (2018)
11. Fournier, H., Lapointe, J.-F., Emond, B., Kondratova, I.: A multidisciplinary approach to enhancing infantry training through immersive technologies e-learning view project virtual reality interaction view project (2011)
12. Fournier, H., Lapointe, J.-F., Kondratova, I., Emond, B.: Crossing the barrier: a scalable simulator for course of fire training. In: Interservice/Industry Training, Simulation, and Education Conference, p. 10. National Training and Simulation Association, Orlando (2012)
13. Munteanu, C., Fournier, H., Lapointe, J.-F.J.-F., Kondratova, I., Emond, B.: We'll take it from here: letting the users take charge of the evaluation and why that turned out well. In: Proceedings of the ACM SIGCHI Conference on Human Factors in Computing Systems, CHI 2013 Extended Abstracts on Human Factors in Computing Systems, Paris, France, pp. 2383–2384 (2013). https://doi.org/10.1145/2468356.2468778
14. Yu, J., Wang, Z.F.: A video, text, and speech-driven realistic 3-D virtual head for human-machine interface. IEEE Trans. Cybern. **45**, 977–988 (2015). https://doi.org/10.1109/TCYB.2014.2341737
15. Hei, Z., Lvi, C., Pengi, D., Yu, D.: A speech recognition-based interaction approach applying to immersive virtual maintenance simulation (2017)

16. Barber, D., Wohleber, Ryan W., Parchment, A., Jentsch, F., Elliott, L.: Development of a squad level vocabulary for human-robot interaction. In: Shumaker, R., Lackey, S. (eds.) VAMR 2014. LNCS, vol. 8525, pp. 139–148. Springer, Cham (2014). https://doi.org/10.1007/978-3-319-07458-0_14

17. Johnson, W.L., Lester, J.C.: Face-to-face interaction with pedagogical agents, twenty years later. Int. J. Artif. Intell. Educ. **26**, 25–36 (2016). https://doi.org/10.1007/s40593-015-0065-9

18. Traum, D., Rickel, J., Gratch, J., Marsella, S.: Negotiation over tasks in hybrid human-agent teams for simulation-based training. In: Proceedings of Second International Joint Conference Autonomous Agents and Multiagent Systems - AAMAS 2003, p. 441 (2003). https://doi.org/10.1145/860575.860646

19. Knerr, B.W., Lampton, D.R., Thomas, M., Corner, B.D., Grosse, J.R.: Virtual environments for dismounted soldier simulation, training, and mission rehearsal: results of the FY 2002 culminating event. Army Research Inst Field Unit Orlando, FL (2003)

20. Candello, H., Pinhanez, C.: The role of dialogue user data in the information interaction design of conversational systems. In: Marcus, A., Wang, W. (eds.) DUXU 2018. LNCS, vol. 10919, pp. 414–426. Springer, Cham (2018). https://doi.org/10.1007/978-3-319-91803-7_31

21. Filar, B., Seymour, R.J., Park, M.: Ask me anything: a conversational interface to augment information security workers. In: Symposium Usable Privacy Security (2017)

22. Barnes, M.J., Chen, J.Y., Hill, S.: Humans and autonomy: implications of shared decision making for military operations (2017)

23. Hamilton, P.L., Cooke, N.M., Brittain, R.D., Sepulveda, M., Cooke, N.M., Sepulveda, M.: simulated operational communications and coordination integration for aircrew learning (SOCIAL). In: AIAA Modeling and Simulation Technologies Conference, pp. 1–21 (2013). https://doi.org/10.2514/6.2013-5228

24. Cooke, N.J., Demir, M., McNeese, N.: Synthetic teammates as team players: coordination of human and synthetic teammates (2016)

25. Clark, L.: Social boundaries of appropriate speech in HCI: a politeness perspective. In: HCI 2018, pp. 1–5. BCS Learning & Development Ltd. (2018). https://doi.org/10.14236/ewic/hci2018.76

26. Weinschenk, S., Barker, D.T.: Designing Effective Speech Interfaces. Wiley, New York (2000)

27. Aylett, M.P., Vazquez-Alvarez, Y., Baillie, L.: Interactive radio: a new platform for calm computing. In: Proceedings of the 33rd Annual ACM Conference Extended Abstracts on Human Factors in Computing Systems, pp. 2085–2090. ACM (2015)

28. Munteanu, C., et al.: Designing speech, acoustic and multimodal interactions, May (2017). https://doi.org/10.1145/3027063.3027086

29. Allison, F., Carter, M., Gibbs, M.: Word play. Games Cult. 155541201774630 (2017). https://doi.org/10.1177/1555412017746305

30. Muller, T.J., Van Den Bosch, K., Kerbusch, P., Freulings, J.H.: LVC training in urban operation skills. In: 2011 Summer Simulation Multiconference, SummerSim 2011, Co-located with 2011 SISO European Simulation Interoperability Work, Euro SIW, pp. 115–120 (2011)

31. Hura, S.L.: Usability testing of spoken conversational systems. J. Usability Stud. **12**, 155–163 (2017)

32. Latorre-Navarro, E.M., Harris, J.G.: An intelligent natural language conversational system for academic advising. Int. J. Adv. Comput. Sci. Appl. **6**, 110–119 (2015)

33. Loddo, I., Martini, D.: The cocktail party effect. An inclusive vision of conversational interactions. Des. J. **20**, S4076–S4086 (2017). https://doi.org/10.1080/14606925.2017.1352909

34. Reeves, S.: Some conversational challenges of talking with machines. In: Talking with Conversational Agents in Collaborative Action, Workshop at the 20th ACM conference on Computer-Supported Cooperative Work and Social Computing (CSCW 2017) (2017)

35. Ortiz, C.L.: The road to natural conversational speech interfaces. IEEE Internet Comput. **18**, 74–78 (2014). https://doi.org/10.1109/MIC.2014.36

36. Haggard, K.M.: Air support control officer individual position training simulation. Naval Postgraduate School Monterey United States (2017)

37. Khooshabeh, P., Choromanski, I., Neubauer, C., Krum, D.M., Spicer, R., Campbell, J.: Mixed reality training for tank platoon leader communication skills. In: 2017 IEEE Virtual Reality (VR), pp. 333–334. IEEE (2017). https://doi.org/10.1109/VR.2017.7892312

38. Ilves, M.: Human responses to machine- generated speech with emotional content (2013)

39. Case, J.E., Twyman, N.W.: Embodied conversational agents: social or nonsocial? In: 2015 48th Hawaii International Conference on System Sciences, pp. 491–496 (2015). https://doi.org/10.1109/HICSS.2015.65

40. Chou, C., Chan, T., Lin, C.: Redefining the learning companion: the past, present, and future of educational agents. **40**, 255–269 (2003)

41. Krämer, N.C., Bente, G.: Personalizing e-learning. The social effects of pedagogical agents. Educ. Psychol. Rev. **22**, 71–87 (2010). https://doi.org/10.1007/s10648-010-9123-x

42. Graesser, A., McDaniel, B.: Conversational agents can provide formative assessment, constructive learning, and adaptive instruction. In: The Future of Assessment, pp. 85–112. Routledge (2017)

43. Mayer, R.E., Moreno, R.: A split-attention effect in multimedia learning: evidence for dual processing systems in working memory. **90**, 312–320 (1998)

44. James-Reynolds, C., Currie, E.: EAI Endorsed Transactions Smart Feedback and the Challenges of Virtualisation. In: EAI Endorsed Transactions on Future Intelligent Educational Environments (2015). https://doi.org/10.4108/fiee.1.2.e6

45. Harvey, P.H., Currie, E., Daryanani, P., Augusto, J.C.: Enhancing student support with a virtual assistant. In: Vincenti, G., Bucciero, A., Vaz de Carvalho, C. (eds.) eLEOT 2015. LNICST, vol. 160, pp. 101–109. Springer, Cham (2016). https://doi.org/10.1007/978-3-319-28883-3_13

46. Von der Pütten, A.M., Krämer, N.C., Gratch, J., Kang, S.-H.: It doesn't matter what you are! Explaining social effects of agents and avatars. Comput. Hum. Behav. **26**, 1641–1650 (2010)

47. Hill, J., Randolph Ford, W., Farreras, I.G.: Real conversations with artificial intelligence: a comparison between human-human online conversations and human-chatbot conversations. Comput. Human Behav. **49**, 245–250 (2015). https://doi.org/10.1016/j.chb.2015.02.026

48. Cafaro, A., Vilhjálmsson, H.H., Bickmore, T., Heylen, D., Jóhannsdóttir, K.R., Valgarðsson, G.S.: First impressions: users' judgments of virtual agents' personality and interpersonal attitude in first encounters. In: Nakano, Y., Neff, M., Paiva, A., Walker, M. (eds.) IVA 2012. LNCS (LNAI), vol. 7502, pp. 67–80. Springer, Heidelberg (2012). https://doi.org/10.1007/978-3-642-33197-8_7

49. Clark, L., et al.: The state of speech in HCI: trends, themes and challenges (2018)

50. Pearl, C.: Designing Voice User Interfaces: Principles of Conversational Experiences. O'Reilly Media, Inc., Sebastopol (2016)

51. Murad, C., Munteanu, C., Clark, L., Cowan, B.R.: Design guidelines for hands-free speech interaction, August 2018. https://doi.org/10.1145/3236112.3236149

52. Nye, B.D., Graesser, A.C., Hu, X.: AutoTutor and family: a review of 17 years of natural language tutoring. Int. J. Artif. Intell. Educ. **24**, 427–469 (2014). https://doi.org/10.1007/s40593-014-0029-5

53. Rus, V., Graesser, A.C., Hu, X., Cockroft, J.L.: Standardizing unstructured interaction data in adaptive instructional systems. In: Sottilare, R.A., Schwarz, J. (eds.) HCII 2019. LNCS, vol. 11597, pp. 217–226. Springer, Cham (2019). https://doi.org/10.1007/978-3-030-22341-0_18

54. Freiman, M., Myers, C., Caisse, M., Halverson, T., Ball, J.: Assessing cognitive fidelity in a situation awareness process model. In: 2019 IEEE Conference on Cognitive and Computational Aspects of Situation Management, pp. 100–106 (2019). https://doi.org/10.1109/COGSIMA.2019.8724256

55. Deriu, J., et al.: Survey on evaluation methods for dialogue systems (2019). http://arxiv.org/abs/1905.04071

56. Walker, M.A., Litman, D.J., Kamm, C.A., Abella, A.: PARADISE: a framework for evaluating spoken dialogue agents (1997)

57. Schmitt, A., Ultes, S.: Interaction quality: assessing the quality of ongoing spoken dialog interaction by experts—and how it relates to user satisfaction. Speech Commun. **74**, 12–36 (2015). https://doi.org/10.1016/j.specom.2015.06.003

58. Wolska, M., et al.: An annotated corpus of tutorial dialogs on mathematical theorem proving. In: The International Conference on Language Resources and Evaluation (LREC), pp. 1007–1010 (2004)

59. Serban, I.V., Lowe, R., Henderson, P., Charlin, L., Pineau, J.: A survey of available corpora for building data-driven dialogue systems: the journal version. Dialogue Discourse **9**, 1–49 (2018). https://doi.org/10.5087/dad.2018.101

60. Graesser, A.C., Chipman, P., Haynes, B.C., Olney, A.: AutoTutor: an intelligent tutoring system with mixed-initiative dialogue. IEEE Trans. Educ. **48**, 612–618 (2005). https://doi.org/10.1109/TE.2005.856149

Abstract Thinking Description System for Programming Education Facilitation

Yasutsuna Matayoshi[✉] and Satoshi Nakamura[✉]

Meiji University, Nakano, Tokyo, Japan
yasutsuna.matayoshi@gmail.com, satoshi@snakamura.org

Abstract. Programming courses in universities generally teach how to solve problems. However, there are many beginners who fail to make programming well. This is because the beginners cannot be aware of abstract thinking related to the structure of the program, and cannot share abstract thinking with their instructors. In this paper, we propose a method to describe the structure of a program with native language comments in the code tree view and to simply change the structure of the program and the source code by drag-and-drop operation in the code-tree. With this method, beginners can easily organize their thoughts, and instructors can understand the level of understanding and thinking of beginners. We constructed a prototype system using our proposed method. The experiment indicated that it was possible to deepen the understanding of the beginners and utilize it for teaching.

Keywords: Abstract thinking · Programming education · Programming UX

1 Introduction

Courses on programming at universities often have more than 100 students in a class. In such a situation, it is almost impossible for instructors to teach classes according to the levels of understanding of each student. It is common that teaching assistants (TAs) are hired as support for this problem. However, since the number of TAs is limited in most cases, they often have to take care of multiple students at once. For example, in our department, six TAs are hired for supporting 120 students. In addition, every time they are asked questions, they need to read and understand source code their students wrote, which is often difficult to understand as it has variable declarations, variable initializations, description order, function scope, indentation, and functions and there are various ways to solve the problem. These are huge burdens to TAs (see Fig. 1).

On the other hand, many students do not fully understand the contents of the lectures and become frustrated at and find difficulty in programming. In other words, programming education has problems in that TAs have a hard time reading source code their students wrote and that students often find difficulty in programming.

© Springer Nature Switzerland AG 2020
P. Zaphiris and A. Ioannou (Eds.): HCII 2020, LNCS 12206, pp. 76–92, 2020.
https://doi.org/10.1007/978-3-030-50506-6_7

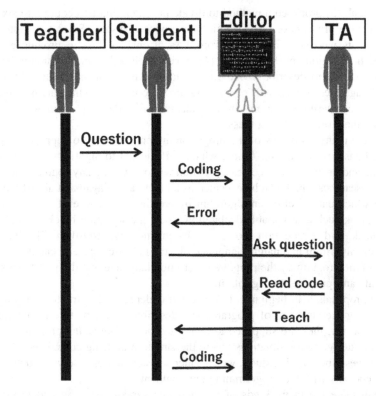

Fig. 1. Teaching flow of programming in the class at the university.

What is important in improving programming skills is to develop the ability to abstract and generalize complex processes. This process is called abstract thinking [1]. This paper focuses on abstract thinking at the time of programming as a solution to the problem in programming education. In general, TAs have excellent programming ability and are trained for abstract thinking. Therefore, if their students' abstract thinking can be directly shared with TAs, their burden to read the students' source code would be reduced. In addition, by trying to incorporate abstract thinking in source code, students can check on their understanding and improve their abstract thinking.

In this study, we propose a method to describe abstract thinking in the code tree and to enable TAs/students to edit the abstract thinking by drag-and-drop operation. We also implement a prototype system to test the usefulness of our method.

2   Related Work

There are many studies on the support for teachers and TAs in universities to give programming lessons to students. Durrheim et al. [2] proposed a system to guide to a correct answer by pointing out difference between a correct answer source code by a teacher and source code by a student in line units. As a study to improve efficiency of

TA, Kim et al. [3] proposed a method to divide programming procedure into six steps and manage the progress of the steps on their proposed system. Since this system can detect students who need assistance from TAs, it enables TAs to provide effective guidance. In addition, Nishida et al. [4] have developed a programming learning environment PEN to describe *xDNCL* that allows expression in Japanese in a short time. Although these systems have similar purposes to this study, they are not designed to facilitate answering questions from students while allowing them to think and understand the structure during class.

There are many proposals of the programming environment to support beginners. Patrice [5] has developed *AlgoTouch*, which is dedicated to algorithms for searching and sorting and designs and executes a program without writing any source code. There are some researches which can be executed as a block, and Kayama et al. [6] proposed a system which can describe an algorithm by creating a structure of a program as a structure block such as a variable declaration block, a calculation block, a conditional branch block, and a repetition block, and having nesting. *AlgoWeb* [7], which can describe the algorithm in a natural language like the proposed system, can describe the structure of the program by the program description language based on Portuguese and can execute and practice the algorithm.

These proposals help beginners to think and understand the structure of programs by visualizing the structure of programs and describing the structure in natural languages. However, they are supposed to be carried out before actual programming, so they are not designed for situations where the structure is being considered while the program is described. In this study, we consider a system to describe the structures in a way that coexists with the programming environment.

Though there are many kinds of research that support teaching and learning of programming, they have not succeeded in simultaneously supporting abstract thinking and programming of beginners. Therefore, in this study, we aim to realize a method to simultaneously support abstract thinking and programming from which both beginners and educators can benefit.

3 Proposal Method

3.1 Abstract Thinking and Its Script

In programming education, beginners first learn the easy level of basic variables, functions and simple arithmetic operations. As they learn, they go on to the more difficult levels of contents with conditional branches, arrays, repeat and creating classes. In addition, they need to be conscious of the goals of the program. In other words, they have to think about the flow of variables, the structure of classes, the decomposition of functions and reuse for efficient source code while writing the code. These ways of thinking are called abstract thinking [1]. In programming education, Abstract thinking is often required when solving advanced problems or new unit problems, so it is important to train this thinking.

A flowchart is often used as a description of abstract thinking. By modeling and designing with flowcharts, we can determine the structure and specifications and write high-quality programs without bugs. However, it is difficult and unrealistic for beginners because they need to learn a unique notation. On the other hand, a comment which can be described directly in the source code of a program can work as a method to describe processing simply. It can also be used easily by beginners because it can be described by a natural language which they use daily. However, there are problems such that it is troublesome to comment, specifications are not decided, and it is insufficient to show the structure.

Pseudocode is known as a notation for simply expressing the structure of a program. Pseudocode is described in both a natural language and source code, and is used to express algorithms. Figure 2 shows an example of the use of pseudocode for FizzBuzz. However, there is a problem that design errors can occur as the pseudocodes cannot confirm and execute the behavior in a real programming environment. Therefore, it is difficult for beginners to program while describing both pseudocode and source code.

In describing abstract thinking for considering program structure, it is important to comment on source code and to describe the structure of source code in correspondence with a natural language like pseudocode. In this paper, we propose a code tree method which displays the same structure as the actual source code by using natural language comments as tree nodes.

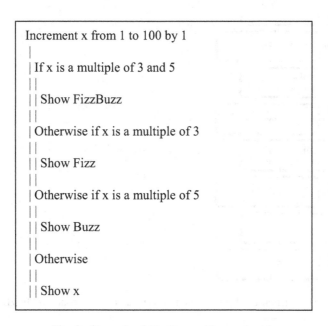

Fig. 2. Example of FizzBuzz with pseudocode

3.2   Code Tree

In order to realize abstraction of programs and abstraction-based teaching by TAs, we propose a programming mechanism in which each process of the source code is diagramed as a tree node and the program is abstracted by associating it with the node operations (see Fig. 3). In Fig. 3, the conditional branches in lines 3 to 7 of the right source code correspond to the nodes described as "If x is a multiple of 3 and 5" in the node of the left code tree. There are nesting and parent-child relation in the program, as the node of "Show Fizz" is the child node and "Otherwise if x is a multiple of 3" is the parent node. These nestings are especially important in the structure of the program, and it seems to lead to the understanding of abstract thinking to grasp these relations visually.

By making it possible to handle the code tree technique with the editor of the source code at the same time, it is expected that the understanding of the structure is deepened because of the substitution of nodes and the editing of parent-child relationships are possible with the nesting in mind. In addition, it is possible for educators to check how far beginners recognize the structure of the program by looking at the relationship between nodes of the code tree, which would make communication with students more smoothly than before.

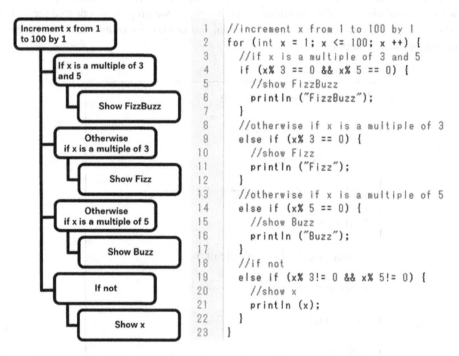

```
1   //increment x from 1 to 100 by 1
2   for (int x = 1; x <= 100; x ++) {
3       //if x is a multiple of 3 and 5
4       if (x% 3 == 0 && x% 5 == 0) {
5           //show FizzBuzz
6           println ("FizzBuzz");
7       }
8       //otherwise if x is a multiple of 3
9       else if (x% 3 == 0) {
10          //show Fizz
11          println ("Fizz");
12      }
13      //otherwise if x is a multiple of 5
14      else if (x% 5 == 0) {
15          //show Buzz
16          println ("Buzz");
17      }
18      //if not
19      else if (x% 3!= 0 && x% 5!= 0) {
20          //show x
21          println (x);
22      }
23  }
```

Fig. 3. The relationship between the tree view and source code (ex. FizzBuzz).

4   Prototype System

We developed a prototype system (see Fig. 4) with Processing [8], which is used in many universities.

The prototype system was implemented as a Web application. It was implemented using JavaScript and MySQL. The client-side is implemented in JavaScript, with an editor for inputting nested comments and code that can describe abstract thinking. It also edits and executes source code. The server-side is implemented in Node.js and MySQL, and stores the source code inputted by the user and performs syntax checking of the source code inputted.

A code tree showing the structure of the program is displayed on the left side of the system, an editor for writing source code in the center of the system, a processing execution screen on the right side of the system, and a console at the bottom of the system. A button at the top of the system lets you execute, stop, code completion, enable and disable code tree, and save. The code tree and editor are always synchronized, and if you rewrite one, the other is automatically updated. In the code tree, the text of the node can be rewritten, the node can be replaced, the nesting can be deepened, and new nodes can be added by a newline. When you swap nodes in the code tree, the source code is also swapped (see Fig. 5 and Fig. 6). The editor allows direct editing of source code. However, when the tree structure of the code tree such as "The number of open brackets does not match the number of close brackets" and "lack comments" is broken, the function of the code tree stops and it becomes impossible to change nodes. To solve this problem, it is necessary to work on the cause from the editor based on the displayed error message.

We also published our system on the Web[1].

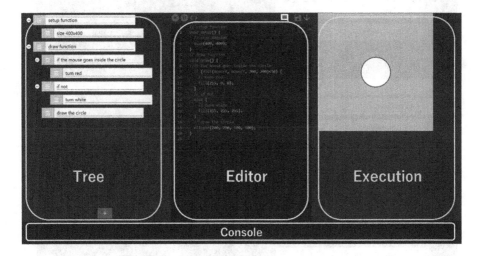

Fig. 4. A screenshot of the prototype system.

---

[1] https://boarditor.nkmr.io/.

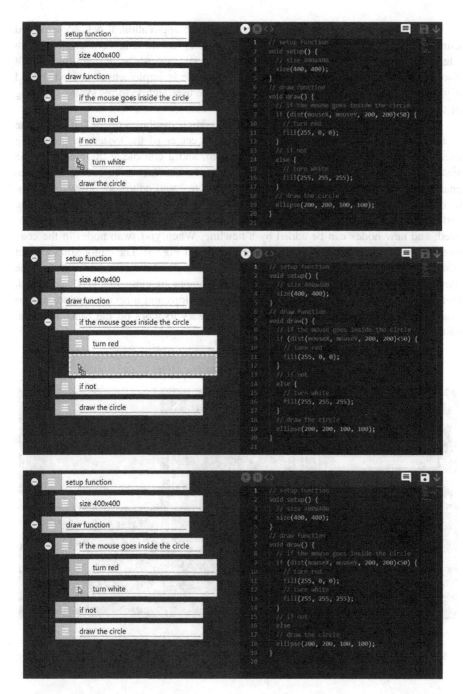

Fig. 5. An example of moving [turn white] node by drag-and-drop operation in the code tree. Then, the system automatically modified the source code.

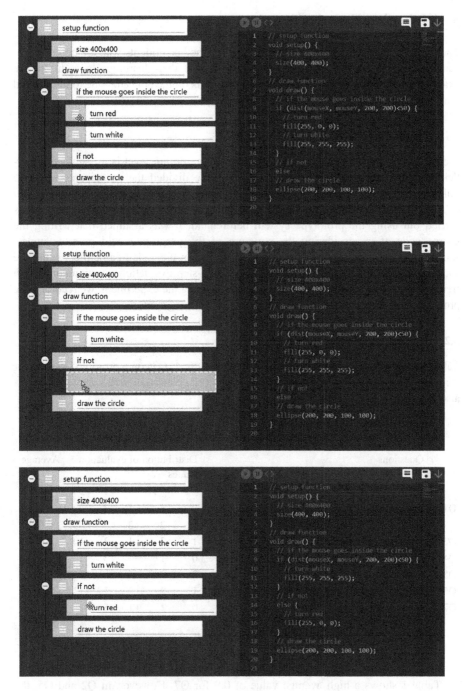

Fig. 6. An example of moving [turn red] node by drag-and-drop operation in the code tree. Then, the system automatically modified the source code.

5   Evaluation Experiment

The purpose of this experiment is to investigate whether students who are beginning to learn programming can use the system to support their learning. In addition, we examine whether the system makes it easier for TAs on the educator side to understand their students' thoughts and intentions in their questions.

5.1   Content of the Evaluation Experiment

We recruited nine university students whose programming level is a beginner as participants, and three graduate students as TA. We divided the participants into two different groups, one with the prototype system and the other without it. We asked them to solve two tasks with a time limit of 30 min per task. In addition, the tutorial was carried out using the prototype system beforehand. It was assumed that writing the source code after considering the structure of the program would promote understanding, so we instructed them to write comments in the code tree before writing the source code. At the end of the experiment, a five-step evaluation questionnaire and a free description questionnaire were conducted. During the experiment, we recorded the programming screen and checked the contents and programming.

5.2   Results of the Evaluation Experiment

Table 1 shows the results of a questionnaire survey (Q1–Q7) on a prototype system for students. The distribution evaluated by 5 stages (−2: Not at all well - 2: Very well) is also listed.

Table 1. Questionnaire survey on our system for students.

	Questions	Distribution of evaluation values					Average
		−2	−1	0	1	2	
Q1	Ease of use of the system	0	4	1	2	2	0.2
Q2	Ease of resolving of the system	2	2	2	3	0	−0.3
Q3	Smoothly solved in the system	1	3	1	3	1	0.0
Q4	Deeper understanding of the system	0	1	4	3	1	0.4
Q5	Speed of resolution in the system	2	2	4	0	1	−0.4
Q6	Do you want to continue using the system?	1	2	4	1	1	−0.1
Q7	Do you think you can improve your programming skills by continuing to use the system?	0	1	1	5	2	0.9

Table 1 shows a high average value of 0.9 for Q7. However, in Q2 and Q5, the average value became negative, and the result showed that the existing method was better than the proposed method.

Table 2 shows the average value of each question item obtained by subjectively dividing the students into a group that uses the code tree frequently (four participants) and a group that uses the code tree infrequently (five participants). The result found that the average value was higher in the group which used the code tree more frequently than in the group which used it less frequently.

We received many positive comments from students, such as "It was easy to write comments and understand what to do." and "It was easy because I could operate it intuitively". However, we also received proposals for better UI of the system and comments on other improvements such as "make programs tend to belong", "When it becomes long, it is difficult to correspond source code and comments."

Table 2. An average of each survey result depending on the usage frequency of the code tree.

	Q1	Q2	Q3	Q4	Q5	Q6	Q7
Group of high frequency in use	1.50	0.50	0.75	0.75	0.50	0.50	1.25
Group of low frequency in use	−0.80	−1.00	−0.60	0.20	−1.20	−0.60	0.60

Table 3 shows the results of a questionnaire survey (Q8–Q10) of TAs who used the system to answer questions from students. The result evaluated by 5 stages (−2: Not at all well - 2: Very well) is also listed. The result showed that only Q8, which is related to the discovery of mistakes, showed negative values. Q9 (about understanding) and Q10 (about classroom use) were positive.

There were favorable comments from TAs such as "It was easy to judge whether the students were worried about syntax or had difficulty in understanding the problem." "It was easy to check the code." and "The bug was easy to find". On the other hand, there were also negative opinions and reflection points such as "I actually had to see the source code.", "TAs can't fix code tree without understanding system specifications", and "I can't judge because there were few questions."

Table 3. Questionnaire survey for TA.

Questions		Average
Q8	The system is easier for students to spot mistakes	−0.3
Q9	The system is easier to understand the intent of the student's question	0.7
Q10	Do you want to use the system in the actual lesson?	1.0

5.3   Consideration of the Evaluation Experiment

Regarding the comparison between the existing method and the proposed method, the fact that Q4 on understanding the problem and Q7 on continuous use gained positive averaged evaluation values would be because the programming structure of the proposed method can be operated intuitively. On the other hand, the distribution of the evaluation values for Q2, Q3, and Q6, which are related to the ease of solving problems, was widened, and there may be individual differences. Q5 on the speed of the solution of the problem gained a negative evaluation value presumably because it took time to write comments in the proposed method. In addition, as a result of comparing the questionnaire results of two student groups divided by the frequency of code tree use, it was found that the group of high frequency in use gave high evaluation and felt the system favorably. This suggests that the proposed method can support programming learning of the beginners.

As a reason why the questionnaire evaluation Q8 of TA was low, it seemed to be a cause that there were many students who were good at programming and that there were not many questions on programming to TA. In addition, sometimes the system could not output errors due to bug, and thus the TAs could not answer questions from the students. The reason why the evaluation results of Q9 on understanding intentions and Q10 on use of the system in classes were high would be that it was possible to grasp the structure of the program in natural language thanks to the code tree. This suggests that the code tree of the prototype system was useful for TAs.

Observation on how the students used the system for programming from the video recording of the screen, the use of the system was divided into two types of comment preceding description type and source code preceding description type. In the comment preceding description type, the code was written after the program flow was input from the code tree or comments in Japanese. On the other hand, in the source code preceding description type, all comments were written just before the end of the experiment. In the experiment, all participants were instructed to write comments first. However, there ended up being 4 participants of comment preceding description type and 5 participants of source code preceding description type. This corresponded to the group structure of the frequency of use of the code tree, and the students who used the code tree frequently were the comment preceding description type. Based on this observation, it was possible to consider that the participants of the comment precedence description type were able to think the structure of the program by writing comments first using the code tree. Some students wrote detailed comments, noticed mistakes in their source code and corrected the mistakes themselves, and often replaced the nodes. On the other hand, for the source code preceding description type, the evaluation value of Q1 was less than zero, and the question items comparing the existing method and the proposed method were also evaluated low. This may be because they wrote the source code in the editor and then commented, and the code tree stopped and could not be restored because of insufficient comments. Some students didn't use the code tree at all. Based on the above fact, it is considered that the source code precedence type had already acquired the skill to consider the structure of the program by themselves without depending on the system, and thus felt the system troublesome. This suggests that these participants were not the beginners the proposed method is supposed to support.

5.4   Summary of the Evaluation Experiment

We examined whether students who started using the prototype system to learn programming could intuitively manipulate the structure of the program and deepen their understanding. Furthermore, we examined whether it is easy for educators and TAs to understand students' understanding and thoughts. The result showed regarding how the participants used the system that there were two types of users, comment preceding description type and source code preceding description type, and it was possible to support the former for their abstract thinking for programming. On the other hand, the latter turned out not to be beginners who the system can benefit, because they had already acquired a skill needed for abstract thinking without using the system. In addition, the result of the questionnaire for TAs indicated a possibility that the system helped educators smoothly understand their students' comprehension and intentions on structures. However, there were few questions from students to TAs during the experiment, so it is not clear how the system affected the educational communication between them. In the next chapter, we investigate the effect of the system on TAs by conducting additional experiments focusing on communication between TAs and students.

6   Additional Experiment

The evaluation experiments revealed that the prototype system can support students' abstract thinking. However, it is unclear how the system affects educators. In this additional experiment, we clarify the effect on TAs by observing the communication between students and TAs.

6.1   Content of the Additional Experiment

We recruited four university freshmen as students and two graduate students as TA. This experiment was carried out for a long period of time so that the participants become so familiar with the prototype system that they do not have to ask questions about the operation and behavior of the system. We asked the participants to solve four tasks in two days. We set a time limit of 40 min per task to solve the problem. Additionally, the problem was made more difficult than the previous experiments in order to increase the communication frequency between the students and the TAs. In addition, we asked the TAs to take care of their students when there was no key input within 1 min and when they had less than 15 min to solve the problem. We also instructed the participants to write comments in the code tree before writing the source code. At the end of the experiment, a free description questionnaire was conducted. During the additional experiment, we recorded the programming screen and confirmed the contents and programming.

6.2   Classification of Questions from Students

The questions on the communication between students and TAs were first classified into five types: "questions on the solution", "questions on program errors", "questions on understanding the purpose of the problem", "questions on the specification of the problem" and "questions on the specification of the prototype system" (see Table 4).

Question on the solution is a question asked when students did not know how to write source code for the task or when they did not get the desired results. This type of questions was most frequently asked during the experiment.

Question on program errors is one asked if students did not understand the rules of the program, such as syntax or compilation errors of the program. In the experiment, there were compilation errors due to variable declarations outside the scope and errors due to typing errors in variable names.

Table 4. The number of questions in each category.

Classification of questions	Count
Questions on the solution	11
Questions on program errors	7
Questions without understanding the purpose of the problem	0
Questions on the specification of the problem	3
Questions on the specification of the prototype system	4

Question on understanding the purpose of the problem refers to questions asked when students did not understand at all about the problem of the source code, and it was difficult for them to formulate a way of solving the problem. The system was supposed to work in such a situation. However, this type of question was not asked during the experiment because the students had already taken programming classes and had some knowledge and experience in programming.

Question on the specification of the problem refers to questions on the behavior of the program which was not clear in the problem sentence and for which the TAs only had to give explanation orally without reading the students' source code. In the experiment, a question on the behavior of the click was asked.

Question on the specification of the prototype system refers to questions to ask for solutions for a halt of the code tree on the system or bug of the system, etc. In the experiment, the code tree of the system stopped when the number of nesting did not match.

6.3   Results of the Additional Experiment

The answers in the questionnaire from the students included much positive feedback such as "I am glad that I could change the order of the source code at once." and "I was able to confirm each action in words, so my understanding was deepened.". However, regarding the support from TAs, there was no comment showing that the system helped it.

In the questionnaire to the TAs, there were positive opinions such as "Although there was a possibility of individual differences, it was easier to answer because the students had more questions than in the actual class." and "I think the students now have a habit of writing comments thanks to this system.". On the other hand, there were also opinions on problems of the system such as "When I was asked a question because I couldn't do certain calculations or processes, I didn't look at the code tree much because I didn't have to look at the entire source code." and "I felt resistance to the number of nodes in the code tree.".

6.4   Consideration of the Additional Experiment

Among the classified questions, "questions on the solution" were most frequently asked. This would be because it often happens while programming that the source code does not work as expected. The purpose of this study is to help TAs and students to communicate smoothly about how to solve such programming problems. In the experiment, there was no scene of instructing these questions using the code tree. In the interaction between the students and the TAs, sometimes the students were pointing to the editor when asking questions and the TAs' eyes were directed toward the editor. The TAs in such a situation were assumed to provide the same usual instruction as to when they were not using the system. Therefore, it was considered to be necessary for the TAs to be familiar with or instructed about the use of the code tree.

"Question on understanding the purpose of the problem" was also questions the proposed method was supposed to support, but there was no question of this type in the experiment. It is considered that the question was not asked because all students had already taken programming classes.

"Question on program errors" was not assumed to be supported by the present study because it usually comes from syntax error of programming language, and "question on the specification of the problem" and "question on the specification of the prototype system" were also not question classifications on which the purpose of the present study, the visualization of the abstract though, has effects. However, these questions were asked in the experiment. This would be because some parts of the problems were difficult for the students to understand and there were insufficient tutorials for them to get used to the system.

The result of the questionnaire revealed that the students did not have the impression that the system helped them with communication with the TAs, and the TAs felt that the contents of the questions were consistent though there might be individual differences. This may be because the students' thinking was supported as explained in the Sect. 5, so they were able to accurately summarize their questions.

The reason why the code tree was not used when the students asked questions to the TAs would be because they had already taken a year-long programming courses and they did not need to ask questions about the whole program. Moreover, as the problem was made to be difficult and the severe time limit was set, the students had to write shorter comments with little information quantity as the remaining time got shorter. Then, it was impossible for the TAs to understand the whole program by looking at the code tree in this situation, so they probably did not use the code tree for questions.

This experiment could not clarify whether using the prototype system would help TAs teach and understand questions from students because the student participants had mastered the basics of programming and questions to understand the purpose of the problem were not asked. Then, the next chapter introduces a user study carried out to investigate what kind of effect the system has on beginners who just started learning programming.

7 User Study with Beginners

We conducted a user study with beginner students who had only three-month-long experience in programming.

7.1 Content of the User Study

We recruited twelve university students as participants and two graduate students as TA. We asked the students to solve two questions about the content of the conditional branch that they had learned in their programming class. They also completed a tutorial to familiarize themselves with the system and completed a free-form questionnaire after the experiment. During the experiment, the video recording of the screen using the system and the video recording of the whole room were carried out, and the communication between the students and the TAs was checked. We also asked the TAs to use the code tree to answer students' questions as much as possible.

7.2 Result of the User Study

Many students gave positive opinions such as "It is easy to do as if you are writing notes on the side.", "I write it in Japanese first, so it's good for studying.", and "It is easy to change the order of the program by changing the order of the comments.". On the other hand, there were also negative opinions such as "It was difficult to operate", "The comment function is troublesome.", and "It was difficult to determine how many nodes are in the same tree or the order of the trees".

7.3 Consideration of the User Study

In the questionnaire for the student, similar opinions to the ones mentioned in the Sects. 5 and 6 were obtained. In addition, there was an opinion that it was difficult to decide the order of the trees, and it seemed to be a cause for this that the ability to construct the structure of the program, that is, abstract thinking was not yet trained. The recording and the confirmation of the communication between the students and the TAs showed that the student who expressed the opinion above asked a question to a TA who was giving an explanation using the code tree. This fact indicates that the system enabled the student to share their abstract thinking with the TA even though they were not trained enough in it. This suggests that the system can be used to help to teach.

In this user study, the TAs were actually able to easily understand the intention of the question because the number of contents covered in the programming class the students had taken was limited and the problem was simple. Therefore, the question on understanding the purpose of the problem was not asked.

In the user study, it was clarified that the system worked effectively for beginners who had just learned programming. It was also suggested that the system can be utilized for teaching as it facilitates communication between TAs and students who are not trained in abstract thinking by visualizing and sharing abstract thinking.

8   Summary and Future Work

In this paper, we propose a method to visualize abstract thinking in a natural language with a similar structure to source code by making a tree from comments in the source code and to enable TAs and students to edit source code by drag-and-drop operation in the code tree.

In the experiment using the prototype system based on the proposed method, the proposed method worked for the beginner participants and assisted them in considering the structure of the programming.

It was also indicated that the system can be useful for educators because it helped the TAs understand their students' understanding of the programming structure and intentions of their ideas. However, we could not obtain enough evidence to clarify this because there was no question on understanding the purpose of the problem from the students in the additional experiment and the user study.

In the experiment, there was a situation in which a TA unilaterally taught the structure (Required variables, etc.). In such a situation, it is considered that the understanding of the student is deepened by not teaching the answer but making the student read and the flow of the program and develop their ideas. However, it is necessary for TAs to induce correct answers from the structure of the source code their students wrote. We will investigate whether the prototype system can make this easy in our future research. It is also necessary to investigate the effect after the system support such as whether the habit of writing appropriate comments is acquired after the users stopped using the system.

Acknowledgements.   This work was supported in part by JST ACCEL Grant Number JPMJAC1602, Japan.

References

1. Kanamori, H., Tomoto, T., Akakura, T.: Development of a computer programming learning support system based on reading computer program. In: Yamamoto, S. (ed.) HIMI 2013. LNCS, vol. 8018, pp. 63–69. Springer, Heidelberg (2013). https://doi.org/10.1007/978-3-642-39226-9_8
2. Durrheim, Mark S., Ade-Ibijola, A., Ewert, S.: Code pathfinder: a stepwise programming E-tutor using plan mirroring. In: Gruner, S. (ed.) SACLA 2016. CCIS, vol. 642, pp. 69–82. Springer, Cham (2016). https://doi.org/10.1007/978-3-319-47680-3_7
3. Kim, S., Kim, W.J., Park, J., Oh, A.: Elice: An online CS education platform to understand how students learn programming. In: L@S 2016: Proceedings of the Third (2016) ACM Conference on Learning @ Scale, UK, pp. 225–228. ACM (2016)
4. Nishida, T., Nakamura, R., Shuhara, Y., Harada, A., Nakanishi, M., Matsuura, T.: A programming environment for novices with visual block and textual interfaces. J. Int. Sci. Publ. **14**, 470–478 (2016)
5. Patrice, F.: A teaching assistant for algorithm construction. In: ITiCSE 2015: Proceedings of the 2015 ACM Conference on Innovation and Technology in Computer Science Education, Lithuania, pp. 9–14. ACM (2015)

6. Kayama, M., Satoh, M., Kunimune, H., Niimura, M., Hashimoto, H., Otani, M.: Algorithmic thinking learning support system with eAssessment function. In: 2014 IEEE 14th International Conference on Advanced Learning Technologies, Athens, Greece, pp. 315–317. IEEE (2014)
7. Dorneles, V.R., Picinin, D.J., Adami, G.A.: ALGOWEB: a web-based environment for learning introductory programming. In: 2010 10th IEEE International Conference on Advanced Learning Technologies, Sousse, Tunisia, pp. 83–85. IEEE (2010)
8. Processing Homepage. https://processing.org/. Accessed 22 Feb 2020

Supporting Student-Teacher Interaction Through a Chatbot

Sonia Mendoza[1]([✉])(iD), Manuel Hernández-León[1],
Luis Martín Sánchez-Adame[1](iD), José Rodríguez[1](iD), Dominique Decouchant[2,3],
and Amilcar Meneses-Viveros[1](iD)

[1] Computer Science Department, CINVESTAV-IPN, Mexico City, Mexico
mhernandez@computacion.cs.cinvestav.mx, luismartin.sanchez@cinvestav.mx,
{smendoza,ameneses,rodriguez}@cs.cinvestav.mx
[2] Information Technologies Department, UAM-Cuajimalpa, Mexico City, Mexico
[3] C.N.R.S. - Laboratoire LIG, University of Grenoble, Grenoble, France
decouchant@correo.cua.uam.mx

Abstract. Nowadays, an important part of academic education comes from online information, such as class topics, homework, and practices. In this sector, chatbots can be a valuable tool in the teaching/learning process by providing information about courses, procedures, and school services. Thus, the deployment of chatbots in schools and universities starts having a high priority for the academic staff. Nevertheless, most chatbots lack mechanisms to adequately integrate into the educational activities, since they should be useful for teachers, students, and educative assistant personnel (e.g., social workers, psychologists, pedagogues, and prefects). In this article, we propose a chatbot whose primary objective is to serve as an extra-school tool and as an intermediary between teachers and students. In this way, students could express themselves more freely, since the chatbot acts as a bridge with their teachers and other involved personnel. Our prototype was developed as a Web application that provides a text-based user interface and defines several interaction profiles to encompass the specific functions of the different actors in the teaching/learning process. We evaluated the proposed chatbot with the participation of third-year middle school students and teachers. In particular, we measured the workload perceived by our participants after performing a series of tasks. According to our results, our chatbot mostly obtained positive impressions from the test participants.

Keywords: Chatbots · Teacher-student interaction · Middle school · Academic support

1 Introduction

In the last years, we have seen a growing interest in chatbots, i.e., computer programs that use natural language processing to interact with humans under different contexts [24]. According to a recent Business Insider report, it is expected

P. Zaphiris and A. Ioannou (Eds.): HCII 2020, LNCS 12206, pp. 93–107, 2020.
https://doi.org/10.1007/978-3-030-50506-6_8

that by 2020, around 80% of companies have plans to use them [14]. Chatbots can be found as support in various sectors such as business [21], tourism [11], frequently asked questions [20], procedures [2], and recommendations [3]. Typically, chatbots work by searching for keywords, phrases, and examples that have been customised in their knowledge bases, in order to offer information about products, services, activities, and places in social networks and online sales services [20].

In this era of hyperconnectivity and immediate responses, education cannot be left behind. Offering accurate and timely feedback is essential for learning [19]. That is why educational systems around the world are increasingly investing in technology; they do not intend to replace teachers but provide more helpful tools to obtain better-prepared students [7,16,26].

Thus, in the education sector, we can find chatbots as a means to provide information about courses, procedures, and school services [23]. Nowadays, students receive a significant part of their education through online information, such as class topics, homework, and practices. For this reason, chatbots can provide valuable help in the teaching/learning process [18]. Also, the development and use of chatbots begin to be of great interest to schools and universities [1,17].

However, most chatbots in education do not have mechanisms to integrate organically into the teaching/learning process, i.e., they should be useful for both teachers and students. In this article, we propose a chatbot that was built around those purposes. The primary objective of this chatbot is to serve as an extra-school tool and, at the same time, as an intermediary between teachers and students: advising them, monitoring them, and facilitating communication between them. In this way, students could express themselves more freely, as the chatbot serves as a bridge with their teachers and other personnel involved in this process, e.g., social workers, psychologists, pedagogues, prefects, and administrative staff.

The proposed chatbot was designed and implemented as a Web application, using a text-based user interface. We define several profiles, e.g., teacher, student, and administrative staff, to interact with the chatbot, since each one has specific functions in the teaching/learning process. For instance, in the case of the student profile, the chatbot gives suggestions for their classes, as well as exam dates and project deadline reminders. As for the teacher profile, the chatbot allows the teachers to receive student questions, as well as to suggest exercises and complementary material for reinforcing some specific topics. In this way, students can have several sources and different ways to understand a topic and enrich their knowledge.

To test the mechanisms that we propose, we evaluate the chatbot with the help of end-users, i.e., third-year middle school students, and teachers. After explaining the essential operation of the chatbot, we let them interact with it. After this small familiarisation, we asked them to complete a series of simple tasks, so that later they could evaluate with the help of the NASA-TLX questionnaire [13]. We also invited them to comment on their overall experience with the chatbot. In this way, we measured the perceived workload, which gave us an idea of the impact that our proposal could have on the education sector.

This paper is organised as follows. After presenting related work (see Sect. 2), we describe the research methodology that we adopted in order to develop our proposal (see Sect. 3). Then, we detail each step of the methodology (see Sect. 4), from understanding the problem to validating the first version of our chatbot with final users. Finally, we provide a conclusion of the achieved work as well as some ideas for improving it (see Sect. 5).

2   Related Work

In this section, we present some works that serve to demonstrate the importance of our proposal, as well as the use of chatbots in education is a domain worth investigating.

Benotti et al. [6] created a chatbot designed to foster engagement while teaching basic Computer Science concepts such as variables, conditionals, and finite state automata, among others to high school students. The tests they performed show that a chatbot can be a valuable tool to interest and help students with school issues.

Fonte et al. [12] implemented a system consisting of two parts, an Android application and a server platform. The Android application implements a chatbot which interacts with both the student and the server. The objective for the system was to enable the student to carry out several actions related to their studies like consult exam questions, receive recommendations about learning materials, ask questions about a course, and check their assessed exams. Although the architecture and characteristics of the system are presented, they did not perform tests with end-users.

Basogain et al. [5] reviewed the limitations of the current education systems, in particular, in the area of mathematics. They discussed a set of fundamental changes in curriculum and teaching methodology. Finally, they examined the role of e-learning as an integral part of the transition from traditional education systems to modern systems. While this work does not propose any work with chatbots, it makes clear that digital tools are valuable for the teaching-learning process.

Clarizia et al. [8] presented a chatbot architecture to manage communication and furnish the right answers to students. They proposed a system that can detect questions and gives the answers to a student, thanks to the use of natural language processing techniques and the ontologies of a domain. Although tests were done with students, they consisted in determining the correctness of the chatbot's responses, and not of the experience or usefulness it had.

Cunningham-Nelson et al. [10] made an exploratory literature review of both chatbots in general use and chatbots in education. Two preliminary chatbots applications are presented; a FAQ chatbot for answering commonly asked student questions, and a short response quiz chatbot designed to facilitate and provide automated feedback based on student responses. They concluded that the chatbots provide a promising area for potential application in the future of education, as they have the capability of streamlining and personalising components of learning.

All these works show that the use of chatbots in education is a promising field with many issues to explore. However, they are also examples of a knowledge gap that we try to fill with our work.

3 Research Methodology

As a research methodology, we decided to shape a little the "Google Design Sprint" technique consisting of five steps [4]:

1. **Understand:** Participants evaluate the problem they are trying to solve, the personas they are designing for, and the form factor they are going to use.
2. **Diverge:** Participants are encouraged to let go of all their presumptions and engage in different activities to generate as many ideas as they can, regardless of how feasible or far-fetched they are.
3. **Decide:** Through different activities, participants decide which ideas to pursue further.
4. **Prototype:** Participants rapidly sketch, design and prototype their ideas, concentrating on User Interface (UI) flow.
5. **Validate:** Participants put their product in front of users, test and are encouraged to show and tell when possible.

Although it is not a research methodology *per se*, we decided to adopt it because it is a way to create valuable products, i.e., that they are not only usable and aesthetically pleasing but that generate a change of skills and a way of thinking [22], as it is that we finally look for with our proposal. This technique, in particular, seeks to reach a viable solution within five days, this is something we decided to modify because we were interested in user-oriented design focus, but we considered that the time would constrict us.

4 Development

In this section, we describe each stage of the methodology that involved the development of the chatbot. All the work described here is the first iteration of the methodology.

4.1 Understand

The collaboration between the middle school and our university took place in the context of a special project between both institutions. The objective of this project was to create a technological tool so that students could have additional support in their classes, a means of information on procedures, as well as a means of communication between them, teachers and administrative staff.

After spending some days familiarising ourselves with the most common processes that students have to perform, conducting interviews with students, teachers and administrative staff, we create three personas who represent these three critical profiles of end-users of the system (see Fig. 1).

The second part of this stage was to refine our interviews to discover the requirements and characteristics of each user profile [15,25], and then apply this knowledge in user stories format [9] to each persona (see Tables 1, 2, and 3).

Table 1. User stories for persona Adriana

Requirements	Must-have	Nice to have
Functional	I want to be able to see all my information classified by class and grade. I want to be able to upload extra material for my classes. I want to be able to see the questions of my students	I would like it to allow me to post information notices periodically for my students. I wish it to allow me to organise activities in and out of class
User interaction	I want it to be simple to use. I want to be able to access the system from my home and smartphone	I would like it to have a register of each student, in order to write down the strengths and weaknesses of each one, so I could help them better
Social context	I want it to help me communicate better with my students. I want it to be a tool to improve my classes	I would like it to improve the work between teachers and administrative staff

Based on the personas and their user stories, we were able to discuss multiple scenarios. Fortunately, the needs of the end-users agreed and complemented each other, so we finally chose a scenario that would guide the design of the system: *The school needs a highly available web application that is easy to use for both experienced users and those struggling with technology. Response times need to be fast and, in some cases, immediate, so some processes need to be automated. The system must recognise the three profiles of the personas created.*

4.2 Diverge and Decide

Taking into account the requirements of the users and the guide scenario, and relying on various brainstorm techniques (e.g., mind maps and storyboards) each participant designed multiple solutions for the scenario in question. All proposals were presented without considering the possible limitations or criticisms and were widely discussed. Table 4 summarises some of the ideas we reached, their corresponding verdict and the reason for it.

To finally choose the solution proposal, each participant chose their favourite proposal and the reasons for their choice. After a debate between the alternatives, it was chosen by a joint agreement that a chatbot would be the most viable option.

4.3 Prototype

After choosing a chatbot as the best option, we decided to make a quick implementation, because we wanted to know to what extent our solution met the requirements of the end-users, the flexibility of the chosen technology, as well as giving us an outline of how it would be to develop the system altogether. Had we tried a functional or paper prototype, we would probably have ended up with an incomplete picture of whether a chatbot was the best solution or not.

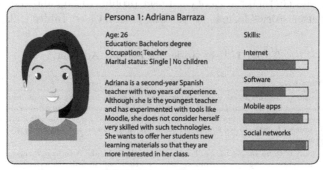

(a) Adriana - Teacher

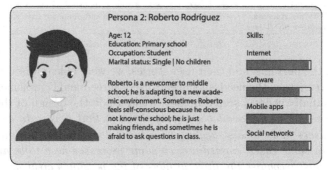

(b) Roberto - Student

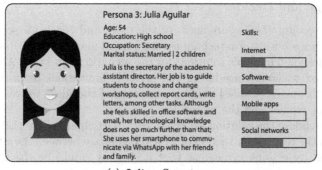

(c) Julia - Secretary

Fig. 1. The three personas we develop through interviews play the leading profiles of the system: teacher 1a, student 1b, and administrative staff 1c.

Table 2. User stories for persona Roberto

Requirements	Must-have	Nice to have
Functional	I want it to know the schedule of my classes and exams and other important events. I want it to have additional material and explanations to the topics seen in class. I want to be able to send messages to my teachers so they can answer my questions	I wish I could check my grades. I would like the system to explain to me complete topics of classes
User interaction	I want it to be simple to use. I want to be able to access the system from my home and smartphone	I wish I could send my homework through the system
Social context	I want it to help me communicate better with my teachers. I want it to help me improve in class	I wish I could share my problems and concerns

Table 3. User stories for persona Julia

Requirements	Must-have	Nice to have
Functional	I want students to receive reminders about important dates (e.g., enrolment). I want them to download formats for the various procedures. I want the system to answer the FAQs	I would like the system to guide the students in each step of their paperwork
User interaction	I want it to be simple to use. I want to be able to access the system from my home and smartphone	I would like the system to direct students with the corresponding person and office for each paperwork
Social context	I want the system to help us get closer to the students	I would like the system to help me to provide the necessary attention to those students who need it most

Table 4. Objective solving proposals

Proposal	Verdict	Reasons
Use Moodle	Rejected	Some teachers commented that they tried to implement it in their class but lacked the training and motivation to keep the platform up to date
Use Gradelink (or similar)	Rejected	Although initially it can be expensive, a prefabricated and tested system usually gives good results. However, it would require training, interaction with students is usually limited, and as with Moodle, motivation is a significant obstacle
Custom system (such as Gradelink or similar)	Rejected	Developing a school administration system is a huge task. While the school can save on licenses, development and maintenance can be very expensive. To make sure that development is on track, multiple tests are needed throughout the process, and this also increases the cost
Use social networks	Rejected	Although social networks allow us to communicate very quickly (as that is one of their objectives) they would probably fall short of fulfilling the persona's requirements. Besides, there is an inherent issue of privacy and information security
Chatbot	**Accepted**	The main challenge of developing a chatbot is its training, i.e., that the answers it provides are consistent with what was asked, in order to have a meaningful conversation. A chatbot is a good option since it will always be available, anyone can use it, many processes can be automated, and it allows all users to participate equally

In this way, using Angular, Node.js and Dialogflow, we develop an initial version of the chatbot with the functionalities that meet the main requirements of the end-users (see Fig. 2).

(a) Login   (b) Scheduling an exam

Fig. 2. The chatbot is a web application. We create a user-friendly interface for mobile devices.

Until now, the chatbot has the following features:

– There are three types of profiles: teacher, student, and administrative staff. At the moment, the registration and classification of all users are done manually by the chatbot administrator.
– The teacher profile contains their assigned groups and classes, as well as a list of students classified by those areas.
– The student profile contains the classes, teachers and assigned schedules.
– At the moment, the profile of the administrative staff is the same as that of the teacher.

- Teachers and administrative staff can schedule events with mandatory date and time.
- Students can ask for previously scheduled events.
- The chatbot can make automatic event reminders.
- Teachers can tell the chatbot to save links (e.g., websites, files, youtube videos) and assign them to a subject so that students can then ask for them.
- If a student asked for material from a subject and the chatbot found nothing, it tells the teacher that the student asked for that material.
- The teacher can send a message to all students who belong to the same group.
- Teachers and students can send files to each other, for example, to send homework.
- The chatbot can respond to basic conversions on subjects and personal matters.
- The chatbot is trained to answer the FAQs of the essential administrative procedures.

4.4   Validate

In this section, we describe the first set of tests conducted with end-users. We evaluated the workload perceived by the participants after performing some tasks. We gathered eight end-users: two teachers (one male-36, one female-28) and six students (three male, three female, between 14 and 15 years old) from middle school. It is essential to mention that all of them were using a chatbot for the first time. To accomplish our tests, we first let them explore the user interface of the chatbot for a few minutes, in order to get acquaintance with the different kinds of widgets and their corresponding functionalities. Then, according to their profile, we asked them to perform the tasks listed below.
For both profiles:

- Asking a specific person for some material in the form of a file or of a simple answer to a question.
- Sending a file to a given person or group.
- Receiving a file from a specific person.

For students:

- Establishing a personal or academic conversation with the chatbot.
- Receiving some suggestion from the chatbot about a personal or academic question.
- Asking for information about a course (e.g., doubts or questions).

For teachers:

- Adding information about a course, in order to be shared with the concerned students (e.g., extra-instructional material, project schedules, and reminders of homework deadlines or examen dates).
- Receiving some warning from the chatbot about the instructional materials that a given student is needing.

To measure the workload perceived by our eight users of the chatbot, we used the *NASA Task Load indeX* (NASA-TLX) [13]. This is a subjective assessment tool that uses six scales (also called dimensions) to measure the workload perceived by an individual or a group in the execution of some task. The test has two parts. In the former, the users evaluated a task in the following scales: *mental demand, physical demand, temporal demand, performance, frustration,* and *effort.*

For each scale, the user selected a value in the interval $[0, 100] \subset \mathbb{N}$ with ticks of 5 units, giving 21 possible qualifications.

On the left of Figs. 3 and 4, the given ratings for the six scales are shown. It is important to mention that we measured the whole workload for the set of tasks described above, so a big value means a lot of workload, which is considered as bad. On the other hand, a small value close to zero means a small workload, which is considered as good.

In the latter part, each user assigns a custom weight for the six scales, which is used to adjust the previous qualifications, as shown on the right of Figs. 3 and 4.

The average adjusted qualifications for the six scales are shown in Table 5. The scale with the smallest average rating was *Physical Demand,* followed by *Frustration.* It is interesting to observe that practically all users gave very little importance to the physical aspect, while interacting with the user interface of the chatbot. The ratings in this scale were small *per se,* but also the given weight was zero for almost all users. The scale with the biggest average rating was *Performance.*

Finally, we calculated the pondered rating from the adjusted ratings in the six scales. Figure 5 shows the pondered ratings given by each participant. The average of pondered ratings for the perceived workload given by the eight users is 23.67. The minimum pondered rating was 14 and the maximum was 36.33, in the range $[0, 100]$. These qualifications are in the "good" region of the scale, i.e., around the first quarter, and give us an approximate idea about how good was the perception of the participants about the burden of performing tasks while using our chatbot.

Table 5. Average adjusted ratings

Mental demand	76.875
Physical demand	8.125
Temporal demand	65.625
Performance	108.125
Frustration	46.875
Effort	49.375

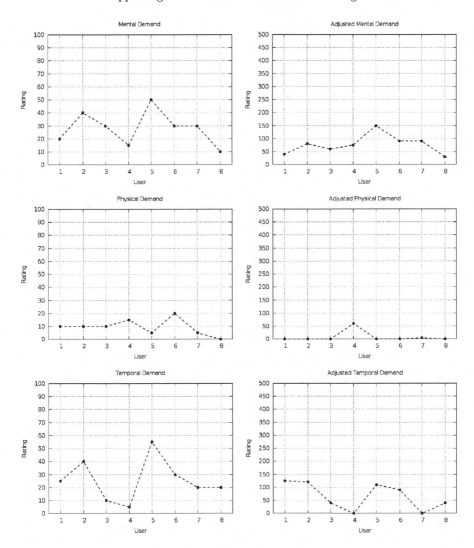

Fig. 3. Mental, physical, and temporal demand perceived by each user (left) and adjusted by the assigned weight (right).

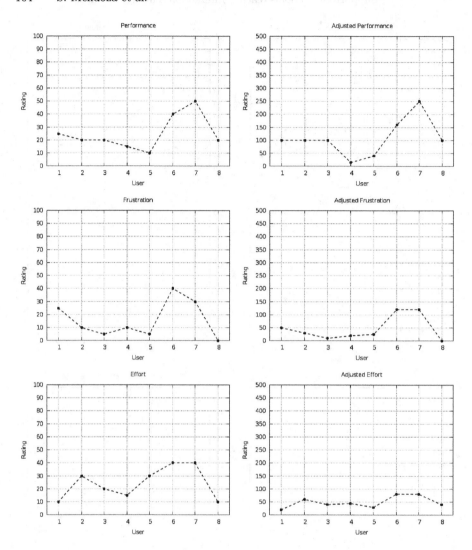

Fig. 4. Performance, frustration, and effort per user (left) and adjusted by the assigned weight (right).

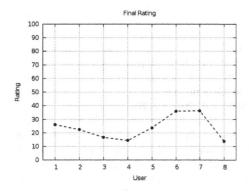

Fig. 5. Weighted rating per user.

5 Conclusions and Future Work

In this paper, we presented a chatbot to support the teaching/learning process in a middle school environment. The work presented here is the first iteration of the "Google Design Sprint" methodology that we adapt. This methodology allowed us to know the wishes and requirements of the end-users in the profiles of student, teacher, and administrative staff.

Although we only develop a scenario in the Understanding phase (see Sect. 4.1) we are already in the process of reviewing alternative scenarios, because we are interested in whether our approach to the chatbot as a tool is the best alternative for the school.

We know well that the tests and the population we use is scarce, but our purpose was to perceive the acceptance of the end-users: observe whether the chatbot met their requirements, whether it had the possibility of being a tool for everyday use, and above all whether the features it has were the indicated to improve communication between stakeholders.

We believe that this first iteration was helpful and will allow us to move forward with the development. As all user stories of our personas suggest that the chatbot should be easily accessible from their smartphones, we consider the possibility that, in the future, we can provide the chatbot service through one (or some) of the most popular instant messaging applications on the market (e.g., WhatsApp, Messenger, Telegram). Of course, security and privacy issues should be taken into account. A possible alternative is to offer a limited service, i.e., that it does not include sensitive information, but merely academic activities in general.

Acknowledgements. The work described in this paper was funded by "Fondo SEP-CINVESTAV de Apoyo a la Investigación (Call 2018)". Number of project 120 titled "Desarrollo de un chatbot inteligente para asistir el proceso de enseñanza/aprendizaje en temas educativos y tecnológicos".

References

1. AdmitHub: Admithub (2019). https://www.admithub.com/. Accessed Oct 2019
2. Agus Santoso, H., et al.: Dinus intelligent assistance (DINA) chatbot for university admission services. In: 2018 International Seminar on Application for Technology of Information and Communication, pp. 417–423, September 2018. https://doi.org/10.1109/ISEMANTIC.2018.8549797
3. Argal, A., Gupta, S., Modi, A., Pandey, P., Shim, S., Choo, C.: Intelligent travel chatbot for predictive recommendation in echo platform. In: 2018 IEEE 8th Annual Computing and Communication Workshop and Conference (CCWC), pp. 176–183, January 2018. https://doi.org/10.1109/CCWC.2018.8301732
4. Banfield, R., Lombardo, C.T., Wax, T.: Design Sprint: A Practical Guidebook for Building Great Digital Products. O'Reilly Media Inc., Newton (2015)
5. Basogain, X., Olabe, M.A., Olabe, J.C.: Transition to a modern education system through e-learning. In: Proceedings of the 2017 International Conference on Education and E-Learning, ICEEL 2017, pp. 41–46. Association for Computing Machinery, Bangkok (2017). https://doi.org/10.1145/3160908.3160924
6. Benotti, L., Martínez, M.C., Schapachnik, F.: Engaging high school students using chatbots. In: Proceedings of the 2014 Conference on Innovation and Technology in Computer Science Education. ITiCSE 2014, pp. 63–68. Association for Computing Machinery, New York (2014). https://doi.org/10.1145/2591708.2591728
7. Biancarosa, G., Griffiths, G.G.: Technology tools to support reading in the digital age. Future Child. **22**(2), 139–160 (2012)
8. Clarizia, F., Colace, F., Lombardi, M., Pascale, F., Santaniello, D.: Chatbot: an education support system for student. In: Castiglione, A., Pop, F., Ficco, M., Palmieri, F. (eds.) CSS 2018. LNCS, vol. 11161, pp. 291–302. Springer, Cham (2018). https://doi.org/10.1007/978-3-030-01689-0_23
9. Cohn, M.: User Stories Applied: For Agile Software Development. Addison-Wesley Professional, Boston (2004)
10. Cunningham-Nelson, S., Boles, W.W., Trouton, L., Margerison, E.: A review of chatbots in education: practical steps forward. In: Australasian Association for Engineering Education 2019, Brisbane, December 2019. https://eprints.qut.edu.au/134323/
11. Dian Sano, A.V., Daud Imanuel, T., Intanadias Calista, M., Nindito, H., Raharto Condrobimo, A.: The application of AGNES algorithm to optimize knowledge base for tourism chatbot. In: 2018 International Conference on Information Management and Technology (ICIMTech), pp. 65–68, September 2018. https://doi.org/10.1109/ICIMTech.2018.8528174
12. Fonte, F.A.M., Nistal, M.L., Rial, J.C.B., Rodríguez, M.C.: NLAST: a natural language assistant for students. In: 2016 IEEE Global Engineering Education Conference (EDUCON), pp. 709–713, April 2016. https://doi.org/10.1109/EDUCON.2016.7474628
13. Hart, S.G., Staveland, L.E.: Development of NASA-TLX (task load index): results of empirical and theoretical research. In: Hancock, P.A., Meshkati, N. (eds.) Human Mental Workload, Advances in Psychology, vol. 52, pp. 139–183. North-Holland (1988). https://doi.org/10.1016/S0166-4115(08)62386-9
14. Kar, R., Haldar, R.: Applying chatbots to the Internet of Things: opportunities and architectural elements. Int. J. Adv. Comput. Sci. Appl. **7**(11) (2016). https://doi.org/10.14569/IJACSA.2016.071119

15. Keijzer-Broers, W.J.W., de Reuver, M.: Applying agile design sprint methods in action design research: prototyping a health and wellbeing platform. In: Parsons, J., Tuunanen, T., Venable, J., Donnellan, B., Helfert, M., Kenneally, J. (eds.) DESRIST 2016. LNCS, vol. 9661, pp. 68–80. Springer, Cham (2016). https://doi.org/10.1007/978-3-319-39294-3_5

16. Kumar, V., Bhardwaj, A.: Role of cloud computing in school education. In: Handbook of Research on Diverse Teaching Strategies for the Technology-Rich Classroom, pp. 98–108. IGI Global (2020)

17. Maderer, J.: Jill watson, round three (2017). https://www.news.gatech.edu/2017/01/09/jill-watson-round-three. Accessed Oct 2019

18. Molnár, G., Szüts, Z.: The role of chatbots in formal education. In: 2018 IEEE 16th International Symposium on Intelligent Systems and Informatics (SISY), pp. 000197–000202, September 2018. https://doi.org/10.1109/SISY.2018.8524609

19. Ndukwe, I.G., Daniel, B.K., Amadi, C.E.: A machine learning grading system using chatbots. In: Isotani, S., Millán, E., Ogan, A., Hastings, P., McLaren, B., Luckin, R. (eds.) AIED 2019. LNCS (LNAI), vol. 11626, pp. 365–368. Springer, Cham (2019). https://doi.org/10.1007/978-3-030-23207-8_67

20. Ranoliya, B.R., Raghuwanshi, N., Singh, S.: Chatbot for university related FAQs. In: 2017 International Conference on Advances in Computing, Communications and Informatics (ICACCI), pp. 1525–1530, September 2017. https://doi.org/10.1109/ICACCI.2017.8126057

21. Ravi, R.: Intelligent chatbot for easy web-analytics insights. In: 2018 International Conference on Advances in Computing, Communications and Informatics (ICACCI), pp. 2193–2195, September 2018. https://doi.org/10.1109/ICACCI.2018.8554577

22. Sari, E., Tedjasaputra, A.: Designing valuable products with design sprint. In: Bernhaupt, R., Dalvi, G., Joshi, A., K. Balkrishan, D., O'Neill, J., Winckler, M. (eds.) INTERACT 2017. LNCS, vol. 10516, pp. 391–394. Springer, Cham (2017). https://doi.org/10.1007/978-3-319-68059-0_37

23. Shaw, A.: Using chatbots to teach socially intelligent computing principles in introductory computer science courses. In: 2012 Ninth International Conference on Information Technology - New Generations, pp. 850–851, April 2012. https://doi.org/10.1109/ITNG.2012.70

24. Shawar, B.A., Atwell, E.: Chatbots: are they really useful? In: LDV Forum, vol. 22, pp. 29–49 (2007)

25. Southall, H., Marmion, M., Davies, A.: Adapting Jake Knapp's design sprint approach for AR/VR applications in digital heritage. In: tom Dieck, M.C., Jung, T. (eds.) Augmented Reality and Virtual Reality. PI, pp. 59–70. Springer, Cham (2019). https://doi.org/10.1007/978-3-030-06246-0_5

26. Zhong, S.H., Li, Y., Liu, Y., Wang, Z.: A computational investigation of learning behaviors in MOOCs. Comput. Appl. Eng. Educ. **25**(5), 693–705 (2017). https://doi.org/10.1002/cae.21830

A Conversational Agent as Facilitator: Guiding Groups Through Collaboration Processes

Navid Tavanapour$^{(\boxtimes)}$, Daphne Theodorakopoulos,
and Eva A. C. Bittner

University of Hamburg, Hamburg, Germany
{tavanapour, theodorakopoulos,
bittner}@informatik.uni-hamburg.de

Abstract. Till now, conversational agents (CA) are often utilized as assistants to answer FAQs, but can they also be involved in other tasks with humans such as guiding them through a process as a group? We cooperate with an editorial office of an online journal and conduct an action design research project to instantiate a CA to facilitate their meetings. We design and develop the digital collaboration process (CP) of the meeting and a CA facilitator based on IBM Watson to integrate it in the digital environment to execute the CP. We conduct a pilot study and expert interviews to evaluate the CP and the derived design principles to facilitate the group during it and through its thinkLets. Our results show positive perception of the CA's capability as a facilitator for a group within its limitations and its neutrality during group discussions perceived as one strengths compared to human facilitators.

Keywords: Automated facilitation · Chatbot · IBM watson · Collaboration engineering · Action design research · Machines as teammates · thinkLet

1 Introduction

Collaboration has shown to be efficient for the accomplishment of complex tasks that exceed individuals' capabilities [1–4]. In this study, we investigate a typical case of such a complex knowledge-intensive task: a team of five editors of a politico-economic journal, who have to negotiate a consensus on their journal's content on a recurring, monthly basis.

Structuring collaboration and designing effective sequential processes towards a common goal for recurring, high-value tasks is in the scope of collaboration engineering (CE) [5]. The repeatability of the designed collaboration process (CP) is based on and enabled by the collection and application of reusable facilitation techniques, called "thinkLets" [6], which lead practitioners towards predictable and re-producible "patterns of collaboration" [5, 6]. The idea behind it is that neither (collaboration) experts nor further training and other prerequisites are needed to execute the CP [7, 8]. The execution of CPs often involves facilitators [5, 6]. Human facilitators have been considered extensively in collaboration research for the facilitation of small collaborative groups working on specific tasks till now [6, 9–13]. Traditional human facilitation of (human) actors is usually characterized by facilitative acts over natural

© Springer Nature Switzerland AG 2020
P. Zaphiris and A. Ioannou (Eds.): HCII 2020, LNCS 12206, pp. 108–129, 2020.
https://doi.org/10.1007/978-3-030-50506-6_9

language (text or speech). The "facilitator in the box" [12] paradigm extends this by considering digital systems for facilitation, which execute facilitation scripts for guiding users automatically [12]. These scripts with different states and prompts enable the facilitation of CPs digitally and automatically without a human facilitator.

However, in contrast to static system prompts, human facilitators can support practitioners in real time conversations by considering their socio-emotional state. Research has shown that socio-emotional support can have an influence on the process outcome [14, 15]. Furthermore, unlike human facilitators, scripted systems cannot adapt flexibly to practitioners' needs or approach them proactively and they lack natural conversation and language skills.

Digital environments face a multitude of challenges to provide human facilitation in real time, which is very cost intensive and hardly scalable for digital group settings. Therefore, with advances in natural language processing (NLP) and machine learning, automated facilitation executed by conversational agents (CAs), which can access and apply natural language in form of text and speech, can deliver a solution to overcome the challenges limited to specific tasks [16, 17]. Although providing first promising results concerning the satisfactory perception of CA facilitators [17], knowledge on group facilitation is limited [16], as recent research mainly focuses on CAs facilitating one individual through a process [17–21]. At this point, scholars call for prescriptive design knowledge for CA facilitators for groups [16]. To address this constituted research gap, we present the results from an action design research (ADR) project, in which we cooperate with the editorial office of a politico-economic journal to design a digital CP for their monthly editorial meeting, which will be facilitated by a designed and developed CA. This research is led by the following research questions: **Q1:** *How does the CP of the monthly editorial meeting need to be designed for digital execution? Q2: How can a CA facilitator be integrated in the CP to facilitate the monthly editorial meeting? Q3: Which differences between the CA facilitation and human facilitation are perceived by the group?*

This research aims to contribute with prescriptive knowledge according to Gregor and Hevner [24] towards the "theory of design and action" [25] with the designed CP for the monthly meetings of the editorial office and a CA facilitator to guide groups through the CPs.

This paper is structured to follow with the theoretical background and related research, before presenting the research approach. Subsequently, we design the CP, before diving in the design and development of the CA facilitator to guide the group through the activities and thinkLets of the designed CP. Finally, the design validation and the discussion section evaluate our design and deliver insights into the CP and the CA facilitation, before this paper closes with a conclusion and contribution section.

2   Theoretical Background and Related Research

John McCarthy's idea of Artificial Intelligence (AI) was "how to make machines use language, form abstractions and concepts, solve kinds of problems now reserved for humans, and improve themselves" [26]. Research from the field of natural language processing (NLP) investigates with the so called conversational agents the capabilities of machines to construct humanlike conversation to communicate with humans. CAs' main concept is based on the access to and processing of natural language in form of speech or text [27]. Text-based CAs are also called chatbots and defined in various ways in research. In this paper, with CAs we mean chatbots as in the definition of Curry and O'Shea: "Chatbots are computer programs that simulate intelligent human conversation. There are typically three parts to any CA. The typed input from the user in natural language, the typed output from the CA and the process of passing the input through the program so that an understandable output is produced. This whole process is repeated until the end of the conversation is reached" [28]. The third part of a chatbot, which processes the input, is also called Natural Language Understanding (NLU). NLU is considered a part of NLP. The aim of NLU is to interpret an input text fragment and translate it into a formal language that represents the text content. This is further processed to perform specific tasks requested by the user and to respond [29]. Weizenbaum [30] introduced the initial CA called ELIZA in 1966. ELIZA examines user's input for keywords to extract certain words to utilize for the construction of its response. A more advanced CA than ELIZA is PARRY (from 1971), which has a model of its own mental state imitating artificial paranoia [31]. The special thing about PARRY is that it was the first system to pass a restrictive Turing test [32]. After ELIZA and PARRY there were a lot of other CAs created. One, that is particularly relevant for this work, is the first version of IBM Watson [33]. The objective of the initial use case was to develop a question-answer system that could answer questions from any domain and win the game show Jeopardy [34]. In 2011 Watson won the game against two champions [35]. Watson was then made commercially available on the IBM platform. It is used in many different fields of application [33].

The improvements of CAs are significant with the ability to process large amounts of data and learn patterns from them [36]. This improvement can be observed in today's CAs, e.g. Apple's Siri, Amazon's Alexa etc., that are involved in human lives and support them in daily tasks [37]. The adaptions of CAs to different domains and scopes such as platform navigation, behavioral influences, learning and education [19, 38–40], improved response construction [41–43] or supporting users to reach a goal [18–20, 44] often consider the interaction of one CA with an individual and are far from facilitating a CP. We follow the aim to facilitate a group through a CP with a CA as facilitator. Thus, our scope is not limited to the facilitation of an individual through the CP. On the one hand, scholars investigate CAs that interact with a group, but not in the role of a facilitator. They often contribute with general CAs not limited to a domain [42] or domain specific CAs as tutors [18, 19, 45–48], administrator [20] or quizmaster [49]. On the other hand, CAs have been investigated to facilitate an individual human during a process [17, 21] but not a group [87]. Albeit scholars report promising results of CAs facilitating individuals, it should be noted that the strengths of a human facilitator, who can react to unplanned situations and provide in depth remarks to elaborated content, can hardly be met by a CA [17]. Nonetheless, the CA's strengths lie in calculating and processing of data in real-time and in the construction of conversations in natural language to proactively respond to users [17, 21, 50, 51]. Consequently, we position our research between these research streams and combine insights from the field of group facilitation and research on the interaction between individuals and CAs to design and develop automated group facilitation via a CA, thereby extending the facilitator-in-a-box paradigm.

The concept of facilitating groups has proven to have an impact on the group outcome in face-to-face meetings [1–3]. Scholars identified the key behind the facilitation concepts in interventions applied by human facilitators during a process [9, 10, 52–62]. Additionally, Clawson et al. [11] investigated the influence of facilitators' skills on the group outcome and contributed with the facilitator dimensions to consider when training a facilitator. These dimensions outline the behavior of a facilitator when guiding and supporting a group and can be valuable to consider for a CA facilitator. Additionally, Dickson et al. [63] identified and classified facilitative acts executed by a facilitator into "task interventions" and "interactional interventions". Task interventions refer to facilitative acts to direct the group's focus to reach the group goal. Interactional interventions refer to facilitative acts to improve and stimulate the group dynamics and communication by considering its members' socio-emotional state. In our case, the CA facilitator should consider the socio-emotional needs of practitioners in the conversation during the CP. This can be reached by the CA's application of social rules and norms and is in the scope of the Computers are Social Actors (CASA) paradigm [51]. According to CASA, people automatically apply social rules as soon as they are confronted with human characteristics [51]. CAs in particular cause this by applying natural language in form of text or speech, which is a very human feature. People therefore behave humanly towards CAs and expect in return human behavior with social rules from them, which are influential on humans' perception and behavior [51]. Anthropomorphized CAs with social cues such as task specific appearance [64, 65], human-likeness [64, 66], age [64], gender [51, 67–69], humor [70], ability to small talk [71] and friendly smiling [72] and their effect on the human perception are not limited to natural language in form of text. Albeit CAs can be perceived more humanlike by considering theses social cues, research outlines this to raise the human expectations towards the CA to have more humanlike capabilities [50]. According to Mori [50], if these raised expectations are not met, a shift from the perception of "likable" to "unsettling" is recognized and known as the "uncanny valley".

In sum, the risk of dropping into the uncanny valley should be considered for the CA facilitator and its task interventions, while the CASA should guide the interactional interventions to avoid raising expectations the CA cannot meet. Additionally, the facilitator dimensions of Clawson et al. [11] should be considered to derive the skills a CA needs to fill in the role of a facilitator.

3   Research Approach

We conducted an Action Design Research project (ADR) [22] with the editorial office of a politico-economic journal. The ADR by Sein et al. [22] defines the four stages (1) "Problem Formulation", (2) "Building, Intervention and Evaluation", (3) "Reflection and Learning" and (4) "Formalization of Learning". Additionally, we followed the Collaboration Process Design Approach (CPDA) [73] (Fig. 1) to design a digital collaboration process (CP) for the monthly meetings of the editorial office (to address Q1). To address Q2, we implemented, integrated and trained a CA to facilitate the complete CP. Eventually, we examined the suitability of the CA for the facilitation of groups and evaluated the final CP in a pilot study. By doing so, stage 2 of the ADR with Building (we built the CP), Intervention (executed by the CA facilitator, see agenda description) and Evaluation (simulation, walkthrough, expert evaluation and pilot study) is covered.

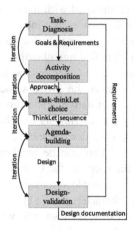

Fig. 1. Collaboration process design approach (CPDA) [73]

Furthermore, we conducted five expert interviews after the pilot study and analyzed them by also conducting a qualitative content analysis according to Mayring [23] to gain insights on differences between the CA facilitation and the human facilitation (to address Q3). Additionally, we reflected (see stage 3) on the designed interventions for the collaboration process and the CA. This reflection was done after each evaluation phase (see section six design validation).

Stage 1 is described in the introduction and the description of our observations. Finally, for stage 4 we generalize our learnings and report the contributions of this research.

4 Designing the Collaboration Process

The following section summarizes our observation of the meeting (face to face) of the editorial office in summer 2018. We audio-taped and transcribed one session with the approximate duration of 60 min for reflection. Furthermore, we conducted a content analysis according to Mayring [23] to gain insights into the activities and deliverables of the CP and to extract training data for the CA facilitation. Therefore, we coded phrases for the four main categories: Deliverables, Activities, Facilitator Interventions and Practitioner's Support Needs. We utilized the latter two categories to extract conversation snippets to train the CA, while the first two categories lead to the design of the CP.

The editors of the politico-economic journal meet once a month to discuss the new comments for the next issue. Everyone has prepared a list with suggestions for possible topics before the meeting. During the meeting, the ideas are gathered by a facilitator without including redundant ideas. The group then discusses the proposed topics. If there are more topics than planned for the next issue, it comes to a vote. One of the topics will be the editorial, in addition there will be four comments. If there is a tie, the group discusses again until an agreement is reached. Subsequently, the group looks for authors to assign to the topics. For this, the team often uses their database, where all previous comments are annotated by keywords. Additionally, they search the internet for further authors who could fit the topics. Finally, a group member is assigned for each article, who contacts the author and is responsible for the comment.

We can conclude that the collaboration goal of the CP is a monthly decision by the editors of the journal for an editorial and four comments. Each of them deals with a different current topic, with at least one author to be asked per article and one person responsible for the realization of the article. The outcome is a document that records these decisions.

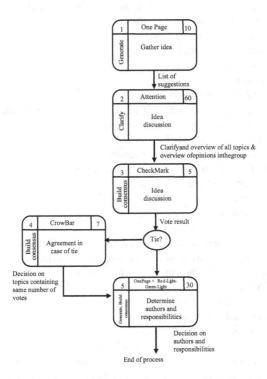

Fig. 2. Collaboration process design for the monthly editorial meetings

Based on these observations, we design the CP by following the CPDA (see Fig. 2) and derive an agenda containing the description of the CA's facilitation when guiding a group of practitioners through each thinkLet.

Table 1 shows the developed agenda with specific questions and assignments for the individual steps made by the CA facilitator. The agenda describes the facilitative acts of the CA in regard to the activities and thinkLets, which is relevant to consider for the design of a specific CA that fulfils the facilitative role in this specific case.

Table 1. Agenda format: collaboration process for the monthly editorial meeting

	Activity	Question/assignment (CA)	Deliverable	thinkLet (Pattern)	Time (minutes)
0	Introduction: presentation	Short explanation of the software and the procedure without detailed instructions (later given by the CA). The goal and result are known, only the procedure has changed	Rough understanding of the changed procedure	–	15
1	Gather ideas	Individual chat: Varying: Which suggestions do you have?/Please suggest an idea/You can suggest your ideas here. (The participants know the type of suggestions)	List of suggestions for the next issue	OnePage (generate)	10
2	Idea discussion	Group chat: We will now discuss all suggestions one after the other. When a topic is finished, please let me know. (No detailed instructions on the content because it remained the same)	Clarity and overview of all topics, an overview of opinions in the group	Attention (clarify)	3 per idea ~60
3	Vote on the articles	We have discussed everything and can now continue with the vote in the individual chats. Individual chat: Vote: Editorial, afterwards: Vote: Comments	Decision on the editorial and four comments, if there is no tie	CheckMark (evaluate)	5
4	Agreement in case of a tie	Group chat: Tie: <articles list> (Votes each: <number of votes>) Reach an agreement and let me know the result	Decision on the topics with the same number of votes	CrowBar (build consensus)	7

(continued)

Table 1. (*continued*)

	Activity	Question/assignment (CA)	Deliverable	thinkLet (Pattern)	Time (minutes)
5	Determine authors and responsibilities	Group chat: At the beginning: We will now go through the articles one after the other. I will suggest authors to you and you can then agree on an author. Of course, it doesn't have to be one of my suggestions. Let me know when you've agreed Alternately: - I assigned the keyword <keyword> to the article <article> and found the following authors: <author list> . Now agree on an author for <article> - Now please agree who is responsible for <article> and inform me about the person	Decision on the authors and responsibilities for the selected articles	Combination of the thinkLets OnePage (generate) + Red-Light-Green-Light (build consensus)	30

5 Design of the CA Facilitator

The role of a facilitator requires different aspects of human behavior than the role of an assistant, which a CA often takes on. Therefore, we derive the design of the CA in form of 19 meta-requirements (**MR**) from the Facilitator Dimensions defined by Clawson et al. [11] and assign them to the facilitative acts of Dickson et al. [63], which are "*task interventions*" and "*interactional interventions*". While task interventions in our case refer to the facilitative acts to reach the deliverables with the thinkLets during the execution of the CP (Table 1) and should consider the concept of the uncanny valley, the interactional interventions refer to the facilitator's expressions over natural language when communicating with the group and should consider CASA. Eventually, based on the MRs, we formulate action-oriented corresponding design principles (**DP**) according to Chandra et al. [74], which are listed in Table 2.

Task Interventions: In line with the uncanny valley, the capabilities of the CA should meet the user's expectations and therefore be reliable in its limitations of an artificial intelligent automated facilitator of the CP. The main objective of the CA is to be capable to facilitate the digital meeting, which mainly are the thinkLets. Therefore, we derive the first three MRs (MR1-3) to address general task interventions for the facilitation from the Facilitator Dimensions of Clawson et al. [11]. Eventually, we zoom into the thinkLets of the CP to derive MR4-8 to consider process demands in the CA facilitation. In line with the Facilitator Dimensions *"developing and asking the right questions"* and *"presents information to the group"* of Clawson et al. [11] the CA should be capable to construct and lead the conversation by asking questions and providing necessary information [18, 79, 88] (**MR1**). Furthermore, the facilitator's responsibility is to *"keep the group focused on outcome"* [11], which in our case is to achieve the deliverables by executing the thinkLets. If the practitioners start to lose focus, the CA's reaction is needed. Therefore, the CA should be capable of preventing deviations from the current thinkLet [88, 90] (**MR2**). Clawson et al. [11] outline the facilitator's capability to *"direct and manage the meeting"* completely. In our case the complete meeting is the execution of the CP, which means guiding and supporting the practitioners through each thinkLet by producing the deliverables in the right logical order (**MR3**).

The first thinkLet to be facilitated is **OnePage** of the first activity "gather ideas" to collectively brainstorm on the next possible articles. The participants work simultaneously on one electronic list to collect topic suggestions [75]. The output of OnePage, *"a collection of contributions"* [76], corresponds to the output of the activity. We conclude for the facilitation of OnePage that the CA should be capable to guide and support each practitioner individually to generate and place brainstormed items on one shared list (**MR4**).

The second activity "idea discussion" needs the generated list of ideas (idealist) as input to execute the thinkLet **Attention**. *"With the help of Attention, the participants elaborate their ideas further, react to the suggestions of others, zoom into certain aspects and discuss which suggestions they do not understand."* [76]. In this thinkLet, the focus is always put on the next point on the list. As this thinkLet describes, the participants can discuss the topic until they signalize that the next point can be addressed. No new topics should be suggested here. Proposed topics should only be elaborated on in order to get a better understanding. The CA should be capable to lead the practitioners through every point on the list to edit them. If one point is unclear to someone, the CA can open and moderate a discussion with all group members to clarify this point on the list (**MR5**).

The next activity is the "vote on the articles" and is executed with the thinkLet **CheckMark**. *"In this thinkLet, you give each participant a ballot, and allow them to checkmark their favorite items. Usually, you limit the number of items that can be marked on a given ballot."* [75]. In our case, the list of positions is the clarified and elaborated idealist from the thinkLet Attention. Analogically to the observed meeting we limit for each practitioner the number of checkmarks to one for the editorial and four for the comments to order the idealist by participant preferences [75]. The ideas on top of the list will be set as articles. Hence, the CA should be capable to guide and support practitioners in marking their five most favorite ideas on the list (**MR6**).

The thinkLet **CrowBar** might be executed next in the activity "agreement in case of a tie" if there is a tie on the marks for the first five ideas on the list. The thinkLet CrowBar *"let the group address the reasons for a lack of consensus on certain issues."* [75]. The intended input is *"Voting results [...] in which agreements and* *disagreements were uncovered*" [76], which would be our case if there is a tie. After the discussion, if there is a change, the list will be modified. For the facilitation of CrowBar, the CA should be capable to recognize existing ties within the first five ideas on the list, open, and moderate the group discussion to find consensus and respectively modify the list afterwards, if applicable (**MR7**).

Finally, the activity "determine authors and responsibilities" is performed via a combination of the thinkLets **OnePage** and **Red-Light-Green-Light**. First, the participants brainstorm possible authors to assign to one article. At the same time, they discuss the proposed authors and evaluate them until everyone agrees. This part is done with a slightly modified version of the thinkLet Red-Light-Green-Light. "*Participants render opinions or evaluations [...]. As the argument ebbs and flows, the participants change their votes in real time. Discussion continues until the group agrees they have sufficient consensus to proceed.*" [75]. This thinkLet provides an overview with changing green and red cells as a symbol for agreement or rejection. Only if all participants agree, the process will continue. The responsibility will then be agreed upon in the same way. This happens for all five articles consecutively. The output of the first thinkLet (OnePage) is the input for the second (Red-Light-Green-Light). The output of Red-Light-Green-Light is, as in the description, a consensus in the group and a prioritized list of authors [75]. Here, too, the top author positions are directly adopted as decisions. It will reduce the workload of practitioners, if the CA would utilize NLP capacity to recommend authors, by checking, analyzing and matching previously written content similar articles and their authors to the top five ideas on the list. At this point, the practitioners should be able to decline the suggestions and add further authors. Hence, the CA should be capable to suggest authors for the five articles, support the generation of additional authors, open and moderate the group discussion to find a consensus about and evaluate the proposed authors until everyone in the group agrees (**MR8**). By utilizing the CA's NLP strength to facilitate and assist practitioners, we stay in line with practitioners' expectation and also in line with the uncanny valley [50].

Interactional Interventions: The main objective of the interactional interventions is to improve the group dynamics. In line with CASA the CA facilitator should apply social cues when confronted with humans to meet their expectations of a very human communication instrument [50, 51], which is the natural language (in our case) in form of text. Scholars found anthropomorphized CAs considering the social cues of friendliness (**MR9**), neutrality (**MR10**) [77], empathy (**MR11**) and without judgment (**MR12**) [78, 79] to have an influence on an individual's perception. Additionally, errors in grammar or spelling [79] (**MR13**) and wrong response to users [80, 81] (**MR14**) have been identified to leave a negative impression of the CA. The CA benefits from a positive perception, which would support the CA to "*build and rapport a relationship*" [11] with the group and is helpful to "*create an open, positive and participative environment*" [11]. In our observations the human facilitator reached this in the meeting by trying to consider the practitioners' socio-emotional needs [63, 78, 82–84] (**MR15**). That is, by treating the practitioners equally (**MR16**), encouraging them (**MR17**) to participate through explicit and precise questions and granting the same amount of time to everyone in the meeting, if needed (**MR18**) and was persuasive especially in the discussions. Additionally, the facilitation in the meeting was characterized by *"listening to, clarifying and integrating information"*, which the human facilitator explained patiently in an understandable way [77, 79, 85] (**MR19**).

Table 2. Design principles (DP) and their corresponding sources: meta-requirements (MR)

Design Principles (DP)	Source
DP1: Provide the CA with NLP capabilities to construct and lead a conversation with perfect grammar and spelling skills in order to direct and manage the digital meeting by executing thinkLets according to the moderation agenda and actively asking questions, providing instructions and information and recognizing drifts from the process to react to them to guide and support practitioners in the collaboration process to reach a common goal	MR1, 2, 3, 13
DP2: Provide the CA with NLP capabilities to guide practitioners to reach elaborated outcomes by considering their socio-emotional state to encourage them to participate and contribute to generate deliverables or to elaborate on produced deliverables with friendly and nonjudgmental empathic statements, strategies to outline and value their contribution in any form during the thinkLets and the capability to recognize and react correctly to practitioner's utterances to support them with strategies to offer explanations about the process, vocabulary and thinkLets	MR4, 5, 8, 9, 11, 12, 14, 15, 17, 19
DP3: Provide the CA with NLP capabilities to guide and support practitioners individually to brainstorm items on a shared group list or calculate and recommend an item to put on the list, update and visualize the list with every modification, lead and encourage practitioners to check and edit every point on the list for clarification and allocate voting instruments to produce an ordered list by practitioners' preferences	MR4, 5, 6, 7, 8
DP4: Provide the CA with NLP capabilities to recognize practitioners respond if a list item is unclear and calculate if the votes for relevant list items are even to initiate a group discussion with all practitioners, moderate the discussion with precise questions and explanations and construct a positive atmosphere to participate in the discussion by being neutral towards any position, treating each practitioner equally, granting similar amount of time or opportunity to discuss and comment to each practitioner to clarify a list item or find a consensus for a list item	MR5, 7, 8, 10, 16, 17, 18, 19

6 Development

We instantiated and trained IBM Watson (with the extracted data we derived from the content analysis) for the facilitation of the CP in line with the derived DPs. We utilize the chat environment Slack to construct the thinkLet environment. Furthermore, we implement the process flow with different functionalities into Slack, the interface between Slack and the trained IBM Watson for this specific case. The training data for

IBM Watson were constructed from the transcript of the oral meeting in summer 2018. We extracted intents, entities and slots for the training. Each utterance sent to Watson contains an intent of the user. Entities refer to identified information for Watson to utilize from the utterances. These can be saved in slots for further processing.

The following will describe the states and process flow of the CA application.

States: The process is divided into states to avoid unwanted behavior of the CA. For example, after the vote no new suggestions can be made because the state has changed. This allows to recognize entities and to assign them to different entity types in different states in order to save and process them differently. The states are "suggest_ideas" → "discussion" → "vote_mainarticle" → possibly   "tie_mainarticle" → "vote_comments" → possibly   "tie_comments" → "authors" → "end". Whenever something depends on how far the collaboration process has progressed, the state is checked. The state changes when the process moves to the next stage.

Gather Ideas: First, everyone is in an individual channel with the CA. Participants are asked to make a suggestion, if they send a message without an idea. In this state (suggest_ideas), if the intent suggesting ideas is recognized, the CA saves the idea in a slot to create and maintain an idea list. As required, the ideas are collected centrally as a list on a server without exact duplicates. The participants work on creating one electronic list by contributing list items by and by as described in the thinkLet OnePage. During the conversation with the participant, if the intent "End" is recognized, a confirmation question is sent to the user, redirecting to the group chat.

Idea Discussion: When all participants have joined the group chat, the discussion about the collected ideas is started. According to the thinkLet Attention, the focus is always on one topic and the participants can further elaborate on it. That is implemented by the CA asking the group to discuss the topics on the list by and by. Each partial discussion ends with the intent "End" and a subsequent confirmation question. This repeats itself to the end of the list. After that, the participants are directed back to their individual chat. The whole discussion happens in the state "discussion".

Vote on the Articles: The end of the discussion triggers the change to the state "vote_mainarticle". The CA requests in each individual chat to vote for an editorial. It contains a drop-down menu with all ideas from which the users can pick their favorite. When the user has made a choice, a modal window appears with a confirmation question. If the user is sure of his/her decision, the message is updated and only contains his/her favorite. This means that users can no longer change their decision or vote more than once. Once all users have voted, the result is displayed. It contains the decided editorial and the number of votes. If there was no tie, the vote for the comments is triggered. The state changes to "vote_comments". The procedure is the same, the only difference is that the users have four decisions to make, i.e. four drop-down-menus. An article disappears from the other menus once it has been selected to avoid voting multiple times for an idea. Of course, that is user-dependent.

Agreement in Case of a Tie: If there was a tie, the users will be shown the result. Additionally, the articles having the same number of votes are displayed and everyone is redirected back to the group chat. The state then changes to "tie_mainarticle" or "tie_comments". For the comments, the articles that had more votes than others are set as comments, and only the remaining comments are discussed. Since the group did not agree, there is obviously a lack of consensus. Thus, the thinkLet CrowBar is carried out in the group chat. The voting results are shown again and the group is asked to agree on the remaining articles. The concept of "agreement" is used, which is triggered by the intent of the same name. If the users have agreed on the missing number of articles and are in the state "tie_mainarticle", they are directed back to their individual chats, otherwise the users remain in the group chat.

Determine Authors and Responsibilities: In the group chat, the selected article topics are now discussed one after the other. For each article, the CA automatically searches for authors on the website of the editorial office to recommend authors for each of the selected articles. The practitioners can suggest more or other authors during the thinkLet OnePage for each of the selected articles. They are asked to come to an agreement again. This is done with the execution of the thinkLet Red-Light-Green-Light. In order to be able to agree, they evaluate suggestions and provide their opinion. In addition, the "Agreement" concept is used again, which allows the team members to change their opinion in real time and only continues the discussion, if there is a common consensus (everyone agrees). After the subsequent prompt of the CA, it is similarly agreed upon who is responsible for this article. The process is repeated for all five articles. The process takes place in the state "authors", which is afterwards set to "end".

Finally, everyone is redirected back to their channel and receives the result document in the same format as it was in the original process. The CA notifies the participants that the meeting is over now and the application terminates.

7 Design Validation

In accordance to the iterative nature of the ADR, we designed the digital CP and its adjustment to CA facilitation in an iterative manner. This is also compatible with the CPDA and its design validation. We utilized four methods for the evaluation as displayed in Fig. 3. The first is the simulation for the collaboration engineer to check for the consistency by conducting a step-by-step analysis. Second is the search for deficits in each building block of the CP by an expert in an expert evaluation. Third is a walkthrough by executing the CP with the problem owner and a practitioner. In this

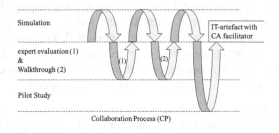

Fig. 3. Evaluation phases of the collaboration process

case they were one of the participants of the monthly meeting and the editorial office manager. Fourth and finally we conducted a pilot study [73], which was executed with space displaced participation. After the pilot study, we conducted guideline-oriented semi-structured expert interviews according to Meuser and Nagel [86] with each of the five practitioners who were members of the group that was facilitated by the CA. We considered questions in the guideline to evaluate the DPs and questions to gain insights on perceived differences between the human facilitation and the CA facilitation. We transcribed each of the interviews. The approximate duration of the interviews is 43 min. To evaluate the CA facilitation, we analyzed the interviews by conducting a qualitative content analysis according to Mayring [23]. By doing so, we categorized content similar phrases of each interviewee (**I**) to the DPs. Additionally, we categorized content similar phrases to the three categories pro CA facilitation, pro human facilitation and unbiased to gain insight into practitioners' different perceptions.

Evaluation and Findings: The interviewees agreed and outlined the capabilities of the CA to facilitate their meeting entirely digitally (I1, I2, I3, I4, I5) and to some extent and within its limitations reliably (I1, I4, I5). The CA was praised to guide and lead the practitioners to the goal of the meeting by executing the thinkLets in the right order and providing support in every step (**DP1: thinkLet execution, directing and managing**). Especially, the CA's allocated capabilities and functionalities for "voting, getting author suggestions (**DP3: voting and calculating**), agreeing on authors in a group discussion and the forwarding between individual and group chats" (I1, I5) (**DP4: initiate group discussion, clarify and finding consensus**) were highlighted positively and argued to be efficient for the digital meeting. Additionally, interviewees I1 and I5 liked the processing capabilities of the CA to sort, modify and logically visualize every produced point (ideas or authors) on the list for the practitioners to elaborate on (**DP2: (produce or edit) deliverables**), which is beneficial and more efficient than in the oral session (I1, I5). The human facilitator gathers, orders and than visualizes in the oral meeting, which is cumbersome, costs time and hinders the practitioners to maintain an overview when something is modified or changed during the elaboration. Furthermore, the CA guides very thoroughly to every point and encourages to think twice about "every point on the list" (I4, I5) to encourage practitioners to participate, contribute and improve them, while in the oral session topics sometimes are skipped (I2) due to lack of interest by practitioners and facilitator (**DP2: Encourage**). Overall, the CA left a positive impression and facilitated the process in line with the participants' expectations (I5). The CA was perceived to create a "more democratic session virtually" (I3) compared to the oral meetings. In the discussion and the entire process "everyone has a say" (I2) and "has the same right to speak" (I4). In sum, the CA is perceived as "neutral, nonjudgmental and more objective" (I5) compared to the human facilitator (**DP4: atmosphere and behavior in the discussion**). Additionally, the CA convinces practitioners with its behavior over natural language by expressing friendliness (I1, I3, I5) (**DP1: friendly**) and considering practitioners' socio-emotional states with empathic statements (**DP2: socio-emotional**) as the participants outline the CA's language to be understandable and excellent in form of text (I2 I5) (**DP1: grammar and spelling**) and it was "not missing much" (I1) for the CA to be like a human facilitator. This outlines the CA's balance between the concepts of CASA and the uncanny valley to be anthropomorphized with natural language and not raising expectations of human capabilities it cannot meet. On the one hand, the human facilitator benefits from the capability to understand the content of the conversation better and provide in depth support. Additionally, human facilitators can summarize what was said more quickly (I1), changing the topic is easier (I1). She/he takes the group forward in the discussion (I2), can perceive the relevance of the topics (I2) and "recognizes... where we should discuss further" (I2). The participants also noted that there is no level of relationship with the CA as there is with humans (I5) and that humans are not as cold as the CA was perceived (I5). On the other hand, the CA as moderator is neutral (I4) and thus supports a more objective decision (I5). It was further said that it is similar to the human being (I4), for example it summarizes, too (I1). One participant stated that the neutrality of the moderator, which is guaranteed by the CA, is often missing with humans (I4). It was also perceived positively that the CA repeatedly asks for a decision and thus brings the discussion to an end (I2) without making anyone feel offended because its behavior is neutral (I1).

Overall, the behavior among each other is perceived as more attentive in a digital environment, because group members hear each other out (I3) and listen more carefully (I5). There is a stronger decisiveness in the group because the CA frequently asks for a decision (I3) and the relationship level is less influential in the chat (I5).

Almost everyone agreed on the CA solution would be more suitable, if not all participants were at the same location (I4). A participant found the virtual session more efficient due to the shorter exchange and thus faster communication (I3). Another statement was that all parts of the process are more efficient except for the discussion (I1). For example, clarification is quicker orally than written (I3). Additionally, the shorter duration of the overall process speaks for more time efficiency of the oral session (I1).

The interviewees provided a criticism and a suggestion for improvement. On the one hand, the discussion via chat was criticized to take long and perceived as cumbersome. On the other hand, interviewees praised the result-oriented approach of the CA to reach the goal during the discussion by asking and encouraging practitioners during the chat. Additionally, their suggestion is to perform an automatic research in real time on the typed topics and to assign them to the top five ideas for a better overview of existing content (I4) to consider by practitioners during the discussion.

8 Discussion

The aim of this work was to find out, whether a CA can be utilized as a facilitator to guide a group through a CP. In order to evaluate this, as an example of such a process, the monthly meeting of an editorial office of a journal was transformed into a digital CP (to address Q1) and executed by a designed, developed and integrated CA facilitator (to address Q2). In sum, the CA facilitation was successful. The CP and its thinkLets were implemented as it was designed and described (Fig. 2 and Table 1). The pilot study confirms that the participants went through all phases as planned and the deliverables were produced. A final document was produced, which recorded the decision by the editors of the journal for an editorial and four comments with different topics and assigned authors. This is in line with the collaboration goal. Therefore, we can report from the pilot study that this goal was definitely achieved, as the group agreed on all the necessary information. The resulting document as a product was sent and contained all the necessary information. Furthermore, during the pilot study, the process was not terminated prematurely, no group activity was skipped and the selected thinkLets were executed accordingly. We were able to evaluate the CP in the pilot study and our design of the CA facilitator by conducting expert interviews. By doing so, we gained insights into the group's perception of the CA facilitator compared to the human facilitator (to address Q3). The expert interviews revealed that the CA was perceived and accepted as a facilitator. The main strengths of the CA, as perceived by the particapants, were its neutrality (I4) and its capability to support the group by guiding it to its goal through explicit questions for decisions, and further support in documenting the results, providing authors suggestions and simplifying the decision with a specific voting mechanism. This implies targeting a group goal, providing efficient group support elements to reach that goal and fairly expressing similar behavior to each participant should be considered for the design of CAs for groups and lead in our case to a positive practitioner's perception of the CA. The major weaknesses of the CA in comparison to a human facilitator were its limitations to support the group more in depth regarding the content of the deliverables and the content of the group discussions, which implies that the design of the CA has a scope on process guidance, calculation and pattern recognition capabilities to assist and facilitate the group and less capabilities to assist in tasks, which require creativity and logical argumentation to reach certain quality such as contributing to the content of an idea by editing or extending it or qualitatively contributing value to a group discussion by analysing the chat history.

During the analysis of the expert interviews, we were especially interested in whether we had been successful to balance the CA's behavior between human likeness and its capabilities to not raise expectations that the CA cannot meet, thereby considering the CASA paradigm while avoiding the uncanny valley. Concerning this balance, we found that the CA was perceived as only moderately humanlike, as the participants still noted that the CA was "colder" than a human facilitator and that relationship level among humans (I5) is not comparable to the relationship among humans and bots. However, this obvious limitation in humanlikeness also came with perceived advantages of the CA over some human facilitators, namely its neutrality (I4) and the fact that it brings the discussion to an end by asking for decisions (I2). Interestingly, while this behavior executed by the CA was perceived as neutral, it was perceived negatively, if a human facilitator showed it. In terms of performance, the participants noted the CA's limitations in understanding the semantics of each statement to respond and provide deeper content support, but this did not lead to a general rejection of the CA, possibly due to its distinct strengths and the awareness that it does not try to mimic a human facilitator. These counterintuitive insights point to an interesting field of investigation for future research. Future work on CAs might not only take a deficit-oriented perspective on the performance of CAs compared to humans, but look at their very own strenghts.

It can also be seen positively that all users participated in the whole process. If the software would not be applicable for this use case, it would probably have been made noticeable by showing disinterest or non-participation of the participants. So, there is no general rejection against a CA as facilitator. Additionally, we can report that even though the CA facilitator pushed the group towards a decision by asking multiple times, the group perceived this as neutral behavior. Our observation in the oral meeting shows a more negative perception when the human facilitator asks multiple times for a decision. This needs to be investigated more in future research.

This research comes with limitations. The training of Watson had limited extracted data from human-to-human conversation of one meeting. Furthermore, our results are restricted to one virtual meeting with five group members and need to be considered with caution. Nonetheless, we could successfully design and develop a CP and a CA to facilitate a group through it and reached the goal of this research.

9   Contribution

The practical contribution of this work is an IT-artifact in form of an application that contains the CP and an integrated CA facilitator that the team of the editorial office can continue to use for its monthly session in the future. Furthermore, we presented one possible way for CAs to take over the execution and facilitation of the thinkLets OnePage, Attention, CheckMark, CrowBar and Red-Light-Green-Light. As this general type of ideation and decision process is quite common for many team meetings, where ideas should be generated, enriched and collectively selected, the process design can most likely be adapted for the composition of these thinkLets in other CPs.

This research contributes with prescriptive knowledge [24] towards a "theory for design and action" [25] with the designed CP, MRs and DPs for a CA to facilitate a group through the CP and thus enriches the still underdeveloped field of automated group facilitation. Furthermore, we describe, how to integrate a CA facilitator in the CP and how to implement it to execute facilitative acts during the CP's activities and thinkLets in a group setting. Thus, this research also contributes to the research on the integration of intelligent collaborative agents and automated facilitation for groups towards better collaborative work practices [16]. Our results can be utilized to deploy improved group procedures by leveraging the potential of CAs.

References

1. Bittner, E.A.C., Leimeister, J.M.: Creating shared understanding in heterogeneous work groups: why it matters and how to achieve it. JMIS **31**, 111–144 (2014)
2. Bowers, C.A., Pharmer, J.A., Salas, E.: When member homogeneity is needed in work teams a meta-analysis. Small Group Res. **31**, 305–327 (2000)
3. Langan-Fox, J., Anglim, J., Wilson, J.R.: Mental models, team mental models, and performance: process, development, and future directions. Hum. Factors Ergon. Manuf. **14**, 331–352 (2004)
4. Wegge, J., Roth, C., Neubach, B., Schmidt, K.-H., Kanfer, R.: Age and gender diversity as determinants of performance and health in a public organization: the role of task complexity and group size. J. Appl. Psychol. **93**, 1301–1313 (2008)

5. Kolfschoten, G.L., Briggs, R.O., de Vreede, G.-J., Jacobs, P.H.M., Appelman, J.H.: A conceptual foundation of the thinkLet concept for collaboration engineering. Int. J. Hum.-Comput. Stud. **64**, 611–621 (2006)
6. Briggs, R., Vreede, G.-J., de Nunamaker, J., Tobey, D.: ThinkLets: achieving predictable, repeatable patterns of group interaction with group support systems (GSS). In: 34th HICSS, Maui (2001)
7. Briggs, R., Kolfschoten, G., Vreede, G.-J., Albrecht, C., Dean, D., Lukosch, S.: A seven-layer model of collaboration: separation of concerns for designers of collaboration systems. In: ICIS 2009, Phoenix (2009)
8. Vreede, G.-J. de Briggs, R.: Collaboration engineering: designing repeatable processes for high-value collaborative tasks. In: 38th HICSS, Big Island (2005)
9. Nunamaker, J., Vogel, D., Heminger, A., Martz, B., Grohowski, R., McGoff, C.: Experience at IBM with group support systems: a field study. Decis. Support Syst. **5**, 183–196 (1989)
10. Clawson, V.K., Bostrom, R.P.: Research-driven facilitation training for computer-supported environments. Group Decis. Negot. **5**, 7–29 (1996)
11. Clawson, V.K., Bostrom, R.P., Anson, R.: The role of the facilitator in computer-supported meetings. Small Group Res. **24**, 547–565 (1993)
12. Briggs, R.O., Kolfschoten, G.L., Vreede, G.-J. de Albrecht, C.C., Lukosch, S.G.: Facilitator in a box: computer assisted collaboration engineering and process support systems for rapid development of collaborative applications for high-value tasks. In: 43rd HICSS, Honolulu (2010)
13. Briggs, R., de Vreede, G.-J., Nunamaker, J.F.: Collaboration engineering with thinklets to pursue sustained success with group support systems. JMIS **19**, 31–64 (2003)
14. Perry-Smith, J.E., Mannucci, P.V.: From creativity to innovation: the social network drivers of the four phases of the idea journey. Acad. Manag. Rev. **42**, 53–79 (2017)
15. Schweitzer, F.M., Buchinger, W., Gassmann, O., Obrist, M.: Crowdsourcing: leveraging innovation through online idea competitions. Res.-Technol. Manag. **55**, 32–38 (2012)
16. Seeber, I., et al.: Machines as teammates: a collaboration research agenda. In: 51st HICSS, Waikoloa Village (2018)
17. Tavanapour, N., Bittner, E.A.C.: Automated facilitation for idea platforms: design and evaluation of a chatbot prototype. In: 39th ICIS, San Francisco (2018)
18. Tegos, S., Demetriadis, S., Karakostas, A.: Leveraging conversational agents and concept maps to scaffold students' productive talk. In: International Conference of Intelligent Networking and Collaborative Systems, Salerno (2014)
19. Tegos, S., Demetriadis, S., Karakostas, A.: Promoting academically productive talk with conversational agent interventions in collaborative learning settings. Comput. Educ. **87**, 309–325 (2015)
20. Kumar, R., Rosé, C.P.: Triggering effective social support for online groups. ACM Trans. Interact. Intell. Syst. **3**, 24 (2014)
21. Tavanapour, N., Bittner, E.A.C.: Supporting the idea generation process in citizen participation - toward an interactive system with a conversational agent as facilitator. In: 27th ECIS, Portsmouth (2019)
22. Sein, M.K., Henfridsson, O., Purao, S., Rossi, M., Lindgren, R.: Action design research. MIS Quart. **35**, 37–56 (2011)
23. Mayring, P.: Qualitative Inhaltsanalyse: Grundlagen und Techniken. Beltz Verlag, Weinheim Basel (2010). (in German)
24. Gregor, S., Hevner, A.R.: Positioning and presenting design science research for maximum impact. MIS Quart. **37**, 337–355 (2013)
25. Gregor, S.: The Nature of Theory in Information Systems. MIS Quart. **30**, 611–642 (2006)

26. McCarthy, J., Minsky, M.L., Rochester, N., Shannon, C.E.: A proposal for the Dartmouth summer research project on artificial intelligence. AI Mag. 1–17 (1955)
27. Otto, B., Lee, Y.W., Caballero, I.: Information and data quality in networked business. Electron. Markets **21**, 79–81 (2011)
28. Curry, C., O'Shea, J.: The implementation of a storytelling Chatbot. In: Agent and Multi-Agent Systems: Technologies and Applications - 5th KES International Conference, KES-AMSTA, Manchester (2011)
29. Ovchinnikova, E.: Integration of World Knowledge for Natural Language Understanding. Atlantis Press, Springer (2012)
30. Weizenbaum, J.: ELIZA - a computer program for the study of natural language communication between man and machine. Commun. ACM **9**, 36–45 (1966)
31. Colby, K.M., Weber, S., Hilf, F.D.: Artificial paranoia. Artif. Intell. **2**, 1–25 (1971)
32. Jurafsky, D., Martin, J.H.: Speech and Language Processing. Prentice Hall, NY (2008)
33. IBM Cloud: Watson Assistant (2016). https://cloud.ibm.com/catalog/services/conversation
34. Jeopardy Productions: Jeopardy (2018). https://www.jeopardy.com/
35. Ferrucci, D.A.: Introduction to "This is Watson". IBM J. Res. Dev. **56**, 1:1–1:15 (2012)
36. Tegos, S., Psathas, G., Tsiatsos, T., Demetriadis, S.N.: Designing conversational agent interventions that support collaborative chat activities in MOOCs. In: EMOOCs-WIP, Naples (2019)
37. Yoffie, D.B., Wu, L., Sweitzer, J., Eden, D.: Voice War: Hey Google vs. Alexa vs. Siri. https://files.transtutors.com/cdn/uploadassignments/2835385_1_voice-war.pdf
38. Eisman, E.M., López, V., Castro, J.L.: A framework for designing closed domain virtual assistants. Expert Syst. Appl. **39**, 3135–3144 (2012)
39. Roda, C., Angehrn, A., Nabeth, T., Razmerita, L.: Using conversational agents to support the adoption of knowledge sharing practices. Interact. Comput. **15**, 57–89 (2003)
40. Xu, K., Lombard, M.: Persuasive computing: feeling peer pressure from multiple computer agents. Comput. Hum. Behav. **74**, 152–162 (2017)
41. Hill, J., Randolph Ford, W., Farreras, I.G.: Real conversations with artificial intelligence. Comput. Hum. Behav. **49**, 245–250 (2015)
42. Porcheron, M., Fischer, J.E., Sharples, S.: "Do animals have accents?": talking with agents in multi-party conversation. In: ACM Conference on CSCW and Social Computing, Portland (2017)
43. Angeli, A.D., Brahnam, S.: I hate you! Disinhibition with virtual partners. Interact. Comput. **20**, 302–310 (2008)
44. Louvet, J.-B., Duplessis, G.D., Chaignaud, N., Vercouter, L., Kotowicz, J.-P.: Modeling a collaborative task with social commitments. Procedia Comput. Sci. **112**, 377–386 (2017)
45. Tegos, S., Demetriadis, S.N., Karakostas, A.: Conversational agent to promote students' productive talk: the effect of solicited vs. unsolicited agent intervention. In: 14th International Conference on Advanced Learning Technologies, Athens (2014)
46. Tegos, S., Demetriadis, S., Tsiatsos, T.: Using a conversational agent for promoting collaborative language learning. In: 4th International Conference on Intelligent Networking and Collaborative Systems, Bucharest (2012)
47. Tegos, S., Demetriadis, S.N., Karakostas, A.: Exploring the impact of a conversational agent when triggering students' discourse in online collaboration. In: 12th International Conference on Advanced Learning Technologies, Rome (2012)
48. Kumar, R., Rosé, C.P.: Engaging learning groups using social interaction strategies. In: HLT-NAACL, Los Angeles (2010)
49. Dohsaka, K., Asai, R., Higashinaka, R., Minami, Y., Maeda, E.: Effects of conversational agents on human communication in thought-evoking multi-party dialogues. In: Healey, P.G.

T., Pieraccini, R., Byron, D., Young, S., Purver, M. (eds.) 10th ACL SIGDIAL, pp. 217–224, Morristown (2009)

50. Mori, M.: The uncanny valley. Energy **7**, 33–35 (1970)

51. Nass, C., Moon, Y.: Machines and mindlessness: social responses to computers. J. Soc. Issues **56**, 81–103 (2000)

52. Adkins, M., Burgoon, M., Nunamaker, J.F.: Using group support systems for strategic planning with the united states air force. Decis. Support Syst. **34**, 315–337 (2003)

53. Ayoub, J.L., Vanderboom, C., Knight, M., Walsh, K., Briggs, R., Grekin, K.: A study of the effectiveness of an interactive computer classroom. Comput. Nurs. **16**, 333–338 (1998)

54. Bostrom, R.P., Anson, R., Clawson, V.K.: Group facilitation and group support systems. In: Jessup, L., Valchich, J. (eds.) Group Facilitation and Group Support Systems, pp. 146–168. Macmillan, New York (1993)

55. Briggs, R.O., Adkins, M., Mittleman, D., Kruse, J., Miller, S., Nunamaker, J.F.: A technology transition model derived from field investigation of gss use aboard the U.S.S. CORONADO. JMIS **15**, 151–195 (1998)

56. Dennis, A.R., Nunamaker, J.F., Vogel, D.R.: A comparison of laboratory and field research in the study of electronic meeting systems. JMIS **7**, 107–135 (1990)

57. Fjermestad, J.S.R.H.: Group support systems: a descriptive evaluation of case and field studies. JMIS **12**, 115–159 (2000)

58. Hosler, K.A., Arend, B.D.: The importance of course design, feedback, and facilitation: student perceptions of the relationship between teaching presence and cognitive presence. Educ. Media Int. **49**, 217–229 (2012)

59. Kelly, G.G., Bostrom, R.P.: Facilitating the socio-emotional dimension in group support systems environments. JMIS **14**, 23–44 (1997)

60. Mosvick, R., Nelson, R.: We've Got to Start Meeting Like This! A Guide to Successful Business Meeting Management. Scott Forseman, Glenview (1987)

61. Niederman, F., Beise, C.M., Beranek, P.M.: Issues and concerns about computer-supported meetings: the facilitator's perspective. MIS Quart. **20**, 1–22 (1996)

62. Vogel, D.R., Nunamaker, J.F., Martz, W.B., Ronald, G., McGoff, C.: Electronic meeting system experience at IBM. JMIS **6**, 25–43 (1989)

63. Dickson, G.W., Lee-Partridge, J.E., Limayem, M., Desanctis, G.L.: Facilitating computer-supported meetings: a cumulative analysis in a multiple-criteria task environment. Group Decis. Negot. **5**, 51–72 (1996)

64. Keeling, K., Beatty, S., McGoldrick, P., Macaulay, L.: Face value? Customer views of appropriate formats for embodied conversational agents (ECAs) in online retailing. In: 37th HICSS, Big Island (2004)

65. McBreen, H.: Embodied conversational agents in e-commerce applications. In: Dautenhahn, K., Bond, A., Cañamero, L., Edmonds, B. (eds.) Socially Intelligent Agents, vol. 3, pp. 267–274. Kluwer Academic Publishers, Boston (2002)

66. Pak, R., Fink, N., Price, M., Bass, B., Sturre, L.: Decision support aids with anthropomorphic characteristics influence trust and performance in younger and older adults. Ergonomics **55**, 1059–1072 (2012)

67. Beldad, A., Hegner, S., Hoppen, J.: The effect of virtual sales agent (VSA) gender – product gender congruence on product advice credibility, trust in VSA and online vendor, and purchase intention. Comput. Hum. Behav. **60**, 62–72 (2016)

68. Forlizzi, J., Zimmerman, J., Mancuso, V., Kwak, S.: How interface agents affect interaction between humans and computers. In: Koskinen, I., Keinonen, T. (eds.) DPPI 2007, p. 209. ACM Press, New York (2007)

69. Krämer, N.C., Karacora, B., Lucas, G., Dehghani, M., Rüther, G., Gratch, J.: Closing the gender gap in STEM with friendly male instructors? On the effects of rapport behavior and gender of a virtual agent in an instructional interaction. Comput. Educ. **99**, 1–13 (2016)
70. Braslavski, P., Blinov, V., Bolotova, V., Pertsova, K.: How to evaluate humorous response generation, seriously? In: Shah, C., Belkin, N.J., Byström, K., Huang, J., Scholer, F. (eds.) CHIIR 2018, pp. 225–228. ACM Press, New York (2018)
71. Endrass, B., Rehm, M., André, E.: Planning small talk behavior with cultural influences for multiagent systems. Comput. Speech Lang. **25**, 158–174 (2011)
72. Ochs, M., Pelachaud, C., Mckeown, G.: A user perception-based approach to create smiling embodied conversational agents. ACM Trans. Interact. Intell. Syst. **7**, 1–33 (2017)
73. Kolfschoten, G.L., de Vreede, G.-J.: A design approach for collaboration processes: a multimethod design science study in collaboration engineering. JMIS **26**, 225–256 (2009)
74. Chandra, L., Seidel, S., Gregor, S.: Prescriptive knowledge in IS research: conceptualizing design principles in terms of materiality, action, and boundary conditions. In: 48th HICSS, Kauai (2015)
75. Briggs, R., de Vreede, G.-J.: ThinkLets: Building Blocks for Concerted Collaboration (2009)
76. Leimeister, J.M.: Collaboration Engineering: IT-gestützte Zusammenarbeitsprozesse systematisch entwickeln und durchführen. Springer Gabler, Berlin (2014). (in German)
77. Jenkins, M.-C., Churchill, R., Cox, S., Smith, D.: Analysis of user interaction with service oriented chatbot systems. In: Jacko, J.A. (ed.) HCI 2007. LNCS, vol. 4552, pp. 76–83. Springer, Heidelberg (2007). https://doi.org/10.1007/978-3-540-73110-8_9
78. Medhi Thies, I., Menon, N., Magapu, S., Subramony, M., O'Neill, J.: How do you want your chatbot? An exploratory wizard-of-oz study with young, urban Indians. In: Bernhaupt, R., Dalvi, G., Joshi, A., Balkrishan, Devanuj K., O'Neill, J., Winckler, M. (eds.) INTERACT 2017. LNCS, vol. 10513, pp. 441–459. Springer, Cham (2017). https://doi.org/10.1007/978-3-319-67744-6_28
79. Morrissey, K., Kirakowski, J.: 'Realness' in chatbots: establishing quantifiable criteria. In: Kurosu, M. (ed.) HCI 2013. LNCS, vol. 8007, pp. 87–96. Springer, Heidelberg (2013). https://doi.org/10.1007/978-3-642-39330-3_10
80. Ghose, S., Barua, J.J.: Toward the implementation of a topic specific dialogue based natural language chatbot as an undergraduate advisor. In: International Conference on Informatics, Electronics and Vision, Dhaka (2013)
81. Salomonson, N., Allwood, J., Lind, M., Alm, H.: Comparing human-to-human and human-to- AEA communication in service encounters. J. Bus. Commun. **50**, 87–116 (2013)
82. Avery, M., Auvine, B., Streibel, B., Weiss, L.: Building UnitedJudgment: A Handbook for Consensus Decision Making. The Center for Conflict Resolution, Madison (1981)
83. Adams, S., et al.: Mapping the landscape of human-level artificial general intelligence. AI Mag. **33**, 25 (2012)
84. Egen, G.: Face to Face: The Small Group Experience and Interpersonal Growth. Brooks/Cole, Monterey (1971)
85. Nimavat, K., Champaneria, T.: Chatbots: an overview, types, architecture, tools and future possibilities. J. Sci. Res. Dev. **5**, 1019–1026 (2017)
86. Meuser, M., Nagel, U.: ExpertInneninterviews—vielfach erprobt, wenig bedacht. Theorie, Methode, Anwendung. In: Bogner, A., Littig, B., Menz, W. (eds.) Das Experteninterview, pp. 71–93 (2002). (in German)
87. Bittner, E.A.C., Oeste-Reiß, S., Leimeister, J.M.: Where is the bot in our team? Toward a taxonomy of design option combinations for conversational agents in collaborative work. In: 52nd HICSS, Maui (2019)

88. Montero, C.A.S., Araki, K.: Enhancing computer chat: toward a smooth user-computer interaction. In: Khosla, R., Howlett, R.J., Jain, L.C. (eds.) KES 2005. LNCS, vol. 3681, pp. 918–924. Springer, Heidelberg (2005). https://doi.org/10.1007/11552413_131

89. Kusber, R.: Chatbots – conversational UX platforms. In: Smolinski, R., Gerdes, M., Siejka, M.,Bodek, M.C. (eds.) Innovationen und Innovationsmanagement in der Finanzbranche, pp. 231–244. Springer Gabler, Wiesbaden (2017). https://doi.org/10.1007/978-3-658-15648-0_11

90. Ramesh, K., Ravishankaran, S., Joshi, A., Chandrasekaran, K.: A survey of design techniques for conversational agents. In: Kaushik, S., Gupta, D., Kharb, L., Chahal, D. (eds.) ICICCT 2017. CCIS, vol. 750, pp. 336–350. Springer, Singapore (2017). https://doi.org/10.1007/978-981-10-6544-6_31

Cognition, Emotions and Learning

Anti-procrastination Online Tool for Graduate Students Based on the Pomodoro Technique

Kholood Almalki[✉], Omnia Alharbi[✉], Wala'a Al-Ahmadi[✉],
and Maha Aljohani[✉]

Jeddah University, Jeddah, Saudi Arabia
{Kalmalki0127.stu, oalharbi0095.stu, walahmadi0031.stu,
mmaljohani}@uj.edu.sa

Abstract. Procrastination is the inclination to postpone or delay performing a task. Graduate students face challenges during their academic studies or when working through their thesis process, which affects their performance. This research aims to develop a tool that helps the graduate students to manage their time by using the Pomodoro technique. The Pomodoro technique suggests 25 min of studying, following five minutes break. Moreover, the tool calculates the required time to complete a subject or assignment considering the exam date or the assignment due date, the complexity of the material and how many materials to study. Furthermore, to avoid wasting time, the tool suggests resources based on the uploaded materials, for example, In the case of reading a paper related to your thesis, the tool suggests similar papers based on the keywords or the title of the current paper you're reading. Finally, if the student procrastinates, the tool senses delaying and warrens the student to take immediate action.

Keywords: Time management · Procrastination · Pomodoro Technique

1 Introduction

Procrastination is the action of postponing appointments, tasks, thoughts, making decisions, important discussion or taking a degree for another day, month or year (Gargari et al. 2011). Studies have shown that a huge number of individuals are affected by procrastination and some of the reasons relate to mental health problems (Lukas and Berking 2017) (Stead et al. 2010) (Ferrari and Díaz-Morales 2014). Academically, procrastination has significant effects on the student's behavior, health, and psychology (Hooda and Saini 2016). Procrastination has a variety of forms, for example, some students delay the submission of an assignment, complete a project, or prepare for an exam until the deadline is approaching. The underlying reasons for students' procrastination include, first, the students at some point tend to be showing a lack of motivation, due to the fear of failure (Hooda and Saini 2016). Second, time management for a graduate student is critical starting from reading numerous papers,

© Springer Nature Switzerland AG 2020
P. Zaphiris and A. Ioannou (Eds.): HCII 2020, LNCS 12206, pp. 133–144, 2020.
https://doi.org/10.1007/978-3-030-50506-6_10

wandering the internet and libraries searching for papers and books to the preparing for the thesis require a vast amount of time and effort, one of the reasons that lead graduate students to procrastinates is perfectionism (Onwuegbuzie 2000).

Pomodoro Technique is a historical technique invented in the early 1900s by Francesco Cirillo, he named the technique Pomodoro after the timer shaped like tomato he used when he was a university student to track his work (Henry 2019). The tool has proven its effectiveness for time management and self-regulate (Cirillo 2006). Pomodoro technique methodology is simple, if you have a large task, break it down into smaller ones with a short break between each task (Henry 2019). Therefore, the technique is very useful to use to decrease procrastination facing graduate students. In this research, due to the presented reasons, we develop a tool that focuses on graduate students who are suffering from procrastinating during the work on a graduate thesis or completing graduate courses, and they have minimum experience in using technology.

The Pomodoro Technique is 25 min of focused studying, following 5 min break (Cirillo 2006). The tool calculates the required time to complete a subject or assignment considering the exam date or the assignment due date, the complexity of the material and how many materials to study. Furthermore, to avoid wasting time, the tool suggests resources based on the uploaded materials. Finally, if the student procrastinates, the tool senses delaying and warrens the student to take immediate action.

2 Related Work

The research of (You 2016a) focuses on the use of the predictive value of the learning management system (LMS) in examining the academic performance. The study focuses on how the student often studies, the total viewing time for the course's videos, attending the sessions, and late submissions of assignments. The data from the 530 underground students were collected. As a result, the total viewing time and messages created were found not significant. Furthermore, the results indicated the importance of self-regulated learning, particularly regular study according to the course schedule, the time to complete assigned tasks, frequent accessing of course materials, and the reading of relevant course information. The study proves the advantages of regularly accessing course material and keeping track of the learning schedule.

Likewise, the research of (You 2016a), this research (You 2015b) uses the absence, and late submission of assignments was used to investigate the relationship between the academic procrastination and the course achievement in the e-learning. The study was conducted on approximately 600 students. The absence score in this study counted when the student did not look at the scheduled learning materials within the predetermined time or incomplete viewing of the required lecture videos. The results showed that students' achievement is negatively affected if the absence score is high and/or submission of assignments is late.

LAD is another example that is a tool that visualizes the information of the students' online course performance. The main goal of LAD is to help students to be aware of their studying habits. By self-assessing and self-reflection, students change their studying strategies to improve their performance. The tool gives real-time feedback which motivates the student to do better and give more effort. The tool could be helpful not only for students but also for teachers who want to track their student performance. (Park and Jo 2015).

A visualized dashboard is designed to help students and teachers. The tool is inspired by jogging and sports applications, these types of applications trace users' activities to motivate them to get better at getting better, the same goal goes for this tool. The tool tracks and then demonstrates the learner online activities including social network and peer activities so that the learner can improve his/her learning habits and strategy. Also, the tool recommends resources, activities, people, and activities of other learners based on the data gathered about user behavior (Duval 2011).

To measure the academic procrastination, the researcher in (Bakhtiar and Kasim 2017) uses quantitative analysis on the data collected from students using pre-experimental design. The objective is to define the student's academic procrastination behavior before and after the given cognitive restructuring techniques. The research was conducted on 14 students. Moreover, to collect the data, questionnaires and observation techniques were used. The results showed that the level of academic procrastination behavior of the students is high for several reasons, like the tendency to procrastinate to start working, completing academic assignments, completing tasks difficulty, problematic to prioritize tasks. Next, after conducting cognitive restructuring techniques, academic procrastination behavior of students has reduced.

The data do not converge between procrastination and academic performance in many studies, that may occur for many reasons. The use of small samples is one of the most critical influences on the study's results. Therefore, to positively affect the accuracy of the outcome, the researchers should use the meta-analysis technique. It is a statistical analysis combining the outcomes of many scientific types of research for the same subject. Kim and Seo (2015) use this technique on 33 relevant studies and more than 38500 participants to aggregation the outcomes of previous studies of the connection between procrastination and academic achievement and recognize factors that influence the relationship. The result of this study proposes that procrastination was negatively related to GPA, the grade of assignment and quiz degrees. Additionally, it has related to cheating, plagiarism and low academic performance (Roig and DeTommaso 1995) (Whitley 1998).

E-Learning environment allows students to have freedom and flexibility in education when compared to traditional methods. At the same time, it increases the procrastination rates in the completion of projects and academic work. Generally, the effect of procrastination tends negatively for students. The procrastination rates change from person to person, depending on several factors like motivation and self-efficacy. Motivation gives the student a stimulating feeling to do the work. In a study by Yang et al. The research of Yang et al. (2012) represents that self-efficacy has a significant impact on the students when using the e-learning environment and facilitates system design and perceived usefulness have the opposite influence on procrastination.

Steel (2007), estimated procrastination rate among undergraduate students is 70–95%. A study by Entezari et al. (2018) has specified the procrastinating behavior of students by tracking their activities in an undergraduate engineering course and observation the relationship with their course degree. By using tools to measure the learning of students during the course. The outcome of the study clarifies the excellent performance of the students' works one- or two-days early deadline. Compared to students who do their work 24 h before the deadline, where have poor results. Therefore, this work helps to improve students' academic performance and monitoring their learning habits.

2.1 Summary

The procrastination affects passive to the performance of student results (Kim and Seo 2015), primarily when they work in the 24 h before the deadline (Entezari et al. 2018). Additionally, there are many factors that depend on procrastination rates, such as motivation and self-efficacy (Yang et al. 2012).

The factors used in the (You 2016a, 2015b) are related to students' time management. Even with providing the pre-planned schedule, and a reasonable time to complete a task, the student is still procrastinating. Moreover, (Park and Jo 2015) and (Duval 2011) aim to inform students of their studying habits, the results show a significant impact on students' performance.

The study presented by (Bakhtiar and Kasim 2017) has a positive effect on reducing the academic procrastination behavior of the students by using cognitive restructuring techniques. Besides, the study provided by (Duval 2011) used a tool to suggest resources, activities, people, and activities according to the learning habits and strategy of the student. The studies presented by (Bakhtiar and Kasim 2017) and (Duval 2011) are attempted to enhance student productivity and performance by applying various techniques and tools.

In the proposed study, we attempted to reduce academic procrastinating by using a time management technique which is the Pomodoro Technique. Moreover, the proposed work conducts tools for facilitating the studying process by suggesting a material related to student studies and calculate the required time to complete the necessary tasks.

2.2 Comparison

The following comparison table describes the similarities and differences between our study and other related studies (Table 1).

Table 1. Comparison between our study and other related studies

Reference	Similarities	Differences
(You 2016a, 2015b)	• All are related to study academic procrastination • All are aims to improve academic performance	• Focus on reducing academic procrastination by applying techniques and tools for enhancing the studying process
(Park and Jo 2015)	• Both are designed for students in general • Both are tools to increase productivity	• For graduate students Uses Pomodoro Technique to increase productivity
(Duval 2011)	• Both targeted students • Both intended to increase students' productivity • Both recommend activities based on the student's activities pattern	• Focused on graduate students • Intended to increase Academic productivity with the use of the Pomodoro technique • Recommends similar Scientific papers
(Bakhtiar and Kasim 2017)	• Both are measuring the academic procrastination • Both are using techniques to reduce the academic procrastination	• Uses a tool that helps students to manage their time
(Entezari et al. 2018)	• Both are designed for students in general • Both encourage to read	• For graduate students • The average reading speed of paper
(Yang et al. 2012)	• Both are designed for students in general • Both encourage to read • Both are tools to increase productivity	• For graduate students • Suggesting similar papers

3   Research Objective

This research aims to develop a tool that helps graduate students to manage their time, increase their productivity and decrease procrastination by using the Pomodoro Technique. Our research questions that drew the research objectives are:

- Does the proposed Anti-Procrastination tool that adopts the Pomodoro technique is effective in increasing the productivity of graduate students?
- How does the proposed Anti-Procrastination tool adopt the Pomodoro technique is different from any other remainder tool?
- How can the complexity of a paper be measured by the proposed Anti- Procrastination tool?
- How can the content of the material be identified if it is subjective or objective by the proposed Anti-Procrastination tool?

4 Design and Methodology

The methodology of the research is divided into two sections: first, we designed the Anti-Procrastination Online Tool for graduate students based on the idea of the Pomodoro Technique. Second, we conducted a diary study with the intended participants. Figure 1 illustrates the diary studies phases and what we covered in each phase.

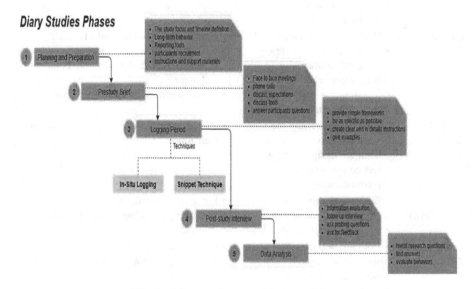

Fig. 1. Diary studies research methodology

4.1 Study Design

The proposed research is adopting a diary study that employs a mixture of quantitative and qualitative data. The study consists of three Stages. The First Stage is a series of well-structured questionnaires to evaluate the students studying behaviors before conducting the study. The Second Stage is a daily report by the participants about their experience. The last Stage is questionnaires to obtain the participants' feedback on using the tool.

The research concentrates on graduate students. A total of 15 graduate students in the Faculty of Computer Science and Engineering at the University of Jeddah are participating in the study.

The time the Pomodoro technique takes for one session of concentrated studying is 25 min long followed by a short break of 5 min or a long break for 15 min. The minimum time to complete one session is only 30 min. Therefore, the expected time to do the study is at least one hour for each participant.

4.2 Study Process

Diary studies are conducted to obtain participants' studying and researching behaviors while using the tool. The study consists of three stages. Table 2 shows the tasks, time, type of data collection, and researcher roles in each stage. The second stage is the on-going study consist of multiple tasks as shown in Table 3.

Table 2. Study process stages

Data collection type	Time	Tasks	Stages
Quantitative and qualitative	The average questionnaire time takes 7 min	An online questionnaire to explore the graduate students' studying behavior The questionnaire contains both open-ended and close-ended questions	Pre-study
Quantitative and qualitative	This stage takes 4 weeks period, the participants send daily feedback reflecting their experience on using the tool	Clear and detailed instructions are provided	On-going study
Quantitative and qualitative	The average time to answer the questionnaire is about 7 min	An online questionnaire, to obtain the participants' reflections about the tool	Post-study

Table 3. The on-going study tasks

Tasks	Description
Introduction	A brief introduction at the beginning to describe what is the used technique and what the tool is intended to do
Instruction	Instructions are provided, for example: how many hours they must spend on using the tool, they should send daily feedback… etc.
Using the tool	Each participant uses the tool on a given material
participant's review	Each participant sends daily online feedback reflecting on their experience during the 4 weeks of using the tool

Study Equipment. The equipment being used through the study are shown in Fig. 2.

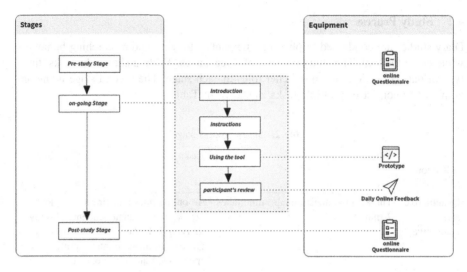

Fig. 2. Study equipment

Study Instruments. Figure 3 shows the interfaces of the tool, (1) is the home page showing the tool name and the instructions on how to use the tool. (2) shows the uploaded materials and the suggested materials based on the uploaded materials. (3) shows the timer, where the user can click work to start the timer, short break for 3 min, long break lasts for 7 min, and the stop button to stop the timer.

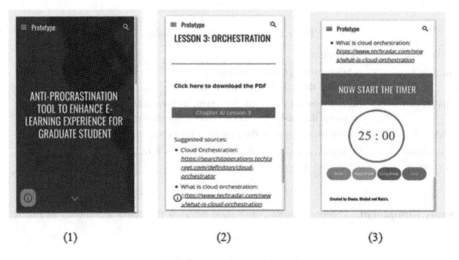

(1)   (2)   (3)

Fig. 3. Website interfaces

5 Data Analysis and Results

Quantitative and qualitative data were collected during the study process. In terms of the quantitative, the data is collected based on a success rate, time to complete a task, error rate, and end-user's satisfaction. In terms of the qualitative data, it is collected from the reflection notes resulted from the diary study. The results of the study have shown that the tool increases productivity and decreases the procrastination time of graduate students. Moreover, the tool helps find similar papers, calculates the complexity. Participants were stratified in using the technology which is reflected by the success rate and the time to complete the tasks.

5.1 Pre-study

The pre-study questionnaire shows that 100% of participants have a time management problem while studying for an exam or reading a paper. The participants rated their time management problems and their tendency to procrastinate on scale 1 to 5, where five means that they have a severe problem with time management and procrastination. Figure 4 shows the results, 62.5% of participants have a time management problem on level 3, while 25% at level 5. Moreover, 75% of participants have the tendency to procrastinate at level 3, while 12% at level 5. Additionally, 62% admit that their tendency to procrastinate is because they avoid or delay difficult tasks. Finally, only 50% of participants have heard about the Pomodoro Technique.

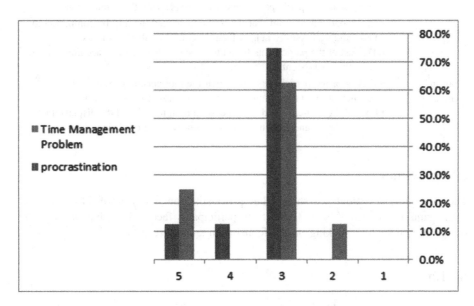

Fig. 4. Time management and procrastination relationship.

5.2　On-Going-Study

The daily feedback from the participants was collected and categorized into four categories which are related to the following areas:

- Time
- Breaks
- Tasks
- Tool in general

Table 4 shows the daily feedback from the participants.

Table 4. Daily feedback

Feedback area	Feedback
Time	• All participants used the tool for three to four hours per day • One of the participants had a problem to be within the time limit • Three participants indicated that they are using the tool as it is, but they suggest changing the focusing time to be more than 25 min • Eleven participants agreed that the tools help them to manage their time and complete their tasks at the required time
Break	• One of the participants did not take the first break at all (5 min) • Two of the participants had a problem with the restriction of the break time • One participant found that 5 min break is not enough • The rest of the participants were comfortable with the 5 min break
Tasks	• Seven participants said that the tool encouraged them to be committed to tasks and successfully helped them to complete all target tasks • The rest of the participants found that the tool helped them accomplish their tasks to some extent
Tool in general	• Eleven of the participants found that the tool encouraged them to accomplish the tasks, motivates them and organizes their work • Four of the participants did not get used to it, they found the displayed timer very stressful, and it distracts them from focusing on their tasks

5.3　Post-study

The post-study questionnaire shows that procrastination behavior of 71.4% of the participants is reduced. Also, 28.6% of the participants faced some challenges while using the tool such as sticking on the focusing time and break time.

6　Limitations

The study has some notable limitations, as follows: The study was conducted on 15 graduate students which may be considered as a small sample size. Accordingly, as future work, a large number of participants will be involved in the study to obtain more data. The process of gathering qualitative data from the on-going and post surveys is a time-consuming process that needs an appropriate amount of time to analyze the data to obtain accurate results.

7 Conclusion

The proposed tool helps graduate students on managing their time, increase their productivity and decrease procrastination. The proposed tool is adopting the Pomodoro technique, the technique proves its effectiveness in time management. The tool applies the technique on activities concerns graduate students such as reading papers, recommending papers related to their thesis, warns them if any delay detected.

References

Bakhtiar, M.I., Kasim, S.N.O.: Cognitive restructuring application techniques to reduce student behavior in academic procrastination (2017)

Cirillo, F.: The Pomodoro Technique (2006)

Duval, E.: Attention please!: learning analytics for visualization and recommendation. In: LAK 2011, pp. 9–17 (2011)

Entezari, N., Darvishzadeh, A., Stahovich, T.: Using an instrumented learning environment to understand procrastination. In: 2018 IEEE Frontiers in Education Conference (FIE), pp. 1–8. IEEE, October 2018

Ferrari, J., Díaz-Morales, J.F.: Procrastination and mental health coping: a brief report related to students. Indiv. Differ. Res. **12**(1), 8–11 (2014)

Gargari, R.B., Sabouri, H., Norzad, F.: Academic procrastination: the relationship between causal attribution styles and behavioral postponement. Iran. J. Psychiatry Behav. Sci. **5**(2), 76 (2011)

Henry, A.: Productivity 101: An Introduction to The Pomodoro Technique. Lifehacker. https://lifehacker.com/productivity-101-a-primer-to-the-pomodoro-technique-1598992730. Accessed 12 July 2019

Hooda, M., Saini, A.: Academic procrastination: a critical issue for consideration. J. Educ. Psychol. Res. **6**(8), 98–99 (2016)

Kim, K.R., Seo, E.H.: The relationship between procrastination and academic performance: a meta-analysis. Pers. Individ. Differ. **82**, 26–33 (2015)

Lukas, C.A., Berking, M.: Reducing procrastination using a smartphone-based treatment program: a randomized controlled pilot study. Internet Interv. **12**, 83–90 (2017)

Onwuegbuzie, A.: Academic procrastinators and perfectionistic tendencies among graduate students. Soc. Behav. Pers. **15**(5), 103 (2000)

Park, Y., Jo, I.H.: Development of the learning analytics dashboard to support students' learning performance. J. Univ. Comput. Sci. **21**(1), 110 (2015)

Roig, M., DeTommaso, L.: Are college cheating and plagiarism related to academic procrastination? Psychol. Rep. **77**(2), 691–698 (1995)

Stead, R., Shanahan, M., Neufeld, R.: "I'll go to therapy, eventually": procrastination, stress and mental health. Pers. Individ. Differ. **49**(3), 175–180 (2010)

Steel, P.: The nature of procrastination: a meta-analytic and theoretical review of quintessential self-regulatory failure. Psychol. Bull. **133**(1), 65 (2007)

Whitley, B.E.: Factors associated with cheating among college students: a review. Res. High. Educ. **39**(3), 235–274 (1998)

Yang, C.Y., Lai, A.F., Chen, M.C., Hwang, M.H., Li, C.Y.: An investigation on procrastination in the e-learning environment. In: 2012 8th International Conference on Information Science and Digital Content Technology (ICIDT 2012), vol. 3, pp. 616–620. IEEE, June 2012

You, J.W.: Examining the effect of academic procrastination on achievement using LMS data in e-learning. J. Educ. Technol. Soc. **18**(3), 64 (2015)

You, J.W.: Identifying significant indicators using LMS data to predict course achievement in online learning. Internet High. Educ. **29**, 23 (2016)

Semantically Annotated Learning Media for Reduced Cognitive Load

Zainb Dawod[(✉)] and David Bell

College of Engineering Design and Physical Sciences,
Computer Science Department, Brunel University London,
Uxbridge UB8 3PH, UK
zainb003@hotmail.com

Abstract. The use of Semantic Web in education has become more significant in recent years. A topic that has received less attention to date is the use of such technologies for supporting special educational needs (SEN). Semantic annotation is now one of the challenges for building the semantic web and dealing with all the different data that exist on the web such as text, pictures or media. Research tries to annotate educational web resources with concepts and relations from explicitly defined formal ontologies. This formal annotation is usually created manually, semi-automatically or automatically. The Semantic Web initiative has had an impact in the educational field and offers potential support for better understanding of learning content. This paper presents an augmented World Wide Web (WWW) vision utilising annotation to more effectively support special educational need students. Students are supported in part by a SEN Teaching Platform (SENTP). This platform is designed with additional support for cognitive load using specific annotation formats within the Amaya annotation tool and coordinated with web application. We present details of the SENTP structure, design and practically how this SENTP is implemented for a poetry topic in literacy lesson. The potential of our approach has been confirmed by a positive user evaluation building on field-testing study at seven UK schools and interviewing twenty-three participants. The findings indicate that applying cognitive load principles to annotated content can improve both learning and class behaviour.

Keywords: Semantic web · Semantic Web annotation (Amaya) · Cognitive Load Theory · SEN Teaching Platform (SENTP) · Effective teaching · Design Science Research

1 Introduction

It has been hypothesized that special need students' understanding, engagement, behaviour and concentration are among the main problems in teaching those with special educational needs. Understanding is especially difficult when learning material with a high cognitive load. Hence, an inappropriate instructional design can impose a high extraneous cognitive load that interferes with the students' level of understanding any learning content. Cognitive Load Theory (CLT) focuses on presenting educational instruction to decrease extraneous cognitive load by considering split attention effect,

© Springer Nature Switzerland AG 2020
P. Zaphiris and A. Ioannou (Eds.): HCII 2020, LNCS 12206, pp. 145–164, 2020.
https://doi.org/10.1007/978-3-030-50506-6_11

redundancy effect and modality effect [43]. Errey et al. [20] stated that high extraneous load occurs when the learner tries to extract information from multiple sources and subsequently integrate it. More importantly, complicated or irrelevant information should be reduced when designing multimedia messages for special needs children, even more than for typically developing learners [28].

Building on Mayer s' theory [32], people can learn more deeply from words and pictures than from words alone. Hence, we can reduce extraneous process by presenting text with near corresponding pictures [32].

The most popular methods to teach special needs in UK are symbol systems (Blissymbolics, Picture Communication Symbols (PECS), Widgit, Signalong and Makaton) as well as images and Diagrams. Building on our previous work [14, 15], we refined the previous platform from a pilot study by employing cognitive load theory principles. In this study, we employ split attention effect, redundancy effect and modality effect on educational content. This assumption challenged our research; hence, we suggested re-designing educational instructions in a specific way, which could reduce extraneous cognitive load, then improve the learning outcomes. We achieve our goals by using semantic annotation techniques by allowing the staff to select the required metadata or add the metadata of their choice. The motivations for promoting semantic annotation tools and cognitive load theory (CLT) motivated the design of a new platform which could support students with a variety of learning needs.

Therefore, we designed the SEN Teaching Platform (SENTP) ontology model using protégé 5, select semantic annotation tool (Amaya) coordinated with a web application.

We contributed with a detailed practical evaluation at seven schools caring for special needs in the UK. So during the study of real analysis, we applied new SENTP framework based on cognitive load theory to increase the understanding ability of concept affecting at the better able to learn, engage and concentrate.

2   Research Design and Platform Process

The study follows a design research approach that starts with learning about the problem space leading through to design artefact evolvement and evaluation. Hevner [24] described the process as an effective solution to a problem. The effectiveness of the solution must be provable through an iterative evaluation of the design artefact(s). The artefact resulting from the Design Science Research (DSR) in this work was to induce the characterisations of the SENTP model. This study aims to build and refine a number of micro-designs (content, annotation and process). Importantly, core theories of learning and memory systems, including those related to cognitive load, direct the design of the SENTP [31, 34]. Artefacts (such as web content and the SENTP architecture) are refined to minimise the cognitive load and enable efficient use of working memory in order to improve communication, aid understanding, and reduce the effort and time needed for resource preparation. Typically optimal performance can be achieved by offering presentation strategies that reduce cognitive load [29]. Consequently, the annotation techniques used with the Amaya [2] tool offer a number of types of annotation for field testing such as images, information, symbol systems, pictures, information, and audio. The final refined framework can be summarized in four main steps, as illustrated in Table 1. The table presents the Iteration Steps, Method and Input-Output Model.

Table 1. Iteration steps, method and input–output model

Steps	Method	Input artefact	Output artefact
1. Identify problems/user requirements identification **An awareness of the problem**	Review the pilot study results	Pilot study results **(Instantiation)**	A proposal for extending the SENTP Redesign the SENTP UI **(construct)**
2. Employ CLT to the design of the SENTP **Suggestion**	literature review (CLT-Redundancy effect, Split Attention effect and Modality effects)	A proposal for extending the SENTP Redesign the SENTP UI **(construct)**	An improved educational poetry website with CLT **(model)**
3. Refine and extend the SENTP model by incorporating CLT principles **Development**	Extend SENTP Annotation process	An improved educational poetry website with CLT **(model)**	Annotated web page text and extended prototype application **(method)** **(instantiation)**
4. Observe the SENTP in action, with proof of concept **Evaluate SENTP**	Semi structured interviews **(Qualitative method)**	Annotated web page text and extended prototype application **(method)** **(instantiation)**	A SENTP **(Instantiation)**

3   Design and Build SENTP Framework

This section describes the design of a SENTP framework and subsequent development of content. The design based on our previous studies [14, 15]. In response to the users' requirements from previous studies and based on further research in literature, we listed a set of objectives, which is described in Table 2.

Table 2. SENTP framework with CLT principles

No	Description	Literature
1	Reduce behaviour problems	'They are too often disruptive in the regular classroom; thus, you are depriving the regular students of the complete education they deserve. 'An autistic child has difficulty with social interaction, communication skills, imagination and they can be easily distracted' [23] 'Teachers showed awareness of the need for low-attaining pupils to be able to focus on the task in hand' [19]
3	Improve students' understanding	'They are incapable of doing the same work as their peers, and begin to act out' [16]
4	Save class preparation time,	'The reports mark a radical response to concerns that workload is one of the major challenges affecting teachers' [17]
6	Easy to use, edit and maintain	'SEN students have low tolerance level and a high frustration' level [21]
7	Used in different subjects	'Visual learning techniques are used widely in schools across the country to accomplish curriculum goals and improve student performance' [3]
8	To integrate two types of sources such as image and text or symbol cards and text	'They find integration of information is difficult. It can be difficult and physically overloaded' [30]
9	Reduce repeated or similar messages from different resources	'The use of images, along with words, diminishes the overwhelming nature of text and helps the student to manage the cognitive load, which increases retention' [43]
10	Present each web page as a combined learning materials such as visual (image, symbols) with sound	'Replace a written explanatory text and another source of visual information such as a diagram (unimodal) with a spoken explanatory text and a visual source of information (multimodal)' [43]
11	Support/replace manual teaching methods	'Students are under-performing because of the inconsistency between teachers, teaching styles and students' learning styles' [45]
12	Displaying visual materials during verbal demonstration or using audio	'Words process in the verbal channel and pictures process in the visual channel. Thus, both verbal and pictorial information require being integrated [12]

(*continued*)

Table 2. (*continued*)

No	Description	Literature
14	Support students with differing severities of autism	'People with autism they demonstrate excellent performance on visually presented tasks and other tasks that support direction. However, they find integration of information is difficult. It can be difficult and physically overloaded' [30]
15	Increase class engagement	'For students with disabilities, engagement (participation of the child in learning) is the single best predictor of successful learning' [10, 25]

Cognitive load (CL) refers to the amount of cognitive demand imposed by a particular task on a person, which is related to the limited capacity of working memory [11, 12] The rationale behind CLT is that the quality of instructional design is enhanced if attention is paid to the limitations of working memory. The objective of using ideas surrounding CL in the SENTP is to examine a key question: "To what extent can semantic annotation techniques reduce the burden of CL for SEN learners?"

There are two aspects to CL, explained by Sweller [39]:

- Reducing intrinsic load: The design of the SENTP should consider the ability of semantic annotation to lower the cognitive load by reducing task complexity, as explained by Ayres [4]. This will be done by adding different forms of annotations, real images, and improving the presentation layout of the User Interface (UI) by using different colours and fonts relevant to the needs of the SEN user.
- Reducing any extraneous Cognitive Load (CL) imposed by the instructional design itself through the integration of the annotations.

Figure 1 illustrates the proposed SENTP framework. Amaya is certainly a good starting point for creating educational content. In this design, it is an annotation tool that supports the teaching and learning of SEN students. However, it needs to be modified to meet the SENTP requirements listed in Sect. 3. The features that need to be modified are as follows:

1. The SENTP should have an option to display visuals (images, symbol systems such as Makaton, PECS, and Widgit) while verbally demonstrating the platform or the provision of audio annotation using headphones with visuals to reduce the contiguity effect [40].
2. A combination of text and visuals, such as images or symbol systems or text and sound, can reduce the split-attention effect. Cognitive capacity in working memory is limited so that if a learning task requires too much capacity, learning will be hampered. The recommended solution is to design instructional systems that optimize the use of working memory capacity and avoid cognitive overload. These results in reducing the time required to keep information active in working memory, without the need to integrate information resources mentally.

3. The learning content should include short text to re reduce the intrinsic load.
4. Visuals should include enough information to reduce the redundancy effect. Importantly, educational content enables exploration of the influences of semantic annotation on SEN teaching and learning, including motivation, understanding, communication and satisfaction. Field testing was used to examine the effectiveness of the SENTP.

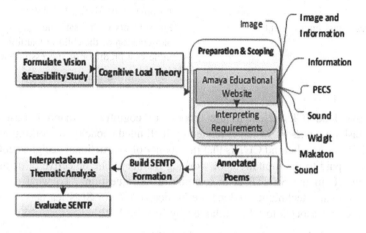

Fig. 1. SENTP **Framework**

Figure 2 presenting a SENTP diagram of employing CLT principles channel, diagrams and spoken text that rely on both auditory and visual modalities can be used.

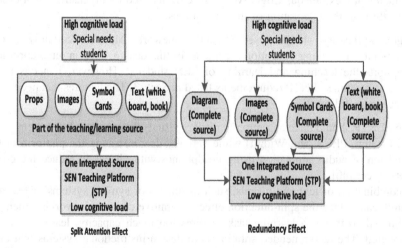

Fig. 2. SENTP with cognitive load theory (CLT) framework

4   Building SENTP Ontology

The architectural approach of the semantic web is relatively straightforward, creating a layer on the existing web that enables advanced automatic processing of the web content so that data can be shared and processed by both humans and computers [27]. Ontologies from part of the semantic web and provide a mean for defining a domain-specific language for education- Special Educational Needs (SEN) in particular.

The basic components of the semantic web are; metadata, semantic web languages, ontologies, semantic mark-up of pages and services [18]. They can be summarised as follows:

4.1   Metadata

Metadata is data about data which means the data that describes another piece of data as shown in Fig. 3. Some developers consider the Metadata as the heart of e-learning [38].

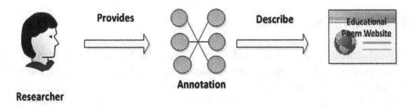

Fig. 3. Representation of metadata

4.2   Semantic Web Languages

The basic ontology language and simple models used for combining data and representing information on the web. They have typically used the Resource Description Framework (RDF), which could be represented as a labelled graph [18, 8, 22, and 1] and are based on XML (then called RDF/XML). Many of the languages based on XML. Resources are described using RDF statements, which are represented as subject, predicate and object (see Fig. 4). SENTP ontology is designed and implemented for a wider design using desktop system (Protégé 5). Protégé has become widely used software for building and maintaining ontologies [36].

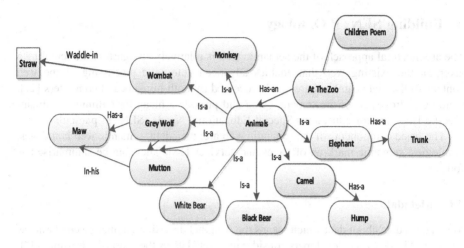

Fig. 4. Representation of RDF statement

5   SENTP Implementation

We designed educational ontology and website using HTML that integrates with the selected annotation tool 'Amaya'. The selection was based on the cost and the school convenience. First, the class teacher selects a poem, style, and type of annotation required for the class demonstration. The platform is prepared beforehand with the kind of annotation required (e.g. images or Makaton symbols). The annotation options are wide-ranging, depending on SEN age and needs. Figure 5 presents the poetry webpage with different annotation options.

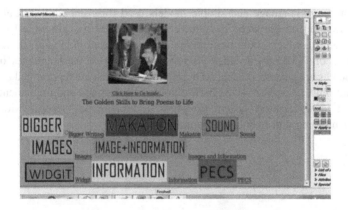

Fig. 5.   SENTP Graphical User Interface (GUI)

Figure 6 presents the 'Bedtime' poem with the selected words for annotation and an annotation symbol 'I' with Makaton.

Fig. 6. Presents the 'Bedtime' poem annotations

Figure 7 presents another annotation with text and image.

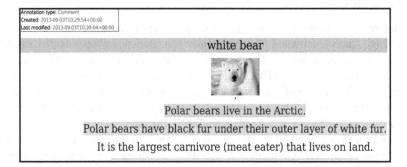

Fig. 7. Illustrate the integration of the picture with the text

6 Data Collection

Data were collected whilst field testing the designed artefacts. The aim was to gather data in order to assess and further develop the SENTP framework and educational content. Data collected from February 2013 to October 2013 and follow qualitative approach. Semi-structured interviews were used, in addition to field notes and researcher/staff observation. The interviews provided an opportunity to explore personal experiences that may otherwise have been hard to observe [31, 41]. The data collection activities are described below.

6.1 Participant Recruitment

Field-testing annotation interviews were carried out at seven schools in the UK. Table 3 provides an overall description of the participants.

Table 3. The overall description of the participants

Description	Total
Sample size	23
Female	21
male	2
Age range SEN children	(2.5-19 years)
Teacher (T)	7
Preschool teaching assistant (TA)	7
Preschool manager/deputy manager and T/TA	3
Special High school/teaching assistant	5
Head teacher (HT)	1
Special school for SEN (secondary)	2
Special school for SEN (pre-school)	1
Nursery cares for SEN	3
State school cares for SEN (speech and language)	1

6.2   Research Instruments

The main research tools were the interview questions framework, and the website supported by Amaya software. The questions were direct and open-ended to allow participants to be more engaged and detail their experiences. An example learning website was designed using HTML, supported by Amaya, containing poetry of different styles as the sample of teaching materials. The NVivo11 [37] software package was employed to carry out thorough and reliable qualitative data analysis. It is a very reliable management tool that can aid in analysing the data [44].

A prototype was presented in schools on a laptop and a projector in a classroom. A digital voice recorder, "Olympus VN-8600PC" was used along with a small notebook and a pen for extra notes.

All the interviews were managed by the researcher using the interview sheet. All recordings were transferred onto a personal laptop and two USB drives secured with a password known only to the researcher.

7   Data Sources

Following the ethical approval given by Brunel University, sixty-one schools caring for SEN students were approached via email, telephone and the postal service. Each school was sent a covering letter along with an information sheet. Seven schools agreed to participate in the research. Of those seven, six completed the interview procedure, and one subsequently withdrew. The data was collected over a six-month period due in part to the scheduling and timing pressures within a typical school. In total, twenty-three interviews were conducted. Table 4 Group demographics are included in Table 5.

Table 4. Group demographic data

NO	Code	Job	Experience
1	T1-M-SMA	T	All SEN, all Subjects, 11–19 years, 16 years teaching experience
2	T2-M-P	T	EYFS curriculum, 3 months - 5 years
3	TA1-M-SMA	TA	SEN ICT support, support 11–19 years
4	TA2-M-SMA	TA	All SEN, all Subjects, 11–19 years
5	TA3-M-P	TA	Early Years Foundation Stage (EYFS), 3 months - 5 years
6	TA4-M-SN	TA	EYFS, 3 months - 5 years
7	TA5-M-SN	TA	EYFS, 2–5 years
8	T3-M-SN	T	EYFS, 2–5 years
9	T4-M-SR	T	EYFS, 3–5 years
10	TA6-M-SR	TA	All subjects, 2–5 years
11	T5-M-SM	HT/T	Nursery manager, 2–5 years, teaching adults
12	T6-M-SMO	T	All SEN
13	TA7-M-SMO	TA	All SEN
14	T7-M-SMO	T	All SEN, all subjects. age 6–19 years
15	TA8-M-SMO	TA	All SEN, experience with 5-30 years. Worked in school and outside with community
16	TA9-M-SP-CH	TA	EYFS, 2 years and 9 months - 5 years, language and communication delay, Makaton
17	T9-M-SP-CH	T/Manager	EYFS, 2 years and 9 months - 5 years, language and communication delay
18	TA10-M-SP-CH	TA	EYFS, 2 years and 9 months to 5 years, language and communication delay
19	TA11-M-SP-CH	TA/Deputy Manager	EYFS, 2 years and 9 months - 5 years, language and communication delay. Other school experience includes teaching year 1–4
20	TA12-M-SP-CH	TA	EYFS, 2 years and 9 months - 5 years, language and communication delay
21	T8-M-PI	T	Support teaching, reading and comprehension skills, writing groups for gifted and talented group, children with additional language, gifted and talented children, worked in infant schools 7–12 years
22	T10-M-SMO	HT	ALL SEN, age 6–19 years

8 Thematic Analysis

Thematic analysis is used as part of the wider design process to elicit future requirements and more importantly determine artefact effectiveness. Consequently, the SENTP design with the Amaya annotation is assessed during interviews, using CLT principles to examine reductions in cognitive load. All interview data were analysed using thematic analysis [7, 9]. After gaining familiarity with the data, the transcription analysis process involved listening to the interviews, reading through the data and uncovering possible themes [7]. First codes were generated from the transcript information. The qualitative data analysis software NVivo11 was used to facilitate the thematic analysis, and transcript data was exported to NVivo11 that then coded the features from the entire dataset. Themes were identified and reviewed. Each theme captured something important about the data in relation to the requirements and problems being addressed. All data relevant to each theme was extracted and matched with specific codes. A model of themes is presented to show the connections and relationships between the themes and the subthemes [6, 7]. Below, nine codes are describing the themes and sub-themes. Table 4 outlines the details of the themes and sub-themes.

Table 5. Open-coding concepts categorization

Codes	Theme	Sub-themes
Current Teaching Methods	Manual (21), Computer with application (14), Support (2), Preparation (8), Differentiation (12)	Internet, visual (12), Images (10), Symbol systems (5), Application (4), Sound (3), Flashcards (7), Games (4), Sign language (4), One-to-one support (1), Preparation time (8), Difficult to support (1)
Important Factors for Teaching SEN	Type of Resources (4), Reduce preparation time (16), Independency, differentiation (5), Mood, class management (2), Understanding (9), Group size (one-to-one or small group) (13), Communication (3)	Visual and audio (12), Simplicity (5), Attractive layout (i.e. font, colour, design) (5), Resources are easy to use (1), Counting the ability level (2), Design, style and type of resources (4), Attention and listening (3), Individual needs (2), Engaging (2), Vocabulary (1), Prepare text and images for each topic (2), Preparation time, support ASD, staffing
Cognitive Load Awareness and Resource Preparation	Individual needs (3), Simplicity (2), Language (2), Resources (2), Group work (1), Behaviour problems (1)	Combine the options and present them in the same area (text, image, sound, symbols), simplify the content-short text (3), The design of the resources (1)
SENTP for Autism spectrum disorder) (ASD)	Visual (3), Combination of resources (11), Emotion (2), Symbols (1), Class management (1), Communication (1), Availability (1), Preparation (1)	One-to-one support (1), Can Express Emotions (1), Support untrained staff (1), Support severe autism (1), Better communication (1), Vocabulary (2)

(continued)

Table 5. (*continued*)

Codes	Theme	Sub-themes
Poetry	Difficult to understand (4), Good Teaching Material (5), Interpretation Required (2), Required Expression of Emotion (1)	Simplify the lesson (1), Difficult to understand the underlying meaning (1), Visuals are essential (2), Challenging (1), Figurative language (2), Imaginary and inference is greater (3), Interpretation (2)
SENTP Evaluation	Aid for Individual Needs (7), Preparation Time and Effort (13), Class Management (14), Reduce/Replace Resources (20), Enhance Teaching and Learning (21), Benefit Autistic Students (5), Engagement (10), Resource Availability (4), Support Teaching staff (21), Understanding (2), Behaviour Problems (13), Availability (3), Support Different Groups of SEN (4), Easy to Use (7), Communication (7), Simplicity (2), Effective Lesson - with combination of image, text and/or symbol (10), Better Teaching Results (12), Reduce Split Attention (10), Design (8)	Reduce Resources (19), Replace resources (1), Increase motivation (14), Increase engagement (10), Increase concentration (4), Save preparation time (12), Better class management (14), Support different types of SEN-ASD (5), Visual learners (4), Hearing impairments (1), Mood (4), ADHD (1), Reduce boredom (3), Frustration (1), Physical special needs (1), Support speech delay (1), Replace teaching, staff (3), Reduce teaching staff (8), Reduce pressure on teaching staff (11), Available any time (3), Support group (4), Better understanding (1), Effective teaching tool (3), Simple instruction required (11), A tool that can be chosen in the future (21), Offer independence in facility use (1), SEN impression of the idea (5), Interesting idea (21), Simplify the topic (1), Support when short of staffing (6), Offer successful delivery of poetry lesson (5), Support untrained staff (9), Support children with additional language (2), Offer efficient way of teaching when presenting a combination of image, text and/or symbol in the same area of the screen (5), Enhance SEN teaching/learning in: Science (2), Maths (3), Humanities (1), Storytelling, literacy (1) and special projects (1)

9 SENTP Evaluation

The evaluation shows that SENTP within the SEN domain makes significant contributions towards SEN teaching and learning. One of the most important visits was to the special needs secondary school where a demonstration was conducted by T7-M-SMO. This was a challenging classroom, with different levels of severity of special needs. The teacher presented the class with four poems, asking students if they wanted more content after each poem, instead of teaching just one, as agreed before the lesson. The immediate feedback from the students and the teacher reaction demonstrated that the entire class was engaged and motivated during the demonstration as noted by T2-M-P: 'they were well involved, they can take part with their actions, with their hands, fingers, very engaged and looking at the computer screen and watching all the images, very involved' and part of the email sent by T7-M-SMO '. In consultation with the class staff, it was felt that the session was very successful. This was made clear by the high level of pupil engagement during the lesson '… the design of the prototype shows promise'. Also, T8 confirmed that some children they may lose their attention because of their physical disability and the traditional way they are using to teach them 'TA8-M-SMO: 'It does make it easier because our children will not have the ability and understanding of turning pages and going there because they lose their attention, their attention is only a couple of seconds'. This shows that SENTP can keep the concentration and engagement of SEN student with physical disability last longer. This can propose a better understanding of the learning materials.

Using the SENTP encouraged group work method as well. The class teacher, T7-M-SMO reported that he will suggest group work method for his class in addition to the current approach of independent learning as the headteacher attended and observed the demonstration and establish that the demonstration was successful: 'I am going to have a word with him and see what he thought because our English and Maths is usually done at workstations and I think there is space for group work as well; they work very well'. He confirmed that in his email when he said 'The prototype could be used for target groups during teaching and would be a valuable resource when finalised. This shows that SENTP can support group work to reduce the one-to-one staff demand and to overcome the difficulty in learning with others in small or large group settings.

Furthermore, the tool was shown to be useful for class management, as indicated by T1-M-SMA, a teacher in the special secondary school. Her class includes children with a mix of severe issues, and she has good background experience: 'we have children with severe learning difficulties, including children with Down's syndrome. I have experience teaching autistic children; we also have children with genetic disorders and severely challenging behaviour; we have a huge range of children'. T1-M-SMA commented on classroom management: 'all the students were quiet and listened when the lesson started'. This shows that SENTP support teachers with managing the special need class that they could easily distracted with behaviour problems.

All the participants agreed that visuals are important to SEN. The manager at the pre-school indicated that the image annotations within the SENTP could improve engagement and attention 'It's visual, isn't it? It keeps their attention'. The teaching assistant at the pre-school indicated that having different options for annotation types can offer various types of teaching methods: 'They give a broad range of ideas and thinking, and we can use different ways to teach children'. This point was furthered in an email sent by the teacher from a special secondary school: 'The ability to have instant access to images etc. and not have to rely on on-the-spot searching would contribute to the pace of the lessons and thereby minimise anxious behaviour and increase understanding'. Hence, SENTP could reduce the student cognitive load because it increases attention.

Most of the participants pointed out that the annotation included within the SENTP is fun and interesting, as indicated by the teaching assistant from the special secondary school: 'I think it is quite engaging; children enjoy looking at the images in the classes'. The teaching assistant from the special secondary school agreed: 'Actually, the student sitting next to me actually participated because he was signing what he saw, what you said […] he seemed to be enjoying it, so yes'. The teacher from the pre-school said: 'The session went quite well. It was very easy-going, the children really enjoyed it, and I think they benefited from it'. SENTP can reduce a behaviour problem which is one of the main concerns in teaching special needs. SENTP could reduce student frustration and improve their mood as noted by many participants, and the teaching assistant from the special secondary school confirmed that 'It takes away quite a lot of the frustration of not understanding. It takes out the boredom of not understanding until all of them have understood'. These benefits of the SENTP are of particular importance in reducing behaviour problems of special need students as they tend to have low tolerance levels and high frustration levels.

The participants agreed that the SENTP could be adapted to subjects other than poetry such as Religious Studies, Science, History and Math, as indicated by the teacher from the special secondary school: 'I think it is really good; that is what I am left with today. That the concept of a click in the text and it pops up with a photo is very good, something we could use for poems, for all kind of things, anything that has text'. This demonstrates that SENTP can be utilised in teaching different learning content to support SEN students such as the one who struggles with their poor handwriting skills and the difficulty in following complicated directions or remembering directions for extended periods of time.

The teachers consider the SENTP as an 'easy to use' tool, which the teaching assistant touched on: 'Yes, I would like to use it because it is the simpler way to teach and grab children's attention, and [it works] on different levels for different children'.

Many participants believed that the SENTP can save preparation time; the teaching assistant from the special secondary school said: 'it's good for teaching; we can concentrate on assessing more students because we have to assess them on regular bases'. This shows that SENTP can save the staff time and effort to free them for other significant work.

Other points related to the ability of the SENTP to support the teaching staff were noted by some of the interviewees who said: 'I think the speech therapist would be very interested to see this software' [...] 'it's interesting'.

In summary, since student's capacity to learn a concept is directly associated to how much cognitive load is used to comprehend the material and their working memory is fixed size. The significant problem is when learning is impaired when processing requirements exceeds the capacity of working memory. We designed the educational content instruction with semantic annotation to minimise cognitive load. To measure cognitive load we used. Not many of the teaching staff aware of the cognitive load theory and its effect on learning, which makes measuring not precise. Hence, ten (50% of the participants) believed that SENTP could reduce spilt attention effect, and then enhance learning (see Fig. 8). Only five (25% of the participants) believed that SENTP could reduce redundancy effect (see Fig. 9).

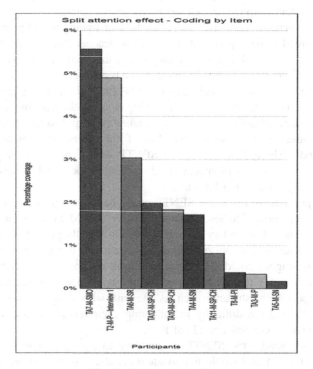

Fig. 8. Split attention effect

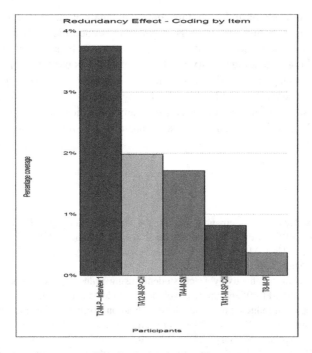

Fig. 9. Redundancy effect

10   Conclusion and Future Works

A considerable gap exists between Semantic Web utilisation in the field of mainstream education when compared to special educational needs education. The teaching methods available in a special needs school are typically based on time-consuming, manual methods. SEN can affect a child's ability to learn, their behaviour and ability to socialise. Reading, writing, understanding, concentration and physical abilities are also more limited (Chen, 2011). This paper presents a novel approach to special needs teaching and learning and finds that Semantic Web annotation techniques can reduce the SEN cognitive load within the classroom. Consequently, the designs and resulting system (developed using Amaya) and the usage methodology enhances the learning process of SEN through the use of a range of annotation types.

Design practice and contributions underpinned all of this research. Design Science Research methods directed the constructs, models, methods and instantiations employed. The artefacts include both larger frameworks (e.g. SENTP) and smaller media content. Furthermore, SENTP ontology is designed and implemented for a wider design using Protégé 5.

Participant requirements defined the application of CLT principles within a number of technological artefacts. The platform was extended by following a set of method-ological guidelines to reduce the SEN cognitive load, reducing the split-attention and redundancy effects. Interviews were conducted to identify the impacts of semantic annotation techniques when teaching poetry for students with a wide range of SENs and with different levels of understanding. Interview analysis supported a combination of text with images, sound, or symbols in order to reduce the SEN cognitive load. Consequently, the classroom benefitted from reductions in behavioural problems and increasing SEN understanding. Poetry teaching material was used that supported CLT, increasing SEN engagement and motivation. The platform can also support teaching staff with class management techniques, including resource preparation. Schools use different types of sign and symbol systems, many of which are integrated into the platform. Children with additional languages are also possible end-users of the proposed approach.

References

1. Allemang, D., Hendler, J.: Semantic Web for the Working Ontologies. Effective Modelling in RDFS and OWL. Elsevier Inc., Amsterdam, The Netherlands (2008)
2. Amaya: Amaya User Manual (2015). https://www.w3.org/Amaya/User/doc/Manual.html. Accessed 21 May 2015
3. Aurthor, G.: How to effectively teach students using video, 15 September 2011. http://gettingsmart.com/2011/09/how-to-effectively-teach-students-using-video/
4. Ayres, P.: Impact of reducing intrinsic cognitive load on learning in a mathematical domain. Cognit. Psychol. **20**(3), 287–298 (2006). https://doi.org/10.1002/acp.1245
5. Baddeley, A.: Working Memory. Am. Assoc. Adv. Sci. **255**(5044), 556–559 (1992)
6. Braun, V., Clarke, V.: Using thematic analysis in psychology. Qual. Res. Psychol. **3**(2), 77–101 (2006). ISSN 1478-0887
7. Braun, V., Clarke, V.: Teaching thematic analysis, look at overcoming challenges and developing strategies for effective learning. Psychologist **26**(2), 9120–9124 (2013)
8. Berners-Lee, T.: The next web. TED (2009) http://www.ted.com/talks/tim_berners_lee_on_the_next_web.html
9. Castleberry, A., Nolen, A.: Thematic analysis of qualitative research data: is it as easy as it sounds? Curr. Pharm. Teach. Learn. PubMed **10**(6), 807–815 (2018). https://doi.org/10.1016/j.cptl.2018.03.019
10. Carpenter, B.: Children with complex learning difficulties and disabilities. Specialist Schools and Academies Trust (2010). www.ssatrust.org.uk
11. Chen, F.: Automatic Multimodal Cognitive Load Measurement (AMCLM) (2011)
12. Chen, O., Castro-Alonso, J.C., Paas, F., et al.: Extending cognitive load theory to corporate working memory resource depletion: evidence from the spacing effect. Educ. Psychol. Rev. **30**, 483–501 (2018). https://doi.org/10.1007/s10648-017-9426-2
13. http://www.dtic.mil/dtic/tr/fulltext/u2/a547654.pdf. Accessed 03 Mar 2016
14. Dawod, Z., Bell, D.: Adaptive Special educational needs (SEN) education on the Semantic Web. In: Proceedings of the U.K. Academy for Information Systems, 16th Annual Conference (2011)
15. Dawod, Z., Bell, D.: Designing effective teaching interventions with semantic annotation. In: Kurosu, M. (ed.) HCI 2016. LNCS, vol. 9733, pp. 505–518. Springer, Cham (2016). https://doi.org/10.1007/978-3-319-39513-5_47

16. Dawo, F.: Special education teaching: teaching students with special needs in inclusive classroom (2015). https://www.youtube.com/. Accessed 04 Dec 2015
17. MP, N.: Teacher Workload: New Measures Announced. Department for Education and Morgan (2016)
18. Devedzic, V.: Education and the semantic web. Int. J. Artif. Intell. Educ. **14**(2), 39–65 (2004a)
19. Dunne, M., Humphreys, S., Sebba, J., Dyson, A., Gallannaugh, F., Muijs, D.: Effective teaching and learning for pupils in low attaining groups (2007). http://dera.ioe.ac.uk/6622/1/DCSF-RR011.pdf. Accessed 10 Dec 2014
20. Errey, C., Ginn, P., Pitts, C.: Cognitive load theory and respondent user interface. Making software easy to learn and use (Part 1) (2006). http://www.ptgglobal.com/papers/psychology/cognitive-load-theory.cfm
21. Fredericks, E.: Cross-functional involvement in new product development: a resource dependency and human capital perspective. Qual. Mark. Res. **8**(3), 327–341 (2005). https://doi.org/10.1108/13522750510603370
22. Ghaleb, F., Daoud, S., Hasna, A., Jaam, J., El-Seoud, S.A., El-Sofany, H.: E-learning model based on semantic web technology. Int. J. Comput. Inf. Sci. **4**(2), 63–71 (2006)
23. Glazzard, J., Hughes, A., Netherwood, A., Neve, L., Stokoe, J.: Teaching Primary, Special Educational Needs (Achieving QTS Series). Learning Matters Ltd. (2010)
24. Hevner, A.R.: A three-cycle view of design science research. Scand. J. Inf. Syst. **19**(2), 87–92 (2007)
25. Iovannone, R., Dunlap, G., Huber, H., Kincaid, D.: Effective educational practices for students with autism spectrum disorders. Focus Autism Dev. Disabil. **18**(3), 150–165 (2003). https://doi.org/10.1177/10883576030180030301
26. Jeroen, J.G., Merrienboer, V., Sweller, J.: Cognitive load theory and complex learning: recent developments and future directions. Educ. Psychol. Rev. **17**(2), 147–177 (2005). https://doi.org/10.1007/s10648-005-3951-0
27. Jung, B., Yoon, I., Lim, H.: Ramirez-Weber, F.A., Petkovic, D.: Annotizer: user-friendly WWW annotation system for collaboration in research and education environments. In: Proceedings of the IASTED International Conference on Web Technologies, Applications and Services, pp. 113–118 (2006). http://www.lw20.com/201202175670121.html
28. Khan, T.M.: The effect of multimedia learning on learners with different special education needs. Soc. Behav. Sci. **2**, 4341–4345 (2010)
29. Kalyuga, S., Chandler, P., Sweller, J.: Incorporating learner experience into the design of multimedia instruction. J. Educ. Psychol. **92**(1), 126–136 (2000). https://doi.org/10.1037//0022-0663.92.1.126
30. LoPresti, E.F., Bodine, C., Lewis, C.: Assistive technology for cognition [understanding the needs of persons with disabilities]. IEEE Eng. Med. Biol. Mag. **27**(2), 29–39 (2008). https://doi.org/10.1109/emb.2007.907396
31. Marshall, C., Rossman, G.: Designing Qualitative Research. Sage, Newbury Park (1989)
32. Mayer, R.E.: Multimedia Learning. Cambridge University Press, Cambridge (2009)
33. Mayer, R.E.: Multimedia Learning. Cambridge University Press, Cambridge (2001). https://doi.org/10.1017/CBO9781139164603
34. Mayer, R.E.: Cognitive theory and the design of multimedia instruction: an example of the two-way street between cognition and instruction. New Dir. Teach. Learn. **2002**(89), 55–71 (2002). https://doi.org/10.1002/tl.47
35. Mayer, R.E., Heiser, J., Lonn, S.: Cognitive constraints on multimedia learning: when presenting more material results in less understanding. J. Educ. Psychol. **93**(1), 187–198 (2001)

36. Musen, M.A.: The protégé project: a look back and a look forward. AI matters **1**(4), 196–359 (2015). https://doi.org/10.1145/2757001.2757003
37. NVivo qualitative data analysis software. QSR International Pty Ltd. Version 11 (2014)
38. Sammour, G.N.: E-learning systems based on the semantic web. Int. J. Emerg. Technol. Learn. (IJET). **1**(1) (2006)
39. Sweller, J., Chandler, P.: Why some material is difficult to learn. Cognit. Instr. **12**(3), 185–233 (1994)
40. Sweller, J.: Visualisation and instructional design. In: Ploelzner, R. (ed.) Proceedings of the International Workshop on Dynamic Visualizations and learning, pp. 1502–1510. Tubingen, Germany (2002)
41. Patton, M.Q.: Qualitative Evaluation Methods. Sage Publications Inc., Newbury Park (1980)
42. Protégé. https://protege.stanford.edu/. Accessed 11 Dec 2016
43. Van Merriënboer, J.J.G., Sweller, J.: Cognitive load theory and complex learning: recent developments and future directions. Assoc. Adv. Comput. Educ. J. **17**, 147–177 (2005)
44. Zamawe, F.C.: The implication of using NVivo software in qualitative data analysis: evidence-based reflections. Malawi Med. J. **27**(1), 13–15 (2015)
45. Zane Education: discover the educational benefits of visual learning and its value to students in education, Zane (2015). http://www.zaneeducation.com. Accessed 04 Dec 2015

Learner's Mental State Estimation with PC Built-in Camera

Shinobu Hasegawa[1](✉), Atsushi Hirako[1], Xianwen Zheng[1],
Shofiyati Nur Karimah[1], Koichi Ota[1], and Teruhiko Unoki[2]

[1] Japan Advanced Institute of Science and Technology,
1-1 Asahidai, Nomi, Ishikawa 923-1292, Japan
hasegawa@jaist.ac.jp
[2] IMAGICA GROUP/Photron, 1-105 Jinboucho, Kanda, Chiyoda,
Tokyo 101-0051, Japan

Abstract. The purpose of this research is to estimate learners' mental states such as difficulty, interest, fatigue, and concentration that change with the time series between learners and their learning tasks. Nowadays, we have many opportunities to learn specific topics in the individual learning process, such as active learning and self-directed learning. In such situations, it is challenging to grasp learners' progress and engagement in their learning process. Several studies have estimated learners' engagement from facial images/videos in the learning process. However, there is no extensive benchmark dataset except for the video watching process. Therefore, we gathered learners' videos with facial expression and retrospective self-report from 19 participants through the CAB test process using a PC built-in camera. In this research, we applied an existing face image recognition library Face++ to extract the data such as estimated emotion, eye gaze, face orientation, face position (percentage on the screen) by each frame of the videos. Then, we built a couple of machine learning models, including deep learning methods, to estimate their mental states from the facial expressions and compared them with the average accuracy of prediction. The results demonstrated the potential of the proposed method to the estimation and provided the improvement plan from the accuracy point of view.

Keywords: Mental state estimation · Machine learning · PC built-in camera

1 Introduction

In recent education, Information and Communication Technology (ICT) has a primary role in daily instruction. Besides, the rapid development of the Internet increases new learning opportunities beyond the school, such as Open CourseWare (OCW) and Massive Open Online Courses (MOOCs). Also, ICT has the potential to accelerate Active Learning that involves actively engaging students with their own pace through problem-solving, group-work, case-studies, and discussions. In these situations, learners need to make their learning activities in a self-directed/-regulated way.

Due to such a paradigm shift with ICT in education, instructors face a problem in learners' assessment and support. In the traditional classroom, instructors could grasp

© Springer Nature Switzerland AG 2020
P. Zaphiris and A. Ioannou (Eds.): HCII 2020, LNCS 12206, pp. 165–175, 2020.
https://doi.org/10.1007/978-3-030-50506-6_12

learners' engagement from the atmosphere, interaction, and examinations. In the context of ICT in education, on the other hand, it is hard for instructors to assess learners' engagement since individual learning goals, place, and process are different. Therefore, our challenges to support ICT in education are how to estimate the mental state of learners during such individual learning process.

The purpose of this research is to estimate learners' mental states such as difficulty, interest, fatigue, and concentration that change with the time series between learners and their learning tasks. One of the basic ideas is to use facial expressions that convey the mental state of human beings and express how well they engage at the current moment. This topic is attractive to many researchers in this research area, such as computer vision and affective computing scientists. Thus, facial expressions are applicable to many kinds of applications, such as mental state estimation of an e-learning platform.

Nowadays, most laptop/tablet PCs used as learning terminals at ICT in education have a built-in camera used only for specific purposes such as video conferences. This challenge is to estimate the learners' mental states from the learners' external state (facial expression) through the PC built-in camera image (without any additional devices). This research would be necessary for realizing immediate feedback in the individual learning process of a modern learning environment.

The rest of this article is organized as follows. Section 2 introduces the recent related work for engagement/mental state estimation in the learning process. Section 3 addresses a data collection that includes facial expression and PC screen videos from 19 participants who answered 30 puzzle-like questions. Section 4 describes a developed neural network from the gathered data to compare the average accuracy of prediction by using some traditional machine learning methods. Section 5 concludes this article and discusses future improvement plans from the accuracy point of view.

2   Related Work

In the related work, there are diverse approaches to estimate learner's mental states from: (1) facial expressions, including eye gaze and head pose, (2) body motion and postures, and (3) biometric signals such as blood pressure, galvanic skin response, heart rate, and electroencephalographic (EEG) signals.

2.1   Estimation by Facial Expressions

Whitehill et al. explored automatic engagement recognition by Gentle-Boost with Box Filter features, support vector machines with Gabor features, and multinomial logistic regression with expression outputs of 10 s video clips captured from 34 undergraduate students who participated in a "Cognitive Skills Training" experiment, in which the Computer Expression Recognition Toolbox was utilized [1].

Dewan et al. employed deep belief network (DBN) for engagement classification using the features obtained from Local Directional Pattern (LDP) to extract person-independent edge features for the different facial expressions and Kernel Principal Component Analysis (KPCA) to capture the nonlinear correlations among the extracted features [2]. They conducted experiments on the Dataset for Affective States in E-Environments (DAiSEE) that includes 112 individuals and 9068 video snippets while watching educational video (approximately 10 s with 1920 × 1080 pixels at 30 fps) [3]. Win et al. also tried to apply the style transfer technique with the VGG-16 face model to obtain the basic features of the facial expressions and eliminates the non-related features for engagement estimation by differing peak and neutral frames with DAiSEE dataset [4].

In this research, we use facial expressions because of their consideration as non-verbal communication [5], which plays a significant role in recognizing the learner's mental state, such as difficulty, interest, fatigue, and concentration.

2.2   Estimation by Body Motions

Kaur et al. proposed an unsupervised topic modeling technique for engagement detection as it captures multiple behavioral cues such as eye gaze, head movement, facial expression, and body posture with DAiSEE and Engagement in the Wild datasets [6]. Engagement in the Wild contains 264 videos captured from 91 subjects (around 5 min with 640 × 480 pixels at 30 fps) [6].

Chang et al. proposed a cluster-based framework for fast engagement level predictions, a neural network using the attention pooling mechanism, heuristic rules using body posture information, and model ensemble for more accurate and robust predictions in the EmotiW dataset [7]. They adopted OpenFace [8] to track head pose, gaze directions, and action units and OpenPose [9] to track head, body, and hands as feature extractions. EmotiW dataset contains 197 video clips in which students watch the educational video with about 5 min long [10].

These researches showed that learner's body motion and postures are essential factors to detect their mental state. In addition, they utilized facial expressions for their detections. To distinguish the impact of facial expressions in mental state estimation, we mainly focus on facial videos.

2.3   Estimation by Biometric Signals

Fairclough et al. investigated the convergent validity between psychophysiological measurements and changes in the subjective status of the individual. 35 participants performed a demanding version of the Multi-Attribute Task Battery (MATB) and were collected EEG, ECG, skin conductance level, EOG, and respiratory rate and correlated with changes in subjective state as measured by the Dundee Stress State Questionnaire [11].

Monkaresi et al. challenged an engagement prediction method while writing activity with concurrent and retrospective self-reports from 22 participants by Updatable Naive Bayes using ANimation Units by Face tracking engine on Kinnect SDK, local binary pattern in three orthogonal planes, and heart rate [12].

One of the difficulties in learners' mental state estimation is to label their state reasonably. In some datasets such as DAiSEE, EmotiW, and Engagement in the Wild, multiple external reviewers put engagement (or other affective) labels for each scene. On the other hand, Monkaresi et al. collected concurrent and retrospective engagement self-reports from the participants [12]. Biometric signals have the potential to make such mental state labels without external reviewers and self-reports. However, video-based detection is more scalable due to the widespread availability, low cost, and lower intrusiveness of cameras compared to physiological sensors. Therefore, we decided to utilize the video collected through the built-in camera on the laptop/tablet PCs as the input for developing a mental state estimation system in challenging real-world environments typically used for education.

3   Dataset

One of the crucial requirements in developing such estimation systems is the reliability of the dataset. The public datasets such as DAiSEE, EmotiW, and Engagement are valuable as a benchmark for proposed estimation methods. However, there are some limitations to these datasets. First, the situation in these datasets is educational video watching that is usually a passive learning process. Second, most of the participants in the public datasets are Westerners, but our target participants are Orientals. Hence, it makes unclear whether the previous datasets could be applied to a more active learning process. Therefore, in this research, we first collected a dataset as training and test data for our target learning process.

3.1   Learning Task

As a learning task in this research, we adopted a "CAB test", i.e., the logical reasoning questions in Cognitive Assessment Battery (CAB) test (we call it "CAB test") [13]. The typical format in the CAB test is that there is a missing one of the five figures arranged based on a specific rule, and the remaining four figures are used to predict the rule and select the figure that matches. Figure 1 shows an example of this question.

The reasons for adopting this learning task are as follows. This task is a non-verbal exam rather than a self-directed learning activity. However, compared with video watching tasks in the previous work, this task allows learners to think and answer the questions at their own pace. This situation is closed to the expected learning process. Besides, this type of question has less variation in response time. Therefore, it is not so hard to apply a retrospective self-report to gather their mental state for each question.

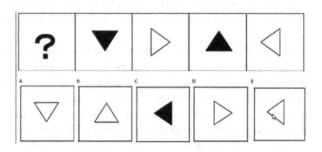

Fig. 1. Example of CAB test.

3.2   Procedure for Data Collection

The procedure for data collection in this research is as follows.

1. Introduction for data collection to participants.
2. Practice with low difficulty examples of the CAB Test in front of a laptop with a built-in camera.
3. Exam with the CAB Test within 12 min, in which there are maximum 30 questions, while capturing their faces (640×480 pixels at 30 fps) and the PC screen (1366×768 pixels at 30 fps).
4. Retrospective self-report after finishing the exam session by providing the correct answers and explanations.

Figure 2 shows examples of scenes in the dataset. In the retrospective self-report, we asked the participants to report their difficulty, interest, fatigue, and concentration for each question with a 5-Likert scale, respectively. The equipment used in this data collection process is a Lenovo E560 laptop PC, and the main specifications are as follows.

- CPU: Intel Celeron 3855U 1.60 GHz
- RAM: 8 GB
- HDD: 1 TB
- Monitor: 15.6 in. Full HD
- Built-in camera

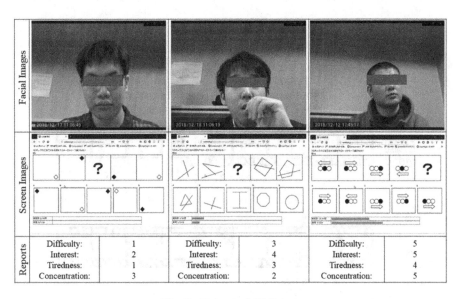

Fig. 2. Dataset of CAB test.

3.3   Feature Extraction

In estimating the learners' mental state from the facial video acquired in the previous section, extracting features for machine learning is one of the critical points. In this research, we applied an existing face image recognition library Face++ [14] to extract the data such as estimated emotion, eye gaze, face rectangle (face size on the screen), head pose, and mouth, as shown in Table 1. Figure 3 shows the procedure for extracting feature parameters from a facial video. The procedure for feature extraction is as follows.

1. Getting still images from facial video frame.
2. Acquiring feature parameters using Face++.
3. Dividing facial video into ones for each question.
4. Dividing the parameters into ones for each question.
5. Linking the parameters with self-report results.

Table 1. Feature parameters from Face++.

Category	Item	Value range
Emotion	Sadness, Neutral, Disgust, Anger, Surprise, Fear, Happiness	0–100
Eye gaze	Right Eye x, y, z, Left Eye x, y, z	−1 to 1
Face rectangle	Width, Height	0–1368
Head pose	Pitch, Roll, Yaw	−90 to 90
Mouth	Close, Open, Other	0–100

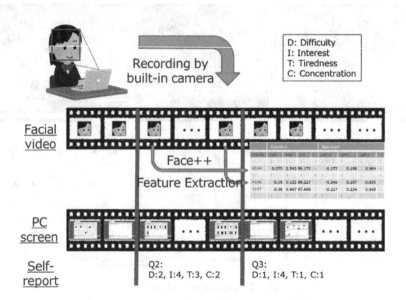

Fig. 3. Outline of feature extraction from facial video.

3.4   Data Collection

We conducted the actual data collection from June to December 2018. 19 participants (13 male and 9 females, from 20 to 46 years old) attended in this process. Due to self-report limitations (some participants did not answer a specific mental state), finally, we obtained the following dataset, difficulty: 453, interest: 453, fatigue: 452, and concentration: 285, respectively.

4   Model Building

4.1   Development Environment

In this research, we adopted TensorFlow [13] and Keras [14] for building analytical models because it supports a simple description for constructing a neural network and has enough functions for image analysis.

4.2   Estimation by Neural Network

To build the neural network (NN) from the data obtained in Sect. 3, the number of input data must be equal. The length of the data was different since the response time for each question by each participant was different. Therefore, we first compressed the data into four statistical values, i.e., average, variance, minimum, and maximum values for each series of all the feature parameters included in every question. The reason why the minimum and maximum values were used was that facial expressions that appeared only momentarily, such as surprises and disgusts, were not easily reflected in the average value. Regarding the variance, the average value could not distinguish between the eye gaze was moving from side to side and stopped at the center. We also made normalization (0–1) for each series in the compressed data to reduce the effect of numerical deviation in the neural network. In this research, the NN learning was performed under the following conditions.

- 83 input layer nodes (same as input data dimensions).
- Hidden layer used sigmoid function and had 83 nodes.
- Output layer used a softmax function and had 5 nodes (according to the 5-scale self-report).
- Learning rate was 0.2.
- The number of hidden layers changed from 0 to 5.
- 30 samples were randomly extracted as test data, and the rest were assigned to training data.
- Extracted test data was changed 50 times.
- The average of the correct answer rate for each test data was calculated.

Figure 4 shows the confusion matrix in this experiment. Here, the correct answer is colored blue, the incorrect answer with one point of difference is colored yellow, and the other incorrect answers are colored red.

D — Difficulty

Prediction	Self-report 1	2	3	4	5	Σ
1	105	53	50	28	30	266
2	30	19	29	9	5	92
3	24	44	97	83	42	290
4	42	25	81	93	73	314
5	39	15	75	80	293	502
Σ	240	156	332	293	443	1464

I — Interest

Prediction	Self-report 1	2	3	4	5	Σ
1	7	2	6	5	5	25
2	12	111	10	16	11	160
3	16	36	331	115	43	541
4	12	49	139	186	80	466
5	7	27	29	93	108	264
Σ	54	225	515	415	247	1456

T — Tiredness

Prediction	Self-report 1	2	3	4	5	Σ
1	191	60	34	34	4	323
2	21	34	50	23	7	135
3	53	58	240	88	16	455
4	22	17	91	223	56	409
5	7	9	12	52	61	141
Σ	294	178	427	420	144	1463

C — Concentration

Prediction	Self-report 1	2	3	4	5	Σ
1	335	79	24	49	12	499
2	74	119	60	39	13	305
3	24	46	127	81	18	296
4	32	29	49	112	40	262
5	2	11	8	8	33	62
Σ	467	284	268	289	116	1424

Fig. 4. Confusion matrixes in NN condition. (Color figure online)

In addition, Table 2 shows a comparison of the accuracy rates using Support Vector Machine (SVM) and k-Nearest Neighbor (KNN). For these two methods, test data was extracted 50 times at random, and the average accuracy of each test data was compared. In the KNN method, the K value (number of neighbors) was varied from 1 to 199, and the highest average accuracy rate was used for comparison.

Table 2. Comparison of average accuracy rate.

Method	Difficulty	Interest	Tiredness	Concentration
NN	0.42	0.55	0.52	0.51
SVM	0.32	0.50	0.42	0.52
KNN	0.38 (k = 4)	0.53 (k = 18)	0.51 (k = 1)	0.66 (k = 1)

4.3 Analysis by Maximal Information Coefficient

To analyze the relevance between the self-report data and the normalized data for each question described in Sect. 4.2, we calculated the nonlinear correlation coefficient using the Maximal Information Coefficient (MIC) [15]. As shown in Table 3, we can confirm weak correlations between the eye gaze parameters and all the mental states. On the other hand, the emotion parameters do not show specific correlations.

4.4 Discussions

According to the confusion matrix in Fig 4, there were around 30% "small prediction error" in which the range was ±1 even when the model could not correctly estimate from facial expressions. In this research, we used a softmax function in the output layer of NN and solved it as a five-class classification problem. However, our final goal is to detect the timing of a change in the learners' mental state. Thus, the straightforward idea is to reduce the classification labels like engaged and not-engaged (2 classes) or easy, so-so, difficult (3 classes) so that "small prediction error" can be informative for the actual application.

As a remark, we might consider the difference between the learners' mental states while learning and while retrospective self-reporting. The self-report adopted in this research has a risk that their answers would change depending on the memory or passage of time. There are other methods, such as concurrent self-report, interview, and annotation by external reviewers, each of which has advantages and disadvantages. Therefore, it is one of vital points to determine the appropriate annotation method for their mental state labeling carefully.

Table 3. Overview of nonlinear correlation coefficient by MIC

Mental state	MIC	Correlated items
Difficulty	>0.3	–
	>0.2	Emotion: Anger, Fear Eye gaze: Right Eye x, z, Left Eye x, z Face rectangle: Width, Hight
Interest	>0.3	Eye gaze: Right Eye z, Left Eye x, z
	>0.2	Emotion: Disgust, Surprise, Fear Eye gaze: Right Eye x, y, Left Eye y Face rectangle: Width, Height Head pose: Pitch, Roll, Yaw Mouth: Close
Tiredness	>0.3	–
	>0.2	Emotion: Anger, Happiness Eye gaze: Right Eye x, y, z, Left Eye x, y Face rectangle: Width, Height Head pose: Pitch, Roll, Yaw Mouth: Close, Other
Concentration	>0.3	Eye gaze: Right Eye x, z Face rectangle: Width, Height
	>0.2	Emotion: Sadness, Neutral, Disgust, Surprise, Happiness Eye gaze: Right Eye x, Left Eye x, y, z Head pose: Pitch, Roll, Yaw Mouth: Open, Other

5 Conclusion

In order to achieve the estimation of learners' mental state in a self-directed learning context, we gathered a new dataset that included facial and PC screen videos in answering the CAB test and retrospective self-report about difficulty, interest, tiredness, and concentration for each question of the CAB test from 19 participants. Then, we built an NN model to estimate their mental states from facial expressions with compressed data, i.e., average, deviation, minimum, and maximum values. As a result, the correct prediction rates for the mental states are Difficulty: 0.41, Interest: 0.55, Tiredness: 0.52, and Concentration: 0.51. We also found that eye gaze is more important than emotion, face distance, head pose, and mouth shape to estimate their mental state.

In the field of machine learning, we should prepare a massive dataset to avoid overfitting in the prediction model. In this research, we collected over 300,000 images, but only 453 paired data from the viewpoint of the number of questions. Therefore, it is one of the critical future work to gather more data in a good quality thought the development of web applications. We also have a plan to apply the Recurrent Neural Network (RNN) for the future estimation method. The RNN, which is a kind of neural network, enables to store past data in the hidden layer and to predict the time-series data. Since the data before processing in Sect. 4.2 was time-series data from continuous frames of the facial videos, the RNN would be applicable to this task if we can gather enough data. Therefore, we will try some RNN approaches such as Gated Recurrent Unit (GRU) and Quasi Recurrent Neural Network (QRNN) in the near future.

References

1. Whitehill, J., Serpell, Z., Lin, Y., Foster, A., Movellan, J.R.: The faces of engagement: automatic recognition of student engagement from facial expressions. IEEE Trans. Affect. Comput. 5(1), 86–98 (2014)
2. Dewan, M.A.A., Lin, F., Wen, D., Murshed, M., Uddin, Z.: A deep learning approach to detecting engagement of online learners. In: 2018 IEEE SmartWorld, Ubiquitous Intelligence Computing, Advanced Trusted Computing, Scalable Computing Communications, Cloud Big Data Computing, Internet of People and Smart City Innovation, pp. 1895–1902 (2018)
3. Cunha, A.D., Gupta, A., Awasthi, K., Balasubramanian, V.: DAiSEE: towards user engagement recognition in the wild (2016). arXiv preprint arXiv:1609.01885
4. Khine, W.S.S., Kotani, I., Hasegawa, S.: Study of engagement estimation with application to e-learning environment. In: the 13th International Conference on Advances in Computer-Human Interaction (ACHI2020), (2020, in press)
5. Ramya, R.: Student engagement identification based on facial expression analysis using 3D video/image of students. TAGA J. 14, 2446–2454 (2018)
6. Kaur, A., Mustafa, A., Mehta, L., Dhall, A.,: Prediction and localization of student engagement in the wild. In: Digital Image Computing: Techniques and Applications (DICTA) 2018 International Conference on IEEE (2018). https://doi.org/10.1109/dicta.2018.8615851
7. Chang, C., Zhang, C., Chen, L., Liu, Y.: An ensemble model using face and body tracking for engagement detection. In: Proceedings of the 20th ACM International Conference on Multimodal Interaction, pp. 616–622 (2018)
8. Baltrusaitis, T., Robinson, P., Morency, L.P.: Constrained local neural fields for robust facial landmark detection in the wild. In: IEEE International Conference on Computer Vision Workshops, pp. 354–361 (2013)
9. Cao, Z., Simon, T., Wei, S., Sheikh, Y.: Realtime multi-person 2D pose estimation using part affinity fields. In: The IEEE Conference on Computer Vision and Pattern Recognition (CVPR), pp. 7291–7299 (2017)
10. Dhall, A., Kaur, A., Goecke, R., Gedeon, T.: EmotiW 2018: audio-video, student engagement and group-level affect prediction. In: Proceedings of the 20th ACM International Conference on Multimodal Interaction (ICMI2018), pp. 653–656 (2018)
11. Fairclough, S., Venables, L.: Prediction of subjective states from psychophysiology: a multivariate approach. Biol. Psychol. 71(1), 100–110 (2006)
12. Monkaresi, H., Bosch, N., Calvo, R.A., D'Mello, S.K.: Automated detection of engagement using video-based estimation of facial expressions and heart rate. IEEE Trans. Affect. Comput. 8(1), 15–28 (2017)

13. Nordlund, A., Pahlsson, L., Holmberg, C., Lind, K., Wallin, A.: The cognitive assessment battery (CAB): a rapid test of cognitive domains. Int. Psychogeriatr. **23**(7), 1144–1151 (2011)
14. Megvii Technology Inc. Face++ Cognitive Services. https://www.faceplusplus.com/
15. Reshef, D.N., et al.: Detecting novel association in large data sets. Science **334**(6062), 1518–1524 (2011)

Virtual Reality as a Stress Reduction Measure – Chilling Out on the Beach in My Living Room

Kevin Pfeffel[(⊠)], Megi Elezi, Philipp Ulsamer,
and Nicholas H. Müller

University of Applied Sciences Würzburg-Schweinfurt, Würzburg, Germany
{kevin.pfeffel,phillip.ulsamer,
nicholas.mueller}@fhws.de, megi.elezi@student.fhws.de

Abstract. Digitization has many advantages, but it also creates an ever-increasing burden on people due to constant availability and a flood of information, which then results in an increased level of stress. Therefore, the study tries to use the advantages of digitalization by using Virtual Reality (VR) to create calming virtual environments, in which users can take a break from their everyday life to relax. In this special case, a 360° VR video of the city beach in Würzburg was recorded and the subjects watched it through a Head Mounted Display (HMD) while they were relaxing in a sunbed. In addition, skin conductivity was measured as an indicator of stress to find out whether the VR session had a positive influence on the stress level of the subjects. In addition, before and after the VR session the subjects should indicate their subjectively perceived stress level by means of a color scale. Although, there was a decrease in the values of electrodermal activity (EDA) during the VR session, it was not significant. On the other hand, the subjective perceived stress level before and after the VR session showed a clear difference and this difference was highly significant. Subjects felt less stressed after a VR session on the city beach than before.

Keywords: Virtual reality · Behavioral neuroscience · Stress · Skin conductance · Electrodermal activity presence · Immersion

1 Introduction

Due to the digitization of society, the term "stress" has become more important than ever. Although mobile communication facilitates everyday life in many areas, there is a continuous modus of constant activity within human beings. New external demands are driving people to be online all the time [1]. As a result, humans no longer feel able to comply to all requirements. For example, a study from a statutory health insurance in Germany showed that absences due to mental health problems such as depression, anxiety and stress disorders has risen by almost 90 percent over the past 15 years [2]. Stress does not have to be bad primarily. From an evolutionary-biological point of view, it ensures that maximum performance is achieved in emergencies. However, this can only be healthy for a limited period, as stress situations require an increased energy

© Springer Nature Switzerland AG 2020
P. Zaphiris and A. Ioannou (Eds.): HCII 2020, LNCS 12206, pp. 176–189, 2020.
https://doi.org/10.1007/978-3-030-50506-6_13

input. Therefore, if you do not plan regular time-outs, you quickly run on reserve [2]. The demands of everyday life at work, in the family and during leisure time can hardly be avoided. Without breaks, the stress level increases more and more and one's own performance and health deteriorates [1]. So the question is in which way can someone reduce stress in his or her daily life? There are many different options, for example short breaks [3–5], short breaks in particular with physical activity [6] or professional stress management or mind body techniques [7, 8]. One of the most important and effective pillars of professional stress management are relaxation techniques [9]. Relaxation techniques are techniques, which produce a relaxation response, which is the physiological opponent of a stress response [9]. In addition, these relaxation techniques can be experimentally and clinically measure how on a physiological level the stress reduction is performing [10, 11]. Relaxation techniques include classical procedures like autogenic training or progressive muscle relaxation or more motion-oriented programs such as "Taichi", "Qigong" or "Yoga" and different meditation techniques [9]. Another option to reduce stress would be going on vacation. According to a meta-analysis, it is ensured that vacations decrease health problems and exhaustion and – to a lesser extent – increase life satisfaction [12]. These effects can be observed immediately after the vacation and then subside again in the next two to four weeks [13]. Unfortunately, it is not possible to be on vacations all the time, so for everyday life one has to resort to short breaks and relaxation techniques. Nevertheless, these two forms of relaxation can also complement each other. The idea here is to take a virtual short trip with the help of Virtual Reality (VR) technology. Virtual travel could also be a relaxation technique and therefore reduce the stress level. Furthermore, the number of virtual trips are unlimited and the user is immediately situated on a beach in the Maldives or a mountain cabin in Switzerland. The user only has to wear a Head Mounted Display (HMD) and start the simulation.

Therefore, the following study will investigate whether participating in a VR simulation on a virtual beach has a significant impact on stress reduction.

2 Related Works

In this part of the study, the term "stress" should be explained exactly. Furthermore, it will be explained which physiological characteristics can occur under stress and how the human being is influenced by it. Afterwards, a relaxation reaction will be examined in more detail as an antipole. In particular, we will look at how such a relaxation reaction can be triggered. In addition, it will be briefly explained why skin conductivity was used as a measuring instrument. Finally, VR will be explained further.

2.1 The Term "Stress" and It's Physiological Mechanisms

The term "stress" is versatile and has already been defined several times [14]. One definition describes stress as everything that is perceived by the individual as stressful and unpleasant [15]. In a narrower sense, stress is a stressor-oriented reaction, whereby stressors or burdens are seen as any requirements that cause a stress reaction in humans [15]. Stressors can be physical nature, such as chronic pain or intense heat, but they can also be mental nature, such as pressure of exams or time pressure that arises in connection with performance requirements. In addition, stressors can also be of a social nature, such as in severe conflicts or separations [1].

More generally, stress reactions occur when an individual is confronted with events that threaten physical and/or mental balance [1]. This is also illustrated by the transactional stress concept. Here, psychological stress is defined as a reaction to a specific event that has a significant impact on the well-being of an individual and at the same time demands or overtaxes the individual to cope with the event that occurs [16].

The physiological mechanisms of stress affect all important organ systems and functions. In particular, it has been shown that organisms react to different stressful events with the same characteristic physical changes [17]. Therefore, it can be assumed that stress is unspecific and general. The organ systems and functions affected are respiratory tract, cardiovascular system, musculature, metabolism, sexuality, immune system, pain perception and skin in the sense of the electrodermal system. The most important organ systems affected include cardiovascular system, respiratory system and electrodermal system [18].

Stress increases blood flow and the performance of the heart, resulting in a faster heartbeat. In addition, the blood vessels of the heart, brain and working muscles constrict, causing blood pressure to rise. The bronchial tubes dilate and breathing becomes faster. Sweating, preferably on the hands, forehead and armpits, cools the body and prevents overheating [1].

The purpose behind the physical stress response is to prepare for a fight or a flight [1]. This fight-or-flight reaction activates the body in the event of imminent danger of any kind and increases the body's ability to defend itself and escape [19]. Stress is generated in the brain, where alarm signals release stress hormones in the brain to promote a rapid emergency reaction [18]. The bodily functions required for the coping strategies are stimulated, while less important and more regenerative and reproductive bodily functions are slowed down [1]. These changes in the body encourage a fight or flight and are part of the evolutionary emergency program [18].

2.2 The Triggering of a Relaxation Reaction

The relaxation reaction is a specific psychophysiological process and is characterized by feelings of calm, well-being and relaxation. It is the antithesis to the characteristic reactions of stress. Various relaxation techniques can be used to elicit a desired relaxation reaction [20].

Many relaxation techniques directly or indirectly stimulates ideas. These techniques make use of the human talent to imagine scenarios. For example, this can be seen in the instructions of relaxation exercises. Indirectly, attempts are made to evoke ideas of relaxation and well-being in order to promote a relaxation reaction [20].

Relaxation measures can be characterized by some uniform components, which have a comparable psychophysiological effect. They are divided into phases of initiation, the creation of certain external conditions that promote relaxation and relaxation induction. The initiation phase contains information about the procedure and gives advice on the sequence of the relaxation technique. The phase of external conditions provides the framework for the exercises. The execution should usually take place in interference-free and externally low-stimulus environments and in a comfortable posture. The aim of both phases is to avoid activation-increasing internal and external stimuli. In the phase of relaxation induction, a pleasant resting posture is aimed, because this is particularly conducive for relaxation [20].

2.3 Skin Conductivity as an Indicator of Stress-Related Changes

As explained in Sect. 2.1, stress triggers physical reactions. The skin, as the largest human organ, is one of the affected organ systems and it is the most important factor in the functionality of skin conductivity or electrodermal activity (EDA) [1]. EDA is a measure of neural mediated effects on sweat gland permeability, observed as changes in the resistance of the skin to a small electrical current, or as differences in the electrical potential between different parts of the skin [21].

In consequence, we use the EDA as an instrument for measuring the physical reactions triggered by stress. A great importance to EDA in the psychophysiology of the autonomous system is attached [22]. Moreover, impulses recorded with the help of EDA describe the conductivity and potential changes of the skin and show a clear correlation with mental processes [22].

2.4 Virtual Reality (VR)

VR is a technology that allows the user to immerse and interact within a psychophysical experience with a computer-generated virtual environment. This experience is elicited with a combination of hardware, software and interaction devices [23, 24].

A virtual reality can have different levels of immersion. The most interesting one is the immersive system. The user is given the opportunity to immerse fully into the computer generated world by means of a HMD which allows a stereoscopic view based on the user's position through a small display screen in front of the users eyes. These systems are mostly enriched by audio and sometimes by haptics and/or sensory interfaces [23, 25].

Virtual environments are used to simulate a real world, therefore it is also very important to "fool the user's senses" [26]. Humans use their five senses approximately as follows: Sight 70%, Hearing 20%, Smell 5%, Touch 4% and Taste 1% [27]. It becomes apparent that above all, the sense of sight plays a major role. A well simulation can therefore be recognized by the following characteristics: Field of View, Visual Acuity, Temporal Resolution, Luminance and Color, and Depth Perception [28].

But the interplay between people and technology is also important. In the so-called 3I model of VR, the most important characteristics of VR are taken into account. These are Immersion, Imagination and Interaction [29]. Immersion is like getting soaked into something or here to immerse in the virtual environment, Imagination means the ability to think oneself into the virtual world and Interaction is the ability of the user to interact within the world, i.e. dynamically change the environment, for example to open doors in a virtual room [29].

3 Methods

This study used a laboratory experiment to investigate if participating in a VR simulation on a virtual beach has a significant impact on stress reduction. In preparation, a 360° video of the city beach in Würzburg was recorded. There were no people to be seen and in the background was a typical soothing bar music. The laboratory was prepared to be regulated to exactly 23 °C. Furthermore, a foot tub was filled with sand and an original sunbed of the city beach was provided. The view of the subjects within the HMD is shown approximately in Fig. 1.

Fig. 1. The view from the city beach within the HMD.

The following hypothesis H1 was made:

H1: When a subject participate in a VR session of the city beach, the stress level will be reduced in the course of the experiment.

For the evaluation, the skin conductivity of the subjects were measured and the 30-min video of the city beach was divided into five measurement times. These were at minute 5, 10, 15, 20 and 25. The mean of the 5-min EDA value is formed from the interval of minute 4 to 6. According to this scheme, the other EDA averages were determined. With several dependent t-tests, it was examined whether there was a change in the EDA value between the individual time intervals and whether the stress level of the subject thus decreased during the session.

As a support, the individually perceived stress level was checked before and after the experiment using a color scale from green to yellow to red. Moreover, a standardized questionnaire was used to determine the degree to which the test subjects were able to empathize with the virtual environment.

3.1   Participants

All data were collected in a laboratory at the University of Applied Sciences Würzburg-Schweinfurt and the subjects were taken directly from there. It involves both technical staff, scientific staff and students of computer science and e-commerce. 40 subjects participated in the study and none of them had to be excluded from the final analysis. The age of the subjects was between 18 and 35 years and the average age was 24, 38 years.

3.2   Materials and Measuring Instruments

During the experiment, the subjects had to wear a HMD. This was a HTC Vive Pro. The screen of the HTC Vive Pro is a Dual AMOLED with a 3.5″ diagonal. The resolution is 1440 × 1600 pixel per eye (2880 × 1600 pixel together). The refresh rate is 90 Hz and the field of view is 110°. The used sensors are SteamVR Tracking, G-Sensor, Gyroscope, distance sensor and an IPD sensor.

The subjects also had to wear an Empatica E4 wristband. This was used to measure the EDA through the skin. This is achieved by passing a tiny amount of electric current between two electrodes in contact with the skin. The two electrodes are attached to the wrist. In contrast to conventional measurements on the palm or fingers, phase signals from the wrist may be less distinct with lower SCR strength [30]. However, the Empatica E4 sensors have additional sensitivity to better detect wrist phase responses.

In addition, the subjects had to complete the "Igroup Presence Questionnaire" (IPQ) [31]. The IPQ is a scale for measuring the sense of presence experienced in a virtual environment.

3.3   Procedure

First, the subjects were welcomed and got a detailed guide to further action. Afterwards, the subjects had the task of indicating how stressed he or she felt at the moment. Then each individual was asked to lie down on the sunbed. There the HTC Vive Pro were put on and adjusted correctly. Moreover, the Empatica E4 was attached to the dominant hand for physiological measurement of EDA. Before the test began, the test subjects were asked to remain in a relaxed and comfortable position for the entire duration of the test. Then the subjects had to watch the 360° video of the city beach. Afterwards, each participant had to fill out a questionnaire again, in which the current stress state was queried using a color gradient scale. Furthermore, it was asked how often subjects experienced VR in the last year and how the handling was. They were also asked how often they visited the city beach in the last year. In the last part of the questionnaire, the IPQ had to be completed.

4   Results

For the evaluation of the results, a correlation of the individual measuring points in time was first carried out. This was followed by the individual dependent t-tests of the respective measurement times ("minute5", "minute10", "minute15", "minute20" and "minute25"). Finally, another dependent t-test was performed to determine the difference in subjectively perceived stress levels.

4.1   Correlation of the Measuring Times

As can be seen in Fig. 2, the correlations of all measurement points were first compared. These were between r = .990 and r = .999 (p = .000, n = 40).

Messzeitpunkte	Min5/ Min10	Min5/ Min15	Min5/ Min20	Min5/ Min25	Min10/ Min15
r	0,998	0,998	0,990	0,997	0,999
p	0,000	0,000	0,000	0,000	0,000
n	40	40	40	40	40

Messzeitpunkte	Min10/ Min20	Min10/ Min25	Min15/ Min20	Min15/ Min25	Min20/ Min25
r	0,993	0,998	0,995	0,999	0,994
p	0,000	0,000	0,000	0,000	0,000
n	40	40	40	40	40

Fig. 2. The correlations between all measuring times.

This shows that there is a strong positive linear correlation between the EDA values of the respective compared measurement points. It can therefore be concluded that there is a strong positive correlation between the VR session and stress reduction.

4.2   Average Value Comparisons

Next, several dependent t-tests were performed. First, the measuring time "minute5" was compared with the measuring time "minute10". The results can be seen in Fig. 3.

Statistik bei gepaarten Stichproben

		Mittelwert	N	Std.-Abweichung	Standardfehler des Mittelwertes
Paaren 1	Minute5	1,01721877	40	3,45610665	,546458443
	Minute10	,90723722	40	3,15710278	,499181780

Test bei gepaarten Stichproben

		Gepaarte Differenzen							
		Mittelwert	Std.-Abweichung	Standardfehler des Mittelwertes	95% Konfidenzintervall der Differenz		T	df	Sig. (2-seitig)
					Untere	Obere			
Paaren 1	Minute5 – Minute10	,109981547	,373426841	,059043968	-,00944615	,229409244	1,863	39	,070

Fig. 3. Comparison of the measuring time "minute5" and "minute10".

It can be seen that higher EDA values were found at measurement time "minute5" (M = 1.02, SD = 3.46) than at measurement time "minute10" (M = 0.91, SD = 3.16). Nevertheless, this difference in EDA values is not significant, t(39) = 1.863, p = .070.

Then the measuring time "minute10" was compared with the measuring time "minute15". The results can be seen in Fig. 4.

Statistik bei gepaarten Stichproben

		Mittelwert	N	Std.-Abweichung	Standardfehler des Mittelwertes
Paaren 1	Minute10	,90723722	40	3,15710278	,499181780
	Minute15	,87947722	40	2,98101193	,471339372

Test bei gepaarten Stichproben

				Gepaarte Differenzen					
					95% Konfidenzintervall der Differenz				
		Mittelwert	Std.-Abweichung	Standardfehler des Mittelwertes	Untere	Obere	T	df	Sig. (2-seitig)
Paaren 1	Minute10 – Minute15	,027760000	,202620620	,032037133	-,03704122	,092561218	,866	39	,392

Fig. 4. Comparison of the measuring time "minute10" and "minute15".

It can be seen that higher EDA values were found at measurement time "minute10" (M = 0.91, SD = 3.16) than at measurement time "minute15" (M = 0.88, SD = 2.98). This difference in EDA values is not significant, t(39) = 0.866, p = .392.

Next the measuring time "minute15" was compared with the measuring time "minute20". The results can be seen in Fig. 5.

Statistik bei gepaarten Stichproben

		Mittelwert	N	Std.-Abweichung	Standardfehler des Mittelwertes
Paaren 1	Minute15	,87947722	40	2,98101193	,471339372
	Minute20	,87210152	40	2,64803407	,418690949

Test bei gepaarten Stichproben

				Gepaarte Differenzen					
					95% Konfidenzintervall der Differenz				
		Mittelwert	Std.-Abweichung	Standardfehler des Mittelwertes	Untere	Obere	T	df	Sig. (2-seitig)
Paaren 1	Minute15 – Minute20	,007375696	,427514552	,067595986	-,12935009	,144101483	,109	39	,914

Fig. 5. Comparison of the measuring time "minute15" and "minute20".

It can be seen that minimal higher EDA values were found at measurement time "minute15" (M = 0.88, SD = 2.98) than at measurement time "minute20" (M = 0.87, SD = 2.65). Nevertheless, this difference in EDA values is not significant, t (39) = 0.109, p = .914.

Then the measuring time "minute20" was compared with the measuring time "minute25". The results can be seen in Fig. 6.

It can be seen that lower EDA values were found at measurement time "minute20" (M = 0.87, SD = 2.65) than at measurement time "minute25" (M = 1.06, SD = 3.69). This difference in EDA values is not significant, t(39) = −1.072, p = .290.

Statistik bei gepaarten Stichproben

		Mittelwert	N	Std.-Abweichung	Standardfehler des Mittelwertes
Paaren 1	Minute20	,87210152	40	2,64803407	,418690949
	Minute25	1,05829857	40	3,68935314	,583337951

Test bei gepaarten Stichproben

		Gepaarte Differenzen			95% Konfidenzintervall der Differenz				
		Mittelwert	Std.-Abweichung	Standardfehler des Mittelwertes	Untere	Obere	T	df	Sig. (2-seitig)
Paaren 1	Minute20 – Minute25	-,18619705	1,09819472	,173639832	-,53741676	,165022663	-1,072	39	,290

Fig. 6. Comparison of the measuring time "minute20" and "minute25".

Finally, another dependent t-test was performed, which compared the measurement time "minute5" with the measurement time "minute20". These measurement times were selected because the highest EDA values were available at the beginning at measurement time "minute5" (excluded from measurement time "minute25"), while the lowest EDA values were found at measurement time "minute20". The results can be seen in Fig. 7.

Statistik bei gepaarten Stichproben

		Mittelwert	N	Std.-Abweichung	Standardfehler des Mittelwertes
Paaren 1	Minute5	1,01721877	40	3,45610665	,546458443
	Minute20	,87210152	40	2,64803407	,418690949

Test bei gepaarten Stichproben

		Gepaarte Differenzen			95% Konfidenzintervall der Differenz				
		Mittelwert	Std.-Abweichung	Standardfehler des Mittelwertes	Untere	Obere	T	df	Sig. (2-seitig)
Paaren 1	Minute5 – Minute20	,145117243	,913922301	,144503804	-,14716929	,437403775	1,004	39	,321

Fig. 7. Comparison of the measuring time "minute5" and "minute20".

It can be seen that higher EDA values are present at measurement time "minute5" (M = 1.01, SD = 3.46) than at measurement time "minute20" (M = 0.87, SD = 2.65). Nevertheless, also this difference in EDA values is not significant, t(39) = 1.004, p = .321.

The course of the mean values of the individual measuring points can finally be seen in Fig. 8.

4.3　Subjectively Felt Exhaustion

First, descriptive statistics show in Fig. 9 that the mean values of the subjectively perceived stress level before (M = 5.24, SD = 3.38) and after (M = 2.68, SD = 2.46) the VR session differ.

This descriptive difference was then tested for significance using a dependent t-test as shown in Fig. 10.

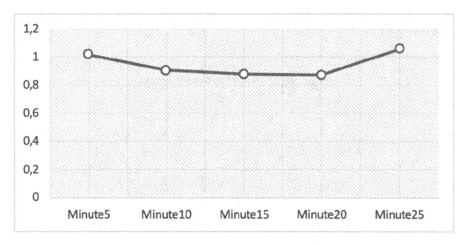

Fig. 8. Course of the EDA mean values of all measuring points.

Statistik bei gepaarten Stichproben

		Mittelwert	N	Std.-Abweichung	Standardfehler des Mittelwertes
Paaren 1	vorher	5,2350	40	3,38265	,53484
	nachher	2,6800	40	2,45735	,38854

Fig. 9. Descriptive statistics of the subjectively perceived stress level.

Test bei gepaarten Stichproben

| | | | | | 95% Konfidenzintervall der Differenz | | | | |
		Mittelwert	Std.-Abweichung	Standardfehler des Mittelwertes	Untere	Obere	T	df	Sig. (2-seitig)
Paaren 1	vorher - nachher	2,55500	2,67466	,42290	1,69960	3,41040	6,042	39	,000

Fig. 10. Dependent t-test for the subjectively perceived stress level before and after the VR session.

It was shown that the VR session had a statistically highly significant influence on the subjectively perceived stress level, $t(39) = 6.042$, $p = .000$.

4.4 Feeling of Presence

As already explained, the feeling of presence in the virtual world was queried using the IGP. There are different items. The item "G" asks for the general impression of the virtual world, the items "SP1" to "SP5" ask for the spatial presence, the items "INV1" to "INV4" for the involvement and the items "REAL1" to "REAL4" for a judgement of reality. In this case, a 5-point Likert scale was used to answer the items. The results are visible in Fig. 11.

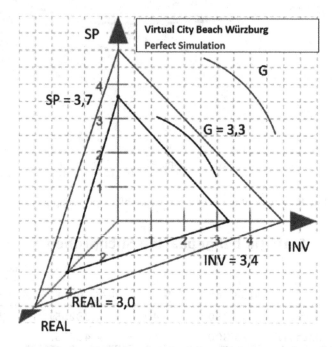

Fig. 11. Comparison of a hypothetical perfect simulation and the mean values of the city beach simulation.

The general impression of the virtual world (G) had a mean value of M = 3.3, n = 40, the spatial presence (SP) had a mean value of M = 3.7, n = 40, the involvement (INV) had a mean value of M = 3.4, n = 40 and judgement of reality (REAL) had a mean value of M = 3.0, n = 40.

5 Discussion

This study demonstrates that the hypothesis H1 can be accepted and rejected.

The more important part of the work in the form of the EDA measurement over the period of the VR session at the city beach showed a reduction of the EDA values, but it was not statistical significant. Therefore, the hypothesis has to be rejected. Even though the values for the sense of presence were in the upper middle range, a further survey after the study showed that test persons would have wished above all for better video quality. In addition, some also complained about the lack of wind and sunlight. The lack of personal contact with fellow human beings was also rated negatively. In addition, many subjects stated that they would have preferred more variety in the virtual world. This could also explain why the EDA values increased again significantly after 25 min. The question arises whether if the modern human is still used to sit still for a longer period of time in this case of 30 min and simply just relaxing without other input or if someone first need a training for this.

On the other hand, the subjects subjectively felt much more recovered after participating in the VR session and this difference was statistically highly significant. Hypothesis H1 can therefore be assumed. This could be mainly due to the fact that every break from everyday life is subjectively perceived as a relaxation technique and is considered to reduce stress [3–5, 9]. Furthermore, it can be assumed that the subjects have different levels of stress competence and are therefore differently susceptible to the VR session. In addition, the correct form of recovery depends on the form of the stress experienced previously [32]. Mostly people who work in the office etc. tend to be more likely to reduce stress when they do short breaks in particular with physical activity [6]. Since the participants probably go through different forms of stress in their everyday life, the VR session could be more relaxing for some subjects than for others. It can therefore be assumed that these differences had a strong influence on the final result, especially since the test group was quite homogeneous. In a follow-up study, it could be examined in advance what kind of stress the test persons bring along and what the respective experience value with stress competences is, in order to ensure group comparisons. To be more precise, the experiment should also be conducted with people who are more likely to be confronted with physical stress in their everyday lives. In addition, other known methods of stress reduction should also be tested to see if they have a proven effect. Alternatively, a comparison with the original city beach in Würzburg would be very interesting. Also noteworthy are the different attitudes of the test subjects towards the VR session. The individual's willingness and ability to recover is particularly important [33]. Measures to reduce stress should therefore be based on voluntariness and not on a sense of obligation [1]. As a result, subjects who are not able to engage in the VR session will have less chance of recovery.

6   Conclusion

The study showed based on the examination of skin conductivity that participation in a VR session of a relaxing virtual environment has an effect on the EDA values, which however did not reach any significance. However, the findings determined by the color gradient scale showed a highly significant stress reduction. Therefore, some effect already seems to be present and it seems worthwhile to conduct potential follow-up studies to further explore or eliminate the limitations of this study. In particular, an inclusion of the type of everyday exposure seems promising. A comparison with the real environment is also interesting. In addition, due to the further development of VR glasses and stereoscopic 360° cameras, in future it will be possible to use higher quality equipment to produce an even more realistic simulation.

Nevertheless, as already mentioned, the ever-increasing demands of society lead to a deterioration in performance and health [2]. Therefore, it is all the more important to reduce stress through recovery measures. VR as a measure for stress reduction is a new innovative relaxation possibility, which offers an eventful and interactive VR experience and can be applied without limits. Furthermore, in the course of digitization, it can be concluded that VR will continue to develop positively, leading to a larger user base due to future decreasing costs and increasing content.

References

1. Kaluza, G.: Gelassen und sicher im Stress - Das Stresskompetenz-Buch: Stress erkennen, verstehen, bewältigen. Springer, Berlin (2014). https://doi.org/10.1007/978-3-642-41677-4
2. Wohlers, K., Hombrecher, M.: Entspann dich, Deutschland – TK-Stressstudie, Hamburg (2016)
3. Henning, R.A., Jacques, P., Kissel, G.V., Sullivan, A.B., Alteras-Webb, S.M.: Frequent short rest from computer work: effects on productivity and well-being at two field sites. Ergonomics **40**, 78–91 (1997)
4. Dababneh, A.J., Swanson, N., Shell, R.L.: Impact of added rest breaks on the productivity and well being of workers. Ergonomics **44**, 164–174 (2001)
5. Boucsein, W., Thum, M.: Design of work/rest schedules for computer work based on psychophysiological recovery measures. Int. J. Ind. Ergon. **20**, 51–57 (1997)
6. Sundelin, G., Hagberg, M.: The effects of different pause types on neck and shoulder EMG activity during VDU work. Ergonomics **32**, 527–537 (1999)
7. Esch, T., Stefano, G.B.: The neurobiology of stress management. Neuroendocrinol. Lett. **31** (1), 19–39 (2010)
8. Komaroff, A.L.: Mind-Body Medicine: A Special Health Report. Harvard Health Publications, Boston (2001)
9. Esch, T.: (Neuro)biologische Aspekte der Regeneration: Entspannung als Instrument der Stressregulation. Z. Arb. Wiss. **65**, 125–135 (2011). https://doi.org/10.1007/BF03373826
10. Esch, T., Stefano, G.B., Fricchione, G.L.: The therapeutic use of the relaxation response in stress-related diseases. Med. Sci. Monit. **9**, RA23–RA34 (2003)
11. Stefano, G.B., Esch, T.: Integrative medical therapy: examination of meditation's therapeutic and global medicinal outcomes via nitric oxide. Int. J. Mol. Med. **16**, 621–630 (2005)
12. de Bloom, J., Kompier, M., Geurts, S., de Weerth, C., Taris, T., Sonnentag, S.: Do we recover from vacation? Meta-analysis of vacation effects on health and well-being. J. Occup. Health **51**(1), 13–25 (2009)
13. Kühnel, J., Sonnentag, S.: How long do you benefit from vacation? A closer look at the fade-out of vacation effects. J. Organ. Behav. **32**, 125–143 (2011)
14. Schwarzer, R.: Psychologie des Gesundheitsverhaltens – Einführung in die Gesundheitspsychologie (Bd. 3. Überarbeitete Auflage). Hogrefe Verlag, Göttingen (2004)
15. Boucsein, W.: Electrodermal activity, 2nd edn. Springer, Heidelberg (2012). https://doi.org/10.1007/978-1-4614-1126-0
16. Lazarus, R.: Emotion and Adaption. Oxford University Press, New York (1991)
17. Selye, H.: The Stress of Life. McGraw-Hill, New York (1956)
18. Müsseler, J., Rieger, M.: Allgemeine Psychologie, vol. 3. Springer, Berlin (2017). https://doi.org/10.1007/978-3-642-53898-8
19. Cannon, W.B.: The James-Lange theory of emotions: a critical examination and an alternative theory. Am. J. Psychol. (39), 106–124 (1927)
20. Vaitl, D., Petermann, F.: Handbuch der Entspannungsverfahren: Grundlagen und Methoden. Psychologie Verlags Union, Weinheim (2000)
21. Critchley, H., Nagai, Y.: Electrodermal Activity (EDA). In: Gellman, M.D., Turner, J.R. (eds.) Encyclopedia of Behavioral Medicine. Springer, New York (2013). https://doi.org/10.1007/978-1-4419-1005-9_13

22. Fere, C.: Note sur les modifications de la resistance electrique sous l'influence des excitations sensorielles et des emotions. Comptes Rendus des Seances de la Societe de Biologie **8**, 217–219 (1888)
23. van Dam, A., Forsberg, A., Laidlaw, D., LaViola, J., Simpson, R.: Immersive VR for scientific visualization: a progress report. IEEE Comput. Graph. Appl. **20**(6), 26–52 (2000)
24. Cruz-Neira, C.: Virtual reality overview. In: SIGGRAPH 1993 Course, no. 23, pp. 1.1–1.18 (1993)
25. von Schweber, E., Linda: Virtually here. PC Mag. 168–198 (1995)
26. Holloway, R., Lastra, A.: Virtual environments: a survey of the technology. In: SIGGRAPH 1995 Course, no. 8, pp. A.1–A.40 (1995)
27. Heilig, M.L.: El Cine del Futuro: the cinema of the future. Presence **1**(3), 279–294 (1992)
28. Mazuryk, T., Gervautz, M.: Virtual reality – history, applications, technology and future (1999)
29. Coiffet, P., Burdea, G.: Virtual Reality Technology. Wiley, Hoboken (2003)
30. Fowles, D.C., Christie, M.J., Edelbe, R.: Publication Recommendations for Electrodermal Measurements. Psychophysiologie **5**, 232–239 (1981)
31. Schubert, T.W.: The sense of presence in virtual environments. Z. für Medienpsychologie **15**, 69–71 (2003)
32. Kallus, W.K., Erdmann, G.: Zur Wechselbeziehung zwischen Ausgangszustand, Belastung und Erholung. Beltz Psychologie Verlags Union, Weinheim (2000)
33. Allmer, H.: Psychophysische Erholungseffekte von Bewegung und Entspannung. Beltz Psychologie Verlags Union, Weinheim (1994)

Brain Activation in Virtual Reality
for Attention Guidance

Philipp Ulsamer[✉], Kevin Pfeffel, and Nicholas H. Müller

Socio-Informatics and Societal Aspects of Digitalization, Faculty of Computer Science
and Business Information Systems, University of Applied Sciences
Wuerzburg-Schweinfurt, Sanderheinrichsleitenweg 20, 97074 Würzburg, Germany
{philipp.ulsamer,kevin.pfeffel,nicholas.mueller}@fhws.de
https://www.fhws.de

Abstract. Virtual Reality (VR) not only offers great opportunities in
terms of entertainment, it is also widely applicable in the field of attention guidance, medicine and psychology. The distinction between VR and
ordinary media is the $360°$ - also known as omnidirectional - environment.
When applying the option of an omnidirectional platform with auditory
as well as visual actions, the focus on the right story line within VR is
crucial. In order to analyze whether attention guidance in VR activates
the same brain regions as in the real world, data of both topographical
brain views must be compared. To do so, functional near-infrared spectroscopy (fNIRS), a brain imaging technology, is being utilized. fNIRS is
a non-invasive neuroimaging technique, which measures brain oxygenation and by that identifies brain activity. The fNIRS method offers a fast
and convenient application and is easily adaptable to the field of VR. In
this experiment, the brain activity of 23 participants was examined under
two scenarios. The first scenario required the location of click noises when
being present in the real world, while the second scenario demanded the
same in the virtual reality. The environment of both settings - in the
real world as well as in the virtual world - were identical. Each brain
picture was analyzed on the basis of a within-subject design. Therefore,
all participants were required to experience both settings while wearing
fNIRS in order to compare similarities and differences of the recordings.
Once all 46 recordings were allocated and broken down by milliseconds,
a cortex view through Oxysoft - a software that analyzes and evaluates
NIRS recordings - was generated. Despite fNIRS limited recording depth,
increased brain activity was detected during the subject's click orientation. The greatest disparity between the resting phase and the stimula-
tion was visible in the temporal as well as the parietal lobe. Findings
also showed that in spite of the stimulated brain regions, the hemoglobin
level remained the same in both environments, the real world and the
virtual world.

Keywords: Virtual reality · fNIRS · Storytelling · Attention
guidance · Cognitive neuroscience · Brain imaging

© Springer Nature Switzerland AG 2020
P. Zaphiris and A. Ioannou (Eds.): HCII 2020, LNCS 12206, pp. 190–200, 2020.
https://doi.org/10.1007/978-3-030-50506-6_14

1   Introduction

In VR the user is, unlike in traditional 2D environments, not limited to the regular line of sight in front of them [1]. VR takes the user on an artificial journey and makes them experience their surroundings as if they were real. In order to allow the user to experience a high sense of immersion, current forms of application-, movie- and video-game-creation have to be rethought and applied to the specific format of VR. Usually, storytelling is a narrative tool that incorporates viewers into a narration and thereby creates a high level of immersion. Story content is linked to a narrative event which guides the user in a specific direction. Therefore, users tend to not just hear the story, but merge into it. One significant problem in terms of viewer guidance within VR is the omnidirectional (360°) canvas. The viewer has the freedom to experience the virtual space freely and is not limited to a frame view. This leads to an increased difficulty when trying to guide the users attention towards the main events. In the case of cinematic virtual reality (CVR) movies, traditional film techniques like blurring [2,3] or stylistic rendering [4] cannot be adapted to steer the viewers' attention [5]. The gaze fixation pattern of movies is often consistent across viewers [6,7], though in an omnidirectional view less effective. In addition, viewers experience a so called fear of missing out (FOMO) due to the abundance of images [8,9]. This problem can be avoided by attention guidance. Moreover, the user should have an immersive experience without being forced into a desired direction. By forcing the user towards a desired point of interest (PoI), the motion sickness result can lead to a loss of immersion. The user should have the feeling to direct their gaze at their free will. Therefore, attention guiding techniques are required to enhance the user experience and redefine the way stories are narrated [8–11].

The use of immersive VR in the field of medical and psychological treatments [12] as well as in the field of neural correlations that subtend VR experiences [13] are continuously increasing. Most research that captures mental workload in the brain has focused on the use of electroencephalography (EEG) [14] or on the functional magnetic resonance imaging (fMRI). While these techniques come with several limitations, functional near-infrared spectroscopy (fNIRS) is a new technique for brain imaging during the users VR experience [13]. fNIRS monitors changes in cerebral blood oxygenation related to human brain functions. It is also used by neuroscientists to find out how human beings react to various conditions in the virtual world. Recent studies have shown that brain activities in VR interactions are identical to the brain activities in corresponding real-life situations [15,16]. Nonetheless, there is also evidence that different brain areas are activated in both scenarios [17].

In 2019, we presented a paper for indoor navigation through storytelling in virtual reality [18]. We tested various techniques to guide the users attention in the virtual world. We used storytelling at different junctions to make it easier for the users to memorize the path within the maze they were virtually put in. In this paper it is to be examined, whether the same brain areas are affected during the orientation search in the virtual world while wearing fNIRS, as they are during the orientation search in the real world.

First, we will summarize related work and confirm that attention guidance in VR needs to be further researched. Afterwards, we will propose our used material and methods for this experiment. Furthermore, we will explain our results in more detail. Finally, we will discuss our future work and give a short outlook.

2   Related Work

In order to get an understanding of brain activity in virtual reality when searching for orientation, an understanding of attention guidance in VR and of the concepts of the mental workload of our brain is preconditional.

2.1   Attention Guidance/Storytelling in Virtual Reality

Rothe et al. [5] wrote a taxonomy that qualified and quantified different methods for attention guidance in CVR. It compares the possibilities in traditional films for implementation in virtual reality. Their findings concluded that most of the possibilities cannot be taken over entirely, because filmmakers no longer decide where to look, the viewers do. While they ignored the interaction in virtual reality in terms of attention control, they come to the conclusion that many methods cannot be implemented because the PoI is not always in the field of view (FoV) and in a 360-degree environment, a forced orientation for the purpose of maintaining immersion is not suitable. This paper is intended to check whether the methods that are suitable for attention guidance in a 360-degree video differ in brain activity from conventional movies.

Sheikh et al. [10] have tested various acoustic and visual techniques to direct the viewer in the VR towards a desired direction. They found that the mixture of different techniques led to the best results for their subjects. The advantage of ambisonic or spacial sound is that the viewer's attention can be drawn from any position. If there is a visual focus point, attention can be focused on the action as quickly as possible. In this paper, we want to describe the method of using visual and ambisonic cues to direct the viewer in the VR and real world in a desired direction. For this purpose, our subjects wore an fNIRS, which checks whether the activity in the brain differs in both scenarios.

Since we are not simply watching movies or playing games in the VR environment, but are virtually placed in the middle of all events, impressions have a much greater impact. In order to remember story content accordingly and to find one's way around the VR world, the way of telling a story is of great importance. In Ulsamer et al. [18] we used storytelling elements in order to remember a path in a virtual environment. However, it remains necessary to check how the elements used affect brain stress. It is crucial to know how high the cognitive workload of remembering story content is within an immersive VR experience.

2.2 Cognitive Science in Virtual Reality

Spectroscopy is a group of physical methods that breaks down radiation according to a specific property such as wavelength, energy, mass, etc. fNIRS is a non-invasive imaging technique based on the fact that changes in brain activity lead to changes in the optical properties of brain tissue which are then quantified. Just like fMRI and positron emission tomography (PET), the physiological basis of fNIRS measurement is neurovascular coupling - only that in the case of fNIRS, the changes in the optical properties of the brain tissue that are triggered by neurovascular coupling are recorded [19].

Kober et al. [20] measured the brain activity during spatial navigation in VR using a combined EEG-NIRS study. They placed their subjects in a virtual maze, in which they had to find the shortest way to the exit. Among those who could solve the maze and those who could not, participants were divided into two groups to test brain activity. They discovered that navigation tasks in VR show an increased activity in the parietal lobe, which correlates with previous fMRI studies that examined spatial navigation.

In this paper we want to test the brain regions that are responsible for orientation and navigation. We are going to apply the fNIRS to check brain activity during orientation tasks in the virtual world as well as in the real world. Since other techniques turned out to be inflexible and cumbersome and, according to Kober et al. [20], fNIRS is a suitable method for testing spatial navigation in VR, we decided to follow this approach.

3 Method

3.1 Brain Imaging

A major advantage of using fNIRS for brain imaging studies is that, in contrast to other methods, it carries low costs, is user-friendly, more portable and offers an increased accessibility. Other methods (like fMRI or PET) reduce the immersion effects of VR due to their nature [20]. fNIRS is a non-invasive optical neuroimaging technique that measures the differences between oxygenated hemoglobin (oxy-HB) and deoxygenated hemoglobin (deoxy-HB) in the brain and uses this to deduce brain activity. Spatial orientation is a complex task that is processed by our brain. This multi-sensory processing requires the cooperation of spatial and temporal information [21]. Another advantage that VR allows is that in the study of spatial knowledge, different attention guidance methods can be tested independently of one another, which is not always possible in the real world [20]. Recent studies in the field of brain activity using VR depict that several regions for spatial navigation processes are activated in humans. Object-location associations activates the parahippocampal gyrus [22]. The hippocampus provides an allocentric representation of space or cognitive maps, with its navigational accuracy being located in the right hippocampus [23]. Detection of single tones are activated in the superior temporal gyrus [24]. The visuomotor control, the egocentric representation of space, as well as the accuracy of navigation through VR are provided by the parietal lobe [23,25,26]. Continuous wave fNIRS uses infrared light which emits light at a constant frequency and amplitude. It uses the modified Beer-Lambert law to assign changes in light intensity to changes in the related concentration of hemoglobin. Due to the low penetration depth [14,27,28], fNIRS is an adequate method for measurements in the cortical areas [29].

3.2   Participants

Twenty-three participants (14 male, nine female) between 20 and 42 years old performed the orientation task in the real environment (RE) and virtual environment (VE), in which they had to react to sound and locate where it came from. All subjects had normal or corrected-to-normal vision and prior experience with virtual reality applications. During the orientation task in both scenarios, the participants brain activation was assessed with fNIRS.

3.3   Materials

All fNIRS recordings during the orientation task in the VE and RE were performed using a 27-channel optical topography system (Brite24, Artinis Medical Systems).

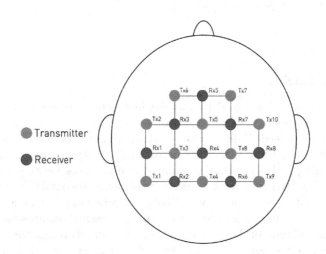

Fig. 1. Details of the fNIRS setup. Brite24 with 27 channel using eight receivers and ten transmitter to capture brain oxygenation.

The Brite is a plug-and-play, user-friendly NIRS device with almost no set-up time. It has a sample rate of up to 50 Hz and works with multi-wavelengths LED's for continuous and real-time feedback. It comes with a soft neoprene head cap which, with the Bluetooth-compatible measuring device, ensures high portability as well as a simplified and more comfortable way to monitor the brain oxygenation of children and elderly patients. There are ten transmitters (Tx) each transmitting two wavelengths, one being approximately 760 nm, while the other is found at approximately 850 nm. The distance between optodes of the head cap grid is approximately 30 mm. The infrared light is scattered through the human tissue and is sent back to then be interpreted via eight receivers (Rx) (see Fig. 1). Oxysoft (Artinis) is used as an analysis tool to interpret and evaluate the NIRS recordings. It provides the calculation of oxygenation, total hemoglobin and tissue saturation index (TSI) in real time. The VR video was shot with the GoPro Fusion Black 360. Two internal cameras each record a 180-degree video, which is then stitched into a 360-degree film. In addition, the camera records spatial audio in order to perceive sounds from different directions in a VE with the HTC Vive Pro virtual reality glasses.

3.4 Process

For our test, we used a within-subject design. Our participants were given the task of reacting to attention guidance methods in a RE and in a VE in order to measure possible changes in hemoglobin. The probands were sitting on a chair and were supposed to react to different clicks and locate them with their eyes (see Fig. 2). We have reproduced exactly the same environment in a VR video as it was in real life and presented it to the subjects. A separate measurement was created for each subject and each environment. The subjects were first made aware of their task. They got the HTC Vive Pro glasses and watched two initial videos for acclimatization purposes. The soft neoprene head cap is very quick and easy to put on and the optodes can be attached quickly, but it took a lot of preparation time to manually adjust the hair so that each transmitter can send enough light for the measurement. For each subject, a parameter, the differential path-length factor (DPF), must be used. This ensures a correct measurement depending on the participants age, which measures the actual distance covered by the NIRS light [30]. Oxysoft calculates the DPF from age by the formula derived from the data of Duncan et al. [31]. This equation is valid for measurements on brain tissue for 17–50 year old human subjects (See Eq. 1).

$$DPF = 4.99 + 0.067 * (Age^{0.814}) \tag{1}$$

After the set-up was completed, participants were asked to perform cognitive tasks for a pretest. Here, we measured further configurations in oxysoft and their basic values in oxygenated and deoxygenated hemoglobin.

4   Descriptive Results

To monitor changes in brain activity, we looked at different time intervals for specific events during the test. We measured oxygenated hemoglobin in cortical areas, because fNIRS only cover this limited range. In particular, we examined differences between the initial state, the click noise and the course of this state

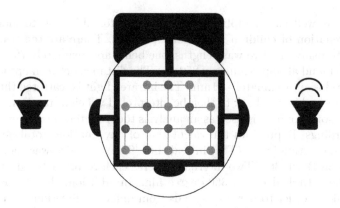

Fig. 2. Set up for fNIRS recordings in virtual reality. Subjects hear different clicks from different directions, which they have to locate with their eyes.

and orientation. We have recorded these results for the RE and the VE. Therefore, we took the data from all participants and generated a cortex view in Oxysoft. This image of the cortex is a summary of all 27 channels and displays the results visually in micromol values (µmol).

4.1 Brain Activation in Real and Virtual Environment

In Fig. 3 we see the initial state of the brain at the beginning of the test. We used this picture in order to compare this base value with later changes. The time of the initial state until the first event was a period of 20 s. During this time no significant changes in blood oxygen saturation occurred. Once hearing the click sound, significant changes in parts of the parietal lobe (values between 80 and 110 µmol) and the superior temporal gyrus (values between 120 and 180 µmol), could be seen.

In comparison to RE and VE, Fig. 4 shows that at the time of click, the same regions of the brain are active and show a similar level of activity. There is a constant activation in the red area in both environments. The activation in the parietal lobe has extended (values between 40 and 80 µmol), while the activation in the superior temporal gyrus has decreased (values between 95 and 150 µmol) (Fig. 5).

Finally, Fig. 6 shows the activation in different areas of the brain. While the parietal lobe (values between 20 and 60 µmol) is responsible for orientation and navigation the superior temporal gyrus (values between 90 and 160 µmol) is responsible for the spatial orientation of sound, the motor cortex (values between 30 and 50 µmol) is used for the movement of the head to locate the object.

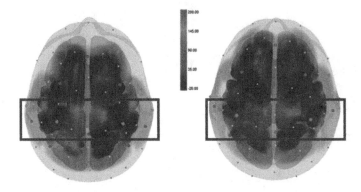

Fig. 3. Cortex view showing the activation of the brain regions at the initial state in the RE (left) and in the VE (right).

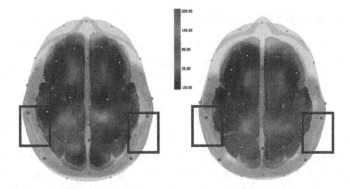

Fig. 4. Cortex view showing the activation of the brain regions at sound detection in the RE (left) and in the VE (right). (Color figure online)

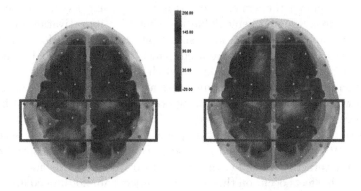

Fig. 5. Cortex view showing the activation of the brain regions between sound detection and moving to the object in the RE (left) and in the VE (right). (Color figure online)

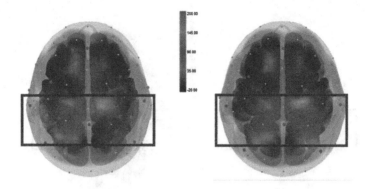

Fig. 6. Cortex view showing the activation of the brain regions while moving to the object location in the RE (left) and in the VE (right).

5   Discussion and Conclusion

In summary, the fNIRS data indicates that higher auditory and visual stimulus correlated with increased concentration portrays changes in the oxygenated hemoglobin. These correlations tended to be stronger in the parietal and temporal cortex. Our test contained a number of clicks from different directions. However, when looking at the topographical images of Oxysoft, no descriptive differences can be made in terms of the direction from which a click originates. As a basis for the investigation, it is given that all test persons could react correctly to various clicks in the RE and VE. During an interview after the test, it was discovered that the reaction to sound effects in the VE seemed to be more difficult for some test persons than in the RE. Nevertheless, no differences in hemoglobin values could be detected in any of the subjects' performance.

The main goal of the experiment was to find out whether the same brain regions are addressed in RE and VE during orientation search and whether these vary or remain the same. The possibility of using fNIRS to check oxygenated and deoxygenated hemoglobin together with its activation in different areas of the brain makes fNIRS an easily applicable method. However, for the orientation search other regions are used, which cannot be checked with fNIRS alone. Therefore, we have focused our research only on the cerebral cortex. Our investigation has shown that the same areas are active at different times in the virtual as well as in the real-world during orientation search by spatial hearing. In further research, we now want to determine the degree of oxygen saturation and observe this at further orientation possibilities. Due to its easy setup and mobility, fNIRS also poses a good method to conduct attention control experiments in an interactive virtual environment. In further experiments we want to examine which effects occur on the user when objects are not immediately found during orientation search in an omnidirectional environment. It is interesting to find out which methods can be used to retrieve the user under such FOMO experiences, which lead to a high cognitive load.

References

1. Bucher, J.: Storytelling for Virtual Reality: Methods and Principles for Crafting Immersive Narratives. Taylor & Francis Group, New York (2017)
2. Smith, W.S., Tadmor, Y.: Nonblurred regions show priority for gaze directon over spatical blur. Q. J. Exp. Psychol. (2013). https://doi.org/10.1080/17440218.2012722659
3. Hata, H., Koike, H., Sato, Y.: Visual guidance with unnoticed blur effect. In: Proceedings of the International Working Conference on Advanced Visual Interfaces - AVI 2016. ACM Press, New York (2016)
4. Cole, F., DeCarlo, D., Finkelstein, A., Kin, K., Morley, K., Santella, A.: Directing gaze in 3D models with stylized focus. In: Proceedings of the 17th Europgraphics Conference on Rendering Techniques (2006). https://doi.org/10.2312/egwr/egsr06/377-387
5. Rothe, S., Buschek, D., Hussmann, H.: Guidance in cinematic virtual reality-taxonomy, research status and challenges. Multimodal Technol. Interact. **3**, 19 (2019). https://doi.org/10.3390/mti3010019
6. Subramanian, R., Shankar, D., Sebe, N., Melcher, D.: Emotion modulates eye movement patterns and subsequent memory for the gist and details of movie scenes. J. Vis. **14**, 31 (2014). https://doi.org/10.1167/14.3.31
7. Dorr, M., Vig, E., Barth, E.: Eye movement prediction and variability on natural video data sets. Vis. Cogn. **20** (2012). https://doi.org/10.1080/13506285.2012.667456
8. Tse, A., Jennet, C., Moore, J., Watson, Z., Rigby, J., Cox, A.L.: Was i there? In: Proceedings of the 2017 CHI Conference Extended Abstracts on Human Factors in Computing Systems. ACM Press, New York (2017)
9. MacQuarrie, A., Steed, A.: Cinematic virtual reality: evaluating the effect of display type on the viewing experience for panoramic video. In: Proceedings of the 2017 IEEE Virtual Reality (VR), Los Angeles, CA, USA (2017)
10. Sheikh, A., Brown, A., Watson, Z., Evans, M.: Directing attention in 360-degree video. In: IBC 2016 Conference (2016)
11. Rothe, S., Hussmann, H., Allary, M.: Diegetic cues for guiding the viewer in cinematic virtual reality. In: Proceedings of the 23rd ACM Symposium (2017). https://doi.org/10.1145/3139131.3143421
12. Bohil, C., Alicea, B., Biocca, F.: Virtual reality in neuroscience research and therapy. Nat. Rev. Neurosci. **12**, 752–62 (2011). https://doi.org/10.1038/nrn3122
13. Seraglia, B., Gamberini, L., Priftis, K., Scatturin, P., Martinelli, M., Cutini, S.: An exploratory fNIRS study with immersive virtual reality: a new method for technical implementation. Front. Hum. Neurosci. **5**, 176 (2011). https://doi.org/10.3389/fnhum.2011.00176
14. Peck, E.M., Afergan, D., Yuksel, B.F., Lalooses, F., Jacob, R.J.K.: Using fNIRS to measure mental workload in the real world. In: Fairclough, S.H., Gilleade, K. (eds.) Advances in Physiological Computing. HIS, pp. 117–139. Springer, London (2014). https://doi.org/10.1007/978-1-4471-6392-3_6
15. Cansiz, Y., Tokel, S.T.: Effects of way finding affordances on usability of virtual world environments in terms of users' satisfaction, performance, and mental workload: examination by eye-tracking and fNIR. In: Amiel, T., Wilson, B. (eds.) Proceedings of EdMedia + Innovate Learning 2012, pp. 1073–1079. Association for the Advancement of Computing in Education (AACE), Waynesville (2012)

16. Campbell, Z., Zakzanis, K., Jovanovski, D., Joordens, S., Mraz, R., Graham, S.J.: Utilizing virtual reality to improve the ecological validity of clinical neuropsychology: an fMRI case study elucidating the neural basis of planning by comparing the Tower of London with a three-dimensional navigation task. Appl. Neuropsychol. **16**, 295–306 (2009)

17. Perani, D., et al.: Different brain correlates for watching real and virtual hand actions. Neuroimage **14**, 749–758 (2001)

18. Ulsamer, P., Pfeffel, K., Müller, N.H.: Indoor navigation through storytelling in virtual reality. In: Zaphiris, P., Ioannou, A. (eds.) HCII 2019. LNCS, vol. 11591, pp. 230–239. Springer, Cham (2019). https://doi.org/10.1007/978-3-030-21817-1_18

19. Boecker, M., Schroeter, M.L.: Signal-und bildgebende Verfahren: Nahinfrarot-Spektroskopie. In: Gauggel, S., Hermann, M. (eds.) Handbuch der Neuro-und Biopsychologie, pp. 211–219. Hogrefe, Goettingen (2008)

20. Kober, S., Wood, G., Neuper, C.: Measuring brain activation during spatial navigation in virtual reality: a combined EEG-NIRS study. In: Virtual Environments: Developments, Applications and Challenges, pp. 1–24 (2013)

21. Siegel, A.W., White, S.H.: The development of spatial representations of large-scale environments. Adv. Child Dev. Behav. **10**, 9–55 (1975). https://doi.org/10.1016/s0065-2407(08)60007-5. PMID: 1101663

22. Janzen, G., van Turennout, M.: Selective neural representation of objects relevant for navigation. Nat. Neurosci. **7**, 673–677 (2004). https://doi.org/10.1038/nn1257

23. Maguire, E.A., Burgess, N., Donnett, J.G., Frackowiak, R.S., Frith, C.D., O'Keefe, J.: Knowing where and getting there: a human navigation network. Science **280**(5365), 921–4 (1998)

24. Molholm, S., Martinez, A., Ritter, W., Javitt, D.C., Foxe, J.J.: The neural circuitry of pre-attentive auditory change-detection: an fMRI study of pitch and duration mismatch negativity generators. Cereb. Cortex **15**, 545–551 (2005)

25. Wolbers, T., et al.: Neural foundations of emerging route knowledge in complex spatial environments. Cogn. Brain. Res. **21**(3), 401–411 (2004)

26. Grön, G., Wunderlich, A., Spitzer, M., et al.: Brain activation during human navigation: gender-different neural networks as substrate of performance. Nat. Neurosci. **3**, 404–408 (2000). https://doi.org/10.1038/73980

27. Scholkmann, F., Kleiser, S., Metz, A.J., Zimmermann, R., Pavia, J.M., Wolf, U., et al.: A review on continuous wave functional near-infrared spectroscopy and imaging instrumentation and methodology. Neuroimage **85**, 6–27 (2014). https://doi.org/10.1016/j.neuroimage.2013.05.004

28. Siegel, A.M., Marota, J.J.A., Boas, D.A.: Design and evaluation of a continuous-wave diffuse optical tomography system. Opt. Express **4**, 287–298 (1999). https://doi.org/10.1364/OE.4.000287

29. Weiskopf, N.: Real-time fMRI and its application to neurofeedback. NeuroImage **62**, 682–692 (2012)

30. Kamran, M.A., Mannann, M.M.N., Jeong, M.Y.: Differential path-length factor's effect on the characterization of brain's hemodynamic response function: a functional near-infrared study. Front. Neuroinform. **12**, 37 (2018). https://doi.org/10.3389/fninf.2018.00037

31. Duncan, A., Meek, J., Clemence, M., et al.: Measurement of cranial optical path length as a function of age using phase resolved near infrared spectroscopy. Pediatr. Res. **39**, 889–894 (1996). https://doi.org/10.1203/00006450-199605000-00025

Visualizing Students' Eye Movement Data to Understand Their Math Problem-Solving Processes

Shuang Wei, Yan Ping Xin, and Yingjie Chen[(✉)]

Purdue University, West Lafayette, IN 47906, USA
{wei93,yxin,victorchen}@purdue.edu

Abstract. Eye-tracking technology has been widely used in educational research to access students' learning processes. However, analyzing and comprehending students' eye movements is a big challenge as eye movement data is enormous and complex. This paper attempts to develop a visualization system presenting students' eye movements to educational researchers to understand students' problem-solving processes. More specifically, the visualization system is developed to illustrate how the visualization method can present students' eye movement data for educational researchers to achieve insights and make hypotheses about students' problem-solving strategies. Elementary school students' problem-solving data, including performance and eye movement data, were collected and visualized. Two educational researchers and one visualization designer were recruited to evaluate the visualization system and compare it to the traditional e-learning analysis method – video recordings. The evaluation results show that the visualization is easy to understand and can help evaluators to identify students' attention patterns and problem-solving strategies quickly. However, the visualization system provided less information than video recordings, e.g., problem-solving context and mouse movement. Our work shows a promising future of using visualization to help researchers and teachers to provide targeted intervention to help young students learn the correct strategy of math problem-solving.

Keywords: Visualization · Eye-tracking · Word problem solving

1 Introduction

Eye-tracking technology has been intensively used in educational research as access to comprehend students' learning process. Many recent studies have used eye-tracking data to analyze students' attention, on-task behaviors, and comprehension processes [1–3]. Understanding students' problem-solving processes is one application of eye-tracking technology. De Corte and Verschaffel [4] used eye movement data to reveal the solution processes of addition and subtraction word problems. Bolden et al. [5] adopted eye movement heatmaps to depict how young children group mathematical representations using different strategies. These studies illustrated that eye movement can reflect students' problem-solving strategies.

© Springer Nature Switzerland AG 2020
P. Zaphiris and A. Ioannou (Eds.): HCII 2020, LNCS 12206, pp. 201–213, 2020.
https://doi.org/10.1007/978-3-030-50506-6_15

However, analyzing and comprehending students' eye movements is a big challenge as eye movement data is enormous and complex. Traditionally, there are two methods of analyzing eye movement data. The first method is using heatmaps or gaze plots to get an intuitive impression of students' eye movements [6, 7]. But this method can't deliver accurate metrics such as the number of fixations to educators. Another method adopts statistical models to analyze eye movement metrics such as fixation duration to compare whether significant differences exist between different groups of students [8, 9]. This method gives statistical conclusions about different students' eye movement patterns. But the statistical results are determined based on groups of students, making it impossible to reflect an individual student's problem-solving strategy.

Data visualization, using graphics to depict quantitative data information, is a method that, to some extent, combines the strengths of the above two methods. This paper presents a visualization system for educational researchers to understand students' problem-solving processes. More specifically, the visualization system presents a novel method for presenting students' eye movement data and performance data. The visualization can help educational researchers form hypotheses and identify insights about students' problem-solving strategies.

2 Research Approach

The research approach of this study is:

1. Identify possible eye movement patterns that may indicate problem-solving strategies from the math literature. In other words, for a specific problem-solving strategy, the student will be more likely to have specific eye interaction patterns with the computer. This research focuses on identifying possible interaction patterns while a student is reading math problems.
2. Base on the possible eye movements, determine what data should be employed in this visualization study, e.g., fixation counts, regression counts.
3. From these data, we need to design/develop some visualization methods to let educators see a student's problem-solving process. Descriptive statistical methods (e.g., average fixation counts of a text) may be used in the visualizations.
4. After the visualization development, we invited target users – educational researchers to evaluate the visualization prototype. The purpose of the evaluation is to examine the usability of the visualization system to see if it can help researchers to gain insights about students' problem-solving strategies.

3 Theoretical Framework

According to the literature, there are two types of mathematical thinking, sequential thinking and holistic thinking [10]. Researchers pointed out that successful problem-solving requires interplay between both ways of thinking. Sequential thinking enables problem-solvers to understand a situation as a process/event while holistic thinking enables problem-solvers to understand the situation as "a system of relationships or a structure" [10].

Different problem-solving strategies may result from two mathematical thinking types. Hegarty et al. [11] contrasted two general strategies: direct-translation strategy and problem model strategy. Direct-translation strategy is a short-cut approach in which the problem-solver "attempts to extract the numbers in the problem and key relational terms (such as "more" and "less") and develops a solution plan that involves combining the numbers in the problem using the arithmetic operations that are primed by the keywords" (p. 19). Different from direct-translation strategy, the 'problem model' strategy is an approach based on situation comprehension. Problem solvers translate the problem statement into a situation model which is an object-based representation rather than text-based representation in the direct-translation strategy. Moreover, some teachers noticed students solving the math word problem linearly which means they only drag/fill numbers in the equation in sequence without any effort to comprehend keywords nor to understand the problem.

Based on mathematical thinking theory and previous studies, three types of problem-solving strategies and their possible reflections on eye movement patterns are summarized below:

The first strategy is 'linear drag', which means students just mechanically put the numbers into the diagram equation without mathematically thinking. In this case, a student may put numbers sequentially, with few fixations to the question, and ultimately failed the task.

The second strategy is 'keyword' strategy. Students may identify keywords, and based on the keywords such as total, to decide which number is whole. In this case, students may pay much attention to the numbers and keywords. Schoot et al. [12] indicated that longer and more regressions on the numbers and keywords are typical for keyword strategy.

The third strategy is 'problem model' strategy. In this stage, students are able to understand the problem as a complete structure and build the corresponding situation model. Reflected in students' eye movement data, problem solvers who likely use problem model strategy tend to fixate not only on numbers and keywords but also on variable names when they reread the problem [11].

The fourth strategy is 'guess and check', which strategy students use to solve mathematical problems by guessing the answer and then checking the guess with feedback [13]. In this case, the student may directly use guess and check strategy with few fixations, or the student may try to understand the problem with many fixations but failed, then he/she use guess and check strategy to finish the problem.

4   Method

4.1   Participants and Stimuli

33 2nd or 3rd-year elementary school students were recruited to participate in this study for data collection. Eight students' data were excluded from data visualization due to experiment incompletion or absence of eye movement data. Students completed a set of

arithmetic word problems, including two demos, six problems in random order. These demos and problems come from a Conceptual Module Based Problem Solving (COMPS-RtI) computer program, which was developed to promote the additive mathematics problem-solving of students [14]. The criteria to choose problems are – 1. Students can't get the correct answer if they drag name tags/number tags to the equation in sequence (e.g., Drag the first tag to the first box, drag the second tag to the second box). 2. Students can't get the correct answer by using the keyword (e.g., using plus when seeing "more", using minus when seeing "left"). These problem choosing criteria may, to some extent, improve the probability of finding problematic behavior/problem-solving strategies/struggles.

Figure 1 is one of the word problems students solved: "Bobby had a total of 87 cards in a box. He gave some cards to his brother, Jeff. Then Bobby had 62 cards left in his box. How many cards did he give to his brother Jeff?" The program let students drag name tags: "gave," "left," and "total" from the question to the Part-Part-Whole (PPW) diagram equation. Then, students were asked to drag numbers from the question to the PPW equation. Students had two chances to answer each question. After two failures, the program would demonstrate the correct answer.

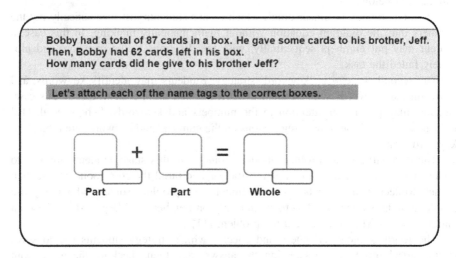

Fig. 1. An illustration of the math problem-solving tasks.

4.2 Data Collection and Data Preparation

Student performance data, including correctness and time spent on the tasks, were recorded. Their eye movement data was captured by a Tobii Pro X3-120 and stored in Tobii Pro bundled software – Tobii Pro Studio. The eye movement data such as fixation positions in X and Y directions (in pixels), timestamp, and fixation duration (in milliseconds) were recorded. Each student's eye movement data was imported into a MySQL database for further analysis. The areas that students expected to focus on were defined as AOIs, and the coordinates of AOIs were recorded in the database too.

A SQL database was built on a server to store students' interaction in real-time. The information registered in the database includes user id, task, prompt (question/instruction), action, feedback, segment, and timestamp. Students' interaction data was split into segments. Each segment was defined by a period of start time and end time. For example, a prompt start time and a prompt end time define a reading segment during which students read the problem. An operation start time and an operation time define an operation segment during which students drag the tags into the equation to solve the problem. Students' action was specifically defined in the program. When students dragged a name tag to the equation, the database recorded two records: "click number tag 30" and "put into part box1". The feedback column recorded students' answer correctness.

Students' interaction, performance, and eye movement data were recorded simultaneously when students were using the computer program.

4.3   Visualization Design

Based on the literature review, we concluded that students' correctness, time spends on each problem, fixation count, fixation duration, and regressions are important metrics that may indicate students' problem-solving strategies [14–16]. These metrics were selected and visualized as Fig. 2. It consists of two views. The performance view in the left shows student's performance data, including time spent on the task and the correctness of problem-solving. On the right side of the visualization is the 'Eye movement' view.

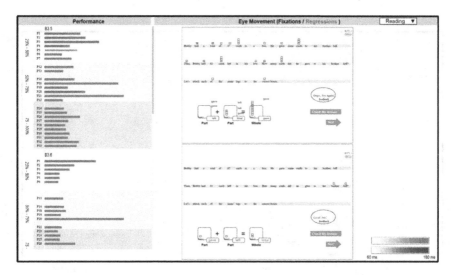

Fig. 2. A screenshot of the visualization system. (Color figure online)

Students were divided into three groups according to their performance in the eight math problems (correctness percentages: 25%–50%, 50%–75%, 75%–100%). In Fig. 2

'Performance' view, different shades of gray background indicate different performance groups. Bars show student's time taken on the problem. Student P5 in task B3.5 failed in the first try (red bar) and correct in the second try (green bar). The time spent on the second try is shorter than the first try.

There are three interaction methods. For different interaction methods, the 'Eye movement' view presents the corresponding content. The first interaction method is clicking on an individual performance bar to observe the student's eye movement during problem-solving. For example, in Fig. 2, the student P5's bar in the 'Performance' view was selected, the 'Eye Fixation' view presents the student's two attempts of problem-solving which is called individual task visualization. Figure 3 is the enlarged view of the individual task visualization. The problem elements such as question texts and equation boxes are defined as Areas of Interests (AOIs). The square bar chart on each AOI represents student eye fixations. The number of squares is the number of eye fixations located on the AOI, and the shades of color represent the duration of eye fixations. The deeper the color, the longer the fixation duration. The color of squares represents the problem-solving correctness. Students' drag performance is also presented in individual task visualization. In Fig. 3, the text on the diagram equation presents the tags that the student dragged into the diagram equation. From top to bottom is the earlier to the later of the operation. It can be observed that the student put 'gave' into the whole box at first, then put 'gave' to the first part box instead and put 'left' in the middle part box. Later, the student changed his/her mind again, put 'gave' into the whole box, put 'total' in the middle part box, and put 'left' in the first part box. The student failed (red color) and had a few fixations on the word 'total', 'cards', and numbers.

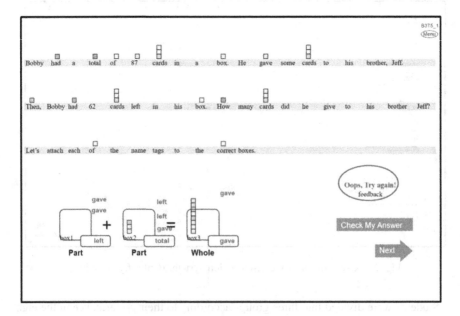

Fig. 3. The individual task visualization in the Eye Movement view. (Color figure online)

Besides that, there is a drop-down box in the 'Eye movement' view (see Fig. 2). Users can designate a specific segment to observe students' eye movements during the period. In Fig. 2, the reading segment is selected, which means the eye fixations presented in the 'Eye Movement' view happened in the problem reading period.

The second interaction method is clicking on multiple student bars in the 'Performance' view to compare the eye fixation differences among different students. For example, if the performance bars of student P2 and student P32 are selected, their eye fixations will be depicted in the 'Eye Movement' view using comparison visualization. Figure 4 is the comparison visualization in the Eye Movement view. Each text of problem content is defined as AOI and listed in sequence. The square bar chart following each AOI depicts the number of fixations and the duration of fixations. In Fig. 4, it can be observed that P2 fixated a lot on numbers (e.g., 87 cards) and keywords (e.g., total). While P32 fixated more evenly on the question content. Users can mouse over an AOI name to get the AOI's fixation/regression count and total fixation/regression duration. If the user mouse over an individual square, the corresponding fixation/regression's duration will pop out.

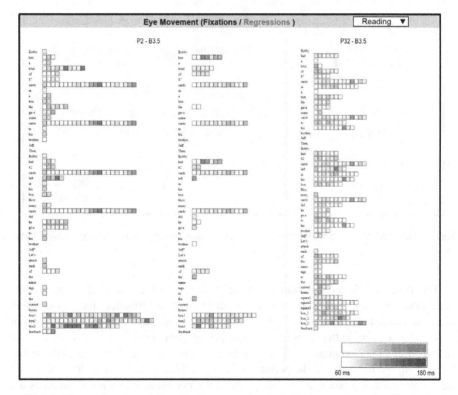

Fig. 4. Comparing the eye fixations between two students (comparison visualization).

The third interaction method is clicking on the index of the problem in the 'Performance' view to observe the whole group students' eye fixations. For example, if problem index 'B3.5' in the 'Performance' view in Fig. 2 is clicked, the 'Eye Movement' view presents the heatmap matrix of all students' eye fixations (Fig. 5). The horizontal axis is AOI and the vertical axis is student indexes. Each square represents the total duration of fixations located on the AOI. The deeper the color shade, the longer the duration. The color represents the correctness of student problem-solving (first try).

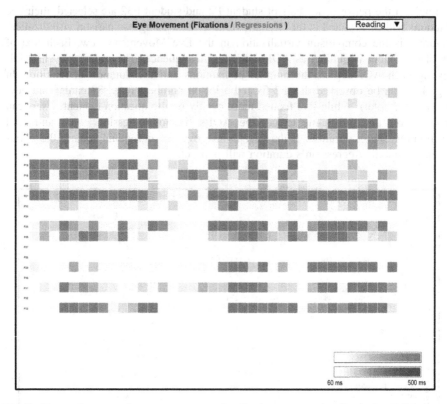

Fig. 5. The student group's eye movement visualization (group visualization). (Color figure online)

Based on the theoretical framework of students' problem-solving strategies, we developed the visualization system to present student performance, fixation duration and count for educational researchers to make hypotheses and achieve insights about students' attention patterns and problem-solving strategies. For example, as we described in Fig. 2, student P5 spent a relatively long time to solve the problem but failed (long red bar of P5 in the performance view). Then in her second try, she solved the problem quickly (short green bar of P5 in the performance view). Figure 3 is the enlarged view of the student's first problem-solving attempt, the student only had a few fixations on some words of the problem (e.g., 87, cards), but fixated on the diagram equation many times for a long time. The student didn't read the problem carefully but tried to solve the diagram equation directly. The visualization shows the student dragged tags everywhere with little attention to the problem context which indicates the student applied 'guess and check' strategy. Later, she may get some hints from the feedback, helping her get the correct answer in her second try.

Another example is in the Fig. 4. It shows student P2 looked at the diagram equation for relative long time and regressed many times on keywords 'total', 'cards', and numbers. But his fixations on other words are limited which indicates the student employed 'keyword' strategy. While student P32 had many fixations on almost every problem element showing the student paid attention to the whole problem context and applied 'problem model' strategy.

In the next section, we evaluate if the visualization can help educational researchers form hypotheses and achieve insights about students' attention patterns and problem-solving strategies.

5   Evaluation

Video recording is the traditional and frequently used method to analyze student problem-solving processes. To evaluate our visualization method, we invited two educational researchers and one visualization designer to go through the visualization system and compare it with the video recordings. The educational recruit criteria were: 1) Having math teaching experience. 2) Familiarity with the computer-assisted math learning program. 3) Having an educational background (with a master's or Ph.D. degree in education). The visualization designer recruit criteria were: 1) Having visualization design and development experience. 2) Being familiar with learning data visualization.

Each evaluator spent about forty minutes on the evaluation experiment, which included two sessions. In one of the sessions, evaluators were asked to identify two students' visual attention patterns and problem-solving strategies using the visualization system. In another session, evaluators were asked to identify another two students' visual attention patterns and problem-solving strategies using video recordings. The student tasks were randomly selected from the 25 student tasks (B3.5). Researchers first introduced the theoretical framework of student problem-solving strategies to evaluators and explained the visualization system to evaluators. After that, evaluators completed the two evaluation sessions. The four questions below were used to support the evaluators' analysis.

I. What was the pattern of the student's visual attention when solving this problem?
   1) Viewing most part of the problem
   2) Focusing only on keywords and/or numbers
   3) Paying little attention to the problem
   4) Other – Please describe
   5) Not sure
II. How was the student's performance? How was the student's performance?
   1) Correct on the 1st try
   2) Incorrect on the 1st try; Correct on the 2nd try
   3) Incorrect on the 1st try; Incorrect on the 2nd try

III. What was the problem-solving strategy the student used when solving the problem? What was the problem-solving strategy the student used when solving the problem?
1) Model-based problem-solving strategy
2) Direct translation strategy (keyword strategy)
3) Linear drag with little attention to the question
4) Guess and Check
5) Other - Please describe
6) Not sure

IV. What were the struggles/difficulties that the student meet when solving the problem? What were the struggles/difficulties that the student meet when solving the problem?
1) No struggles/difficulties
2) Difficulty in understanding the problem (literally)
3) Difficulty in understanding the diagram equation
4) Paid little attention to the problem
5) Careless drags/clicks
6) Other – Please describe
7) Not sure

After evaluators' evaluations, they were interviewed below questions:

1. Are you able to identify students' attention patterns? How did you identify it?
2. Are you able to identify students' problem-solving strategies on the math problem? How did you identify it?
3. Are you able to identify any unexpected patterns or characteristics of student learning behavior? If so, what are they?
4. What suggestions do you have for the visualization?

Additionally, evaluators were asked to rate their preferences for the visualization using a 7-point Likert Scale (1 = strongly disagree, 7 = strongly agree). The Likert items are in Table 1.

Table 1. Likert questions

#	Question
1	I found it easy to understand the visualization prototype
2	I found the visualization prototype help me understand the learning behavior of students
3	I can explore students' problem-solving activities efficiently
4	I am able to identify the attention patterns of students
5	I am able to identify the problem-solving strategies that a student used
6	I am confident I found all the problem-solving strategies that a student used
7	I am confident I can identify the student problem-solving strategies correctly
8	I am able to identify some other learning patterns of students (except attention and problem-solving strategies)
9	I am able to identify the learning difficulties/struggles of students

6 Results

The Likert scale survey results are presented in Table 2. Evaluation results show that evaluators strongly agreed that the visualization could help them understand students' learning behavior (average-point = 6.25), including students' problem-solving strategies (average-point = 5.75). They agreed that the visualization system is easy to understand (average-point = 6) and they could identify students' problem-solving strategies efficiently (average-point = 5). Evaluators stated that bar charts and square bar charts are easy to understand, and the individual student eye movement visualization presents the problem-solving context, which is beneficial to their situation understanding.

Table 2. Average points of Likert questions

Likert question	Q1	Q2	Q3	Q4	Q5	Q6	Q7	Q8	Q9
Average points	6	6.25	5	6.75	5.75	2.75	4.5	6	5.25

But they did not think all students' problem-solving strategies can be identified using the visualization (average-point = 2.75), which is consistent with the authors' expectation as problem-solving is a complex process involving many factors and some students may not present obvious eye movement patterns. In this case, researchers need more information to identify students' problem-solving strategies. But for the students who present clear eye movement patterns, evaluators agreed that they could identify their problem-solving strategies. For the problems in which students did not show obvious eye movement patterns, evaluators showed less confidence in the correctness of identified problem-solving strategies. Additionally, evaluators agreed that the visualization, to some extent, can help them get insights about students' difficulties and struggles, for example, a student fixated on the equation boxes for a relatively long time, and gazed between question content and equation may indicate his difficulty in building connections between question content and the equation.

The evaluation results show that the visualization system can help researchers understand students' problem-solving processes, get insights about students' problem-solving strategies, and make hypotheses about students' difficulties in solving the problems. Compared to video analysis, the visualization system enables users to analyze student problem-solving data quickly as visualization presents all data points through graphics at once. Besides that, visualization presents the data quantity clearly, such as the time students spend on the task, the number of fixations, while video recordings can't present such data quantity directly. With clear data quantity, evaluators can make more reliable diagnoses on student problem-solving strategies. However, evaluators pointed out that video recording can present student mouse movement, which is an important data source to depict student problem-solving operations, especially in the problems that need mouse operation as the problems in this study.

Students' frustration, uncertainty, and hesitation may be reflected from their mouse move forth and back. It is necessary to present student mouse movement in the visualization. Besides that, the square bar chart and heatmap matrix in the Comparison visualization and Group visualization are too abstract to depict the problem-solving context.

The visualization designer advised: 1. visualizing within the problem-solving context, which means using the problem layout as the visualization background (as was done for the Eye movement visualization in Fig. 2). 2. Use line elements instead of squares to visualize eye fixations to save space.

7 Conclusion and Future Work

Based on the theoretical framework of problem-solving strategies, and by employing eye movement and performance data from interactive mathematics problem-solving programs, this study developed a visualization approach for researchers to understand students' attention distributions, get insights about students' problem-solving strategies, and further comprehend students' difficulties in solving problems. More than that, this approach can also be generalized and applied to other educational areas such as reading, to help researchers better understand students' comprehension process.

However, more work should be done to strengthen the visualization, including presenting more data both in terms of quantity and variety, depicting student problem-solving context, and simplifying visualization graphics. Moreover, a more in-depth evaluation with more evaluators is needed. Nevertheless, our visualization design can help researchers and educators aware of a student's problem-solving strategy in a much faster way than traditional video recording methods. Using the visualization, it is possible for educators to quickly identify individual student's learning difficulties and thus develop more targeted interventions to help students learn correct ways of solving math problems.

References

1. Tsai, M.-J., et al.: Visual attention for solving multiple-choice science problem: an eye-tracking analysis. Comput. Educ. **58**(1), 375–385 (2012). https://doi.org/10.1016/j.compedu.2011.07.012
2. Che, X., Yang, H., Meinel, C.: Automatic online lecture highlighting based on multimedia analysis. IEEE Trans. Learn. Technol. **11**(1), 27–40 (2018)
3. Liu, C.J., Shen, M.H.: The influence of different representations on solving concentration problems at elementary school. J. Sci. Educ. Technol. **20**(5), 621–629 (2011). https://doi.org/10.1007/s10956-011-9293-4
4. De Corte, E., Verschaffel, L.: Eye-movement data as access to solution processes of elementary addition and subtraction problems. In: 67th Annual Meeting of the American Educational Research Association, 16–20 April, San Francisco, CA (1986)
5. Bolden, D., et al.: How young children view mathematical representations: a study using eye-tracking technology. Educ. Res. **57**(1), 59–79 (2015). https://doi.org/10.1080/00131881.2014.983718

6. Yoon, D., Narayanan, N.H.: Mental imagery in problem solving: an eye tracking study. In: Proceedings of Eye Tracking Research and Applications Symposium (ETRA), pp. 77–83 (2004)

7. Kabugo, D., et al.: Tracking students' eye-movements when reading learning objects on mobile phones: a discourse analysis of luganda language teacher-trainees' reflective observations. J. Learn. Dev. **3**(1), 51–65 (2016) http://files.eric.ed.gov/fulltext/EJ1107314. pdf

8. Chen, S.C., et al.: Eye movements predict students' computer-based assessment performance of physics concepts in different presentation modalities. Comput. Educ. **74**, 61–72 (2014). https://doi.org/10.1016/j.compedu.2013.12.012

9. Moutsios-Rentzos, A., Stamatis, P.J.: One-step "change" and "compare" word problems: focusing on eye-movements. Electron. J. Res. Educ. Psychol. Universidad de Almeria **13**(3), 503–528 (2015). https://doi.org/10.14204/ejrep.37.14133

10. Polotskaia, E., Savard, A., Freiman, V.: Duality of mathematical thinking when making sense of simple word problems: theoretical essay. EURASIA J. Math. Sci. Technol. Educ. **11** (2), 251–261 (2015). https://doi.org/10.12973/eurasia.2015.1325a

11. Hegarty, M., Mayer, R.E., Monk, C.A.: Comprehension of arithmetic word problems: a comparison of successful and unsuccessful problem solvers. J. Educ. Psychol. **87**(1), 18–32 (1995). https://doi.org/10.1037/0022-0663.87.1.18

12. van der Schoot, M., et al.: The consistency effect depends on markedness in less successful but not successful problem solvers: an eye movement study in primary school children. Contemp. Educ. Psychol. **34**(1), 58–66 (2009). https://doi.org/10.1016/j.cedpsych.2008.07. 002

13. Taspinar, Z., Bulut, M.: Determining of problem solving strategies used by primary 8, grade students' in mathematics class. Proc. – Soc. Behav. Sci. **46**(1998), 3385–3389 (2012). https://doi.org/10.1016/j.sbspro.2012.06.071

14. Tai, R.H., Loehr, J.F., Brigham, F.J.: An exploration of the use of eye-gaze tracking to study problem-solving on standardized science assessments. Int. J. Res. Method Educ. **29**(2), 185–208 (2006). https://doi.org/10.1080/17437270600891614

15. Catrysse, L., et al.: How are learning strategies reflected in the eyes? Combining results from self-reports and eye-tracking. Br. J. Educ. Psychol. **88**(1), 118–137 (2018). https://doi.org/10.1111/bjep.12181

16. Lai, M.L., et al.: A review of using eye-tracking technology in exploring learning from 2000 to 2012. Educ. Res. Rev. **10**, 90–115 (2013). https://doi.org/10.1016/j.edurev.2013.10.001

Games and Gamification in Learning

A Co-design Approach for the Development and Classroom Integration of Embodied Learning Apps

Yiannis Georgiou[1]([⊠]) and Andri Ioannou[2]

[1] Research Center on Interactive Media, Smart Systems and Emerging
Technologies, Nicosia, Cyprus
y.georgiou@rise.org.cy
[2] Cyprus Interaction Lab, Cyprus University of Technology, Limassol, Cyprus
andri.i.ioannou@cut.ac.cy

Abstract. The development of embodied learning apps has gained traction in the recent years. However, current design approaches present two main limitations: (a) the inadequate involvement of teachers in the design process, and (b) the development of embodied apps, neglecting the context-specific requirements. It is, therefore, no surprising that teachers are often reluctant to integrate such innovations in their classrooms. In this paper we present a co-design approach to address these limitations, thus contributing to the smoother introduction of embodied apps in mainstream education. The suggested design approach was applied for the co-design of the "Young cardiologists" embodied app, including three sequential stages: Teachers as (a) "Users", (b) "Content experts", and (c) "Technology integrators". The co-design approach ensured the active involvement of primary school teachers and guided the development of the app in alignment with the teachers' educational curriculum. The evaluation of the co-designed app reported learning gains in children's conceptual understanding.

1 Introduction and Theoretical Background

Embodied learning apps, which compose an emergent category of educational digital apps that integrate bodily movement into the act of learning, are argued to have the potential to revolutionize K-12 education [1]. These innovative apps that leverage the power of motion-based technologies and natural interfaces, have created new educational possibilities [2]. Embodied learning apps are usually equipped with motion tracking systems (e.g., Wii, Xbox Kinect, or Leap Motion) to enable hand gestures or body movements that are closely mapped to the educational content to be learned. The springboard for the development of these cutting-edge apps is that bodily involvement can support learning by allowing (a) multimodal interaction, (b) dynamic feedback, and (c) the creation of physical representations [3, 4].

Despite the tremendous educational opportunities related to embodied learning apps, their integration in authentic educational settings is still in slow pace [5–9]. According to Karakostas, Palaigeorgiou, and Kompatsiaris [10] embodied learning apps, are mainly developed for research purposes and do not follow the curriculum. In

© Springer Nature Switzerland AG 2020
P. Zaphiris and A. Ioannou (Eds.): HCII 2020, LNCS 12206, pp. 217–229, 2020.
https://doi.org/10.1007/978-3-030-50506-6_16

particular, existing embodied apps have usually derived from a designer-oriented approach, in which teachers are excluded from the development process [4]. As such, it is not a surprise that teachers do not have confidence in integrating embodied learning apps within their classrooms and teaching practices [10]. Quick et al. [11] have pointed out that supporting teachers in adopting embodied learning apps, requires teachers to obtain a sufficient understanding of technology-enhanced embodied learning, on a personal level.

Participatory design, as a bottom-up approach allows the co-design of educational technologies with the involvement of teachers and can contribute to the successful development of embodied learning apps. Participatory design is a common practice outside the field of education and aims to involve the users of a product in the design process, to ensure the usability, acceptability and effectiveness of the final product [12]. Re-contextualizing this practice in education, the co-design of educational technologies can allow teachers to result in more effective final products, as it allows a better understanding of the relationship between the underlying pedagogy and its instructional goals [13].

While participatory design methods have been mainly used in the past for the development of desktop computer apps [14], researchers have argued that the design of novel embodied interaction interfaces require different modalities of interaction with the technology and provide opportunities that are essentially different from traditional desktop-based interfaces [15]. However, existing research efforts on the participatory design of embodied learning apps are still fragmented and limited. These efforts have focused on the involvement of children, excluding the voices of teachers [16, 17]. At the same time, existing participatory frameworks, often neglect the context-specific requirements in which the co-designed embodied apps will be used [15], which is a crucial factor in ensuring that the produced embodied learning apps can be integrated effectively in teachers' classrooms. In this paper we introduce a co-design approach to the development and classroom integration of embodied learning apps in order to address previous limitations concerning the quality of the outcome and possibilities of successful integration.

2   The Co-design Approach

The identified limitations in the design and introduction of embodied learning apps in teachers' practices point out to the need for taking a critical stance on the development of embodied learning apps. We propose a co-design approach for the development of embodied learning apps which involves teachers throughout all the stages of the design process. The proposed co-design approach requires a shift from the decontextualized design of embodied learning apps to a serious consideration of the educational context in which they will be used, to ensure that the produced embodied learning apps are aligned with the educational curriculum and its underlying learning goals.

From a methodological point of view, the proposed approach borrows from: (a) participatory design, to gain useful insights in teachers' needs, to then be integrated in the design process [18], and (b) design-based research to organize teachers' contributions within an iterative design and assessment cycle [19]. The proposed co-design approach can be visualized as an iterative design process enacted by a protype and aiming at its transformation into a fully functional embodied learning app, aligned with the educational curriculum and teachers' expectations. The workflow includes three-stages: Stage 1: Teachers as "Users", Stage 2: Teachers as "Content experts", Stage 3: Teachers as "Technology integrators" (Fig. 1). The proposed co-design approach was enacted in the context of the INTELed European project (INnovative Training via Embodied Learning and multi-sensory techniques for inclusive Education) [20].

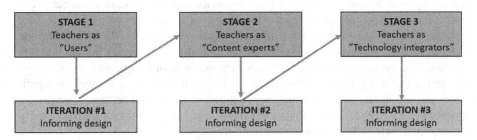

Fig. 1. Diagrammatic representation of the co-design approach for the development and classroom integration of embodied learning apps

3   The "Young Cardiologists" Embodied App

In this work, we applied the proposed co-design approach to the development of the "Young cardiologists" embodied app, to support 5th–6th graders' conceptual under-standing about the heart circulatory system. The co-design approach was enacted by a prototype of an embodied learning app of the heart circulatory system, controlled by a leap-motion sensor (Fig. 2). The leap motion sensor was initially set up so as to identify users' hands enacting two types of sequential gestures (a) a close/open fist gesture simulating the heart's pumping action, followed by (b) a hand flipping gesture simulating the heart valves' open/closing movement allowing the blood transition to the rest of the body (i.e. right atrium, right ventricle, pulmonary artery, lungs, left atrium, left ventricle, aorta, rest of the body) (Fig. 3). What follows is the presentation of the three stages as well as the main aims, methods, findings and iterations, per stage.

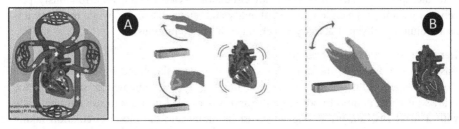

Fig. 2. Screenshot of the embodied app

Fig. 3. The combination of close/open fist gesture (A) and the flipping gesture (B)

3.1   Stage 1: Teachers as "Users"

Aims
Having a prototype at hand, the first stage had the goal of eliciting teachers' preferences and viewpoints on the modes of embodied interaction, during a co-design workshop.

Methods
The co-design workshop had a total duration of 1,5 h and was carried out at our university premises with a total of nine in-service primary education teachers. The workshop comprised of two main sessions. As part of the first session, which lasted for approx. 30 min, the teachers were initially requested to act as "Users" to test the prototype and familiarize themselves with the embodied app. During this session, the participating teachers were introduced to the embodied learning approach and the goals of the particular app as an example case. Subsequently they were allowed to experiment and use the embodied learning app. As part of the second session, which had a duration of 1 h, the teachers took part in a focus group in which they were requested to reflect upon their embodied interaction with the app.

Findings
We analysed the video-recordings of the workshop using the multi-modal framework analysis suggested by Maliverni, Shaper and Pares [21] for the co-design of embodied learning environments analysing and synthesizing: (a) teachers' sensorimotor engagement with the prototype version, focusing on their in-situ interactions with the embodied app, (b) teachers' verbal interactions, focusing on their spontaneous speech acts during their in-situ interaction with the prototype and (c) teachers' productions, focusing on teachers' written reports and discussions, produced during the post-activity focus group.

This analysis of the in-situ physical and verbal interactions as well as the following group interview revealed that the embodied interaction with the prototype version of the app was perceived as relatively complex by the teachers. As we found from the sensorimotor explorations, the teachers had difficulty in combining the flipping gesture with the open/close fist gesture repeatedly to control the app. Instead, the teachers proposed to retain a more simplified gesture, such as the open/close fist gesture, which could be more intuitive as a heart pumping action. The teachers had also highlighted, that as the heart "pumping" was depended exclusively on user's embodied interaction with the app, the function of the heart circulatory system could be erroneously perceived by some of the children as a voluntary and intended activity, while in reality it is an involuntary physical activity which takes place continuously.

Iteration #1: Informing Design
Based on our findings, the embodied interaction was simplified by keeping just the close fist/open palm gesture, as a more intuitive type of interaction simulating the heart's pumping action. In addition, the app was revised in order to run automatically with a heart rhythm, presenting the heart pumping and the blood circulation taking place on a continuous basis. Additionally, in the revised version, the users could intervene in the operation of the human circulatory system via their hand gestures, speeding up the heartbeat by moving their fists faster (Fig. 4).

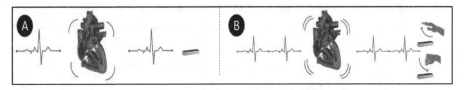

Fig. 4. The automatized version of the app with a heart rhythm (A), which also allowed users to intervene with their gestures to speed up the heartbeat (B)

3.2 Stage 2: Teachers as "Content Experts"

Aims
A second co-design workshop aimed at evaluating the educational content of the prototype, focusing on teachers' perceived affordances and limitations of the app.

Methods
The co-design workshop had a total duration of 2 h and was carried out at the university premises with the same cohort of in-service primary education teachers (n = 9). As part of the workshop the teachers were requested to act as "Content experts" after they had the opportunity to interact with the revised app of Stage 1. This time their aim was to evaluate the emerging opportunities and limitations of the app in promoting students' conceptual understanding on the topic. To achieve this goal, during the workshop the teachers took part in a group interview activity, which was grounded on the nominal technique [22]. According to this technique, the teachers were initially asked to write down and justify their viewpoints individually regarding their perceived learning affordances and limitations of the embodied app. As a second step, the teachers were asked to share their ideas with the group and the interview ended with a debriefing discussion.

Findings
The data were qualitatively analysed using thematic analysis [23], in order to identify the main themes discussed by the teachers. According to our findings the teachers' discussion evolved around two main themes, as follows: (a) the level of embodiment afforded by the learning app, and (b) the circulatory system representation supported by the app (Table 1).

The embodiment category involved ideas around the embodied and motion-based affordances of the app. As part of their discussion the teachers evaluated positively the affordances of the app for students' bodily involvement (i.e. learners' kinaesthetic activity), gestural congruency (i.e. gestures alignment with the concepts to be learned) as well as the degree of interactivity (i.e. gesture-based interaction and experimentation with the app). However, the teachers noticed and evaluated negatively the lack of bodily congruency (i.e. misalignment between their body and the simulated heart), as the circulatory system in the app was presented via a mirrored view. According to the teachers this misalignment could provoke a confusion to the students.

Discussing about the circulatory system representation afforded by the app, the teachers evaluated positively its realism (i.e. fidelity of the circulatory system representation). However, the teachers evaluated negatively the lack of key terminology (i.e. terms indicating the structure of the circulatory system), suggesting the

Table 1. Overview of the main themes discussed, as these were evaluated by the teachers.

Themes	Factors discussed *(teachers' comments)*	Evaluation
Embodiment	Gestural congruency *(gestures' alignment with the educational concepts)*	√
	Bodily involvement *(learner's kinesthetic activity)*	√
	Interactivity *(gesture-based interaction & experimentation with the app)*	√
	Bodily congruency *(alignment of real body with the simulated heart)*	X
Circulatory system representation	Realism *(fidelity of the circulatory system representation)*	√
	Key terminology *(terms indicating the structure of the circulatory system)*	X
	Dynamic features *(zoom in-out, Selective focus)*	X
	Sound effect *(heartbeat sound)*	X

addition of all the key terms in the app. The teachers evaluated negatively the static nature of the representation, suggesting the addition of more dynamic features such as a macro (zoom out) to a micro (zoom-in) transition within the circulatory system, and the selective focus on the different types of blood circulation which was deemed as a topic of high difficulty for their students. Finally, the teachers noticed the lack of any sound effect (i.e. heartbeat sound) and suggested how the integration of the "heartbeat" sound in alignment with the pace of the simulated heart could result in a more immersive learning experience.

Iteration #2: Informing Design

Based on our findings, the embodied app was updated with a zoom-in and zoom out feature, in order to allow children's transition from the human heart (micro-level), to a holistic overview of the blood circulation within the body (macro-level) (Figs. 5a–b). Likewise, a selective focus feature was added allowing children to activate the systemic or the pulmonary blood circulation, or both of them (Figs. 6a–b). The embodied app was also revised to match the users' position of his/her heart location as opposed to a mirror view. Finally, key terminology was integrated in all the representations, while the heartbeat sound effect was added to the app.

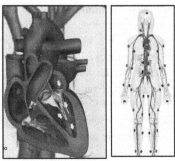
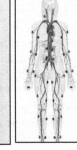
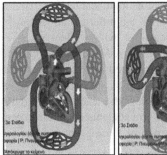
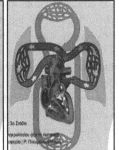

Fig. 5. a–b. The zoom-in/-out   **Fig. 6.** a–b. The selective focus feature

3.3   Stage 3: Teachers as "Technology Integrators"

Aims
The third co-design workshop had the goal to evaluate whether the revised design was aligned with the educational curriculum, thus allowing teachers to integrate it within their science classrooms.

Methods
The co-design workshop had a total duration of 2,5 h and was carried out at the university premises with a total of 5 of the primary education teachers, who had also participated in the previous two stages. As part of this workshop the teachers were asked to take the role of "Technology integrators" in order to discuss and reflect on whether the revised version of the embodied app could be integrated successfully in their classrooms. In order to do so, the teachers were provided access to the refined from Stage 2 embodied app as well as to the national educative materials used to teach the human circulatory system.

Findings
The co-design meeting was video-recorded and fully transcribed. The emerging data corpus was analysed via an open coding approach [24], focusing on teachers' verbal interactions around their efforts to develop a technology integration scenario using the embodied learning app in their curriculum. Teachers' discussion in this stage, focused on whether the learning goals underlying the app were aligned with the national educational standards and current learning activities, as these were presented in their educative materials (i.e. teacher and student guidebooks).
Based on our findings, according to the teachers, the embodied app was in alignment with most of the national education standards as it could contribute to students' understanding about: (a) the basic organs of the human circulatory system, (b) the position and size of the heart within the human body, (c) the structure of the heart, (d) the role of the heart as a pumper sending blood to all the parts of the human body, (e) the systemic and pulmonary circulation, and (f) the role of blood in the systemic and pulmonary circulation to transfer oxygen and carbon dioxide within the human body. However, according to the teachers, the embodied app was not capable of responding

to the educational national standards related to students' understanding about: (a) how the heartbeat varies and differentiates according to the pace of the physical exercise and (b) everyday customs which affect positively or negatively the human circulatory system (e.g. smoking, sedentary life, food and diet, physical exercise). As the teachers discussed, the embodied app could not support students' understanding about the impact of various physical exercises (e.g. walking Vs running) on the pace of the heartbeat. In addition, the teachers highlighted that in its current form, the embodied app could not inform students about basic concepts such as atherosclerosis, cholesterol, heart attack, stroke or thrombosis which are related with lifestyle and bad habits.

Iteration #3: Informing Design

Based on our findings, a motion-based human figure was added on the upper right corner of the app, acting responsively to the pace of the children's gestures, as captured by the leap motion e.g. walking, jogging, running (Fig. 7). In addition, a new section (Lifestyle & Bad habits) was added to the app, illustrating atherosclerosis with the build-up of cholesterol which can block gradually the blood vessels, thus resulting in thrombosis, stroke or heart attack (Fig. 8). As part of this section the children could encounter on the left part of their screen various bad habits (e.g. lack of exercise, junk foods, sedentary lifestyle). Subsequently, via their embodied interaction with the app the children could observe the negative impact of these habits, via the gradual accumulation of cholesterol in the blood vessels, resulting in thrombosis, stroke or a heart attack episode.

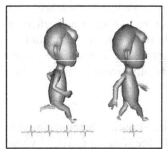

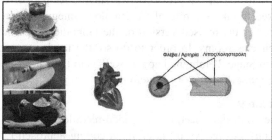

Fig. 7. The motion-based figure   **Fig. 8.** The lifestyle & bad habits section

4   The Evaluation of the "Young Cardiologists" App

The final version of the "Young cardiologists" was evaluated with children, with a focus on children's learning experience and learning gains. The evaluation study was a pilot before classroom integration of the embodied learning apps, as the ultimate goal of the project.

4.1   Methods

The evaluation was conducted in the context of a summer club for children which took place at the university. As part of the implementation, a class group of 21 children (12 boys and 9 girls; age: M = 11.9, SD = 1.29) participated in three 45-min lessons (Figs. 9a–b). The children were randomly assigned in groups of 2–3 and were invited to use the final version of the embodied app to investigate the following guiding questions: (a) How does our heart function?, (b) How does the blood flow within the human body?, and (c) How can our everyday habits affect the human circulatory system?. A pre-post conceptual test was developed, adopting a combination of multiple-choice items and open-ended tasks from a published conceptual test on the topic [25]. The test had a maximum score of 10 marks and was allocated to investigate children's conceptual understanding, before and after the learning intervention, on the three thematic areas addressed by the embodied app (Structure and function of the heart, Systemic and pulmonary blood circulation, Lifestyle and bad habits). After the intervention, a semi-structured interview was also conducted with 11 of the children, to discuss their impressions about their learning experience.

Fig. 9.   a–b. Snapshots from children using the final version of the embodied learning app

4.2   Findings

To investigate the impact of the embodied app on children's learning we analysed the pre-post tests using the Wilcoxon signed-rank test, as the data did not follow a normal distribution. The test revealed a statistically significant increase in children's total learning scores as well as in all the three conceptual aspects: (a) Structure and function of the heart, (b) Systemic and pulmonary blood circulation, (c) Lifestyle and bad habits (Table 2).

The qualitative analysis of children's interviews reinforced and shed light on the quantitative findings. In particular, the children reported their perceived learning gains in all the three conceptual aspects. At the same time, the children highlighted that the embodied app was user-friendly, highly interactive, enabled visual feedback according to their movements, and promoted a playful learning experience.

Table 2. Pre-post-test comparison of students' conceptual understanding

	Pre-test scores		Post-test scores		Z
	Mean rank	Sum of ranks	Mean rank	Sum of ranks	
Total learning scores	**8.00**	**10.11**	**8.00**	**182.00**	**−3.51***
Structure and function of the heart	0.00	0.00	7.50	105.00	−3.32***
Systemic and pulmonary blood circulation	5.00	20.00	8.50	85.00	−2.11*
Lifestyle and bad habits	4.50	9.00	6.90	69.00	−2.44**

Note. *p < .05, **p < .01. ***p < .001

5 Discussion

In this study, we have presented a co-design approach to the development and classroom integration of embodied learning apps. The approach aimed at allowing teachers' contributions to guide the design of embodied learning apps in alignment with their educational curriculum and therefore, increase the potential for their successful integration in mainstream education. This work informed the development of the "Young Cardiologists" embodied learning app, capable of supporting students' learning about the human circulatory system. The suggested co-design approach acknowledges the importance of engaging teachers in the design of products aligned with their expectations and their teaching practices [18]. In addition, the suggested approach responds to the call for the development of embodied learning apps aligned with the educational curriculum [10], thus addressing the lack of participatory approaches that ground the design of embodied learning apps within context-specific requirements [15].

Focusing on the structure of the proposed approach, each one of the three stages enabled access to the further development of the embodied learning app. The first stage of the co-design approach (Teachers as "Users") focused on the improvement of the embodied interaction with the app. According to our findings, teachers' contributions in this stage indicated how the initial embodied interaction with the learning app was deemed as complex and as such, was replaced with a more intuitive embodied interaction, simulating the heart "pumping" action. This finding is aligned with prior research supporting that while movement-based interfaces often provide a venue for more natural interactions than mouse and keyboard, such interfaces could also be criticized by the users when they do not resemble movements in real life, when not responding to users' expectations or when there is no gestural congruency with the educational content to be learned [2, 26, 28]. The second stage of the co-design approach (Teachers as "Content experts") focused on teachers' input about the educational content and its delivery via the app. Teachers' contributions in this stage were vital in revising and improving the content of the app. This finding is in agreement with our prior research, suggesting that teachers' involvement in the co-design of educational technologies can result in final products, aligned with students' needs and capable of supporting learning [13, 27, 28]. Finally, according to our findings, teachers' contributions in the third stage (Teachers as "Technology integrators") were crucial for the refinement of the app, ensuring its readiness to enter the school classroom. Overall, the suggested co-design approach can provide an alternative opposed to the top-down design approach for the development of research-oriented embodied learning apps [10], geared towards the development of embodied apps which match the curriculum goals as well as teaching and learning needs.

The evaluation of the final version of the app with children, allowed the investigation of the opportunities emerged of the app in promoting students' learning. According to our findings, the embodied app could support learning on all the intended conceptual aspects while it was also positively perceived by the children. Our positive findings are aligned with previous studies in the field which presented participatory design efforts with the involvement of children, resulting in final products capable of engaging young students and promoting their learning [15, 29].

Overall, the suggested co-design approach moves beyond top-down and designer-driven development approaches, which depend on the intuition of researchers and designers, excluding the contribution of other stakeholders. Instead, the involvement of teachers, which is found in the core of the proposed co-design approach, is of paramount significance for the design of meaningful modes of embodied interaction, appropriate educational content and successful contextualization of the app in teachers' educational curriculum and classrooms.

6   Limitations and Future Studies

Overall, the co-design approach appeared to be successful for the development of embodied learning apps aligned with both teachers' needs and the educational curriculum as well as capable of supporting children's learning. A limitation is that, by addressing the design approach to in-service teachers, we did not include the actual end-users in the design process, namely 5th–6th graders. While the final product was embraced by the children and promoted their learning, future studies should focus on the expansion of the proposed approach to include both teachers' and their students. At the same time, the evaluation study presented in this work was a pilot in a summer school programme, before formal classroom integration of the embodied learning app could take place; the forthcoming research plans of this project are directed towards the integration and investigation of the co-designed learning app within authentic educational contexts. Last but not least, the "Young cardiologists" apps a just a specific example of an embodied gesture-based app. Future studies should investigate the co-design of a broader range of embodied learning apps.

Despite these limitations, this study has presented a successful design approach which moves beyond the designer-driven approaches, involving in-service teachers in the design process, and embracing cycles of refinements to optimize the design and contextualization of embodied learning apps in the educational curriculum. The co-design method can contribute to the design of embodied learning apps for classroom integration, taking into account the teachers' needs and expectations as well as the context-specific requirements in which the app will be used.

Acknowledgements. This work is part of the project that has received funding from the European Union's Horizon 2020 research and innovation programme under grant agreement No 739578 (RISE-Call:H2020-WIDESPREAD-01-2016-2017 TeamingPhase2) and the government of the Republic of Cyprus through the Directorate General for European Programmes, Coordination and Development. This work is also part of the INTELed Project [INnovative Training via Embodied Learning and multi-sensory techniques for inclusive Education] (Project 2017-1-CY01-KA201-026733), which is co-funded by the Erasmus + Programme of the European Union.

We would kindly like to thank the INTELed consortium, the KINEMS (https://www.kinems.com/) for supporting the INTELed's endeavours, as well as all the teachers and their students, who participated in the project.

References

1. Georgiou, Y., Ioannou, A.: Embodied learning in a digital world: a systematic review of empirical research in K-12 education. In: Díaz, P., Ioannou, A., Bhagat, K.K., Spector, J.M. (eds.) Learning in a Digital World. SCI, pp. 155–177. Springer, Singapore (2019). https://doi.org/10.1007/978-981-13-8265-9_8

2. Johnson-Glenberg, M, Megowan-Romanowicz, C: Embodied science and mixed reality: how gesture and motion capture affect physics education. Cogn. Res. Princ. Implic. $2(1)$ (2017). Article number: 24. https://doi.org/10.1186/s41235-017-0060-9

3. Abrahamson, D., Lindgren, R.: Embodiment and embodied design. In: Sawyer, R.K. (ed.) The Cambridge Handbook of the Learning Science, 2nd edn, pp. 358–376. Cambridge University Press, Cambridge (2014)

4. Antle, A.N.: Research opportunities: embodied child-computer interaction. Int. J. Child-Comput. Interact. $1(1)$, 30–36 (2013)

5. Georgiou, Y., Ioannou, A., Ioannou, M.: Investigating immersion and learning in a low-embodied versus high-embodied digital educational game: lessons learned from an implementation in an authentic school classroom. Multimodal Technol. Interact. $3(4)$, 68 (2019)

6. Ioannou, M., Georgiou, Y., Ioannou, A., Johnson, M: On the understanding of students' learning and perceptions of technology integration in low-and high-embodied group learning. In: 13th Conference of Computer-Supported Collaborative Learning, pp. 304–311. ISLS (2019)

7. Georgiou, Y., Ioannou, A., Ioannou, M.: Investigating children's immersion in a high-embodied versus low-embodied digital learning game in an authentic educational setting. In: Beck, D., et al. (eds.) iLRN 2019. CCIS, vol. 1044, pp. 222–233. Springer, Cham (2019). https://doi.org/10.1007/978-3-030-23089-0_17

8. Ioannou, M., Ioannou, A., Georgiou, Y., Boloudakis, M.: Orchestrating the technology enhanced embodied learning classroom via learning stations rotation: a case study. Paper presented at the Hybrid Learning Spaces - Design, Data, Didactics (HLS: D3) Workshop of the 14th European Conference on Technology Enhanced Learning (ECTEL), Delft, The Netherlands

9. Ioannou, M., Ioannou, A., Georgiou, Y., Retalis, S.: Designing and orchestrating the classroom experience for technology-enhanced embodied learning. In: Proceedings of International Conference of the Learning Sciences (ICLS 2020). ISLS (2020)

10. Karakostas, A., Palaigeorgiou, G., Kompatsiaris, Y.: WeMake: a framework for letting students create tangible, embedded and embodied environments for their own STEAM learning. In: Kompatsiaris, I., et al. (eds.) INSCI 2017. LNCS, vol. 10673, pp. 3–18. Springer, Cham (2017). https://doi.org/10.1007/978-3-319-70284-1_1

11. Quick, J., et al.: Understanding and supporting the teachers involved in adopting a mixed-reality embodied K-12 environment (RTD). In: The Annual Meeting of the AECT Convention (2010)
12. Simonsen, J., Robertson, T.: Routledge International Handbook of Participatory Design. Routledge, London (2012)
13. Kyza, E.A., Georgiou, Y.: Developing in-service science teachers' ownership of the profiles pedagogical framework through a technology-supported participatory design approach to professional development. Sci. Educ. Int. **25**(2), 57–77 (2014)
14. Wang, F., Hannafin, M.J.: Design-based research and technology-enhanced learning environments. Educ. Technol. Res. Dev. **53**(4), 5–23 (2005). https://doi.org/10.1007/BF02504682
15. Malinverni, L., Schaper, M.-M., Pares, N.: An evaluation-driven design approach to develop learning environments based on full-body interaction. Educ. Technol. Res. Dev. **64**(6), 1337–1360 (2016). https://doi.org/10.1007/s11423-016-9468-z
16. Giaccardi, E., Paredes, P., Díaz, P., Alvarado, D.: Embodied narratives: a performative co-design technique. In: Proceedings of the Designing Interactive Systems Conference, pp. 1–10. ACM (2012)
17. Schaper, M.M., Malinverni, L., Pares, N.: Participatory design methods to define educational goals for full-body interaction. In: Proceedings of the 11th Conference on Advances in Computer Entertainment Technology, p. 50. ACM (2014)
18. Muller, M.J., Druin, A.: Participatory design: the third space in HCI. In: HCI: Development Process, vol. 4235, pp. 1–70 (2003)
19. Anderson, T., Shattuck, J.: Design-based research: a decade of progress in education research? Educ. Res. **41**(1), 16–25 (2012)
20. Martínez-Monés, A., Villagrá-Sobrino, S., Georgiou, Y., Ioannou, A., Ruiz, M.J.: The INTELed pedagogical framework: applying embodied digital apps to support special education children in inclusive educational contexts. In: Proceedings of the XX International Conference on Human Computer Interaction, pp. 1–4 (2019)
21. Malinverni, L., Schaper, M.M., Pares, N.: Multimodal methodological approach for participatory design of Full-Body Interaction Learning Environments. Qual. Res. **19**(1), 71–89 (2019)
22. MacPhail, A.: Nominal group technique: a useful method for working with young people. Br. Educ. Res. J. **27**(2), 161–170 (2001)
23. Attride-Stirling, J.: Thematic networks: an analytic tool for qualitative research. Qual. Res. **1**(3), 385–405 (2001)
24. Patton, M.Q.: Qualitative Research and Evaluation Methods. Sage, London (2002)
25. Ozgur, S.: The persistence of misconceptions about the human blood circulatory system among students in different grade levels. Int. J. Environ. Sci. Educ. **8**(2), 255–268 (2013)
26. Pasch, M., Bianchi-Berthouze, N., van Dijk, B., Nijholt, A.: Immersion in movement-based interaction. In: Nijholt, A., Reidsma, D., Hondorp, H. (eds.) INTETAIN 2009. LNICST, vol. 9, pp. 169–180. Springer, Heidelberg (2009). https://doi.org/10.1007/978-3-642-02315-6_16
27. Georgiou, Y., Ioannou, A.: Teachers' concerns about adopting technology-enhanced embodied learning and their mitigation through Professional Development. J. Technol. Teach. Educ. **27**(3), 335–371 (2019)
28. Georgiou, Y., Ioannou, A.: Investigating in-service teachers' concerns about adopting technology-enhanced embodied learning. In: Scheffel, M., Broisin, J., Pammer-Schindler, V., Ioannou, A., Schneider, J. (eds.) EC-TEL 2019. LNCS, vol. 11722, pp. 595–599. Springer, Cham (2019). https://doi.org/10.1007/978-3-030-29736-7_47
29. Malinverni, L., Mora-Guiard, J., Padillo, V., Valero, L., Hervás, A., Pares, N.: An inclusive design approach for developing video games for children with autism spectrum disorder. Comput. Hum. Behav. **71**, 535–549 (2017)

Play to Learn! Nurturing Fundamental Digital Skills of Romanian Preschoolers by Developing Edutainment Applications

Adriana-Mihaela Guran[1]([⊠])[iD], Grigoreta-Sofia Cojocar[1][iD],
and Anamaria Moldovan[2][iD]

[1] Babeş-Bolyai University, M. Kogalniceanu 1, Cluj-Napoca, Romania
{adriana,grigo}@cs.ubbcluj.ro
[2] Albinuţa Kindergarten, G. Alexandrescu 27, Cluj-Napoca, Romania
anabeekindergarten@gmail.com
http://www.cs.ubbcluj.ro

Abstract. From their early age, children are exposed to technology, mainly used for entertainment. It is considered that the current generations possess the so-called lifestyle digital skills (focused on entertainment goals), while their work-related skills are missing. In this paper we describe our approach in changing preschool children's attitude towards technology by developing and integrating edutainment applications in their teaching-learning activities. The approach was used for preschoolers in the public formal educational system. We describe our experience in designing and implementing edutainment applications over a period of three years, the challenges encountered and the solutions we have used.

Keywords: Edutainment · Digital skills · Preschooler · User centered design

1 Introduction

Nowadays, considerable efforts are made to transfer different human performed activities to computer supported tasks. In the European Union (EU) there is a high interest in society digitization, that is why a Digital Agenda for Europe (DAE) has been set since 2010 [14]. Along with the digitization goals, statistics about the level of EU citizens digital skills have been made. Unfortunately, our country ranks the last positions from the 28 states of EU [15]. The statistics show that Romanian citizen possess the so called *lifestyle digital skills* related to playing multimedia content and social networking, but they do not possess the digital skills needed for the future workforce market. It is considered that education should be at the forefront of the process of improving the digital skills of the citizens and that equality of chances should be provided to all of them. To ensure equality of chances, intervention in the public formal educational system seems appropriate. In this paper we describe our approach in designing and

© Springer Nature Switzerland AG 2020
P. Zaphiris and A. Ioannou (Eds.): HCII 2020, LNCS 12206, pp. 230–240, 2020.
https://doi.org/10.1007/978-3-030-50506-6_17

implementing edutainment applications for Romanian preschoolers that can be used as a support to classical teaching-learning activities. The paper is structured as follows. Section 2 describes the challenges of early childhood digital education. Section 3 presents our experience in designing and implementing edutainment applications for preschoolers. The paper ends with conclusions and future development in Sect. 4.

2 Early Childhood Digital Education

In order to act optimally in favour of the children's growth during their preschool age, it is necessary to implement appropriate working methods with them, to use validated modalities and to use the experience gained in the field. The need to integrate technology into education to support 21st century pedagogy and learning environments is frequently emphasized nowadays and teachers need to be "at the forefront of designing and implementing the change" [11]. Today, using the computer in the classroom is considered to be equally important to reading, writing and maths.

At preschool stage, kindergarten time is dominated by discovering the world through games and playing [12]. This stage is the proper start in building new skills for using devices in a joyful and pleasant way. The development of the communication skills of the preschoolers occupies a main place in the educational process from kindergarten, the language being one of the essential conditions of the personality formation of the child. Still, many practitioners find it difficult to integrate digital technology into their practice due to several constraining factors, such as: a curriculum focused on literacy as primarily paper-based, lack of time to explore available digital resources, absence of guidance about the potential of new technologies to promote early literacy and low confidence in using digital devices effectively in the classroom [5,9,13]. In Romania there is a lack of digital materials for educational goals dedicated to preschoolers, as there is just one publisher that creates and sells educational applications together with magazines. We could not find any information about the development process of the provided materials or if the products adhere to the National Curricula for preschool children.

3 Developing Edutainment Applications - Children and Kindergarten Teachers Participation

3.1 Edutainment Applications

Edutainment applications are a class of applications intended for playing, but at the same time for educational purposes. Building edutainment applications for preschoolers needs to integrate the learning goals with their main activity, namely playing. Although there are some guidelines on designing for children, it is difficult to choose the appropriate ones for preschoolers, which are a special kind of users. The existing guidelines consider children aged 0 to 8 years as a homogeneous group [3,8]. However, there are essential differences between children belonging to different ranges of age. Romanian preschoolers are 3 to 6/7 years old. At this age, the children cannot read or write, they need the guidance of an adult in performing tasks and they need rewards for accomplishing them. All these characteristics bring new constraints on designing interactive applications for children. These applications need to be conceived as games or, at least, they need to expose game-related objects, they must provide output through audio messages and to gather input only using the basic computer skills the children possess. In the following we present our experience in designing, developing and evaluating edutainment applications for Romanian preschoolers.

In 2017 we initiated it as a to-do project for undergraduate computer science students attending the Human-Computer Interaction optional course. Each year, more than 20 teams have participated to the course, each team consisting in 3–5 members, as shown in Table 1. In the first year we tried a general approach, so the applications were addressed to all 3 ranges of preschool children. In 2018 the applications were addressed to the children in the middle group (4–5 years old), and in 2019 the final users were children in the older group (5–6/7 years).

Table 1. Teams participating in the project.

Academic year	Number of teams	Themes for edutainment applications
2017–2018	27	Colours, Human body, Fruits, Spring, Summer
2018–2019	24	Wild animals, Insects and small beetles, By boat on waves
2019–2020	26	Moneys, Space, Dinosaurs, Earth

3.2 Designing with/for Preschoolers - An Iterative Process

We decided to use a User Centered Design (UCD) [10] approach in order to build interactive applications suitable for a special group of final users, the preschoolers. As they are very young, the UCD has been adapted through our experience. In the first year we have involved the children only during the evaluation phase. In the second year we have involved the children in the requirements step and, also, in the evaluation step, while in the last year we have succeeded to involve the children in every step of the design process.

The design teams have benefit the participation of educational experts, of interaction designers, and of software engineers. In the design process the preschoolers and their parents have been involved in different phases. In this section we describe the design process that was followed and the challenges encountered during our experience. The first challenge was the fact that we could not extract the requirements from our final users, as they are preschoolers, so we decided to elicit them from an educational expert. The participation of the educational expert was mandatory in this phase, as it is the only stakeholder who can answer the question WHAT. In order to gather the requirements we have organized interviews with kindergarten teachers. Valuable information was elicited from the interviews regarding the following aspects:

- How the teaching process is organized in the kindergarten? We have found out that the curricula domains are taught in an integrated manner, as integration proves to be a real solution for a better correlation of science with society, culture, technology and "supposes the establishment of close, convergent relations between the following elements: concepts, skills, and values, belonging to the distinct schools disciplines" [7];
- What did the children already studied from the curricula for preschoolers, especially in terms of counting, comparisons, vocabulary, and emotions?
- What is the duration of teaching activities? We found it is between 20 and 45 min, but the time span increases accordingly to the children's age.

In the first iteration of the process, in 2017, we have considered that involving the kindergarten teacher is sufficient. Also, we have considered that the design and development teams have understood what it meant to teach in an integrated manner. As such we did not involved the kindergarten teacher nor the children in the next phases of design and development. We found out that it was not true. In the evaluation phase, the kindergarten teacher discovered that most of the applications were addressed to a single curriculum domain, mainly mathematics, and that the rest of the domains remained uncovered. Also, most of the developed applications did not provide audio interaction, only written messages, which could not be understood by the children. In order to be used by the children, the assistance of an adult user was mandatory. In 2018, we have considered that we need to improve the design process, in each phase. First, the requirements needed to be more clear for the design teams. As a consequence, the kindergarten teacher has formulated from the beginning the problem statements, establishing also the age range, the curricula domains that have to be integrated and the activities types that must be covered (teaching, review, practice or consolidation). Examples of the problem statements used in 2018 are given in Table 2. During the design step, the kindergarten teacher has discussed with the design teams the proposed designs. The kindergarten teacher's feedback was influenced by how the design alternatives were presented. Some design teams have provided abstract design sketches and the kindergarten teacher needed a lot of explanations. Other teams have prepared for this step executable prototypes of the application. The more effort has been spent on developing the prototypes, the more detailed was the feedback given by the client and the design team already knew more things about the interaction structure and how the content should be presented to the children.

After receiving the feedback on the design alternatives, the design teams have built the prototypes for their applications. These prototypes have been evaluated by the kindergarten teacher. She has reported some possible problems that children could encounter while interacting with the application. The observations were related to how the tasks were formulated, the position of objects on

Table 2. Project statements examples.

Theme	Domain	Goal
By boat on waves	Environmental study, Mathematics	Number 5 - teaching
Insects and small beetles	Environmental study, Mathematics	Numbers from 1 to 5 - review and practice

the screen, and the widgets that were used. In the end, we have performed the evaluation of the obtained applications with a few kindergarten children. Three kindergarten boys have participated in the evaluation session. Observation, interviews and smileyometers have been used to assess the children's attitude towards their experience with the applications. During the evaluation phase we have discovered new problems that were not predicted during the prototypes evaluation. The most encountered issue was related to the synchronization of the audio messages. Most of the applications gave audio feedback while children were hovering the objects on the screen. No one had imagined that children would move the mouse cursor on the entire screen, intentionally or non-intentionally. Thus, more audio files were playing at the same time, making the content not understandable. From the children's point of view, it was fun, but from the educational point of view it was a big problem. Another drawback of the applications was the formulation of tasks. For example, when the children were required to count the number of objects on the screen or recognize the digit corresponding to the number of objects shown, they just said the answer or pointed with their finger on the screen, without interacting with the applications. As a consequence, tasks needed to be reformulated by clearly stating how to choose the correct answer: *Select with a click the number of....*

After the second experience of designing edutainment applications, we have drawn the conclusion that children should be included more during the design process. The previous experience proved us that involving only the kindergarten teacher during the design process does not completely substitute the children's participation in this phase. Many of the problems encountered during the evaluation sessions could have been identified earlier if the children had been included in the design process. In the third design and development iteration, we have centered the design process on the children. The participation of the kindergarten teacher was still essential regarding the content and tasks, but for a realistic evaluation of engagement, fun and efficiency, children would be more involved. Thus, we have involved the children from the beginning of the design process. During the requirements step, we have included children as informants. They provided us information on their digital skills, their interests and their level of knowledge on the subject of the edutainment applications. Their participation was facilitated through field studies in the kindergarten. Members of the design teams have visited the kindergarten and have observed the children during their every day activities, interviewing them and playing with them.

The design team members have considered that they need to spend more time with the children to understand their interests and to assess their digital skills. They came with the idea of volunteering in the kindergarten and they have proposed to organize optional classes for preschoolers related to computers and technology. With the guidance of kindergarten teachers, they have prepared 45 min classes, with a teaching part related to computers, their components and roles followed by consolidation games. All the activities (teaching and consolidation) were conceived as games using paper based mock-ups, balloons, pencils and other objects familiar to the children and available in the kindergarten classroom (see Fig. 1), followed by interaction with the laptops brought by the volunteers.

Fig. 1. Optional computer class with preschool children.

During the meetings with the children, the members of the design teams have given the children the opportunity to interact with the prototypes of the applications. This way, the children have started to become design partners. Being already familiar with the members of the design teams, the children dared to ask them to change the objects from the applications based on their preferences (one little boy asked a developer to replace the bicycle from the game with cars). Then, the same boy had the same requirement to other teams, but for some of the applications, where the theme was different, it was impossible to incorporate this kind of change. Other children wanted to change the narrator character during the games, and because there wasn't a consensus, the design teams have decided to let the children choose the character accompanying them during the interaction with the application. They can choose the character when they start interacting with the application (see Fig. 2).

Fig. 2. First window of an application - choose your character.

3.3 Evaluation

Evaluation is an essential development step, as it provides feedback on the measure to which the product satisfies users needs. In the case of educational applications the assessment of a product includes multiple aspects. It is important to have satisfied users (i.e., preschoolers), but at the same time the product should prove its effectiveness. For this goal we needed to also include the educational experts.

Evaluation with Preschoolers. Evaluation with preschoolers is challenging due to the constraints imposed by their cognitive and communication skills. Most of the assessment methods used with adults are not applicable with small children. Many products for children are still analytically evaluated by adult experts [2] instead of using observation on children. The observational evaluation methods that work with adults cannot always be applied with children [6]. However, "it is not easy for an adult to step into a child's world" [3], [4], and sometimes the children's behaviour with a game it is very difficult for adult experts to predict.

Children between four and eight years old are part of the youngest and the middle age group. The characteristics of these age groups according to Hanna et al. [6] are:

- 2 to 5 years: Preschool children's attention span is rather low. Furthermore, their motivation to please adults and their ability to adjust to unfamiliar surroundings and new people may change from one moment to the next, making the course of the test session unpredictable. Therefore, this age group requires the most extensive adaptations of user testing.
- 6 to 10 years: Children in this age group are used to going to school. Therefore they can successfully perform tasks and follow directions from adults. They will answer questions and try out new things, and they are not very concerned about being observed when they play with the computer. Still, the youngest children of this age group (6 and 7 years old) may be a little shy or inarticulate when talking about the computer.

The children participating in our study were part of the category 2 to 5 years. Through the years we have applied different approaches in trying to evaluate the developed applications. In the first iteration, we have organized play-testing sessions and we have allowed children to interact in groups with the applications to simulate think-aloud protocols. In 2018 we have introduced the smileyometers to assess the subjective opinion of the children towards our products, and post-test interviews containing simple questions as: *Would you like to show this game to your best friend? Would you like to play again?*. The children have always chosen the happiest face on the smileyometer, even though we have observed some situations when they did not manage to interact with the application as expected. Although the children were enthusiastic about their experience of interacting with the proposed applications, we considered that we needed a validation of our conclusions. That is why we have considered that by involving the parents during the evaluation we will gather supplementary information. Moreover, we have considered that an objective evaluation of children's emotions will also help us extract their attitude towards our products.

Evaluation with Other Education Experts. In 2017 we have considered that in order to be used by more kindergarten teachers, the developed applications must be perceived as appropriate and useful. We have had in view that the most efficient way of finding out kindergarten teachers' opinion about the developed applications was to apply heuristic evaluation. As there is no heuristics set for small children edutainment applications, we have adapted Heuristic Evaluation of Children E-learning (HECE) [1]. HECE contains three heuristics sets, as it follows. NUH is the subset related to navigability, CUH is the subset related to children, and LUH is the subset related to learning. We have involved 12 kindergarten teachers in the evaluation process. The results for the CUH and LUH heuristics evaluation were very clear. All kindergarten teachers have evaluated with the highest scores the heuristics from these sets. But, when evaluating the NUH subset the results were very diverse, such that we could not draw a conclusion about their opinion. We consider that the results were so unconvincing because the kindergarten teachers did not clearly understand the heuristics.

Evaluation with the Parents. In 2019 we have added complementary approaches in usability assessment. We have organized workshops with the children's parents. We wanted to find out how the children have reported (presented) their experience at home. The parents have told us that children presented their interaction as "playing with the computer" and that children have mentioned different objects from the applications they had interacted with (the bathroom, the cat under the table, etc). Some parents have also mentioned their concern about the children's enthusiasm. They considered that children would never stop playing if they had unrestricted access to the presented computer games. From the experience of observing the children while interacting, we have assured them that children had not spent more than 10 min in front of the computer. They often returned to their usual play activities with the toys, and only some of them returned for another game if it was interesting. Children haven't played the same game more than twice. Related to children's development of digital skills, parents have reported improvements on the use of mouse to select an object on the screen, clicking, recognizing usual widgets as the play button, exit option and the use of arrow keys. At home, some children initiated discussions about computer's components, their role, and differences between desktop and laptop computers.

Automatic Satisfaction Evaluation. At this age the children are trying to please the adults, so when they say that they have enjoyed playing the games, it is not always relevant. We have tried another approach in evaluating children's satisfaction. We wanted an objective measurement of children's attitude towards their interaction with the games. So, we have used an emotion recognition automatic tool, provided by Google Vision API. During the interaction with one application, we have captured pictures of children's faces every 30 s with the help of a webcam software system. Five children have participated at this evaluation session and 134 pictures have been collected. The pictures have been analyzed by the before mentioned API. Mainly, we were interested in finding if the children experienced negative emotions as anger or sorrow. The results are encouraging, as the presence of negative emotions was 100% very unlikely, as Fig. 3 shows.

Fig. 3. Statistics for Anger and Sorrow likelihood

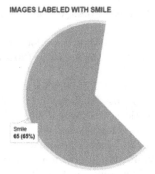

IMAGES LABELED WITH SMILE

Smile
65 (65%)

Fig. 4. Statistics on the number of pictures labeled with **smile**

Moreover, a number of 91 pictures have been labeled with smile, representing 65% of the total number of pictures (see Fig. 4). This shows us that children had a great time interacting with our product.

4 Conclusions and Future Work

In this paper we have described our experience in designing, developing and evaluating edutainment systems for preschoolers. We have organized the entire activity as playing activities, such that children have been part of the design process by playing. In the future we intend to enhance the products by adding new functionalities for:

- children authentication;
- automatic analysis of children emotions while interacting;
- applications adaptation based on children's emotions.

Acknowledgement. We would like to express a special thanks to the kindergarten teachers who guided us through the design process, to the kindergarten management and teaching staff and to the children and their parents participating in our study. We would like to thank to the students for accepting the challenge of designing for a very special kind of users.

References

1. Alsumait, A., Al-Osaimi, A.: Usability heuristics evaluation for child e-learning applications. In: Proceedings of the 11th International Conference on Information Integration and Web-Based Applications & Serviced, pp. 425–430 (2009)
2. Buckleitner, W.: The state of children's software evaluation-yesterday, today and in the 21st century. Inf. Technol. Child. Educ. **1999**, 211–220 (1999)
3. Druin, A., Solomon, C.: Designing Multimedia Environments for Children. Wiley, New York (1996)

4. Druin, A.: The role of children in the design of new technology. Behav. Inf. Technol. **21**(1), 1–25 (2002)
5. Flewitt, N.K.R., Messer, D.: New directions for early literacy in a digital age: the iPad. J. Early Child. Lit. **15**(3), 2014 (2014). https://doi.org/10.1177/1468798414533560
6. Hanna, L., Risden, K., Alexander, K.: Guidelines for usability testing with children. Interactions **4**, 9–14 (1997). https://doi.org/10.1145/264044.264045
7. De Landsheere, V.: L'éducation et la formation. In: Recherche & Formation, No. 13, 1993. Quelle formation en commun pour les enseignants, pp. 201–203 (1992)
8. Markopoulos, P., Bekker, M.M.: How to compare usability testing methods with children participants. In: Workshop Interaction Design for Children, Proceedings of the IFIP 9th International Conference on Human-Computer Interaction - INTERACT 2005, Rome, pp. 153–158. Shaker Publishing, Maastricht (2005)
9. Marsh, J.A.: The digital literacy skills and competences of children of preschool age. Media Educ.: Studi Ricerche Buone Pract. **7**(2), 197–214 (2016)
10. Norman, D.A.: User-centered system design: new perspectives on human-computer interaction (1986)
11. OECD: Inclusive Growth, Digitalisation 21st Century Skills: Learning for the Digital Age A look back at the Forum 2017 session. The Organisation for Economic Co-operation and Development (2018). https://www.oecd-forum.org/users/50593-oecd/posts/20442-21st-century-skills-learning-for-the-digital-age
12. Piaget, J.: The Construction of Reality in the Child. Basic Books, New York (1954)
13. Robertson, J.W.: Usability and children's software: a user-centred design methodology. J. Comput. Child-Hood Educ. **5**(3–4), 257–271 (1994)
14. Digital Agenda for Europe. https://www.europarl.europa.eu/factsheets/en/sheet/64/digital-agenda-for-europe. Accessed 12 Feb 2020
15. European Commission:The Digital Economy and Society Index (DESI). https://ec.europa.eu/digital-single-market/en/desi. Accessed 12 Feb 2020

Teachers' Adoption of Embodied Learning Digital Games with an Inclusive Education Approach: Lessons Learnt from the INTELed Project in Spain

Alejandra Martínez-Monés[✉], Sara Villagrá-Sobrino,
Eva María Fernández Faundez, and María Jiménez Ruiz

GSIC-EMIC Research Group, Universidad de Valladolid, Valladolid, Spain
amartine@infor.uva.es

Abstract. Embodied learning digital games have been used with success in the past to support students with special education needs, but their application by teachers in mainstream classes with an inclusive approach is still a challenge. This paper presents the results of a set of pilots in which a suite of embodied digital games was applied into pre-school and primary school classrooms. The findings of the studies provide insights into the conditions that facilitated and/or impeded the adoption of the technology by the participant teachers. These results are then elaborated to define a first set of strategies that could be used by third-party teachers to fulfill the same objectives, and to identify concrete design challenges for the application of embodied digital games in classrooms.

Keywords: Embodied digital games · Classroom management · Primary education · Inclusive education

1 Introduction

Embodied learning is a contemporary theory of learning which emphasizes the use of the body in the educational practice [2]. Inspired by this theory, there has been intensive research on the use of embodied digital technologies, with special focus on special education [1]. Existing research on embodied digital technologies

This work is part of the INTELed Project [INnovative Training via Embodied Learning and multi-sensory techniques for inclusive Education] (Project 2017-1-CY01-KA201-026733), which is co-funded by the Erasmus+ Programme of the European Union. This research has been partially funded by the European Regional Development Fund and the National Research Agency of the Spanish Ministry of Science, Innovation and Universities, under project grant TIN2017-85179-C3-2-R (SmartLET) and by the European Regional Development Fund and the Regional Council of Education of Castilla y Leon under grant VA257P18 (CASSUALearn)).

P. Zaphiris and A. Ioannou (Eds.): HCII 2020, LNCS 12206, pp. 241–253, 2020.
https://doi.org/10.1007/978-3-030-50506-6_18

has taken place in laboratory settings or one-to-one sessions in Special Education Units [4]. It is still a challenge how to integrate these embodied games and their associated pedagogical approaches into mainstream classrooms, specially in inclusive educational contexts with students with and without disabilities [6]. To face this challenge, the EU-funded INTELed project[1] aimed at training teachers in the use of embodied digital games, with a focus on promoting the inclusion of children with special education needs (SEN). The research question driving this work is: *How can teachers adopt embodied learning games into their classrooms, considering principles of inclusiveness?*

This paper reports the results of a study carried out on the INTELed pilots, where teachers, supported by the research team, designed and implemented activities supported by embodied digital games in their classes. The study followed a qualitative case study research design. The results of the study show how the teachers manage to overcome the obstacles they found to apply the INTELed methodology, and in which ways they integrated this new methodology into their classrooms: how they designed the lesson plans and how they enacted the activities. The results describe strategies that could be used by other teachers applying embodied digital games, and design challenges that have to be met to improve the introduction of these technologies into classrooms with an inclusive approach.

The structure of the paper is as follows: The following section reviews the main challenges of the application of embodied digital games to mainstream classrooms. Then, we present the context of the study, with information about the INTELed project and the conditions in which the pilot experiences were carried out. Then we present the results and their discussion. The paper finishes with conclusions and future work lines.

2 Embodied Digital Games in the Classroom: Challenges

Embodied learning constitutes a contemporary pedagogical theory of learning inspired in the principles of embodied cognition (EC), which emphasizes the benefits of the use of the body in the educational practice [2,10].

From all the technologies that enable embodied learning, motion-based body-gesture technologies appear as some of the best suited to implement the principles of embodiment, based on the taxonomy proposed by [5]. Moreover, these technologies may have an advantage for their use by students with special needs, because full body interaction is more convenient for students that are not able of performing fine-grained gestures, such as the ones required by tablets and mice. These technologies are represented by commercial products such as Wii, Leap Motion and Kinect.

In a comparative study between these technologies [9], Kinect cameras were chosen as the most appropriate ones for their use in special education, due to their accuracy in identifying the body movements, the existence of an open

---

[1] http://www.inteledproject.org.

API, the voice-recognition and RGB camera, and the fact they do not need calibration. Moreover, Kinect cameras are relatively affordable, and cheaper than other specific technologies that are used in special education. These reasons may explain why most of the applications based on the idea of embodied learning are Kinect games [8].

The application of embodied digital games to children with SEN has provided initial evidence of success, although many issues remain unexplored about the effectiveness of this approach to enhance learning [4]. Additional challenges arise when addressing the application of these technologies, which are normally designed for one-to-one and personalized interaction, to formal education in schools. It is necessary to examine which are the best practices in the design and set up of learning environments that take full advantage of embodied learning [3]. Specific challenges are how teachers adopt these technologies, which are not of common use in the classroom; how do teachers integrate the tools in their curriculum; and how they setup and manage the classrooms to take full advantage of the embodied games. The work carried out in the INTELed project provided the opportunity to explore these issues in the four countries where the project was implemented. Next section describes the context of the study reported in this paper, based on the pilots that were set up in Spain.

3   Context of the Study

3.1   INTELed Project

The INTELed project is an EU-funded project that run between the years 2017 and 2019. Its main goal was to support in-service teachers in acquiring knowledge and skills about the use of embodied digital learning games for addressing the needs of SEN children in inclusive educational settings.

The project defined a teacher professional development (TPD) program, consisting of 4 phases. In the first phase ("teachers as learners"), the participant teachers received an initial training on the principles of embodied learning, including tools that support it in the classroom. In a second phase ("teachers as designers"), teachers acted as co-designers with the researchers, creating their lesson plans seeking to transfer the embodied learning pedagogy from theory into praxis. Then, the lesson plans were put in practice ("teachers as innovators") and finally, the pilots were evaluated with the help of the research team ("teachers as reflective practitioners").

Throughout these four phases, one researcher worked closely with the participant teachers, acting as a companion, and helping them in all the issues that appeared in the design and implementation of the pilots. She co-designed the lesson plans with the teachers, and gave them ideas about how to overcome the difficulties they found. This process was documented in a diary, which, as will be described later on, constitutes one of the most valuable data sources of the study.

3.2 The Local Setting: The Teachers' Workgroup and the Participating Schools

In Spain, the implementation of INTELed school pilots took place in three schools with pre-school and primary school education: CEIP Gómez Bosque, CEIP Antonio García Quintana, CEIP Francisco Pino. In the three of them, SEN students (i.e., pupils with moderate motor disabilities and/or learning difficulties) attend mainstream classes, and have a dedicated team of specialists that work in special units with them at certain times during the week.

In order to carry out the project, we established a collaboration with the Specific Team for Children with Motor Disabilities (EOEP for its acronym in Spanish). This team is composed of several specialists (physiotherapists, psychologists, language and hearing, etc.) that work in an interdisciplinary way with the children with SEN. In collaboration with the EOEP and the CFIE (the Centre in charge of in-service teacher training in our region) we set up in May, 2018 a "working group". This working group provided official recognition to the activities that the participant teachers and specialists carried out in INTELed.

The local coordinator of the working group was a psychologist that works in the EOEP, who could easily reach all teachers and specialists in the aforementioned schools. He launched two internal "calls for participation", one in May, 2018, that served to initiate the proposal of the working group, and another one in September 2018, when the working group started to run, and the research team was preparing the first phase of the INTELed TPD. As a result of these two calls, an initial group of 25 teachers and SEN specialists joined the working group. From these 25 participants, 7 where teachers (5 pre-school and 2 primary school). They are the focus of this paper, as they are the ones that faced the challenge of integrating the embodied digital games in their classes with an inclusive approach.

This group of teachers worked semi-autonomously, organized into three subgroups (one for each school). For example, in one of the schools, the teachers set up regular meetings after the initial training to keep on learning about the tools and help each other in the implementation of the pilots. They were supported by one of the members of the research team, who was in permanent contact with them. She had a main role in helping the teachers achieve their goals and reach the implementation of the pilots.

4 Pilots' Setup

As defined by the INTELed TPD, once the participating teachers had been introduced to the INTELed's pedagogical framework of embodied learning [7] ("teachers as learners"), they were asked to lead a set of school pilots in their classrooms ("teachers as innovators"). As an intermediate step, they had to design the lesson plans that were to be enacted in the classes ("teachers as designers").

4.1   Design of the Lesson Plans

From February to May 2019, the participant teachers and the research team worked together in the co-design of the lesson plans. The teachers were asked to integrate the embodied digital games they chose into their classes, in order to engage all the students (with and without disabilities) in the learning activities. These activities had to be related to learning goals defined in the curriculum. Each lesson plan included a description of the context on which it is applied (level, learning goals and competences); the connection with the curriculum (contents, assessment criteria); a description of the sessions and the activities to carry out in them; the resources needed; and, finally tips for its implementation[2].

We carried out 4 pilots, involving 7 classrooms, 6 in-service and 3 pre-service teachers. Two of the pilots took place in pre-school education. One of them involved three classes in the same school (3, 4, and 5-year-old children), where the in-service teachers and a member of the research team proposed a similar design for all the classes; the second one involved a teacher of 5-year-old children in a different school, who was able to design the intervention by herself. The other two pilots were carried out in primary education. One of them took place in 1st and 4th grade of Physical Education at a third school. A fourth pilot was led by a special education teacher who collaborated with a Primary School teacher of 3rd grade to plan the educational design and the ways the SEN student could participate in the activity following an inclusive approach.

4.2   Selection of the Embodied Learning Tools

One decision that had to be taken was to decide which application(s) would be used in the pilots. After analysing the repository of embodied learning tools that had been created by the INTELEd project[3], the teachers chose to use Kinems learning games[4]. Kinems offers a suite of movement-based educational kinect games for children with special education needs, such as dyspraxia, autism, ADHD and motor difficulties. It aims to improve children's eye-hand coordination, visual perception, motor planning and execution skills, and can be used by children with and without disabilities, as the games help achieve different levels of school performance. In the underlying conceptual model of the tool, each school working with Kinems has a number of teachers. Each teacher is responsible of a number of students, for whom s/he must configure personalized sessions a priori. To that aim, the teacher can browse the whole set of games and possible configurations, or use a new feature that recommends a subset of games, based on the learning goals and the educational level. A session may contain one or several games with different configurations. During the enactment,

---

[2] Examples of two lesson plans can be found in https://platform.inteled.org/wp-content/uploads/2019/07/Lesson-plan-1-Tika.pdf and https://platform.inteled.org/wp-content/uploads/2019/07/Lesson-plan-2-Do-like.pdf (In Spanish).

[3] https://www.inteled.org/repository/.

[4] http://www.kinems.com.

the teacher selects the child, and the application runs the programmed session (which the teacher can modify on the fly in response to the evolution of the session). The system monitors the performance of the child and provides reports to the teachers based on learning analytics.

Kinems provides a large offer of games. It was necessary to devote time to select the specific games that were to be used in the pilots. The teachers and the research team collaborated in order to find the most suitable ones for each class, taking also into account the characteristics of the SEN children who assisted to those classes. The final selection was composed of the following games:

Tikka Bubble: In this game, the child is asked to recognize matching pairs of objects, grab the corresponding bubbles at each side of one totem and bang them simultaneously at the center. This game helps a child to improve the way of coordinating both sides of the upper body, which is an indication that both sides of the brain are communicating and sharing information with each other. There are different categories of matching pairs which can be chosen. In our pilots, the teachers of pre-school education found it appropriate for the ages of their students and matching with the content about animals and plants they were developing at that moment. They used the Tikka Bubble game with different categories for each class. Tikka Bubble was also used with a more complex configuration in the pilot that took place in 3rd grade, where the game was set up in this case so that students could identify the animal with an associated product (eg, Bee with Bee-wax).

Lexis: Lexis has the objective of becoming familiar with the spelling of words of different length and conceptual categories. This game is translated into Spanish, making it suitable for its application in our classrooms. The educator can choose the length of words or the conceptual category that will be shown to a child, the number of missing letters, as well as the time limit that might exist. Also, the educator can allow the child to see the picture of the given word thus helping the child to correlate the way an object is written. This game was used by the teachers in pre-school education with different configurations depending on the course (3–5 years old).

Do Like: Do like proposes interactive gross motor activities to help children improve their postural control and balance. With "Do Like" the child is asked to replicate a body movement or a sustained position by listening or reading a given instruction. The educator can choose from a variety of specified postures or movements. This game was used by the Physical Education teachers with 1st and 4th graders. In these cases, teachers employed Do Like game to help children improve their gross motor skills, body awareness, laterality, and balance. The game was configured with a different degree of difficulty for the two classes, with a specific profile for the SEN children in those classes.

5   Methodology

In order to address our research objective, we followed a qualitative case study guided by the following issue: *How did teachers integrate the use of Kinems games based on embodied technologies into their classroom considering principles of inclusiveness?* This issue involved studying which was the support needed by the teachers for the design of the activities; and which were the solutions proposed to overcome the difficulties they encountered.

The following data sources were used: the diary taken by the researcher during the co-design process and the implementation of the pilots; classroom observations during the enactment of the pilots and the interviews with the participant teachers that took place after the pilots.

These data were analysed with content analysis using a mixed approach, that combined predefined (etic) and data-driven (emic) categories that emerged during the coding process. The main two topics that structured the analysis correspond to the two themes derived from the research issue that have been mentioned above: *T1. Support needed by the teachers*; and *T2: Solutions proposed.*

5.1   Results

This section describes the main findings that emerged from the coding process. These findings are supported by excerpts of evidence from the data collected. To facilitate a better readability, these excerpts are codified in the text and their content is presented in Tables 1 and 2.

Support Needed by the Teachers. The first topic explored up to which point teachers needed support, and what was the nature of their needs, both at design and enactment time.

Support at Design-Time. Right after the initial training, the working teams formed by teachers organized themselves to analyze the games, and generated templates in which they made explicit which were the most relevant aspects of the games for them: goals, students' characteristics, difficulties ($[Diary]_A$). This approach was deemed necessary by the teachers, as they reported that the knowledge acquired during the training had not been sufficient be aware of the possibilities offered by the tool ($[IntPhys]_A$, $[IntPrimSchool]_B$).

The templates were geared to study which games were appropriate for which SEN children in each school, but they did not help the teachers find ways to integrate the games into their lessons ($[Diary]_B$). This led to a higher involvement of the assistant researcher, who had to provide more advice and support to the teachers than expected ($[Diary]_C$). The assistant researcher maintained one to two co-design sessions with most of the participant teachers before the implementation. In these sessions, the research assistant facilitated the interchange of ideas and the reflection by the teachers, to i) make explicit the educational goals they pursued and the identification of the most appropriate games to reach them, and ii) provide the teachers information about the possibilities of the tool, depending on the characteristics of the students with and without specific education needs ($[Diary]_D$).

Support at Enactment. During the development of the pilots, the teachers perceived that the support provided by the external researcher, both at the technical and the methodological level was crucial to setup the activities in their classrooms ($[IntPhys]_{CD}$). In two cases, they also benefited from the presence of pre-service teachers during their internship, as a help to the design and implementation of the activities ($[IntPrimSchool]_E$).

Solutions and Strategies to Apply the Tool in Classrooms. The teachers found different ways to address the problems that were posed at the outset of the project, that are discussed below:

Generic Accounts for the Classroom and Specific for SEN Students. Kinems offers personalized support for each child, which has proven to be appropriate for special education units. However, this feature was considered problematic for its application in classrooms with about twenty students each. The teachers stated that the time devoted to change the user for each child could affect the rhythm of the class and led to a loss of children's engagement. As a solution it was decided that the teachers selected the features of the corresponding game for each class, using a unique generic user, and created only a specific user with adapted settings for the special education students ($[Diary]_E$). This resulted in more dynamic sessions in which the students followed each other and could be almost autonomous using the tool.

This turnaround solved the problem of having to configure too many children profiles in advance and to change the user for each child, but has important drawbacks. It impeded the use of valuable features provided by the tool, especially the monitoring support, which could have provided useful information about the progress and performance of the students. However, these aspects of personalisation and monitoring were not at the focus of the teacher and they did not pay attention to them, even for the special education children, who did have a profile.

Work in Stations. A second challenge was the fact that Kinems, as many other tools, is thought for individual interaction between the player and the game. When applied to a classroom with more than 20 children, this may mean that one child has to wait almost an hour to enjoy a few minutes with the tool. In response to this problem, the students were organized in small groups that worked in parallel activities. Thus, each class was structured in learning stations (or "corners") where the children had to rotate to carry out each one of these parallel activities. Students worked in small groups and when they had finished one activity, they passed to the next one ($[IntPrimSchool]_F$).

Provide Clear Directions. At the beginning of the session, each teacher explained the contents and the activities that would be done. In all the cases, the teachers provided very clear instructions to the students about how they had to interact with the tool, and the precision of the movements they had to make in order to avoid potential mistakes ($[Obs]_A$).

Specific Focus on Inclusion. An additional challenge, relevant for the project and for the classes where the pilots were implemented, was to promote collaboration, peer-help and the participation of all the students, conditions that were fundamental to guarantee inclusion in the class ($[IntPrimSchool]_G$). In the aforementioned stations, the students were asked to work in groups (5–6 children) to learn from their peers, carrying out the activities at the same time as their mates who were working in front of the game. For example, in the Physical Education pilot, where the game used was DoLike, the children in each group were asked to do the same movements as the one in front of the Kinect camera) ($[Obs]_B$; $[IntPrimSchool]_G$). This strategy enabled the children that had problems interpreting the instructions of the game to learn from their peers ($[IntPrimSchool]_{HI}$) or by imitation when solving doubts ($[Obs]_C$). In the case of the SEN students, the teachers decided to configure the program adapting the needs of each student. They were satisfied with this solution, and stated this allowed the SEN children feel more integrated into the classroom, as they had been able to play the same game as the others (which is not always possible).

5.2   Discussion

The results presented above help illuminate the issue addressed in the study, i.e., how did teachers integrate Kinems games into their classrooms with an inclusive approach.

The fact the tool offered many games and configuration possibilities enabled its use at different educational levels and for different learning goals. The flexibility of the tool enabled the SEN children to use the same games than the rest of the class, which was pointed out by the teachers as a key factor to favour inclusion.

However, this complexity also posed some problems. Teachers needed extra support to be able to identify the right games for their contexts. Even though they were encouraged to use the Kinems feature that helped to select the game and the configurations based on the learning goals, teachers did not use it. Their approach to get acquainted with the tool was to try to get familiar with all the games, and then, propose ways of applying them to their practice. This probed to be a very demanding task, that needed the intervention of the research assistant to help them select the games and the most suitable configurations. These results point out to the need of a longer and more focused initial training period, due to the complexity of the tool and the number of possibilities it provides to its users. Moreover, further work is needed to gain insight into the reasons why the goal-based selection approach was not followed by the teachers. This could be due to a lack of alignment between the goals offered by the games and the ones used in the Spanish context, or to deeper differences in the way teachers face the design of their classroom activities.

In spite of the difficulties, and thanks to the extra support given by the researcher, the teachers were eventually able to think of appropriate designs

Table 1. Excerpts of data evidence from the Interviews. The code refers to the speciality of the interviewee (Physiotherapist [IntPhys] or Primary School Teacher [IntPrimSchool])

Code	Excerpt
$[IntPhys]_A$	[...] I think we devoted quite a long time to the theoretical talks and too little time to the practical part [...] but for the people that did not know anything about the tools, perhaps the practical part was too short to be able to put it in practice"
$[IntPrimSchool]_B$	In the training course I think we could have seen more games, because it is the only way in which I can have an idea. I need to know more games, which is what I need to work out
$[IntPhys]_C$	[...] At the beginning we were very negative and reluctant, because we say it very difficult to bring the theoretical proposal to the ground. And the poor lady [the researcher] found at the beginning "no, this is not possible, this is not possible ...", and eventually, thanks to her support and all the logistics and so on, we have been able to implement the project
$[IntPhys]_D$	Well... the difficulties that schools have: a bad wi-fi network, a bad Internet, bad computer logistics, etc. But, well, we have had the luck that the university has solved it
$[IntPrimSchool]_E$	We were lucky to count on two in-service teachers, and thanks to their help we could bring INTELed to the gym (which seemed not feasible at the beginning)"
$[IntPrimSchool]_F$	I think that if you do not work by stations or small groups, I cannot think of any other way of carrying out one of these activities in a mainstream classroom
$[IntPrimSchool]_G$	I think that what has prevailed has been the focus on inclusion. At least, as we have designed it. I wanted to use the Kinect in Physical Education and to work cooperative learning. Then, it was like ... how do I do to work on cooperative learning if in this moment only one child was working in the game. Then, what was difficult was to find a way so that they helped each other to reach the final goal, which was the inclusion of all the children
$[IntPrimSchool]_H$	To make it more collaborative, we have asked the classmates who were in the Kinems station to make the same movements as the one who was playing with the game. Moreover, we said that if they saw somebody with difficulties, they could give them hints to help them [...]. But that they should not be alone looking at the screen
$[IntPrimSchool]_I$	Then, maybe they give indications of how to improve, or the ones that are doing the movement, so that their mate sees them and has them a reference. I think they are the ones that help each other. It is positive. Maybe they do not have the competitiveness because they are out of the game, its not their turn

that enabled all the children, with and without disabilities, use the tool and engage in the activities with success. Some of the ideas point out to patterns of use that could be generalized to other contexts, like the use of rotating stations that help to divide the whole class in groups of 4–6 children, where the children carry out different activities, but not all of them at the same time. This pattern was complemented with additional instructions, to enable help between peers, and learning by imitation, which probed to be helpful for the success of the activities, and for the inclusion of the SEN students.

Table 2. Excerpts of data evidence from the Observations and the Diary.

Code	Excerpt
$[Diary]_A$	Once they have tried it [the game] they will produce a template where they will state: Minimum skills that the student has to have to play the game; Goals of the game; Potential (SEN) students for which it applies; Difficulties; Possibilities
$[Diary]_B$	We can observe in the teachers that the games are not responding to the contents they teach
$[Diary]_C$	We are providing more help, they are not as autonomous as we would have desired
$[Diary]_D$	(e-mail from the researcher to a teacher). In the template you wanted to work with memory and logic reasoning with M. For you to have more resources to work with, I propose you the following games: (Memory): "UnboxIT", a game that [...]
$[Diary]_E$	How do we apply games to a full class? Shall we create a profile for each student? Do we have to exit and enter again each time a child plays? The rest of the partners have solved this problem by using the same account for all the class [...] although for the SEN students specific profiles are created
$[Obs]_A$	The teacher explains how they have to put their hands, and how to hold the object. The first time it is difficult for them, but motor control gets better with time."
$[Obs]_B$	XXX, the in-service teacher, is configuring the application and will receive each group and explain to them what they have to do. He asks the children that, while they are waiting for their turn, they may try to follow the instructions given by the game"
$[Obs]_C$	XXX is a child with intellectual and hearing disabilities. At the time of performing the coordination activities with "Do Like", a classmate helps him, telling him what to do. The second time he repeats the exercise, he does it well

6   Conclusions

The use of embodied digital games in classrooms is a promising educational approach, supported by the theories of embodied cognition. However, the existing technologies that have proven to be beneficial in one-to-one settings, need adaptation for their use in mainstream classrooms. Classrooms have conditions that differ from the special units were individualized support is the norm, and teachers have different ways of working than the specialists that treat children in those special units.

The pilots carried out in the INTELed project have given us the opportunity to explore the ways in which embodied digital games can be integrated in the classroom, with a focus on educational inclusion, and to identify challenges to reach that aim.

One outcome of the study is the identification of the use of "stations" as a good practice, that can be reused by other teachers in the future as a pattern. A second conclusion is that inclusive classrooms can benefit from configurable tools, that allow teachers adapt their content to the capabilities of the students. This probed to be true in our study, even though teachers were not able to use all the customization capabilities offered by the application.

The experience gained with these pilots points out to design challenges that remain unsolved. Further work needs to be done to deal with the trade-off between the full personalised support offered by the applications (with individual profiles defined by the teacher in advance) and the needs of providing a system as simple and efficient as possible so that teachers and students can integrate it into their classroom dynamics without additional burdens. Other design challenges, such as providing more facilities to adapt the content of the games to the curriculum, providing a kind of authoring tool for teachers, were also mentioned. This study should be put in contrast with the results obtained by the pilots in the rest of the countries that implemented INTELed, to find similarities and differences between the different educational contexts, and derive from them more generalisable results.

Acknowledgements. The authors want to thank Prof. Yannis Dimitriadis for his valuable feedback, and specially, to the teachers that worked in the INTELed project, and the students who eagerly participated in the activities carried out in the pilots reported in this paper.

References

1. Altanis, G., Boloudakis, M., Retalis, S., Nikou, N.: Children with motor impairments play a Kinect learning game: first findings from a pilot case in an authentic classroom environment. Interact. Des. Archit. J. - IxD&A **19**, 91–104 (2013)
2. Anderson, M.L.: Embodied cognition: a field guide. Artif. Intell. **149**(1), 91–130 (2003). https://doi.org/10.1016/S0004-3702(03)00054-7
3. Evans, M.A., Rick, J.: Supporting learning with interactive surfaces and spaces. In: Spector, J., Merrill, M., Elen, J., Bishop, M.J. (eds.) Handbook of Research on Educational Communications and Technology, pp. 689–701. Springer, New York (2014). https://doi.org/10.1007/978-1-4614-3185-5_55
4. Fu, Y., Wu, J., Wu, S., Chai, H., Xu, Y.: Game system for rehabilitation based on Kinect is effective for mental retardation. In: MATEC Web of Conferences, vol. 22, p. 01036. EDP Sciences (2015). https://doi.org/10.1051/matecconf/20152201036
5. Johnson-Glenberg, M.C., Megowan-Romanowicz, C., Birchfield, D.A., Savio-Ramos, C.: Effects of embodied learning and digital platform on the retention of physics content: centripetal force. Front. Psychol. **7**, 1819 (2016). https://doi.org/10.3389/fpsyg.2016.01819
6. Kourakli, M., Altanis, I., Retalis, S., Boloudakis, M., Zbainos, D., Antonopoulou, K.: Towards the improvement of the cognitive, motoric and academic skills of students with special educational needs using Kinect learning games. Int. J. Child-Comput. Interact. **11**, 28–39 (2017). https://doi.org/10.1016/j.ijcci.2016.10.009
7. Martínez-Monés, A., Villagrá-Sobrino, S., Georgiou, Y., Ioannou, A., Ruiz, M.J.: The INTELed pedagogical framework: applying embodied digital apps to support special education children in inclusive educational contexts. In: Proceedings of the XX International Conference on Human Computer Interaction, pp. 1–4 (2019)
8. Martínez Monés, A., Sibrini, T., Villagrá Sobrino, S., Jiménez, M., Georgiou, Y., Ioannou, A.: O1–T3. A collection of existing ICT multi-sensory educational resources and tools for learning and assessment for the support of SEN students. Technical report, INTELed Erasmus+ Project. European Commission (2018)

9. Ojeda-Castelo, J.J., Piedra-Fernandez, J.A., Iribarne, L., Bernal-Bravo, C.: KiNEEt: application for learning and rehabilitation in special educational needs. Multimed. Tools Appl. **77**(18), 24013–24039 (2018). https://doi.org/10.1007/s11042-018-5678-1
10. Wilson, M.: Six views of embodied cognition. Psychon. Bull. Rev. **9**(4), 625–636 (2002). https://doi.org/10.3758/BF03196322

Do Individual Differences Modulate the Effect of Agency on Learning Outcomes with a Serious Game?

Julien Mercier[✉], Kathleen Whissell-Turner, Ariane Paradis, Ivan Luciano Avaca, Martin Riopel, and Mélanie Bédard

NeuroLab, University of Quebec at Montreal, 405 Sainte-Catherine East, Montreal, QC H2L 2C4, Canada
mercier.julien@uqam.ca

Abstract. In order to support and promote new ways of learning, educational technology should be based on sophisticated theories and models of learning. Many issues are raised in the current understanding of learning by the constant evolution of educational technology and the burgeoning of educational contexts using these technologies. By examining the relation between agency and learning gains using a Serious Game for learning Physics, the present study focuses on a main issue of technology use: whether actively playing the game or watching someone play is beneficial for learning. Thirty-seven dyads participated in the study. Randomly assigned, one participant played a Serious Educational Game for learning Physics, *Mecanika* (Boucher-Genesse et al. 2011), for 120 min, while the other participant watched the player's gameplay in real-time on a separate screen. As pretest and posttest, the *Force Concept Inventory* (FCI; Hestenes et al. 1992) was administered to measure learning gains in Physics. Analyses of answers on the FCI demonstrate that a Serious Game, such as *Mecanika*, is beneficial to learning, regardless if learning is conceived as relatively coarse shifts from wrong to good answers (scientific conceptions) or as more nuanced shifts from fillers/misconceptions to scientific conceptions. Also, individual differences in learning gains across dyads were found, which can be explained by the gameplay of a dyad created by the active player. Furthermore, the effect of agency is systematic and not modulated by individual differences: watchers learn more than players. These results need to be further explained by modeling the learning process.

Keywords: Agency · Learning gains · Serious educational game

1 Introduction

According to Stephanidis, Salvendy and their group of experts (2019), how technology can be used to its full potential to foster learning is still vastly an open question after decades of research and technological evolution. Technology use for learning encompasses old as well as new issues including privacy and ethics, learning theories and models, and pedagogical aspects. These issues translate into current challenges for applied research.

© Springer Nature Switzerland AG 2020
P. Zaphiris and A. Ioannou (Eds.): HCII 2020, LNCS 12206, pp. 254–266, 2020.
https://doi.org/10.1007/978-3-030-50506-6_19

With respect to learning theories and models, educational technology should strive to support and promote new ways of learning, creative learning and lifelong learning for all learners, avoiding to focus on tech-savvy generations. The field should aim to design technologies focusing on the needs of learners and educators that are gracefully embedded in the educational process and do not disrupt learners and teachers, and to design serious games featuring the appropriate balance between seriousness and fun, and be driven by tangible educational needs and not by new technological capabilities. The field should address unprecedented challenges related to privacy and ethics, such as the extensive monitoring of students (potentially under-age) by data-gathering software, sensors and algorithms, such as the parent issues of data ownership, and such as management as well as human rights concerns (e.g. potential for excessive control restricting the freedom of the individual). In terms of pedagogical aspects, key aspects still in need of improvement include the involvement of educators in the design of learning technologies, a serious and multi-faceted assessment of long-term impact of learning technologies, support for personalized creativity and for the amplification of human creative skills, for the entire spectrum of creative activities including in smart environments, blending digital and physical artifacts.

Despite more or less direct ramifications regarding the previous issues, the present work focuses on learning theories and models. In particular, the study presented examines the accepted notion that active learning fosters learning gains.

In learning about real-world phenomena from observations without having acquired scientific conceptions, one develops misconceptions which wrongly predict phenomena that do not correspond to current scientific knowledge. Such misconceptions are constructed through interactions with the environment, which do not provide all the information necessary to construct scientifically-valid explanations. In this context, Clark's (2013) prediction-action model posits that learning occurs when these misconceptions are surmounted by input that make prediction errors manifest. In this view, teaching and fostering learning involve providing input that will ultimately lead a learner to formulate predictions adequately representing the state of the world.

An interactive learning environment providing simulations of Physics phenomena should help learners test their worldview against scientific conceptions embedded in the simulations. In this context, agency should also be beneficial to learning because the possibility to control the simulations should optimize the testing of predictions. To the contrary, it was shown elsewhere that agency was detrimental to learning (Mercier, Avaca, Whissell-Turner, Paradis and Mikropoulos, this volume, submitted). The objective of this study is to refine the previous results by examining if a computer-based interactive learning environment is beneficial to learning, and to verify if the effect of agency on learning is modulated by individual differences.

2 Theoretical Framework

2.1 A Prediction-Action View of Learning and Agency

In the context of a prediction-action framework, Lupyan and Clark (2015) provide a pivotal question for the design of serious games for learning by suggesting what one knows ought to change what one sees. Globally, a prediction-action framework explains learning as the production of representations at multiple levels of abstraction, so that a given level predicts the activity in the level below it. Also, reducing prediction error in the present enable better predictions in the future.

That is, higher-level predictions currently used are informed by priors (prior beliefs, usually taking the form of nonconscious predictions or expectations) concerning the environment. Prior beliefs or lower-level neural expectations are statistically optimal in the sense that they represent the overall best method for inferring the state of the environment from the ambient conceptual and sensory evidence. A prediction-action framework seems to articulate perception and attention as optimal (Bayesian) ways of combining sensory evidence with prior knowledge in the process of learning. Predictive-processing models are based on an asymmetry between the forward and backward flow of information: The forward flow computes residual errors between predictions and the information from the environment, while the backward flow delivers predictions to the appropriate level. The forward flow also escalates high-information contents upward by pushing unexplained elements of the lower-level sensory signal upward so that the appropriate level selects new top-down hypotheses that are better able to accommodate the present sensory signal. One can sometimes become aware of them when they are violated (Lupyan and Clark 2015). This long-term error-reduction mechanism can be thought of as responsible for academic learning.

In sum, Lupyan and Clark (2015) propose that the learning of a symbolic language (verbal or mathematical) may modulate the recruitment of prior knowledge and the artificial manipulation, at any level of processing, of the relative influence of different top-down expectations and bottom-up sensory signals. These manipulations, which can be communicated to others, could selectively enhance or mute the influence of any aspect, however subtle or complex, of our own or another agent's world model. Exposure to and the acquisition or learning of a symbolic language (whether shared or self-produced) leverages the exploration and exploitation of our own knowledge as well as the knowledge of others. In the context of designer learning environments, the possibility to manipulate their features by directly interacting with them should optimize the prediction-action by improving the fit between the predictions formulated and the predictions tested by the learner. In contrast, without this possibility of agency, the fit between the predictions tested and the current predictions of a learner is necessarily lessened.

2.2   Learning Analytics and the Design of Serious Games for Learning

Learning Analytics and their Potential Uses. Serious Games have already showed their advantages in different educational environments (Stephanidis, Salvendy et al. 2019). Game Learning Analytics can further improve serious games, by facilitating their development and improving their impact and adoption (Alonzo-Fernandez et al. 2019).

Game Learning Analytics (hereafter GLA) is an evidence-based methodology based on in-game user interaction data, and can provide insight about the game-based educational experience and outcomes, like validating the adequation of the game design to the educational goals. Besides providing a visual in-game follow-up, GLA can verify if the game in question is accessible to the target population as expected. Another great advantage of GTA that could redefine educational assessment is its capability to predict in-game learning gains.

Alonzo-Fernandez and her colleagues (2019) used GTA for serious games in order to evaluate game design and deployment processes. Alonzo-Fernandez et al. (2019) asserts that the design of games should be based on clear goals, and specify how the attainment of these goals are to be measured with interaction data adequately collected. Additionally, the use of learning analytics is greatly facilitated if, from the very beginning, games are designed so that data can be extracted from them and provide the information required to validate the games and assess the process and outcomes of learning with students using them. Early uses of GTA in designing Serious Games are also possible. Effectively GTA allows to remotely collect and analyze data and feedbacks during a beta testing on target users. This way, potential problems could be quickly solved and the game can be largely deployed. In addition, improvements for subsequent versions of an already deployed game could be leveraged by players' interaction data.

Optimal Serious Games' criteria emerged from Alonzo-Fernandez and her colleagues (2019) observations regarding assessment. A main recommendation is to keep in mind that Serious Games are not only created to play and learn, but ultimately to collect data on evidence-based learning assessment. To do so, conception of Serious Games need to take into account the types of data wished to be collected and the standard format of GLA data.

The work of Alonzo-Fernandez et al. (2019) showcases the importance of game learning analytics in different contexts, even when being used as the sole means to obtain players feedback. While his experiments of GLA were conducted in various reals contexts pursuing diverse goals, Alonzo-Fernandez et al. (2019) suggest the exploitation of GLA in the context of Serious Educational Games.

Westera (2018) presents a computational model for simulating how people learn from serious games based on simulation studies across a wide range of game instances and player profiles for demonstrating model stability and empirical admissibility. While avoiding the combinatorial explosion of a game micro-states, the model offers a meso-level pathfinding approach, which is guided by extant research from the learning sciences. The model can be used to assess learning from (or with) the serious game and for investigating quantitative dependences between relevant game variables, gain deeper understanding of how people learn from games, and develop approaches to improving serious game design. With this in mind, simulation models can also be used as an alternative to using test players as the only source of information, to improve game design. To reduce overall complexity and to avoid model overfitting and the combinatorial explosion of game states and player states, the model focuses on meso-level aggregates that constitute meaningful activities. It accounts for discrete-time evolution, failure, drop-out, revisit of activities, efforts made and time spent on tasks.

According to Westera (2018), advances in learner data analytics, stealth assessment, machine learning and physiological sensors for capturing such data represent new additional ways to enrich the constituents of the model. Ultimately, the computational modelling approach would help to design serious games that are more effective for learning. So far, however, conditions for empirical validation with real players are only partially met, since some of the learner model's variables are still hard to record without the appropriate interdisciplinary work in cognitive science merging psychology, neuroscience and education, such as the real-time progression of motivation and flow.

Real-world, authentic experiments should be based on discrete events at longer time scales and aggregates of finer-grained events constituting an approximation of the model rather than the full discrete-time evolution version (Westera 2018). At a given, typically longer, temporal grainsize, self-report instruments and performance measures can be used to capture additional data.

Modeling for Assessing Learning Gains. The main interlinked constituents of the model are the knowledge model, the player model and the game model. The productive outcomes of a serious game need to be expressed as knowledge gains Westera (2018). As such, they are the easiest aspect to model, requiring only the knowledge model. The knowledge model is generally expressed as a knowledge tree of operationalized learning goals or learning outcomes (e.g. skills, facts, competences) while child nodes in the tree have a precedence relationship with their parent nodes. While the game is represented as a network of meso-level activity nodes, each activity in the game is allowed to address one or more nodes from the knowledge tree. Each activity in the game is characterized by prior knowledge requirements and by an inherent complexity.

To explain learning gains, the player model accounts for the player's mental states, preferences and behaviors. Only few primary player factors will be taken into account: overall intelligence, knowledge state, and motivation. While both intelligence and prior knowledge refer to the player's learning capability, motivation is linked to personal attitudes, emotions and ambitions. Westera (2018) purports that these are exactly the key dimensions that reflect the potential of serious games: learning new knowledge from serious games, while benefitting from their motivational power. These elements can be further detailed to reflect the state of the art in the learning sciences.

Then, after updating the player's knowledge states, the whole cycle is repeated for the next time step, while the player progresses in the game. In each time step (Δt) the player's knowledge state must be updated to account for the knowledge gained during that period of time.

Following the classic approach in intelligent tutoring systems research, a node in the knowledge tree, as a parent, combines, integrates and extends all child nodes, the process of mastering a parent node inherently contributes to the further mastery of all subordinate nodes in the parent tree. Hence, the updating process should also be applied for updating the respective child node states and deeper subordinate levels. As a consequence, mastering a parent node in the game, be it partially, will directly contribute to knowledge gains in all conditional nodes in the knowledge tree.

Each activity is supposed to somehow contribute to the mastery of learning goals, which means that a mapping of knowledge nodes to game activities is needed. Such mapping is not always straightforward, depending on the type of serious game (educational simulations, Serious Games, Serious Educational Games). Educational simulations as interactive representations of real-world phenomena used to practice tasks to be eventually performed in the real world and may be the least easy to map. Serious

Games are designed to develop skills in performing tasks using realistic situations and may contain by design a mapping of the knowledge. Serious Educational Games may be easiest to map in that they are similar to Serious Games but incorporate specific a priori pedagogical approaches to not only develop skills but teach specific learning content as well (Lamb et al. 2018). In all cases, various methodologies are available for defining the mapping, for instance Evidence-Based Design and Bayesian nets for stealth assessment (Shute 2011).

Modeling for Improving Game Design. To bolster efficiency, serious game design should be paired with instructional design, to optimize the use of game mechanics from entertainment and instructional principles. Appropriate modeling is essential to grasp the complexity of learning from and with serious games, in order to construct the required research base so that game design and instructional design cease to be viewed as ill-structured, artistic domains.

Improving game design through modeling is much more complex than modeling for assessing learning gains, requiring all three main interlinked constituents of the model (the knowledge model, the player model and the game model). The model Westera (2018) provides a proof of principle of a computational modelling methodology for serious games involving the three constituents that provides stable, reproducible and plausible results. Leveraging this approach however will require more detailed game states and player states, and careful tradeoffs to contain the combinatorial explosion of possible states.

Within the player model, players are characterized by intelligence, prior knowledge and susceptibility to flow, while their motivation and learning progress is evaluated and continually updated during their progression in the game. One limitation identified by Westera (2018) is that the model does not include cognitive models of human learning, but instead just relies on the phenomenology of the process of play. Connecting with existing models of human cognition would allow for including a multitude of psychological constructs, be it at the expense of simplicity.

Finally, the game model requires a knowledge tree indicating the learning objectives, and a set of game activities, possibly annotated with complexity and attractiveness indices. One limitation identified by Westera (2018) is that the model bypasses the complexities of instructional content and didactics by postulating that engagement in a game activity entails a productive learning experience. Second, although "game activities" are a key concept in the model, the meso-level indication does not say much about their grainsize. In fact, the model is ignorant and indifferent about the grainsize.

2.3   Hypotheses and Research Questions

In light of the previous considerations, this study investigates three hypotheses and two research questions:

Hypothesis 1: A serious game is beneficial to learning when learning is conceived of as shifts to scientific conceptions.
Hypothesis 2: A serious game is beneficial to learning when learning is conceived of as shifts among misconceptions, fillers and scientific conceptions.
Hypothesis 3: There are individual differences in learning across dyads.

Is the effect of agency on learning modulated by individual differences when learning is conceived of as shifts to scientific conceptions?

Is the effect of agency on learning modulated by individual differences when learning is conceived of as shifts among misconceptions, fillers and scientific conceptions?

3 Method

3.1 Sample

For this study, 82 paid volunteers (60$) were recruited in undergraduate programs (primary education, special education, philosophy, and sociology) at University of Quebec at Montreal by the research coordinator who presented the research project in numerous classes. Only one participant is studying in another French-language university, University of Montreal, and was recruited by word of mouth. Since participants could volunteered individually or with a teammate, some participants were also recruited by snowball effect with respect of all including criteria. Participants volunteering in pairs formed a dyad for the experimentations, while individual volunteers were matched based on lab schedule and their respective availabilities. Students who attended a Physics class after high school, had severe skin allergies, had a pacemaker or had epilepsy were not included in the study. Moreover, the exclusion criteria included being under 18 years old or graduate students. Hence, 41 dyads of undergraduate students with novice background in Physics participated in the study.

The mean age of the remaining sample was 25.7 years old (ages ranged from 18 to 45 years old). There was 43 (58.10%) females and 31 males (41.89%). Most of the participants were right-handed (87.8%). Even though few players were left-handed, they reported using their right hand while using the computer mouse. A total of 22 players (29.73%) and 23 watchers (31.08%) declared a 10th grade knowledge level in Physics, and 13 players (17.57%) and 13 watchers (17.57%) in 11th grade. It was decided to kept the participant (player) who took a basic physic class at college in the sample, as well as the two participants (1 player and 1 watcher) who were previously educated in another school system because those two reported that they did not attend any Physics class after high school.

3.2 Task and Settings

Mecanika is a serious computer game developed by Boucher-Genesse et al. (2011). The game addresses 58 widespread misconceptions in Newtonian Physics (see Hestenes et al. 1992). Each of the 50 levels involves making an object move according to a given trajectory by applying different types of force to it. This involves choosing the right type(s) of force, the quantity of sources, and their appropriate positioning. The level is completed when the requested trajectory is entirely respected. In the view presented earlier, *Mecanika* is a tool to command a generative model of Newtonian mechanics and to test predictions about how physical objects behave.

In our paradigm, participants either played *Mecanika* or watched the player on a separate screen in real time. Their respective roles were randomly assigned. Participants progressed through the levels by achieving them or by being instructed to skip them after 20 min of play. This stop rule was apply in rare cases, in average, dyads skipped a level 4.3% of the total number of levels played. The task length was 2 h precisely (120 min); participants were stopped from playing without notice and research assistants entered the room, immediately talking to the participants and beginning their uninstallation. In average, each dyad played through 28.7 levels.

3.3 Measures

The *Force Concept Inventory* (FCI; Hestenes et al. 1992) is a widely used questionnaire designed to measure Newtonian's physic knowledge through six main concepts which are the three laws (first, second, and third), superposition principle, kinematics, and kinds of forces (see Fig. 1 for an example). Hestenes et al. (1992) has shown its equivalence to its predecessor, the *Mecanics Diagnostic*, and argued for its use as a diagnostic tool to identify misconceptions and for evaluating instruction, both in practical settings as well as research. The French adaptation of the FCI was administered immediately pre and post gameplay to establish learning gains attributable to the intervention.

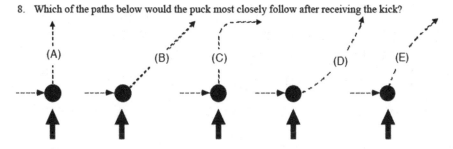

Fig. 1. Example of question from the *Force Concept Inventory* (FCI; Hestenes et al. 1992)

The FCI comprises 30 multiple-choice questions in which the choices reflect either the scientific conception underlying the question, documented misconceptions regarding the target knowledge, or fills that are wrong but not related to documented misconceptions. As can be seen in Figs. 2 and 3, the knowledge model of the game corresponds exactly to the structure of the FCI. It should be noted that each of the levels in *Mecanika* are specifically designed to address at least one conception/misconception within the FCI.

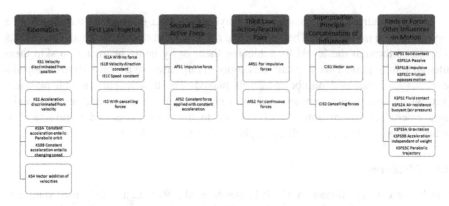

Fig. 2. The knowledge model underlying the levels in *Mecanika* – scientific conceptions.

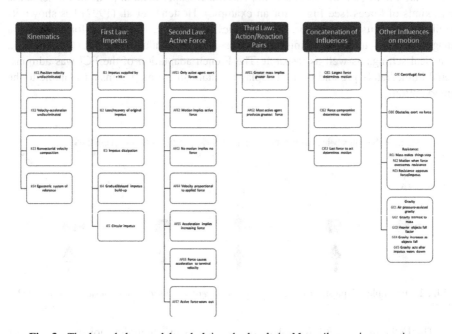

Fig. 3. The knowledge model underlying the levels in *Mecanika* – misconceptions.

3.4   Data Preparation and Plan of Analysis

For each question in the FCI, transitions between the pretest and posttest were coded. Learning is operationalized in two manners in the present study, because both ways provide complementary evidence by either insisting on learning gains or on the nature of conceptual change.

In the first coding, the nine possible transitions from pretest to posttest were: *Fill* to *Fill*, *Misconception* to *Fill*, *Scientific* to *Fill*, *Fill* to *Misconception*, *Misconception* to *Misconception*, *Scientific* to *Misconception*, *Scientific* to *Scientific*, *Fill* to *Scientific*, and *Misconception* to *Scientific*.

Then, in the second coding, *Fills* and *Misconceptions* were collapsed as wrong answers (*Error*), leaving only the following 4 transitions: *Error* to *Error*, *Error* to *Scientific*, *Scientific* to *Error*, *Scientific* to *Scientific*.

Statistical tests according to the hypotheses and research questions were constructed using the loglinear approach since the data are categorical. The SAS CATMOD procedure was used (SAS Institute 2013), which provides a test of the influence of each factor, much like a usual factorial analysis of variance, but without an indication of effect size.

4 Results

The analysis shows that hypothesis 1 is accepted. A serious game is beneficial to learning when learning is conceived of as shifts to scientific conceptions. ($\chi_3^2 = 1558.02$, $p < .0001$). In addition to the 16.44% of answers already correct at pretest, combined for players and watchers, 12.04% of wrong answers at pretest transitioned to good answers at posttest.

Hypothesis 2 is also accepted. A serious game is beneficial to learning when learning is conceived of as shifts among misconceptions, fillers and scientific conceptions ($\chi_3^2 = 2808.86$, $p < .0001$). In addition to the 16.44% of answers already correct at pretest, wrong answers transitioned from fillers (1.36%) and misconceptions (10.69%) to good answers.

Finally, hypothesis 3 is accepted. There are individual differences in learning ($\chi_{81}^2 = 149.22$, $p < .0001$). Dyads did not perform equally, and this is attributable to the unique experience created by the gameplay of the player of a given dyad.

The results for the question "Is the effect of agency on learning modulated by individual differences when learning is conceived of as shifts to scientific conceptions?" show that the effect of agency is not modulated by individual differences in learning ($\chi_{81}^2 = 77.90$, $p = .58$). Systematically, watchers learn more than players (see Table 1).

Finally, the question "Is the effect of agency on learning modulated by individual differences when learning is conceived of as shifts among misconceptions, fillers and scientific conceptions?" could not be tested because of empty cells. Some of the nine possible transitions from pretest to posttest were too few or nonexistent.

Table 1. Transitions between pretest and posttest on the *Force Concept Inventory* (collapsing fills and misconceptions as wrong answers) by agency (player or watcher).

	Agency	Transitions between pretest and posttest				
		EtoE	EtoS	StoE	StoS	Total
Frequency	Players	786	134	95	197	1212
Percent		32.31	5.51	3.90	8.10	49.82
Row %		64.85	11.06	7.84	16.25	
Col %		50.51	45.73	51.63	49.25	
Frequency	Watchers	770	159	89	203	1221
Percent		31.65	6.54	3.66	8.34	50.18
Row %		63.06	13.02	7.29	16.63	
Col %		49.49	54.27	48.37	50.75	
Frequency	Total	1556	293	184	400	2433
Row %		63.95	12.04	7.56	16.44	100.00

E = Error
S = Scientific conception

5   Discussion

The hypotheses and questions examined in this study jointly reveal that a serious game is beneficial to learning when learning is conceived of as shifts to scientific conceptions or as shifts among misconceptions, fillers and scientific conceptions. There are individual differences in learning in the sense that dyads did not perform equally, and this is attributable at least in part to the unique experience created by the gameplay of the player of a given dyad. Systematically, watchers learn more than players.

The findings regarding learning are in line with the theory and previous work. Because the impact of Serious Games may be highly dependent on the educational environments I which they are used (Stephanidis, Salvendy et al. 2019), it is interesting to note that the present learning gains attribution to a single, short gameplay episode complements a previous study by another team about the effectiveness of *Mecanika* (Boucher-Genesse et al. 2011), involving the same population used in this study but repeated play over weeks, which showed that playing the game was associated with a 30% gain in good answers on corresponding items of the same knowledge test, the *Force Concept Inventory*.

This clear and repeated empirical demonstration of the efficiency of the game is certainly facilitated by the clear relationship between game design and measures of knowledge gains in the form of the same knowledge model and supports Alonzo-Fernandez et al. (2019) assertion that the design of games should be based on clear learning goals.

By also stressing a need to specify how the attainment of the learning goals embedded in a Serious Game are to be measured, especially with interaction data, Alonzo-Fernandez and her colleagues (2019) corroborates the key elements required to further explain the patterns of results reported in the present study. This explanation is especially required in the case of the present observation that active players systematically learn less than the passive watchers, which goes against prevalent intuitions in education as well as a major psychophysiological and cognitive theory of human functioning and learning that is highly relevant to the study of Serious Games, namely a prediction-action framework as recently discussed by Lupyan and Clark (2015).

Since some dyads did significantly better than others in terms of individual learning, and thus that this learning is influenced by the common experience provided by the gameplay of the dyad's player, is it possible to pinpoint the influence of the gameplay on the individuals' learning by using a fine-grained record of affective and cognitive processes of the players and watchers, constructed from continuous psychophysiological measures of cognition and affect?

It was shown elsewhere (Mercier et al., in press) that comparing means of around 7200 data points per participant representing second by second variations in cognitive load and cognitive engagement between groups (players and watchers) using traditional analysis of variance methods was hampered by a lack of statistical power. This realization, along with the present results showing individual differences in learning and the commonalities of this learning within dyads sharing a common gameplay experience, points to the need for within-subject analytic approaches linking aspects of performance (number of trials, time on task, etc.) with psychophysiological indexes such as cognitive load and cognitive engagement measured during a *Mecanika* level that ultimately led to a shift to a scientific conception. These analytic approaches could lead to a better understanding of the gaming experience that, in turn, could lead to a deeper understanding of relevant issues about the design of serious games. Extending the model developed by Westera (2018) is key in this endeavor. Now that a computationally tractable model has become available, the next research steps involve strengthening the construct validity and ecological validity of the model by including theoretically-sound concepts from extent research from the learning sciences. Then, additional studies are needed for the empirical validation of the model across a wide range of serious games, along with serious game theory development and ultimately the development of predictive systems and tools.

Extensions of the present work should contribute to the aims identified by Alonzo-Fernandez et al. (2019) by thickening the information that can be collected online during gameplay. The use of self-administered questions measuring knowledge gains attributable to gameplay could be an additional source of precious data. In addition, the manipulation of the context of use (agency), there is also a need to improve upon data sources used in learning analytics. Gains in information about the learner and the learning process are generally accompanied by efforts in gathering, preparing, transforming and interpreting data. Following Westera (2018), the present study should be finally extended by explorations of the relationships between the available knowledge model, the player model currently under development and the game model, which remains underdeveloped at this time.

Acknowledgements. The authors would like to acknowledge the important technical development work of Anthony Hosein Poitras Lowen underlying the study reported in this paper. The study was conducted with the support of the Social Sciences and Humanities Research Council of Canada and the Canada Foundation for Innovation.

References

Alonso-Fernández, C., Calvo-Morata, A., Freire, M., Martínez-Ortiz, I., Fernández-Manjón, B.: Applications of data science to game learning analytics data: a systematic literature review. Comput. Educ. **141** (2019). https://doi.org/10.1016/j.compedu.2019.103612

Boucher-Genesse, F., Riopel, M., Potvin, P.: Research results for Mecanika, a game to learn Newtonian concepts. In: Games, Learning and Society Conference proceedings, pp. 31–38, Madison, Wisconsin (2011)

Stephanidis, C., Salvendy, G., et al.: Seven HCI grand challenges. Int. J. Hum.-Comput. Interact. **35**(14), 1229–1269 (2019). https://doi.org/10.1080/10447318.2019.1619259

Clark, A.: Expecting the world: perception, prediction, and the origins of human knowledge. J. Philos. **110**(9), 469–496 (2013)

Hestenes, D., Wells, M., Swackhamer, G.: Force concept inventory. Phys. Teach. **30**, 141–158 (1992)

Lamb, R.L., Annetta, L., Firestone, J., Etopio, E.: A meta-analysis with examination of moderators of student cognition, affect, and learning outcomes while using serious educational games, serious games, and simulations. Comput. Hum. Behav. **80**, 158–167 (2018)

Lupyan, G., Clark, A.: Words and the world: predictive coding and the language-perception-cognition interface. Curr. Dir. Psychol. Sci. **24**(4), 279–284 (2015)

Mercier, J., Avaca, I.L., Whissell-Turner, K., Paradis, A., Mikropoulos, T.A.: Agency affects learning outcomes with a serious game. In: 22nd International Conference on Human-Computer Interaction, Copenhagen, Denmark (2020, in press)

SAS Institute Inc.: SAS/ACCESS® 9.4 Interface to ADABAS: Reference. SAS Institute Inc., Cary (2013)

Shute, V.: Stealth assessment in computer-based games to support learning. In: Tobias, S., Fletcher, J.D. (eds.) Computer Games and Instruction, pp. 503–523. Information Age Publishing, Charlotte (2011)

Westera, W.: Simulating serious games: a discrete-time computational model based on cognitive flow theory. Interact. Learn. Environ. **26**(4), 539–552 (2018)

Agency Affects Learning Outcomes
with a Serious Game

Julien Mercier[1]([∞]), Ivan Luciano Avaca[1], Kathleen Whissell-Turner[1],
Ariane Paradis[1], and Tassos A. Mikropoulos[2]

[1] NeuroLab, University of Quebec at Montreal, 405 Sainte-Catherine East,
Montreal, QC H2L 2C4, Canada
`mercier.julien@uqam.ca`
[2] University of Ioannina, 451 10 Ioannina, Greece

Abstract. Clark's (2013) prediction-action cognitive architecture predicts that
active learners are more likely to learn. Even though this vision is widely spread
in education, it has not been rigorously tested yet. This study investigated if
agency while playing Mecanika, a serious educational game about Newtonian
Physics knowledge, is beneficial to learning. Participants were 74 French-
speaking undergraduate students with a novice background in Physics. Participants were paired and randomly designated as an active player or a passive
watcher. Players played Mecanika for two hours while watchers were looking in
real time on a separate screen a duplicate of the player's screen. Dual-EEG was
recorded to derive cognitive load and cognitive engagement metrics. Before and
after the experiment, participants filled a Physics knowledge questionnaire, the
Force Concept Inventory (Hestenes et al. 1992), where each of the five multiple
choices for every item was either representing a scientific conception (good
answer), and common misconceptions or fillers (wrong answers). Transitions
occurring from pretest to posttest according to those three types of answers were
analyzed. One unanticipated finding was that agency is less beneficial to
learning than passively watching: watchers are more likely than players to
transition from a wrong answer (either misconception of filler) to a good answer
(scientific conception) between the pretest and the posttest. Statistical analyses
of continuous psychophysiological measures of cognitive load and cognitive
engagement didn't show differences between players and watchers. Results
point to a need for further research aiming at finer-grained decompositions of the
performance and the learning context.

Keywords: Agency · Learning gains · Serious educational games · EEG

1 Introduction

The notion that making learners active fosters learning is pervasive in educational
settings. This claim has not been tested empirically under the most strictly controlled
conditions. Learning in scientific domains can be understood as conceptual change, in
which misconceptions interfere with scientific conceptions (Potvin 2013). Cognitive
science offers powerful accounts such as Clark's (2013) prediction-action cognitive
architecture, regarding how making learners active, or providing agency, may foster

© Springer Nature Switzerland AG 2020
P. Zaphiris and A. Ioannou (Eds.): HCII 2020, LNCS 12206, pp. 267–278, 2020.
https://doi.org/10.1007/978-3-030-50506-6_20

learning especially in the context of interaction between learning materials and prior knowledge.

What causes learning in Clark's (2013) view of cognition is that prediction errors drive change in (memory structures in) the brain. Indeed, when sensory input is different from prediction, change must take place in a) memory structures or b) in the source of sensory input. The latter depends on the possibility to act upon stimuli, which may be provided by agency. In other words, agency can be seen as the potential to use a generative model to test predictions about the world by acting upon it.

The objective of this study is to examine if agency is beneficial to learning. If so, can this effect be explained by fine-grained psychophysiological measures of cognitive processes, by controlling every other aspect of the learning situation using a computer-based interactive learning environment (see below for the hypotheses and the research question)?

2   Theoretical Framework

The theoretical framework presents a view of learning integrating various levels of explanation, the nature and implications of agency in learning contexts, as well as a brief review of serious educational games.

2.1   A Prediction-Action View of Learning Scientific Concepts

In the context of his prediction-action framework, Clark (2013) characterizes human learning as the most basic necessity. His proposals encompass extremes such as physical survival and a love of the arts and everything in between as "three 'basic elements'—predictions (flowing from a long-term multi-level top-down 'generative model'), prediction error signals (calculated relative to active predictions), and the estimated, context-varying 'precision' of those prediction error signals" (Clark 2018, p. 522).

His insistence on the curious, novelty-seeking human mind and its underlying mechanism arising from evolutionary and ongoing lifetime learning pressures provides insights into learning academic domains.

Prediction-action mechanisms implemented using hierarchical, multi-level brain machinery automatically uncover structure in information at multiple scales of space and time. This information can be as specific as sensory input or as aggregated as a scientific principle, where higher levels contain the more generic, powerful predictions.

The brain thus uses top-down prediction to bootstrap knowledge acquisition: the structured world knowledge from past iterations is later used to generate increasingly better predictions. Pedagogy thus involves providing "just-novel-enough" situations through what Clark calls designer-engineered contexts of culture, technology, and exchange through language. "Our prediction-error-minimizing brains are thus immersed in exotic statistical baths that enforce exploration and novelty-seeking…" (Clark 2018, p. 532) such as learning from a computer simulation.

2.2   Agency in Learning

The notion of agency as contributing to cognitive processes involved in learning comes primarily from Piaget (1967) where the Piagetian notion of constructivism implies that agency can shape both the process and the outcomes of student learning. In relationship with the prediction-action framework, the development of knowledge occurs through taking actions and modifying knowledge structures based on the outcome of those actions (Lindgren and McDaniel 2012).

Across domains, the concept of agency expresses the sentient and intentional character of human nature, describing in turn one's ability to exert control over one's course of actions, to determine how to apply one's will in concrete acts and possibility of autonomy within the environment; intentionality as the core aspect of agency: purposefulness of action, determination of the course of actions, and reflective regulation of the activity; ability to act through goal-directed and purposive action using mediating means to perform this action; creativity and intersubjectivity by selectively reactivating known patterns of thought and action; to find new ways to express their ideas.

Of special interest with respect to the prediction-action framework above, Damşa et al. (2010) insisted on the human capacity to generate future trajectories of action in a creative manner; and to make practical and normative judgments of possible trajectories of action. They posited that both habitual and innovative, creative actions can account for agentic behavior. Agency emerges in problematic situations through newly emerging actions or through the (re)adjustment of existing patterns of action that "may allow for greater imagination, choice, and conscious purpose" (Damşa et al. 2010, p. 149).

Exploring the subjective experience of agency, Moore et al. (2012) concluded that there is an implicit and explicit aspect of the sense of agency, which are separable, and based on relatively independent agency processing systems. Intentional binding is an indicator of low-level, implicit, sense of agency and explicit prediction of action outcomes is an indicator of a higher order, explicit, sense of agency.

Snow et al. (2015) showed the impact of agency in the case of learning with open interface serious games. Since these systems contain different activities and features providing students opportunities to create their own learning trajectory, the authors concluded that "the impact of students' interactions on learning has less to do with what they choose, but how they choose to do it" (p. 387). Students need to make meaningful choices by taking agency to design optimized learning trajectories according to their needs. Since this conclusion can also indicate that more structured interactions could be responsible for learning instead of agency, they also showed that the degree of control in students' interaction patterns had a greater impact on performance, with the potential to enhance performance, over and above the potential effect of better structured interaction. Overall, Snow et al. (2015) suggest that the best optimization of learning with open interface serious games occurs when students actively control their interaction pattern based on their own choices.

2.3   Educational Games

Serious educational games can be defined in relationship with other related computer tools for learning: educational simulations, and Serious Games. Lamb et al. (2018) define educational simulations as interactive representations of real-world phenomena used to practice tasks to be eventually performed in the real world. More precisely, a simulation is constituted of a computational model simulating a phenomenon or process and an interface enabling the learning to interact with the computational model (de Jong et al. 2018). The gains in using simulations for learning include practicing skills in safe and various circumstances, without the need to learn elaborate procedures as would be required in using real-world apparatus. In contrast, Serious Games are games designed to develop skills in performing tasks using realistic situations. Serious Educational Games are similar to Serious Games but incorporate specific a priori pedagogical approaches to not only develop skills but teach specific learning content as well (Lamb et al. 2018).

Mayer (2019) distinguishes between three types of research conducted with educational computer games: value-added research, cognitive consequences research, and media comparison research. His review of value-added research suggests five promising features to include in educational computer games: modality, personalization, pretraining, coaching, and self-explanation. The outcomes of extent cognitive consequences research appear relatively downsized: he suggests that games (first-person shooters and spatial puzzle respectively) are good only to foster perceptual attention and two-dimensional mental rotation skills. According to Boyle et al. (2016), the most frequently occurring outcome reported for games for learning was knowledge acquisition, in a variety of topics predominantly within STEM and health sciences.

Media comparison research suggests that science, mathematics, and second-language learning benefit from games more than conventional media, concluding that additional research should address the cognitive, motivational, affective, and social processes underlying learning with educational computer games. In particular, future research should replicate earlier findings with different games, examine factors such as types of learners, types of content, types of learning objectives, and learning contexts. Further research should also determine the optimal ways to integrate games within existing formal and informal educational settings, use fine-grained measures such as eye tracking, physiological measures, and brain-based measures to determine how game playing affects learning, through cognitive and affective processing during learning, and how cognitive and affective processing are related. This last aspect has been reviewed by Lamb et al. (2018), who conducted a meta-analysis of the learning outcome of games taking into account the following moderators: affect, engagement, motivation, self-efficacy, cognition, skill development, and dimensionality.

Lamb et al. (2018) concluded that three-dimensional environments help to increase affective and cognitive engagement. Also, serious educational games had the greatest effect size when compared to serious games and educational simulations, and in turn educational simulations have stronger effects than serious games. With no surprise, they attribute these results to the inclusion of specific pedagogical approaches.

With respect to the moderating variables, the greatest effect for games resides in the development of skills related to task, followed by cognitive changes. This result is expected given the interrelationship between tasks and cognition. This suggests that the most important factor in using these educational technology tools for learning gains is the focus on content; the how and when of using these tools should be contingent on the need to train specific skills related to specific content.

2.4 Hypotheses and Research Question

According to Clark's (2013) prediction-action framework and the brief literature review on agency in learning presented above, two hypotheses were formulated and tested by controlling every other aspect of the learning situation using a computer-based interactive learning environment. The operationalization of learning alluded to in the hypotheses will be presented in conjunction with the measures.

Hypothesis 1: Agency is beneficial to learning when learning is conceived of as shifts to scientific conceptions.
Hypothesis 2. Agency is beneficial to learning when learning is conceived of as shifts among misconceptions, fillers and scientific conceptions.

A research question follows the above hypotheses as far as it regards the eventual effect of agency. Can this effect be explained by fine-grained psychophysiological measures of cognitive processes?

3 Method

3.1 Participants

Eighty-two recruited volunteered students showed their interest in participating in this study and were paid for their involvement ($60). The recruitment procedure was direct, by a short presentation of the research coordinator in classes or by snowball effect. The recruited participants were from various undergraduate programs of the same French-Canadian university (education, philosophy, and sociology), except one participant from a neighbor French Canadian university. Recruited participants had to be at least 18 years old and didn't attend to a Physics class after their high school education. For the participant's wellness, they couldn't participate if they were reporting having severe skin allergies, a pacemaker or epilepsy. Unfortunately, two participants didn't respect the exclusion criteria based on their education but were kept in the sample. Indeed, one participant was studying in a graduate program, but not related to science, and another one attended a single Physics class in college. Prior to testing, all participants signed a written consent form preapproved by the ethic committee. This form offers a detailed explanation of the research including the objectives, the risks and advantages as well as the anonymity and confidentiality policy.

After data preparation, four dyads were excluded from the study because of their incomplete or overall poor EEG or eye-tracking data. For the same reasons, partial data also had to be excluded for some dyads, even though the dyad was kept in the analysis. EEG data was excluded if the recording contained too many artefacts or if the impedance of an electrode of interest was unstable or too high. Eye-tracking data was also sometimes hard to record because of difficulties occurring during calibration. Also, one dyad didn't complete the whole experiment because one participant asked to end the experiment prematurely due to an important personal appointment. Thus, thirty-seven dyads (seventy-four participants) remained in the sample. Participants' (31 males [41.89%], and 43 females [58.11%]) ages ranged from 18 to 45 years (mean = 25.7).

3.2   Design

Progressively with recruiting, the volunteers were paired, allowing participants volunteering in pairs to form a dyad for the experimentations. Within a dyad, one participant played *Mecanika*, while the other was watching exactly what the player was doing in real time on a separate screen. Participants were randomly assigned to their respective roles prior to the experimentation. Teammates were seated in the experimental room side by side, each in front of a computer, and they were instructed not to communicate.

Mecanika is a serious computer game developed by Boucher-Genesse et al. (2011). Through 50 levels, the game addresses 58 widespread misconceptions in Newtonian Physics (see Hestenes et al. 1992) at a conceptual level—no calculations are involved. Each of the 50 levels in the game systematically addresses one (and sometimes two) of these 58 misconceptions by provoking cognitive conflicts (Dreyfus et al. 1990), one way to foster conceptual change (Potvin 2013).

The players were asked to play for two hours, and progress through the multiple levels. In the allocated time, players completed an average of 29 levels. A 20 min stop rule for every level was added during data collection to avoid discouragement, even though it was rarely necessary (about 4.3% of levels).

3.3   Measures

The French version of the *Force Concept Inventory* (FCI; Hestenes et al. 1992) was administered immediately before and after the gameplay to establish learning gains attributable to the intervention, both for the player and the watcher. This test is a 30 items multiple choice format targeting main scientific conceptions about Newtonian Physics also addressed in *Mecanika*. Among the five multiple choice answers, only one corresponds to a scientifically-valid, correct conception (hereafter *Scientific*), the other ones were common misconceptions regarding Newtonian Physics (hereafter *Misconception*) or generic distractors (hereafter *Fill*). An example of question extracted from FCI is showed in Fig. 1.

A 64-channel digital electroencephalography system was used to derive cognitive load and cognitive engagement metrics (see Holm et al. 2009, and Pope et al. 1996). The desired impedance for scalp electrodes was 10 KΩ or lower and 5 KΩ or lower for ground and reference electrodes to maximize data quality over the whole testing period. Unfortunately, those stringent expectations were difficult to achieve for some participants. In those specific cases, the impedances were kept below 25 KΩ for all the scalp electrodes, which is the threshold recommended for the system used to ensure a good signal throughout the prolonged testing period.

12. **A ball is fired by a cannon from the top of a cliff as shown in the figure below. Which of the paths would the cannon ball most closely follow?**

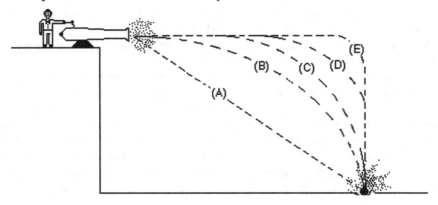

Fig. 1. Example of question from the *Force Concept Inventory* (FCI; Hestenes et al. 1992)

3.4   Data Preparation and Plan of Analysis

For the FCI, the type of answer (*Scientific, Misconception, Fill*) was first coded for each item, and each participant. Then, changes occurring from pretest to posttest answers were documented. The possibility to answer *Scientific, Misconception* or *Fill* at pretest associated with the possibility to, again, answer all three types of responses at posttest allows 9 potential transitions: *Fill* to *Fill, Misconception* to *Fill, Scientific* to *Fill, Fill* to *Misconception, Misconception* to *Misconception, Scientific* to *Misconception, Scientific* to *Scientific, Fill* to *Scientific*, and *Misconception* to *Scientific*. Another coding was also performed to collapse *Misconception* and *Fill* answers to *Error*.

To ensure a perfect synchrony of the data, the EEG of both participants in a dyad was recorded in a single file. At the data preparation step, this file was split for player and watcher to allow for individual analyses. On all files, a rigorous semi-automatic inspection was performed to remove all big artefacts. Blinks and saccades were automatically removed with an Independent Component Analysis (ICA), referenced on electrode FP1 and F8, respectively for vertical and horizontal eye activity.

Derived from the EEG recording of all participants, cognitive engagement was measured by means of the Index of Cognitive Engagement (ICE) focusing on electrodes F3, F4, O1, and O2. The standard reference electrodes were kept as the reference for this analysis. Three Fast Fournier Transform (FFT) full spectrum bands were extracted: alpha (8–13 Hz), beta (13–22 Hz), and theta (4–8 Hz).

The Cognitive Load metric necessitates a re-referencing to the right mastoid (TP10) before isolating the electrodes of interest: Fz, Cz, and Pz. This being done, alpha (8–12 Hz) and theta (4–8 Hz) full spectrum FFT bands were performed. The alpha rhythm for the participants was checked and found to be normal (8–12 Hz, 10 Hz peak).

4 Results

It has been shown elsewhere (Mercier, Whissell-Turner, Paradis, Avaca, Riopel and Bédard (this volume), submitted) that *Mecanika* fostered learning in this experiment: in addition to the 16.44% of answers already correct at pretest, 12.04% of the wrong answers at pretest transitioned to good answers at posttest.

Hypothesis 1 is rejected. Contrary to the hypothesis, agency is detrimental to learning when learning is conceived of as shifts to scientific conceptions ($\chi^2_8 = 2.55$, $p = .47$). When considering all types of transitions in an omnibus test, agency does not globally affect transitions. The transitions *Error* to *Error*, *Scientific* to *Error*, *Scientific* to *Scientific* are equally distributed among players and watchers, but interestingly, watchers produce more *Error* to *Scientific* compared to the players (54% vs. 46%) (see Table 1). Thus, agency is detrimental to learning in the sense that players learn more than players, but playing does not decrease the performance between pretest and post-test.

Table 1. Transitions between pretest and posttest on the *Force Concept Inventory* (collapsing fills and misconceptions as wrong answers) by agency (player or watcher)

	Agency	Transitions between pretest and posttest				
		EtoE	EtoS	StoE	StoS	Total
Frequency	Players	786	134	95	197	1212
Percent		32.31	5.51	3.90	8.10	49.82
Row %		64.85	11.06	7.84	16.25	
Col %		50.51	45.73	51.63	49.25	
Frequency	Watchers	770	159	89	203	1221
Percent		31.65	6.54	3.66	8.34	50.18
Row %		63.06	13.02	7.29	16.63	
Col %		49.49	54.27	48.37	50.75	
Frequency	Total	1556	293	184	400	2433
Row %		63.95	12.04	7.56	16.44	100.00

E = Error

S = Scientific conception

Hypothesis 2 is also rejected. The results point to the opposite direction: Agency is detrimental to learning when learning is conceived of as shifts among misconceptions, fillers and scientific conceptions is rejected ($\chi^2_8 = 13.93$, $p < .08$). The players produce more transitions *Fill* to *Fill* (60.5% vs. 39.5%), *Misconception* to *Fill* (60.8% vs. 39.2%) and *Scientific* to *Fill* (80% vs. 20%) than the watchers. The transitions *Fill* to *Misconception*, *Misconception* to *Misconception*, *Scientific* to *Misconception* and *Scientific* to *Scientific* are in equal proportions among players and watchers. The watchers produce more transitions *Fill* to *Scientific* (63.6% vs. 36.4%) and more transitions *Misconception* to *Scientific* (53% vs. 47%) compared to the players. Again, contrary to the hypothesis, watching produce more learning than playing, no matter if participants previously held misconceptions or not with respect to targeted concepts but as noted previously playing leads to a stagnation and not a decrease in knowledge (see Table 2).

Table 2. Transitions between pretest and posttest on the *Force Concept Inventory* (distinguishing between fills and misconceptions) by agency (player or watcher)

	Agency	Transitions between pretest and posttest									
		FtoF	FtoM	FtoS	MtoF	MtoM	MtoS	StoF	StoM	StoS	Total
Frequency	Players	46	27	12	31	682	122	12	83	197	1212
Percent		1.89	1.11	0.49	1.27	28.03	5.01	0.49	3.41	8.10	49.82
Row %		3.80	2.23	0.99	2.56	56.27	10.07	0.99	6.85	16.25	
Col %		60.53	51.92	36.36	60.78	49.53	46.92	80.00	49.11	49.25	
Frequency	Watchers	30	25	21	20	695	138	3	86	203	1221
Percent		1.23	1.03	0.86	0.82	28.57	5.67	0.12	3.53	8.34	50.18
Row %		2.46	2.05	1.72	1.64	56.92	11.30	0.25	7.04	16.63	
Col %		39.47	48.08	63.64	39.22	50.47	53.08	20.00	50.89	50.75	
Frequency	Total	76	52	33	51	1377	260	15	169	400	2433
Row %		3.12	2.14	1.36	2.10	56.60	10.69	0.62	6.95	16.44	100.00

F = Fill
M = Misconception
S = Scientific conception

Can the effect of agency be explained by continuous psychophysiological measures of cognitive load and cognitive engagement? Repeated measures ANOVA with data averaged for each of the first 10 levels show no difference between players and watchers: for cognitive load ($F9,59 = 1.00$, $p = .45$) and for cognitive engagement ($F9,59 = 0.91$, $p = .52$). Likewise, group comparisons of the data averaged over the entire 2-hour gameplay (players vs. watchers) irrespective of the dyads (MANOVA: $F2,70 = 0.18$, $p = .83$) or taking into account the nesting in dyads (repeated measures MANOVA with players and watchers as repeated measures of a common learning experience [the dyad] [$F2,43 = 0.45$, $p = .64$] show no difference between players and watchers).

Unfortunately, the highest statistical power was .45 for the repeated measures MANOVA with cognitive load as dependent variable. The explanatory potential of these very low-level psychophysiological measures needs to be leveraged by linking them with a finer-grained decomposition of the learning context. This involves looking at how a specific level was solved by a series of actions.

5 Discussion

Contrary to our initial hypotheses based on Clark's prediction-action framework (2013), agency is less beneficial to learning Physics in the context of *Mecanika*, the serious computer game used in this study. Effectively, watchers, passive participants, produce more learning regardless of the type of errors (*Fillers* or *Misconceptions*), held before the gameplay. Not only the players do not learn more than their associate pair, but their performance on the Physics knowledge test decreases from pretest to posttest; they produce more errors. These results will be discussed from the point of view of cognitive consequences research (Mayer 2019).

Although the results tend to challenge the relevance of active learning in educational settings, a few points must be considered. Globally, these borderline results command a finer examination of learning gains, by focusing on each of the scientific conceptions targeted by the game. The strong tendencies observed in this study go against the theory indicating that to command a generative model of Newtonian mechanics and to test predictions about how physical objects behave would be more conducive to learning.

Firstly, it may be possible that the game length (2 h) was a source of fatigue that affected differently the player and the watcher. In this experiment, agency is determined by the fact that a participant is required to play and, by doing so, he acts upon the source of sensory input. This may provide an additional source of fatigue affecting mostly the player. In the same time, the watcher may benefit from additional time to test his own predictions by watching the player's actions, without mobilizing the cognitive resources needed to play, which may have resulted in more learning.

Secondly, while the player had to first develop knowledge about how to play and then about the Newtonian Physics scientific conceptions addressed in the game by their misconceptions, the watcher may have devoted more cognitive resources for the latter since he doesn't need to learn how to play. It is interesting to examine the fact that, to complete a level, the "physical" orientation of the various elements to be manipulated in the game had to be perfect. However, in case of a lack of precision, barely a few millimeters even, the player devotes his energy to correctly orient the force (for example), even if in theory the problem is already solved in his mind, while the watcher is less focused on these details. The watcher may take this time to understand that the force must be in a given direction, and not that it must be moved 1 mm upwards, 1 mm downwards, etc. there is also a possibility for the player to revert to a strategy of trial and error. This may explain why watching produce more learning in Newtonian Physics. If we posit that the greatest effect for games resides in the development of skills related to task, could it be possible that part of the knowledge acquisition of the player was task-specific? The transfer of this type of knowledge (more task-specific) to the knowledge posttest may be limited. It must be noted, however, that even if these results point to a need to refine the interface, a simulation such as *Mecanika* produces learning gains over 2 h that are unparalleled to real-world simulations.

The lack of difference in cognitive load and cognitive engagement for the first 10 levels might be due to differences across dyads in terms of gameplay. For example, a dyad may have spent two hours completing the first 10 levels, while another may have spent only an hour to do the same. This difference between dyads should be investigated. As said before, a finer-grained decomposition of the learning context into specific levels may be more relevant. Another way would be to analyze the learning context in different periods of time to examine the cumulative effects of gameplay on cognitive load and cognitive engagement, for example by segmenting the gameplay into four episodes of 30 min.

Taken together, these results may orient the design of serious games. It may be possible that the link between the 58 widespread misconceptions in Newtonian Physics and their scientific conception isn't clear enough for the player as suggested by the more frequent transitions to errors than misconceptions for the players. Making this link more explicit may foster players' learning. In addition, directing his attention by providing direct clues on the gameplay may give him a better opportunity to make the shift between misconception and scientific conception by reducing the cognitive resources needed to learn how to play. In this sense, it would be interesting to compare eye-tracking data from the player and the watcher to understand which elements of the game attract their respective attention.

Acknowledgements. The authors would like to acknowledge the important technical development work of Anthony Hosein Poitras Lowen underlying the study reported in this paper. The study was conducted with the support of the Social Sciences and Humanities Research Council of Canada and the Canada Foundation for Innovation.

References

Boucher-Genesse, F., Riopel, M., Potvin, P.: Research results for Mecanika, a game to learn Newtonian concepts. In: Games, Learning and Society Conference Proceedings, pp. 31–38, Madison, Wisconsin (2011)

Boyle, E.A., et al.: An update to the systematic literature review of empirical evidence of the impacts and outcomes of computer games and serious games. Comput. Educ. **94**, 178–192 (2016)

Clark, A.: Expecting the world: perception, prediction, and the origins of human knowledge. J. Philos. **110**(9), 469–496 (2013)

Clark, A.: Surfing Uncertainty: Prediction, Action, and the Embodied Mind. Oxford University Press, New York (2018)

Damşa, C.I., Kirschner, P.A., Andriessen, J.E.B., Erkens, G., Sins, P.H.M.: Shared epistemic agency: an empirical study of an emergent construct. J. Learn. Sci. **19**(2), 143–186 (2010)

de Jong, T., Lazonder, A., Pedaste, M., Zacharia, Z.: Simulations, games, and modeling tools for learning. In: Fischer, F., Hmelo-Silver, C.E., Goldman, S.R., Reimann, P. (eds.) International Handbook of the Learning Sciences, 1st edn, pp. 256–266. Routledge, New York (2018)

Dreyfus, A., Jungwirth, E., Eliovitch, R.: Applying the "Cognitive Conflict" strategy for conceptual change – some implications, difficulties, and problems. Sci. Educ. **74**(5), 555–569 (1990)

Hestenes, D., Wells, M., Swackhamer, G.: Force concept inventory. Phys. Teach. **30**, 141–158 (1992)

Holm, A., Lukander, K., Korpela, J., Sallinen, M., Müller, K.M.I.: Estimating brain load from the EEG. Sci. World J. **9**, 639–651 (2009)

Lamb, R.L., Annetta, L., Firestone, J., Etopio, E.: A meta-analysis with examination of moderators of student cognition, affect, and learning outcomes while using serious educational games, serious games, and simulations. Comput. Hum. Behav. **80**, 158–167 (2018)

Lindgren, R., McDaniel, R.: Transforming online learning through narrative and student agency. Educ. Technol. Soc. **15**(4), 344–355 (2012)

Mayer, R.E.: Computer games in education. Annu. Rev. Psychol. **70**, 531–549 (2019)

Mercier, J., Whissell-Turner, K., Paradis, A., Avaca, I.L., Riopel, M., Bédard, M.: Do individual differences modulate the effect of agency on learning outcomes with a serious game? In: 22nd International Conference on Human-Computer Interaction, Copenhagen, Denmark (2020, in press)

Moore, J.W., Middleton, D., Haggard, P., Fletcher, P.C.: Exploring implicit and explicit aspects of sense of agency. Conscious. Cogn. **21**(4), 1748–1753 (2012)

278   J. Mercier et al.

Piaget, J.: Biologie et Connaissance (Biology and Knowledge). Gallimard, Paris (1967)
Pope, A.T., Bogart, E.H., Bartolome, D.S.: Biocybernetic system evaluates indices of operator engagement in automated task. Biol. Psychol. **40**, 187–195 (1996)
Potvin, P.: Proposition for improving the classical models of conceptual change based on neuroeducational evidence: conceptual prevalence. Neuroeducation **2**(1), 1–28 (2013)
Snow, E.L., Allen, L.K., Jacovina, M.E., McNamara, D.S.: Does agency matter? Exploring the impact of controlled behaviors within a game-based environment. Comput. Educ. **82**, 378–392 (2015)

Experiential Learning and STEM in Modern Education: Incorporating Educational Escape Rooms in Parallel to Classroom Learning

Leonidas Papadakis[1] and Modestos Stavrakis[2]([⊠]) [iD]

[1] Hellenic Open University, Patras, Greece
lpapadak@sch.gr
[2] Department of Product and Systems Design Engineering,
University of the Aegean, Syros, Greece
modestos@aegean.gr

Abstract. The rapid technological development of our society requires the revision of the traditional teaching methods. In many developed countries a new educational framework, Science Technology Engineering and Mathematics (STEM) is currently being emphasized. Traditional seminar style lecturing is not reaching up to students who seek more active participation as in most interactive aspects of their lives. A new educational framework is required to encourage students to overcome stress, anxiety and build strong personalities. This case study examines the effects on applying modern learning theories such as social constructivism, activity theory with STEM, in an educational escape room context that incorporates game-based learning. Finally, we present results from a 2-year ongoing evaluation of the developed framework. Leave no doubt on the added value and positive experience of both students and teachers.

Keywords: STEM education · Educational escape rooms · Experiential learning

1 Introduction

In the past decade the STEM educational and game-based learning considered educational concepts in an interdisciplinary way, and enabled students to become researchers and makers in an interactive playful learning experience [1, 2]. Moreover, the evolution of role-playing games has led to interactive rooms where participants collaborate to solve puzzles in order to escape, stop a "threat", find treasure etc. In this research we consider a number of current learning theories, interaction design and user experience, methods and techniques used in physical computing and the Maker Movement for implementing an educational activity [3–9]. Based on educational material of the Greek secondary education that is related to science, technology, engineering and mathematics, we developed and evaluated game-based learning scenarios centered around the concept of STEM escape room. Our purpose was to engage students in STEM education in a playful and engaging context of an escape room [2, 10–12]. The students had 2 roles a) the makers, computer science course students of the

© Springer Nature Switzerland AG 2020
P. Zaphiris and A. Ioannou (Eds.): HCII 2020, LNCS 12206, pp. 279–295, 2020.
https://doi.org/10.1007/978-3-030-50506-6_21

2nd Vocational High School of Heraklion in Crete and b) the participants, students of various K12 levels who were invited to participate in the educational escape room. The results were very encouraging in all areas. Both makers and participants experimented with the constructions and eventually conveyed the key concepts in a pleasant and entertaining way. The direction of the room with the scenarios and the teamwork eliminated the students' stress (especially by the achievement addicts), providing a positive educational experience for both groups of students and the instructors.

In the following sections we provide a review about the necessity for a new educational model based on student engagement through playful use of technologies and educational concepts, the purpose and goals of our research, a brief analysis of STEM education, game-based learning in escape rooms, design and development as well as a preliminary evaluation and results.

1.1   The Necessity for a New Model in Teaching and Learning

It is widely documented that teaching and learning are highly stressful activities for both teachers and students [13, 14]. Stress can be defined as the unpleasant emotional condition characterized by feelings of oncoming danger, tension and anxiety. It commonly leads to both biological, behavioral and social changes [15, 16]. Moreover, socio-environmental events, cognitive and emotional processes along with their reactions to them, in interaction with parental behaviors have been implicated in causing anxiety disorders to students that in turn transfer to the classroom. This epidemic condition affects almost all modern societies. Student stress is characterized by feelings of insecurity, uncertainty, failure, defeatism, frustration, resignation and constant anxiety. One of the main reasons of student stress and anxiety is the preparation for their future academic and eventually professional development. Students are overwhelmed by the demands of the globalized work environment and often develop career anxiety and indecision [17]. Students are forced to work for long, out of school hours, in order to maximize their chances of becoming successful according to social demands and professional competences required. Grade-seeking is thought as the key to success rather than a tool for improvement. Many students become achievement addicts and perfectionists who can't cope with failure, an important aspect of adult development. The 2015 PISA results regarding the average life satisfaction for 15-year-old students is surprisingly low for many developed countries. USA and Germany are at OECD average while European countries greatly affected by recession like Greece and Italy are below the average. These findings should be considered more important than any skill performance.

Stress does not only affect students but also teachers whose profession involves responsibility for the safety, well-being and prosperity of their students. Teachers, practicing a mainly humanitarian profession, are subject to stressful conditions that often lead to professional burnout [14]. Traditional teaching places the teacher in a seminar-based lecture position where the "expert" (teacher) verbally conveys the knowledge to the "novice" students in sessions that often last 45 min. A study in chemistry class showed that "Contrary to common belief, the data in this study suggest that students do not pay attention continuously for 10–20 min during a lecture [18].

Instead, their attention alternates between being engaged and non-engaged in ever-shortening cycles throughout the lecture segment. Some students reported lapses of

30 s after the class began, followed by more lapses about four-and-a-half minutes into the lecture". The main reasons for teacher's stress are the lack of incentives on behalf of students, the lack of time to solve problems that arise daily, the lack of discipline, communication issues among the teachers and even the lack of physical infrastructure [19]. The teacher's stress can be manifested by confusion, aggression, avoidable behavior, increased tendency for absences, reduced performance of both the learner and the student. The development of the above is the "professional burnout" [20], a complete personality degradation. Burned out professionals suffer from emotional exhaustion, depersonalization and a reduced sense of personal achievement [21]. Students' stress reacts as a catalyst to teachers' stress creating a dead loop of misery. It is quite clear that traditional teaching methods should be avoided as much as possible.

To stop this vicious circle of "student - negativity - creation of family - transmission of negativity etc.", the students should be given a perspective. Mistakes should not be punished, but on the contrary, educators should explain the practical benefits, compensatory positive elements even in failures. Fear, along with anxiety and phobia is one of the most painful emotions. The opposite of fear and anxiety is courage, ecstasy and hope. The role of the educators and the parents is to prevent the effects of anxiety. In order to cope with this great challenge, the teacher should also be in a stable and balanced psychological state. The fragile mental process of participating in personality formation should be taking placing in an environment of peace, tranquility, trust in personal abilities and most important optimism. This research is an attempt to combine modern learning theories, STEM and escape rooms, in order to provide a new educational model that will activate healthy teachers to provide the best conditions for building strong, independent and free personalities. Students that anticipate participating to courses and learn via an innovative, friendly and stress free approach.

2   Purpose and Goals

The purpose of the research work is to investigate whether students get encouraged/enthused when experimenting with STEM scenarios in an escape room and if that contributes to a better understanding of the concepts. In addition, whether this leads to an interdisciplinary attitude when dealing with academic or real-life issues.

Goals of this work include:

- investigation of the design requirements of STEM scenarios in escape rooms.
- to investigate whether relevant activities contribute positively towards further engagement with STEM
- to analyze the behavior of the students in a group experimenting in a close environment.
- to investigate the percentage of students that understood the key concepts.
- to investigate whether a "close" experiment room acts as added value in student motivation and whether it potentially encourages or discourages students from understanding the key concepts in comparison to the classical learning method of reading.

- to introduce students to a new way of learning that is not based on grading but on understanding through observation, experimentation and mistakes.

Students not only participate in escape room's activities, but also act as makers. All STEM constructions should be designed and implemented within the classroom. The goals, regarding the maker's role, include:

- problem analysis and division into smaller tasks.
- investigation of possible solutions, combination of different science fields.
- introduction of 3D printing, microcontrollers, mechanical engineering etc.
- implementation of real-world prototype constructions.
- development of social skills, communication between school mates.

In this case teachers should have a more active role as advance technical knowledge is required to build STEM constructions. Students should be asked to investigate a specific task via webquests, build conceptual maps through brainstorming and express their opinion e.g., regarding the selection of soil humidity sensors. 3d printing, coding and even soldering tasks can be given to the students. Current publication focuses on escape room's participation. The makers' role will be analyzed in following paper. In both cases, the main goal is to eliminate the stress of both students and professors during the learning process, leading to a relationship of mutual respect in order to create an ideal environment to build and exchange mental models. This research can eventually offer a new research field to the academic society.

3   STEM, Cognitive Theories, IoT - Automation, and Escape Rooms

STEM (Science Technology Engineering and Mathematics) is an educational framework that offers a pleasant, interactive experience which simplifies the learning process. It is imperative for students to be able to deal with open-ended problems found in trigger material. to analyse and explore, to invent, innovate and find solutions in real conditions. Morrison outlined several functions of a STEM education [22]. She suggested that students participating in STEM scenarios should be: problem-solvers, innovators, inventors, self-reliant, logical thinkers, technologically literate - understand and explain the nature of technology, develop the skills needed and apply technology appropriately.

The above skills can be developed in a social constructivism environment where knowledge is built through social activities in the "outer" world. In other words, social constructivists consider that human nature is developed socially and it's meaning has to depend on the cultural and social framework through which the knowledge was grown. Bruner's Discovery Learning draws on these principles as well as Aristotle's and Sofocle's learning theories. Interactive participation helps to discover knowledge (rules, principles, skill development) by experimenting, testing or refraining, enhancing the discovery of internal structures that contribute to deeper understanding by the student [23]. Sofocles quoted "someone has to learn by doing it, because if you know that you have the knowledge, you are not certain till you try it". In the same line

Aristotle quoted "These that we have to learn to do, we should learn them by doing them". Modern philosophers like Galileo "You cannot learn anything to a person. You can only help him to find them himself". STEM, in combination with the above modern learning theories create an innovative and explorative environment for students to develop their construct and convey their mental models in order to create knowledge. The teacher is not the center of the world as in a Behaviorist model where obedience, repetition and success are rewarded. Failure is punished by low mark and repetition. On the contrary the role of the teacher is observatory and supportive to the students to discuss the findings and exchange their mental models in order to build knowledge. Failure is considered welcome as it creates further discussion, experimentation and eventually knowledge.

The emerging open hardware communities like Arduino and 3D printing have given the ability to innovate and create constructions in a very trivial and friendly way. Providing low cost, low voltage microcontrollers like Arduino enables students to get involved in a safe and experiential way. These technologies alongside Internet of Things, an autonomous digital entity within the internet framework, provide all the necessary tools to create and explore STEM scenarios.

Last but not least, escape rooms provide an exciting place where participants live the experience, not just observing as in cinemas. Various individuals team-up to solve puzzles, stop threats, find treasures and finally escape the room. The escape room industry is currently flourishing in an exciting new entertainment field.

4   Design

Several frameworks were investigated in order to acquire data for the design of the interactive elements of the escape room. The scoping technique PACT was selected as it is mainly human centered [24]. PACT is a useful framework for designing interactive systems and it is based on 4 entities (People, Activities, Context and Technologies) (Table 1).

Table 1. Table topic.

Subject	Design
Physiological characteristics	K12, level 7–11 students are expected to attend, even possibly levels 5 and 6, height approx. 1.5 m to 2 m, various weight sizes
Age	From 12 to 17 years old
Physical abilities	No physical strength is required
Motives and how pleasure is involved - affected	Knowledge discovery through game, mistakes, without grading but via discussion with other team members
Cognitive characteristics	Knowledge transfer in a very simple and practical way
Level and duration of attention	In order to maintain a balance in the level of attention each STEM scenario should last no more than 15 min. Subject variety causes new interest

(continued)

Table 1. (*continued*)

Subject	Design
Perception	Trivial constructions and scenarios to easily interpret and convey the concept
Memory	Ease in understanding and practical participation is intended to facilitate the transition from working memory to long-term memory
Learning abilities	Initially, their desire to join the room is needed. Social interaction would enhance this feeling
Fears	Escape rooms may not be suitable for claustrophobic people. In this case, however, the accompanying teacher is reducing this feeling. Room should be in white/light blue – green - purple colors than darks
Personality characteristics	Participation in groups often causes behavioural changes (e.g. shame or a sense of threat). The accompanying teacher encourages all students to participate and, if necessary, gives roles to relieve possible pressure

During the design process several teachers and escape room owners were interviewed. Both teachers and owners stressed out the need of small groups, as they favor relationship building and involved all members. The room's activities were designed based on common key concepts that students have difficulties in understanding (calculating an area, transmission – energy conversion etc.). Through the PACT framework analysis special safety measures were considered to provide an appropriate environment for students. The final room design is shown on Fig. 1, p. 9.

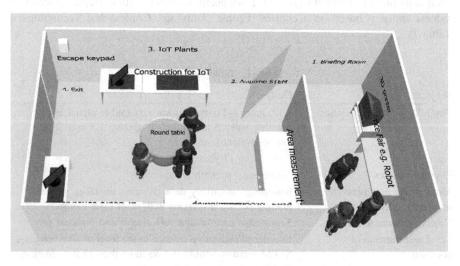

Fig. 1. Escape room layout and design

The round table is the most important concept of the room. At the end of each activity, students are invited to gather around and exchange their mental models. This is the point where knowledge and relationship are built. It symbolizes the equality of members as well as the equality in sharing views - opinions. Every student can freely join the conversation without oppression or intimidation. Humor is especially welcome.

4.1 Scenarios

The first STEM scenario should investigate the concept of measuring an area's surface. Students are often confused with perimeter and area measurement. Initially, 1×1 cm wooden blocks should be used to fill in a 3D printed rectangle frame and try to calculate the area and deduct the formula. Upon completion they should use a robot to draw a requested area. In order to further practice coding (and have more fun) students should drive the robot across countries on a 2-dimensional printed map. The robot will be programmed using a custom, logo like environment. The main components of the robot include an Arduino uno r3 microprocessor and stepper motors. The Arduino environment has been designed to be easy for use for beginners who have no software or electronics experience [25]. Stepper motors will be used to drive the wheels as they provide greater accuracy than dc motors. They can be regarded as polyphase synchronous motors with salient stator poles [26].

The second STEM scenario should investigate the concept of transmission through gears. At least 2 gears should be designed in order to experiment and explore their characteristics like number of teeth, pitch diameter etc. The construction should also include electronics to monitor the rotations. 3D printing will be used to provide the designed gears. Magnets with hall-effect sensors will be used to track the rotations. Hall-effect sensors operate in the basic principle where If current in a conductor and a magnetic field is applied perpendicular to the direction of the current, a voltage will be generated in the conductor [27]. Node.js, johnny-five.io and web-sockets are some of the technologies to display the rotations in a web browser without refreshing.

The third STEM scenario should investigate the concept of Internet of Things. Students will use a device to measure soil humidity and remotely send the data to a server. Latest measurements and statistics should be displayed to drive conclusions on the status of the plants. ESP8266 ESP-12E UART Wi-Fi chip will be used to transmit the data via Wi-Fi to a custom built RESTful webservice.

4.2 Implementation and Participation

The school library was finally modified according to PACT design in order to host the escape room's STEM scenarios. The idea of hosting an escape room inside a library was eventually an added value as it provided a known, "safe" and stress-free environment to the students. The escape room became very popular from the first visit. Students had a surprising and fun learning experience, eager to share on social media. The direction of the room with the role-playing factor immediately inspired the students to get involved and experiment with the scenarios. Prior to the entry, students were asked to wear robes, name tags and glasses as real scientists in laboratories (Fig. 2). A folder containing simple instructions was also given in order to provide basic flow. The accompanying teacher (researcher) discussed the room scenario and explained issues related to safety. This was the only time of intervention. Students were left free to discuss and experiment with the scenarios and deduct their own conclusions. At the end of the experiments, participants were asked to enter a random number in a fake keypad to leave the room. Surprisingly this fake mechanism was accepted as real. Students did not express any negative feelings, on the contrary excitement that led to reluctance in leaving the room (Fig. 3).

Fig. 2. Students prior entry

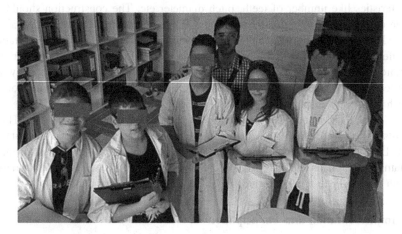

Fig. 3. During the 1rst round table meeting students appear to enjoy the process

Scenario 1 involved the usage of robotics and programming to convey the idea of area measurement. Students initially used wooden blocks to measure an area's surface. The 1×1 cm blocks gave a quick understanding on what area measurement actually means and how to calculate it. Students were able to deduct the rectangle area formula by themselves. Following the discovery, students formed areas by programming PADE, a remotely controlled drawing robot. The second part involved the reverse case where an area of 18 cm² was given and students were asked to draw the sides. They had to think of possible solutions like 6 × 3, 2 × 9, 1 × 18 etc., all accepted. PADE was built by the maker's team using 3D printing for the robot's chassis, wheels etc. and app inventor for the Bluetooth programming interface. In the last part of the first scenario students were given a random route through famous destinations to drive the robot via programming, providing the chance to relax and enjoy the experiment (Figs. 4 and 5).

Fig. 4. Using wooden blocks to discover area, drawing rectangles with PADE

Fig. 5. Driving PADE across famous destinations

The 2nd scenario involved the idea of transmission through gears, as well as energy transformation. The makers designed and built a construction were students could move gears and visually track the rotations. The participants had the opportunity to experiment and deduct the relation between the teeth of the gears and the rotations. Furthermore, the usage of a hair dryer demonstrated the idea of energy transformation (Figs. 6 and 7).

Fig. 6. 3D printed gears and 3D printed LOL ward (hosted hall sensor for rotation measurement)

Fig. 7. Gears construction, using hairdryer for energy conversion

The 3rd and final scenario involved the Internet of Things concept. The makers created 3 flowerpots and a device that could measure and remotely transmit soil humidity values to a server. Various technologies like node.js, johnny-five.io, websockets etc. were used that provided a rich experience to the maker's team. An attractive, responsive web interface was designed to show the measurements (Figs. 8 and 9).

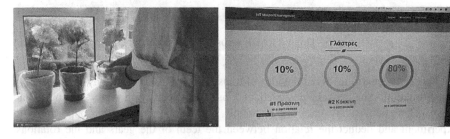

Fig. 8. Humidity measurement, display

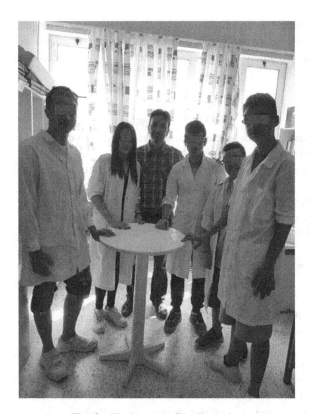

Fig. 9. Final round table discussion

5 Preliminary Evaluation

The case study's evaluation included rubrics questionnaires alongside empirical observation by the accompanying, experienced teacher. As already mentioned, the main role of the teacher was to encourage students to participate and not to teach the concepts. Another role was to observe and note student's behavior without being noticed in order to cause stress.

5.1 Rubrics

"Cognitive rubrics" help us make decisions based on our past knowledge and our current goals. Most people use cognitive rubrics to evaluate a variety of situations [28]. At the end of the scenarios, scientists (participant students) were asked to fill in a rubric questionnaire. Numerous researches have proven the validity and objectivity of the results obtained through the assessment of student performance with rubrics. The purpose of the rubrics, along with the neutral observation by the accompanying teacher, was to evaluate the goals of the case study. The rubrics requested feedback for all STEM activities as well as general evaluation. Table 2 shows all questions per topic and Table 3 the final General Evaluation rubric questionnaire. The questionnaires were designed to be as concise and comprehensive as possible in order to reduce fill in time to the minimum possible (students are reluctant in long questionnaires).

Table 2. Questions per topic

Topic	STEM 1. Area surface and robotics
Question 1. Understanding the concept of area measurement via the scenario (added value)	
Question 2. Usage of robot PADE for embedding the concept of area measurement	
Question 3. Usage of driving map to embed programming	
Question 4. Combination of simple materials like wooden blocks with robots to understand area measurement and programming	
Topic	STEM 2. Transmission through gears. Energy transformation
Question 1. Usage of STEM construction to understand the concept of transmission via gears	
Question 2. Understanding of Gear Transmission Ratio	
Question 3. Rotation application interface	
Question 4. Usage to electronics and computer science to display rotations	
Topic	STEM 3. I.o.T. humidity
Question 1. Usage of moisture measurement and computer science to comprehend the concept of Internet of Things	
Question 2. Humidity application interface	
Question 3. As to the interest in using such structures for the good of mankind	
Topic	Social activity participation evaluation
Question 1. Room effect on ability to co-operate	
Question 2. Ability to solve problems within the team	
Question 3. As regards to freedom of individual initiative	

Table 3. General evaluation rubric questionnaire

General evaluation				
	Very satisfying	Satisfying	Average	Uninteresting
1. Your participation in STEM scenarios	Very pleasant and fun experience, concepts were understood better than reading from book	Concepts were understood but the constructions were not simple enough	Concepts were understood but I would prefer book reading	Concepts were not understood and I was uninterested in the scenarios

(*continued*)

Table 3. (*continued*)

General evaluation				
	Very satisfying	Satisfying	Average	Uninteresting
2. Your participation in experiments with no obligation to find a specific solution in order to exit the room	It was very entertaining and not stressful as it was about participation and questioning. The concept of puzzles encouraged our efforts	Nice experience and time passed pleasantly	Puzzles were not required	I did not like to experience and the puzzles to escape the room were stressful
3. Would you recommend this experience to your friends?	Definitely, I had a really unique and nice experience	I would tell them	I might mention it	I did not enjoy it and I would not recommend it
4. Would you prefer such interactive activities than reading from books?	Definitely, all concepts were easily understood in an entertaining way	I would prefer it	In either way the result is the same	I would prefer books
5. Would you be interested in making your own S.T.EM.?	Definitely, it was fun and educational	I would do it	Maybe, but I would not be that interested	Not at all

Overall 60 students visited the escape room. All of the them were K12 students: 15 level 8 (13–14 years old), 25 level 9 (14–15 years old), 35 level 10 (15–16 years old, vocational High school). The average number of students per group was 5, so approximately 12 hourly visits to the room were made. The results of the case study were overwhelming. In most questions the positive answers exceeded 90% and 100%. A sample of results is shown in the following figures.

In the first scenario, level 8 and 9 students answered 100% "Excellent" in the added value of the scenario to understand the concept of area. Level 10 vocational high school students answered 80% "Excellent" and 20% "Good". Above 93% of all levels answered "Excellent" in "Usage of robot PADE for embedding the concept of area measurement." and an impressive 96% of all levels in question 3. "Usage of driving map to embed programming". As to question 4, level 8 and 9 students answered 100% "Excellent". Level 10 students answered 88% "Excellent" and 12% "Good".

In the second scenario, "Excellent" was selected by 100%, level 8 students, 95% level 9 and 84% level 10 for question 1 "Usage of STEM construction to understand the concept of transmission via gears." and remaining "Good". In question 2 "Understanding of Gear Transmission Ratio", "Excellent" was selected by 93%, level 8 students, 90% level 9 and 84% level 10 (remaining "Good"). In question 3 "Rotation application interface", "Excellent" was selected by 100%, level 8 students, 100% level 9 and 88% level 10 (remaining "Good"). In last question "Usage to electronics and computer science to display rotations" students answered "Excellent" at an impressive 100%.

In the third scenario, "Excellent" was selected by 100% of all levels for questions 1 and 2. In question 3 "As to the interest in using such structures for the good of mankind", "Excellent" was selected by 87%, level 8 students, 90% level 9 and 88% level 10 ("remaining Good").

Social activity results were also very impressive. All students answered 100% "Excellent" in all questions, apart from level 10 students that answered 92% in question 3 (remaining "Good").

It is very important to mention the high percentages in general section questions. Students would prefer interactive experiences over traditional classical reading in almost 100%. The escape room factor (without having to find a specific answer) reaches 100%. Finally STEM experience reached 100%. The case study findings leave to doubt regarding the positive experience of the students and the added value of the STEM – escape room combination.

The results of the above analysis are quite impressive and agree with the empirical observation, especially regarding socialization.

5.2   Observation

Students were truly surprised by the different roles of the teacher. Instead of attending a lecture room, they were welcomed outside a mysterious escape room. The teacher, as an actor, introduced the scenario and asked them to become part of a science team, in order to escape a room. Students dressed up with lab coats and teacher joined in i.e. by wearing glasses. It was very important was to make them feel safe, as most of them had never met the teacher and never attended an escape room. Inside the room, the teacher observed the actions and reactions of the students. Students were so absorbed in the scenario, even believing that a disconnected keypad locked and unlocked the room. This also proves how easily convinced students are in a "know everything, question nothing" teacher expert model.

In the first few minutes students were reluctant to using the constructions, so the teacher had to encourage them to get involved. This feeling was easily overcome as they quickly built confidence by understanding the concept of area measurement without learning by the "expert" but by themselves. The gradual built of confidence led to a more open discussion and fun. Driving the robot PADE across destinations gave an excellent chance for socializing as students were asked to choose which route to take based on their appetite, site seeing preference etc. Mistakes in driving was taken as "drunk" programmer - driver offering a few laughs. Upon completion, second and third scenario were considered more straightforward as students knew exactly what was expected, no more than exploration and conversation. Nevertheless, during the entire session, students reached for the confirmation of the teacher. The reply was always in the direction of further exploration and questioning. A few times, teacher simply replied "I am now aware, please run your test and let me know as well". All students got involved, even the ones initially considered shy. This role playing game created an atmosphere of equality where questions were replied by questions. It provided an excellence chance for socializing.

At the end of the visit students were quite excited and eager for more exploration. It was very interesting when they requested permission to upload photos to their social media pages, presumably adding such content for their first time in their life. It proved quite difficult to ask them to return to their classroom. One could easily identify the feeling of disappointment for returning to the reality of the classroom.

Overall the results of the observation matched the results of the rubric question-naires. Students did learn all key concepts without stress, in much less time. Teacher and students built an environment of mutual respect that all parties enjoyed.

6 Conclusions

The case study provided a very interesting and challenging experience due to the multifaceted and complex research that included the study of learning theories such as Behaviourism, Constructivism, Social Constructivism, frameworks like PACT, STEM, escape room design, electronic boards, sensors and many more. The originality of the subject bared a certain risk as it required the setup of the escape room, the design and implementation of STEM constructions using state-of-the-art hardware and open source frameworks. All STEM scenarios were designed from scratch using minimal ready-made 3D models (chassis, wheels) robots. Makers innovated, experimented and ultimately became very keen on further developing the devices. At the same time, they were introduced to Internet of Things, various open source/hardware technologies that helped them realize their advantages. Makers and participants developed their critical thinking and the ability to explore and experiment without any fear, ultimately becoming more self-sufficient in taking initiatives. The round table offered member equality, spontaneous responses, face to face open conversation without the need for leadership.

The STEM scenarios reduced student and teacher stress and anxiety levels, com-mon feelings that appear in typical classroom teaching. In this project we identified a number of factors that supported this goal including, the sense of participation in the educational scenarios that focus on learning by doing, the focus on self-assessment and peer to peer collaboration, the shift towards learning rather than hunting for grades, the simplification of course content for supporting understanding rather than memorizing concepts, and the development of confidence, safety and inspiration for innovation among class members. The evaluation results demonstrate that the overall experience of the participants led to the elimination of anxiety, insecurity, uncertainty, failure, defeatism, frustration, resignation and constant agony and negativity. On the contrary, participants expressed feelings of increased courage, enthusiasm for participation. They became more engaged and motivated in participating to class activities. Even in this very short period of time, students changed perspective about the class participation and experimented with knowledge exploration, reflected upon their learning outcomes and shifted from task completion to understanding.

This research and case study showed the advantages of using current education methods based on STEM and game-based learning. Results show that it widened the participants' cognitive field, introduced makers to innovation and reduced stress. Based on the findings this work we currently evaluate the development of new educational curricula that support and amplify traditional teaching practices.

References

1. Bybee, R.: Advancing STEM education: a 2020 vision - ProQuest. Technol. Eng. Teach. **70**, 30–35 (2010)
2. Murphree, C., Vafa, S.: Escape rooms in education (2019). https://doi.org/10.31124/advance.8947430.v1
3. Hsu, Y.-C., Baldwin, S., Ching, Y.-H.: Learning through making and maker education. TechTrends **61**, 589–594 (2017). https://doi.org/10.1007/s11528-017-0172-6
4. Richard, G.T.: Employing physical computing in education: how teachers and students utilized physical computing to develop embodied and tangible learning objects. Int. J. Technol. Knowl. Soc. **4**, 93–102 (2008). https://doi.org/10.18848/1832-3669/CGP/v04i03/55887
5. Blikstein, P., Krannich, D.: The makers' movement and FabLabs in education: experiences, technologies, and research. In: Proceedings of the 12th International Conference on Interaction Design and Children, pp. 613–616. ACM, New York (2013). https://doi.org/10.1145/2485760.2485884
6. Martin, L.: The promise of the maker movement for education. J. Pre-Coll. Eng. Educ. Res. (J-PEER) **5** (2015). https://doi.org/10.7771/2157-9288.1099
7. Worsley, M., Blikstein, P.: Children are not hackers: building a culture of powerful ideas, deep learning, and equity in the maker movement. In: Makeology, pp. 78–94. Routledge (2016)
8. Martinez, S.L., Stager, G.S.: Invent to learn: makers in the classroom. Educ. Digest **79**, 11 (2013)
9. Martinez, S.L., Stager, G.S.: Invent To Learn: Making, Tinkering, and Engineering in the Classroom. Constructing Modern Knowledge Press, Torrance (2013)
10. Clarke, S., Arnab, S., Keegan, H., Morini, L., Wood, O.: EscapED: adapting live-action, interactive games to support higher education teaching and learning practices. In: Bottino, R., Jeuring, J., Veltkamp, R.C. (eds.) GALA 2016. LNCS, vol. 10056, pp. 144–153. Springer, Cham (2016). https://doi.org/10.1007/978-3-319-50182-6_13
11. Järveläinen, J., Paavilainen-Mäntymäki, E.: Escape room as game-based learning process: causation-effectuation perspective. Presented at the Proceedings of the 52nd Hawaii International Conference on System Sciences, Hawaii, 8 January 2019 (2019)
12. Lopez-Pernas, S., Gordillo, A., Barra, E., Quemada, J.: Examining the use of an educational escape room for teaching programming in a higher education setting. IEEE Access **7**, 31723–31737 (2019). https://doi.org/10.1109/ACCESS.2019.2902976
13. Kyriacou, C.: Teacher stress: directions for future research. Educ. Rev. **53**, 27–35 (2001). https://doi.org/10.1080/00131910120033628
14. Burke, R.J., Greenglass, E.R., Schwarzer, R.: Predicting teacher burnout over time: effects of work stress, social support, and self-doubts on burnout and its consequences. Anxiety Stress Coping **9**, 261–275 (1996). https://doi.org/10.1080/10615809608249406
15. Pearlin, L.I., Menaghan, E.G., Lieberman, M.A., Mullan, J.T.: The stress process. J. Health Soc. Behav. **22**, 337 (1981). https://doi.org/10.2307/2136676

16. Fink, G.: Encyclopedia of Stress. Academic Press, San Diego (2000)
17. Daniels, L.M., Stewart, T.L., Stupnisky, R.H., Perry, R.P., LoVerso, T.: Relieving career anxiety and indecision: the role of undergraduate students' perceived control and faculty affiliations. Soc. Psychol. Educ. **14**, 409–426 (2011). https://doi.org/10.1007/s11218-010-9151-x
18. Bunce, D.M., Flens, E.A., Neiles, K.Y.: How long can students pay attention in class? A study of student attention decline using clickers. J. Chem. Educ. **87**, 1438–1443 (2010). https://doi.org/10.1021/ed100409p
19. Kloska, A., Ramasut, A.: Teacher stress. Mal. Ther. Educ. **3**, 19–26 (1985)
20. Freudenberger, H.J.: The staff burn-out syndrome in alternative institutions. Psychother. Theory Res. Pract. **12**, 73–82 (1975). https://doi.org/10.1037/h0086411
21. Maslach, C.: Burned-out. Human behavior. Recuperado En. **2**, 2016 (1976)
22. Morrison, J.: Attributes of STEM education: the student, the school, the classroom. TIES (Teaching Institute for Excellence in STEM) **20** (2006)
23. Bruner, J.S.: The Process of Education. Harvard University Press, Cambridge (2009)
24. Benyon, D.: Designing Interactive Systems: A Comprehensive Guide to HCI and Interaction Design. Pearson Education, Harlow (2010)
25. Margolis, M., Weldin, N.R.: Arduino Cookbook. O'Reilly Media (2011)
26. Khorrami, F., Krishnamurthy, P., Melkote, H.: Modeling and Adaptive Nonlinear Control of Electric Motors. Springer, Heidelberg (2003). https://doi.org/10.1007/978-3-662-08788-6
27. Luecke, G., Luecke, J.: Analog and Digital Circuits for Electronic Control System Applications: Using the TI MSP430 Microcontroller. Newnes, Burlington (2005)
28. Quinlan, A.M.: A Complete Guide to Rubrics: Assessment Made Easy for Teachers of K-College. R&L Education, Lanham (2012)

EDUGAME4CITY. A Gamification
for Architecture Students. Viability Study
Applied to Urban Design

Ernest Redondo[1,3](✉) , David Fonseca[2,3] ,
Mónica Sánchez-Sepúlveda[2,3] , Héctor Zapata[1,3] ,
Isidro Navarro[1,3] , Lluís Gimenez[1,3] ,
and Miguel Angel Pérez[1,3]

[1] Universitat Politècnica de Catalunya-BarcelonaTech, 08028 Barcelona, Spain
{ernesto.redondo,hector.zapata,isidro.navarro,
lluis.gimenez}@upc.edu, maps@azc.uam.mx
[2] Arquitectura La Salle, Universitat Ramón Llull, 08022 Barcelona, Spain
{david.fonseca,
monica.sanchez-sepulveda}@salle.url.edu
[3] Universidad Autónoma Metropolitana, Unidad Azcapotzalco,
02200 Ciudad de México, Mexico

Abstract. Hereby we present the first results of a Financed Research Project that focuses on the use of (Serious games) SG for training future architects and urban planner in the urban design context. After the first viability studies and tests in the creation of urban scenarios at intermediate scale, virtual simulation, vegetative environment and lighting, as well as basic gamification, the complete development of the teacher's methodology proposal of the research project is outlined. First five urban scenarios have been selected in which the students of Máster y Grado de Arquitectura of the ETSABarcelona-UPC of landscape and urban design have developed of urban intervention projects from the local administration and neighborhood associations. These projects have been completed subsequently in different optional courses ICT, in which 3-D virtual scenarios have been created and rehearsed under a first basic gamification. Following with the project it has continued with other courses of Architectonic Representation degree, where final settings and designs have been created, according to the students´ interest in using Virtual Reality Technology. Afterwards the virtual models and scenarios were transferred to La Salle-Barcelona URL Architecture students in different courses of Representation tools, in order to continue with advanced gamification, HMD and analysis of its usage and their motivation. The results of these instructed processes have reached the administration, neighbors, professionals and general public.

Keywords: Gamification · Urban design · Educational research · Interactive learning environment

P. Zaphiris and A. Ioannou (Eds.): HCII 2020, LNCS 12206, pp. 296–314, 2020.
https://doi.org/10.1007/978-3-030-50506-6_22

1 Introduction

The work hereby presented is part of the project BIA2016-77464-C2-1-R & BIA2016-77464-C2-2-R7/AEI-EU FEDER, both of the National Plan for Scientific Research, Development and Technological Innovation 2013–2016, Government of Spain, focused in the use of SG (Serious Games) when training future architects and urban planner in the area of urban design. It is a complement of another work that focuses in using strategies for citizen's participation of future public spaces users.

This subproject is coordinated with the previously mentioned one, it is titled EDUGAME4CITY and has been created by the following research groups, ADR&M, Architecture, Design, Representation & Modeling of the Universitat Politècnica de Catalunya BarcelonaTech (UPC) and GRETEL, Group of Research in Technology Enhanced Learning from the Architecture La Salle Center, Universitat Ramón Llull, (URL), Barcelona, funded by the National Plan for Scientific Research, Development and Technological Innovation 2013–2016, Government of Spain.

The first part of the communication is the introduction and general presentation of the project. The second part shows the current status of VR (Virtual Reality) usage in the gamification of serious urban games, applied to the processes of training future architects and urban planner. The third part describes the methodology of this work that includes: various experiences from the research team when using SG (Serious Games) applied to reinforce ICT (Information and Communication Technologies) usage in the architectonic educational field. In addition, the methodology for diverse urban scenarios designs is explained as well as their gamification. All these within the study plan of a master's degree in the ETSAB, Superior Technical School of Architecture from Barcelona (Escuela Técnica Superior de Arquitectura de Barcelona), the Polytechnic University of Catalonia-BarcelonaTech (Universitat Politècnica de Catalunya-Barcelona Tech) and from the La Salle-Barcelona Architecture center from Llull Ramon University (Centro Arquitectura-La Salle-Barcelona de la Universidad Ramón LLull). In the fourth part our conclusions are explained, and the first results of the project are discussed, since it is still in the execution phase.

In order to understand better this project, we will begin by explaining in complete summary both subprojects. The project is a cross-sectional research at the intersection of computer science and urban policies in the cities of the future, where public participation is crucial. It fits the challenge defined in the "Social changes and innovations" theme, whose five main scientific and technical priorities perfectly match our gamification for urban design proposal. For the study of the working hypotheses, we have identified four main action areas: 1. Focused on the training and interaction with students in an area with a substantial visual component as well as social impact such as Architecture, specially urbanism in the design of urban public spaces. 2. The education of Multimedia Engineers, where gamified processes using ICTs will be designed and implemented. 3. Focused on the emotional component of the users of the project. The motivation and degree of satisfaction about the use of ICT and the gamified proposal of students, professionals and the general public. 4. The study and the improvement of public participation involvement in this kind of projects and proposals. Although some precedents of gamification and public participation in urban planning processes exist, there are none on urban design. Neither exists an experience involving formal and informal education processes of future architects. There is not a single example with such degree of realism in the definition of the virtual environment or visual immersion. In addition, none of them did evaluate scientifically the motivation and user satisfaction, or the effectiveness and efficiency in an academic setting of the integrative and collaborative urban design processes.

The main hypothesis of the project is based in proving the following affirmation: "The implementation of virtual gamified strategies in the field of urban design will provide an improvement in public participation since they are a more dynamic, realistic and agile collaborative environment, thanks to the augmented and immersive visual technologies". In addition, a secondary hypothesis is defined: "gamified strategies for the comprehension of three dimensional space improve the spatial competences of non-expert users (general public) as well as students and professionals, providing a greater motivation in their use and a higher degree of satisfaction". The general objective of this work consists on promoting the use of digital technologies, in particular to evaluate the inclusion of serious games strategies and virtual reality in several areas of formal and informal teaching of collaborative urban design, in order to improve it, streamline it and increase its positive social impact. The other objectives of the project are: test and assess the teaching of urban design using collaborative design, immersive ICTs, gamification and public participation. Simulate, test and evaluate public participation in urban projects through online gamification.

2   The State of Art

2.1   Serious Games Applied to Urban Design

Some examples of gamification and citizen participation can be found in planning processes, but there are none in urban design. Neither are there any examples in the formal and informal processes of teaching future architects. No example has such a high level of realism in the definition of the virtual scenario, nor such a high level of visual immersion. None of them scientifically assessed the motivation and satisfaction of users, nor the efficacy and efficiency in an academic simulation of integrated and collaborative processes of urban design.

The main hypothesis of this project is based on proving the statement: the implementation of "gamified" strategies in the area of urban design will improve citizen participation as gamification creates more dynamic, real, flexible collaborative environments through augmented and immersive visual technologies. Some examples of the use of gamification in urban planning processes are associated with citizen participation. One of these is Blockholm: a Minecraft-based planning game on Stockholm. A total of 100,000 users, urban design technicians and experts, and citizens were invited to participate in Blockholm [1].

Other examples are Play the City, from the Play the City Foundation, [2] implemented throughout 2012 in various cities in Holland, Belgium, Turkey and South Africa and based on a game like World of Warcraft, or the use of the game SimCity in its various versions in urban planning workshops, notably in Cape Town in 2013.

Finally, we can mention the experience of gamification of the urban planning process in the game PLANIT, [3] developed in 2013 in Detroit. This is an internet-based game designed to increase the attractiveness of citizen participation, by making planning fun. However, ultimately the game is an organiser of mind maps of how users understand the city. The aim is to involve elderly people and challenge them to give their opinions of urban planning and bring new residents into the process. In this regard, the experience is closer to our approach, given that challenges have been defined for users to resolve, which generate complementary information prior to creating the design, which can be interpreted as support or rejection of a proposal.

2.2   Serious Games Applied to Urban Design for Architect's Education

Architects are trained to have the ability to build abstract relationships and understand the impact of ideas based on research and analysis, including the facility with a wider range of media used to think about architecture and urbanism including writing, research skills, speaking, drawing and model making. Linked to these skills are visual communication skills [4–7]. Architecture students tend to express primary by visual representation and throughout their academic career learn to represent through various representation technologies incorporating them in their design process to better communicate their proposals.

Technologies that model in 3D, Virtual Reality and even video games, represent progress to enhance the capacity of spatial and graphic vision and therefore facilitate the process of project conception [8]. Architects should have the ability to use appropriate representational media, such as traditional graphic and digital technology skills, to convey essential formal elements at each scenario of the programming and design process [9].

The use of ICTs in educational methods is defined in the courses of many undergraduates and master's degrees, including the architecture degree [10, 11]. From an educational perspective, these methods are applied to enhance the acquisition of spatial competences to analyze the visual impact of any architectural or urban project [12]. Architecture students must learn to be proficient in these representation technologies throughout their studies [13, 14].

For this paper, we will focus on the new interactive systems based on video games. Video Games/Gamified Systems have tasks that have a high spatial component (rotate, move, scale, etc.) are present in video games, as well as in serious games applied to the visualization of complex models, where we can find actions in which the user must move the character in a multitude of possible combinations [15, 16]. These interactive applications have favored the performance and speed of learning as well as the personal and intrapersonal skills of students. The contents that are based on these formats are closer to the means of everyday use of students and end-users. For this reason, this type of system is more attractive, increase the motivation and favor the performance [17].

For this, we created a virtual reality game in which through interactive elements, the students shaped the urban public space, following previous case studies focused on similar approaches [18]. Students were in charge of modelling the space with different software and then analyzing the proposed methods, their profile and learning experience. Students were first introduced to emerging technologies such as augmented and virtual reality in a course that is focused on using videogame technology for architecture representation [19], taking advantage of improvements in real-time rendering to produce interactive content.

2.3 Digital Technologies (DT) in Urban Design and Architectural Education

Recent Studies [20] that can be consulted in the specialized biography are focused in adapting its contents and application using ICT in the architecture and urban design fields. This work focuses in evaluating students' profiles as well as their satisfaction and motivation when using ICT in their design processes.

From an academic perspective, ICT improves the acquisition of space skills for studying the impact of architectonic or urban projects of visual impact. Particularly in architecture and urban design courses, there is a need to evaluate if a design is appropriate before it could be built, which leads educators to reconsider how students represent the designs and learn how to perform this evaluation.

Therefore, it is important that students develop skills in different emerging technologies so that they can integrate them in their designing process, with the purpose of better communicating their proposals and facilitate the analysis when it comes to the spaces they are designing [21].

Along the history of Architectonic Education, the comprehension and visualization of 3D spaces has been done through drawings and models, even though recently it is very common to use 3D models and virtual displays [22]. The use of these new methods is emerging due to the generation change and continuous technology improvement and development [23]. In particular, the new generations have technology knowledge and are familiarized with the use of computer systems and immersive visualization, the VR through HMD.

In education, gamification is a new standpoint that transforms the way in which students deal with the information they learn. In the specific context of Urbanism, where the scenarios to be designed are quite extensive and are planned to be visited and discovered from multiple points of view, VR along Serious Games SG, seem to be a natural and logic solution. If we add the immersive capacity and the possibility to modify the design in real time and before our own eyes and ears, because VR is multisensory, the educational paradigm change is very big.

That is the reason why we have considered this research project, in a teaching context, in master's degree studies from ETSAB-UPC from La Salle-Barcelona Architecture center (Centro Arquitectura La Salle-Barcelona), in which urban design is one of the identity brands of the Catalonian architectonic culture.

3 Methodology

3.1 Generating the 3D Urban Scenario and the Urban Design Studio

The urban projects we work on, promoted by the Barcelona Metropolitan Area, aims to generate spaces that are designed to meet what the users' wants: spacious, pleasant spaces with vegetation, with dynamic uses, spaces for children's games, urban gardens, lighting, recreational and cultural activities, among others.

The 4–5 selected sites, streets and squares that are closed to the vehicle for the pedestrian and outdoor activities of the neighbors. The objective is to create a large public space that prioritizes the people instead of the vehicles [24]. By closing the street to vehicles and allowing it to pedestrians, the program to be situated there is design according to their criteria. Collaboratively, along with the neighbors, was stated the following conditioners: Address the street primarily to pedestrians; give spaces for a stay and neighborhood living. Increase the low vegetation while maintaining the alignment of trees typical. Increase the surface of rainwater catchment on the terrain. Establish criteria for the location of furniture and services (garbage bins, bar terraces, etc.).

We work with two groups of students. In the first group, the students were selected from a 4th year subject at the Superior Technical School of Architecture of Barcelona, Polytechnic University of Catalonia (UPC). They used Sketch Up for modelling and rendering applications like, 3DSmax-Arnold, Sketch Up-Vray, Cinema4D-Corona or Blender-Cycles/EVEE for creating visual simulations or renders; real time render engines like Twinmotion or Lumion for creating interactive virtual scenarios, and game engines like, Unreal or Unity with HMD for creating the interactive virtual environment of the space. The second group has students from a 2nd year subject at the Superior Technical School of Architecture of La Salle, Ramon Llull University, where the students used 3DMax and Unreal reproduced the same spatial area that the first group and gamify the scenarios using HMD. In this section the scenarios here are optimized and completed in their functionalities by the students and teachers of the degree in Multimedia Engineering of La Salle-Barcelona-URL.

In the other communication presented here, the citizens participation is described, according to the initial hypothesis, only one test was carried out in the neighbor's association premises from the first studied environment. The Illa Germanentes of Barcelona. Where the reorganization project content was shown on a virtual reality device HMD (Head Mounted Display) and a laptop during just one visit. Users visualize the hyperrealist interactive urban environment where the urban proposal is developed. Before that first failure a contingent plan was applied which better results are widely described in the bellow quoted document under the acronym GAME4CITY.

On the other hand, for the study performed in this research, the number of students involved was larger. Overall 1300 students from the ETSAB-UPC have participated and 210 from La-Salle-URL Architecture.

3.2 Project Development Study in the Architecture and Urbanism Education

Continuing with the project, the relation among the courses involved from Architecture and Urbanism are explained. Each course contains some of the images that portray the work carried out by students in regard to the project theme and a description of their course, level, year or semester, number of students, scenario or urban environment studied, and technology apps used.

Subjects at the Bachelor and Master in Architecture Level at the ETSAB-UPC.
The subjects where teaching related to this project has been taught are the following.
MBLandArch. Subject. Landscape Design 3. Course 2. Compulsory. Semester 1
Credits ECTS, 6. Year. 2017–2018. Urbanims Department. Max. 25 Students for
group. Groups 1. Urban scenario 1. Superblock Germanetes-Barcelona. Action. Urban
design and furniture project based on a preliminary project of the (Metropolitan Area of
Barcelona). AMB Superblock Barcelona and the Neighborhood Association of
"L'Esquerra de L'Eixample". Traditional architectural drawing CAD, Freehand
Drawing, Digital Collage, etc. (see Fig. 1).

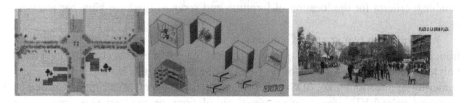

Fig. 1. Images of the intervention project in Scenario 1

GArqBCN. Degree in Architecture Studies. Subject: Urban Design III. "Public
Space". Course 3. Compulsory. Semester 1. Credits ECTS, 5. Year. 2018–2019.
Urbanism Department. Maximum 180 students per group. Groups 2. Urban scenario 3.
Cataluña Square and Generalitat Square. Sant Boi de Llobregat. Action. Urban design
and reorganization project based two urban plans promoted by the Sant Boi City
Council and the neighborhood associations "El Poblet" and "La Plaça Catalunya".
Graphical Techniques CAD, Freehand Drawing, Digital Collage, (see Fig. 2).

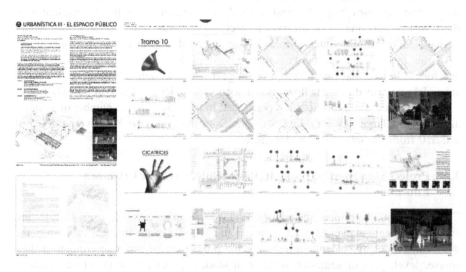

Fig. 2. Images of the intervention project in Scenario 3

To conclude, the work is being done for the last urban scenario planned for this project. We have pending the rehearsal with the new touch screen system in the Gameplay Exhibition at the CCCB, in the Rambla Modolell de VIladecans scene, where the neighbors and shopkeeper's association is immersed in a participative process for its redesign. The goal is to place our videogame in the city hall of this neighborhood for a long period of time so that users can engage in the design itself based on a municipal draft.

GArqBCN. Degree in Architecture Studies. Subject: Multimedia. Architectural Information and Communication Technologies ICT. Elective. Semester 2. Credits ECTS 3. Year. 2017–2018. Architectural Representation Department. 15 Students per group. Groups 1. Subject that served to conduct a feasibility study of the teaching process and based on the data obtained request the financing of the Project. Urban scenario 00. Barcelona Knowledge Campus. Conversion in residence of students the building of the ETSEIB. Construction of the 3D scenario and study of basic gamification. Reconversion in residence of students of the ETSEIB building. Construction of the 3D scenario and study of basic gamification ICT Techniques. 3D modelling. Photogrammetry, rendering, gaming with unreal-unity (see Fig. 3).

Fig. 3. Images of the basic representation and gamification project in Scenario 00. BKC. Barcelona

GArqBCN. Degree in Architecture Studies. Subject: Multimedia. Architectural Information and Communication Technologies ICT. Elective. Semester 2. Credits ECTS 3. Year. 2018–2019. Architectural Representation Department. Max. Students for group. 15. Groups 1. Urban scenario 1. Construction of the 3D scenario and basic gamification project. ICT Techniques. 3D modelling. Photogrammetry, photoscan, photomodeler, rendering, gaming with unreal-unity (see Fig. 4).

Workshop UPC+URL. Gamification for urban scenario. Urbanism Department + Architectural Representation Department. 2018–2019. Subject. Elective. ECTS 3. Max. Students for group. 15. Groups 1. Urban scenario 2. Plaza Baró. Santa Coloma de Gramenet. Barcelona. Action. Construction of the 3D scenario and basic gamification project based on a preliminary project defined by the City Council and the Neighborhood Association "Barri Center". ICT Techniques. 3D modelling. Photogrammetry, photoscan, photomodeler, rendering, gaming with unreal-unity (see Fig. 5).

GArqBCN. Degree in Architecture Studies. Subject: Multimedia. Architectural Information and Communication Technologies ICT. Elective. Semester 2. Credits ECTS

304   E. Redondo et al.

Fig. 4. Images of the Basic Gamification Project in Scenario 1. Germanetes. Barcelona

Fig. 5. Images of the intervention and virtual simulation project in Scenario 2. Sta. Coloma de G. Barcelona.

3. Year. 2018–2019. Architectural Representation Department. Max. Students for group. 15. Groups 1. Urban scenario 2. Construction of the 3D scenario and basic gamification project. ICT Techniques. 3D modelling. Photogrammetry, photoscan, photomodeler, rendering, real time rendering, gaming with Unreal-Unity (see Fig. 6).

Fig. 6. Images of the intervention and virtual simulation project in Scenario 2. Sta. Coloma de G. Barcelona.

GArqBCN. Degree in Architecture Studies. Subject: Workshop Interactive-Urban-scenario. Year. 2018–2019. Curse 4. Elective. Credits ECTS 3. Semester 2. Architectural Representation Department+Urbanism Department. Max. Students for group. 15. Groups 1. Urban scenario 2. New construction of the 3D scenario and advanced gamification project. ICT Techniques. 3D modelling, photogrammetry, rendering, gaming with unreal-unity (see Fig. 7).

Fig. 7.   Images of the Gamification Project in scenario 2. Sta. Coloma de G. Barcelona

GArqBCN. Degree in Architecture Studies. Subject: Interactive Urban scenario. Elective. Semester 1. Credits ECTS 3. Year. 2019–2020. Architectural Representation Department. Max. Students for group. 15. Groups 1. Urban scenario 5. Exhibition assembly project in the "Pati de les Dones" of the CCCB, Center of Contemporary Culture of Barcelona. Part 1. Construction of the 3D scenario. Part 2. Advanced gamification project. ICT Techniques. 3D modelling. Photogrammetry, photoscan, photomodeler, rendering, real time rendering, gaming with Unreal-Unity (see Fig. 8).

Fig. 8.   Images of the virtual simulation and gamification project in scenario 5. CCCB. Barcelona.

In these optional courses, volumetric definition of 3D model textures is emphasized in the urban scenario. Just as it is defined by the municipal administration, neighbors and landscape or urbanism students, we proceed to insert new elements, evaluating its location, scale, materials, with a low level of gamification, alternating interactive navigation through a mouse when using HMD.

As for the mandatory courses, they use the 3D model defined in the optional courses, as well as the designing projects with small changes that affect the insertion of new elements of urban furniture and remodeling of existing buildings, etc. On the other hand, the insertion of vegetative elements and nigh lighting are also included, all this in the first part of the course, using the usual rendering programs. Since the 2018–2019 course, a third exercise was included in which the modified urban scenarios are seen through a rendering engine in real time, Enscape, Twinmotion or Lumion. GArqBCN. Degree in Architecture Studies. Subject: Arquitectural Representation 3. Course 2. Compulsory. Semester 1 and 2. Credits ECTS, 5. Year. 2017–2018, S1 and S2. Architectural Representation Department. Max. Students for Group/Semester. 90. Groups 2. Urban scenario 1, studied by the students of the MBLandArch course. Subject. Landscape Design 3. ICT Techniques. 3D modelling, rendering, photomontage (see Fig. 9).

Fig. 9. Images of the virtual simulation project and setting in scenario 1. Germanetes. Barcelona.

GArqBCN. Degree in Architecture Studies. Subject: Arquitectural Representation 3. Course 2. Compulsory. Semester 1 and 2. Credits ECTS, 5. Year. 2018–2019, S1 and S2. Architectural Representation Department. Max. Students for Group/Semester. 90. Groups 2. Urban scenario 2, studied by the students of the Workshop Gamification for Urban scenario. Urbanism Department+Architectural Representation Department. 2018–2019. ICT Techniques. 3D modelling, rendering, photomontage (see Fig. 10).

Fig. 10. Images of the virtual simulation and setting project on the scenario 2. Sta. Coloma de G. Barcelona.

GArqBCN. Degree in Architecture Studies. Subject: Arquitectural Representation 3. Course 2. Compulsory. Semester 1 and 2. Credits ECTS, 5. Year. 2019–2020, S1

Architectura Representation Department. Students for group. 90. Groups 2. Urban scenario 3. Virtual simulation and ambience project based on an urban environment design and reorganization project developed by GArqBCN students. Subject: Urban Design III & IV. ICT Techniques. 3D modelling, rendering, real time rendering, photomontage (see Fig. 11).

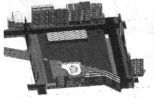

Fig. 11. Images of the virtual simulation and setting project on scenario 3. Sant Boi de Llobregat. Barcelona.

PART 1. Rendering+Visual Analysis.
PART 2. Real Time rendering methodologies in interactive urban scenarios (see Fig. 12).

Fig. 12. Images of the virtual simulation project and interactive atmosphere on scenario 3. Sant Boi de Llobregat. Barcelona.

MBArch. Master's Degree in Advanced Studies in Architecture-Barcelona. Line of specialization: Contemporary Project. Subject: Urban Project. Ideas and Praxis. Compulsory. ECTS 5. 2 2018–2019. Students for Group. 20. Groups 1. Urban scenario 4. La Rambla Modolell. Viladecans, Barcelona. Action. Project for the reorganization of uses and redesign of urban furniture based on an urban plan promoted by the City Council of Viladecans and the neighborhood and merchant associations of "La Rambla Modolell". ICT Techniques. 3D modelling, rendering, real time rendering, photomontage. PART 1. Urban project. Ideas. Project for the reorganization of uses and redesign of urban furniture based on an urban draft promoted by the City Council and neighborhood and merchant associations. PART 2. Urban Project. Praxis. Virtual simulation project and setting. Real time rendering methodologies in interactive urban scenarios (see Fig. 13).

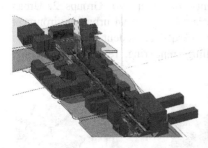

Fig. 13. Images of the virtual simulation project and interactive atmosphere on scenario 4. Rambla Modolell. Viladecans, Barcelona.

Courses of Architecture Master's Degree in Architecture -La Salle Barcelona-URL. Courses where topics relating this project have been taught. In these subjects the Architecture-La Salle students, have the support of Multimedia instructors who also use such gamification digital tools in the process of urban design, introduction menus and interactive objects. Degree in Architecture Studies. Subject: Computer Tools. 2, Course 2. 6 ECTS. Compulsory. Semester 2. Year. 2017–2018. Max. Students for Group. 35. Groups 2. Urban scenario 1. Gamification in interactive urban scenario. Advanced gamification of urban settings with the use of HMD. ICT Techniques. 3D modelling, gamification, unreal-unity. HMD glasses (see Fig. 14).

Fig. 14. Images from the Advanced Gamification Project of scenario 1. Germanetes. Barcelona.

Degree in Architecture Studies. Subject: Computer Tools. 2, Course 2. 6 ECTS. Compulsory. Semester 2. Year. 2018–2019. Max. Students for group. 35. Groups 2. Urban scenario 2. Gamification in interactive urban scenario. Advanced gamification of urban settings with the use of HMD. ICT Techniques. 3D modelling, gamification, unreal-unity. HMD glasses (see Fig. 15).

Degree in Architecture Studies. Subject: Computer Tools. 2, Course 2. 6 ECTS. Compulsory. Semester 2. Year. 2019–2020. Students for group. 35. Groups 2. Gamification in Interactive Urban scenario 3. Advanced gamification of urban settings with the use of HMD. ICT Techniques. 3D modelling, gamification, unreal-unity. HMD glasses (see Fig. 16).

Fig. 15. Images from the Advanced Gamification Project of scenario 2. Sta. Coloma de G. Barcelona.

Fig. 16. Images from the Advanced Gamification Project of scenario 3. Sant Boi de Llobregat. Barcelona.

Particular attention was paid to this experiences in order to reflect the right scale of new buildings and the effect of the sun in public spaces; the right night lighting in squares and the safety feeling transmitted to the neighbors; the amount of vegetation elements to add to the projects, as well as the different paved zones hard or soft. On the other hand, the correct location of furniture elements and urban equipment is not always controlled.

3.3   Students Courses Evaluation

Students from ETSAB-UPC Evaluated Their Experience. Based on the data gathered from the teaching information system. UPC University Using the telematics survey model has performed these questionnaires every six months for all the courses. These surveys are for students taking the classes who volunteer to participate.

Aspects to consider by the University: in the context of surveys on subjects and teaching activity, and in the face of the problem of low participation in surveys, we saw the need to create a model in order to statistically define the minimum responsiveness to be able to consider survey results as representative of teaching performance and subjects. The purpose of this work is to provide a criterion to ensure that the hypotheses tested can be resolved with sufficient guarantees of sensitivity and specificity. It is decided to propose a hypothesis test on finite size population and with variable size sample. The methodology developed must allow the diagnostic test to be characterized based on its ability to correctly decide the test. Based on the number of registrations and responses, the reliability of the survey is classified in bad/regular/normal/very good/excellent. Then: both faculty and subject surveys will be eliminated automatically with confidence regular or bad. In this case the number of registrations and responses is normal or very good.

The questions about the courses considered in the survey are: Q1 Have the subject contents been interesting? Q2. Does de program evaluation align with the objectives and level of the course? Q3. Am I overall satisfied with the course? The evaluation criteria for the questions are as follows: Q1: The average response per course or subject for Q1. In a scale of 1 (Strongly Disagree) to 5 (Strongly Agree). Answer-Q1. Number of answers to each question Q1. Participation %. Question 3 is used as the core to evaluate its quality and continuity (Table 1).

Table 1. Evaluation of the compulsory and optional courses of architectural representation at the ETSAB-UPC

Subject: Architectural Representation 3										
Subject	Year	Sem.	Stud.	Val. P1	Val. P2	Val. P3	R. P1	R. P2	R. P3	%
Arch. Rep 3	2016/17	2	126	4,03	4,17	4,03	29	29	29	23,02
Arch. Rep 3	2017/18	1	223	3,81	3,68	3,39	88	87	87	39,46
Arch. Rep 3	2017/18	2	101	3,32	3,81	3,37	28	27	27	27,72
Arch. Rep 3	2018/19	1	163	4,05	3,66	3,48	58	58	58	35,58
Arch. Rep 3	2018/19	2	111	3,91	3,74	3,62	35	35	34	31,53

The type of work addressed by students, as well as traditional virtual simulation methodologies and some Real Time rendering for the course, Architectural Representation 3,57 above 5 is Good or Very Good. This improvement is done in parallel with Real Time rendering programs that speed up the processes and allows you to look over the scenarios internally and discover different points of view. In the case of the multimedia course where basic gamification is used in urban settings, the results for question 3 are greater than 4 over 5 in average. In this case the need to program an urban scenario by the students and its difficulties, was not always properly solved by them. The participation rate, even though low, is considered representative by the UPC according to the criteria previously outlined and due to the optional character of the surveys.

Experience Evaluation by Students from the Architecture LaSalle-Barcelona-URL. **La Salle URL's case in evaluating the experiences has been done by a research team, based in specific questionnaires documented in different publications.** [Experts Systems] Utility perception of interactive and gamified systems: Post-test.

The structure of the post-test is based on the International Organization of Standardization (ISO) 9241-11 and make achievable to assess the usability of the VR technology and interactive-gamified methods in educational environments. Table 2 shows the students' main perceptions (P1 to P7), including their valuation the proposed

Table 2. Subject: multimedia. ICT for the architecture.

Subject	Year	Sem.	Stud.	Val. P1	Val. P2	Val. P3	R. P1	R. P2	R. P3	%
MultiM ICT	2016/17	2	19	4,33	3,67	4,00	3	3	3	15,79
MultiM ICT	2017/18	2	10	4,75	4,75	4,75	4	4	4	40,00
MultiM ICT	2018/19	1	15	4,20	3,80	3,80	5	5	5	33,33

methodology, perceived usefulness, and level of satisfaction. In addition, we have incorporated their assessment of gamification processes (GA UPC students. GB URL students). GA students del Workshop Gamification for urban scenarios. Urbanism Department+Architectural Representation Department. 2018–2019. UPC-URL (Table 3).

The best-valued aspect is the P1 that affirms the importance of 3D visualization for the understanding of space, but the motivation of the students for their use in architectural projects can be defined as low. An aspect that is related to the difficulty of use and needs to perceive the quality of the model (P5), in mobile devices with small screens. The perception of the usefulness of sound and the gamification of the interaction are the aspects least valued by the students, and that reflect as there was a lack in the need to take into account other variables of the project in the academic presentations beyond of the visual. Just the opposite of users who are not experts in the development or education of architectural or urban projects, an aspect that reflects a gap to be resolved internally in current educational plans.

Table 3. Means of perception and gamification by students group

Variables	Mean GA (34, 21 m-13 f)			Mean GB (39, 12 m-17 f)		
Perception of the proposal	GA	Males	Females	GB	Males	Females
P1 – Digital 3D visualisation of Architecture/Urban projects is very important to understand the space	**4.28**	4.13	4.44	**4.28**	4.33	4.24
P2 – The use of Virtual Reality to display A/U projects is useful for their understanding	**4.08**	4.38	3.78	**4.02**	4.17	3.88
P3 – Based on the proposal used, I am motivated to use VR in my future projects for their presentation and understanding	**3.72**	4.00	3.44	**3.77**	3.67	3.88
P4 – Models scale are suitable to manipulate virtual elements	**3.73**	3.56	3.89	**4.24**	4.25	4.24
P5 – The materials, textures, and lighting of a virtual environment	**3.24**	3.25	3.22	**3.42**	3.67	3.18

(*continued*)

Table 3. (*continued*)

Variables	Mean GA (34, 21 m-13 f)			Mean GB (39, 12 m-17 f)		
Perception of the proposal	GA	Males	Females	GB	Males	Females
must always be the most realistic possible						
P6 – The existence of background music is better and satisfies the user in the interaction with virtual spaces	**2.47**	2.38	2.56	**3.35**	3.75	2.94
P7 – The visualisation device has a considerable influence in the virtual quality perception	**4.08**	4.38	3.78	**3.79**	4.17	3.41
Gamification indicators						
G1 – The use of gamified environments (with missions and achievements) are better than simple free navigation in a virtual space	**3.77**	3.88	3.67	**3.28**	3.33	3.24
G2 – Playing games, I prefer one-to-one games vs. multiplayer environments	**3.16**	2.88	3.44	**2.85**	2.75	2.94
G3 – I consider that using games in educational environments can help to understand better the typology and correction of the materials used in the scenes	**3.80**	3.81	3.78	**3.10**	3.08	3.13

4   Conclusions

With the information gathered until now and since the Project ends by the end of the year 2020, we can mention that among the positive aspects of these academic experiences we have an increase of motivation from the Architecture and urbanism students when using the ICT and in particular gamification of urban scenarios. This happened in students from ETSAB-UPC and from Architecture-LaSalle-Barcelona.

In second place, the graphic courses where Real Time rendering is given and that allowed exploring in a continuous way and designing at the same time, are better evaluated than the use of conventional techniques. The immersive capacities of HMD linked to programs previously described of Real Time rendering are valued when gamification is used. It is also highly valued the realism of the scenarios, since it adds credibility to the proposals; therefore, it is considered an agile tool for exploring ideas suitable to precise contexts. The condition of night lighting in the scenarios is positively evaluated.

On the negative side: once the urban scenario were completed with all the vege-tative environment, facades with textures, etc. they were quite heavy; files with fre-quency hard to handle were created for the use of traditional virtual simulation programs. The aspect will increase when simulating artificial lighting and its reflection. The use of Real Time rendering programs, are limited to students who own personal laptops for gaming or very powerful and expensive. Very few students have HMD goggles for their designing process. If they use the ones provide by the Institute, their use is time limited. Gamification is considered very useful; however, we lack the possibility of building new virtual objects in real time because we can only use the ones previously defined.

Acknowledgments. This research was supported by the National Program of Research, Development and Innovation aimed to the Society Challenges with the references BIA2016-77464-C2-1-R & BIA2016-77464-C2-2-R, both of the National Plan for Scientific Research, Development and Technological Innovation 2013–2016, Government of Spain, entitled "Gam-ification for the teaching of urban design and the integration of citizen participation (Arch-GAME4CITY)", & "Gamified 3D visualization design with virtual reality systems for the study of the improvement of the user's motivational, social and spatial skills (EduGAME4CITY)". (AEI/FEDER, EU).

References

1. Blocholm. https://arkdes.se/en/utstallning/blockholm-den-fantastiska-staden. Accessed 12 Feb 2020
2. Play de City. https://www.playthecity.nl/page/3435/play-the-city-foundation. Accessed 12 Feb 2020
3. Cooper Hewitt Org. https://www.cooperhewitt.org/2017/02/20/22454. Accessed 12 Feb 2020
4. Cho, J.Y., Suh, J.: Understanding spatial ability in interior design education: 2D-to-3D visualisation proficiency as a predictor of design performance. J. Inter. Des. (2019). https://doi.org/10.1111/joid.12143
5. János, K., Gyula, N.K.: The CAD 3D course improves students' spatial skills in the technology and design education. YBL J. Built Environ. **7**(1), 26–37 (2019)
6. Lobovikov-Katz, A.: Methodology for spatial-visual literacy (MSVL) in heritage education: application to teacher training and interdisciplinary perspectives. Revista Electronica Interuniversitaria de Formacion Del Profesorado (2019). https://doi.org/10.6018/reifop.22.1.358671
7. Piga, B.E.A., Salerno, R.: Non-conventional representation for urban design: depicting the intangible. In: Cocchiarella, L. (ed.) ICGG 2018. AISC, vol. 809, pp. 1694–1705. Springer, Cham (2019). https://doi.org/10.1007/978-3-319-95588-9_152
8. Martín-Dorta, N., Saorín, J.L., Contero, M.: Development of a fast remedial course to improve the spatial abilities of engineering students. J. Eng. Educ. (2008). https://doi.org/10.1002/j.2168-9830.2008.tb00996.x
9. Champion, E.M.: Otherness of place: game-based interaction and learning in virtual heritage projects place and interaction in virtual heritage projects. Int. J. Herit. Stud. (2008). https://doi.org/10.1080/13527250801953686

10. Reffat, R.: Revitalizing architectural design studio teaching using ICT: reflections on practical implementations. Int. J. Educ. Dev. Inf. Commun. Technol. (IJEDICT) 3(1), 39–53 (2007)
11. Sariyildiz, S., Der Veer, P.: The role of ICT as a partner in architectural design education. In: Design Studio Teaching EAAE (1998)
12. Valls, F., Redondo, E., Fonseca, D., Torres-Kompen, R., Villagrasa, S., Martí, N.: Urban data and urban design: a data mining approach to architecture education. Telemat. Inform. (2017). https://doi.org/10.1016/j.tele.2017.09.015
13. Navarro, I.: Nuevas tecnologías de visualización para la mejora de la representación arquitectónica en educación. Universidad Ramon Llull, España (2017). https://www.tesisenred.net/handle/10803/403374
14. Sanchez-Sepulveda, M.V., Marti-Audi, N., Fonseca Escudero, D.: Visual technologies for urban design competences in architecture education. In: Proceedings of 7th International Conference on Technological Ecosystems for Enhancing Multiculturality, Leon, Spain, pp. 726–731. ACM, New York (2019). https://doi.org/10.1145/3362789.3362822
15. Gagnon, D.: Video games and spatial skills: an exploratory study. Educ. Commun. Technol. 33(4), 263–275 (1985). https://doi.org/10.1007/BF02769363
16. Sedeno, A.: Video games as cultural devices: development of spatial skills and application in learning. Comunicar 17(34), 183–189 (2010). https://doi.org/10.3916/C34-2010-03-018
17. Martín-Gutiérrez, J., Saorín, J.L., Contero, M., Alcaniz, M.: AR_Dehaes: an educational toolkit based on augmented reality technology for learning engineering graphics. In: 2010 10th IEEE International Conference on Advanced Learning Technologies, pp. 133–137 (2010). https://doi.org/10.1109/ICALT.2010.45
18. Stauskis, G.: Development of methods and practices of virtual reality as a tool for participatory urban planning: a case study of Vilnius City as an example for improving environmental, social and energy sustainability. Energy Sustain. Soc. (2014). https://doi.org/10.1186/2192-0567-4-7
19. Calvo, X., et al.: Qualitative assessment of urban virtual interactive environments for educational proposals. In: Proceedings of the Sixth International Conference on Technological Ecosystems for Enhancing Multiculturality, Salamanca, Spain, 24–26 October 2018 (2018)
20. Riera, A.S., Redondo, E., Fonseca, D.: Geo-located teaching using handheld augmented reality: good practices to improve the motivation and qualifications of architecture students. Univ. Access Inf. Soc. 14, 363–374 (2015). https://doi.org/10.1007/s10209-014-0362-3
21. Suwa, M., Tversky, B.: What do architects and students perceive in their design sketches? A protocol analysis. Des. Stud. 18, 385–403 (1997)
22. Sanchez-Sepulveda, M.V., et al.: Innovation in urban design education. In: Proceedings of the Sixth International Conference on Technological Ecosystems for Enhancing Multiculturality, Salamanca, Spain, 24–26 October 2018 (2018)
23. Valls, F., Redondo, E., Fonseca, D., Torres-Kompen, R., Villagrasa, S., Martí, N.: Urban data and urban design: a data mining approach to architecture education. Telemat. Inform. 35, 1039–1052 (2017)
24. Sanchez-Sepulveda, M.V., et al.: Collaborative design of urban spaces uses: from the citizen idea to the educational virtual development. In: Kurosu, M. (ed.) HCII 2019. LNCS, vol. 11568, pp. 253–269. Springer, Cham (2019). https://doi.org/10.1007/978-3-030-22636-7_18

GAME4CITY. Gamification for Citizens Through the Use of Virtual Reality Made Available to the Masses. Viability Study in Two Public Events

Ernest Redondo[1]([⊠]) [iD], Héctor Zapata[1] [iD], Isidro Navarro[1] [iD],
David Fonseca[2] [iD], Lluís Gimenez[1] [iD], Miguel Ángel Pérez[3] [iD],
and Mónica Sánchez-Sepúlveda[2] [iD]

[1] Universitat Politècnica de Catalunya-BarcelonaTech, 08028 Barcelona, Spain
{ernesto.redondo,hector.zapata,isidro.navarro,
lluis.gimenez}@upc.edu
[2] Arquitectura La Salle, Universitat Ramón Llull, 08022 Barcelona, Spain
fonsi@salle.url.edu, maps@azc.uam.mx
[3] Universidad Autónoma Metropolitana, Unidad Azcapotzalco,
02200 Ciudad de México, Mexico
monica.sanchez@salle.url.edu

Abstract. Hereby we present the first results of a Research Funded Project that focuses on the use of SG (Serious Games) with citizen's participation in urban design projects. After the early trials of HMD devices used by the neighbors in three urban scenarios, the complexity of obtaining results was confirmed due to the system limitations and users' mistrust in spite of the scenes realism. Therefore, a contingency plan was defined, with a strategic variation, participating in events and expositions with big audience; a monographic hall of the architecture professional environment and an international exposition focused on video games. We were able to validate SG usefulness by testing the new use of HMD (Head Mounted Display) in great public gatherings and also a new interaction methodology through touch screens joined with screenings of great size in a semi immersive environment. By this means the user designs and modifies the scene in third person, navigating through it with the help of a joystick or using HMD as an alternative. The result of the screening has proven to be robust and stable along the time, it is accessible to all types of users and very encouraging. With this installation and the participation of the citizens in our project has increase exponentially, allowing us to validate the agility of itself by having different people playing simultaneously with it and taking data by automatically taking screen captures.

Keywords: Gamification · Urban design · Educational research · Public participation · Usability

© Springer Nature Switzerland AG 2020
P. Zaphiris and A. Ioannou (Eds.): HCII 2020, LNCS 12206, pp. 315–332, 2020.
https://doi.org/10.1007/978-3-030-50506-6_23

1 Introduction

This work is part of a project of the National Plan for Scientific Research, Development and Technological Innovation 2013–2016, Government of Span, focused on the use of SG (Serious Games) and the citizens participation in the process of urban design, as a complement of the other, that focuses on the use of strategies in teaching future architects and urbanists. This project with the title Game4City has been created by the following research groups, ADR&M, Architecture, Design, Representation & Modeling- de la Universitat Politècnica de Catalunya-BarcelonaTech (UPC) y el GRETEL, Group of Research in Technology Enhanced Learning del Centro Arquitectura La Salle, Universität Ramón Llull, (URL), Barcelona.

The first part of the communication shows the status of VR (Virtual Reality) use in the gamification of serious urbanistic games applied to the process of citizen's participation. On the second part, different experiences from the research team about the use of SG (Serious Games) applied to increase citizens participation in designing urban spaces are described as a complement of the use of them in the education of future architects and urbanists. On the third part the poor results of these experiences are discussed; we barely got twenty neighbors of one of the three urban projects to use immersive VR through HMD (Head Mounted Display) devices. We also describe the strategies used to caught their attention, the representation and public consultation of their proposals, carried out in a traditional way by participative processes, debates, mental and scheme maps, in the capturing data phase and through itinerant or general renders for new proposals in three urban scenarios.

In the fourth section, the two strategic changes are described after confirming the issues presented with different approaches, one exhibiting, a public spectacle type but using VR+HMD, and the other museum like with a touch screen in a semi-immersive environment. In the fifth section we extract the first conclusions of one project, still in progress phase.

2 The State of Art

2.1 Serious Games Applied to Urban Design

Some examples of gamification and citizen participation can be found in planning processes, but there are none in urban design. Neither are there any examples in the formal and informal processes of teaching future architects. No example has such a high level of realism in the definition of the virtual scenario, nor such a high level of visual immersion. None of them scientifically assessed the motivation and satisfaction of users, nor the efficacy and efficiency in an academic simulation of integrated and collaborative processes of urban design.

The main hypothesis of this project is based on proving the statement: the implementation of "gamified" strategies in the area of urban design will improve citizen participation as gamification creates more dynamic, real, flexible collaborative environments through augmented and immersive visual technologies. Some examples of the use of gamification in urban planning processes are associated with citizen participation. One of these is Blockholm: a Minecraft-based planning game on Stockholm. A total of 100,000 users, urban design technicians and experts, and citizens were invited to participate in Blockholm [1].

Other examples are Play the City, from the Play the City Foundation [2], implemented throughout 2012 in various cities in Holland, Belgium, Turkey and South Africa and based on a game like World of Warcraft, or the use of the game SimCity in its various versions in urban planning workshops, notably in Cape Town in 2013.

Finally, we can mention the experience of gamification of the urban planning process in the game PLANIT, [3] developed in 2013 in Detroit. This is an internet-based game designed to increase the attractiveness of citizen participation, by making planning fun. However, ultimately the game is an organiser of mind maps of how users understand the city. The aim is to involve elderly people and challenge them to give their opinions of urban planning and bring new residents into the process. In this regard, the experience is closer to our approach, given that challenges have been defined for users to resolve, which generate complementary information prior to creating the design, which can be interpreted as support or rejection of a proposal.

2.2 Serious Games Applied to Urban Design for the Education of Architects

Architects are trained to have the ability to build abstract relationships and understand the impact of ideas based on research and analysis, including the facility with a wider range of media used to think about architecture and urbanism including writing, research skills, speaking, drawing and model making. Linked to these skills are visual communication skills [4–7]. Architecture students tend to express primary by visual representation and throughout their academic career learn to represent through various representation technologies incorporating them in their design process to better communicate their proposals.

Technologies that model in 3D, Virtual Reality and even video games, represent progress to enhance the capacity of spatial and graphic vision and therefore facilitate the process of project conception [8]. Architects should have the ability to use appropriate representational media, such as traditional graphic and digital technology skills, to convey essential formal elements at each stage of the programming and design process [9].

The use of ICTs in educational methods is defined in the courses of many undergraduates and master's degrees, including the architecture degree [10, 11]. From an educational perspective, these methods are applied to enhance the acquisition of spatial competences to analyse the visual impact of any architectural or urban project [12]. Architecture students must learn to be proficient in these representation technologies throughout their studies [13, 14].

For this article, we will focus on the new interactive systems based on video games. Video games/gamified Systems have tasks that have a high spatial component (rotate, move, scale, etc.) are present in video games, as well as in serious games applied to the visualisation of complex models, where we can find actions in which the user must move the character in a multitude of possible combinations [15, 16]. These interactive applications have favoured the performance and speed of learning as well as the personal and intrapersonal skills of students. The contents that are based on these formats are closer to the means of everyday use of students and end-users. For this reason, this type of system is more attractive, increase the motivation and favour the performance [17].

For this, we created a virtual reality game in which through interactive elements, the students shaped the urban public space, following previous case studies focused on similar approaches [18]. Students were in charge of modelling the space with different software and then analysing the proposed methods, their profile and learning experience. Students were first introduced to emerging technologies such as augmented and virtual reality in a course that is focused on using videogame technology for architecture representation [19], taking advantage of improvements in real time rendering to produce interactive content.

2.3 Digital Technologies (DT) in Urban Design and Public Participation

In Urban Planning there are four important issues: it is for and about people; the value and importance of the "place"; operates in the "real" world, with its field of opportunity limited and limited by economic (market) and political (regulatory) forces; and the importance of design as a process. It is about building a scenario for urban evolution, imagining the conditions of transformation and proposing a process capable of incorporating new experiences in the human-environment relationship [20].

Using technological innovation has an effect on the mode through which social movements and the diverse forms of active citizenship operate from below as agents of innovation, inclusion and social development [21]. In the last decade, there have been various initiatives conducted by researchers as well as all type of organizations to explore methods and technologies to foster the public participation in the design and implementation processes of social projects. One of the strategies, increasingly used, has been the implementation of these projects through new digital media. However, the use of new tools has not generated a digital transformation (DT) as was expected, among other things because of the novelty of the proposals, or even because of the use of technologies that are not commonly used by users [22].

Taking advantage of technology from the visual simulation and virtual reality, provide a delivery system for organizations to get closer to final users. Virtual reality has rapidly become one of the most exciting new computer technologies exercising a strong hold on the popular imagination, attracting hundreds of researchers, and spawning a booming industry [23]. Working on the spatial transformation virtually is a supporting dimension of the overall process of a structural change. We are in the need of new collaborative design processes, adapted to the new social, technological, and spatial context in which we live. The active design feedback from a city's inhabitants is an essential way towards a responsive city. This article describes the role and use of technological innovations in DT that involve the social reappropriation of urban spaces and contribute to social inclusion in the city of Barcelona. It is focused on studying the motivation, engagement, and overall experience of the participants with the technology.

Combining the innovative technologies to reach citizen participation in decision-making about the construction of the city is an essential condition for urban ecological regeneration. The act of "urbanizing" a project through DT requires a vision for what parts of the process need to be transformed. In face of the enormous amount of urban data that is needed to develop a proposal, the field of Urbanism is yet to incorporate many sources of information into their workflow. Whether it is in the way students are trained and professionals work and collaborate, the way processes are executed, or in the way, it relates to the users, digital technology provides a meaningful opportunity.

Regardless of the enormous amount of urban data to incorporate, representation technologies bring ideas into reality, allowing communication between designers, clients, contractors and collaborators. This is the same as for the professionals in the field and organizations should commit to incorporate these technologies (or research questions) to approach the following topics: Combining model with real-scale proposals using Virtual Reality in open spaces makes, is it possible to define a new space-participation model, guided, on the local scale, by single citizens, and by a local community. It is inferred that these initiatives could facilitate public decisions through the social re-evaluation of real and virtual spaces, in order to respond to unsatisfied needs. Organizations can be able to incorporate informal data obtained from citizens, urban and architecture professionals, students, and consequently, designs can be executed with a suitable design, adapted to space and combining the functionality, needs, and interests of all of them.

3   Methodology

3.1   Generating the 3D Urban Scenario and the Urban Design Studio

The urban projects we work on, promoted by the Barcelona Metropolitan Area, aims to generate spaces that are designed to meet what the users' wants: spacious, pleasant spaces with vegetation, with dynamic uses, spaces for children's games, urban gardens, lighting, recreational and cultural activities, among others.

The 3 selected sites, streets and squares that are closed to the vehicle for pedestrian and outdoor activities of the neighbors. The objective is to create a large public space that prioritizes people instead of vehicles [24]. By closing the street to vehicles and allowing it to pedestrians, the program to be situated there is design according to their criteria. Collaboratively, along with the neighbors, was stated the following conditioners: Address the street primarily to pedestrians; Give spaces for a stay and neighborhood coexistence. Increase the low vegetation while maintaining the alignment of trees typical. Increase the surface of rainwater catchment on the terrain. Establish criteria for the location of furniture and services (garbage bins, bar terraces, etc.).

We work with two groups of students. In the first group, the students were selected from a 4th year subject at the Superior Technical School of Architecture of Barcelona, Polytechnic University of Catalonia (UPC). They used Sketch Up for modeling and unity for creating the interactive virtual environment of the space. The second group has students from a 2nd year subject at the Superior Technical School of Architecture of La Salle, Ramon Llull University, where the students used 3DMax and Unreal reproduced the same spatial area that the first group.

This virtual three-dimensional scenario becomes an environment that users can interact with, to recreate new spaces. These spaces are meant to show maximum realism, including materials, textures, movements, and even sounds of the environment. Using VR glasses, the users experimented and shaped the urban public space. The idea is that now neighbours and the city council can visualize the scale, the textures, the lights, and shadows, amongst other elements, in the context of the needs and uses of citizens. The VR let users understand in an immersive way how their actions and changes affect the environment in real-time. The focus of this evaluation of this project is to study the motivation, engagement, and overall experience of the students and the citizens with the used methodology, more than the effectiveness of the approach, as the complete urban design process still ongoing.

Only one test could be carried out in the social premises of the neighborhood association of the first environment studied: the Illa Germanetes de Barcelona. It showed the content of the project of reorganization of the area with a virtual reality device HMD (Head Mounted Display) and a laptop during a single visit. Users visualized a hyperrealistic urban interactive environment, where the proposal is developed.

The three participants of the video game, valued the experience showing low interest regarding the project proposal and the distribution of urban furniture, as well as the configuration of the projected spaces, since they lost the urban gardens and the dome where they developed activities in common. However, the possibility of observing an environment that was familiar and very easy to understand was positive, but as we have described [25], it was clear that gamification using VR with glasses was not very effective in terms of promoting greater participation and increase the number of users.

3.2 New Strategy for Promover the Public Participation

After noting the difficulty of using these methodologies in citizen participation processes, the three case studies were evaluated by only a dozen residents because the municipal elections prohibited certain acts of institutional publicity. This prevented further experimentation in the other two scenarios, Plaza Baró in Santa Coloma de Gramenet and Plaza de la Generalitat in Sant Boi de Llobre-gat. Therefore, it was decided to disseminate the experience to the general public. Thus the three case studies were presented at the stand of the COAC (College of Architects of Catalonia) in the Barcelona Building Construmat 2019 hall, an installation in the form of a Pop-Up Store, in which the group of researchers of the project participated in its design and materialisation.

The BBConstrumat held from May 14 to 17, 2019, is an international construction industry exhibition and was the place where the use of virtual reality and gamification was proposed for a majority public use.

The proposal was to design a stand together with the COAC. This stand had a double purpose, on the one hand to show the activities of the institution together with a virtual visit to its facilities; on the other hand to show new lines of research of the architecture professionals. In addition to generating the design and contents of the first part, our contribution was to build a set where we could evaluate our Game4City game in the three virtual scenarios described above, using the HMDs connected to the same computer.

At the same time, it was proposed to formalize the structure of the video game applied to the design of the stand, which allowed interacting with it in third person and be visualized in first person, all this using the HMD and its specific controls. The formalization of the stand allowed duplicating the projection screens and the game points. This event had 422 exhibitors and was attended by over 54,000 people, an average of 128 people per exhibitor according to official figures from the Fira de Barcelona organisation.

The second event was participation in the joint exhibition of the CCCB+ZKM, the Centre of Contemporary Culture "Culture of Videojoc", which took place from 19 December 2019 to 3 May 2020. The project team was invited as a special guest, along with two other projects also created by university research groups.

The exhibition has 28 game points and 9 artistic montages, divided into five areas: 1. Replay. Origins of the Video Game, 2. Liquid Narratives, 3. Art and Playful Essay, 4. Breaking the Magic Circle, our proposal at Level 5.

Beyond the entertainment in which some video games created for educational purposes are shown, Serious Games can have certain sensitive implications, and therefore require expert advice. For example, educational video games intended for formal education, video games for professional training or to support the development of minors with some special difficulty, video games used for military training and three in particular, derived from research and development at Catalan universities. In recent years, EduGame4City from the UPC-URL is our contribution of a software based on games for the study and exercise of architecture; Virtual Perfusionist, also from the UPC, for virtual training in choir operations, and Terres de Niebla, from the Universitat Pompeu Fabra, UPF of Barcelona, a game that promotes the playful socialization of autistic children.

Our proposal is the only interactive of the three that have emerged from the university research groups; the other two are limited to video projections of digital content in a cyclical manner.

3.3 First Processes of Citizens Participation

On each urban scenario we have modeled a proposal coming from the process of citizens participation, with Architecture students from ATSAB-UPC help or Architecture La Salle-URL based on a local government draft. With this basis a new variation of the videogame GAME4CITY is formalized.

The neighbors grouped in associations, presented improvement proposals an also of the use of public spaces that they usually enjoy. These processes have been performed through experts on these subjects; they are in charge of the performing the meetings and gather the proposals in different ways. We found in all these meetings that drawing in an intuitive or professional way; along with small work mockups are very agile procedures. This process has been conducted in three places. At the Super manzana Germantes del Ensanche de Barcelona; on the Baro de Santa Coloma de Gramenet Square 13[12–33] and on the Generalitat de Sant Boi de Llobregat Square (see Fig. 1) (see Fig. 2) (see Fig. 3).

Fig. 1. Images of the citizen participation process in the Germanetes area, Barcelona 2017.

Fig. 2. Images of the process of citizen participation in the Baró square of Santa Co-loma de Gramenet during 2017 carried out at the Torre Balldovina School.

Fig. 3. Images of the process of citizen participation in the Plaza de la Generalitat in Sant Boi de Llobregat during the year 2018 promoted by the Association of Neighbors "El Poblet" Marianao.

The common point of these three processes was the neighbors desire of not missing any of the activities self-managed by them and help on each of the three places, such as urban vegetable patches, rest and conversation areas, places for the youth, etc. On Second place confirm the over exploitation of the place by giving many uses at the same time often generating conflict by clashing activities, for instance the playground area with pet's area. The third, the demand of paved zones with land suitable for games, sitting down and walking, covered with trees of easy maintenance.

3.4   Interaction Urban Designers-Citizens, in Our Three Case Studies

The response to these premises by the municipal technicians' managers has provided draft projects fill up with activities and excessive urban furniture. Spaces with lot architecture to meet all the demands at once. This aspect can be corroborated with the images of the first interaction between neighbors and designers. Virtual scenes and photomontages as the ones showed below, as well as diagrams and sketches following the usual methodology for the process of informing the public (see Fig. 4) (see Fig. 5).

Fig. 4. Renders of the proposals of the neighbors, interpreted by the technicians and students of architecture in the square block of Germanetes, in the Ensanche of Barcelona.

This work allowed the neighbors to adjust their opinion, although it also generated some misinformation because the visits were little realistic and idealized in some cases. The represented projects, in their opinion, were interventionists, the public space was filled up with too many designed objects. In parallel, requested by the administration, the Project Research team, developed various photomontages and virtual simulations of the urban places while they were creating each urban scene as a way to set the changes of neighbors premises on the urban projects promoted by local administrations. These representations were generated with the maximum severity possible, either by precision on the point of views, scale an element presented materials, the real layout condition simulation and night lighting (see Fig. 6) (see Fig. 7).

These images payed particular attention in showing the correct scale of new buildings and their influence in the lay out of public spaces; with the correct night lighting of the squares and safety feeling that it transmitted to the neighbors; the amount of vegetative to incorporate in the projects, as well as the different paved areas, hard or soft.

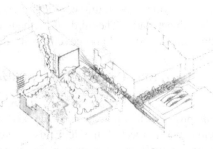

Fig. 5. Sketches of the proposals of the neighbors, interpreted by the technicians and architecture students of the Plaza Baró de Santa Coloma de Gramenet and the Plaza Sant Boi de Llobregat.

Fig. 6. Precise photomontages of the interior of the Germanetes superblock of the Ensanche, Barcelona.

Fig. 7. First street views of the virtual stages of the video game GAME4CITY for Plaza Baró de Santa Coloma de Gramenet, Generalitat de Sant Boi, Llobregat.

3.5　The Presentation of the Urban Projects to the Public for Their Evaluation and Definition Through the Interaction with a Gamified Virtual Model

As we have previously described, after evaluating the difficulty of testing with the neighbors the three urban projects and the use of HMD in a virtual gamified scene, we opted for a different strategy. It is worth mentioning that the use of this gamification strategy was sometimes interpreted as a way of trivializing the problems or that a voice was only given to the young ones or well versed in these technologies.

The first case was the COAC stand in BBConstrumat 2019. In this case the installation was done in a dual space destinated to exposure with Led screens and two installations of virtual and augmented reality with Chroma key Technique in order to combine the real video and the virtual background and therefore create a mixed reality. The users saw the different urban scenarios of the project interacting with them in third or first person depending on their location with the HMD controls, adding, removing or relocating urban furniture. The use of a Chroma background allowed the creation of a final image in which you could see the HMD user immerse in the hacienda scene more attractive to the eye for external users and two great projection screens located behind the chroma parameters and simultaneously in various high quality monitors distributed along the stand. These projection systems were alternatively used for presentations and conferences that were also held in the stand.

The required technology for this installation consisted of two screens 3 × 4 m and a puzzle of synchronized monitors along with 5 web cameras that picked all the scenes. Two of those were dedicated to film the player, 3 fixed computers to play the video-game, 2 high quality monitors, 2 HMD googles with its controls, movement sensors, etc. and two video signal mixers to create the combined signal of the videogame and the player. A complex installation that at one point collapsed, caused by the excessive heat generated by the computers, executing the games after running uninterrupted for more than 8 h (see Fig. 8).

Fig. 8. Images of the COAC stand at the BBConstrumat 2019 exhibition.

On the bright side it is worth mentioning that this event, help 422 speakers, according to Fira de Barcelona organization official number, more than 54,000 people participated, which gives us an average of 128 persons per speaker. The experience was greatly accepted by the audience. In total the stand was visualized by over 4,000 people, according to COAC data, who counted the people who approached the stand to inquire information, without counting the ones that crossed by and saw the virtual scenes. In parallel and alternating the videogame screening, different conferences were organized, which counted over 1,500 attendee trough out the days, with over 80 professional visitors who experienced the HMD and the videogame with a positive evaluation, pointing out the possibility to see the action from the outside and share the interaction of the user with the virtual reality device. These evaluations were gathered in surveys that were analyzed, the results have been published [26] and attached herby in a summary.

We divided the group of users in two. The first group (professionals) was composed of 28 women between 20 and 57 years old (age average, AA: 31.89 and standard deviation, SD: 14.31) and 51 men (AA: 33.86, SD: 14.31, between 20 and 68 years old). In the second group, (architecture students), there were 17 women (AA: 20.76, SD: 1.56, between 19 and 24 years old) and 14 men (AA: 21.14, SD: 2.77, between 19 and 25 years old). For this work we only consider professional users. On the negative side, it is necessary to mention the long waiting times and the slowness of changing users each time a visitor wanted to test HMD, as well as the problem of the stability of programs and equipment after more than 36 h of non-stop operation.

The second event as previously described has been the participation in the joint exhibition of CCCB+ZKM, the Centro de Cultura Conteporánea de Barcelona+Center for Art and Media Karlsruhe (Zentrum für Kunst und Medien). Which is our center game focused of this work. For this matter, Architecture students from the ETSAB-UPC created a new virtual scenario of the CCCB inner patio and designed some special furniture elements by following the same principles mentioned before and fitted to the requirements of the International Commission of the exposition.

It consisted in the installation of a project with a touch screen scene in third person, with a menu that contained several elements that could be pulled or dragged to a virtual scenario. This installation shows an environment that reproduces the main patio of the museum, "Pati de le Dones" specifically, where the users distributed virtual panels in order to create a brief architectonic structure. In this case the virtual scenario proposed focused in simulating the CCCB patio, following the same realism criteria that in the previous urban scenario, using orthorectified images that have been mapped over a simple volumetric. The elements to be added in this occasion, since it is a public space where temporary exhibitions are set up, we had to create a series of illustrated panels with the work of the research group, which had assorted volumetric and real scale pavilions, based on the game of House of Card by Charles and Ray Eames, 1952.

Four games of 12 cards were designed, each one represented different visits to Barcelona scenarios, Sta. Coloma de G. and Sant Boi, and always a video and a presentation cover with a different back image specific to each set of cards. The second card game represented images from the ETSAB-UPC historic Archive; the third had images of La Salle-URL students' projects, the fourth included the renovation process of the COAC building and a fifth game with images of architectonic parameters in general. The user can combine the cards propose a set up assembling assorted representations of the temporary exhibitions pavilion located in the Patio de les Dones. The setting of the scene is completed with characters that wander (see Fig. 9).

Fig. 9. Images of the various urban scenarios studied, collected in the letters and the CCCB video game.

While a user interacts with the touch screen, the result could be seen in a vertical screen of 2.5 × 5 m where the image is broadcasted from a high positioned projector or at ground level. Navigating though the scenario could be done with the game console joystick. In a different configuration, the user can interact with the virtual reality device and the controls through some HMD googles and it's controls. In this installation we have used desk computers set for an uninterrupted performance of 6 months, the length of the exposition, charged with a SAI electric system, a 25″ touch screen, the projector (laser for a better autonomy, over 20,000 h), a videogame controller, a HMD device with controllers and a vertical screen for auxiliary projection (see Fig. 10).

This type of exposition is favorable for catching a bigger attendance, in two months 8000 people have visited the facility with a more positive response that in previous proposals. The system captures the final screen of user' proposals through an attached

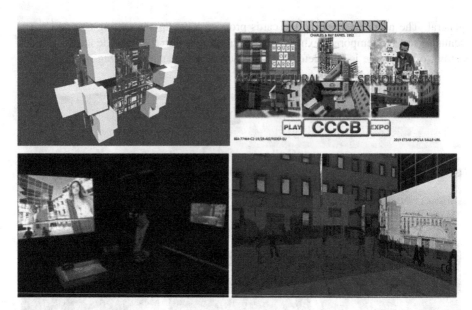

Fig. 10. Images illustrating the possible links of the cards, the cover, the installation of the video game and a proposal built by the public in the CCCB gameplay exhibition.

survey, such installation could be accessed with a QR code, favorably the simple interaction with the touch screen and the high quality visualization in real time from a first person point of view facilitates the interpretation of the results. Additionally by being a dark environment and a high quality projection, it becomes a semi-immersive experience very gratifying with great interaction capacity, it could even be played by two people at the same time, one manages the elements added to a scene while the other one can navigate through the scenario, even climbing over the pavilions. As a supplementary option and for smaller groups, the system allows to share the interface from some HMD.

3.6   The Version of the GAME4CITY Game Developed for the CCCB

For the creation of the serious game "House of Cards", after considering multiple options, it was decided to develop the application using the Unity environment, due to its versatility and compatibility with all types of devices, including touch screens and VR displays. The main challenge was to create an application that would allow the creation of constructions as rich and complex as possible, including the use of several groups of cards, but at the same time be easy enough to use, so that anyone without previous experience could enter data on the touch screen. This challenge led to important design decisions.

First, with respect to scenario navigation, the most commonly used navigation operations in modeling and visualization software, such as panning or zooming, were discarded. It had to be a system so simple that it did not need combinations such as keys plus mouse clicks. Therefore, a system combining manual rotation and automatic position was chosen: the user could change the point of view using four buttons that rotated the camera at 15-degree intervals. The position of the camera was then automatically calculated according to the space available on the Pati de les Dones 3D model.

In the case of card selection, the possibility of combining cards of different types was ruled out. Instead, a much simpler, more direct approach was made, which also had many possibilities. The option chosen was to create 5 groups of 11 cards each (5 images in horizontal, 5 in vertical, and a video), easily selected by the user through two buttons. Having all the collections of identical number of cards, it allowed to exchange them even after starting the construction and to change the aspect of the designs already made, multiplying the possibilities.

In any case, the most difficult part of the design and programming of the application was the construction system. In order to achieve a user-friendly and direct interface, operations such as deleting letters, changing position or reorienting were ruled out. Even the position or orientation was not directly determinable by the user. The solution was to create a series of areas of influence around the slots off each card. Each of these areas of influence pointed in one of the three available directions and corresponded to the three slots of the possible new card (six slots were not considered because the cards were symmetrical and choosing only three made the construction system much clearer). This meant that each card had 18 different connection possibilities, which were carefully represented by selection areas invisible to the user, but which covered those areas around each card where it would be logical to place a new one.

The apparent complexity of this system contrasts with its enormous simplicity of use: all the user had to do was move their finger on the touch screen. When the finger was moved closer to an existing card, the possible positions of the new card were automatically displayed. By lifting your finger off the screen, the card is fixed in its final position. One last important aspect of designing was the ability to correct errors. Without tools to select and delete cards, a simple system was chosen, undoing the last card created. In this way, users could go back in time and resume their creation from the point they chose.

As important was the creation of the constructions as their experimentation. For this reason, two navigation systems were designed: one using a first-person camera and a video game that can be controlled by a gamepad, and the second based on teleportation, for Virtual Reality devices. Both options allowed users to move around their creations, including climbing to any height by leaning on the charts.

4   Conclusions

Since the CCCB exposition will end until May 3rd we cannot provide further data of the usage and impact of this installation. Nevertheless, based on the data compiled until now we can conclude that:

On the negative side: The set ups to evaluate user's participation in urban design processes using Serious Games, are perceived with mistrust by some neighbors of certain ages of the areas studied. They consider it as something trivial compared to the real problems of the neighborhood. They have difficulties to handle the HMD devices and understanding the operation of the game. On the other hand, younger neighbors feel attracted by these strategies. The fact that urban scenarios must be modernized in a very detailed level even in parts not quite visible could also be a problem for designers, since the navigation through a scenario could lead the users to see aspects unsolved from the urban project. It is also difficult sometimes to define the game rules and how to manifest that some elements are not well located. The long wait and changing users when using the HMD slowed down the process, creating a vertigo feeling, problems with the googles hygiene, difficulty when using conventional googles. It is also complicated to gather all the surveys from the users in a rapid way.

On the Positive side: the realism of the scenarios give credibility to the proposals. The fast way in which variations in real time can be added to the project, relocating elements or changing its appearance, has proven to be a very agile tool to set ideas. It is positively evaluated in the night lighting simulation scenarios and the possibility to increase the number of lamps and lampposts. The fact that a scenario is animated with moving cars is also highly appreciated, in such a way that you see the user immerse in the scene of the videogame. That is also thought of the sound added to the scene. The new type of installation through a touch screen combined with a video console and the HMD googles as optional is also highly evaluated.

To conclude, we are currently working in the last urban scenario for this project. We have a pending rehearsal of the new touch screen system, the scenario of the rambla Modolell de Viladecans where the association of neighbors and shopkeepers are immersed for its design in a participative process. The objective is to place in the city hall of this location our videogame adapted to the scenario in order to have users participate for a long period of time in the design of itself based on a draft of the local government.

Acknowledgments. This research was supported by the National Program of Research, Development and Innovation aimed to the Society Challenges with the references BIA2016-77464-C2-1-R & BIA2016-77464-C2-2-R, both of the National Plan for Scientific Research, Development and Technological Innovation 2013-2016, Government of Spain, titled "Gamificación para la enseñanza del diseño urbano y la integración en ella de la participación ciudadana (ArchGAME4CITY)", & "Diseño Gamificado de visualización 3D con sistemas de realidad virtual para el estudio de la mejora de competencias motivacionales, sociales y espaciales del usuario (EduGAME4CITY)". (AEI/FEDER, UE).

References

1. Blocholm. https://arkdes.se/en/utstallning/blockholm-den-fantastiska-staden. Accessed 12 Feb 2020
2. Play de City. https://www.playthecity.nl/page/3435/play-the-city-foundation. Accessed 12 Feb 2020
3. Cooper Hewitt Org. https://www.cooperhewitt.org/2017/02/20/22454. Accessed 12 Feb 2020
4. Cho, J.Y., Suh, J.: Understanding spatial ability in interior design education: 2D-to-3D visualisation proficiency as a predictor of design performance. J. Inter. Des. (2019). https://doi.org/10.1111/joid.12143

5. János, K., Gyula, N.K.: The CAD 3D course improves students' spatial skills in the technology and design education. YBL J. Built Environ. **7**(1), 26–37 (2019)

6. Lobovikov-Katz, A.: Methodology for spatial-visual literacy (MSVL) in heritage education: application to teacher training and interdisciplinary perspectives. Revista Electronica Interuniversitaria de Formacion Del Profesorado (2019). https://doi.org/10.6018/reifop.22.1. 358671

7. Piga, B.E.A., Salerno, R.: Non-conventional representation for urban design: depicting the intangible. In: Cocchiarella, L. (ed.) ICGG 2018. AISC, vol. 809, pp. 1694–1705. Springer, Cham (2019). https://doi.org/10.1007/978-3-319-95588-9_152

8. Martín-Dorta, N., Saorín, J.L., Contero, M.: Development of a fast remedial course to improve the spatial abilities of engineering students. J. Eng. Educ. (2008). https://doi.org/10. 1002/j.2168-9830.2008.tb00996.x

9. Champion, E.M.: Otherness of place: game-based interaction and learning in virtual heritage projects place and interaction in virtual heritage projects. Int. J. Herit. Stud. (2008). https:// doi.org/10.1080/13527250801953686

10. Reffat, R.: Revitalizing architectural design studio teaching using ICT: reflections on practical implementations. Int. J. Educ. Dev. Inf. Commun. Technol. (IJEDICT) **3**(1), 39–53 (2007)

11. Sariyildiz, S., Der Veer, P.: The role of ICT as a partner in architectural design education. In: Design Studio Teaching EAAE (1998)

12. Valls, F., Redondo, E., Fonseca, D., Torres-Kompen, R., Villagrasa, S., Martí, N.: Urban data and urban design: a data mining approach to architecture education. Telemat. Inform. (2017). https://doi.org/10.1016/j.tele.2017.09.015

13. Navarro, I.: Nuevas tecnologías de visualización para la mejora de la representación arquitectónica en educación. Universidad Ramon Llull, España (2017). https://www. tesisenred.net/handle/10803/403374

14. Sanchez-Sepulveda, M.V., Marti-Audi, N., Fonseca Escudero, D.: Visual Technologies for urban design competences in architecture education. In: Proceedings of 7th International Conference on Technological Ecosystems for Enhancing Multiculturality, Leon, Spain, pp. 726–731. ACM, New York (2019). https://doi.org/10.1145/3362789.3362822

15. Gagnon, D.: Video games and spatial skills: an exploratory study. Educ. Commun. Technol. **33**(4), 263–275 (1985). https://doi.org/10.1007/BF02769363

16. Sedeno, A.: Video games as cultural devices: development of spatial skills and application in learning. Comunicar **17**(34), 183–189 (2010). https://doi.org/10.3916/C34-2010-03-018

17. Martín-Gutiérrez, J., Saorín, J.L., Contero, M., Alcaniz, M.: AR_Dehaes: an educational toolkit based on augmented reality technology for learning engineering graphics. In: 2010 10th IEEE International Conference on Advanced Learning Technologies, pp. 133–137 (2010). https://doi.org/10.1109/ICALT.2010.45

18. Stauskis, G.: Development of methods and practices of virtual reality as a tool for participatory urban planning: a case study of Vilnius City as an example for improving environmental, social and energy sustainability. Energy Sustain. Soc. (2014). https://doi.org/ 10.1186/2192-0567-4-7

19. Calvo, X., et al.: Qualitative assessment of urban virtual interactive environments for educational proposals. In: Proceedings of the Sixth International Conference on Technological Ecosystems for Enhancing Multiculturality, Salamanca, Spain, 24–26 October 2018 (2018)

20. Carmona, M., Heath, T., Tiesdell, S., Oc, T.: Urban design today. In: Public Places Urban Spaces, pp. 3–19 (2010). http://dx.doi.org/10.1016/B978-1-85617-827-3.10001-X

21. Di Bella, A.: Digital urbanism in Southern Italy. Int. J. E-Plan. Res. **1**, 73–87 (2012). https:// doi.org/10.4018/ijepr.2012100105

22. Thiel, S.K., Fröhlich, P.: Gamification as motivation to engage in location-based public participation? In: Gartner, G., Huang, H. (eds.) Progress in Location-Based Services 2016. LNGC, pp. 399–421. Springer, Cham (2017). https://doi.org/10.1007/978-3-319-47289-8_20

23. Schroeder, R.: Ralph Possible Worlds: The Social Dynamic of Virtual Reality Technology. Westview Press Inc., Boulder (1996)

24. Sanchez-Sepulveda, M.V., et al.: Collaborative design of urban spaces uses: from the citizen idea to the educational virtual development. In: Kurosu, M. (ed.) HCII 2019. LNCS, vol. 11568, pp. 253–269. Springer, Cham (2019). https://doi.org/10.1007/978-3-030-22636-7_18

25. Calvo, X., Fonseca, D., Sánchez-Sepúlveda, M., Amo, D., Llorca, J., Redondo, E.: Programming virtual interactions for gamified educational proposes of urban spaces. In: Zaphiris, P., Ioannou, A. (eds.) LCT 2018. LNCS, vol. 10925, pp. 128–140. Springer, Cham (2018). https://doi.org/10.1007/978-3-319-91152-6_10

26. Sanchez-Sepulveda, M., Torres-Kompen, R., Fonseca D., Franquesa-Sanchez, J.: Methodologies of learning served by virtual reality: a case study in urban intervention. Appl. Sci. **9**, 5161 (2019). https://doi.org/10.3390/app9235161

StickAndClick – Sticking and Composing Simple Games as a Learning Activity

Andrea Valente[1]([⊠]) [iD] and Emanuela Marchetti[2] [iD]

[1] Mærsk Mc-Kinney Møller Instituttet, Embodied Systems for Robotics
and Learning, University of Southern Denmark (SDU), Odense, Denmark
anva@mmmi.sdu.dk
[2] Media, Department for the Study of Culture, University of Southern Denmark
(SDU), Odense, Denmark
emanuela@sdu.dk

Abstract. StickAndClick is a new digital tool meant to support teachers and pupils to define simple interactive digital contents. We propose to use a minimalistic and asset-based redefinition of coding to support algorithmic thinking, focusing on the creative and design-like aspects of Computational Thinking. Here we discuss the design and implementation of 3 prototypes of Stick-AndClick, and present the results from the first of a series of tests, and address the games developed by the children, game mechanics, usability and engagement with the prototype. We observed the emergence of game design dialogue, use-modify-create thinking, both important in a tool for scaffolding Computational Thinking. Our study is placed at the intersection between Computational Thinking and multimodal literacy, as both combine problem solving with the use of digital tools and the creation of digital content with the goal of fostering critical thinking and creativity.

Keywords: Game-based learning · Game design · Learning ecosystems · Computational Thinking

1 Introduction

The creation of simple paper-based games and multimodal narratives has become a broadly accepted practice in Danish schools, enabling forms of active learning. At the same time, systems like Minecraft[1] and Powtoon[2] (a digital platform to create animated comics) have become popular, as they enable the pupils to express digitally their creativity. Moreover, these systems have been introduced in the classroom with the goal of supporting learning of Computational Thinking (CT for short) in the classroom, defined as a set of skills from computer science [19].

A typical scenario that we observed in Danish primary schools' classrooms involves the teachers assigning groups of pupils the task to create a board game, related to a topic they have studied. For example, after having read and discussed a topic from

---

[1] Official website: www.minecraft.net.

[2] Official website: www.powtoon.com.

© Springer Nature Switzerland AG 2020
P. Zaphiris and A. Ioannou (Eds.): HCII 2020, LNCS 12206, pp. 333–352, 2020.
https://doi.org/10.1007/978-3-030-50506-6_24

a textbook or novel, the pupils might be given the task to design a game based on the discussed topic, modifying the classic goose game so to require the player to answer questions about the book or its author, in order to play and win. Typically, the pupils are divided into small groups (from 3 to 5 pupils) and are given the task to design and test a variation a board game based on a topic introduced by the teacher. The games are then played by all, in turns, and feedback is given by the teachers and the other pupils. Sometimes the best games are also rewarded or given acknowledgement, but that is not the usual goal of the activity. In other cases, we observed competitions among classes, where one of the games per class is played by pupils of other classes. Again, winners might be rewarded or simply acknowledged, according to good-hearted forms of gamification.

Interestingly some of these activities have been digitized in recent years, by adopting free online tools, like *Kahoot!*,[3] which are appealing to schools because of their high usability, and because they afford easy-to-setup, class-wide networked games. However, we find the game aspects in these tools to be severely limited. Kahoot! in particular was originally only capable of supporting multiple choice questionnaires, even if recently it has been extended with more features, precisely to cope with the in-class-games we have observed [18].

Minecraft offers more possibilities to design and implement large worlds-like games, but to our knowledge it is mainly used in time-boxed workshops, often in connection to experts' visits (such as researchers or master students from universities, or professionals from IT companies). In these cases, the teachers host a workshop with their classes for the duration of a week, the experts take over the teaching and focus on demonstrating the CT potential of Minecraft. However, when the experts leave at the end of the workshop period, the teachers have issues with keeping using Minecraft in their normal teaching and revert to their usual lecture modalities.

In the past 10 years we have worked with Danish institutions, developing and testing e-learning tools [6], to expand the creative spectrum of learning practice in the classroom. Our goal has been to empower digital creativity and close the gap between tinkering in the physical world and authoring of game-like digital materials, which normally require a significant degree of programming skills. In this sense, our previous studies suggest that digital games are experienced by teachers and pupils as less creative than paper-based games, which can be easily redefined based on social agreement among teachers and pupils. Digital games on the other hand, come as black boxes, which can be played only in a particular way, decided by the developers, and cannot be customized to follow pedagogical needs nor created from scratch without advanced programming skills [6, 16]. However, during our studies [6, 15, 16] teachers have systematically expressed the desire to edit or at least customize existing digital games, and to enable their pupils to customize or design digital games, to better meet their pedagogical needs. Moreover, Danish primary schools have engaged in different

---

[3] Official website: www.kahoot.com.

initiatives to enable their pupils to learn how to program, using systems like MIT's Scratch[4], Minecraft or Google's Blockly[5], and are currently in the process of formalizing CT as a subject. But these systems were often found too complex to use in the learning of curricular subjects, therefore they remained limited to the practice of teaching pupils programming fundamentals.

Based on these insights, we have been working on re-contextualization and re-conceptualization of interactive digital contents, to make them more accessible to teachers, pupils and young students, in and outside the classroom. In this respect, we are investigating a new tool called *StickAndClick* (as documented in [14]) to support creative authoring of simple digital games, aimed at teachers and pupils, and to meet new curricular requirements, in introducing computational thinking as a subject and in connection to other curricular subjects. So far, we developed 3 different high-fidelity prototypes, our goal: to empower teachers and pupils, enabling them to create interactive content, and to expand the creative affordances offered by digital games and learning platforms.

In Sect. 2 we present related work and studies that provide the basis for the design and implementation of the new tool. The requirements and inspiration are presented in Sect. 3; our first and second prototypes are discussed in Sect. 4, and the current one in Sect. 5. Tests and discussion are in Sect. 6, and Sect. 7 concludes the paper, presenting ongoing and future work.

2   Related Work and Theoretical Foundations

In our study we are working at the intersection of CT and multimodal literacy, as we aim at:

- promoting CT as a creative thinking approach that could be applied to the analysis and representation of any field of knowledge,
- supporting forms of multimodal literacy in schools, enabling teachers and pupils to create multimodal texts, seen as interactive representations of knowledge.

In our study we approach CT as an emergent competence in a symbiotic relation to multimodal literacy, combining problem solving with the use of digital tools and the creation of digital content. We see CT and multimodal literacy as rooted into each other. In this sense, CT can be cultivated and applied in schools, to the representation of knowledge across curricular disciplines.

CT has been defined as a subset of knowledge, mindset and skills from the computer science and engineering domain [19]. CT has been proposed as a fundamental component of literacy, together with writing and counting, including skills like: problem solving, design thinking, understanding human behavior drawing on fundamental concepts from computer science that would be desirable for "everyone" and not only IT professionals [19]. However, this perspective has been criticized for being

---

[4] Official website: scratch.mit.edu.

[5] Official website: developers.google.com/blockly.

"arrogant", suggesting that everybody should aspire to learn to "think like a computer scientist", no matter what they do [13]. Moreover, so defined computational thinking appears as overlapping, including or included within soft skills or the of the 21st century, such as: digital literacy, innovation and creativity, critical thinking, communication and collaboration, and also (digital) citizenship, self-regulated learning [17].

However, we believe that CT should involve also hardcore computational skills, such as: understanding of "algorithmic thinking, navigating multiple levels of abstraction, decomposing problems into manageable pieces, and representing data through models" [3, p. 1]. Hence, CT can be seen defined as "a collection of computational ideas and habits of mind" that are acquired by learning to make "software, simulations, and computations performed by machinery" [13]. In this sense, we argue that CT should include competent use of software tools and coding, at different levels of proficiency, applied to a set of problems originated within other fields than computer science. An interesting example is represented by digital humanities, in which CT is already applied to solve problems from the domain of the humanities [7].

Considering the multitude of definitions that have emerged in recent years, the meaning of CT is going through a complex elaboration process and it is still ambiguous [13]. We find that the main issue is represented by ambition levels for hardcore computational skills, such as proficiency level in the use of software and if coding should be a requirement at all. In our view, CT is emerging as an interdisciplinary field, including also creative thinking skills from the design field and collaboration from the management field. However, if CT is deprived of specific skills related to the process of using, testing, and constructing software, as it is defined in [19], CT becomes a mix of design and management skills, with superficial relation to Computer Science. Therefore, in our view, CT should strive to include understanding of the distinction between static code and running code (i.e. program versus process), the practice of coding, and the role of testing and debugging practices. We see CT as including passive competences of coding practice, similarly to comprehension skills in language learning, where pupils should gain an understanding of how software is being planned and constructed, and how programmers can imagine the program in action by looking at its code. In this way, pupils should become expert users of technologies, aware of how software works and how programmers think, able to communicate effectively and negotiate with programmers, according to their needs.

Starting from these premises, the relation between CT and multimodal literacy appears blurred and overlapping. Multimodal literacy is in fact defined as a set of abilities in creative and design thinking, communication, and competent use of digital tools for audio-visual production in collaborative settings [5]. In this way, CT and multimodal literacy can include one another. During our previous studies, we observed Danish teachers leveraging multimodal literacy as a complex entanglement, related to the analysis and creation of multisensory texts [5]. This takes place through creative activities, such as: design of games, quizzes on Kahoot, comics or simple animations, videos, paper based boardgames, and artistic artefacts such as posters, drawings, and sculptures. These activities leverage an ecological understanding of multisensory media creation [10], entangled with learning and sense-making processes. These activities are aimed at training critical thinking skills, bridging between children's the living ecologies and their free-time interests and their learning ecology in schools [10].

Recent studies have showed that use of digital games, also commercial games found on Youtube and on the Internet, but not specifically developed for learning, can foster shared forms of critical thinking and sense-making, eliciting motivation and rich social interaction in the classroom [1]. Misfeldt and Zacho [8] have explored how the design of interactive scenarios in relation to open-ended projects in mathematics, can foster creative engagement, collaboration, and peer-learning also supporting understanding. A study on movie editing on iPad has given similar results [9]. Therefore, designing and editing multimodal texts are found beneficial for the children to foster self-expression, collaboration, and creativity, which figure among the 21st century skills. At the same time, the production of multimodal texts provide escape from the black box of commercial digital games, empowering teachers and pupils in create new playful experiences and narratives for them and their mates. Moreover, multimodal literacy deals with critical analysis of complex semiotic messages, for instance engagement with graphic novels was found beneficial in training pupils to decode information in multiple sign systems. In this way, pupils learn how a story can be crafted and conveyed for different audiences [5]. The same study also discusses how teachers encourage pupils to watch movies in the classroom to acquire information and create films on their own, to communicate to the class their personal understanding on a given topic.

This multimodal approach is enabling teachers to provide their pupils with a rich expressive repertoire, also enabling them to become able to decode contemporary media. On this perspective, O'Halloran et al. [11] have proposed MACT, a framework for multimodal analysis aimed at enabling primary school pupils to understand different mediatic genres, identifying main "features, structures, and ideas" in various texts in print and non-print sources, at making pupils able to "plan, organize, summarize and synthetize" information in an aesthetic whole [11, p. 15]. The ability of translating meaning from a school subject into a multimodal text, requires that the pupils gain a deep understanding on the subject. The production process will foster further questions, leading the pupils to iteratively analyze the subject in order to create a good text. According to Jewitt [4], creation of multimodal texts requires the pupils to familiarize with the affordances available in the different sensorial elements and to integrate them harmoniously. This in turn requires the pupils to acquire a meta-language enabling them to shift from one to another, understanding their cognitive, cultural and ideological relations [4], so to create an effective text.

In our study we aim at bridging between CT and multimodal literacy, as we find a significant overlapping between the two concepts and that they complement each other regarding creative and critical thinking, collaboration, and problem solving. At the same time, we find that there is a need to address the appropriate place for hardcore computer science skills (use of software and coding), but little investigation has been conducted on the interdisciplinary foundation of CT and how it is increasingly converging towards the fields of multimodality and digital humanities. Based on these premises, our study explores the connections between Ct and multimodality, through the design of StickAndClick, which we see as a multimodal editing tool, targeted the creation of multimodal texts in the classroom, specifically in the form or point and click games. StickAndClick has to be understood also as a mediational mean [Latour], bridging between CT and multimodal literacy as well as CT and curricular subjects.

Moreover, the rules for editing games are aimed at concretizing a meta-language, in the terms of Jewitt [4], enabling the pupils and their teachers to reflect on how visuals, sound, game mechanics, and envisioned interactions can be harmoniously integrated to create a multimodal text (the game) on a given subject, yet at the same time incorporating key skills in CT.

3 Inspiration and Requirements

The initial idea came from the results of the tests conducted with paper materials and digital games [6] and Fables [7]. In both studies we used web-based prototype tools to let the pupils enact our scenarios, moreover, in previous work we used a set of static HTML pages with hyperlinks and images to reason about non-linear narrative as a designerly way to engage with web programming in higher education [6]. In both cases the pupils were able to author their own materials into digital, non-linear, and visual novels as a resource for learning other subjects.

From the point of view of game design, planning a visual non-linear story is often done via sticky notes and tangible materials, a set of activities that is very close to the typical creative tinkering we observed many times in Danish primary schools. However, the final goal of digital game designers is to create a digital game, while pupils and teachers usually would stop at table-top or pen-and-paper games.

The scenarios of use we define for our authoring tool are: one in which the teacher uses StickAndClick to design, implement and deploy a digital game to be used by her pupils in an augmented class situation or at home, according to flipped classroom teaching. In the second scenario the teacher assigns groups of pupils the task of designing and implementing a digital game about a topic that she covered in class. The pupils will be able to create, deploy and playtest their game with other groups, supporting possible peer-learning. In our attempts to find a metaphor that could help us explain our experiments to primary school practitioners and their pupils, we looked at *action transfers* and *sticker albums*, which despite being toys, can be easily re-appropriated as props and materials to be used in game design.

Based on our scenarios and results from previous studies, we define the requirements for our visual, digital game authoring tool:

- minimalistic computational model (i.e. hopefully easy to understand)
  - based on a variation on hyperlinks
  - no math (or minimal mathematical skills required), which in turn implies no (explicit) coordinates
- no universal programming language, so:
  - instead of imperative instructions, just simple before/after rules
  - limited interaction, which restricts us to simple *point and click* game development, or non-linear visual novels
- asset-first, to ground the meaning of programming in multimedia:
  - the tool should allow pupils and teachers to author only simple digital games, but they can use self-generated, custom images and audio
- focus on the software engineering/design-cycle parts of CT

- visual and possibly for web and/or android; our too should export towards many (and more sophisticated) game development environments

Based on our previous, we decided to base StickAndClick on a tangible metaphor of transferable stickers and the interaction that these can afford, such as pasting stickers on a background picture. These stickers are user-created and can be used to construct narrative and support playful interaction. The games afforded by the system are turn-based and the computer cannot initiate actions, and the only game mechanic allowed is clicking on a sticker. StickAndClick is based on simple conditional rules, according to which pupils can define what happens when a sticker is clicked and also on the state of the stickers (to be specified in the actual prototypes) in the page (i.e. the current room in which the player finds herself in). A central idea in the design of StickAndClick is to look at existing game development environments (such as Scratch or Construct3[6]) and reduce their computational models to a single mechanism, as simple as possible, that we could use as a formal model for digital and interactive artefacts. In this sense, we are searching of a sub-universal meta-language [4] for point and click games, that could be simpler than in existing tools, yet affording the creation of game-like multimodal texts (a similar point of view can be found in the PuzzleScript[7] project). So far, we have developed three different prototypes with different characteristics, in order to explore how we could reach a minimal meta-language, in which children could set the rules for their games, harmoniously integrating multimodal resources. In the following sections we describe all 3 prototypes: the first 2 in Sect. 4, and the latest in Sect. 5. For each we provide insights on our design process as a hands-on continuous exploration of the technological affordances offered by different platforms and programming languages adopted in each prototype.

4   First and Second Prototypes

4.1   First Prototype – A Javascript Library

In our first experiment, conducted in 2018, we implemented StickAndClick as a JavaScript library, so we could start creating simple games. Each game consisted of a collection of rooms, each realized as a separate HTML page, with images representing items in the game. The main interaction mechanism was provided by images with HMLT anchors. We used simple CSS tricks so that all the pages were visualized in full-screen and responsive, allowing us to deploy on mobile devices from the start. Minimal persistence-like support was added, so that the state of every image in the page could be stored and retrieved from LocalStorage, effectively allowing a player to stop and resume playing. Since we were targeting mobile devices, such as tablets which are commonly used in Danish primary schools, we realized that our idea could easily express non-linear digital games in the style of point-and-click games.

---

[6] Official website: editor.construct.net.

[7] Official website: www.puzzlescript.net.

In our scenario, the author of the game would define one of such games by doing the following:

- define a layout for each page, i.e. rectangular regions that we call markers,
- decide which images (i.e. stickers) from a palette of self-created ones, will initially occupy which markers,
- then define rules for the game, so that when the player clicks on an image, 1 of 2 things could happen:
  - the game changes page (i.e. move the player to another room),
  - or the clicked image changes to another

Since this scenario could be summarized as "the game designer places stickers on pages and then the player clicks on them", we named this system *StickAndClick*. The first set of experiments we performed with StickAndClick consisted in the creation of short **point and click** games, using our JavaScript library. We mainly performed functional tests and explored the expressivity of our computational model. One of the earliest games created is shown in Fig. 1. We purposefully kept the low-fidelity quality of the images, to emphasize that pupils will develop games from hand-drawn paper prototypes. In this "escape the room"-type game the player finds herself in a room with a closed cabinet and a locked door. Clicking on the cabinet opens a drawer and reveals a key; when the key is clicked, it disappears and appears to have moved to the status bar (top-left corner of the first room in Fig. 1). Clicking on the door initially has no effect, but when the key is in the status bar, then clicking on the door opens it (using the key, that disappears definitively from the game). The door, now open, can be clicked to go to a second room.

The most difficult part of the design of StickAndClick was to find a good yet simple way to express the rules avoiding the typical difficulties of coding; therefore, we attempted at describing this entire game with just 2 types of rules:

- RULE 1: cabinet-closed => cabinet-open-with-key
- RULE 2: cabinet-open-with-key, status-bar =>cabinet-open-empty, status-bar-key
- RULE 3: cabinet-open-empty => cabinet-closed-empty
- RULE 4: cabinet-closed-empty => cabinet-open-empty
- RULE 5: door-locked, status-bar-key => door_unlocked, status-bar
- RULE 6: door_unlocked JUMP_TO page2

Rule 1 is very simple, it specifies that when the image "cabinet-closed" is clicked, it changes to "cabinet-open-with-key" (all these images, or stickers, are visible on the right of Fig. 1). Rules 3 and 4 are the inverse of each other and allow the player to keep clicking on the cabinet repeatedly, opening and closing its drawer, resulting in a 2-frame animation. Rule 2 is a bit more complex, because it is contextual: it states that when "cabinet-open-with-key" is clicked AND the "status-bar" image appears any-where in the current page, then the first image changes to "cabinet-open-empty" and the second changes to "status-bar-key", at the same time. If both conditions are not met, the rule cannot execute. This purely textual way of expressing before/after rules is inspired by Join patterns [2], and it fits our requirement about avoiding explicit coordinates: to specify which images are involved in a rule, we can simple use its the name. Placement of images on the HTML page still depends on coordinates and sizes, but it can now be

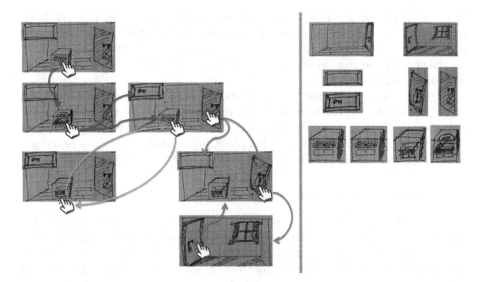

Fig. 1. On the left: the gameplay of the first game. On the right: the manually drawn stickers used in the game; from the top - 2 rooms, an item bar (empty and with a key), the door (opened and closed), and the 4 states of the cabinet (2 closed images, open but empty, and open with key inside).

relegated to the definition of a *page layout*, made of *markers*; furthermore, it is easy to imagine how markers can be defined visually in more advanced prototypes of StickAndClick.

The last rule, Rule 6, is of a different kind: it does not transform one or more images, but instead it makes the game jump to another room (i.e. page). Later in the design we decided to merge these 2 kinds of rules in a single rewrite-and-jump type of rule, where the jumping part is optional: in this way the whole gameplay can be described with just 1 type of rule.

A special situation might arise when the game author wants to make a sticker disappear: this is possible by (for example) changing an image of a dog with a placeholder. In StickAndClick a placeholder is name (in this example it could be "empty-dog") that does correspond to any image. When the dog image changes into the "empty-dog" placeholder, it looks to the player like the dog disappeared since all placeholders are invisible. Moreover, we decided that a placeholder cannot be the target of a click, so no rule can directly change it back into another image. However, it is possible to write rules that change multiple images, including placeholders.

4.2 Second Prototype – A Node.js Generator

After having worked for a few months with this first implementation, we wrote a *generator* in Node.js, capable of taking a JSON specification file and a folder of images, and create an entire website of static webpages, implementing the game described in the JSON file. This file contains a serialization of the rules of a

StickAndClick game, grouped by page; the generator creates one HML page per game-page, and 1 initial page for the game, with a description of the game. When the game is reset, the player finds herself again at the initial page. Parts of the library developed for the first prototype are used by this generator that adds them to the game folder, together with images and HTML pages.

We developed the generator iteratively, and the final iteration was able to create a single-page application (SPA for short) for each game, with the advantage that the player would always resume from the correct place in the game. With the generator we wanted to address two limitations of StickAndClick: global images, and better persistence; we also wanted to explore the expressivity of StickAndClick's rules.

4.3   Exploring Expressivity via Game Creation

We decided to expand the scope and expressivity of StickAndClick by creating few games, each pushing the envelope of what the tool could express, and each game exploring more complex game mechanics. During these iterations, we relied also on feedback from a minimalistic, convenience focus group (a boy and a girl, age 13 and 14 respectively) who were periodically available to performing functional testing and evaluation with us. The games we created were: the "simple game", the "lives" game, the "backpack" game, the "Flip a coin" and the "LCD" game.

The "simple game" has 2 rooms, and its goal is to escape by finding objects and unlocking the door. We used it to test:

- how to work with more than a single room,
- that the state of the game is correctly saved, and the game can be resumed by a single "initial" HTML page, after closing the game at any stage the player desires,
- the navigation between the 2 rooms,
- that rules can express the need for the player to have collected a few items hidden in a room, in any order she wants, in order to unlock the door that leads to the other room,
- that multiple items are place in the first room of the game (e.g. a large carpet and a sofa) in 2.5D, i.e. the order in which places are defined in each room, also defines the z-order of the images. The background images are therefore simply the first images to be added to a room definition.

The "lives" game also has simple rules: the player can click on her lives, represented by the 2 hearts (see Fig. 2), and decide how many should be enabled. The door from the first room to the second works each time it is clicked, but the door in the second room, to come back to the first, only works when the player has exactly 2 hearts. When the player moves from a room to the other, the amount of hearts stays the same: i.e. the hearts are a global value, persistent across rooms. The purpose of this game was to test how to use the StickAndClick rules to express global values. To allow for global values we used a HUD (or global transparent page) that is always drawn "above" the current page. The HUD has its own places that can be transparent or contain stickers, and its own rules. Moreover, the rules of every page can also involve stickers in the HUD; in this

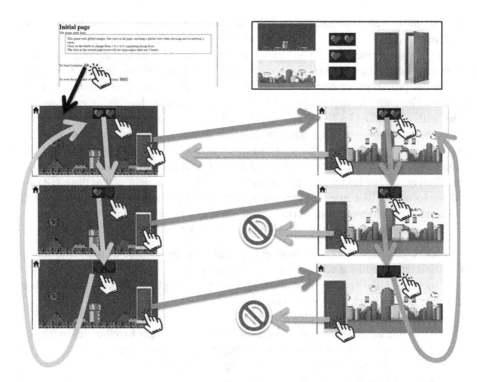

Fig. 2. The gameplay of the "lives" game. The stickers used in this game are visible on the top-right corner.

case the image of the 2 hearts is in the HUD, and not in the 2 pages of the game. The rule that decides whether the door in the second room should open or not looks like this:

- doorClosed, 2lives => doorOpen, 2lives

which reads as "if the **doorClosed** image is clicked, and there is another image anywhere in the page, called **2lives**, then change **doorClosed** into **doorOpen**, and change **2lives** in **2lives**", i.e. the door opens and the 2 lives stay as they were.

The next was the "backpack" game. In this game the player stands in a room with shelves and can zoom in 2 of the shelves. The player also has a "backpack" area on the screen, inspired by head-up display (HUD) and backpacks in RPG games. The player can explore zooming in and out of the 2 shelves, and when "inside" each of the shelves she can decide to leave or pick-up items from her backpack. The goal with this game was to test navigation inside realistic-looking settings (in fact all images in this game are actual photos of shelves and objects) and how the rules can be used to express the workings of a "global" backpack, that moves with the player across multiple rooms.

So far, all rules in StickAndClick are deterministic, which means that it is impossible to express random behavior in games created with our tools. Therefore, we created the game "flip a coin", to clarify how to implement random-choice rules: in this game the player tosses a coin and a random result is displayed. We expect that pupils will be introduced to deterministic rules first, and when they can master them, to random rules.

Finally, we created the "LCD" game, to see if StickAndClick could express much more than just point-and-click game mechanics. The game (shown in Fig. 3) is based on a paper prototype we created and digitalized, and its gameplay is inspired by LCD games[8]. The game is single-page and has 2 possible endings: for this we extended the rules with a "win" and a "lose" command, so that when the player loses (or wins), the game shows a pop-up message and automatically resets. The apparent movement of the player's avatar (the warrior character in Fig. 3) is realized by using placeholders. The game defines markers for the warrior in 5 locations: at the far left of the page, by the on/off lever, on the bridge, under the bridge, and at the far right of the page (i.e. the victory location). The rules are defined in such a way that at any given moment, 4 of these markers are empty and 1 contains the image of the warrior.

To summarize, at this stage of development StickAndClick offers:

- a single-page application, with reset capability and persistence of the game state;
- definition of multiple rooms and custom graphics;
- a special HUD-like page that allows games to have global stickers, useful when implementing backpacks and lives;
- a unified way to express rules for:
    - changing an image (when clicking on it), or many images together depending on the dynamic state of (some of the) images in the same page,
    - jumping to another page (when clicking on an image)
    - choosing randomly among different outcomes
- "invisible" placeholders to be used in place of stickers, to make them disappear

StickAndClick however, does not have audio capabilities nor can express animations, such as an image shaking or rotating. We have received feedback about those issues during our testing with the 2 participants to the focus group. Audio and animations will be added in the P5 prototype, Sect. 5, together with a visual editor for StickAndClick.

5   Current Web-Based Prototype in P5

We considered implementing StickAndClick in various platforms; we made spikes in Processing, Java (using Android Studio), and Python 3 (attempting to take advantage of the Pygame Zero library). However, an important feature of our new tool is that it should be the ability to run online and on mobile devices, so finally we opted for P5[9], a JavaScript implementation of Processing.

The new web-based prototype of StickAndClick is composed of 2 web-apps: an editor and a player. Figure 4 shows an early design of the proposed GUI for editor: this design is mobile-first, so most operations are based on drag-and-drop or tap-like single

---

[8] More information at: archive.org/details/handheldhistory.

[9] Documented at p5js.org.

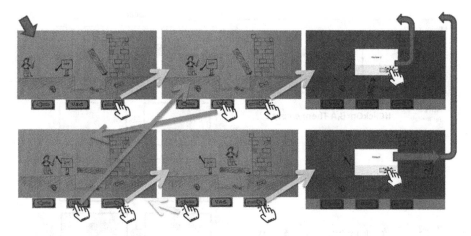

Fig. 3. The LCD-inspired game. The controls appear to the player as functioning buttons, but they are based on the same rules as in all other StickAndClick games. Notice the win and lose pop-ups (on the right side).

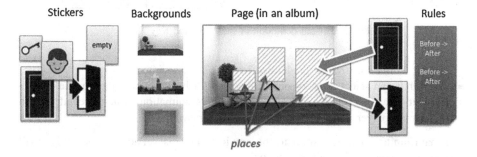

Fig. 4. Early design of the GUI for the new StickAndClick web-editor.

clicks. The actual GUI of the web-editor is visible in Fig. 5, where the game "Boy and Key" is defined visually.

We designed the workflow of a pupil creating a game with the StickAndClick web-editor as follows: first the pupil uploads her custom images to the web editor, then layout and rules are defined, and the game description can be saved. Only games with 1 page can be defined for now, and therefore we did not implement the global HUD-like backpack; rules are defined in a visual before/after fashion, without the use of block-based code. Saving a game generates 2 files: a JSON file with the description of the game, and an image file containing a vertical list of all stickers used in the game (the atlas file). The web-player can then be used to open the game files and play. The save/load capability allows pupils to exchange their games or play games generated by their teachers. Other features are:

- game author can create a game using her custom stickers images,
- only deterministic rules are implemented,

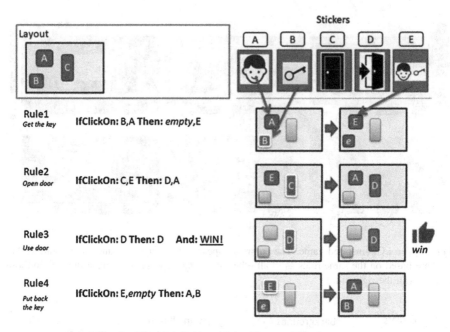

Fig. 5. Visual definition of the "Boy and Key" game.

- a short animation (from a predefined list) can be associated to a rule,
- the author can select a background image and/or background sound in the editor,
- the web-player execution the rules and triggers animations when needed; it also signals the player when she wins or loses the game.

The main limitation with respect to the previous, node.js versions is that only small images (less than 20 kb each) can be uploaded.

6 Tests and Discussion

The latest of our 3 prototypes was tested in spring 2020, with a group of children, from a class of 8 to 12 years old: the test was part of Teknologiskolen (translated as "technology school", TS for short), an afternoon activity organized by SDU to promote digital literacy and skills in the area of CT. Our test aimed at evaluating how the children related to our approach to game design and if they could make sense of the tool. We wanted to verify if primary school children could understand the computational model behind StickAndClick (i.e. a simple extension of the hyperlink). At the same time, we wanted to gather data on the usability of our P5 prototype, in order to improve its features. Finally, we wanted to analyze which kind of games the children would develop, which game mechanics and narratives they preferred and how to better support their engagement with our prototype.

Methodologically the test was based on ethnography [12]: we observed the children while engaging with our system, as we took notes. Since we did not have the permission to film the children, we recorded only their voices, took notes and sketches of their actions. In this way, we could collect data and documentation material for our test without violating their privacy. The test was conducted in a semi-structured fashion, as we gave the children loose tasks in trying out the game examples and in creating their own games.

Preliminary results show that StickAndClick can be understood and used productively by our intended target audience, and that testers attempted to create games beyond the point and click genre. We observed emergence of game design dialogue in the group and use-modify-create thinking, both of which match the intent of our tool; we believe that these elements are important in a tool for scaffolding Computational Thinking. This was only the first of a series of tests we have planned for the TS classes and in local, Danish primary schools; we intend to promptly start a new iteration of development, bringing improvements to the current version of the prototype, based on the gathered data.

6.1 Test Procedure and Results

Our test lasted for about 1 h and involved a group of 6 boys around 12 years old. The test was articulated in approximately three stages, such as:

1. introduction to the interface,
2. free play with one or more of the example games,
3. creation of new games,

During the first step, introduction, the boys were introduced to the interface and basic functionalities of StickAndClick (Fig. 6). We showed StickAndClick projecting from our computer to a big screen on the wall, we ran through the system, describing and demonstrating its functionalities, such as: Player, Game Examples, the Editor and the Assets. The Game Examples included a set of 5 pre-made mini games of different genres and using various visual assets. The first is called "Boy and Key" (a variation of the game defined in Fig. 5) and it is an "escape the room" game showing a closed room with a door and a boy-looking character, who has to find a key in order to open the door and leave the room. The second game is "CastleGame" (a version of the "LCD-inspired game" described in Sect. 4.3), a fantasy platform game in which a character has to discover how to open the drawbridge to enter the castle. The third is called "Mix", a digital toy inspired by dress up games, in which the players have to mix and match heads, torsos and legs of three different robots and/or aliens. The fourth game, called "Animals", is intended as an interactive book about animals, in which a player can learn about the voices of different animals; the *voices* are not actual audio files, but rather images of text bubbles.

The last game is called "Combination" and it requires the players to answer a question to find the combination of a digital lock, and win. All the games are available online[10] and the children could simply access them on their laptops through the URL we gave to them. During the first stage, we also demonstrated how to play the games

---

[10] At StickAndClick's website: http://andval.net/stick_n_click/game_examples.html.

Fig. 6. Introduction of the functionalities of StickAndClick to the children.

and how to edit new games, introducing stickers and setting up rules, as well as how to handle the 2 downloadable files containing the rules and the graphic assets. This part was rather short, about 5 min, as the boys were eager to start engaging with the system on their own.

Moving towards the second stage, we encouraged the boys to start playing on their own. The boys chose among the games based on their own taste: most boys started with the "Boy and Key" game, which one of the boys recognized as an "escape the room game". A couple of boys played mostly with "CastleGame", another boy tried them all but then used his remaining time playing with "Mix", while the other boys spent their time trying all the games. The length of this stage varied according to the children's needs, as soon as they were satisfied with playing around with the games, they shifted into editing the games. Generally, our data shows that the boys did not have any issues with the player's interface, they did not ask for help and that stage ran smoothly. As expected, challenges emerged during the third stage, in which the boys were supposed to create their own games.

During our observations we noticed that the visual assets we provided affected significantly the creativity of the boys, suggesting specific game genres and game mechanics. All the boys started playing with the room background that we employed in the "Boy and Key" game, which shows the inside of an empty room (the background in Fig. 7, on the left). It seemed that they used that background to play around with basic interactions, as a *safe room* to experiment with the basic functionalities of the editor and game mechanics, using only a few of the provided assets. Interestingly, one boy created a platformer game, in which a character had to open a box to find a key; after the key was found it appeared on the top of the open box (Fig. 7 on the right). So instead of an "escape the room" game he ended up creating a third person version of the Jack in the Box toy, in which a character finds a surprise object popping out of an initially closed box.

Afterwards the boys played with the platformer background we employed in the "CastleGame" and the urban background of the "Animals" digital book. One of the boys, made a different version of the "Animals" game: he went searching for images of other animals online and then he had fun mixing them with the wrong sounds. Another boy used the background from "CastleGame", the game he played the most during the second stage. He created an articulated version of an "escape the room" game with many rules, in which a character started near a door, on one side of the screen, and had to go all the way across to collect a key, come back to open a door. This game was structured as a typical bonus level that can be found in platform games, in which a player has the opportunity to collect different bonuses, like coins or lives, without fighting enemies, and once the bonuses have been collected the player can go back to the regular levels.

The children were generally concentrated on engaging with the system and seemed to have understood well the basic functionalities and affordances offered by Stick-AndClick, however, they also encountered a series of difficulties. We need to consider that since the test was conducted in the late afternoon (around 6 to 7 pm), towards the end of the test the boys started to get tired. Hence, a few of them, especially two boys sitting in the back got distracted, one continued to play with StickAndClick while chatting and looking at his mate screen, who instead shifted from testing out our system to watching videos on the Internet, at time playing loud music to be noticed by the others. However, we were able to carry out the test and we got inspiration to improve the interface.

We expected that the children were going to be confused about downloading and uploading the 2 files to edit their games, but in fact they managed that part quite well, without any issues. On the other hand, one of the boys in the back criticized the system for being "too easy". He said this smiling with self-confidence, meaning that it was too easy for him since he said: "I have already tried Python!". He also suggested inserting a dropdown menu for selecting the musical backgrounds, as the one the prototype already has for the background images. Four boys had issues with understanding how to model the sequence of steps in editing the rules for the game, not being sure how much could happen in the same rule. But in general, through trial-and-error experiments they could figure it out; however, we could reflect on how to simplify the process of editing rules or provide an embedded tutorial/guideline.

We noticed that the boys had issues with handling the various kinds of buttons found in the StickAndClick interface. We have a "plus" button on the top left area to add a sticker to the layout panel, and another "plus" button in the bottom area (the palette panel, containing all stickers for the current game), which allows the game author to add new stickers to the stickers' palette. Each sticker in the stickers' palette also has a button, to edit that sticker, i.e. to upload a different image for all copies of that sticker in the current game. Finally, double-clicking on any sticker in the layout (or

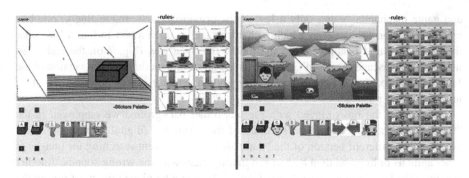

Fig. 7. Two games created by the children during the test. On the left the "Jack in the Box" game. On the right the platformer game, with its many rules.

selecting a sticker and clicking the "edit" button of the layout panel) opens a popup and lets the game author change the size of the selected sticker. We could see that this workflow is quite complex and the boys seemed confused about the different roles of the "plus" buttons, since these buttons look the same but are placed in different areas, therefore, the children expected correctly that these buttons had a different function but were unsure how to relate to them. Hence, we observed them clicking back and forth on those buttons to understand their function. We should re-conceptualize this workflow in future versions, where we think that we should develop a drag and drop system, so that after stickers have been uploaded in the bottom palette, they should be simply dragged to the layout panel.

In conclusion, we found that the workflow in the system provided a meaningful meta-language for engaging in editing multimodal game-like texts, as in [4], however, it needs further simplification; however, the system was fairly easy to learn and understand. Moreover, we found interesting how the provided backgrounds, actively inspired possible game genres and game mechanics, fostering creative thinking. In this respect, in a future test we might add more visual assets, such as backgrounds, characters, enemies and objects, photographed and drawn, to analyze how different visuals can be interpreted as affordances, inspiring specific game concepts and interactions, ultimately contribute to children acquisition of the meta-language needed to effectively engage in the creation of multimodal texts.

7   Conclusion and Future Work

In this paper we have addressed the central challenge of simplifying the practice and logic behind programming simple point-and-click games, to be accessible to teachers and pupils, without previous programming knowledge. Even if StickAndClick is not meant to become a universal programming language, and it not intended to be used in the creation of games outside the point-and-click genre, we have shown how to support multiple rooms, implement global values, and extend the rules to non-determinism.

Our early test data shows that the children did not have problems with the prototype's interface and the save/load mechanism; they also quickly grasped the idea of our simple click-inspired game mechanic and the stickers' model behind it. However, the workflow for adding and editing stickers in the games requires simplification.

Finally, further experiments are planned involving Teknologiskolen and classes of primary school pupils.

References

1. Fenyvesi, K.: English learning motivation of young learners in danish primary schools. Lang. Teach. Res. Sage J. (2018). https://doi.org/10.1177/1362168818804835
2. Fournet, C., Gonthier, G.: The reflexive CHAM and the join-calculus. In: Proceedings of the 23rd ACM SIGPLAN-SIGACT Symposium on Principles of Programming Languages, pp. 372–385 (1996)
3. Jacob, S.R., Warschauer, M.: Computational thinking and literacy. J. Comput. Sci. Integr. **1**(1) (2018). https://inspire.redlands.edu/jcsi/vol1/iss1/1/
4. Jewitt, C.: Multimodality and literacy in school classrooms. Rev. Res. Educ. **32**(1), 241–267 (2008)
5. Lenters, K.: Multimodal becoming: literacy in and beyond the classroom. Read. Teach. **71**(6), 643–649 (2018)
6. Marchetti, E., Valente, A.: Learning via game design: from digital to card games and back again. Electron. J. e-Learn. **13**(3), 167–180 (2015)
7. Marchetti, E.: Bildung and the digital revolution. In: Remenyi, D., Grant, K.A., Singh, S. (Eds.), The University of the Future Academic Conferences and Publishing International (2019)
8. Misfeldt, M., Zacho, L.: Supporting primary-level mathematics teachers' collaboration in designing and using technology-based scenarios. J. Math. Teach. Educ. **19**(2–3), 227–241 (2016)
9. Møller, T.E.: Collaborative learning through film production on iPad: touch creates conflicts. In: The Digital Literacy and Multimodal Practices of Young Children: Engaging with Emergent Research, Proceedings of the First Training School of COST Action IS 1410, pp. 127–134, University of Minho, Braga, Portugal (2016)
10. Nardi, B.A., O'Day, V.: Information Ecologies: Using Technology With Heart. MIT Press, Cambridge (1999)
11. O'Halloran, K.L., Tan, S., E, M.K.: Multimodal analysis for critical thinking. Learn. Media Technol. **42**(2), 147–170 (2017)
12. Pink, S.: Doing Visual Ethnography. Sage, California (2013)
13. Tedre, M., Denning, P.J.: The long quest for computational thinking. In: Proceedings of the 16th Koli Calling Conference on Computing Education Research, Koli, Finland, pp. 120–129 (2016)
14. Valente, A., Marchetti, E.: The road towards friendly, classroom-centered interactive digital contents authoring. In: 27th International Conference on Computers in Education. Asia-Pacific Society for Computers in Education, pp. 38–46 (2019)
15. Valente, A., Marchetti, E.: Kill it or grow it: computer game design for playful math-learning. In: 2012 IEEE Fourth International Conference on Digital Game and Intelligent Toy Enhanced Learning, pp. 17–24. IEEE (2012)

16. Valente, A., Marchetti, E.: Fables for teachers and pupils. In: Zaphiris, P., Ioannou, A. (eds.) HCII 2019. LNCS, vol. 11590, pp. 206–224. Springer, Cham (2019). https://doi.org/10.1007/978-3-030-21814-0_16
17. Van de Oudeweetering, K., Voogt, J.: Teachers' conceptualization and enactment of twenty-first century competences: exploring dimensions for new curricula. Curriculum J. **29**(1), 116–133 (2018)
18. Wang, A.I.: Jumble vs. quiz - evaluation of two different types of games in kahoot! In: Proceedings of the 13th European Conference on Games Based Learning, Academic Conferences International, Odense, Denmark (2019)
19. Wing, J.M.: Computational thinking. Commun. ACM **49**(3), 33–35 (2006)

Facilitating Ideation and Knowledge Sharing in Workplaces: The Design and Use of Gamification in Virtual Platforms

Olga Viberg[1(✉)], Mohammad Khalil[2(✉)],
and Alexandros Lioliopoulos[1(✉)]

[1] The Royal Institute of Technology (KTH), Stockholm, Sweden
oviberg@kth.se, alexislioliopoulos@gmail.com
[2] Centre for the Science of Learning & Technology (SLATE),
University of Bergen, Bergen, Norway
mohammad.khalil@uib.no

Abstract. Large organizations often constrain their innovation quests only inside the silos of dedicated departments. However, in the rapidly changing world, innovation processes need to be opened to wider circles suggesting involving virtual environments in workplaces that trigger employees' to be highly engaged. This empirical study investigates the facilitation of knowledge sharing in large organizations and the effect of gamification elements on the perceived level of engagement of users. The case study takes place in one of the largest banks in the Scandinavian countries, Nordea bank. The case study involves an innovation platform (i.e., a virtual place where the employees can share their ideas) within two variations: a conventional and a gamified one. Despite the contradiction between the results from the quantitative approach and the qualitative one, the outcome of this study suggests that in large organizations, there is a potential of opening up the innovation processes and make employees more engaged.

Keywords: Open-innovation · Gamification · Large organization · Innovation · Ideation · Design-thinking · Prototyping · Workplace learning

1 Introduction

Innovation is the process of translating a new idea or invention into a good or service that creates value for a customer. In order to be considered innovation, an idea needs to be replicable at an economic cost and must serve a specific need [26].

The importance of innovation is at the forefront of every organization's strategy more than ever before [15]. Contrary to what most people have in mind, innovation does not just consist of new, interesting ideas, rather than it is about new ideas with a potential market impact [9]. In order to maintain and improve their position in the fiercely competitive market landscape, many companies are interested in finding effective ways to achieve innovation. But, how is innovation achieved? The conventional way of pursuing innovation - that has been in use for many years and is still used mostly in large non-flexible companies – is by appointing all the innovative processes

© Springer Nature Switzerland AG 2020
P. Zaphiris and A. Ioannou (Eds.): HCII 2020, LNCS 12206, pp. 353–369, 2020.
https://doi.org/10.1007/978-3-030-50506-6_25

to a dedicated division in an organization, i.e., an innovation and experimentation department [12]. The employees of this department are often in charge of ideating, examining and orchestrating the implementation of novel ideas. Such an approach is called 'closed innovation', with its main benefits being that all the knowledge remains inside the organization's silos, maintaining all the competitive advantages of the innovation produced inside the firm [10]. On the other hand, an expanding volume of research has been performed around the so-called 'open innovation', i.e., opening the doors of an organization to outside knowledge and collaboration [13]. An example of such an approach is "Lego Ideas[1]", a website where people can post their innovative Lego ideas and when one reaches 10 k supporters, it is being considered for production. It has been observed that such an approach can provide better results, both in development speed but also concerning the quality of the output, compared to the individual results that each collaborator would have achieved in a closed innovation environment [5].

A very important step in the innovation process is ideation, i.e., the generation of multiple ideas around a field of interest [2]. These ideas are then examined and filtered, until a small number of them that are suitable for implementation are left. Similar to innovation, ideation can also be performed in a closed environment or in an open one.

An important issue that arises when discussing open innovation and/or ideation is how to motivate people to continuously and actively take part in those processes, i.e., share their ideas, give feedback to others and potentially collaborate with different stakeholders. A technique that can facilitate people's motivation and that has recently gathered a lot of attention as well as being applied to a wide range of modern-day products is gamification.

Gamification is the application of game-design elements and principles in non-game contexts [11]. It is used to increase users' engagement with a product or service, as well as make the overall experience fun and addictive [23].

The study at hand examines the effect of gamification in the context of open innovation. To increase our understanding of how we can facilitate employees' engagement in the innovation sharing process in large organizations, an innovation platform including elements of gamification was designed and evaluated. The study tries to measure the effect of gamification on the employees' (or users') perceived engagement. The research question: *Can the use of gamification elements increase users' engagement in an innovation process in a large organization?* The initial hypothesis is that gamification can in fact enhance the perceived engagement.

2   Theory and Related Research

2.1   Innovation Strategy

Restricting the innovation quest around only a limited number of people, even if these people are skilled or talented, cannot be as effective as opening the innovation processes to a wider pool, either that being the general public or just a specific group of

---

[1] https://ideas.lego.com/ (last accessed: 30.01.2020).

people [20]. Following such an approach, an organization can collect a vast amount of ideas, with a secondary benefit being that the value of the best idea generally increases with the variability of the ideas received [5].

However, the larger an organization is, the more difficult it is to open its innovation processes to the public [3]. Employee-Driven Innovation (EDI) [19] is a way to go from a closed innovation model to an open one, by first exploiting the innovation capabilities of a company's own employees, bringing benefits both by boosting the innovation as well as making the working time more interesting for the employees. This can work as a "playground to test novel ways of organizing work by applying open innovation principles to a limited group of people, facilitating the change of work routines and mental models towards open and collaborative modes" [3, p. 17]. In fact, involving all employees of the organization in the innovation process does not only prepare the ground for a future shift to open innovation practices, but it also helps the organization achieve better results. Earlier research has shown that "outperforming organizations are 17% more likely to actively encourage innovation by employees through specific incentives and rewards than underperformers. They are also 31% more likely to engage employees directly in innovation" [2, p. 14]. Moreover, Cotterill [14] claims the value of including all employees in the innovation process may lie not just in helping it to save money, but in encouraging personnel to collaborate with each other, having multiple implications that go well beyond innovation; future employees will choose jobs that challenge them and exploit their capabilities and full potential, allowing them to contribute on multiple levels and develop.

Such an intermediate approach can, to some extent, combine the benefits of both the closed and open innovation approach, in the sense that the number of ideas received will still be great, without the risk of receiving ideas that are far away from the company's strategic direction or interest.

Ideation is not the only benefit that a company can get through opening up its processes. Knowledge sharing is of equal importance to ideation, as it "has a significant effect on employees' innovation capability" [4, p. 107].

This research study focuses on the early critical stage of innovation processes that starts with ideation, including user research and deeper insights, idea generation, selection and final decision [6].

2.2 Motivation

Creating the conditions for internal organization innovation is not enough though. The biggest challenge – that is the main touchpoint of this research project - is how to motivate employees to participate in the innovation process, i.e., to publish their ideas as well as to exchange relevant knowledge and to collaborate with each other. Considering that employees usually have time pressuring work to be done in their day-to-day activities, along with the fact that time and energy is needed to reflect on new ideas, it is clear that relying on the employees' goodwill would not be the best practice [3]. A lot of effort should be directed towards finding ways to make them interested and engaged in the aforementioned process.

Early stage innovation is more unpredictable and unstructured than the consequent product development, and is characterized by informal relationships between stakeholders, complexity and uncertainty [7]. Hence, attempting to effectively structure it requires unconventional methods. A concept that has gained a lot of popularity lately and attempts to solve such problems is gamification.

Gamification aims to increase participation by enhancing engagement, providing an intriguing experience with the purpose of achieving some set goals [21]. Showing the user how s/he ranks compared to other users in a specific task is an example of a positive psychology practice, whereas making an option available for a limited amount of time is considered to be a negative psychology practice [8]. Using elements of the gamification theory in the context of open internal innovation is expected to increase the employee's engagement and motivate them to collaborate, share knowledge and come up with innovative ideas that will benefit the company.

Earlier research around gamification highlights that gamification elements have positive effects on the intended outcomes [see Sect. 4.4]. However, only a small subset of those studies have found a positive effect on all intended outcomes [1]. Those results stress the importance of "context specificity of the motivational affordances of gamification" [1, p. 837].

Research around gamification in the context of internal ideation in large organizations, although scarce, has produced some interesting insights. According to Zimmerling [1], the main drive behind employees willingness to participate in the ideation process, either by sharing their ideas or by exchanging knowledge, is the collection of points for each action, followed by the possibility to influence the evaluation of an idea as well as some virtual prizes in the form of badges etc.

2.3 User Engagement

User engagement in this study refers to the quality of user experience that captivates the user and makes the whole experience feel of importance and interest. According to Simon, engagement is defined as "the emotional, cognitive and behavioural connection that exists, at any point in time and possibly over time, between a user and a resource" [16, p. 2]. In this study, Simon et al.'s [16] framework to study and measure user engagement is adapted.

In line with this framework, user engagement can be measured applying both subjective and objective metrics. Subjective metrics include a user's own perception of the experience s/he had, usually through self-reported input, often the form of post-experience questionnaires or/and interviews. O'Brian et al. [22] tried to create a general purpose user engagement questionnaire, but it turned out that engagement is different among different application domains and user groups. For that reason, they suggested that an exploratory study should take place to reveal engagement characteristics relevant to each particular case.

Two key objective metrics to measure engagement include the Subjective Perception of Time (SPT) and Follow-On Task Performance (FOTP) [16]. SPT measures the estimation of a user in regards to the time it took to complete an action or a task, compared to the actual time passed. Several studies have dealt with the matter from a psychological standpoint [18], with most of them concluding that feelings can indeed influence one's perception of time. Most commonly, positive emotions tend to decrease the perception of time, whereas negative ones usually increase it.

On the other hand, FOTP measures the performance of a user in a puzzle-like task right after an interaction in an engaging context. It has been observed that users have limited performance when they have previously been immersed in an environment [17].

2.4   Gamification Affordances

Gamification has proven to be successfully used in marketing, work organizations, health, and environmental initiatives to achieve desirable outcomes by influencing user behaviors [27, 28]. Games serve no other intention, other than pleasing the user; for that reason, they have mastered the art of engaging, immersing and keeping the user interested throughout the whole interaction. Thus, taking elements of games and bringing them to conventional products or services has gained a lot of attention lately. Chu [23] argues that every game focuses on a certain core drive inside us, and based on that developed a framework for gamification called Octalysis. According to him, the eight core drives of motivation are: Meaning, Empowerment, Social Influence, Unpredictability, Avoidance, Scarcity, Ownership and Accomplishment. Chu categorizes Scarcity, Ownership and Accomplishment as Extrinsic Motivators, suggesting that the user has the desire to obtain something, whereas Empowerment, Social Influence and Unpredictability are considered Intrinsic Motivators; there is no reward here. It has been observed [23] that when you take out the Extrinsic Motivators, the user motivation decreases to a much lower level than the one before its addition.

Another important categorization is between White Hat Gamification and Black Hat Gamification [23]. White Hat refers to the gamification affordances that trigger positive emotions, for instance "talking" to the user's creativity, sense of belonging or self-development. On the other hand, Black Hat affordances are mostly related to fear of losing something, the pursuit of the unknown etc.

3   Case Study and Method

This study focuses on design for, rather than design of, concept [29]. As a part of a Human-Computer Interaction (HCI) study, this research project is performed using the design thinking methodology by Brown [24] within a case study. *"The design process is best described metaphorically as a system of spaces rather than a predefined series of orderly steps. The spaces demarcate different sorts of related activities that together form the continuum of innovation"* (p. 4). This is an iterative design process that includes three main parts: Inspiration, Ideation, and Implementation. several subphases include steps such as: empathizing, defining a problem or opportunity, developing, testing ideas, and refinement. The potential of this method saturates a spectrum of innovation activities with a human-centered design ethos that we believe will help us create a prototype that enhances the spirit of innovation at workplaces.

3.1 Case Description

This study was conducted in collaboration with Nordea-Stockholm, One of the largest Scandinavian banks. Nordea wanted to both enhance its employees' innovative mindset, as well as to increase the actual innovative output of the bank. Thus, as one of the approaches is to develop an ideation (or innovation) platform and place it in the intranet system of the bank. The platform would serve both everyday innovation attempts, as well as work as a tool in the company's innovation hackathons, week-long events that many employees take part in.

One of the main objectives of the proposed platform is to encourage the employees of Nordea to publish their innovative ideas and comment on others' ideas. Posting ideas can happen at any time, however the platform in particular, is designed to facilitate and encourage campaigns. Campaigns are open calls, usually around a concrete thematic area, asking employees to provide ideas only around that topic. Campaigns are important since a company can steer the direction of the innovation around specific interests with strategic focus.

The project followed a business concept called "try fast, fail fast, and adjust fast", as it was a part of the Innovation & Experimentation department of the company. The aim of it is to enhance the knowledge around employee driven innovation, measuring the effect of gamification in the perceived engagement of a large organization's employees, with the use of an ideation platform.

3.2 Method Outline and Data Collection

As part of the first and last stage of the design thinking process, i.e. empathizing and testing with the users, user data was collected in the form of ten user interviews for the former and seven user tests for the latter. In both cases, the employees were randomly selected, based on their availability and willingness to participate. The user tests consisted of a combination of interviews, quantitative metrics as well as observations from the author's part.

In between, a workshop was run, organized and facilitated by the authors of this study, in order to translate the data collected from the first phase into tangible targets for the design of the platform. After that, the actual design work for the two versions of the innovation platform took place. Table 1 depicts the design process of the study.

Table 1. Design process of the study

Stage	Method	Time frame	Participants
Empathize	Workshop & User interviews	2 days	10 interviewees
Define & Ideate	Workshop + Meetings	2 weeks	Own contribution
Prototype	Design work	2 months	Own contribution
Evaluate	User testing	15 days	7 participants

3.3   Empathizing with the Users: User Interviews and Workshop

In order to empathize with the target users (i.e., stage 1), 10 user interviews took place at the premises of Nordea. This was part of an exploratory research aimed at understanding the current landscape when it comes to innovative ideas generated by the employees, as well as to identify their pain-points and preferences around the matter.

The content of the interviews was decided at a 2-day workshop that involved UX designers, web developers and business developers. In this workshop, the participants offered their opinions on the information that needs to be collected to be able to provide a proper solution that answers the users' problems, and thus what should be asked in the interviews. A lot of effort was put on formulating the questions in an open format, leaving space for the interviewees to provide their opinion on the topic, rather than just agreeing or disagreeing with a statement. The number of questions was decided to be kept at a low number, more specifically 11, in order to avoid boring the interviewees, something that could potentially make them answer the last questions without the same energy compared to the first ones.

3.4   Defining the Problem and Ideating on the Solution

A lot of interesting insights and suggestions were collected from the interviews, with some being recurring. We tried to find patterns in the insights collected, focus on the recurring ones and extract relevant features for the platforms that answer to those.

The business direction was to create a simple product, and depending on its reception from the employees, build on that afterwards. That, along with the fact that design thinking, the project's method, focuses on many small iterations of a design (each of them an improvement of the previous), it was decided to go forward with a Minimum Viable Product (MVP), that is a product consisting of only the core functionalities, usually created for a fast launch of a product, instead of creating a full version of the platform. Thus, only a handful of the features that were originally decided were selected to be part of the MVP.

3.5   Prototype - Platform Design

Having a clear plan on what path to take, and consequently which platform features are needed, as well as how the platform would be structured, the focus was given on its actual design. Based on the best practices found while researching other similar products, the structure of the design was decided, and wireframes (Fig. 1) were created to showcase the side-bar layout that was selected to stakeholders and get feedback.

After showing the progress of the project to specific stakeholders (e.g. product owners, managers) the final step was the high-fidelity design of the platform (see Fig. 2). The colors, typography and icons used were Imported from the Bank's libraries.

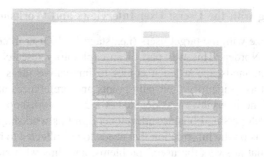

Fig. 1. Wireframe skeleton design

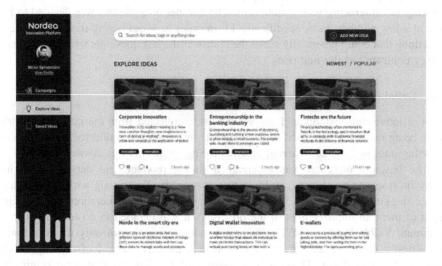

Fig. 2. High-fidelity of the virtual environment homepage design

3.6 Platform Structure

The platform was decided, upon order from the management, to be campaign-centric. This meant that the main focus would be to lead users into participating in campaigns. Campaigns work similar to small idea competitions, having a target area and deadlines for publishing them. However, since this study is heavily tied to Nordea and has a limited time frame related to the course time frames, some shortcuts needed to be applied. As a result, the main page of the innovation platform is the one where all active campaigns are being shown (Fig. 3), with users being able to either see the campaign information, comment on it, check the participating ideas or add an idea of their own.

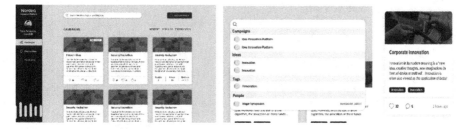

Fig. 3. **Left:** Campaign Page; **Mid:** Search bar; **Right:** Campaign card

When adding one idea, users are presented with a form where they need to fill in some obligatory fields, such as a title, a summary and a pitch, as well as answer some campaign-specific questions, add tags for better discoverability etc.

Visitors of the platform are able to discover ideas in multiple ways: as mentioned before, by entering a campaign, by exploring all available ideas in the "all ideas" section, or by searching for a specific one, either by name, author or tag.

Last but not least, each user has a dedicated personal page, where all ideas and/or campaigns posted are stored and presented.

3.7 Gamification Design

The gamification elements that were included in the design are:

- Leaderboards: exploiting the social influence (Fig. 4).
- Feedback and progress: indicate when filling all the necessary text field before posting an idea (Fig. 5).
- Point system: points for posting ideas and commenting on others' ideas (Fig. 6).

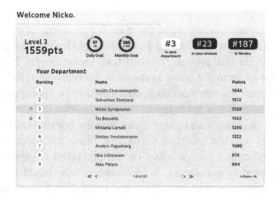

Fig. 4. Leaderboards

Fig. 5. Progress bar and feedback

Fig. 6. The point system

3.8   User Testing

In order to see if innovation is enhanced using such a platform, as well to measure the users' perceived engagement while using the conventional versus the gamified version, the last step of the design process was to test users. Seven Nordea employees were recruited (none of them the same as the ones interviewed in the first stage of the design thinking process), - a number that is considered to be appropriate for qualitative analysis [1]. The platform was intended to be used by two different target users, the managers, who post challenges and judge ideas, and the conventional employees, who share their ideas and provide feedback on others. Since the focus of this project is around whether gamification has an effect on the perceived engagement of the users (and not the super users – managers), the recruitment was based on the rank of the employees, no manager was recruited. No other restriction was put on the selection, with employees being selected in a random way.

The participants were presented with the ideation platform along with its purpose and signed a consent form giving the researcher the right to process the data gathered. Then, the participants were given a scenario and two tasks that they needed to perform, which were the same in both the conventional and the gamified version of the platform. The two tasks that were presented to the users were:

- Find the idea called "Nora opens a new channel in Leaderboard" and post a comment on it.
- Find the campaign called "Fintech Ideas" and publish a new idea on it.

Users were asked to answer questions in a semi-constructed interview structure, right after their interaction with both versions. In order to avoid biased results, the order in which the designs are given to each user is alternated. More specifically, participants were first asked to give their general thoughts on the prototypes, then to describe them with the first three words that comes to their minds and finally state one thing they liked as well as one they did not like when using the prototypes. At the end, after having tried both prototypes, users were asked to compare the prototypes and to choose the one that they would like to use daily.

Apart from the interviews, users were asked to estimate the time they spent using the prototype (SPT, as elaborated in the theory of this research, Fig. 7 and 8) and to solve a simple mathematical equation (FOTP); both of them right after they finished their interaction with each of the designs.

3.9   Ethics

Regarding ethics, participants were chosen voluntarily, participating in the study by giving an informed consent. All personal information, as well as all the data gathered from the interviews was anonymized. The user tests were conducted in an open and honest manner, with the participants being able to opt out from the process at any given time.

4   Results

4.1   Conventional Design

Most users found this prototype to be easy, simple and intuitive, with phrases like "*It was a very smooth process; I didn't find any difficulties*" (Respondent 1, R1) being the norm. However, one user did not share the same feelings, stating that "*It was a bit overwhelming. There was too much information*" (R5).

When asked to describe their interaction with just three words, users gave similar responses. The predominant responses could be categorized as follows: first and foremost, the most common one was simplicity (R1, R2, R3, R6) followed by intuitiveness (R2, R3, R7), and functionality (R4, R6, R7). Replies standing out, and worth mentioning include "*boring*" and "*okayish*".

More specifically, participants pointed out that the design's strongest points were structure, visual style, and simplicity. On the other hand, they felt that the long forms and the absence of visible progress were the prototype's weakest points.

4.2   Gamified Design: Increased Motivation?

The comments gathered while interviewing users after using the gamified version of the design were more extensive and included a wider range of feelings and perceptions. As with the first design, users found the second prototype as well to be easy and intuitive. More specifically users stated that "*the flow is clear, and I can find what I am looking for, using the clues*" (R1) and "*I liked the structure. It was simple, I could easily locate all necessary elements*" (R3). At the same time, users seemed to have their motivation triggered, as seen in comments such as "*I really liked it, it is engaging*" (R7) and "*It is special. Interesting and playful*" (R1). A user actually mentioned that "*I was happier, it was motivating and was actually like a game*" (R5), showing that this version did not just work as a functionality, but rather managed to talk to the feelings of users, triggering them. On the other hand, there were some issues that users brought up, mainly regarding how the personalization was visualized. Some users (R2, R4) would prefer to have a personalized avatar instead of their profile picture.

When asking participants to describe their interaction with 3 keywords the results were: easy (R1, R2, R3, R5, R6) -the most commonly encountered word-, followed by motivating (R1, R4, R7) and interesting (R4, R6, R7).

What users liked the most in this design was by far the implementation of the point system, with some responses mentioning the multi-step form instead. On the other hand, participants had some concerns regarding the misuse of gamification. They mostly pointed out that they could potentially be inclined to use it just for the sake of gathering points, something that could have negative results in the intended outcome of the platform, knowledge transfer and enhancement of innovation.

4.3   Comparison of the Designs

All the participants (100%) chose the gamified prototype when asked about which of the two designs they prefer and would like to use on a regular basis. The vast majority of them (86%) justified their preference on the fact that this version of the platform would motivate them to keep coming back and using it again and again. This is because they liked the idea of having their contributions visualized (and on a second level, gamified) but also "competing" with their colleagues was engaging to them. As one respondent mentioned, "*for sure I would choose the 2nd. It gave me an incentive to be active, perform better and outperform the other colleagues. The most important feature was the comparison with the others*" (R7) Another one (R2) said: "*I would like to use the gamified one. Its triggering, you want to use it more often. I especially liked the point system; I really enjoyed the gift of getting something in return for an action of mine"*. However, some users, even if they preferred the gamified version to the conventional one, were unsure about if the incentives provided would be enough to keep them active in the platform. In fact, one of them stated that *"I would like to use the second one, provided that there are more perks. The level up is cool, but I'd like something more to keep my interest up"* (R4).

4.4   Quantitative Metrics: Subjective Perception of Time

The time that participants spent on each prototype were interesting. At this point it is worth mentioning that any bias due to prior knowledge of the task to be performed, is balanced by the interchange in the prototypes' order of presentation to the users. Although the actual average time that the users took for completing the tasks of each prototype was comparable (54.8 s to 56.7 s, as seen in Fig. 7), the time that the users perceived was around 8 s less in the conventional design, and around 8 s more in the gamified one.

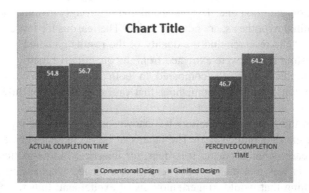

Fig. 7. Actual vs perceived completion time

4.5   Quantitative Metrics: Follow-On Task Performance

Users were presented with a puzzle-like task (FOTP and SPT, see Sect. 2.3), right after their interaction with each prototype. For the context of this research, the puzzle was decided to have the form of a simple arithmetical operation, consisting of basic multiplication and sum.

Once again, the results obtained could be considered interesting, with participants struggling considerably more to succeed in solving the puzzle right after interacting with the gamified design. In fact, as can be seen in Fig. 8, the time difference is substantial, with the time needed after the gamified experience being double than the one after the conventional one.

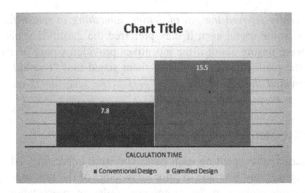

Fig. 8. Calculation time of the puzzle-like tasks

5 Discussion

This research started with the hypothesis that the gamified version would engage users more than the non-gamified one. The results, although strongly towards the direction of receiving the initial hypothesis, are not conclusive. The reasons for that are mainly two: the limitations of the research and the duality of the results gathered.

Very interesting results were extracted from the quantitative metrics. On one hand, SPT gave contradictory results compared to both the interviews and the FOTP, rejecting the initial hypothesis, something that raises questions on how to translate those results.

Research in the field of psychology has shown that specific feelings can alter the perception of time of a human [25]. The latter can be decreased when a person feels excited or increase, when a person feels fear, for instance. In this particular case, the initial hypothesis was that users would feel more engaged when using the gamified version, something that would trigger emotions of excitement; thus the expected perceived completion time would be lower than the actual. Nonetheless, the results clearly contrast the hypothesis for reasons that could range from pure randomness due to the small sample, to the failure of the prototype to engage the users. It needs to be noted though, that further research [18] has also shown that users perceive an increased time duration when faced with novel stimuli. Considering the fact that the research case is an innovation platform, the fact that the users see the gamified design as something novel can only be considered appropriate to the context of it.

On the other hand, FOTP gave the expected results, however there are still some issues that need to be stated; the sample size does not allow the researcher to claim any statistical significance on those results, nevertheless it is an indicator of potential impact of the gamified experience in the processing ability of the user. As explained before, the more immersed a user is in an environment, the longer it takes to adjust to the normal environment. Moreover, it should be mentioned that the two arithmetical operations were different, thus there is always the chance that one of the two was more difficult than the other, although this was attempted to be avoided by the researcher.

One of the limitations of the project was the small number of users that were tested, mainly due to the lack of budget to run an organized user testing session; all the tests took place with Nordea employees that were picked at the bank's reception. This limitation mostly influenced the validity of the statistical data that was collected, such us the Subjective Perception of Time and the puzzle calculation time. More users would be needed in order to have statistically strong results. For the qualitative data that was collected, the number of responses gathered was enough.

Another important limitation of the study was the inability to actually develop and thus test fully working versions for both versions of the platform, due to time constraints regarding the completion of the project. In fact, the conventional version of the innovation platform was actually taken live, whereas the gamified one is, at the moment these lines are being written, only in a non-functional prototype form. In order to avoid testing non-similar versions, all the user tests took place in the prototype state of the designs. This resulted, however, in users only being able to be tested on a brief and pre-set task on the platform, without having the possibility to spend a substantial amount of time on it. In the researcher's opinion, this would be necessary to have a good understanding of the level of engagement that each version managed to achieve with them. Besides, it's impossible to measure engagement, without long-term metrics such as time spent etc. This is in fact the reason behind the choice of measuring the perceived user engagement, instead of the pure user engagement. The former can be extracted from the users' personal opinions but does not come with the same weight.

Regarding the duality of the results obtained, this mostly concerns the Subjective Perceived Time. The initial hypothesis concerning the results collected when measuring the time that the users thought they spent versus the actual time that passed, was that the users would believe that they spent less time when working with the gamified version, compared to when using the conventional one. This hypothesis was strongly rejected though, with the results hinting towards users having more positive emotions when using the conventional version, since they perceived to have spent a smaller amount of time there than they actually did. Considering the fact that in the interviews, each and every one of the participants responded that they preferred the gamified version, one must conclude that either users preferred the version that did not engage them, or, and most probably according to the writer, this particular metric was not appropriate for this kind of study, at least so with as few participants. As mentioned before, the ideal way would have been to have working versions of both designs, and letting people use them for an indefinite amount of time, and then collecting and analyzing time data, behavior patterns, results produced (ideas published, comments made) etc.

Moreover, users clearly liked the gamified design, and in some cases and extent, they were excited by it. This was basically seen in the most prominent gamification element, the leaderboard. Most of the users were intrigued by the idea of competing against their fellow colleagues and thought that this would be a big incentive for them to constantly coming back to the platform. Thus, this setting should always be present in such platform designs, however, it would be preferable if the goal of the competition would be more concretely described, and prizes are set. This could either be in the form of virtual avatars, or in the form of real-life gains for the users; some users mentioned that a note to their higher manager would have been sufficient.

All in all, the outcomes of this study are directly relatable with the ones of relevant literature, and more specifically with Zimmerling [1], who also concluded that the inclusion of gamified elements, and especially the point system, has a big positive impact in ideation IT systems.

6 Conclusion

In this study, an innovation platform was designed and tested with users to enhance the spirit of innovation in the context of a large financial organization, namely Nordea. The focus was on exploiting the large number of employees, that is translated in various and diverse potential innovative ideas. In order for this to happen though, the foundations need to be built, in the form of a usable and inviting platform that will encourage employees to use it on a regular basis. An alternative version of the platform was designed, enhancing the former with elements of gamification, in order to answer the main research question of this project; whether gamification can increase the perceived user engagement. The results showed that the users perceived the gamified platform as much more engaging and motivating for them to use on a daily basis. However, in some of the metrics that were used to try and capture the actual engagement of the users, the results were varying, with the conventional design getting better results in some of them.

In general, though, it was clear that users liked many of the elements of gamification and would certainly prefer to have them when interacting with the platform. The most important gamification element to the users was the point system followed by the leaderboard list.

References

1. Zimmerling, E.: Increasing the creative output at the fuzzy front end of innovation - a concept for a gamified internal enterprise ideation platform (2016)
2. Marshall, K.: How successful organizations drive innovation. Strategy Leadersh. **44**(3), 9–19 (2016)
3. Schneckenberg, D.: Open innovation and knowledge networking in a multinational corporation. J. Bus. Strategy **36**(1), 14–24 (2015)
4. Ologbo, A.: The influence of knowledge sharing on employee innovation capabilities (2015)
5. King, A.: Using open innovation to identify the best ideas (2013)
6. Patricio, R.: Gamification approaches to the early stage of innovation (2017)
7. Cooper, R.: What's next?: After stage-gate (2015)
8. Seligman, M.: Positive psychology progress empirical validation of interventions (2005)
9. Drucker, P.: Innovation and Entrepreneurship. Routledge, Abingdon (2014)
10. Herzog, P.: Open and Closed Innovation: Different Cultures for Different Strategies. Springer, Gabler (2011). https://doi.org/10.1007/978-3-8349-6165-5
11. Deterting, S.: Gamification using game-design elements in non-gaming context. In: CHI 2011 Extended Abstracts on Human Factors in Computing Systems, pp. 2425–2428 (2011)
12. Pisano, G.: You need an innovation strategy. Harvard Bus. Rev. **93**(6), 44–54 (2015)

13. Bogers, M., et al.: The open innovation research landscape: established perspectives and emerging themes across different levels of analysis. Ind. Innov. **24**(1), 8–40 (2017)
14. Everett, C.: Gamification for the public good, the Guardian (2011). https://www.theguardian.com/government-computing-network/2011/jun/27/gamification-principles-public-services-dwp
15. Roberts, A.: Observatory of Public Sector Innovation (N.A.)
16. Attfield, S., Kazai, G., Lalmas, M., Piwowarski, B.: Towards a science of user engagement (position paper). In: WSDM Workshop on User Modelling for Web Applications, pp. 9–12 (2011)
17. Jennett, C., et al.: Measuring and defining the experience of immersion in games. Int. J. Hum. Comput. Stud. **66**(9), 641–661 (2008)
18. Campbell, L.A., Bryant, R.A.: How time flies: a study of novice skydivers. Behav. Res. Ther. **45**(6), 1389–1392 (2007)
19. Kesting, P., Ulhøi, J.P.: Employee-driven innovation: extending the license to foster innovation. Manag. Decis. **48**, 65–84 (2010)
20. Schenk, E., Guittard, C., Pénin, J.: Open or proprietary? Choosing the right crowdsourcing platform for innovation. Technol. Forecast. Soc. Change **144**, 303–310 (2019)
21. Bunchball, I.: Gamification 101: an introduction to the use of game dynamics to influence behavior. White paper, p. 9 (2010)
22. O'Brien, H.L., Toms, E.G.: The development and evaluation of a survey to measure user engagement. J. Am. Soc. Inform. Sci. Technol. **61**(1), 50–69 (2010)
23. Chou, Y.: What is Gamification (2012). https://yukaichou.com/gamification-examples/what-is-gamification/
24. Brown, T., Wyatt, J.: Design thinking for social innovation. Dev. Outreach **12**(1), 29–43 (2010)
25. Dawson, J., Sleek, S.: The fluidity of time: scientists uncover how emotions alter time perception. APS Obs. **31**(8) (2018)
26. http://www.businessdictionary.com/definition/innovation.html
27. Khalil, M., Ebner, M., Admiraal, W.: How can gamification improve MOOC student engagement?. In: 11th European Conference on Games Based Learning, ECGBL 2017. Curran Associates, Inc. (2017)
28. Khalil, M., Wong, J., de Koning, B., Ebner, M., Paas, F.: Gamification in MOOCs: a review of the state of the art. In: 2018 IEEE Global Engineering Education Conference (EDUCON), pp. 1629–1638. IEEE (2018)
29. Viberg, O., Grönlund, Å.: Understanding students' learning practices: challenges for design and integration of mobile technology into distance education. Learn. Media Technol. **42**(3), 357–377 (2017)

VR, Robot and IoT in Learning

Immersive Telepresence Framework
for Remote Educational Scenarios

Jean Botev[1(✉)] and Francisco J. Rodríguez Lera[2]

[1] University of Luxembourg, Av. de la Fonte 6, 4364 Esch-sur-Alzette, Luxembourg
`jean.botev@uni.lu`
[2] University of León, Campus de Vegazana S/N, 24071 León, Spain
`fjrodl@unileon.es`

Abstract. Social robots have an enormous potential for educational applications, allowing cognitive outcomes similar to those with human involvement. Enabling instructors and learners to directly control a social robot and immersively interact with their students and peers opens up new possibilities for effective lesson delivery and better participation in the classroom.

This paper proposes the use of immersive technologies to promote engagement in remote educational settings involving robots. In particular, this research introduces a telepresence framework for the location-independent operation of a social robot using a virtual reality headset and controllers. Using the QTrobot as a platform, the framework supports the direct and immersive control via different interaction modes including motion, emotion and voice output. Initial tests involving a large audience of educators and students validate the acceptability and applicability to interactive classroom scenarios.

Keywords: Social robotics · Education · Immersive telepresence · Teleoperation · Virtual reality · Human-robot interaction · UI design

1 Motivation

Social robots have an enormous potential for educational applications, allowing cognitive outcomes similar to human involvement [6]. Many research efforts focus on aspects related to autonomous and cognitive robotics for education [5,9,18,27]. However, enabling learners and instructors to directly control a social robot and immersively interact with their peers and students opens up further possibilities for effective lesson delivery, participation and tutoring in the classroom.

From an operator's point of view, which could be either a teacher or a tutor (peer) [19], the direct interaction with students is crucial to acquiring non-verbal feedback and observing immediate reactions in order to evaluate their comprehension [15]. Virtual reality (VR) technology here lends itself perfectly as an addition, complementing pure human-robot interaction (HRI) scenarios where a

© Springer Nature Switzerland AG 2020
P. Zaphiris and A. Ioannou (Eds.): HCII 2020, LNCS 12206, pp. 373–390, 2020.
https://doi.org/10.1007/978-3-030-50506-6_26

robot is controlled remotely. Specifically, the combination of a VR headset with motion-based control allows the operator to more naturally translate movements to input. Together with the visual, acoustic and further channels of expression, the interaction between operator and student, despite mediated, becomes much more immersive. In addition, technologies such as emotion recognition and face detection enhance the way in which the operator perceives the student.

Educational research distinguishes various communication mechanisms between students and instructors, i.e., teachers or tutors, which include non-verbal clues that are visible to the instructor during the lesson [15,20]. These clues involve the monitoring and tracking of body movement to different extents, the time watching materials, or students looking away. Other, more subtle clues are more complex to recognize, such as blinking and the lowering of eyebrows. In both cases, many software solutions are able to capture this information from robot sensors, however, certain information and gestures are difficult to generalize and translate to software, as they are based on experiential knowledge originating from the interaction with the students.

Conversely, instructor feedback to students is equally significant to the learning process [11]. A typology based on four types of feedback extending beyond classic reward and punishment feedback by also specifying attainment and improvement is, for instance, proposed in [30]. Such feedback could be transmitted to students using verbal and non-verbal capabilities of the robot; a social robot with diverse interaction modalities thus would increase the quality and amount of feedback delivered to students.

Both of these feedback scenarios have led to several robotic telepresence solutions [8,14,35] along with a plethora of purely experimental approaches. However, this paper goes one step further in that it combines a semi-autonomous social robot with a fully immersive system based on a head-mounted display. We discuss our efforts to create an open-source framework for this kind of scenarios, as well as the exploratory experience evaluating the perception of the system before possible deployment in classrooms throughout the country of Luxembourg. To this end, we set up the fully functional platform at a national science and research fair to evaluate the interaction with students using a quick assessment method designed to capture the succinct interactions generated in events of that kind (30 pupils every 15 min in a noisy environment).

During this first iteration of our research, we intend to answer mainly the following research questions:

- Q1: What are the issues of developing an open-source software framework supported on a commercial social robot and HMD?
- Q2: How can the experience be assessed effectively using a quick evaluation method capturing a complete framework?

The remainder of this paper is structured as follows: Sect. 2 introduces the various components and technologies used in the framework, inclusive of how communication between them is handled. Section 3 then discusses important user interface (UI) and user experience (UX) design aspects along with a dedicated assessment method, followed by the results from an initial evaluation of the system in a larger-scale context in Sect. 4. Finally, we conclude with a brief summary and outlook on future development in Sect. 5.

2   Framework and Components

This paper proposes a telepresence framework for the location-independent operation of a social robot using a VR headset and controllers as schematically illustrated in Fig. 1. Such an approach suggests a twofold communication system: on the one hand, a robot sending relevant data and receiving commands to carry out in order to interact with users and bystanders; on the other hand, a device and a dedicated user interface to present the robot's data/state to the operator and to send commands to the robot.

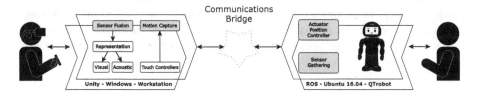

Fig. 1. Telepresence framework; VR-based operation to social robot interaction.

The telepresence framework is purposely designed to be completely location-independent, i.e., the person controlling the robot can either be in the next room or on a different continent altogether. As indicated in Sect. 1, the operator in our case is an instructor, i.e., a teacher or a tutor. Accordingly, and in line with their general use in HRI research, we employ the terms user and bystander for students and peers here [29].

In the following, we first outline the VR technology on operator side in Sect. 2.1, then introduce the robotic platform used on the user/bystander side in Sect. 2.2, and finally discuss the bridge that handles all communication between them in Sect. 2.3.

2.1   Virtual Reality

Historically, there are several definitions for VR, based either on technological means or the different notions of presence [26]. Generally speaking, VR can be described as a real or simulated environment presented to an individual through a mediating technology, so that the environment is perceived with a strong sense of presence. The feeling of immersion can be further intensified by allowing users to interact with the environment and by addressing a larger variety of sensory channels. To this day, the main channel remains visual, usually complemented by spatial audio, motion input and haptic feedback through dedicated hardware.

VR technology is composed of two central elements: the hardware, i.e., all physical components conveying the experience of and interaction with the environment, such as screens, gloves and controllers; and software allowing to develop virtual environments.

Hardware: Oculus Rift Headset and Touch Controllers. The VR hardware employed in this research are the Oculus Rift[1] headset and accompanying Touch controllers. The head-mounted display (HMD) consists of two PenTile OLED displays with an overall resolution of 2160 × 1200 at 90 Hz and a 110-degree field of view. This dual-display arrangement is complemented by two adjustable lenses which rectify the 1080 × 1200 image for each eye to create a stereoscopic 3D image. The headset features rotational and positional tracking and comes with integrated headphones supporting 3D-audio effects. The Oculus Touch controllers utilize the same low-latency tracking technology of the headset, providing a setup with joysticks and buttons for input and the opportunity for haptic feedback. Both the headset and the controllers are tracked using Oculus' Constellation sensors, a pair of external infrared cameras mounted on dedicated desk stands. The Constellation sensors, Touch controllers and Rift headset are depicted in Fig. 2.

Fig. 2. Oculus Rift VR headset, Touch controllers and Constellation sensors.

Software: Unity. Oculus provides several SDKs adding functionality to its core software. However, it can also be integrated easily with existing game engines such as Unity or the Unreal engine to harness their power for creating realistic VR experiences. Particularly Unity provides the flexibility of deploying and developing the software on a wide range of different platforms [10]. Moreover, it has a large community of developers and there are previous results where the engine has been put to good use in robot-VR scenarios [10,23]. This guarantees the scalability of the project, its long-term maintenance and platform independence.

---

[1] https://www.oculus.com/rift/.

2.2   Robotic Platform

The robotic platform utilized for this project is LuxAI's QTrobot[2], a humanoid robot with an expressive social appearance. It has a screen as its face, allowing the presentation of facial expressions and emotions using animated characters, as well as 12 degrees of freedom to present upper-body gestures. Eight degrees of freedom are motor controlled, two in each shoulder, one in each arm plus pitch and yaw movements of the head. The other four, one in each wrist and one in each hand, can be manually configured. As shown in Fig. 3 amongst other features, QTrobot has a close-range 3D camera mounted on its forehead and is provided with a six-microphone array. The QTrobot is powered by an Intel NUC processor and Ubuntu 16.04 LTS providing a native ROS interface.

Fig. 3. QTrobot features and hardware specifications.

QTrobot behaviors can be programmed from two perspectives: a low-level programming perspective, using ROS interfaces for full robot control as in the framework implementation; and a high-level approach, through a visual programming interface presented as an Android application for tablets and smart phones, based on Blockly [21]. The latter mostly aims at users less familiar with programming, enabling them to add motion and behaviors that QTrobot can then assume when operating autonomously.

2.3   Communications Bridge

Due to the heterogeneity of VR and robot software, it is necessary to bridge the information between the different technologies. In particular, it is essential to interface the Unity engine with the ROS-based system.

As described in Sects. 2.2 and 2.1, QTrobot deploys ROS as operational middleware while the Oculus Rift uses the Unity engine; each system has its own communication protocol based on classic approaches. ROS sends messages between nodes using its own protocols called TCPROS and UDPROS. These

---

[2] https://luxai.com/qtrobot-for-research/.

protocols generate the connections through TCP Sockets with a header containing the message data type and routing information.

For simplicity's sake, we use Rosbridge[3] for establishing communication between the QTrobot and the Oculus Rift HMD, i.e., the Unity engine. Rosbridge allows non-ROS systems to access ROS functionality by providing a JSON API. It utilizes the WebSocket protocol as a communication layer, so that any external agent with network access can send messages to the ROS environment. In particular, Rosbridge serializes ROS services and topics using a single socket interface. Figure 4 shows the bridge handling communications from the VR system to the robot and vice versa.

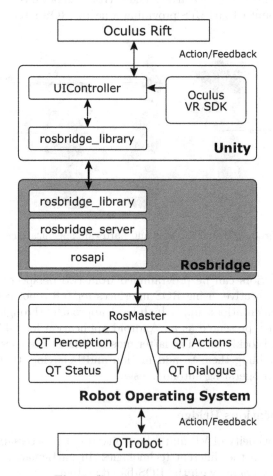

Fig. 4. Communications bridge.

Recent research related to social robotics focuses largely on artificial intelligence and autonomous robotics rather than on immersive teleoperation.

---

[3] https://wiki.ros.org/rosbridge_suite/.

However, various approaches for interfacing VR technology with robotic systems have been proposed in different contexts, covering scenarios from fundamental HRI research aspects [33], over piloting unmanned aerial vehicles (UAV) [23], to industrial applications [25]. For example, an interesting engine for interfacing with and controlling an Arduino board is presented in [4]. It does not, however, connect to ROS. A ROS-based approach is the multi-modal man-machine communication system for remote monitoring of an industrial device as discussed in [25]. Also some UAV-related studies combine ROS with Unity [17,23], yet they often have a proof-of-concept character and focus on simulated or replicated environments rather than social HRI aspects.

The technical approach presented in this paper is an extension of the Unity-ROS interface introduced in [10]. In the same spirit, our source code is released and made available publicly via GitHub. The code has been updated to work with ROS Kinetic and Ubuntu LTS 16.04.5 Desktop which is supported until 2021. This way, it is guaranteed that other researchers can integrate our solution to their robots running ROS with only minor changes, i.e., mainly adding customized messages. Alternatively, with ROS Reality [32], a similar solution exists which aims at offering an interface for performing manipulation tasks on robots rather than predominantly social HRI control as proposed here.

The AI Robolab repository[4] provides our two packages for interfacing QTrobot with the Oculus Rift: the Unity package, called *vr_teleop*, which is the one running on the Unity SDK available in Windows; and the ROS package, called *vr_teleop_server*, which is the one interacting directly with the Unity side. In particular, it takes care of forwarding user requests to correct topics and manages the messages defining the robot status. Consequently, the repository can be considered as one of the main contributions of this study.

3   User Interface and Experience

The design of effective UIs and good UX constitutes a major area in human-computer interaction research [7]. In HRI, which is concerned with complex and dynamic control systems in real-world environments [13], the requirements tighten further as solutions for all individuals interacting with the robot or using the robot need to be considered.

UI design therefore should be seen as a process beyond the engineering development; it is a process that involves the individuals such as operators, users and bystanders, as well as the devices used during the interaction themselves. For instance, in urban search-and-rescue scenarios where different degrees of robot autonomy are supported on remote control, the UI should concentrate on four central elements [2]: 1) enhancing operator awareness of the robot environment, 2) reducing operator cognitive load, 3) minimizing the use of multiple windows/desktops, and 4) assisting with the selection of the correct robotic autonomy level in a given scenario.

---

[4] https://github.com/AIRobolab-unilu.

In a similar vein, we opted for an approach aiming at maximum immersion for the operator in order to alleviate distractions and prevent cognitive overload, as discussed in the following section.

3.1 Immersive Approach

As indicated in Table 1, there are four main elements in an HRI scenario supported on teleoperation interfaces. The various components need to be translated into the system, i.e., the scene rendering, the robotic behavior generator and the remote operation. For instance, the HRI scene is defined by the perceptive sensors integrated in the robot. The number and type of these sensors define the perception of the environment. Besides, this raw input needs manipulation and sensor fusion before it is presented to the operator. The behavior generator is associated with joint positions and the current robot status, which is relevant to a replication of the operator's movements in real time.

The goal is to create a strong sense of immersion and telepresence for the operator as defined in [12], i.e., the perception of being present in the remote environment. To achieve this, our approach suggests the transparent mapping of as many interaction channels to their direct counterparts on the operator side as possible and vice versa; e.g., visual and auditory perception (the operator sees and hears what the humanoid robot sees), or motion (the humanoid robot moves as the operator does). A VR solution composed of a headset able to relay and display robot information and a set of devices to capture operator movements (head and arms) therefore is the natural choice for a teleoperation setting as proposed here.

The HRI interface types discussed in Sects. 3.2 and 3.2 are based on previous experiences involving HMDs with controllers as well as children interacting with QTrobot, where the two modes reflect different design strategies considering individual concerns [28].

3.2 Control Modes and Requirements

When considering employing robots in remote education, all actors present in the scenario need to be taken into account: the educator, the student and any other user potentially involved in the classroom, such as teachers or tutors on site as well as student friends or colleagues. To meet the requirements of these actors, it is imperative to design a solution that involves usability guidelines for teleoperation. A validated and complete taxonomy showing a total of 70 factors associated to HRI, grouped into the following eight categories, is presented in [1]:

1. Platform Architecture and Scalability (5 factors).
2. Error Prevention and Recovery (5 factors).
3. Visual Design (10 factors).
4. Information Presentation (12 factors).
5. Robot State Awareness (10 factors).
6. Interaction Effectiveness and Efficiency (12 factors).

7. Robot Environment/Surroundings Awareness (10 factors).
8. Cognitive Factors (6 factors).

We employed the usability guidelines identified in the validated taxonomy for designing our first prototype, having in mind as actors users with little or no experience of ICT solutions. Still, the proposed control mode design explicitly considers the most frequently employed operational interfaces and the robot skills with the highest impact for the end user.

Explicit: Direct Interaction Control. In general, teleoperation solutions offer control of a platform changing between different autonomous states of the robot to allow flexibility in human control and adaptability to specific scenarios. When taking an explicit approach, the aim is to allow the operator direct control of the robot, i.e., to input and translate intention without the limitations of intermediates such as predefined options. This facilitates appropriate supervision during the interaction allowing to make informed decisions, take alternative decisions, and generate new verbal or non-verbal information, such as to any kind of motion or gestures.

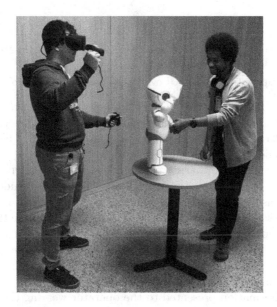

Fig. 5. Explicit control mode.

The explicit control mode as implemented in our telepresence framework is shown in Fig. 5, where the operator's head and arms motion is directly forwarded and translated to the robot interacting with users and bystanders. The operator generally would be at a different location and is only in the picture for illustration purposes. Also other input, such as audio, can be forwarded and processed in real time. Without such direct interaction control and the use of different sensory channels, achieving immersion and telepresence as defined in [12] would be impossible, or at least much harder, to achieve.

Implicit: Social Interaction Control. In addition to the explicit control mode, in an educational context it is imperative to offer a complementary type of control which focuses on human-robot and human-human roles as well as their relationships. This way, the robot can offer predefined voices and prerecorded sentences, gestures or expressions provided not only by educational stakeholders, such as teachers and tutors, but also by individuals with a personal connection, such as family members or friends. Depending on the specific situational context, the operator selects from a set of associated, implicit options.

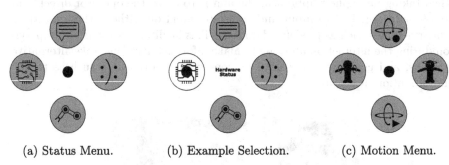

(a) Status Menu.   (b) Example Selection.   (c) Motion Menu.

Fig. 6. Implicit control mode - UI overlays for access to available functions.

The different UI overlays defined in our framework are shown in Fig. 6. When triggered, the different options are displayed in a circle and the operator can use the analog stick to navigate to and select a specific item. In Fig. 6b, for instance, the operator is about to select the hardware option from the status menu to retrieve relevant system information. The status menu is triggered from the left Touch controller. The other options in the status menu include motor/servo status (bottom), as well as dialog (top) and robot motivational variables (right) component controls. The motion menu in Fig. 6c is triggered from the right Touch controller. It provides access to the various motion-related options, e.g., to record (top) or play (bottom) complex motion sequences, as well as fine-grained control of QTrobot's arms (left) or head (right). The latter are displaying options related to the conversation and facial expression modules.

The status information presented to the operator wearing the Oculus HMD has a variety of sources: motor/servo status reflects the different motor positions within a normalized numeric range. The dialog menu opens a new window where a set of variables and facial expressions can be selected and triggered using the QTrobot speech system and display. Motivational variables indicated in the corresponding menu constitute a subset of the variables described in [22] to outline the current mood of the robot: curiosity, frustration, fatigue and pain. This particular option is shown in the screenshot in Fig. 7.

Fig. 7. Transparent status information overlay on reduced camera viewport.

3.3 Measuring UI/UX Impact

Beyond the lab, any kind of HRI scenario suffers from variability and dynamic changes in the environment. When developing the UI design, a number of factors defining HRI scenarios need to be considered because they influence or directly affect interaction [34]:

1) Ratio of People to Robots,
2) Amount of Intervention,
3) Level of Shared Interaction Among Teams,
4) Composition of Robot Team,
5) Human-Robot Physical Proximity,
6) Decision Support for Operators,
7) Space,
8) Interaction Roles,
9) Criticality,
10) Time,
11) Autonomy,
12) Task Type, and
13) Robot Morphology.

These categories comprise most part of the HRI elements for the different actors defining the HRI scenario [3]:

- HRI system: the technological elements involved during interaction, mainly composed of the following three elements: the system that perceives information from and presents information to individuals, which is a robot; the communication system, focusing on the network transmission; and the display system, which makes the operator perceive the remote scene and generate actions to influence bystanders.
- Robot: the mobile or non-mobile agent that interacts in one way or another with the bystander.

- Remote operator: the individual having the capacity to change or manipulate the robot behaviors so as to provide the correct actions in a given scenario. The set of actions is proposed by a supervisor.
- Supervisor: the individual who monitors and controls the overall situation during the HRI scenario, also known as commander or director.
- Bystander: the individual or individuals in the remote environment whose behaviors affect the robot actions (both autonomous and via remote operator).

A good design should enhance the effectiveness, efficiency and efficacy of an HRI approach, but the evaluation is not a straightforward process. In educational environments, this assessment is further complicated by potential ethical and technological implications of working with actual students and professional educators. Finding issues in the system only during the experimental phase might turn costly for both the researchers and the bystanders involved in the process.

Based on validated approaches from the mapping review of the literature that we performed, we propose a set of parameters to be evaluated for measuring UI/UX impact as in Table 1, defining the Quick Assessment Method (QAM). Each parameter has an effect on particular actors and is therefore evaluated independently. The proposed parameters have well-defined metrics, however, interviews with the director and developer can further accelerate evaluation and development. At this point, these interviews assess the impact following a Likert scale that focuses on the level of influence: 1, not at all influential; 2, slightly influential; 3, somewhat influential; 4, very influential; 5, extremely influential.

Table 1 contains four elements: the parameter ID, the parameter name, the expected effect, supported on the proposed scale, and the perceived effect, using the same scale, which is obtained once the design is evolving or tested during development and pre-experimental phases. The expected and perceived parameter values in the table indicate the values obtained during a first evaluation of the proposed telepresence framework discussed in Sect. 4.

4   Evaluation

An initial evaluation of the system in action was conducted at the recent FNR Researchers' Days[5], a two-day national science and research fair. The sixth edition in November/December 2018 attracted more than 6,500 attendees. Visitors from the mostly laymen audience continuously tried the system at our stand.

The photo in Fig. 8 shows part of the stand. Visitors were not only allowed to interact with the robot, but also to take on the role of its operator. The setup included a projector displaying the image routed to the HMD together with other data to the remaining audience, so as to give a detailed impression of what is being captured by the robot's sensors and actuators.

---

[5] http://www.researchersdays.lu/.

Table 1. Quick Assessment Method (QAM), cf. [3,31].

ID	Parameter	Exp.	Perc.
HRI System			
1	Percentage of requests for assistance made by robot	1	1
2	Percentage of requests for assistance made by operator	4	5
3	Number of interruptions of operator rated as non-critical	3	4
4	Effectiveness (objective ratings)	-	-
5	Efficiency (objective ratings)	-	-
6	Efficacy (objective ratings)	-	-
7	Ease of use (subjective rating)	5	5
8	Ease of learning (subjective rating)	5	5
9	Functional primitives decomposition	5	5
10	Interaction effort	3	2
Robot			
11	Robot self-awareness	1	3
12	Human awareness	1	1
13	Autonomy	1	3
Remote Operator			
14	Human-robot situation awareness	5	5
15	Human-human situation awareness	2	1
16	Robot-human situation awareness	5	5
17	Robot-robot situation awareness	1	1
18	Human's overall mission awareness	3	5
19	Robot's overall mission awareness	1	1
20	Workload	3	3
21	Accuracy of mental models of device operation	5	5
Bystander (Student, Educational Professional)			
22	Human-robot situation awareness	1	1
23	Human-human situation awareness	1	1
24	Accuracy of mental models for interaction	3	5
25	Workload	1	1
26	Social acceptance	3	5
27	Effort expectancy	5	5
28	Attitude toward using technology	5	5
29	Self-efficacy	3	5
30	Attachment	1	1
31	Reciprocity	1	1
32	Emotion	3	5
33	Feeling of security	5	5

Fig. 8. System demonstration and assessment at national science and research fair.

Sociodemographic Observations. During the first day, attendance of the fair is limited to high-school pupils, journalists and invited guests, while the second day is open to the general public. 120 school classes registered to the event with, according to the organization recap, a total of 1,907 pupils (excluding teaching staff) visiting the event over the first day. The visits were peaking between 9:30 and 12:00. The Luxembourgish pupils were between 12 and 19 years old. Our stand was visited by approximately one group of students per 30 min, however, every 5–10 min a student or teaching personnel was operating the robot for 5-min time slots during which they interacted with friends and other visitors. The presentations were held in different languages, with the main languages used being German and French, corresponding with the main tongues spoken by visitors. The main language available in QTrobot is English. The second day of the fair comprised around 4,500 visitors with no age limit. The team proceeded with the same established presentation mode of the first day. At the end of each day, there were around 50–60 system tests with pupils, children, parents and teachers contributing to the overall evaluation data.

Objective Observations. Despite operator changes in quick succession and constant operation, the robot was running robustly most of the time. The VR system was used by one visitor every five to ten minutes throughout the day, i.e., around ten individual operators per hour, eight hours per day. Due to the extremely busy environment, there were network issues when using Wi-Fi connections; using Ethernet greatly improved delays, however, some audio delays are related to the first version of the communications bridge, since it delivers the signal in chunks. In terms of UX, due to the minimal interface, there was close to no setting-in period even for users yet unfamiliar with VR or controller-based input. The interaction was natural, and the degree of immersion high, with users putting themselves readily in QTrobot's position to interact with the person opposite.

Subjective Observations. The feedback on both operation and reception sides was very positive and encouraging. There was a strong feeling of presence [24] and embodiment [16], with only few operators displaying slight symptoms of disorientation. The robot was accepted without exception by young and old, with highly focused interaction in particular also from younger children. This group was particularly unbiased towards the robot, however, the visitors generally interacted with the robot as if it were the most natural thing in the world.

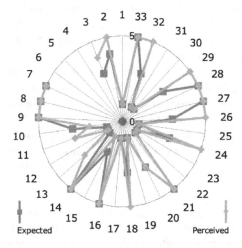

Fig. 9. Expected vs perceived results using the QAM.

QAM Observations. Following the evaluation of the objective and subjective feedback obtained during the tests at the Researchers' Days, the data was correlated with the QAM parameters to show the expected versus the perceived results. The visualization in Fig. 9 clearly indicates that the final users met our expectations and indeed were comfortable with the immersive approach. In particular, parameter 14 (human-robot situation awareness) confirms our approach for reducing the interaction effort, with the operators perceiving low complexity in direct interaction control mode. While deliberately employing an expressive humanoid robot to reduce bystander's reservations about the technology, the high social acceptance (parameter 26) and self-efficacy (parameter 29) assessment results greatly exceeded our expectations. Other factors, such as those related to particular robot skills, indicate that it is important to show also recurring, autonomous behaviors in the robot, as bystanders were expecting familiar or movie-like actions.

5 Conclusion and Outlook

This paper introduces a telepresence framework for the location-independent operation of a social robot using a VR headset and controllers with motion-tracking technology. Such robots have an enormous potential for educational applications: different to employing autonomous techniques, enabling learners and instructors to directly and immersively control a platform like QTrobot and interact with users and bystanders opens up new possibilities for effective participation and tutoring. Throughout, the robot operators exhibited a strong feeling of presence and embodiment.

Besides detailing the technical implementation of the framework along with the various interaction modes, this paper also discusses a multi-phase evaluation approach to assess HRI scenarios in different contexts, including an initial evaluation of the proposed framework. The preliminary tests involved a large and heterogeneous audience, and already helped validating the general applicability to interactive educational settings.

Our vision includes the full experimental evaluation of our approach in ordinary classrooms with professional educators on operator side and regular students on bystander side in order to push forward the inclusion of interactive, social robots and remote presence technologies in schools. Before doing so, however, we would like to further improve the network robustness and optimize servo/motor control, potentially with additional gesture input. Another possible extension would be to add a UI elements to mitigate the disorientation issue we observed at times during the demonstration of the system.

Acknowledgements. The authors would like to thank Thomas Sauvage and Julien Sanchez from the University of Toulouse III - Paul Sabatier, who assisted in this research in the context of an internship at the University of Luxembourg.

References

1. Adamides, G., Christou, G., Katsanos, C., Xenos, M., Hadzilacos, T.: Usability guidelines for the design of robot teleoperation: a taxonomy. IEEE Trans. Hum.-Mach. Syst. **45**(2), 256–262 (2015)
2. Baker, M., Casey, R., Keyes, B., Yanco, H.A.: Improved interfaces for human-robot interaction in urban search and rescue. In: Proceedings of the IEEE International Conference on Systems, Man and Cybernetics (SMC 2004), pp. 2960–2965 (2004)
3. de Barros, P.G., Linderman, R.W.: A survey of user interfaces for robot tele-operation. Technical report, Worcester Polytechnic Institute (2009). http://digitalcommons.wpi.edu/computerscience-pubs/21
4. Bartneck, C., Soucy, M., Fleuret, K., Sandoval, E.B.: The robot engine - making the unity 3D game engine work for HRI. In: Proceedings of the 24th IEEE International Symposium on Robot and Human Interactive Communication (RO-MAN 2015), pp. 431–437 (2015)
5. Belpaeme, T., et al.: Child-robot interaction: perspectives and challenges. In: Herrmann, G., Pearson, M.J., Lenz, A., Bremner, P., Spiers, A., Leonards, U. (eds.) ICSR 2013. LNCS (LNAI), vol. 8239, pp. 452–459. Springer, Cham (2013). https://doi.org/10.1007/978-3-319-02675-6_45

6. Belpaeme, T., Ramachandran, A., Scassellati, B., Tanaka, F.: Social robots for education: a review. Sci. Robot. **3**(21) (2018)
7. Benyon, D.: Designing Interactive Systems: A Comprehensive Guide to HCI, UX and Interaction Design. Pearson Edinburgh (2014)
8. Cha, E., Chen, S., Matarić, M.J.: Designing telepresence robots for K-12 education. In: 26th IEEE International Symposium on Robot and Human Interactive Communication (RO-MAN 2017), pp. 683–688 (2017)
9. Clabaugh, C., Matarić, M.: Escaping Oz: autonomy in socially assistive robotics. Ann. Rev. Control Robot. Auton. Syst. **2**, 33–61 (2019)
10. Codd-Downey, R., Forooshani, P.M., Speers, A., Wang, H., Jenkin, M.R.M.: From ROS to unity: leveraging robot and virtual environment middleware for immersive teleoperation. In: Proceedings of the 11th IEEE International Conference on Information and Automation (ICIA 2014), pp. 932–936 (2014)
11. Crooks, T.J.: The impact of classroom evaluation practices on students. Rev. Educ. Res. **58**(4), 438–481 (1988)
12. Draper, J.V., Kaber, D.B., Usher, J.M.: Telepresence. Hum. Factors **40**(3), 354–375 (1998)
13. Fong, T., Thorpe, C., Baur, C.: Collaboration, dialogue, human-robot interaction. In: Jarvis, R.A., Zelinsky, A. (eds.) Proceedings of the 10th International Symposium on Robotics Research (ISRR 2003), pp. 255–266 (2003)
14. Gallon, L., Abenia, A., Dubergey, F., Négui, M.: Using a telepresence robot in an educational context. In: Proceedings of the 10th International Conference on Frontiers in Education: Computer Science and Computer Engineering (FECS 2019), pp. 16–22 (2019)
15. Jecker, J.D., Maccoby, N., Breitrose, H.: Improving accuracy in interpreting nonverbal cues of comprehension. Psychol. Sch. **2**(3), 239–244 (1965)
16. Kilteni, K., Groten, R., Slater, M.: The sense of embodiment in virtual reality. Presence: Teleoperators Virtual Environ. **21**(4), 373–387 (2012)
17. Meng, W., Hu, Y., Lin, J., Lin, F., Teo, R.: ROS+Unity: an efficient high-fidelity 3D multi-UAV navigation and control simulator in GPS-denied environments. In: 41st Annual Conference of the IEEE Industrial Electronics Society (IECON 2015), pp. 2562–2567 (2015)
18. Miller, D.P., Nourbakhsh, I.: Robotics for education. In: Siciliano, B., Khatib, O. (eds.) Springer Handbook of Robotics, pp. 2115–2134. Springer, Cham (2016). https://doi.org/10.1007/978-3-319-32552-1_79
19. Mubin, O., Stevens, C.J., Shahid, S., Al Mahmud, A., Dong, J.: A review of the applicability of robots in education. Technol. Educ. Learn. **1**, 1–7 (2013)
20. Okon, J.: Role of non-verbal communication in education. Mediterranean J. Soc. Sci. **2**(5), 35–40 (2011)
21. Pasternak, E., Fenichel, R., Marshall, A.N.: Tips for creating a block language with blockly. In: Proceedings of the IEEE Blocks and Beyond Workshop (B&B 2017), pp. 21–24 (2017)
22. Rodríguez-Lera, F.J., Matellán-Olivera, V., Conde-González, M.Á., Martín-Rico, F.: HiMoP: a three-component architecture to create more human-acceptable social-assistive robots. Cogn. Process. **19**(2), 233–244 (2018)
23. Roldán, J.J., Peña-Tapia, E., Garzón-Ramos, D., de León, J., Garzón, M., del Cerro, J., Barrientos, A.: Multi-robot systems, virtual reality and ROS: developing a new generation of operator interfaces. In: Koubaa, A. (ed.) Robot Operating System (ROS). SCI, vol. 778, pp. 29–64. Springer, Cham (2019). https://doi.org/10.1007/978-3-319-91590-6_2

24. Schuemie, M.J., van der Straaten, P., Krijn, M., van der Mast, C.A.: Research on presence in virtual reality: a survey. CyberPsychol. Behav. **4**(2), 183–201 (2001)
25. Sita, E., Horváth, C.M., Thomessen, T., Korondi, P., Pipe, A.G.: ROS-Unity3D based system for monitoring of an industrial robotic process. In: Proceedings of the 10th IEEE/SICE International Symposium on System Integration (SII 2017), pp. 1047–1052 (2017)
26. Steuer, J.: Defining virtual reality: dimensions determining telepresence. J. Commun. **42**(4), 73–93 (1992)
27. Toh, L.P.E., Causo, A., Tzuo, P.W., Chen, I.M., Yeo, S.H.: A review on the use of robots in education and young children. J. Educ. Technol. Soc. **19**(2), 148–163 (2016)
28. Tromp, N., Hekkert, P., Verbeek, P.P.: Design for socially responsible behavior: a classification of influence based on intended user experience. Des. Issues **27**(3), 3–19 (2011)
29. Tsui, K.M., Desai, M., Yanco, H.A.: Considering the bystander's perspective for indirect human-robot interaction. In: Proceedings of the ACM/IEEE International Conference on Human-Robot Interaction (HRI 2010), pp. 129–130 (2010)
30. Tunstall, P., Gipps, C.: Teacher feedback to young children in formative assessment: a typology. Br. Educ. Res. J. **22**(4), 389–404 (1996)
31. Weiss, A., Bernhaupt, R., Lankes, M., Tscheligi, M.: The USUS evaluation framework for human-robot interaction. In: Proceedings of the Symposium on New Frontiers in Human-Robot Interaction at the Adaptive and Emergent Behaviour and Complex Systems Convention (AISB 2009), pp. 11–26 (2009)
32. Whitney, D., Rosen, E., Phillips, E., Konidaris, G., Tellex, S.: Comparing robot grasping teleoperation across desktop and virtual reality with ROS reality. In: Amato, N.M., Hager, G., Thomas, S., Torres-Torriti, M. (eds.) Robotics Research. SPAR, vol. 10, pp. 335–350. Springer, Cham (2020). https://doi.org/10.1007/978-3-030-28619-4_28
33. Whitney, J.P., Chen, T., Mars, J., Hodgins, J.K.: A hybrid hydrostatic transmission and human-safe haptic telepresence robot. In: 22nd IEEE International Conference on Robotics and Automation (ICRA 2016), pp. 690–695 (2016)
34. Yanco, H.A., Drury, J.: Classifying human-robot interaction: an updated taxonomy. In: Proceedings of the IEEE International Conference on Systems, Man and Cybernetics (ICSMC 2004), vol. 3, pp. 2841–2846 (2004)
35. Zhang, M., Duan, P., Zhang, Z., Esche, S.: Development of telepresence teaching robots with social capabilities. In: Proceedings of the ASME International Mechanical Engineering Congress and Exposition (IMECE 2018), pp. 1–11 (2018)

Web-based Teleoperation System for Learning of 3D Prototype Designing and Printing

Siam Charoenseang$^{(\boxtimes)}$ ⓘ, Poonsiri Jailungkaⓘ,
and Chaowwalit Thammatinnoⓘ

Institute of Field Robotics (FIBO), King Mongkut's University of Technology
Thonburi, Bangmod, Thungkru, Bangkok 10140, Thailand
siam@fibo.kmutt.ac.th, pu.poonsiri@gmail.com,
chaowwalit.thammatinno@gmail.com

Abstract. This research proposed the design and development of the web-based teleoperation control system for learning of 3D prototype designing and printing. The system was used as a supplementary education tool that integrated between technology development and learning approaches such as blended learning, project-based learning, and creative-based learning. The proposed system provided a sharing resource and resource utilization via the computer network. The students could access to learn, design, and observe the real process of 3D prototyping via the web pages. The system allowed the user to print 3D prototype via uploading a CAD file to the web server. The CAD file was then approved to be printed as a 3D prototype by the teacher and the admin. Afterward, the system managed the printing queue and displayed 3D printer status including video feedback from the 3D printer for the user. The actual teleoperated 3D printing system was installed at the FIBO building in Thailand and it could be accessed via the website. The proposed system has been used by 265 participants from 5 regions of Thailand, including Thai high school students, vocational students, and teachers. The experimental results showed that the learning achievement of students got improvement up to 30.13% by comparing average T-scores of pretest and posttest. The teachers and students showed a very good level of satisfaction on using the proposed teleoperation system for learning of 3D prototype designing and printing. Finally, this proposed system utilized the advance technology to increase the self-motivation in learning and promoted the concept of resource sharing in order to reduce the educational inequality.

Keywords: Remote learning · 3D printing · Telepresence · Distance learning

1 Introduction

Distance learning or distance education [1, 2] has been making a learning opportunity for anyone who is unable to receive a formal education in education institution. Distance learning means the education system that learners and teachers are far from each other or without face-to-face learning in the classroom. The teachers can utilize the materials or teaching tools such as textbooks, computers and using

P. Zaphiris and A. Ioannou (Eds.): HCII 2020, LNCS 12206, pp. 391–407, 2020.
https://doi.org/10.1007/978-3-030-50506-6_27

telecommunications equipment including radio and television. The teaching tools can help the different levels of students to access to the educational system.

Distance learning television [3] was a policy of the Thai government for resolving the lack of teachers of small-sized schools and increasing access to quality education for rural students in Thailand. In 1995, Khankeo Watcharothai established a distance education project via satellite at Wang Klai Kangwon School [4]. The first teaching and learning procedures were broadcasted on December 5, 1995 and there has been the broadcasted teaching and learning activities via the satellite until now. In 2004, Professor David Yaron and a team from the Carnegie Mellon university proposed a research work on the simulation of a chemical operating system [5]. In 2003, this research was successfully created as a virtual chemical laboratory system.

Teleoperation [5] is the remote operation and means the operation of a robot or a system over a distance. The human operator is a person who monitors the operated machine and makes the needed control actions. For example, Professor Ken Goldberg from the University of California, Berkeley and his team designed and developed robotic systems for gardening [6]. The user was allowed to water the plants and watch the pictures of the growth of plants in the garden via the internet. This system used only one SCARA robot to control all operations. In 2017, the design and development of the telerobotic control system for learning of chemical mixture was proposed to allow the users to learn the chemical mixture process via the web-based telerobotic system [7]. Furthermore, the learning achievement and usability test of teachers and students were investigated using their proposed system. A small articulated robot was used for picking and placing the chemical equipment. The student could easily control the robot at the high level via the web browser. The proposed teleoperation system also provided the video feedback of the real experiments about chemical equilibrium via the web. The student was allowed to choose the type and amount of chemical, view the pH level of chemical, and observe the system operation via the video feedback from the web browser.

In general, the designing of 3D model is a common subject that brings the hands-on experiences. In addition, the 3D printing is a new technology used as a tool for teaching a variety of subjects including science, technology, art, engineering, and mathematics [8, 9]. The 3D printing technology provides students with hands-on experience to accompany the traditional classroom learning. For Thai traditional education, students practiced on creating 3D works by filing, shaping and turning, which is a limitation in creating some complex and creative works. Therefore, using a 3D printer helps students to design many complex and creative models and learn from mistakes without high costs. However, the 3D printer may not be easy for the novice because of the complexity of 3D printing workflows and requirement of professional operators for setting and maintenance. Hence, this research proposes a web-based teleoperation for learning of 3D prototype designing and printing. The system was designed to support the learners from science and art branches as a supplementary education tool that integrated between technology development and learning approaches such as blended learning, project-based learning, and creative-based learning. The system assisted the learners to build knowledge by themselves and supported sharing resources and resource utilization via the computer network.

2 Methodology

2.1 System Overview

The proposed system consisted of both main hardware and software parts. The key components of the hardware part consisted of one 3D printer, two computers for controlling the 3D printer [10], webpage user interface, and user management and three cameras for video feedback of 3D prototyping process. The actual hardware components have been installed at the institute of field robotics, King Mongkut's university of technology, Thonburi as shown in Fig. 1.

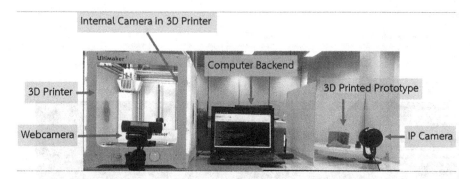

Fig. 1. Hardware components of proposed system

All software components were designed and developed for communication between the user's web-based user interface and the server's remote 3D printing system via the computer network. The overview of the proposed system can be summarized as a diagram of the data transmission between the two sites as shown in Fig. 2.

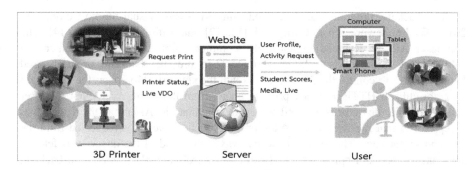

Fig. 2. System overview

First, the server management program was developed for communicating with the 3D printer after the 3D model files were sent into the system. This program read and listed all approved three-dimensional file into the system format via the web page orderly. It converted data from a 3D model file into the STL file format and G-code format, respectively. The G-Code file is a file containing commands that define the movement and operations of a 3D printer. Once the G-code file was created, that file was sent to the 3D printer to produce the 3D prototype via the internet. This program was launched on the backend server and connected to the 3D printer as shown in Fig. 3.

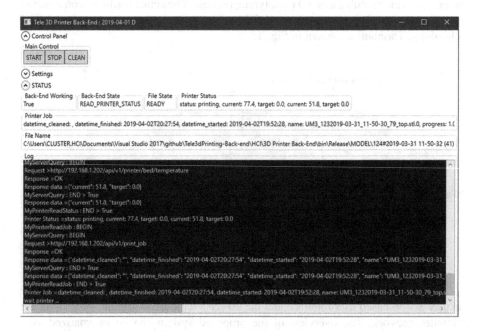

Fig. 3. 3D printer backend server

This backend program was developed using Microsoft Visual Studio Community 2017, Net Framework 4.6.1, Cura 3.2.1 [11, 12] and Ultimaker API [13, 14]. The Ultimaker API is designed to allow the communication between 3D printer and software via REST API in JSON format. Therefore, the backend program used Ultimaker API to control the 3D printer through the network. Moreover, the developed program utilized HTTP to check printing queue from the web server. First, the user submitted .STL file to the server and request to print that file. After that, the request was accepted and that file was added to the printing queue which was requested from the backend server later. The .STL file, which was at the head of the queue, was fetched and sent to the Cura application that directly controls the 3D printer. The backend server then checked the status of the 3D printer to check whether it was ready to print the 3D prototype or not. When the 3D printer was ready, the backend program sent the . Gcode file of the 3D model file to the 3D printer to produce the 3D prototype. While the 3D printer was working on the 3D prototyping process, the backend server program monitored the printer status continuously. When the 3D prototype was printed completely, the 3D model file was then deleted from the queue and the printer status was updated. The operation diagram of the 3D printer controlled by the proposed backend server program can be shown in Fig. 4.

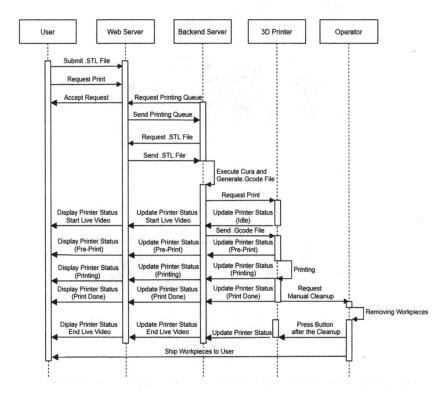

Fig. 4. Operation diagram of the 3D printer controlled by the proposed system

Furthermore, a web-based user interface was developed for communication between users and the server as shown in Fig. 5. Users were able to access the website from any computer or a mobile device via internet. This website provided the learning materials related to 3D printing, online 3D design tools, and 3D model submission function. The user needed to register, log into the proposed system, take a pretest, self-study about 3D printing, design some 3D model file, submit the 3D file, view the 3D printing process, and take a posttest and a usability test.

The user interface of this website consists of 4 main sections, such as the user account, the content and learning progress tracking, the file management and the display. The proposed system's operation flow can be illustrated in Fig. 6.

User Account. The user account section consists of the user register section (Register) and login checking section (Login) which were embedded into the developed website. The user management section (User Management) divided users into 3 groups which are administrators, teachers, and students. Each type of user has different rights to manage files, such as file uploading to the system, file approval for 3D prototype printing, etc.

Fig. 5. Proposed web-based user interface

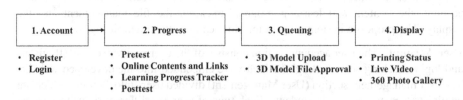

Fig. 6. Proposed system's operation flow of the client side

Content and Learning Progress Tracking. This section provided the contents about 3D prototyping and tracked the user's self-learning progress. This section contained 4 functions as follows.

- Pretest. This section contained questions related to 3D prototyping which was used to test the user's knowledge before using the proposed system.
- Main Website's Contents. This section provided the contents about 3D prototyping, designing tool links, and examples of 3D prototypes for visualization and inspiration purposes.
- Learning Progress Tracker. This section was used to track the user's learning progress by recording the learning state, the amount of spending time, and exam scores. It also showed in the form of progress bar.
- Posttest and User's Satisfaction Evaluation. After using the proposed system, the user can take the posttest and evaluation of user's satisfaction about the system's usage, the provided contents, and the specific values for 3D prototyping

File Management. The file management allowed the student to submit the 3D model file to the system via the file submission menu. Then, the teacher checked and approved those submitted files. Finally, the system administrator authorized the submitted files to be printed orderly.

Display. The display section was used to display the process of 3D printing through live video feedback, 3D printing order, and the gallery of 3D prototype model design and final product.

- Live Video. The users can view the process of creating the 3D prototype from the 3D printer from the live video on the webpage including the working status of the 3D printer. This helps the students to learn and understand the techniques of 3D design and actual 3D printing among shared processes on the webpage.
- Web Gallery. The web gallery allowed the user to visualize the 3D model and final printed product in 360-degree view.

3   Implementation

3.1   Survey

First, many targeted teachers from 3 high schools and 11 technical colleges were interviewed about the forms of activities and teaching media that they normally used and looked for their classes related to 3D prototyping. This helped the development team to design the proposed system overview. For targeted teachers from high schools, they taught the learning areas of art, occupation and technology, mathematics, science, etc. For targeted teachers from technical schools, they conducted the vocational certificate program and higher vocational certificate program in the learning areas of mechanics, mechanical parts design and production, electronics equipment, industrial robot, etc.

The summary of the interview of targeted teachers can be shown in Table 1. It indicates the readiness of school's equipment, learning media, and learning approaches. Those teachers were also interested in using the proposed teleoperation for learning system.

Table 1. Survey data from the targeted teachers by interviewing

Survey topics	Number of schools	Number of colleges
1. Available learning media on manufacturing equipment & machines		
1.1 CNC Machines	–	7
1.2 3D Printer	1	4
1.3 CAD/CAM/CAE Software	3	4
2. Available teaching approach		
2.1 The Lecture-based Learning	3	11
2.2 The ICT-Integrated Learning	3	5
2.3 The Problem-based Learning	–	9
2.4 The Project-based Learning	3	11
2.5 The Project-based Learning with Problems from Industry	–	5

From the interview results, teachers informed that their students were not able to produce the workpieces as designed due to the limitation of building skills and the usage skills of tools for filing, shaping or turning. This limited the student's creativity and it had to pay high service fees for 3D prototyping. Therefore, teachers were interested in using the proposed teleoperation of 3D printer in their classes so that their students would be able to learn technology for 3D designing and create some creative and unique 3D prototypes.

In addition, the surveyed learning approaches in classes were used to design of implementation of the proposed teleoperation for learning system on the targeted groups. It consisted of 3 approaches as follows:

Teaching Media in the Classroom

With this approach, the teachers applied the proposed teleoperation for learning system as a teaching media in the classroom for both lectures in theory and practice. Teaching period took approximately 3-4 weeks. Students could use the proposed system to print their workpieces for about 1 week. The teaching plan can be shown in Fig. 7.

Timeline

1ˢᵗ week	2ⁿᵈ week	3ʳᵈ week	4ᵗʰ week
1. Lecturers teach in classroom 2. Students take the exam and sign in the system.	1. Students sketch the design idea, design 3D model, and upload 3D model file to the system.	1. Lecturers and admin approve student's 3D model files. 2. Students receive printed workpieces within 1 week. 3. Students modify and assemble workpieces.	1. Students present their workpieces within 1 week.

Total about 1 month

Fig. 7. Teaching plan of applying the proposed system in the classroom

In general, the examples of workpieces that students needed to design covered the parts of robot, gripper, structure, parts of body, gears, joints, cutting tool models such as turning knives, milling cutters and models to be embedded with electronics parts or sensors, etc. Figure 8 shows the robot gripper with gears, joints, and links that the students needed to design and build in their classes.

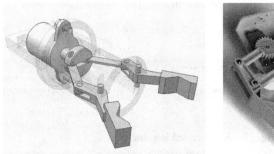

Fig. 8. Examples of designed and printed workpieces [15, 16]

Short Course Training

This teaching approach is a form of short-term training for teachers and students. It took about 1-3 days to learn how to use the proposed teleoperation system from the system development team. The training covered how to design the 3D prototype from the real problem such as a name tag, jig and fixture, etc. All students needed to present their design and send the 3D model files to be printed within 1 week. The teaching plan of this short course training can be shown in Fig. 9.

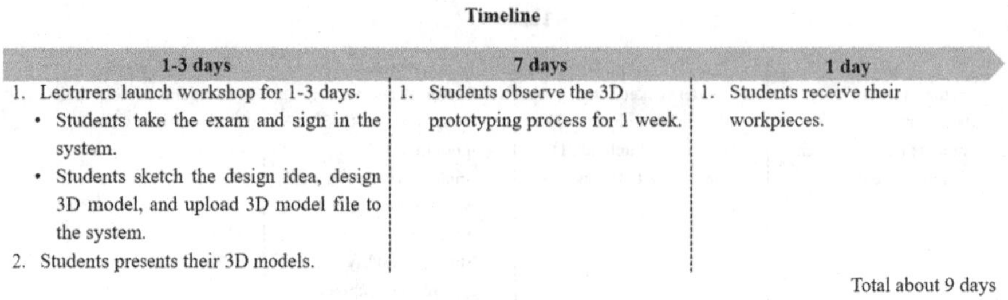

Timeline

1-3 days	7 days	1 day

1. Lecturers launch workshop for 1-3 days.
  • Students take the exam and sign in the system.
  • Students sketch the design idea, design 3D model, and upload 3D model file to the system.
2. Students presents their 3D models.
	1. Students observe the 3D prototyping process for 1 week.	1. Students receive their workpieces.

Total about 9 days

Fig. 9. Short course training approach

Self-directed Learning

With this approach, students needed to log into the proposed teleoperation system to learn about the contents and practice of 3D design by themselves. Teachers needed to reserve the period of printing for their classes with the system administrators. In addition, teachers could utilize the proposed teleoperation system to print the 3D workpieces for teaching media, the product design competition, the roadshow activities, the science project activities or the project activities of vocational students to solve the industrial problems, etc. as shown in Fig. 10.

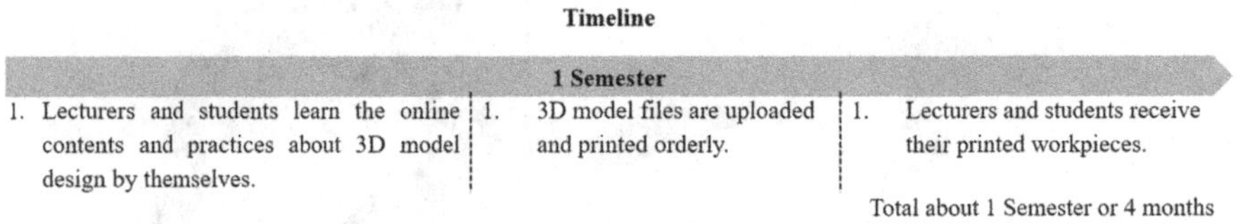

Timeline

1 Semester		
1. Lecturers and students learn the online contents and practices about 3D model design by themselves.	1. 3D model files are uploaded and printed orderly.	1. Lecturers and students receive their printed workpieces.

Total about 1 Semester or 4 months

Fig. 10. Self-directed learning plan

4 Experimental Results

4.1 Participants

The sampled population was 200 high school students, 44 vocational students and 21 teachers in the targeted groups of learning areas related to art, occupation and technology, mathematics, science, mechanics, mechanical part design and production, electronics equipment, industrial robot, etc.

4.2 System Performance

The proposed teleoperation system with one 3D printer was able to support up to 250 users per day with 20 MBytes per user. There were 3 average sizes of the workpieces as shown in Table 2.

Table 2. Average sizes, printing times, and samples of 3D prototypes

Size of workpiece	Details	Sample of 3D Prototype
Small size	20 min/workpiece 24 workpieces/day (8 hrs) 98 workpieces/week	
Medium size	2 hrs/workpiece 4 workpieces/day (8 hrs) 21 workpieces/week	
Large size	10 hrs/workpiece 1 workpieces/day (8 hr) 14 workpieces/week	

4.3 Usage Evaluation

There were three sampled groups of high school students, vocational students, and teachers who evaluated the usage of the proposed teleoperation system. They utilized the proposed system as a supplementary education tool in blended learning activities, project-based learning activities, or creative-based learning activities. The experimental results showed that learning achievement of high school students, vocational students, and teachers received the improvements by 30.13%, 18.3%, and 20.85%, respectively. They were computed based on comparison of average T-scores of pretest and posttest and the statistics of the learning progress can be shown in Table 3.

Table 3. Statistics of learning progress after using the proposed system

Group	N	Pre-test					Post-test					Diff. of avg. T-score	% of avg. T-score
		Min	Max	$\bar{x}$	Avg. T-score	S.D.	Min	Max	$\bar{x}$	Avg. T-score	S. D.		
High school	200	1	10	5.62	43.45	1.91	5	10	8.51	56.55	1.37	13.09	30.13
Vocational	44	4	10	7.11	45.81	1.63	6	10	8.50	54.19	1.37	8.39	18.31
Teacher	21	3	10	7.00	45.28	1.92	7	10	8.67	54.72	1.11	9.44	20.85

In addition, the teachers and students showed a very good level of satisfaction on using the proposed teleoperation system for learning of 3D prototype designing and printing. The participants were asked to fill in the questionnaire to evaluate the level of user's satisfaction. The satisfaction rating started from 1 (strongly disagree) to 4 (strongly agree). The results from the survey are shown in Table 4.

Table 4. User's satisfaction after using the proposed system

Evaluation list	$\bar{x}$		
	High school	Vocational	Teachers
1. Usability	3.45	3.53	3.70
2. Contents	3.57	3.49	3.65
3. Value for specific task	3.62	3.68	3.86
4. Service and support	3.65	3.50	3.61

Finally, this proposed teleoperation system was used widely in 5 regions of Thailand with more than 200 participants. The proposed system increased self-motivation in learning and reduced the educational inequality, supported the resource sharing via internet, and saved the school's budgets.

4.4 Values of Using the Proposed Learning System for 3D Prototyping

Examples of 3D Prototypes from the Student Groups

1. Teaching media in the classroom

   After teachers in the learning area of computer and vocational teachers attended the training how to apply the proposed system as the teaching media, they conducted the classes with 55 high school students and 44 vocational students. After applying this proposed system in the classroom as shown in Fig. 11, it found that students were excited and motivated to learn about 3D printing technology and they gained more confidence about designing of 3D models. Several sampled 3D prototypes for robot application in Fig. 12 were printed successfully using the proposed system.

Fig. 11. System usage in classroom

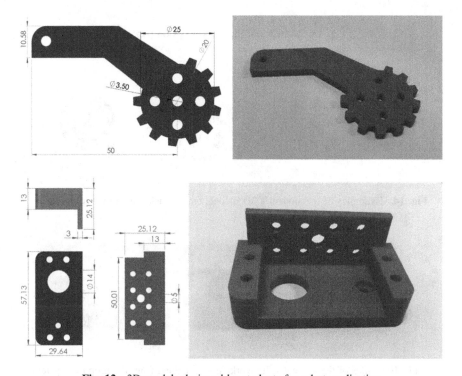

Fig. 12. 3D models designed by students for robot application

2. Short Course Training

After 113 students participated in the short course training about 1–3 days from the system developing team, they were able to design and create some creative 3D prototypes. First, they learned how to sketch the workpiece as shown in Fig. 13. Next, they used the online program linked from the proposed system to design the 3D model as shown in Fig. 14. Then, the designed 3D model files were sent to the proposed system to produce the real 3D prototypes as shown in Fig. 15. Students could observe the online printing process from the live video feedback. After that, students presented the idea and technique of design and showed the printed 3D prototypes in the classroom. This leads the knowledge exchange among the students under the teacher's advices for better improvement in the future.

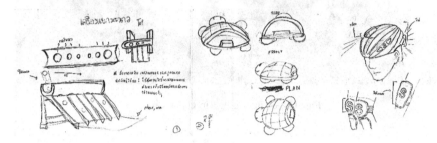

Fig. 13. Sketches of the workpieces on paper

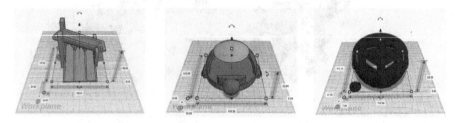

Fig. 14. Examples of the student's 3D models created using the online program

Fig. 15. Examples of the student's 3D workpieces obtained from the proposed system

3. Self-directed Learning

There were 32 users from several Thailand's regions to access the proposed tele-operation system via the webpage to self-study the contents, create 3D models, and submit the designed files to be printed. Samples of workpieces can be shown in Fig. 16. This also confirms the capability of remote access from the different places across the country.

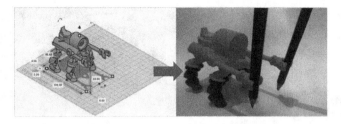

Fig. 16. Examples of the 3D prototypes from the self-directed learning approach

Examples of 3D Prototypes from the Teacher Groups

There were 3 teacher groups that utilized the proposed teleoperation system. The first group designed and built the 3D prototypes from the basic problems such as the name tags as shown in Fig. 17. The second group used the proposed system to create the teaching media for the basic robotics subject and the mechanical part designing subject such as gears and various joints as shown in Fig. 18. The last group utilized the proposed system to create workpiece to solve the industrial problems as shown in Figs. 19 and 20.

Fig. 17. Examples of workpieces for basic problem

Fig. 18. Examples of 3D prototypes as teaching media

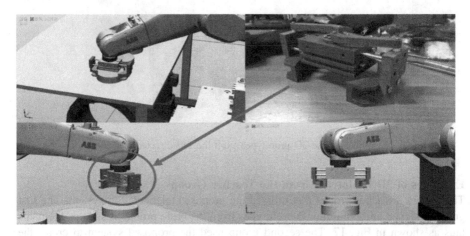

Fig. 19. Example of the Robot Gripper printed from the proposed system

Fig. 20. Example of printed workpiece for the control circuit box

5   Discussion and Conclusion

The teleoperation system for learning was proposed to help both teachers and students about 3D designing and prototyping via the web access. The experimental results showed that the learning achievement of 265 participants from 5 regions of Thailand gained improvement up to 30.13% by comparing average T-scores of pretest and posttest. The teachers and students showed a very good level of satisfaction on using the proposed teleoperation system for learning of 3D prototype designing and printing. From the interviews and online questionnaires, the users informed that the proposed system offered the well-explained contents about the 3D prototyping process, good visualization of the process via the video feedback, and ease to access from anywhere through the webpage. Teachers utilized this proposed system as teaching media about 3D model designing and prototyping. Students got more motivation and gained more confidence about 3D prototyping process. Many creative workpieces such as robot parts, miniature bearings, and joints were built by using this proposed system in classroom remotely. Some prototypes were also used to solve the industrial problems from the classes of technical colleges.

The proposed teleoperation for learning system accelerated the learning activities in the schools with limited budget. Those schools did not have to invest the equipment at school. They needed only internet to access this proposed teleoperation for their classes. This promoted the concept of resource sharing across the country in order to reduce the educational inequality.

In the future, multiple 3D printers can be connected to the server to provide more time-sharing access service. Further, variety of computerized machines could be integrated with the proposed teleoperation system as well.

Acknowledgement. This research work was financially supported by the national research council of Thailand.

References

1. Holmberg, B.: The Evolution, Principles and Practices of Distance Education, vol. 11. BIS-Verlag der Carl von Ossietzky Universität Oldenburg, Oldenburg (2005)
2. Kaplan, A.M., Haenlein, M.: Higher education and the digital revolution: about MOOCs, SPOCs, social media, and the Cookie Monster. Bus. Horiz. **59**(4), 441–450 (2016)
3. Haruthaithanasan, N.M.a.T.: Educational management of distance learning television of small-sized schools for Thai Education 4.0. Acad. Serv. J. **29**(2), 209–218. (2018). (Prince of Songkla University)
4. Distance learning brings education to rural Thailand. http://oknation.nationtv.tv/blog/print.php?id=287331. Accessed 29 Dec 2019
5. Yaron, D., Cuadros, J.. Karabinos, M., Leinhardt, G., Evans, K.L.: Virtual laboratories and scenes to support chemistry instruction. In: National Science Foundation Course, Curriculum, and Laboratory Improvement (NSF-CCLI) Program Conference, pp. 177–182 (2004)
6. Goldberg, K.: The robot in the garden: telerobotics and telepistemology in the age of the Internet by Goldberg, Ken. MIT Press, Cambridge (2000)
7. Charoenseang, S.: Telerobotic Control System for Learning of Chemical Mixture. The Thailand Research Fund, Bangkok (2014)
8. Tillinghast, R.C., et al.: Integrating three dimensional visualization and additive manufacturing into K-12 classrooms. In: 2014 IEEE Integrated STEM Education Conference, Princeton, NJ, USA, pp. 1–7. IEEE, (2014)
9. Straub, J., Kerlin, S.: Development of a large, low-cost, instant 3D scanner. Technologies **2**, 76–95 (2014)
10. Ultimaker-3. https://ultimaker.com/3d-printers/ultimaker-3. Accessed 28 Jan 2020
11. Cura 3.2.1. https://github.com/Ultimaker/Cura/releases/tag/3.2.1. Accessed 28 Jan 2020
12. Ultimaker Cura, https://ultimaker.com/software/ultimaker-cura. Accessed 28 Jan 2020
13. Ultimaker API (yourUltimakerIPaddress). http://10.1.1.1/docs/api/. Accessed 14 Feb 2020
14. Ultimaker Cloud API. https://api.ultimaker.com/docs/. Accessed 28 Jan 2020
15. Robot Gripper 9, Youtube. https://www.youtube.com/watch?v=shUN5VXV8mE. accessed 14 Feb 2020
16. Kwartzlab Makerspace, Robot Gripper Improvements. https://old.kwartzlab.ca/2014/04/robot-gripper-improvements/. Accessed 14 Feb 2020

Building STEM Capability in a Robotic Arm Educational Competition

Lin Chu[1], Yu-Liang Ting[2(✉)], and Yaming Tai[1]

[1] Department of Children English Education,
National Taipei University of Education, Taipei, Taiwan
[2] Department of Technology Application and Human Resource Development,
National Taiwan Normal University, Taipei, Taiwan
yting@ntnu.edu.tw

Abstract. This paper investigated high school students' STEM capability in a robotic arm educational competition. The learning design of the competition based on the pedagogy of copy and redesign, and social creativity framework. Students learned the process of building up robotic arms by copying instructors' examples, discussing possible ways of redesigning the robotic arms. The students need to present their creativity by using robotic arms as boundary objects in a collaboration. After a one-day workshop and another one-day competition, the observation results showed that students were capable of exhibiting unique creativity to solve the problem during the competition, such as refining the robotic arms to grab something which it had not been able to reach, or adding materials on the robots to create a better user experience. Students also applied scientific and mathematical knowledge to improve the robots, performed integrated STEM ability. Furthermore, students' meta-cognitive strategies of taking notes and collaboration were evidenced. It indicated that the copy and redesign, and social creativity framework can facilitate students' creative performance of STEM capability. Moreover, as the study adopted students' attitudes towards STEM survey, the results showed that students' attitudes towards STEM had no significance after the curriculum design. The possible reasons included that short-term learning process might have minor influence on students' STEM attitudes. Other possible reasons might be the ceiling effect, and small number of samples. Future study was suggested to evaluate the learning design into a long-term curriculum, adopt semi-structured interview to investigate more delicate relationship between the learning design and students' performance, and conduct STEM ability test to understand students' performance.

Keywords: STEM · Robotic arm · Copy and redesign · Social creativity · Boundary object · Educational competition

1 Introduction

STEM emphasizes the importance of the integration of science, technology, engineering, and math (STEM). Developing integrative curricular materials has a greater increase in students' scientific expertise [1]. In recent decades, curriculum design of robotics is seen as an important part of STEM education and involves various kinds of

© Springer Nature Switzerland AG 2020
P. Zaphiris and A. Ioannou (Eds.): HCII 2020, LNCS 12206, pp. 408–421, 2020.
https://doi.org/10.1007/978-3-030-50506-6_28

knowledge such as mechanics and electronics, automatic control theory, and software programming of microcontrollers [2, 3]. Rogers and Portsmore [4] also indicated that students can apply mathematical concepts, the scientific method of inquiry, and problem-solving skills in building robots. However, there is no guarantee that a lesson of building robotic arms can lead to successful technology education. Kopcha et al. [5] suggested that robotic lessons should be introduced in a functional environment, which includes problem-solving tasks, explorations, or challenges. A functional environment helps building students' abilities in intangible domains such as math and programming. Students can apply their contextualized STEM knowledge when assembling robots.

In an educational-oriented robotic competition, the tasks for students to work on are related to students' daily life scenarios, and the materials of robots are easy to access [6]. Students can perform tasks, whose challenges in an environment similar to a real situation [7]. Moreover, competition can give students an opportunity to be away from traditional theory-oriented lecture courses. The prize of the competition also can motivate students, resulting in the feeling of accomplishment [8]. The purpose of the competition is to create a functional environment that promotes students' integrative learning and creativity. In short, a well-designed STEM competition can improve students' academic skills, interest, and awareness of STEM. It also emphasized the ability of cooperation as well as respect towards other teams during the competition [9].

However, few studies in robotics education and competition focused on educational methodology and related process of building robots [10], such as students' copying and redesigning from teacher's prior work of how to build a robot and the pedagogy in facilitating students to exercise their creativity and collaboration. In addition, teaching procedures in robotic education mostly focus on programming the robots instead of presenting functional environment for students to exercise their knowledge [5]. Thus the present study was intended to use educational-oriented competition with the adoption of the teaching framework of copy and redesign. By doing so, students copy the making of robotic arms to learn the basic knowledge of robots during a one day workshop. The competition, as a functional environment, then engages students into their STEM learning and performance of social creativity. The current study aims to examine students' performance during the workshop and the competition while experiencing the process of copy and redesign and collaboration. Meanwhile, a survey was conducted to understand students' STEM attitudes towards STEM before the workshop and after the competition.

2 Literature Review

The learning design in the present robotic competition was based on integrated STEM education and was originally proposed for hands-on educational program. Integrated STEM education emphasizes the importance of connections, representations, and misconceptions [11, 12]. The connections not only include the four subjects, but also the relations of real world problems. Teachers should provide multiple representations to scaffold students' learning and address students' misconceptions. As for the hands-on education, it can be seen as the process of tinkering. Tinkering is an exploratory activity that many researchers claim it helps novices learn to program. Tinkering activities include trial and error in using feedback mechanisms. Through repeatedly change and test, students can improve their design with better performance, meanwhile they can learn more about the knowledge and skills behind the design. Borrowing the concept of tinkering in programming learning, this study used the copy-and-redesign structure associated with competition rules to stimulate participants to exercise and integrate their knowledge and skills. In relating to the so-called "alternative programming environments" such as Scratch and in tangible environments such as e-textiles, the proposed learning is an alternative electromechanics STEM learning environments, facilitating participants to integrate and exercise their science knowledge and hands-on skills. When the tinkering is aligned with Kolb's experiential learning cycle, students activate the robotic arms (active experiment), make measurements and experience the phenomena (concrete experience), observe and comprehend (reflective observation), and make assumptions and grasp ideas to plan a new trial (abstract conceptualization). It should be playful and experimental. Students are continually reassessing goals, exploring new paths, and imagining new possibilities [13]. Digital tools applied in hands-on education, which include prototyping tools and microcontrollers, are effective and affordable for students to copy and redesign in various ways. Therefore, the learning design forms a community infrastructure that facilitates students' learning and creativity in social context [14]. The following section presents the framework of copy and redesign of integrated STEM learning, followed by the discussion of social creativity in the robotic competition.

2.1 Copy and Redesign

Research has proposed ways of teaching STEM in hands-on education to build up students' STEM literacy [15–19]. Chou [20] categorized the robotic teaching techniques into three stages: pre-design, in-design, and post-design (Fig. 1).

- Pre-design stage: In this stage, the easily accessed prototyping tools and microcontrollers are introduced to the students to experience the making of robots. By copying teacher's examples, they can have a better understanding of the robotic concept.
- In-design stage: The teacher further introduces a challenge to students in the in-design stage. Students have to base on their discussion to collaboratively tinker and redesign the robots, such as re-programming or testing different materials to tackle the challenge. This is also the step that creativity takes place.
- Post-design stage: The post-design stage aims to wrap up the learning by reviewing and reflecting students' performance. Students can learn from peers' advice and write reflective journals to promote meta-cognition and transfer of learning.

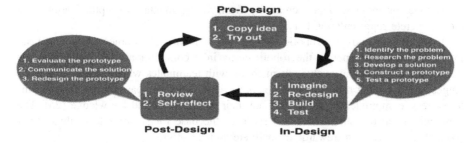

Fig. 1. Instructional maker education program framework proposed by Chou [20].

The present study employs the robotic arm (Fig. 2) and Arduino as the prototyping tool and microcontrollers for the framework of copy and redesign. Two tandem activities, a one-day workshop and a one-day competition, are used as the pre-design and in-design stages to investigate students' performance of creativity. In the workshop, students are hoped to learn to copy teachers' examples to build robotic arms, and acquire the basic knowledge of robots. Two weeks after the workshop, the competition is held and students are assigned tasks to copy the previously learned robot and redesign it to win the champion.

Fig. 2. The robotic arm employed in the present study.

2.2 Social Creativity

The competition design adopts the framework of social creativity. Fischer et al. [21] proposed that creativity has four essential attributes: originality, expression, social evaluation, and social appreciation within a community. These attributes indicate that the ability of creativity is not only within individuals, but related to social context. One's creativity should be evaluated by the society so that others can give feedback and appreciation as rewards, then further motivate more creativities [22, 23]. In addition, creativity within social interactions can be fostered by the boundary objects, which indicates the evolving artifacts can become meaningful as they are used, discussed and evaluated [24]. During collaboration, the boundary objects can trigger related knowledge, promote students' creativity from vague mental conceptualization to a more concrete representation [21].

In the current study, the robotic arms served as the boundary objects. Students need to try to build and operate the robotic arms in a competition. Hence students are engaged into discussing evaluation methods with teammates when encountered challenges, evaluate their robots to win the competition. They can base on the robotic arms to express, communicate, and coordinate their perspectives and knowledge [25]. The competition, on the other hand, can serve as the base for students to evaluate their products and give them rewards to facilitate their creativity.

3   Workshop and Competition Design

A one-day workshop and a one-day competition were adopted in this research. The competition was held two weeks after the workshop. Four experts were responsible for the workshop and competition design, which included a professor in technology education domain, an instructor who specialized in robotic Makers, one undergraduate and one graduate students of technology education as the assistants. The instructor and two assistants were employed to plan and teach the lessons, while the professor designed the structure of the workshop and competition.

The workshop applied pre-design stage of copy and redesign. All of the students learned how to build robotic arms under the guidance of the instructor and two assistants. The instructor demonstrated the making of the robotic arm, students then copied the process through hands-on practices to acquire basic knowledge of robot. Figure 3 shows one of the learning steps that the instructor encouraged students to copy the program codes. To facilitate students' learning, the instructor also gave students clues to try out more possibilities (Fig. 4).

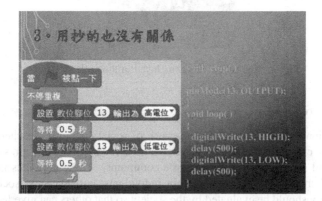

Fig. 3. Workshop design that encouraged students to copy the process.

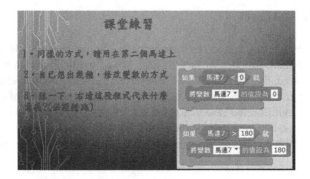

Fig. 4. Workshop design that encouraged students to try out more possibilities.

In the competition, all teams went through the in-design stage of copy and redesign framework. At first, each team had to build the robotic arm as same as the one they had built during the previous workshop. Then, a task was assigned for the teams to put objects (dices) into three different positioned shelves. Each shelf had three different altitude grids that represent various scores (Fig. 5). Students had to look for the best scoring combination to win the competition. If students built the same robotic arms as the one in the previous workshop, they could not operate the arm to reach the highest score grids. Therefore, students had to identify the problem, share and discuss their creative opinions with teammates, and re-design their robots to tackle the challenge. To support students' creativity, the competition provided a piece of foam core board and foam tape. Both of them were dispensable for the making of robotic arms. Students could apply the materials to solve the problem in the competition.

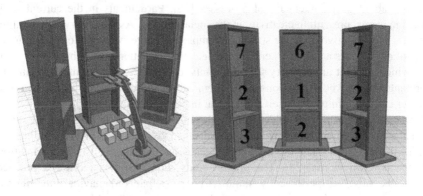

Fig. 5. The task design which was adopted in the competition.

4 Research Method

The present study applied mixed methods research to investigate students' creativity performance and their attitudes toward STEM. Mixed methods research collects and analyzes both quantitative and qualitative data within the same study to explore diverse perspectives and uncover relationships that exist behind the synthesis of both types of data and answer multifaceted research questions. A qualitative observation was conducted in the workshop and competition, and the quantitative method of students' attitudes toward STEM survey was employed before the workshop and after the competition.

4.1 Participants

Participants were 13 teams represented 10 senior high schools in the new Taipei city of Taiwan, and each team consists of 3 students. The age of the participants ranged from 16 to 18 years old and they all showed distinct levels of STEM proficiency. Some of the students had already acquired basic physic knowledge of Grade 10 and 11; but some of them just started to learn it. The participants learned to build the prototype of basic robotic arms in the workshop. After two weeks, the educational competition created a problem-solving situation that encourages students' collaboration of STEM learning and creative thinking.

4.2 Research Instruments

The present study applies the qualitative observation method primarily to understand how students present their ability to copy and redesign and how they exhibit their creativity when facing the challenges. Behavioral observation is useful for answering questions about social interactional processes [26]. Participants in the current study worked in teams, presenting creativity in the social context. As the observation required authentic and objective data, the stance of complete observer was employed during the competition [27]. As a field worker the complete observer attempts to observe people in ways which make it unnecessary for informants to take the observer into account and informants do not know he is observing them. So in the current study, the complete observer entirely removed himself from social interaction with competition participants (informants). The data was collected through photos, video recording, and the observational notes, then analyzed by the method of in vivo coding. In vivo coding is a practice that assigned a label to a section of data, and the label is usually named from participants' own words [28]. The present study didn't apply interviewed practice. Instead, the observer periodically summarized participants' behavior into different categories to create labels during the workshop and competition [26].

Meanwhile, a quantitative method was adopted to measure students' attitudes toward STEM. The survey of attitudes towards STEM aimed to understand the possible improvement of participants' attitudes before and after the workshop and competition.

The survey consists of a total of five sections with 33 items. The first three sections, math, science, and engineering, investigate students' learning experience, self-efficacy, expectancy-value, and motivation towards the three subjects [29, 30]. The fourth section is attitudes toward STEM integrated learning, which refers to Guzey et al.'s [31] study. The last section investigates students' career choice and adopts 4 of 43 items in Erkut and Marx's [30] original survey. The survey adopted 5-point Likert scale in the first to fourth sections, while the fifth section was a 4-point Likert scale to force respondents to take sides.

5   Results and Discussion

This section presents the results of current mix-methods study. Qualitative observation data was encoded into four labels, and quantitative data of attitudes towards STEM survey was analyzed by t test. Followed by the discussion to gain a deeper understanding of the relationship between the present learning design and the results.

5.1   The Qualitative Observation Results

The qualitative observation data, analyzed by in vivo coding, can be labeled as four distinguished features: creativity, STEM integrated performance, meta-cognition strategy, and collaboration. The results are as follows.

- Creativity: To solve the problems in the competition, participants discussed with teammates, showed distinct creative performance (Fig. 6). The participants refined their robots by lengthening the arms, or heightening the base of the robots. Some of the participants improved the controller to better operate the robot in the competition. The materials they used to redesign the robots included not only the foam core board and foam tape, but the remnant of the robotic arms made by the medium-density fiberboard (MDF).

Fig. 6. Participants performed creativity during the competition

- STEM integrated performance: Participants presented integrated STEM skills by extending the grippers on the robots to make it more effective on grabbing objects. Some of the teams added pieces of foam core board beside the joint of the robots to stabilize the motion of the arms and grippers. These performances were related to the theory of the surface friction, which indicated the integrated science and engineering skills (Fig. 7). Furthermore, while participants discussed their strategies of operating the robotic arms, they also performed integrated math and engineering skills. They used measuring tools or their hands to estimate the height of the shelf, and discussed the possible redesign methods (Fig. 8).

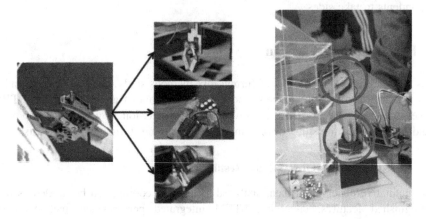

Fig. 7. Participants presenting integrated science and engineering skills

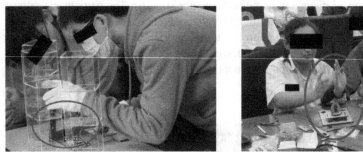

Fig. 8. Participants presenting integrated math and engineering skills

- Meta-cognition strategy: Participants applied the meta-cognitive strategy by taking notes of their programming process to support their learning. Figure 9 showed two teams wrote down the programming content which indicated the robots' operation.

Fig. 9. Participants using the meta-cognitive strategy

- Collaboration: During the competition, participants showed different strategies of collaboration, such as divided operational works to decrease the load of cognition, or gave teammates support (Fig. 10).

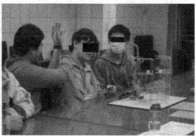

Fig. 10. Participants' strategies of collaboration

5.2 The Survey Results of Attitudes Towards STEM

A total of 29 participants' survey data were collected before the workshop and 56 after the competition, indicated that 27 students didn't participate the pre-test. It was due to the nature of voluntary participation in the survey. Four participants' pre-test data was deleted due to items' vacancy, 5 participants' data were examined as invalid. Therefore, the number of valid sample is 20. The attitudes toward STEM survey results showed in Table 1, suggesting that participants' attitudes toward STEM subjects and integrated STEM instruction had no significant difference after the competition ($t(19) = -1.860$, $p > .05$) on the 5-point Likert scale. The career choice had no significant difference ($t(19) = -0.134$, $p > .05$) on the 4-point Likert scale.

Table 1. Results of the *t* test. (N = 20)

Sections	Pretest mean (SD)	Posttest mean (SD)	Posttest-Pretest mean (SD)	*t*	Sig.
Math	3.21 (0.80)	3.13 (0.81)	−0.71 (0.57)	−0.56	0.582
Science	3.31 (0.71)	3.1 (0.73)	−0.21 (0.46)	−2.008	0.059
Engineering	3.69 (0.48)	3.76 (0.70)	0.07 (0.53)	0.560	0.582
Integrated STEM	3.96 (0.66)	3.66 (0.69)	−0.30 (0.64)	−2.091	0.050
4 sections' total	3.54 (0.38)	3.41 (0.54)	−0.13 (0.31)	−1.860	0.078
Career choice	2.76 (0.47)	2.75 (0.48)	−0.01 (0.42)	−0.134	0.895

5.3   Discussion

The observation results showed that participants did apply integrated STEM knowledge to solve the problem when building robots, such as increased the surface friction of the grippers and joints of robotic arms, also used tools to measure the possible design plan. To win the competition, the participants lengthened the arms and heightened the base of the robotic arms, which indicated their application of problem-solving skills. However, the observation data can only indicate students' performance of integrated STEM knowledge and problem-solving skills. Without further investigation, students' progress of STEM knowledge and problem-solving skills remained unsure in the current study. Therefore, the results showed that the framework of copy and redesign can facilitate the performance of integrated STEM knowledge and problem-solving skills.

Regarding the boundary object, the robotic arm in the present study, it encouraged students to perform social creativity in the workshop and the competition. It seemed to trigger students' knowledge acquired in building the robotic arms, such as STEM integrated knowledge which mentioned previously. Furthermore, students' creativity was no longer vague but shown through the concrete robotic arms [21]. Their performance aligned with the natures of social creativity, which was supported by the boundary object. In the competition, students solved the problem by refining robotic arms with different methods and materials, for example, attaching the controllers to a round shape foam core board to make it easier to use. It seemed that students employed meta-cognitive strategies and their collaboration, showed the nature of social evaluation and appreciation within the community.

Regarding participants' quantitative attitudes toward STEM survey, no significant differences were shown after the competition. In other words, students' learning experience, self-efficacy, expectancy-value, motivation toward the three subjects, attitudes of integrated STEM knowledge, and career choice didn't change significantly after the competition. The possible reason was that the purpose of present workshop and competition design aimed to facilitate participants' integrated STEM skills and creativity. Also, the survey content included learning experience, self-efficacy, expectancy-value, motivation toward subjects, attitudes of integrated STEM knowledge, and career choice, were possibly not suitable for a short-term curriculum design. Consequently, it was difficult for the current study to improve students' attitudes in a one-day workshop and competition. Additionally, most of the participants held high interest in the STEM domain to participate in the competition. Finally, only 20 participants' survey data were valid, it could influence the results of the survey.

6 Conclusions and Further Study

The present study investigated high school students' performances and attitudes towards STEM in a one-day STEM educational workshop and a one-day competition, which were supported by the framework of copy and redesign and social creativity. Regarding students' performance, they showed their creativity through the robotic arms, such as refining the robots to solve the problem in the competition, and using remaining materials to improve the experience of operation. Also, students were able to perform integrated STEM abilities during the process of making robotic arms. As the robotic arms serving as boundary objects, students evaluated the robotic arms with teammates, showed meta-cognitive strategies and collaboration skills. The results indicated that the framework of copy and redesign and social creativity can support the demand of integrated STEM education, which put emphasis on the connection of four subjects and the real world problems [11, 12]. In addition, the learning design facilitated students to form a community infrastructure that encouraged creativity in social context, also aligned with the focus of hands-on education [14]. However, students' attitudes toward STEM survey showed non-significance after the competition due to the difficulty of influencing students' attitudes through a short-term learning activity. Also, most of the students had presented high attitudes towards STEM in the pre-test, the results might be affected by the ceiling effect. Insufficient survey sample can also be the reason for the insignificance.

Further researches could be improved as follows. First, it was a short-term one-day workshop and one-day competition learning design. The results showed that the participants had valuable performances through the learning process. However, further investigation such as a more delicate relationship between learning design and students' performances can be conducted through a semi-structure interview in the future. Second, it was difficult to see students' progress in a short-term learning design, it is suggested that the curriculum can be evaluated in a long-term course, so that the results of the learning design can be more evident. Third, instead of examining students' attitudes toward STEM, a STEM ability test can be conducted in the future research to investigate students' improvement in STEM education.

References

1. Sengupta, P., Kinnebrew, J.S., Basu, S., Biswas, G., Clark, D.: Integrating computational thinking with K-12 science education using agent-based computation: a theoretical framework. Educ. Inf. Technol. **18**(2), 351–380 (2013). https://doi.org/10.1007/s10639-012-9240-x

2. Nagai, K.: Learning while doing: practical robotics education. IEEE Robot. Autom. Mag. **8** (2), 39–43 (2001)
3. Hwang, K.S., Hsiao, W.H., Shing, G.T., Chen, K.J.: Rapid prototyping platform for robotics applications. IEEE Trans. Educ. **54**(2), 236–246 (2010)
4. Rogers, C., Portsmore, M.: Bringing engineering to elementary school. J. STEM Educ.: Innov. Res. **5**(3–4), 17–28 (2004)
5. Kopcha, T.J., et al.: Developing an integrative STEM curriculum for robotics education through educational design research. J. Form. Des. Learn. **1**(1), 31–44 (2017)
6. Avanzato, R.: Mobile robot navigation contest for undergraduate design and k-12 outreach. In: Proceedings of Conference of American Society for Engineering Education (ASEE) (2002)
7. Yanco, H.A., Drury, J.L., Scholtz, J.: Beyond usability evaluation: analysis of human-robot interaction at a major robotics competition. Hum.-Comput. Interact. **19**, 117–149 (2004)
8. Huang, H.H., Su, J.H., Lee, C.S.: A contest-oriented project for learning intelligent mobile robots. IEEE Trans. Educ. **56**(1), 88–97 (2012)
9. Menekse, M., Higashi, R., Schunn, C.D., Baehr, E.: The role of robotics teams' collaboration quality on team performance in a robotics tournament. J. Eng. Educ. **106**(4), 564–584 (2017)
10. Yanco, H.A., Norton, A., Ober, W., Shane, D., Skinner, A., Vice, J.: Analysis of human-robot interaction at the DARPA robotics challenge trials. J. Field Robot. **32**(3), 420–444 (2015)
11. Walker, E.N.: Rethinking professional development for elementary mathematics teachers. Teach. Educ. Q. **34**(3), 113–134 (2007)
12. Stohlmann, M., Moore, T.J., Roehrig, G.H.: Considerations for teaching integrated STEM education. J. Pre-Coll. Eng. Educ. Res. (J-PEER) **2**(1), 4 (2012)
13. Resnick, M., Rosenbaum, E.: Designing for tinkerability. In: Design, Make, Play: Growing the Next Generation of STEM Innovators, pp. 163–181 (2013)
14. Martin, L.: The promise of the maker movement for education. J. Pre-Coll. Eng. Educ. Res. (J-PEER) **5**(1), 4 (2015)
15. Massachusetts Science and Technology/Engineering Curriculum Framework. http://www. doe.mass.edu/frameworks/scitech/1006.pdf. Accessed 3 Mar 2017
16. Bers, M.: The TangibleK robotics program: applied computational thinking for young children. Early Child. Res. Pract. **12**(2), 1–20 (2010)
17. Stone-MacDonald, A., Wendell, K., Douglass, A., Love, M.L.: Engaging Young Engineers: Teaching Problem-Solving Skills Through STEM. Paul H. Brookes, Baltimore (2015)
18. Bagiati, A., Evangelou, D.: Practicing engineering while building with blocks: identifying engineering thinking. Eur. Early Child. Educ. Res. J. **24**(1), 67–85 (2016)
19. Fernandez-Samaca, L., Barrera, N., Mesa, L.A., Perez-Holguin, W.J.: Engineering for children by using robotics. Int. J. Eng. Educ. **33**(1B), 389–397 (2017)
20. Chou, P.N.: Skill development and knowledge acquisition cultivated by maker education: evidence from Arduino-based educational robotics. EURASIA J. Math. Sci. Technol. Educ. **14**(10), 1–15 (2018)
21. Fischer, G., Giaccardi, E., Eden, H., Sugimoto, M., Ye, Y.: Beyond binary choices: Integrating individual and social creativity. Int. J. Hum. Comput. Stud. **63**(4–5), 482–512 (2005)
22. Engeström, Y.: Expansive learning at work: toward an activity theoretical reconceptualization. J. Educ. Work **14**(1), 133–156 (2001)
23. Fischer, G.: Social creativity: turning barriers into opportunities for collaborative design. In: de Cindio, F., Schuler, D. (eds.), Proceedings of the Participatory Design Conference, PDC 2004, Canada, pp. 152–161, July 2004

24. Ostwald, J.: Knowledge construction in software development: the evolving artifact approach. Ph.D. Dissertation, University of Colorado, Boulder (1996)
25. Tai, Y., Ting, Y.-L.: English-learning mobile app designing for engineering students' cross-disciplinary learning and collaboration: a sample practice and preliminary evaluation. Australas. J. Educ. Technol. **36**(2), 120–136 (2020)
26. Heyman, R.E., Lorber, M.F., Eddy, J.M., West, T.V.: Behavioral observation and coding. In: Reis, H.T., Judd, C.M. (eds.) Handbook of Research Methods in Social and Personality Psychology, 2nd edn., pp. 345–372. Cambridge University Press, New York (2014)
27. Gold, R.: Roles in sociological field observations. Soc. Forces **36**, 217–223 (1958)
28. Manning, J.: In vivo coding. In: The International Encyclopedia of Communication Research Methods, pp. 1–2 (2017)
29. Unfried, A., Faber, M., Stanhope, D.S., Wiebe, E.: The development and validation of a measure of student attitudes toward science, technology, engineering, and math (S-STEM). J. Psychoeduc. Assess. **33**(7), 622–639 (2015)
30. Erkut, S., Marx, F.: 4 Schools for WIE (Evaluation Report). Wellesley College, Center for Research on Women, Wellesley (2005)
31. Guzey, S.S., Harwell, M., Moore, T.: Development of an instrument to assess attitudes towards science, technology, engineering, and mathematics (STEM). Sch. Sci. Math. **114**(6), 271–279 (2014)

Using Virtual Reality Simulations to Encourage Reflective Learning in Construction Workers

Eileen Fiala[(⊠)] ⓘ, Markus Jelonek ⓘ, and Thomas Herrmann ⓘ

Ruhr University Bochum, 44780 Bochum, Germany
{eileen.fiala,markus.jelonek,thomas.herrmann}@rub.de

Abstract. Improvement of work safety measures and trainings are important elements to enhance the sensibility for hazardous situations and decrease work accidents. Virtual reality (VR) simulation-based trainings have been shown to be a promising approach to support experience-based learning, as the virtual environments can simulate realistic work environments. To investigate to which extent reflective learning can be supported by using VR simulations, this exploratory study combines a VR simulation on a construction site with subsequent semi-structured interviews to induce reflections in participants. Results of the qualitative content analysis show, that a reflection process about work safety aspects benefits from combining VR simulation with a subsequent interview. Numerous reflections on the content of the simulation coupled to own past (real-life) experience were induced, indicating the tested combination to be a promising learning approach to teach work safety aspects that may help to raise the awareness about work safety at construction sites.

Keywords: Reflective learning · Construction site safety · Virtual reality

1 Introduction

Accidents at work counted 103.775 cases in 2017 and 105.687 in 2018 only in the German construction industry [1]. While construction workers are exposed to greater risks than workers in most other professions, the effective transmission of safety aspects is challenging in all areas of employment [2]. Numerous problems can occur, that may concern the motivation to learn or the lack of awareness and the implementation of learned aspects in the daily workflow [3, 4]. Therefore, further improvement of work safety measures and trainings are essential to decrease work accidents. In this regard, virtual reality (VR) simulations have shown a great potential to be used as training environments for construction site safety trainings [5]. To transfer knowledge into practice, reflective learning has been acknowledged as beneficial in changing routine behavior and foster awareness in critical situations for example through reflecting on or about actions [6, 7].

This explorative study was conducted to investigate the combination of VR-based safety trainings and subsequent interviews as a didactic method to induce reflections about occupational safety among construction site workers. Within the VR simulation,

P. Zaphiris and A. Ioannou (Eds.): HCII 2020, LNCS 12206, pp. 422–434, 2020.
https://doi.org/10.1007/978-3-030-50506-6_29

participants had to fulfill a task with an angle grinder while considering multiple safety aspects to complete the simulation. If participants made a mistake that led to an accident (in the simulation), they received feedback and the simulation restarted. Directly after experiencing the VR simulation, participants were surveyed in semi-structured interviews to gain in-depth knowledge about reflections concerning work safety, their decisions in the simulation and attitudes to safety measures. Reflective learning through interviews combined with a playful approach, hence using VR simulations, are expected to be a promising strategy to overcome low motivation, to better convey learning content and possibly enhance the sensibility for construction site safety. In particular, the semi-structured interview is intended to serve as an essential foundation for encouraging reflections on work safety aspects experienced in the simulation and beyond.

2 Reflective Learning and VR-Based Safety Trainings

Reflective Learning can be described as an internal process that is built on a re-evaluation of former experiences and results in a changed perspective of an issue of concern [8, 9]. By reflecting on former experiences or actions, individuals gain the possibility to better judge, improve and adjust their behavior according to the actual occurring circumstances [8, 10]. Reflection processes occur in learning environments, professional work or the everyday life [8, 10, 11]. Especially with regard to learning in practical work environments, learning oftentimes appears quite different from formal learning in classrooms and faces unique challenges such as continuous adaption to and critical evaluation of new practical situations. Herein, reflective learning methods are expected to offer advantages for professionals which have been confirmed in several studies, e.g. [6, 7, 12], such as an enhanced awareness of own behavior providing a possible foundation to change future behavior.

In the field of professional practice, learning in safety trainings and construction site safety is to be considered with special caution. Work safety trainings may suffer from a low motivation of trainees or a limited attention and awareness due to frequently performed tasks [3, 4]. In this regard engaging methods which include learning by doing and the participatory integration of a learner are recommended rather than only receiving safety trainings conveying information about possible risks [2]. It is also suggested that workers need to be empowered to self-awareness and the ability to act [13]. These suggestions align well with an VR-based reflective learning strategy, which can be considered as highly engaging. Construction site safety receives a specific role when it comes to learning and internalization of safety measures to prevent dangerous situations at work as certain experiences to reflect upon cannot be provided in training settings. The appropriate behavior in dangerous situations can hardly be taught as hazardous situations cannot be experienced in practice without any real danger. Here, VR environments offer a promising approach to create realistic experiences, which may enhance a sensibility for hazardous situations, especially when conducting routine tasks. It has been shown that VR-based safety simulations can result in enhanced attentiveness during the training and support the retrievability of learned aspects [5]. Compared to laboratory settings, VR simulations allow to contextualize work scenarios into the known work environments of trainees or participants and therefore have the potential to increase the ecological validity of experiments [14].

This study examines the combination of VR-based trainings and (post-simulation) interviews as a didactical method to induce reflections about occupational safety. Thereby, the VR simulation served as a realistic work experience to reflect upon, while the interviews were expected to support a learning process through reflecting on (personal) experiences gained in the simulation and on the job.

3   Methods and Data Analysis

3.1   Experimental Procedure

The sample size of the study consisted of 14 machine trainee operators that were in their second year of a three-year training and had already basic knowledge about construction site safety aspects. The participants were aged between 18 and 32 years, 2 females and 12 males. For this study, an HTC Vive Pro Headset was used. Prior to the simulation, participants did not receive any information about the scenario and the content of the simulation which addressed the topic work safety. They underwent a short tutorial at the beginning of the simulation to get familiar with the interaction in the VR environment and the usage of the controllers, e.g. how to operate their working tool, an angle grinder. At this point all participants were asked to verbalize any questions and concerns. Afterwards, the VR safety training started and participants received a short introduction about their work task by a foreman inside the simulation. To finish the simulation participants had to consider all work safety aspects the simulation contained. First, they had to select the appropriate personal protection equipment (PPE), choosing between two helmets of which one had a visual cover and one did not. Next, participants had to decide for a safe work tool from two offered angle grinders whereas only one was equipped with a slide arm. While exploring the simulation, they had to keep their personal workspace clear, notice the operating range of others and keep a construction vehicle (forklift truck) within viewing range. In case a work accident occurred, the simulation restarted. The playtime varied from three to 15 min and after successfully completing the simulation all participants were interviewed by two interviewers. The semi-structured interviews lasted 6 to 33 min and mainly followed 4 aspects:

- Biographical background and former experience with VR and work safety
- Evaluation of the simulation's content and behavior in the simulation
- Evaluation of realism and illustrative depiction
- General experiences and attitudes concerning work safety

3.2   Qualitative Content Analysis

The 14 interviews were transcribed and the qualitative content analysis followed the procedure described by Mayring [15]. The main categories followed a deductive selection while the descriptive subcategories on reflections about work safety were inductively created. The categorization, coding and analysis took part circularly in 3 rounds to ensure an intracoder reliability and was also discussed. Thereby coding units were always considered as a unit of meaning while only passages that concerned the simulation or the topic work safety were included. Reflections were categorized separately according to their origin and reference (main category) and the topics addressed (subcategory; see Fig. 1).

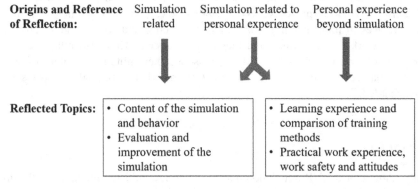

Fig. 1. Experiences reflections originated from or referred to (top row) and topics that arose in the interviews summed up in 4 categories (bottom bullet points).

As reflective learning especially derives from experiences [7, 8, 10], in the main category reflections were classified according to the origin and reference of the experiences (Fig. 1), that either solely concerned the simulation (without personal experience), the simulation's content paired with own practical experience, or experiences of work safety that did not directly relate to the simulation but only derived from personal experience. Thus, the occurring reflections served as a selective and suitable indicator of how or through what experience the reflections were induced. They were analyzed to conclude the richness of reflections occurring in each main category and to gain an insight over the quantitative appearance of the types of reflections.

To gain a deeper insight into the content of the reflections they were organized by the topics that were addressed and summed up in 4 subcategories (Fig. 1, bullet points). The subcategories were created inductively and along the data material. Given the number of cases, only the content of reflections that appeared more than once were included in the interpretation. A more detailed description of the topics the subcategories include are listed below:

1. **Content of the Simulation and Behavior:** Engaging with the simulation participants reflected on the content and concrete experiences made in the simulation. They reflected upon their own performance, their behavior, decisions and especially mistakes made in the simulation.

2. **Evaluation and the Improvement of the Simulation:** (Critical) Reflections contained the improvement of the simulation referring to practical experience and problems experienced in the simulation resulting in ideas to improve the simulation.
3. **Learning Experience and Comparison of Training Methods:** Reflections about the didactical learning experience provided through VR contained e.g. the general learning experience through playing the simulation and the comparison between VR learning and traditional methods like on-the-job-training and theoretical lessons.
4. **Practical Work Experience, Work Safety and Attitudes:** Participants shared experiences in implementing work safety in practice and corresponding problems such as work routines, time, and hierarchical aspects. They also reflected on the impacts of own (near) work accidents, reasoned their attitudes to safety measures and explained how they would handle situations where work safety aspects were disregarded.

4 Results

Results show that the VR simulation and the interview initiated numerous reflections about work safety aspects in all three main categories.

The categorization of the data has shown that the experiences participants referred to and the topics they addressed were not specific for just one main category. Therefore, subcategory 1 (Content of the simulation and behavior) and 2 (Evaluation and improvement of the simulation) contained aspects that were either mainly built on the experience in the simulation or derived from the experience in the simulation including elements of personal experience. Subcategory 3 (Learning experience and comparison of training methods) and 4 (Practical work experience, work safety and attitudes) mainly required personal experiences but also referred to the content of the simulation. An overview of the number of participants that addressed the topics in the 4 subcategories related to the main categories is depicted in Fig. 2.

Overall, a high number of reflections deriving from former, own experiences coupled to the content of the simulation was found, indicating the simulation's utility to improve the reflection process supported by interview questions. Quantitatively, 71 passages of reflections concerning the content of the simulation coupled to own experiences were marked in all 14 interviews, compared to 33 reflections that only concerned the simulation and 27 reflections that did not directly relate to the simulation but referred to own former experiences about work safety.

The provided experience through the VR simulation which was mostly related to own experiences and oftentimes ended in reflections about own ideas and solutions to problems during the interview shows that the combined use of VR and interviews effectively induces reflections. All topics appeared in the main category which captured reflections concerning the simulation coupled to own experience, which further underlines that the simulation serves as an essential foundation for inducing reflections and helps to call on own experiences (Fig. 2).

**Origins and Reference
of Reflection:**

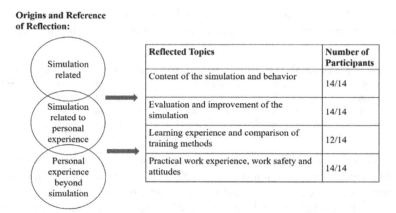

Reflected Topics	Number of Participants
Content of the simulation and behavior	14/14
Evaluation and improvement of the simulation	14/14
Learning experience and comparison of training methods	12/14
Practical work experience, work safety and attitudes	14/14

Fig. 2. Number of participants addressing either one or both of the topics (4 subcategories) listed in the table and relation of the subcategories to the 3 main categories (circles).

The further analyses of the reflected topics and their content revealed aspects such as how the simulation could possibly help to enhance the sensibility for work safety and to clarify (new) problems with work safety measures. All participants were able to reflect upon the content of the simulation and evaluate its setup. They recapitulated experiences made in the simulation, including own mistakes, such as choosing an inappropriate work tool (causing an accident). Most participants also provided a deeper insight into discrepancies of the simulation and practical experiences leading to ideas to improve the simulation. Didactically, on-the-job-training was viewed as the best way to learn whereby participants stated that playing the VR simulation was beneficial and came close to this practical experience as everything was perceived as very realistic. Thus, theoretical lessons were considered as most problematic, e.g. due to difficulties in memorizing learning content. Critically reflecting on their own actions and general knowledge about work safety, participants were able to share their own experiences and disclosed problems in implementing works safety measures into practice such as the lack of time, internalized work routines and hierarchical aspects. A more detailed overview of the 4 most reflected topics (subcategories) and its content, including exemplary excerpts of the interviews is provided below.

Content of the Simulation and Behavior (1): Reflecting on the simulation, all participants evaluated the simulation's setup as coherent and comprehensible, but some noted that some additional information would be helpful. They reflected on the central topic 'work safety' of the simulation. Thereby, participants described the trained aspects, especially when they experienced accidents in the simulation, such as the differences in the PPE, the experience with a moving forklift truck, being attentive to their surrounding (clearing the own workspace) and to the operation range of others, while making their way to their workplace. Furthermore, some participants used the environment to explore possible situations and accidents, apart from their in-game work task, while others had in mind to finish their task as quickly as possible.

When asked about the content of the simulation one participant summarized aspects such as the awareness of other workspaces, the construction vehicle and the accident he experienced:

P: *"Generally, it was about the learning effect. No, it was about, let's say, for example, to not run past the worker, because there you are putting yourself at risk. On the construction traffic route, I reacted as I expected. He would drive back and forth [...]. And that I had to cut it [work piece] there, was clear. But I didn't expect that an accident would happen. That surprised me, but also positively, because it recalls that to the mind. As I said, I peeked at the guy. I thought it would fit, but then it didn't. Overall I think it was quite good implemented."*[1]

Participants stated why they picked a certain work tool (angle grinder) or one of the two helmets, explaining their adjustment in their following runs after mistakes have led to an accident. One example is provided by a participant who focused on the surroundings of his workplace but did not take the missing slide arm on the angle grinder into account and that the disc could burst and hurt coworkers:

P: *"Because there was a grid and, in my opinion, he was in another room and not in my workspace. And as I began to position the angle grinder I realized, the flying sparks did not spread into my direction [...]. In that moment I considered the flying sparks as a safety aspect to consider and not the disc which could burst. That is why I thought the safety clearance would be sufficient."*

Reasoning why a decision in the simulation was made often lead to critical reflections on problems in the simulation and ideas to improve.

Evaluation and the Improvement of the Simulation (2): Critically reflecting on the VR simulation with regard to existing practical experiences, participants came up with various suggestions to improve the simulation to enhance the realism and better transmit certain safety aspects. Thereby many participants considered a broader choice of PPE elements as necessary and noted that the ear protection or a filtering face piece that was missing is very important.

When asked about the content of the simulation and why certain decisions were made another participant summarized the aspects motioned above:

P: *"Yes, I did not choose the helmet without the mask, because I want to protect my face within my VR life. That is why I took the one with the mask. But there was no dust mask, normally there are also dusk masks available. Let's go the whole hog, also considering earmuffs. I figured the work tools were good as well, one with a slide arm, one without. Maybe there should be another one that doesn't function at all, or something like that. That could be implemented, maybe even a check-up, [...]. Maybe one could check the tool itself, for example if its unsteady."*

When another participant was asked about ideas for improvements, he stated that:

P: *"Considering that the simulation was about the safe handling of an angle grinder at the workplace, I think that it was very good. Eventually, if that is noticed is another question. One could provide a third angle grinder with a broken disc, or similar, that needs to be considered. That would be a good idea because it is considered by the least, if the disc is safe. [...] Or*

---

[1] Quotes from this interview were translated from the original German transcript to English for this paper.

maybe a broken cord or something like that, that you have to pay attention to. That is what I would add. [...] Exactly and I would include ear protectors [...], that you have to grab."

Most participants did not have any prior experience with VR before but stated that it was easy to get comfortable with the steering and surroundings. Except for two participants who experienced motion sickness during playing the simulation, all other participants considered the simulation-based training as an enjoyable experience. Almost all participants stated that they perceived the simulation's content and construction site as realistic, except of some missing details. Deriving from personal experience it was mentioned that, even though the simulation was perceived as very realistic, the surroundings could have been more chaotic, dusty and loud to even better mirror a construction site. Also, the forklift truck was experienced as a good element in the simulation, yet some participants noted, that in practice it is instructed to have eye contact with the driver before passing. Yet even though they thought they tried to establish eye contact with the driver, some of them got run down, coming too close to the operating range of the truck in the simulation.

In this context, an important aspect mentioned was that the simulation's content needs to utterly match all defined safety measures, since wrongly taught aspects may be picked up and internalized subconsciously. These unclear aspects also referred to the own avatar that was already wearing protective gloves, whereas a dusk mask and hearing protection (choice of PPE) were missing in the simulation and were therefore often addressed in the interview.

Learning Experience and Comparison of Training Methods (3): While VR learning was mostly perceived as beneficial, some participants also stated to expect to better remember situations experienced in the simulation and the work safety aspects it addressed. Even though participants stated that playing the simulation would not directly affect or change consisting attitudes about work safety, they declared to be more aware of hazardous situations and feel safer after going through the simulation. When asked what was positive about the simulation in general, one participant focused on the closeness to reality and problems of theoretical lessons:

P: *"I liked everything. That you could choose among the tools [...]. That you could make mistakes and learn through them, of course. And not just, 'congratulations', you sharply engaged with the topic and nothing happened. That is what I liked. I think that you better memorize it, also on the construction site. [...]. At least it comes a little closer to practice. If you only hear about it in class and then you're confronted with the situation, then you will never know, okay: What did I have to do again? Since you never learn it this way it and never see it anywhere."*

Whereas two participants that experienced motion sickness while playing the VR simulation and were skeptical about the utility of the VR simulation as a training, all other participants were satisfied with their learning experience.

Comparing different methods, on-the-job training was assessed as the best way to learn whereby nearly all participants stated that playing the VR simulation came close to a realistic experience. However, some participants also mentioned that on the job instructions could, due to effort, not always be provided, especially for simple tasks like quickly cutting something (e.g. with an angle grinder). Some participants further emphasized the realism as an essential feature to their positive learning experience, especially when compared to theoretical lessons. When asked about overall positive features of the simulation another participant stated:

> P: "It was positive, that one's attention is drawn to aspects that one usually doesn't think about. The next time, when using an angle grinder, one would probably more likely look around, to see if there is someone in close distance. Yes, if one only gets a reading lecture or reads scripts, or something similar, one will say "Yes, Yes I got it", read it, but then it is forgotten anyhow. I think, it is better memorized. That's what I like."

Another participant emphasized the closeness to reality when asked about work safety in the educational context:

> P: "That has already been taught in the education center as well as in the vocational college and company-internally. It is something completely different, if you really experience it on a construction site, that's where the simulation has an essential effect, since it is closer to reality compared to sitting in class and being told, 'yes, that is to mind out there, watch this, watch that.'"

Especially compared to theoretical lessons like reading or addressing a topic only in dialogs the experience in the simulation was perceived as superior. Overall theoretical learning was perceived as most problematic and least motivating, whereby participants oftentimes emphasized the huge differences of theoretical safety aspects taught in lessons and the actual work situation in practice.

Practical Work Experience, Work Safety and Attitudes (4): Some participants pointed out that their choice of the PPE on the job would depend on the circumstances, sometimes independently of the advised guidelines indicating a selective importance of PPE. This also derives from reasoning their decisions in the simulation, where participants concluded, that they would choose their PPE in real life according to their own priority list. Thereby ear protection and a visual protection cover were considered to play an important role whilst wearing a helmet or gloves were viewed as less important. This also resonates with general problems implementing theoretical work safety standards into practice. When asked how participants would implement work safety in practice, they often concluded differences between theory and professional practice. In this context, the lack of time, work routines, practical problems and hierarchical aspects appearing within a work situation were exposed to be the most impedimental for following and applying all work safety standards. A quite experienced trainee stated:

> P: "Since I already had a bad experience with these tools [angle grinder], I had a disc that busted while working. I was lucky though, it almost hit me (...). In that situation a helmet or safety glasses do not help. No, the point is, you should definitely use it [angle grinder] with both hands. I did not always do it. [...] It is simply not always possible, you have to, cannot always use the slide arm. [...] Then you are really sitting here like this, in a small corner, [...] because sometimes you simply do not have space. [...] These are such aspects, the theory is nice, but in practice it is always different."

When asked what a participant would do if one would say that safety measures on a construction site are overrated, one participant for example emphasized that considering all work safety aspects would prevent work from getting done and described selective aspects that are important for him:

P: "Let me put it this way, we can be glad, that they [work safety measures] exist and that they are complied with and that there are people who control them, but sometimes it is not possible to work safely. Because otherwise one does not progress with work, in that case no construction site would be functioning. But it is nice, of course. Safety measures are reasonable. Sometimes I think that the requirement to wear a helmet [...], sometimes I think this is stupid, for example when there is no lifting equipment in use, then it is not really necessary. But if superiors are coming, you will get into trouble and will be banned from the construction site. But one can resign to always wear a helmet."

Another participant, when asked how he would react when one makes him aware of missing the side protection of an angle grinder, emphasized that due to work routines one would become unconscious about an unsafe working tool:

P: "Me as a trainee, I wouldn't be allowed to further work with it, I'd say. [...] Yes, sometimes you just do not realize it. I take the angle grinder, cut and yes, when I am completely absorbed in my work, then you are just cutting but if someone pointed that out, of course I should change it."

Routines and selective importance of safety measures are also mentioned from another participant when referring to his statement that playing the simulation was beneficial:

P: "I expected that when I run through the flying sparks, which was a bit overrated, to be honest. Because I work without gloves and helmet, without visual cover and sometimes use the angle grinder then. The only thing that I still protect are my ears because, knock on the wood, they are still safe and sound, even though many things have been flying past them. Consequently, it [the simulation] calls to mind again, what is maybe, especially in my age, oftentimes suppressed, I'd say. No, that is, in my opinion, a really, really good system."

Reflecting on behavior in a hypothetical situation wherein a colleague would disregard safety measures, participants mentioned that hierarchical aspects would play a role. While some participants considered informing or confronting a coworker about missing PPE, others expressed concerns about their position, e.g. being still in education whereas the colleague might be an experienced worker. When assumed that a participant would observe someone who disregards work safety two participants mentioned that the reaction would be different depended on their status as a trainee or an experienced worker:

P: "I would tell him. Yet, as a trainee it is always a bit hard, because you are just the trainee. But I would tell him, straightforwardly. [...]. With other trainees that works well, because you are on the same level, [...]. With old and experienced workers, it depends; it works without [safety measures] for a short while, but I would tell them and I think it will change, if you are a few years on the construction site. If you gained some respect, then it would work, I'd say."

When asked if a participant would use an angle grinder without a slide arm to finish a task quickly, she would rather do what is told instead of insisting on a safe work tool: *"That's hard, I think I would ask if there was another angle grinder with a slide arm. But if he said no, I think, I would still do it. At least while still being in training."* When asked how she would react if someone said that her safety measures are overrated, she stated that:

P: "He can do it differently, but I don't know, nothing is going to happen. [...] I wouldn't care.
But I would rather address it after I have finished my vocational training. [...] I think I wouldn't
say a lot, but only do what I am told to do, yes."

The interpretation of these aspects implies that circumstances such as lack of time, routines, practical and hierarchical problems might interfere with practically implementing work safety standards. When enhancement of occupational safety is considered, a holistic approach not only including improvement of work safety training but also considering improvement of the above-mentioned aspects seems to be crucial.

Being asked about their general attitudes or if someone would disregard work safety aspects, some participants were moderate about wrong behavior, emphasizing again that work safety in practice is always different from theoretical aspects. Others would insist on applying all work safety measures possible. While some participants were less experienced than others who worked with a range of different tools and environments four out of the 14 trainees already had their own experience with (near) work accidents. Interestingly, participants differed in their general attitude on behavioral change after experiencing an accident or a near miss: While one participant who had a real accident stated that he did not make huge changes in his behavior, others, who only experienced a near miss said that they were more careful afterwards.

5   Limitations and Discussion of Results

The reflections combining or including aspects of the simulation and personal experience had an overweight in total when quantified. Yet, results need to be considered critically, since the categorization and the interpretation of the data is subjective itself and relies on the view of the interpreter. However, all interpretations mainly serve to capture the meanings and unique perspectives of the participants, to discover new and important aspects and to gain insights about their reflections and their view on the simulation. The overall positive feedback and a large number of reflections referring to the simulation and personal experiences show the utility of the tested approach, combining VR with interviews to ensure a reflection process. Thus, findings in this qualitative study cannot be generalized but imply a promising background for further studies.

A further limitation might be the interviewers during the study. Interview effects always affect the results of qualitative research like in this case study and it needs to be highlighted that the reflection process also depends on the experience, motivation and knowledge of the interviewer. Although the interviewers were confident with all work safety aspects addressed in the simulation, it can be expected that if a professional or expert is included in the interview situation, participants could profit even more from the interview and simulation induced experiences within their reflection process. On the other hand, qualitative research also benefits from a setting which is not influenced by experts but puts the test subjects themselves in an expert position, like in this case study. This could enforce participants to feel safer and share more aspects they would not mention in a larger group or an interview situation where superiors are present which could be counterproductive and restrict a further reflection process.

6 Conclusion and Outlook

Given the problematic and difficult situations that occur in effectively and sustainably transferring work safety content from theoretical training to practice at construction sites, the hypotheses that a VR simulation combined with an interview can help to induce (critical) reflections and promotes reflective learning can be confirmed. The positive feed-back of participants captured in the qualitative analysis underlines the realism of the simulation coming close to a practical experience. Since a clear preference for practical teaching methods over theoretical lessons were pointed out, this further supports the VR simulation to be a more motivating, enjoyable and engaging learning tool by improving the subjective learning experience. While the simulation served as a realistic experience to engage with work safety aspects and a possibility to open a conversation, the interviews have shown to be an essential part in producing reflective thoughts. During the interview participants remembered and evaluated their behavior in the simulation, referred to own personal experiences and critically discussed implementation of work safety measures. A large amount of (critical) reflections was produced, especially combining personal experience and elements of the simulation, motivating participants to consider problems and solve them. Considering the topics that appeared, this case study does not imply a change of existing attitudes through playing the VR simulation but supports an increased awareness and sensibility for work safety among the construction trainees. Overall, the results underline the potential of combining VR training with reflective learning methods. Further studies are required to elucidate the effectiveness of this approach to lead to a change of attitude and behavior preventing hazardous situations.

References

1. DGUV: DGUV-Statistiken für die Praxis 2018. Deutsche Gesetzliche Unfallversicherung (DGUV), Berlin (2019)
2. Burke, M.J., Sarpy, S.A., Smith-Crowe, K., Chan-Serafin, S., Salvador, R.O., Islam, G.: Relative effectiveness of worker safety and health training methods. Am. J. Public Health **96**, 315–324 (2006). https://doi.org/10.2105/AJPH.2004.059840
3. Wilkins, J.R.: Construction workers' perceptions of health and safety training programmes. Constr. Manage. Economics. **29**, 1017–1026 (2011). https://doi.org/10.1080/01446193.2011.633538
4. Khosravi, Y., Asilian-Mahabadi, H., Hajizadeh, E., Hassanzadeh-Rangi, N., Bastani, H., Behzadan, A.H.: Factors influencing unsafe behaviors and accidents on construction sites: a review. Int. J. Occup. Saf. Ergonomics. **20**, 111–125 (2014). https://doi.org/10.1080/10803548.2014.11077023
5. Sacks, R., Perlman, A., Barak, R.: Construction safety training using immersive virtual reality. Constr. Manage. Econ. **31**, 1005–1017 (2013). https://doi.org/10.1080/01446193.2013.828844
6. Emmanuel, A.: Reflexive learning (2016). https://doi.org/10.4135/9781483318332.n303
7. Prilla, M., Herrmann, T., Degeling, M.: Collaborative reflection for learning at the healthcare workplace. In: Goggins, S.P., Jahnke, I., Wulf, V. (eds.) Computer-Supported Collaborative

Learning at the Workplace: CSCL@Work, pp. 139–165, Springer US, Boston, MA (2013). https://doi.org/10.1007/978-1-4614-1740-8_7

8. Boud, D., Keogh, R., Walker, D.: Promoting reflection in learning: a model. In: Reflection: Turning Experience into Learning. Routledge, London (1985)

9. Boyd, E.M., Fales, A.W.: Reflective learning: key to learning from experience. J. Hum. Psychol. **23**, 99–117 (1983). https://doi.org/10.1177/0022167883232011

10. Schön, D.A.: The Reflective Practitioner: How Professionals Think in Action. Basic Books, USA (1983)

11. Moon, J.: Reflection in Learning and Professional Development Theory and Practice. Kogan Page Limited, London (1999)

12. Fleck, R., Fitzpatrick, G.: Reflecting on reflection: framing a design landscape. In: Proceedings of the 22nd Conference of the Computer-Human Interaction Special Interest Group of Australia on Computer-Human Interaction, pp. 216–223. ACM, New York, NY, USA (2010). https://doi.org/10.1145/1952222.1952269

13. Weinstock, D., Slatin, C.: Learning to Take Action: The Goals of Health and Safety Training. New. Solut. **22**, 255–267 (2012). https://doi.org/10.2190/NS.22.3.b

14. Duarte, E., Rebelo, F., Wogalter, M.S.: Virtual reality and its potential for evaluating warning compliance. Hum. Factors. Man. **20**, 526–537 (2010). https://doi.org/10.1002/hfm.20242

15. Mayring, P.: Qualitative Inhaltsanalyse. Beltz, Weinheim (2010)

First-Person Perspective Physics Learning Platform Based on Virtual Reality

Yu Han[1], Yining Shi[2], Juanjuan Wang[3], Yue Liu[1,4(✉)],
and Yongtian Wang[1,4]

[1] Beijing Engineering Research Center of Mixed Reality and Advanced Display,
School of Optics and Photonics, Beijing Institute of Technology,
Beijing 100081, China
han.yu@outlook.com, {liuyue,wyt}@bit.edu.cn
[2] The High School Affiliated to the Renmin University of China,
Beijing 100080, China
Shiyining@rdfz.cn
[3] Department of Physics, Beijing Normal University, Beijing 100875, China
201611140921@mail.bnu.edu.cn
[4] AICFVE of Beijing Film Academy, Beijing 100088, China

Abstract. This study is aimed at investigating the effects of instructional materials developed with virtual reality (VR) technology on middle school students' learning achievements and motivation towards the course of physics in China. In this study, the authors designed a VR-based first-person perspective physics learning platform for students to learn the "velocity-time graph of uniform variable rectilinear motion". A between-subjects design was used and a total of 23 eighth graders took part in this experiment. The students were assigned to two groups on the basis of their background knowledge. The experimental group adopted VR-based learning platform for the learning activities, while the control group watched a video containing the same learning contents. The results show that students from the VR-based experimental group reported higher learning achievements compared with those from the control group. The results also show that students' levels of motivation in the experimental group were higher than those from control group. The findings of this study imply that VR technology can be utilized as an effective instructional tool for fostering students' learning of the basic physics concepts and laws in middle school.

Keywords: Virtual reality · Uniform variable rectilinear motion · Physics education

1 Introduction

Science, Technology, Engineering, and Mathematics (STEM) subjects are becoming more and more important around the world and are deemed to be the driver for innovation and scientific and technologtical progress [1]. As a core part of STEM education, physics plays an increasingly greater role in our society. However, a large number of Chinese students do not like learning physics. According to the survey from Zhejiang Education Examinations Authority, in 2017, there were 250,100 college

© Springer Nature Switzerland AG 2020
P. Zaphiris and A. Ioannou (Eds.): HCII 2020, LNCS 12206, pp. 435–447, 2020.
https://doi.org/10.1007/978-3-030-50506-6_30

entrance examination candidates in Zhejiang province, whereas only 27% of them chose physics as one of the exam subjects [2]. This is largely due to the teaching ways of physics. In spite of being a widely taught subject for a very long time, it is still a significant challenge to make physics education engaging and exciting to students in today's modern classrooms, many of whom still regard physics to be complex and tedious [3]. As what is already known to all, physics is full of abstract concepts and laws, which are usually given in the form of equations and hard to be demonstrated in real life. When conventional teaching methods are used in physics education, students often struggle to understand the underlying objective laws behind complicated physical phenomena since there is a giant gap between abstract concepts and concrete reality. Even students with a normal abstract thinking ability have to make more efforts when learning physics concepts compared to other types of concepts. Obviously, traditional ways are not suitable for physics education. Students should be helped with the comprehension of the underlying principles and phenomena of often complicated formulas with the support of interactive and hands-on experiences. In addition, existing researches have indicated that high-quality teaching and learning requires active engagement with students. The primary reason for students' losing interests and lower achievements in physics education is the lack of engagement [4].

With the advance of science and technology, VR has been widely applied in learning activities to create a feeling of immersion and engagement. VR provides a highly immersive and simulated environment in which users can interact with various objects generated by a computer [5, 6]. With the help of VR, invisible phenomena (electromagnetic field, etc.) can be made visible to the users and it is possible for students to expand time and space and to conduct experiments that would be too dangerous, expensive, or even impossible in real life. Due to the abovementioned advantages, virtual reality has been adopted, explored, and adapted in STEM education such as anatomy [7], architecture [8], neurosurgery [9], medicine [10] and so on, to improve students' learning achievements. However, physics education has not yet been exposed to thorough research on the potential of VR approach. In prior studies, the main form of VR applied in physics education is virtual laboratories, most of which take the third person perspective [11–15]. According to our survey towards physics education in middle schools, some teachers mentioned that the first person perspective might better build the relationship between physics laws and real life in some cases. Nevertheless, VR-based first-person perspective physics learning platforms have not yet been thoroughly investigated. Therefore, this study is aimed at filling this gap in the literature.

On the other hand, potential benefits of VR technology including its capabilities to promote learners' psychological states, might significantly influence learning achievements [16, 17]. Motivation, which "provides a source of energy that is responsible for why learners decide to make an effort, how long they are willing to sustain an activity, how hard they are going to pursue it, and how connected they feel to the activity" [18], is one of the factors that impact the psychological states of learning. Several researches have reported the effectiveness of VR-based instructional materials for fostering students' motivation [19–21].

The study presented in this paper aimed to investigate the use of first-person perspective VR-based physics learning platform in middle-school physics education.

The research objectives of this study can be listed as follows:

1. To investigate the influence of first-person VR on students' learning achievements in a physics course.
2. To investigate the influence of first-person VR on students' motivation.

This paper starts by presenting the experimental design in Sect. 2. Then, Sect. 3 shows the evaluation results and data analysis of the experiment. Section 4 discusses the experimental results. Conclusions and future work are outlined in Sect. 5.

This study is unique in that it investigates the use of VR-based first-person perspective physics learning platform within real school settings for middle-school physics education. The study can help us learn to what extent first-person VR can be effective in improving students' learning achievements and promoting their motivation.

2 Methodology

In this study, a between-subjects design was adopted to assess the learning performance of physics in the two learning scenarios, with and without the first-person perspective VR-based physics learning platform. Both objective and subjective assessments were adopted. The learners had to complete two sessions during the two days of experiment.

2.1 Participants

A total of 23 eighth graders (aged from 13 to 14 years) from a middle school in Beijing took part in the experiment at the beginning of 2020. All of them had never experienced VR technology before. The demographic characteristics of the students are given in Table 1. A text document was provided to students and their parents outlining the purpose of the research and their right to withdraw at any moment before the start of the experiment and informed consent was obtained from every participant. The students were assigned to two groups on the basis of their scores of pre-test so as to ensure that the students in the two groups had similar background knowledge before the intervention. There were 12 learners in the experimental group, and the control group had 11 learners.

Table 1. Demographic characteristics of the participants.

Groups	Girl	Boy	Total
Experimental group	0	12	12
Control group	0	11	11
Total	0	23	23

2.2 The Design of First-Person Perspective VR-Based Physics Learning Platform

In this study, teachers' thoughts and opinions on the use of VR technology for assisting physics learning were firstly collected, and then teachers were invited to co-design the first-person perspective VR-based physics learning platform. The topic, the "velocity-time graph (v-t graph) of uniform variable rectilinear motion", which is a unit in the physics curriculum, was chosen because this topic involves many abstract concepts and laws which are impossible to be objectified in real life. As the subject matter of the "v-t graph of uniform variable rectilinear motion" is difficult to perceive and requires highly on students' imagination and abstract thinking, teaching should be concretized and enriched. The authors designed a VR-based learning platform following the guidelines set by the official program that Chinese middle schools must use in physics education. The official program defines both the objectives and the key activities that students must perform. The learning platform was designed following these official guidelines with the aim of assisting students in learning uniform variable rectilinear motion. VR-based learning materials followed the course book given by the Ministry of Education of the People's Republic of China.

The first-person perspective VR-based physics learning platform, which was named "v-t Graph Learning System", mainly composes of a gaming PC (the main specifications are 16 GB RAM, NVIDIA GTX 1080 TI, Intel Core i7-8700K 3.70 GHz) with Windows 10, HTC Vive (Pro) and learning system software. Unity, a 3D real-time development platform published by Unity Technologies, is employed to develop the learning system software.

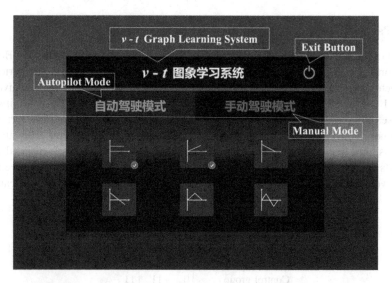

Fig. 1. The screenshot of the menu of the VR-based v-t graph learning system, which contains autopilot mode and manual mode.

The learning scenario is set in a self-driving car and a virtual window which can track the motion of the learner's head is always displayed in front of the learner's eyes. The students can control the car with Vive controller to experience the real-time rendering process of the v-t graph of the car, which can help students build the relationship between the abstract v-t graph and the experience of life. The system also integrates Baidu Speech API to realize real-time voice prompt function. The learning system contains autopilot mode and manual mode, as shown in Fig. 1. In the autopilot mode, students can press the button using the Vive controller to choose a v-t graph from six different typical graphs, and the car will run according to the specified v-t graph. When the car is running, the real-time v-t graph of the car and the state of the car's motion is displayed in the virtual window, as shown in Fig. 2 (a). The students can also hear the information of the state of the car's motion through the headphones of the Vive head-mounted display (HMD). Once the learners complete experiencing the chosen v-t graph, the learners need to return to the menu and the lower right corner of the button will be ticked, as shown in Fig. 1. In the manual mode, students can control the car's forward and backward running with the Vive controller and observe the real-time illustration of the v-t graph, as shown in Fig. 2 (b).

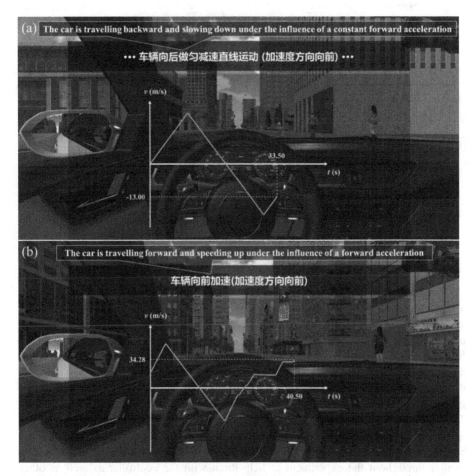

Fig. 2. The screenshots of the (a) autopilot mode (corresponding to the sixth v-t graph in Fig. 1) and the (b) manual mode of the v-t graph learning system.

2.3   Procedure

The study consisted of two sessions, with a day between each session to reduce the cognitive load of the students, the procedure of the experiment is shown in Fig. 3. In the first session, to start with, all students need to watch a video to learn the background knowledge of the uniform variable rectilinear motion such as the basic concepts of vector quantity, displacement, velocity and acceleration. During the last 15 min of the first session, all of them completed the pre-test which is used to evaluate their academic achievements.

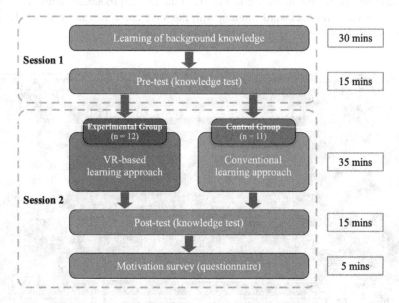

Fig. 3. Experimental design of the learning activities.

The intervention was implemented in the second session. The students were assigned to two groups on the basis of their scores of pre-test so as to ensure that the students in the two groups had similar background knowledge. In the experimental condition, the student received five minutes of instruction from the experimenter on how to use the equipment and it was made clear that they could stop the experiment at any time if they felt dizzy or felt bad. After the instruction, each student in the experimental condition was seated on a chair and put on the VR headset to learn v-t graphs of the uniform variable rectilinear motion using "v-t Graph Learning System". They are asked to first choose the autopilot mode and learn all of the six typical v-t graphs, as shown in Fig. 4. They then switched to the manual mode to control the car and further explore the v-t graph. Each student was always supervised by an experimenter throughout the experiment to help them with the controller as well as other facilities. They will also kind to offer help if students have any discomfort situations (dizziness, nausea, etc.). In the control condition, the students were briefed about the content of the course and then asked to watch a video. The equivalence of the teaching contents in both groups was confirmed by two experienced physics teachers. The learning activity lasted 35 min. On completing the learning activities, students from both groups spent 20 min finishing the post-test and the motivational survey.

Fig. 4. Experimental group students were learning v-t graphs of autopilot mode.

2.4   Measuring Tools

Pre-test and Post-test. To evaluate the effectiveness of the intervention on learners' academic achievements, pre- and post-test were conducted and analyzed. The pre- and post-test comprised 10 multiple-choice questions respectively, each was worth 1 point. Tests were designed by researchers and validated by middle-school teachers taking part in the study. An example of these tests is listed as follows:

Sample question:

"Which of the following statements about acceleration is correct?

(a) There is no necessary relation between the magnitude of acceleration and the magnitude of velocity.

(b) The direction of acceleration may be the same as that of velocity, or it may be opposite to the direction of velocity.

(c) When a body travels with a large magnitude of acceleration, its magnitude of velocity may be small.

(d) If a body travels with a large magnitude of acceleration, its change of the magnitude of velocity must be large."

Motivational Survey. To evaluate students' motivation towards the instructional materials used, students completed the 36 items of the instructional materials motivation survey (IMMS) [16], with 5-point Likert-scale. IMMS consists of 12 items for Attention assessment; 9 items for Relevance assessment; 9 items for Confidence assessment and 6 items for Satisfaction assessment (ARCS).

2.5   Data Analysis

The data analysis was conducted according to the scores of the pre- and post-test as well as the results of the questionnaires. IBM SPSS Statistics 25 was adopted as the main software for statistical analysis. Descriptive statistics were calculated to describe the means and standard deviations, Student's t-test was adopted to compare the level of background knowledge, the learning achievements and the questionnaire results between the two groups.

3   Results

Within the scope of the study, the level of background knowledge before the intervention, the academic achievements after the intervention and motivation of the students were determined. Data is reported as statistically significant at $p < 0.05$. Statistically significant differences are denoted by an asterisk (*) in figures and tables of this session.

3.1   Pre-test

Table 2 indicates that there was little difference between the students in the experimental and control groups in terms of their mean scores of pre-test. A Shapiro-Wilk test for normality indicates that the variables followed a normal distribution (Experimental group: $p = 0.282$; and Control group: $p = 0.100$) and the results of Levene's two-tailed test (F $(1, 21) = 0.125$, $p = 0.727$) show that equality of variances was satisfied. In order to determine any significant difference between the levels of background knowledge of the two groups, an independent samples t-test was carried out and the results indicate that there was no significant difference between the background knowledge of the experimental and control groups which means that the experimental-group students and the control-group students had similar background knowledge before the intervention.

Table 2. The t-test results of background knowledge.

	Groups	M	SD	t	df	p
Background knowledge	Experimental group	7.417	1.165	0.115	21	0.909
	Control group	7.364	1.027			

3.2   Post-test

The mean scores of pose-test from the two groups are illustrated as a bar graph, as shown in Fig. 5, indicating that students in the experimental group had a higher level of academic achievements than students in the control group. Both for experimental and for control groups, the results of Shapiro-Wilk test (Experimental group: $p = 0.407$; and Control group: $p = 0.449$) indicate that the normality was satisfied. The independent samples t-test following Levene's two-tailed test (F $(1, 21) = 0.059$,

$p = 0.810$) of equality of variances was implemented to compare students' academic achievements between students from experimental and control groups. The results indicate that there was a statistically significant difference between the experimental and control groups, as shown in Table 3, which means that students who use VR technology in the experimental group had higher levels of academic achievements compared to those in the control group.

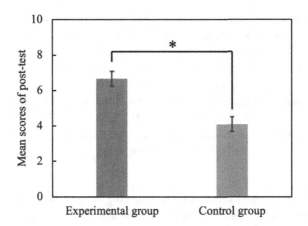

Fig. 5. Academic achievements of students from experimental and control groups. Error bars represent standard errors.

Table 3. The t-test results of academic achievements.

	Groups	M	SD	t	df	p
Academic achievements	Experimental group	6.667	1.435	4.385	21	0.000 *
	Control group	4.091	1.375			

Table 4. The t-test results of motivation towards instructional materials.

	Groups	M	SD	t	df	p
Motivation	Experimental group	3.611	0.211	3.729	21	0.001 *
	Control group	3.194	0.319			

3.3   Motivation Towards Instructional Materials

Technology might contribute to students' motivation towards instructional activities in STEM education. The results of Shapiro-Wilk test (Experimental group: $p = 0.735$; and Control group: $p = 0.085$) and Levene's two-tailed test (F $(1, 21) = 0.137$, $p = 0.715$) indicate that both the normality and the equality of variances were satisfied. Hence, an independent samples t-test was conducted to evaluate the effect of instructional materials on motivation. It can be seen from Table 4 that there was a statistically significant difference between experimental and control groups. The VR experimental group showed a higher level of motivation than the control group. A further analysis was implemented to compare the effects of type of instructional materials on the reporting value of each motivation factor (attention, relevance, confidence and satisfaction) considered in the IMMS [16], and the results are shown in Table 5.

Table 5. The t-test results of motivation factors.

Factors	Groups	M	SD	t	df	p
Attention	Experimental group	3.299	0.165	2.381	21	0.027 *
	Control group	3.023	0.363			
Relevance	Experimental group	3.972	0.419	1.831	21	0.081
	Control group	3.535	0.702			
Confidence	Experimental group	3.185	0.203	0.444	21	0.662
	Control group	3.141	0.268			
Satisfaction	Experimental group	4.333	0.512	5.708	21	0.000 *
	Control group	3.106	0.518			

Attention. An independent samples t-test following Shapiro-Wilk test (Experimental group: $p = 0.364$; and Control group: $p = 0.878$) and Levene's two-tailed test (F (1, 21) = 2.276, $p = 0.146$) was implemented in order to assess the effect of instructional materials on the motivation factor of attention. A statistically significant difference between the VR experimental group and control group (t = 2.381, $p < 0.05$) was found. The VR experimental group showed a higher level of attention compared with the control group.

Relevance. An independent samples t-test following Shapiro-Wilk test (Experimental group: $p = 0.846$; and Control group: $p = 0.843$) and Levene's two-tailed test (F (1, 21) = 2.670, $p = 0.117$) was implemented in order to assess the effect of instructional materials on the motivation factor of relevance. Although the experimental group showed a higher level of relevance than the control group, the difference was not significant (t = 1.831, $p = 0.081$). Therefore, relevance is not influenced by the instructional technology used.

Confidence. An independent samples t-test following Shapiro-Wilk test (Experimental group: $p = 0.831$; and Control group: $p = 0.245$) and Levene's two-tailed test (F (1, 21) = 2.834, $p = 0.107$) was implemented in order to assess the effect of instructional materials on the motivation factor of confidence. However, a statistically significant difference between type of instructional materials was not found (t = 0.444, $p = 0.662$). Hence, confidence is another motivation factor which is not influenced by the instructional technology used.

Satisfaction. An independent samples t-test following Shapiro-Wilk test (Experimental group: $p = 0.220$; and Control group: $p = 0.578$) and Levene's two-tailed test (F (1, 21) = 0.169, $p = 0.685$) was implemented in order to assess the effect of instructional materials on the motivation factor of satisfaction. There was a statistically significant difference between VR experimental group and control group (t = 5.708, $p < 0.05$). The experimental group showed a higher level of satisfaction than the control group.

4 Discussion

This study was aimed at exploring the learning effectiveness and motivation of VR-based learning activities in middle-school physics education. For this purpose, we developed the "v-t Graph Learning System" for students to learn uniform variable rectilinear motion.

With respect to the learning effectiveness of VR-based experimental group compared to the conventional control group, after implementing a statistical analysis on the pre- and post-test scores, results show that VR-based experimental-group students outperformed significantly compared with control-group students. Our findings are in accord with other studies in which VR promoted to achieve better learning outcomes in STEM subjects than other instructional methods [22–25]. Further research effort is necessary for identifying what specific characteristics of VR may influence the effectiveness of learning in physics.

As for the motivation towards instructional materials, the statistical results of the study show that the motivation of participants in the VR-based experimental group was more likely to be stimulated than those in the control group. This result meets outcomes of other studies which claim that VR contributes to improving learners' motivation compared with other teaching methods [19–21].

A further analysis on the four factors composing learners' motivation experiences indicated that VR-based instructional methods was conducive to improving students' levels of attention and satisfaction compared with traditional instructional methods. However, results suggest that VR technology did not foster better levels of relevance and confidence than traditional teaching method. It can be seen from the ARCS model [16] that relevance refers to things which we perceive as instrumental in meeting needs and satisfying personal desires. Since the topic is close to the actual, the learning contents might be considered useful by students from both groups, so that there is no statistically significant difference of relevance between experimental and control groups. Regarding the factor of confidence, the ARCS model suggests that learners should be allowed as much personal control as possible and given an expectancy for success to build their confidence. However, multiple-choice tests used in this study give learners less control compared with short-answer tests. And the tests might be challenging for students since they were not able to master the basics of learning contents in a short time. Further study is necessary to explore whether the multiple-choice tests lead to students' feeling less control, and whether the time of learning is too short for students to achieve better levels of confidence.

There are still some research limitations regarding the present study that should be pointed out. Firstly, there is no time interval between learning activities and knowledge tests. The results of tests may be influenced by the short-term retention of learning content since students did not have enough time for thorough understanding. A long-term retention evaluation is likely to provide more insight into the effectiveness of the VR-based learning activities. Secondly, the video-based learning activities might be less engaging compared with face-to-face teaching. Lastly, it is essential to point out that this study includes a limited sample size, and a larger, multi-centric study must be designed and carried out in order to draw more credible conclusions.

5   Conclusion

This study aimed to investigate whether using first-person perspective VR-based physics learning platform could foster middle-school students' physics learning in Chinese middle schools. Evaluation was conducted to investigate the learners' academic achievements and motivation towards the course after the VR-based learning and traditional learning.

The results of this study demonstrate that the first-person perspective VR-based physics learning was more effective than the traditional learning in both facilitating students' learning achievements and also fostering motivation towards the instructional materials. Results also suggest that VR technology can be used as an effective learning tool within physics courses in Chinese middle schools.

Further studies could focus on examining the effect of VR technology on the permanence of the knowledge acquired. It is suggested that the next study focus on the effect of VR technology on learning achievements of students who have different level of achievements. The effects of first-person and third-person VR on physics learning can be further explored in the future. The study was carried out with eighth graders and similar studies can be conducted with students in different grades. Lastly, it is suggested that future studies recruit more participants of different genders and spend longer implementing the experiment so as to confirm the research findings.

Acknowledgements. This work is supported by the National Key Research and Development Program of China (No. 2018YFF0300802), the National Natural Science Foundation of China (No. 61960206007) and the 111 Project (B18005).

References

1. Olson, S., Riordan, D.G.: Engage to Excel: Producing One Million Additional College Graduates with Degrees in Science, Technology, Engineering, and Mathematics. Report to the President. Executive Office of the President (2012)
2. Guangming. http://news.gmw.cn/2018-06/07/content_29166599.htm. Accessed 21 Jan 2020
3. Gütl, C., Scheucher, T., Bailey, P.H., Belcher, J., dos Santos, F.R., Berger, S.: Towards an immersive virtual environment for physics experiments supporting collaborative settings in higher education. In: Internet Accessible Remote Laboratories: Scalable E-Learning Tools for Engineering and Science Disciplines, pp. 543–562. IGI Global (2012)
4. Reeve, J., Jang, H., Carrell, D., Jeon, S., Barch, J.: Enhancing students' engagement by increasing teachers' autonomy support. Motiv. Emot. **28**(2), 147–169 (2004). https://doi.org/10.1023/B:MOEM.0000032312.95499.6f
5. Burdea, G.C., Coiffet, P.: Virtual Reality Technology. Wiley, Hoboken (2003)
6. Crosier, J.K., Cobb, S., Wilson, J.R.: Key lessons for the design and integration of virtual environments in secondary science. Comput. Educ. **38**(1–3), 77–94 (2002)

7. Jang, S., Vitale, J.M., Jyung, R.W., Black, J.B.: Direct manipulation is better than passive viewing for learning anatomy in a three-dimensional virtual reality environment. Comput. Educ. **106**, 150–165 (2017)
8. Abdullah, F., Kassim, M.H.B., Sanusi, A.N.Z.: Go virtual: exploring augmented reality application in representation of steel architectural construction for the enhancement of architecture education. Adv. Sci. Lett. **23**(2), 804–808 (2017)
9. Pelargos, P.E., et al.: Utilizing virtual and augmented reality for educational and clinical enhancements in neurosurgery. J. Clin. Neurosci. **35**, 1–4 (2017)
10. Pensieri, C., Pennacchini, M.: Overview: virtual reality in medicine. J. Virtual Worlds Res. **7** (1), 34 (2014)
11. Kim, J.H., Park, S.T., Lee, H., Yuk, K.C., Lee, H.: Virtual reality simulations in physics education. Interact. Multimed. Electron. J. Comput.-Enhanc. Learn. **3**(2), 1–7 (2001)
12. Wu, Y., Chan, T., Jong, B., Lin, T.: A web-based virtual reality physics laboratory. In: Proceedings 3rd IEEE International Conference on Advanced Technologies, p. 455. IEEE (2003)
13. Rivas, D., et al.: Virtual reality applied to physics teaching. In: Proceedings of the 2017 9th International Conference on Education Technology and Computers. ACM (2017)
14. Pirker, J., Lesjak, I., Guetl, C., Maroon, V.R: A room-scale physics laboratory experience. In: 2017 IEEE 17th International Conference on Advanced Learning Technologies (ICALT), pp. 482–484. IEEE (2017)
15. Savage, C., McGrath, D., McIntyre, T., Wegener, M., Williamson, M.: Teaching physics using virtual reality. In: AIP Conference Proceedings, vol. 1263, no. 1, pp. 126–129. American Institute of Physics (2010)
16. Keller, J.M.: Strategies for stimulating the motivation to learn. Perform.+ Instr. **26**(8), 1–7 (1987)
17. Csikszentmihalyi, M.: Toward a psychology of optimal experience. In: Csikszentmihalyi, M. (ed.) Flow and the Foundations of Positive Psychology, pp. 209–226. Springer, Dordrecht (2014). https://doi.org/10.1007/978-94-017-9088-8_14
18. Rost, M.: Generating student motivation. WorldView, pp. 1–4 (2006)
19. Liou, W.K., Chang, C.Y.: Virtual reality classroom applied to science education. In: 2018 23rd International Scientific-Professional Conference on Information Technology (IT), pp. 1–4. IEEE (2018)
20. Stepan, K., et al.: Immersive virtual reality as a teaching tool for neuroanatomy. In: International Forum of Allergy & Rhinology, vol. 7, no. 10, pp. 1006–1013 (2017)
21. Bhagat, K.K., Liou, W.K., Chang, C.Y.: A cost-effective interactive 3D virtual reality system applied to military live firing training. Virtual Real. **20**(2), 127–140 (2016). https://doi.org/10.1007/s10055-016-0284-x
22. Hwang, W.Y., Hu, S.S.: Analysis of peer learning behaviors using multiple representations in virtual reality and their impacts on geometry problem solving. Comput. Educ. **62**, 308–319 (2013)
23. Merchant, Z., Goetz, E.T., Keeney-Kennicutt, W., Kwok, O.M., Cifuentes, L., Davis, T.J.: The learner characteristics, features of desktop 3D virtual reality environments, and college chemistry instruction: a structural equation modeling analysis. Comput. Educ. **59**(2), 551–568 (2012)
24. Shim, K.C., Park, J.S., Kim, H.S., Kim, J.H., Park, Y.C., Ryu, H.I.: Application of virtual reality technology in biology education. J. Biol. Educ. **37**(2), 71–74 (2003)
25. Stranger-Johannessen, E.: Exploring math achievement through gamified virtual reality. In: Pammer-Schindler, V., Pérez-Sanagustín, M., Drachsler, H., Elferink, R., Scheffel, M. (eds.) EC-TEL 2018. LNCS, vol. 11082, pp. 613–616. Springer, Cham (2018). https://doi.org/10.1007/978-3-319-98572-5_57

Telepresence Robots and Their Impact on Human-Human Interaction

Lisa Keller[✉] [ID], Kevin Pfeffel, Karsten Huffstadt,
and Nicholas H. Müller

University of Applied Sciences Würzburg-Schweinfurt,
Sanderheinrichsleitenweg 20, 97074 Würzburg, Germany
lisa.keller.it@gmx.de

Abstract. In an increasingly globalized world remote communication becomes ever more crucial. Hence, telepresence robots gain importance as they simplify attending important but distant events. However, research regarding human affinity towards a person by interacting directly or through a telepresence robot with another individual has not been undertaken immensely. Therefore, this work aims to investigate if there is a difference and by what it may be caused. Thus, a concurrent nested mixed method study was performed. A tour guided by a student was conducted with 102 participants through a part of a university building. Forty-one subjects experienced the tour through the telepresence robot Double 2 whereas another 41 subjects did the tour in person. The Multidimensional Mood State Questionnaire was used before and after the tour to detect if the tour has an impact on subjects' mood. Human affinity was measured inter alia through a hypothetical injury scenario of the guide in a questionnaire. In addition, information about the robot and tour were collected. Indications which strengthen that there is no difference in perception of human affinity whether people are interacting through a telepresence robot or in person were found. Moreover, new hypotheses which refine the original were established. Furthermore, the human guide will be replaced by a robot guide in a future study. Thereby, future work aims to lay the foundation of "human-robot-robot" interaction with respect to human affinity which has not yet been undertaken.

Keywords: Human-robot interaction · Telepresence robots · Human affinity

1 Introduction

The number of robots and their impact on today's everyday life has increased immensely. Manifold studies on human-robot interaction (HRI) have been undertaken. Most of them have investigated direct interactions between humans and robots as well as their impacts on humans [1, 2].

As it is not always feasible to be at a certain location due to spacial distance or disabilities, telepresence robots such as Double 2 (seen in Fig. 2) can be used as remote communication platform. Telepresence robots are mobile (mostly wheeled) platforms equipped with microphones, cameras and a screen, which can be controlled remotely via internet. The robot's operator who attends at a distant social event (e.g. a

© Springer Nature Switzerland AG 2020
P. Zaphiris and A. Ioannou (Eds.): HCII 2020, LNCS 12206, pp. 448–463, 2020.
https://doi.org/10.1007/978-3-030-50506-6_31

conference) can communicate through the robot with local attendees, who in turn can see the operator's face on the screen and interact with him or her. A huge benefit of using robots in remote communication instead of regular video conferences (e.g. Skype) is that the distant attendee can change the view and position of the camera by controlling the robot. Thereby, the remote attendee does not depend on an assisting person who turns the camera for him or her locally as it would be necessary during a regular video call.

2 Related Work

This aspect of freedom, as mentioned in the end of the introductory section, was also stated by participants of a study which investigated the impact of using telepresence robots in distance romantic relationships [3]. Other related work indicated that telepresence robots with arms that move accordingly to the operator's movements have a more positive impact on people's engagement, cooperation, and enjoyment compared to people who interacted with a non-arm moving robot [4]. However, co-presence and trust were not affected by movements.

Nevertheless, not only non-humanoid robots but also androids can be used as telepresence platforms. The work of Sakamoto et al. showed that the android was perceived as more present; however, also uncannier as a person on a screen [5].

Similar to the use case in this work, test subjects of Tsui et al.'s study visited an art gallery with a telepresence robot and also in person afterwards. Conversations with a person in the gallery were perceived as normal during the telepresence tour. Moreover, the participants answered that they perceived the gallery through the telepresence robot mostly in the same way as in person [6].

3 Objective

The studies introduced in Sect. 2 examined differences in perception of objects and environment or the appearance of telepresence robots themselves. However, research with respect to human affinity towards a person interacting directly or through a telepresence robot with another person has not been undertaken immensely. Therefore, this works aims to investigate if there is a difference and by what it may be caused. Thus, a concurrent nested mixed method design focusing on quantitative data was chosen.

4 Methods

As use case for the study, a short tour through the university's building with test subjects doing the tour with the telepresence robot or in person, respectively, was chosen. Thereby, test subjects were accompanied by a student guide who explained the stations of the tour. In order to detect if the tour has a significant impact on participants' mood, the Multidimensional Mood State Questionnaire was used before (short version A) and after (short version B) the tour [7, 8]. To measure human affinity as well as to collect information about the telepresence robot and the tour, a questionnaire containing quantitative and qualitative questions was developed.

5 Approach

To gain a broader understanding how test subjects feel during the tour as well as how the telepresence robot is perceived, additional questions besides to measuring human affinity were asked. The main focus of this work, however, remains on human affinity. Thus, it is hypothesized that there is a difference in human affinity depending on, if there is a telepresence robot involved or not. Precisely speaking, it is presumed that subjects who experienced the tour through the telepresence robot show less human affinity towards the human guide than subjects who did the tour in person (see *H1*). Furthermore, it is hypothesized that this may be caused by a distance, test subjects could experience through the telepresence robot. All methods used to collect the data will be discussed in further detail later on in this section.

Hypothesis

H1: If subjects are connected on the telepresence robot and guided by a human, then subjects show less human affinity towards the human guide compared to subjects who were directly guided by the human guide.

To strengthen or weaken *H1* a tour through the university's building was conducted with a total of 102 test subjects. The statistical population was composed of university students as well as employees. The study was performed in the building of the faculty of computer science and business information systems as well as the faculty of visual design. Therefore, most of the test subjects had a background in computer science. The participants were randomly sampled and dived into two groups. Group 1 ($N = 41$) experienced the tour through the telepresence robot Double 2 from Double Robotics (seen in Fig. 2), whereas Group 2 ($N = 41$) undertook the tour in person. Both groups (illustrated in Fig. 2) were guided by a student through a part of the campus' building. All in all, the guide showed and explained seven stations. Also, during moving among the different stations, information about the passing environment was provided by the guide and conversations with subjects were established. An illustration of the tour and its stations can be seen in Fig. 1.

The telepresence robot Double 2 can be either controlled via WASD or arrow keys. Additionally, zooming in and out is feasible through mouse clicking. Also, the robot's telescopic neck can be moved to see objects which may be above or below the range of vision. This can be realized by means of the robot's user interface and the mouse.

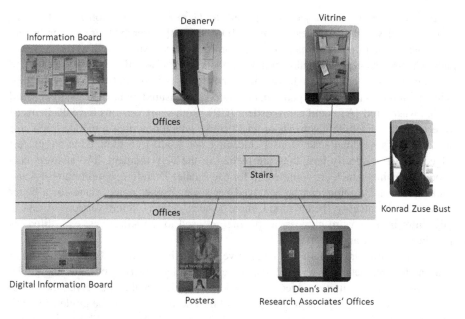

Fig. 1. Tour

Groups

Group 1: Subject connected on telepresence robot and guided by a human guide.
Group 2: Subject directly guided by a human guide.

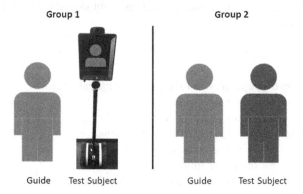

Fig. 2. Groups

First of all, a pretest ($N = 20$) was conducted. This test was performed with subjects being connected on the telepresence robot as in Group 1. However, questions 12 to 16 (see questionnaire enumeration below) of the designed questionnaire were not included in the question catalogue. To measure human affinity further, these questions were added after the pretest.

Before the tour, test subjects completed the German short version A of the Multidimensional Mood State Questionnaire (MDMQ) [7, 8]. After the tour was conducted, test subjects filled in the German short version B of the MDMQ as well as the designed questionnaire (see questionnaire enumeration below). The MDMQ was selected to determine if the tour or the telepresence robot have a significant impact on the participants' mood. Thereby, the participants' mood is measured by three scales: good-bad (GB), awake-tired (AT), and calm-restless (CR). Both short versions have 12 items (4 for each scale). Each item consists of an adjective which describes a mood, "tired" for instance. On an ordinal scale from 1 (meaning not at all) to 5 (defined as very), test subjects have to specify how they are feeling in the very moment. The answers correspond to points which are summed up for each scale. Therefore, a minimum of 4 and a maximum of 20 points can be achieved per scale. Higher points stand for a better mood in each category (better mood, more awake, calmer). Short versions A and B only differ in their word choices, as people get used to the adjectives; e.g. "tired" is used in version A and "awake" in B.

The questionnaire containing quantitative and qualitative methods was designed to examine the interaction among the test subject, the telepresence robot, and the guide. To measure human affinity, subjects were asked how likeable they perceived the guide, why they perceived the guide as likeable, and how well they knew the guide (question 7 to 9). Moreover, a hypothetical scenario of the guide being injured by falling to the ground was chosen to create an uncomfortable emergency situation to measure human affinity further (questions 12 to 16). The complete questionnaire can be seen in the enumeration below. The same scale from 1 to 5 as in the MDMQ was used in closed-ended questions, except question 14, 17, and 20 were nominal measured. Question 5 and 6 written in italic, were only applied in group 1 and the pretest, respectively. Questions including a backslash such as number 8, varied based on the answer of the previous question. If scale 1 or 2 was selected, the right side of the backslash was asked by the survey system.

Questionnaire

1. How much did you enjoy the tour?
2. How well could you understand the guide acoustically?
3. How well could you see the guide?
4. How well could you hold pace with the guide?
5. *How well did you get along with the robot's control?*
6. *How could we improve the robot's control?*
7. How likeable was the guide to you?
8. Why did you perceive the guide as likeable/unlikeable?
9. How well do you know the guide?
10. How annoyed had you been during the tour?
11. If you were annoyed, what did annoy you?
12. How dismayed would you be, if your guide would get injured (e.g. through falling to the ground)?
13. Why would you be dismayed/not dismayed?
14. Would you help the guide?
15. Why would you help/not help the guide?

16. How would you approach to help the guide?
17. Do you work in a STEM (science, technology, engineering, mathematics) field?
18. Would you prefer to experience the tour personally or through a remote control-lable robot? Why?
19. Do you have any suggestions for improvement?
20. What is your gender?
21. How old are you?

6   Evaluation

All quantitative data was evaluated by means of MathWorks' MATLAB. As an ordinal scale was used and also performed Kolmogorov-Smirnov tests pointed out the data to be non-normally distributed, only two-tailed non-parametric tests at the significance level of $p \leq 0.05$ were applied. A sign test with respect to subjects' mood before and after the tour (MDMQ) was performed for each group. Moreover, the Wilcoxon signed-rank method for repeated measurement was applied between the pretest and group 1. For comparing two different populations, the Wilcoxon rank-sum method was used between the pretest and group 2 as well as between group 1 and 2.

For all tests a p and h value are provided. Thereby, p represents the significance level, whereas h indicates whether the test fails to reject the null hypothesis of equal medians. Thereby, $h = 1$ implies that the hypothesis of equal medians can and $h = 0$ that it cannot be rejected, respectively.

Also, correlation for ordinal data was considered by using Spearman's rank correlation coefficient. Thereby, the relations among the perceived likeability of the guide, how well subjects know the guide, and how dismayed they would be (questions 7, 9, and 12) were investigated. The following categories of Spearman's correlation coefficient r will be used in the analysis:

- .00–.19 "very weak"
- .20–.39 "weak"
- .40–.59 "moderate"
- .60–.79 "strong"
- .80–1.0 "very strong"

The mean and standard deviation values of all results are shown in Table 2.

6.1   Results and Analysis

The pretest composed of 20 participants of whom 14 (70%) identified themselves as male, 5 (25%) female, and 1 (5%) other. Subjects were aged 21 to 51 and 29.70 years old averagely. A total of 17 (85%) participants had a STEM (science, technology, engineering, mathematics) background.

On the other hand, a total of 41 subjects participated in group 1 of whom 35 (85.37%) were male and 6 (14.63%) female as well as between the ages of 18 and 57.

The average participant was aged 29.46. Moreover, 37 (90.24%) subjects were occupied in a STEM field.

Likewise, 41 subjects were assigned to group 2 of whom 32 (78.05%) were male and 9 (21.95%) female. The participants were between the ages of 20 and 34 as well as 24.88 years old in average. A STEM background was stated by 27 (65.85%) subjects.

MDMQ. In all groups, participants exhibited a slight increase in their mood on all three scales (GB, AT, CR) averagely. It can be seen though, that the GB and CR values of group 2 (MDMQ difference: $M_{GB} = 0.68$, $M_{CR} = 1.54$) rose marginally more compared to the pretest ($M_{GB} = 0.30$, $M_{CR} = 0.80$) and group 1 ($M_{GB} = 0.10$, $M_{CR} = 0.02$). However, the AT value increased averagely highest in the pretest ($M_{AT} = 2.40$), followed by group 2 ($M_{AT} = 1.54$) and finally group 1 ($M_{AT} = 1.41$). Nevertheless, as all participants regardless of groups showed a slight increase in their mood, it can be implied that the tour has no significant impact on participants' mood. Moreover, this indicates that the telepresence robot was not perceived as disturbing or annoying.

Tour. The tour was enjoyed averagely high in each group, $M = 4.30$ (pretest), $M = 4.07$ (group 1), $M = 4.39$ and (group 2). All participants regardless of groups were only slightly annoyed, $M = 1.8$ (pretest), $M = 1.49$ (group 1), $M = 1.24$ (group 2). Participants who experienced the tour with the telepresence robot specified that they were annoyed by poor video and audio quality, a breakdown of the robot, latency, and the robot's low driving speed. On the other hand, annoyance of the surrounding environment such as noise and the fire door (see threats to validity) were stated by subjects who did the tour in person. Nonetheless, these factors did not seem to affect participants' annoyance level profoundly.

All in all, these insights indicate successful applications of telepresence robotics as well as that those robots are not perceived as highly annoying or disturbing.

Obviously, there is a noticeable difference in acoustical understanding, visibility of the guide, and holding pace between doing the tour in person or through the robot. However, not the knowledge of the difference itself but its magnitude is of interest. Even though the guide showed consideration for the robot's speed and adapted pace, robot participants still perceived holding pace (pretest: $M = 2.90$, group 1: $M = 3.07$) less well than group 2 ($M = 4.73$). However, visibility of the guide through the robot's camera can be considered fairly well (pretest: $M = 3.70$, group 1: $M = 3.82$, group 2: $M = 4.85$). Whereas acoustical understanding is relatively poor compared to group 2 (pretest: M = 2.85, group 1: $M = 2.51$, group 2: $M = 4.85$), which complicated communication occasionally.

Robot's Control. Only 4 out of 61 participants (pretest and group 1) faced major difficulties controlling the robot (scale values 1 and 2). It was proposed by them to broadening the camera view, controlling the robot via joystick, speeding up moving the robot's telescopic neck, and to improving the robot's agility.

On the other hand, the remaining participants were able to deal fairly well with the robot's control. Averagely, the control was rated by $M = 4.10$ (pretest) and $M = 4.07$

(group 1), which emphasizes that the subjects generally perceived the control as sufficiently well. Nonetheless, there is still room for improvement such as less latency, enhanced audio and video transmission, using a 360-degree camera, increased driving speed, moving telescopic neck via keys as well as adding a brake, bumpers, and obstacle handling as suggested by subjects.

Human Affinity. All participants in any group perceived the guide as likeable (scale values 3 to 5). Subjects experienced the guide thereby in average as 4.75 (pretest), 4.78 (group 1), and 4.65 (group 2) likeable. As knowing the guide could have an impact on measuring human affinity this variable was captured (see correlation paragraph). In the pretest, 3 (15%) subjects knew the guide not at all, 3 (15%) only little, 6 (30%) mediocrely, 8 (40%) well and on a scale value of 2.95 averagely; whereas, in group 1 more subjects knew the guide. Therein, 4 (9.76%) subjects knew the guide not at all, 1 (2.44%) only little, 14 (34.15%) moderately, 17 (41.46%) well, 5 (12.20%) very well and on a scale value of 3.44 in average. In group 2 on the other hand, most participants knew the guide only little $M = 2.21$. Sixteen (39.02%) of them knew the guide not at all, 10 (24.39%) only little, 6 (14.63%) mediocrely, 8 (19.51%) well, and 1 (2.44%) very well.

Some participants of the telepresence robot groups specified that they liked the guide because they knew the person. Moreover, some stated that the guide explained well, spoke clearly, showed consideration for them as well as was patient, open-minded, nice, motivated, and informative.

On the other hand, group 2 appreciated the calmness, openness, niceness, eye contact, conversations, and good explanations of the guide. Furthermore, some stated that the guide spoke clearly and also liked the person as they already knew the guide.

Participants who undertook the tour through the robot were dismayed on a scale value of 4.24, averagely. Also, 2 (4.88%) were only little dismayed (scale value 2) as one stated that a distance through the display was given. Another participant specified that the guide seems to be athletic and thereby the risk of injuries should be lower. Subjects who were more dismayed stated that they would feel so as they are not on site and therefore do not know how they could help. Moreover, it was provided that they would feel dismayed as injuries are emergency situations, they would not like to be hurt either or due to compassion. All subjects except for two would help the guide. Reasons and approaches of helping can be seen in Table 1.

Subjects who did the tour in person were dismayed on a scale value of 4.22, in average. Also, 2 (4.88%) were only little dismayed as injuries can happen or because they do not know the guide well. More dismayed participants stated that they would feel so as this would be an emergency situation, the guide was nice, and due to compassion. Furthermore, all subjects would help the guide.

It could be observed that in the way group 1's subjects phrased answers sounded more panicked than group 2's. This insight led to a new hypothesis which will be introduced in Sect. 7.

Table 1. Reasons and approaches of helping.

Group	Reasons for helping	Reasons for not helping	Approach of helping
1	Out of humanity, compassion, liked or knew the guide	Would be too far away to help	Ask how the guide feels, make an emergency call, finding other people by controlling the robot through the building, call university employees
2	Out of humanity, compassion, liked or knew the guide	–	Ask how the guide feels, provide assistance, first aid, call an ambulance if necessary

Finally, the participants were asked, if they would have the choice, whether they would like to experience the tour in person or through a telepresence robot. Additionally, they were requested to specify their decision. In the pretest, 13 (65%) would prefer to do the tour in person as interacting with the guide and environment is simpler as well as more personal. Moreover, 5 (25%) would like to do the tour through the robot as it is less personal, a new experience to control a robot, or similar to a game. Also, 2 (10%) stated that both would be adequately for them; however, a longer tour could get exhausting with the robot according to one participant.

Likewise, 31 (75.61%) of group 1 would like to do the tour in person as it does not feel as distanced as through the robot. Furthermore, 9 (21.95%) would favor to do the tour with the robot as it is an exceptional experience. Also, 1 (2.44%) participant stated that both variants would be fine. In addition, other reasons given resemble those from the pretest.

On the other hand, 31 (75.61%) of group 2's participants would like to conduct the tour in person. Moreover, 7 (17.07%) through the robot and 3 (7.32%) expressed no preference. Reasons stated correspond to those given in the pretest and group 1.

Overall, participants showed a fascination for the telepresence robot which benefits their use. Furthermore, it was mentioned in all groups that the robot would be preferred if the tour would take place at a far distant place, otherwise in person would be preferred. Most interestingly, some subjects would prefer an in-person tour as it is more personal, whereas others prefer the robot as it is less personal. However, most would prefer the personal tour.

Table 2. Means and standard deviations.

Variables	Pretest	Group 1	Group 2
MDMQ before tour (GB, AT, CR)	M: 16.75, 13.55, 15.45 STD: 1.86, 3.19, 2.87;	16.09, 13.24, 14.41 3.22, 3.45, 3.11;	16.56, 13.46, 14.95 2.40, 2.70, 3.06;
MDMQ after tour (GB, AT, CR)	17.05, 15.95, 16.25 1.64, 2.87, 2.55;	16.20, 14.66, 14.44 3.21, 3.01, 2.79;	17.24, 15.00, 16.49 1.82, 2.16, 2.37;
Difference MDMQ	0.30, 2.40, 0.80 1.75, 3.00, 2.29;	0.10, 1.41, 0.02 1.95, 2.45, 2.44;	0.68, 1.54, 1.54 1.68, 2.45, 2.42;
Enjoyed tour (Q1)	M: 4.30, STD: 0.57	4.07, 0.85	4.39, 0.59

(continued)

Table 2. (*continued*)

Variables	Pretest	Group 1	Group 2
Acoustic (Q2)	2.85, 0.75	2.51, 0.78	4.85, 0.48
Visibility (Q3)	3.70, 0.87	3.82, 0.89	4.85, 0.36
Holding pace (Q4)	2.90, 1.21	3.07, 1.13	4.73, 0.59
Robot Control (Q5)	4.10, 1.07	4.07, 0.85	–
Likeable (Q7)	4.75, 0.55	4.78, 0.48	4.65, 0.53
Know guide (Q9)	2.95, 1.10	3.44, 1.07	2.21, 1.24
Annoyed (Q10)	1.80, 1.15	1.49, 0.79	1.24, 0.49
Dismayed (Q12)	–	4.24, 0.80	4.22, 0.85
Help (Q14)	–	M: yes	M: yes
STEM (Q17)	M: yes	M: yes	M: yes
Personally or robot (Q18)	M: personally	M: personally	M: personally
Gender (Q20)	M: male	M: male	M: male
Age (Q21)	29.70, 9.08	29.46, 9.86	24.87, 3.66

MDMQ - Sign Test. Table 3 shows the resulting data of the sign tests with respect to the subjects' mood before and after the tour for each group. According to the sign test, the tour does not seem to have an impact on the GB-scale (refer to Sect. 5) of any group, as the hypothesis of equal medians cannot be rejected ($h = 0$) with a significance of $p = 0.30$ (pretest), $p = 1.00$ (group 1), and $p = 0.06$ (group 2). The tour, however, does seem to have an insignificant impact on people's AT-value as test subjects felt more awake after the tour with respect to all groups (pretest: $p = 0.001$, group 1: $p = 0.01$, group 2: $p = 0.001$). By considering the means (refer to Table 2) of the AT-values before and after the tour though, it can be seen that there is not a vast difference (pretest: 13.55 (before), 15.95 (after); group 1: 13.24, 14.66; group 2: 13.46, 15.00). Therefore, this could be an artifact which occurred. Likewise, the same phenomenon can be observed with group 2's CR-value as subjects felt calmer after the tour ($p = 0.001$, means: 14.95 (before), 16.49 (after)). However, test subjects who used the telepresence robot expressed no change in their calmness level (pretest: $p = 0.08$, group 1: $p = 0.74$). Nevertheless, the increased calmness level of group 2 could also be an artifact.

Overall, the data indicates that the tour has no significant impact on participants' mood in all groups. Also, the MDMQ mean difference (see Table 2) outlines that subjects' mood on all scales increased only slightly averagely, in all groups. Summarizing, this especially indicates that the telepresence robot (pretest and group 1) was not perceived as disturbing or annoying. This pleads for successful applications for further telepresence robot use cases.

Table 3. Sign test: MDMQ before and after tour.

Variables	Pretest	Group 1	Group 2
GB	$p = 0.30, h = 0$	$p = 1.00, h = 0$	$p = 0.06, h = 0$
AT	$p = 0.001, h = 1$	$p = 0.01, h = 1$	$p = 0.001, h = 1$
CR	$p = 0.08, h = 0$	$p = 0.74, h = 0$	$p = 0.001, h = 1$

Hypothesis Testing. To investigate if there is a difference between the repeated measurements (pretest and group 1) Wilcoxon's signed-rank test was applied. Moreover, Wilcoxon's rank-sum was carried out to determine if the independent samples of subjects doing the tour in person or with the telepresence robot have the same distribution. If the MATLAB function calculated Wilcoxon's signed-rank p-value by using a normal approximation, then the Z-statistics is provided. Otherwise, the T-statistics is reported. Likewise, the Z-statistics will be provided if the approximate method of Wilcoxon's rank-sum was used. Otherwise, the W-statistics will be reported instead. Table 4 gives an overview of the tests' results. The MDMQ difference as well as questions 1 to 4, 10, 12, 14, and 17 were examined with the tests.

There could be no difference detected between the pretest and group 1, all $p > .05$ (please refer to Table 4 for the exact results). This strengthens that repeated measurement has no influence on the telepresence robot groups' results.

Comparing the pretest with group 2, only the CR-value differs. Subjects who did the tour in person showed a higher increase of calmness (MDMQ difference: $M = 1.54$) than subjects who used the telepresence robot (MDMQ difference: $M = 0.80$), p < .05, $z = -2.23$. The same phenomenon can be observed between group 1 (MDMQ difference: $M = 0.02$) and 2 (MDMQ difference: $M = 1.54$), $p < .05$, $z = -2.59$. However, this could also be an artifact as earlier discussed in the sign test analysis. Surprisingly, acoustical understanding (Q2) and the visibility (Q3) of the guide do not differ between the pretest and group 2 (Q2: $p > .05$, $W = 24$; Q3: $p > .05$, $W = 23$), even though they do differ between group 1 and 2 (Q2 and Q3: $p < .05$, $W = 26$). This could be an error made by Wilcoxon's rank-sum test, as the guide normally should be less well seen and understood through remote communication than in person. In this case though, not the knowledge of the difference itself but its magnitude is particularly interesting as discussed earlier in this section. Any other investigated variables between group 1 and 2 did not show inequality in medians according to Wilcoxon's rank-sum test (see Table 4).

Most interestingly, the variables measuring human affinity: being dismayed ($p = 1.00$, $W = 1.5$), helping the guide ($p = 1.00$, $W = 1.5$), and likeability of the guide ($p = .40$, $W = 19$) exhibit high p-values with respect to group 1 and 2. Consequently, the null hypothesis cannot be rejected. Also, by considering the mean and deviation values of these three variables, there is almost no difference recognizable (refer to Table 2). Thus, the results strengthen H0, that there is no difference between human affinity shown towards another individual in person or through a telepresence robot. New hypotheses with respect to this aspect and knowing the guide, were established (refer to Sect. 7).

Table 4. Statistical tests.

Variables	Pretest and Group 1 Wilcoxon Signed-Rank	Pretest and Group 1 Wilcoxon Rank-Sum	Group 1 and 2 Wilcoxon Rank-Sum
MDMQ difference (GB, AT, CR)	$p = 0.95, h = 0,$ $z = -0.06$ $p = 0.43, h = 0,$ $z = 0.79$ $p = 0.73, h = 0,$ $z = -0.34$	$p = 0.17, h = 0,$ $z = -1.37$ $p = 0.12, h = 0,$ $z = -1.54$ $p = 0.03, h = 1,$ $z = -2.23$	$p = 0.21, h = 0,$ $z = -1.24$ $p = 0.67, h = 0,$ $z = -0.42$ $p = 0.01, h = 1,$ $z = -2.59$
Enjoyed tour (Q1)	$p = 0.50, h = 0,$ $T = 3$	$p = 1.00, h = 0,$ $W = 20$	$p = 0.43, h = 0,$ $W = 22$
Acoustic (Q2)	$p = 0.13, h = 0,$ $T = 10$	$p = 0.14, h = 0,$ $W = 24$	$p = 0.03, h = 1,$ $W = 26$
Visibility (Q3)	$p = 0.13, h = 0,$ $T = 10$	$p = 0.17, h = 0,$ $W = 23$	$p = 0.03, h = 1,$ $W = 26$
Pace (Q4)	$p = 0.13, h = 0,$ $T = 10$	$p = 0.97, h = 0,$ $W = 17.5$	$p = 0.54, h = 0,$ $W = 20.5$
Likeable (Q7)	$p = 0.25, h = 0,$ $T = 6$	$p = 1.00, h = 0,$ $W = 16.5$	$p = 0.40, h = 0,$ $W = 19$
Annoyed (Q10)	$p = 0.75, h = 0,$ $T = 4$	$p = 0.51, h = 0,$ $W = 13.5$	$p = 0.69, h = 0,$ $W = 14.5$
Dismayed (Q12)	–	–	$p = 1.00, h = 0,$ $W = 1.5$
Help (Q14)	–	–	$p = 1.00, h = 0,$ $W = 1.5$

Correlation. As how well known the guide was to the subjects and how likeable the guide was perceived could have influenced each other as well as the level of being dismayed, a Spearman correlation was performed. Table 5 shows the corresponding results of each group. Spearman's r categories introduced earlier in this section will be applied to describe the results in the following:

The level of being dismayed was significantly weak positive correlated with the likeability of the guide, $r = .33, p < .05$. Furthermore, being dismayed was significantly weak negative related to knowing the guide, $r = -.16, p < .05$. In addition, the level of being dismayed was weak significant positive correlated to knowing the guide, $r = .33, p < .05$. Other variables only exhibited non-significant correlation.

All in all, it can be said that Spearman's correlation only shows a maximum of weak significant relationships among likeability, knowing the guide, and being dismayed. Thereby, it can be implied that the three variables only interdepend to a small degree. However, there could still be a greater or different relationship as Spearman's correlation only investigates monotonic relations.

Table 5. Spearman correlation.

Variables	Pretest	Group 1	Group 2
Likeable (Q7), know guide (Q9)	$r = -.08, p = .73$	$r = -.27, p = .91$	$r = .11, p = .48$
Dismayed (Q12), likeable (Q7)	–	$r = .33, p = .03$	$r = .22, p = .16$
Dismayed (Q12), know guide (Q9)	–	$r = -.16, p = .03$	$r = .33, p = .04$

6.2   Threats to Validity

As the tour was conducted in an open part of the university's building, passers-by interfered with the tour occasionally. Moreover, the mood, appearance, and clothing of the guide may have had an impact on subjects. Also, how well participants knew the guide could have had an impact on the tour and all study settings. Therefore, this factor was considered and examined through Spearman's correlation. Moreover, technical difficulties such as audio disturbances and breakdowns of the telepresence robot occurred. Furthermore, a fire door obstructed a part of the tour's path during the last quarter of conducting group 2. Thus, the tour's path differed slightly from the tours before. The door may have annoyed subjects, which was also stated by one participant. Accordingly, the tour could not be carried out exactly identical.

All in all, these factors may have influenced inter alia: participants' mood, enjoyment of the tour, amount of annoyance, perceived likeability, and level of being dismayed.

7   Conclusion

The results of the MDMQ showed that the tour does not seem to have a significant impact on participants' mood. Thus, it can be implied that using telepresence robots has no significant influence on people's mood as well as the feeling of being annoyed. Also, the measured level of annoyance affirms this. Furthermore, nearly all participants were able to deal well with the robot's control. However, latency as well as audio and video quality should be improved to enhance communication.

With respect to human affinity measuring, a maximum of weak significant relationships among likeability, knowing the guide, and being dismayed could be determined. Furthermore, the hypothesis $H0$ could not be rejected. Also, analysis of the data exhibited insights which strengthen that there is no difference in human affinity shown towards another individual personally or through a telepresence robot. However, subjects who used the telepresence robot seem to be more affected by possible injuries of the guide than participants who did the tour in person. This insight and others of the qualitative data led to the following new hypotheses:

H2: If subjects are connected on the telepresence robot and guided by a human, then subjects are more affected by possible injuries of the guide, compared to subjects who were directly guided by the human.

H3: If subjects are guided by a human they know, then subjects show equivalent human affinity towards the guide, whether they are connected on the telepresence robot or guided directly by the human.

H4: If subjects are connected on the telepresence robot and guided by a human they do not know, then subjects show less human affinity towards the guide, then subjects who are directly guided and do not know the guide.

8 Outlook

Future research will have to evaluate the new established hypotheses *H2*, *H3*, and *H4*, introduced in Sect. 7. Moreover, it is planned to replace the current camera of the Double 2 telepresence robot with a 360-degree camera to improve vision, as suggested by participants. In addition, solutions to enhance audio transmission and to reduce latency will be examined.

As already discussed in the introductory section, most studies on HRI have investigated direct interactions between humans and robots. Also, indirect HCI e.g. through a projector robot [9] or in form of remote "human-robot-human" interaction [4, 5] was studied. Moreover, studies in which humans act as bystander or as instructor of one robot in robot-robot communication was examined [10, 11]. However, studies on "human-robot-robot" interaction, where humans operate a robot which in turn interacts with a robot, have not been undertaken with respect to human affinity, based on extended research.

Therefore, further work aims to lay the foundation of "human-robot-robot" interaction and its influence on human perception of robots. Thereby, the results of this future work could provide new insights into the design of robots and their operating environment. Thus, a new curve may be modeled in the Uncanny Valley hypothesis [12, 13] with respect to "human-robot-human" interaction. Such an effect of perceiving robots differently if seen through another medium than in person could be observed in a study of motivating young women for STEM by using robots [14].

This future study will be undertaken by combining two common use cases, a robotic tour guide [15–19] and telepresence robotics. Thereby, the study is divided in two groups analogous to group 1 and 2 in this current work. However, the human guide will be replaced with Aldeberan Robotics' Pepper, as illustrated in Fig. 3. Thereby, the robot guide will be designed with consideration of the insights of this current study to create the robot as likeable as possible.

Groups

Group 3: Subject connected on telepresence robot and guided by a robot guide.
Group 4: Subject directly guided by a robot guide.

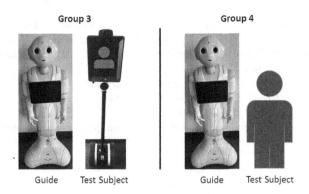

Fig. 3. Additional groups

References

1. Arkin, R.C., Fujita, M., Takagi, T., Hasegawa, R.: An ethological and emotional basis for human-robot interaction. In: Robotics and Autonomous Systems, pp. 191–201 (2003)
2. Rosenthal von der Pütten, A.M., et al.: Investigations on empathy towards humans and robots using fMRI. Comput. Hum. Behav. **33**, 201–212 (2014)
3. Yang, L., Neustaedter, C., Schiphorst, T.: Communicating through a telepresence robot: a study of long distance relationships. In: Proceedings of the 2017 CHI Conference Extended Abstracts on Human Factors in Computing Systems, pp. 3027–3033 (2017)
4. Adalgeirsson, S.O., Breazeal, C.: Mebot: a robotic platform for socially embodied presence. In: Proceedings of the 5th ACM/IEEE International Conference on Human-robot Interaction, pp. 15–22 (2010)
5. Sakamoto, D., Kanda, T., Ono, T., Ishiguro, H., Hagita, N.: Android as a telecommunication medium with a human-like presence. In: Proceedings of the ACM/IEEE International Conference on Human-Robot Interaction, pp. 193–200 (2007)
6. Tsui, K., et al.: Accessible human-robot interaction for telepresence robots: a case study. Paladyn J. Behav. Robot. 6 (2015)
7. Steyer, R., Schwenkmezger, P., Notz, P., Eid, M.: Der mehrdimensionale Befindlichkeitsfrage-bogen (MDBF). In: Hogrefe, Verlag für Psychologie (1997)
8. University of Jena MDMQ questionnaire (English version of MDBF). https://www.metheval.uni-jena.de/mdbf.php. Accessed 06 June 2019
9. Park, J., Kim, G.J.: Robots with projectors: an alternative to anthropomorphic HRI. In: Proceedings of the 4th ACM/IEEE International Conference on Human Robot Interaction, pp. 221–222 (2009)
10. Fraune, M.R., Šabanovic, S.: Robot gossip: effects of mode of robot communication on human perceptions of robots. In: Proceedings of the 2014 ACM/IEEE International Conference on Human-Robot Interaction, pp. 160–161 (2014)
11. Williams, T., Briggs, P., Pelz, N., Scheutz, M.: Is robot telepathy acceptable? Investigating effects of nonverbal robot-robot communication on human-robot interaction. In: The 23rd IEEE International Symposium on Robot and Human Interactive Communication, pp. 886–891 (2014)
12. Mori, M.: The uncanny valley. IEEE Robot. Autom. Mag. **19**(2), 98–100 (2012)
13. Saygin, A.P., Chaminade, T., Ishiguro, H., Driver, J., Frith, C.: The thing that should not be: predictive coding and the uncanny valley in perceiving human and humanoid robot actions. Soc. Cogn. Affect. Neurosci. Oxford University Press 7, 413–422 (2011)
14. Keller, L., John, I.: How can computer science faculties increase the proportion of women in computer science by using robots? In: 2019 IEEE Global Engineering Education Conference, pp. 206–210 (2019)
15. Thrun, S., Bennewitz, M., Burgard, W., Cremers, A.B., Dellärt, F., Fox, D., Haehnel, D., Charles Rosenberg, N.R., Schulte, J., Schulz, D.: Minerva: a second-generation museum tour-guide robot. In: Proceedings of the 1999 IEEE International Conference on Robotics & Automation, pp. 1999–2005 (1999)
16. Burgard, W., et al.: The interactive museum tour-guide robot. In: Proceedings of the Fifteenth National/Tenth Conference on Artificial Intelligence/Innovative Applications of Artificial Intelligence, pp. 11–18 (1998)
17. Daye, D., Gobbe, S., Durairajah, V.: Autonomous tour guide robot using embedded system control. Procedia Comput. Sci. **76**, 126–133 (2015)

18. Shiomi, M., Kanda, T., Ishiguro, H., Hagita, N.: A larger audience, please!: encouraging people to listen to a guide robot. In: Proceedings of the 5th ACM/IEEE International Conference on Human-Robot Interaction, pp. 31–38 (2010)
19. Clodic, A., et al.: Rackham: an interactive robot-guide. In: The 15th IEEE International Symposium on Robot and Human Interactive Communication, pp. 502–509 (2016)

3D Hologram Learning Kit Development for Elementary Education

Youbin Kim[✉] and Dong Yeong Lee

Hanyang University, Seoul, Republic of Korea
{gumi0508, dannylee}@hanyang.ac.kr

Abstract. This paper aims to explain the design for immersive learning resources that include 3D holographic learning content intended to complement basic textbooks. Also, it shows a development process for a portable learning kit that is accessible and universally available for collaborative learning to increase the interest and understanding of elementary school students.

When it comes to designing 3D hologram learning content, we have worked with scientific content based on the national curriculum for fifth and sixth grade levels in elementary school. We used an IAP process (A Design Process based on Iterative Agile Prototyping) for developing a tangible learning kit, which consists of a reflective mirror, a tablet holder, and a height adjustment stand, providing 3D holographic images via a tablet and an app controller.

We have assessed the learning kit in order to define problems and improvements for future development. As a primary test, the 3D learning content was evaluated with student users from the perspectives of immersion, and social interaction. For the secondary test, we conducted a usability analysis from teacher's observation and interviews focusing on tangible interaction, and convenience. As a third test, the kit was evaluated by experts in field of EdTech (Education and Technology) to reveal its weaknesses and strengths in aspects of marketability with feedback and possible improvements. Through this exploratory study, we have identified the strengths and weaknesses of this 3D hologram learning kit and defined further improvements as a universal teaching resource in the future classroom.

Keywords: 3D hologram · Learning kit · Elementary education · EdTech

1 Introduction

In the era of the fourth Industrial Revolution, educational learning systems and methods have changed rapidly, incorporating advanced technologies such as AR/VR, holograms, big data and AI. Traditional education has mostly been carried out by means of didactic instruction, which is a one-way approach to information and cognition. Nowadays, however, educators favor experience-oriented teaching methods and tools that offer learners interactive experiences as well as psychological satisfaction about the fulfillment of essential learning. Going forward, education will expand especially into virtual spaces providing a significantly new kind of learning through interactive device design that includes various interactive contents, something that users have not yet experienced.

This work was supported by the research fund of Hanyang University.

P. Zaphiris and A. Ioannou (Eds.): HCII 2020, LNCS 12206, pp. 464–479, 2020.
https://doi.org/10.1007/978-3-030-50506-6_32

In 2012, the Republic of Korea's Ministry of Education established 41 smart education research schools to provide learning environments for virtual experiences. Also, these schools have developed appropriate curriculums and courses for virtual education via high-tech equipment (KERIS 2012). However, educational tools using AR/VR technology have problems: there is a lack of sufficient content because it is costly and time consuming to develop software. At the same time, it is inconvenient to have educators and students wear headsets while trying to participate in the educational experience.

On the other hand, holographic technology is more valuable because it can directly show virtual objects without any mediating devices. This technology is useful as a tool for collaboration through mutual communication. New forms of virtual learning with various interactive contents, including EdTech products based on holographic technology, will provide new tools for more collaborative learning experiences rather than unidirectional approaches to information and cognition. However, the existing hologram equipment is large, cumbersome, and difficult to install, and the equipment must maintain a Wi-Fi network with a minimum guaranteed constant speed of 20 megabits per second (Ghuloum 2010, p. 698). At the same time, the cost burden and space limitations make it impractical for easy use in the classroom.

Therefore, this paper aims to create resources for designing a 3D hologram learning kit that provides immersive learning experiences meant to complement basic textbooks. In addition, the ultimate goal is to develop a portable learning kit that is accessible and universally available for collaborative learning. The learning kit will display learning content that leads to effective learning, increasing the interest and understanding of elementary school students. Additionally, this learning kit must be evaluated for suitability and feasibility in various aspects that will be assessed to reveal weaknesses and strengths in order to justify any improvements. Thus, this paper aims to achieve the following objectives.

Research Objectives

- To reveal the importance of 3D holograms in the teaching and learning environment.
- To create 3D hologram learning content as science learning resources for elementary education.
- To develop a portable kit for interactive and collaborative team teaching.
- To evaluate the suitability of the content and learning kit from the user's point of view.
- To analyse the market feasibility of the 3D hologram learning kit.

To implement research based on the objectives above, this study is divided into 4 stages: learning content design, learning kit development, primary/secondary test of user experience, and experts' feedback that answers pertinent questions.

Research Questions

- What is the appropriate learning content of elementary science courses?
- Which design is best suited to form a kit shown as a 3D hologram?
- Does the 3D hologram content lead to efficient learning for elementary students?
- What difficulties will elementary instructors face while using this kit?

– What are the 3D hologram kits' strengths and weaknesses compared with traditional methods or competing products?

2 Theoretical Research

2.1 The Importance of 3D Hologram Technology in Learning Environment

A hologram is a three-dimensional projection of laser light. The word, hologram, comes from the Greek terms, "holos" for "whole view"; and "gram" meaning "written". Dennis Gabor, a Hungarian physicist, he researched about electron microscopes, discovered the basic technology of holography in 1947 (Gabor 1948). In 1962 scientists in both the United States and the Soviet Union created 3D holographic technology (3DHT). However, 3DHT has advanced notably since the 1980s owing to low-cost solid-state lasers that have become easily accessible for consumers. The way 3DHT operates is by creating the illusion of three-dimensional imagery. A light source is projected onto the surface of an object and scattered. A second light illuminates the object to create interference between both sources. Essentially, the two light sources interact with each other and cause diffraction, which appears as a 3D image (Ghuloum 2010). The importance of 3DHT on the learning environment has increased due to the instructional advantages of technological services via ICT integration that has successively made novel forms of education. This learning process is interactive beyond merely playing a video in a 3D hologram. Here, hundreds of teaching resources appear as if real materials actually exist in the classroom. Moreover, 3DHT enhances the educational process by bringing in famous characters that speak about themselves as well as explain points of interest, just like an assistant teacher would. As a virtual teacher, the character leads the learners' interest and increases their immersion in the class. According to Sandra Andrews at Arizona State University College of Education, "The virtual world gives a greater sense of presence than discussion boards. The students get a better feel for the teacher, and it is more fun" (Harrison 2009). Hence, the studies have shown that the learning results by virtual materials aid better retention of information and understanding of a given topic.

2.2 Examples of Previous 3D Hologram Technology for H-Learning

Currently, sophisticated technological tools for H-learning have been proposed as different ways of expressing educational content in 3D holograms. The first type is when a virtual teacher, unrestricted by time and space, teaches students. The process goes a step further when the holographic teacher appears to be in the classroom, seeing and speaking to the pupils as if they were all in the same room. For example, this system was demonstrated by Duffie White in Edexcel, the largest supplier of Internet connections to the UK education market, at the BETT2000 Educational Technology Show in London (BBC News 2000). Math teacher Catharine Darnton was digitally teleported into the exhibition center at Olympia from Graveney School in South London. The distance was a few miles; however, since the system used internet protocols, the audience and the teacher could have been anywhere and shared their experience. The second type interacts with philosophers or historical masterminds from the past. This is utilized in museum education. At the TEDx Copenhagen, the founder of the Carlsberg dynasty appeared in front of 300 invited guests over 170 years after his passing. The audience at the world famous Glyptothek museum was stunned to see the founder of the iconic international beer brewery, JC Jacobsen in real time as a hologram.

The third type is when the learner wears a holo-lens and chooses specific resources according to the courses. Here, learners experience embedded 3D images within reality relating to the educational contents. Pearson and Microsoft released HoloPatient and HoloHuman, which provide nursing schools with a series of digitally created healthcare scenarios. Students wearing HoloLens see holograms of professional actors pretending to be ill and learn how to diagnose and treat them (Microsoft 2018). The final type is 3D Studio by Hypervsn, which is an online service with the integrated 3D content marketplace that provides a new way of creating and customizing 3D content for one's own work. Avoiding expensive creative agencies, users are able to take 2D images and convert them into 3D visuals. This program includes a feature that adds stunning animation in a variety of languages, fonts, colors, and textures. The platform allows educators to design custom curricula for their own specific needs. Action recognition systems without additional headsets also demonstrate interactive features which lead to engagement focused on studying and other key interactive offerings (Figs. 1 and 2).

Fig. 1. A holo-lens in use (Source: Microsoft)   **Fig. 2.** 3D studio for 3D content creation (Source: Hypervsn)

3 Development of the 3D Hologram Learning Kit

3.1 Designing the 3D Hologram Learning Content

When it comes to designing 3D hologram learning content, we have utilized scientifically accurate educational sources based on the national curriculum for fifth and sixth grade elementary school levels established by the South Korean Ministry of Education. The revised national science education standards for 2018 stipulate that educators at these grade levels must foster scientific thinking, research skills, problem solving, communication skills, participation, and learning skills as core capacities (Korean Ministry of Education p. 211 2018). The standards for overall learning aim to develop scientific understanding and inquiry ability as well as to stimulate students' interest and curiosity about natural phenomena and objects. The national curriculum for content design adopted the following achievement criteria (Table 1):

Table 1. Setting up the earth science curriculum for content design

Core concept	Core content	Content element	Achievement standards	Specific learning objectives
Composition and motion of the solar system	The solar system is made up of various objects, including the sun, planets, and satellites	Planets in solar system	Understand the types and features of the planets in the solar system	1) Students will observe shapes and distinguish sizes of Mercury, Venus, Earth, Mars, Jupiter, Saturn, Uranus, and Neptune 2) Learners will distinguish the planets' sizes and know distances between them
		The sun	Know the shapes and features of the sun and about solar energy	1) Students will observe the appearance and surface of the sun, and learn about its characteristics and processes 2) Students will understand the importance of the sun for life on earth

In order to build effective learning experiences, we have adapted the mobile application system to control curriculum-based learning. We have designed stereo-scopic images based on this core content for science education in application guidance and services. The content interfaces are clear and user-centered, helping students and teachers obtain information and complete critical tasks easily. The users' experience has been designed by clearly organizing the overall menu composition in order to deliver the main content. In addition, the flow plan and pagination of content has been organized using wireframes. We have also used an iterative prototype of IAP process for developing the app and a tangible learning kit, which is an ICT convergence design process developed by Kim and Lee (2019). It is a way to come up with new ideas while repeatedly drawing on paper, demonstrating that creators can become users who evaluate and improve their apps continuously. The following table depicts the order of interfaces and functions in the easy-to-show 3D holograms (Table 2).

3.2   Designing the 3D Hologram Physical Learning Kit

For the development of a physical learning kit designed for both students and teachers, we have used an IAP process for ICT convergence product design. This is a participatory design process model for innovation as well as an extension of the methodology for developing the learning content. Four design researchers fashioned kit prototypes iteratively using the various given paper resources and found them to work according to the following three principals.

Durability. This is the ability of a physical product to remain functional without requiring excessive maintenance or repair when faced with the challenges of normal operation over its design lifetime (Tim 1994, p 25). We focused on the aspects of the kit's structure stability as well as on sustainable tactile design materials.

Ergonomics. This refers to the understanding of interactions between humans and other elements of a system in order to optimize the performance and effectiveness of the working system, including accessibility, usability, and safety (Wickens C. D. et al. 1998, p. 295). We intended an easy-to-assemble kit that rested on the table at the user's sitting height.

Portability for Collaboration. Portability in product design means the quality of being small and light enough to be easily transported. We aimed for a smaller kit that is also easier to carry than the existing heavy hologram devices. Such portability enhances the potential for teamwork and idea exchange as well as how users can implement cooperation within the academic environment.

In the field prototyping of the IAP process, we discovered potential users' needs and problems by deconstructing the existing hologram devices. We repeatedly attempted to research key questions regarding a product that is more robust and intensive. The "decision prototyping" exploratory phase generated data to clarify the product's ergonomics, usability, and convenience. We defined problems in virtual situations by marking them with post-its. In the stage of "idea prototyping", we applied an iterative agile process. These activities led to the evaluation of prototypes via quick and lightweight feedback. At this stage, we drew wild ideas on existing prototypes as well as created new functions reflecting novel ideas. Rapid feedback about new ideas gave us insights into innovative solutions. At the same time, we continued to experiment with structural forms so that the triangular reflectors could function well technologically at the same time as the learning content was displayed accurately on the tablet screens.

Table 2. Flow and functions according to app pages

Page name	Left bar	Main screen	Content list
Images			
Functions	1) My profile 2) My collection 3) Introduction 4) Learning analysis 5) App information	1) Searching content 2) Selecting a subject 3) Selecting content of a chapter	1) Listing holographic content by curriculum 2) Information section on educational goals and background content
Flows	1) Users register their own profiles as soon as they enter main page. 2) Users check how to utilize app service through introduction in menu bar. 3) Users choose the subjects and sub-topics they want to teach or to learn.		

Page name	3D hologram content 1	3D hologram content 2	Learning Analysis
Images			
Functions	1) Transferring holographic image to tablet 2) Adjusting volume of background music 3) Adjusting image size 4) Adjusting image angle 5) Stopping planet rotation	1) Press 'Like' to select 2) Sharing images with others 3) Saving images in "My Collection" 4) Listening to the information	1) Number of images students "like" 2) Number of images viewed in total learning time 3) Previously viewed image 4) Percentage completed
Flows	1) User sets up contents, rotation, sound, etc. 2) User sends desired contents to the tablet by pressing a specific button. 3) User moves the contents and adjusts size and angle by sliding fingers and using pinch-zoom. 4) User checks amount of the time spent and content learned according to subjects.		

Various prototypes have been made to rise to the technical challenge of presenting holographic resources from different physical angles so that many users can communicate with each other from different positions, postures, and locations in order to stimulate team collaboration. The 3D simulated images that appear on cell phones and tablets use a transparent acrylic pyramid. Projected stereoscopic motion that contains 3D holographic content enhances the viewer's perception and motivates participation (Table 3).

Table 3. Development procedure of 3D hologram learning kit

Process	Field prototyping	Decision prototyping	Idea prototyping	Actualization
Images				
Procedure	1) Deconstructing existing hologram devices. 2) Discovering problems through user interviews and tablet testing. 3) Prototyping possible ideas reiteratively with easy-to-access materials.	1) Defining problems in virtual situations using holograms. 2) Marking size and structure problems on physical prototypes. 3) Clarifying common problems and refining structure shape.	1) Generating wild ideas regarding shapes and materials. 2) Simulating the different ideas. 3) Selecting the final texture and form. 4) Demonstrating functionality through feedback.	1) Branding and character design for marketability. 2) Designing all-in-one portable packages for easy portability and collaboration. 3) Examining the manufacturing process to consider mass production and economic feasibility.

The package—the whole kit—consists of a reflective mirror, a tablet holder, and a height adjustment stand. The various data in the 3D app link to the tablet's screen through a Wi-Fi connection. This allows educators and students to view and project high quality holographic images in a universal learning environment. In addition, the controlling function of the app enables students to rotate and zoom in on or out of 3D holographic images for interactive learning and new experiences. The interconnected operating system for the final output via Wi-Fi can be represented by the following Fig. 3:

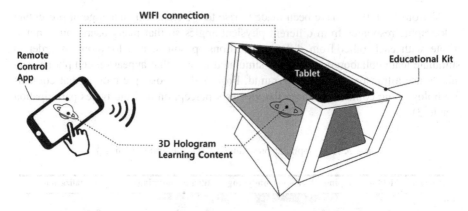

Fig. 3. The 3D hologram learning kit's cross connecting system (Drawing by Youbin Kim)

4   Evaluation

4.1   Methodology

The methodology of evaluation adapted for this study is comprised of three tests, analyzing qualitative and quantitative data as a method of mixed research. We specifically focused on one formative evaluation case utilizing of Kantosalo's (2015, p. 280) criteria for interaction design evaluation methods. As with all human studies, ethical issues arose in relation to child participants; thus we used the consent forms of Waller et al. (2009, p. 27) to obtain agreement with the children's parents.

For the primary test, we conducted a comparative evaluation of 2D textbooks and 3D learning content. The evaluation focused on how and to what extent the 3D content affects a student's understanding and interactive participation. We recruited fifth and sixth grade students and divided them into two teams, each of which had five students. Educators facilitated a real educational situation, and the student teams became involved with the content and tools while researchers observed. We assessed the level of high/middle/low from the perspectives of perceptual coupling, configurability, legibility, high concentration, letter perception, and continuous interaction. Also, in aspects of social interaction we evaluated the encouragement of participation, collaboration, physical focus, social awareness, and effective communication.

The secondary test evaluates usability of the learning kit as a teaching tool for elementary school teachers. A sample of five primary school teachers individually implemented the 3D hologram in a teaching environment with the help of a kit guide. A researcher checked the teachers' behavior and noted the details on an observation sheet to determine important factors in relation to tangible interaction and convenience. The checklists were quantified through a one to five on the Likert scale where "one" indicates a level of strong disagreement while "five" indicated strong agreement. Afterward, the teachers completed an experience survey according to the interview protocol.

As a final assessment, the kit was evaluated at the Consumer Electronics Show (CES 2020) to reveal its weaknesses and strengths from the perspective of market suitability. Forty-one experts in the fields of university academia, and EdTech related professionals provided feedback pointing out possible improvements. The questionnaire focused on evaluating the 3D hologram learning kit's for educational institutions by identifying advantages and disadvantages.

Results of Primary Test. First, in order to measure content immersion, Team A received a 2D textbook to learn about the solar system and planets. Team B was given a 3D hologram kit that covered the same material. An instructor explained the same guide to both teams for the same length of time. Both teams had 30 min of study time, and after a ten-minute break, they took an exam about the features and components of the planets Jupiter and Saturn, as well as about the order of the solar system. This was done to understand how well they concentrated on the content.

Team A read for only 10 min and paid no other attention to the material for up to 15 min. On the other hand, Team B focused on the 3D holograms, manipulating the application until time was up. During those 30 min they were immersed in the experience as if playing a game, which demonstrates augmented concentration and continuous interaction through high participation. To identify the aspect of legibility, five students of Team A wrote short answers to the questions, answering on average only three of the five questions; also, the students drew very simple pictures of Jupiter and Saturn. Team B correctly answered all five questions, and their responses were much more expansive and creative. At the same time, their descriptions and expressive drawings were quite detailed. Team A had no problems recognizing the letters in the textbook in terms of letter perception. However, Team B found it difficult to recognize the rotating 3D letters. They asked their teacher three questions during the 40-min learning period. This revealed the connection between letter recognition and learning, and it seems to reveal that the difficulty in perceiving 3D characters lowers the perceptual coupling and interrupts the flow of learning.

In order to evaluate the results of cooperation and interaction between team members, comparative analysis was performed through video recording. During the given time, Team A's communication about the subject was minimal and the students made no attempt to collaborate with one another in order to solve any problems. However, in the case of Team B, one student assumed a leadership role and suggested participation to another student, and together they informed the others about how to adjust the 3D content; inter-student communication continued until the end of the study period. Therefore, this demonstrates how the 3D hologram kit encourages participation and effective communication during learning. Regarding collaboration, Team B showed a higher degree of teamwork in that they cooperatively solved problems, using the discussion time to share their opinions about the questions. However, since the students took so much time communicating and cooperating rather than answering the end-of-period questions, the value of the physical focus score is low (Tables 4 and 5).

Results of Secondary Test. For the secondary test, a sample of five primary school teachers implemented the 3D hologram kit with the help of a kit guide while we conducted observation, checking the usability checklist. Statistically, the results show high scores for direct haptic manipulation, lower thresholds of physical interface, and accurate movements in the aspect of tangible interaction. Also, the in-depth interviews revealed that almost all the teachers were satisfied with adjusting their own apps and

Table 4. Results of comparative test between 2D textbook and 3D hologram learning kit

Criteria	Sub-factors	Team A	Team B
Immersion	High concentration	Low	High
	Legibility	Middle	High
	Letter perception	High	Low
	Continuous interaction	Low	High
	Perceptual coupling	Middle	Middle
Social interaction	Encouragement of participation	Middle	High
	Collaboration	Low	High
	Physical focus	Middle	Middle
	Social awareness	Low	High
	Effective communication	Low	High

explaining the content. The 3D hologram kit was also effective in delivering learning content because of its rapid and accurate operation, as well as its response from its interface operation. However, it received low scores for spatial and continuous interaction because there is little interactive response in conjunction with its surrounding situations and environments (Table 4).

In the aspect of convenience, the kit could be set up by following the simple instructions on the package and worked according to the teachers' needs without any problems. Also, it was possible for multiple users to operate the hologram at the same time because of the multiple input points. The educators had no problems utilizing whatever holographic content they wanted to store in their collections. They also felt that the kit was easy to move and assemble for use, which generated high scores for the sub-factors of convenience.

Results of the Third Test. Forty-one experts at the Consumer Electronics Show (CES 2020) responded to our questionnaire about the advantages and disadvantages regarding the learning kit's marketability. Remarkably, the respondents identified "universal compatibility" and "ease of distribution by effective packaging" as the main strengths with percentages reaching more than 30%. This is because, unlike traditional hologram devices, the kit is able not only to easily utilize any tablet and phone but also to access any global market. Additionally, the experts believed that the learning kit is suitable as a classroom product offering educational instruction with a significant level of over ten percent for both "low initial cost of infrastructure in schools" and "applicability of various teaching resources" because it is effective in both theoretical and practical subject content delivery. Also, two responders mentioned "possible language translation for global retail", which shows that the 3D hologram content and kit are expandable regardless of national or language barriers.

However, the experts overwhelmingly pointed out "difficulty of self-development for new content" as the main disadvantage, with a score that reached more than 40%. At the same time, over 20% of the sample believed that there are technical limitations in the categories of "Wi-Fi access constraint" and "platform limitation" because the kit cannot be used in a non-Wi-Fi area or can only be used by downloading the

Table 5. Outcomes of comparative test between Team A and Team B

	Team A	Team B
Outcome images		
Test images		

Table 6. Results of usability test captured via observations and interviews

Criteria	Sub-factors	A	B	C	D	E	Average	Comments
Tangible interaction	Haptic direct manipulation	5	5	4	5	5	4.8	Users are able to hold and operate movement according to haptic interface
	Accurate movement	4	5	4	4	4	4.2	Depending on the degree of operation, the hologram images respond accurately
	Realtime feedback	2	4	3	3	3	3	Work instructions provide quick feedback in real time
	Lightweight interaction	4	3	3	4	2	3.2	Even with the lightest touch, the kit tends to respond well
	Environmental interaction	2	1	1	2	2	1.6	There is little interactive response in conjunction with surrounding situations and environments
Convenience	Control constraints	3	3	4	4	3	3.4	Holographic movements can be controlled according to users' needs
	Multiple access points	4	3	3	2	4	3.2	Due to multiple input points, multiple users can operate the hologram at the same time
	Configurability	3	2	3	4	3	3.0	The installation is simple and the setting function is conveniently

(*continued*)

Table 6. (*continued*)

Criteria	Sub-factors	A	B	C	D	E	Average	Comments
								configured without an instructional manual
	Lower thresholds of physical interface	4	5	5	5	3	4.4	It is easy to utilize holographic content that educators want to store in their collection
	Portability	5	5	5	5	4	4.8	It is easy to move and easy to assemble for use

application. Additionally, "lack of technical know-how" was also identified as a relatively unimportant barrier in the aspect of personal ability, due to users' possible slowness to adapt to new technical devices or innovative trends (Fig. 4).

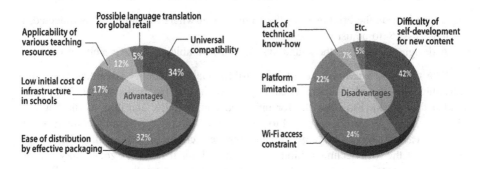

Fig. 4. Advantages and disadvantages of 3D hologram learning kit

5   Discussion and Conclusion

The 3D hologram learning kit is a medium that more effectively enhances interaction between students and teachers for collaborative education compared to traditional 2D textbook learning. Through our intensive research we have designed 3D hologram learning content and created the 3D hologram images based on educational resources in accordance with the national curriculum for fifth and sixth grade elementary school levels. Using iterative prototyping we developed a portable kit, consisting of a reflective mirror, a tablet holder, and a height adjustment stand. After that, we assessed the kit's learning content's user interaction, usability for teachers, and marketability as a school product. Through exploratory tests, we identified the learning kit pros, cons, and needs for improvement. We will also discuss possible improvements for further development in order to enable the learning kit to become a universal teaching resource.

In the first test, we assessed the learning content regarding immersion and social interaction. The results revealed that most of the learning content is well designed in terms of legibility, effective communication, high concentration, encouragement of participation, and collaboration. However, we found some problems with the letter perception, perceptual coupling, and physical focus. Hence, we suggest the following improvements:

- To increase perception of three-dimensional letter, the titles should be limited to five words. Assistive backgrounds will also improve text readability.
- Storytelling through holographic will enhance physical focus and thus attract viewers as well as complement perceptual coupling.

The second test evaluated the physical learning kit from the perspectives of tangible interaction and convenience of educators' usability. Observational research revealed mostly high scores about almost all sub-factors such as haptic direct manipulation, lower thresholds of physical interface, precise movement, and portability. However, there was a lack of environmental interaction regarding the spatial feature. Therefore, in order to consider environmental interaction, the kit's inside design should apply the following elements and take into account reactions to the potential surroundings:

- Depending on the brightness of the environment where the hologram is reflected, it is necessary to adjust the light.
- A design solution for the sound system must be able to manage ambient noise.

The third test surveyed 41 EdTech professionals to identify advantages and dis-advantages of the 3D hologram learning kit regarding its marketability. They con-cluded that the kit has strengths for universal compatibility and ease of distribution. However, the main problem related to the expandability of the learning content is that teachers cannot incorporate any of their own new content. Additionally, the experts pointed out the kit's technical limitations, which limit it to Wi-Fi zones only. More-over, the content only operates through downloading the application. The following solutions will resolve these problems:

- Through technical developments, customized app functions should make it easy for educators to include their own content.
- In addition to connecting the tablet to a mobile phone via a Wi-Fi connection, Bluetooth access should be added for more than one device.
- Establishing open source systems will allow users to download new content from online web sites without application accounts.

In conclusion, this study conducted several tests for the initial development of new ideas for a 3D hologram learning kit. Moreover, we defined the above problems and suggested enhancements. Continuing improvements will help the kit become a more reliable educational tool for students and educators. At the same time, we defined the kit's various strengths and potentials. Below, we will discuss how the kit has expansive possibilities for the future.

As a new medium, a 3D textbook in forward-looking education, the concept of the learning kit can be applied to a variety of basic subjects beyond science education. Furthermore, STEM based convergence education of national curriculum subjects like technology, mathematics, engineering, and art can also be accessed through similar 3D hologram kits. At the same time, these kits can be used as collaborative educational tools for different institutions; not only elementary education but also higher levels such as middle school, high school, and university will benefit greatly. Furthermore, it is possible to expand this concept beyond educational institutions and include industrial organizations and company education programs by displaying stereoscopic 3D content in the medical, architectural, and engineering fields.

As mentioned previously and as a result of this study, the kit will become useful global teaching material due to its translatability and easily distributed portable packaging. We ultimately intend that the kit lead to great social impact that provides interactive experiences for teachers and students as well as enhances cooperative teamwork and collaboration through enthusiastic participation.

References

BBC News: Meet the hologram teacher (2000). http://news.bbc.co.uk/2/hi/in_depth/education/2000/bett2000/600667.stm

Gabor, D.: A new microscopic principle. Nature **161**, 777–778 (1948)

Ghuloum, H.: 3D hologram technology in learning environment. In: Proceedings of Informing Science & IT Education Conference 2010, pp. 693–704 (2010)

Harrison, D.: Real-Life teaching in a virtual world. Campus Technology (2009). https://campustechnology.com/Articles/2009/02/18/Real-Life-Teaching-in-a-Virtual-World.aspx

Kantosalo, A., Toivanen, J.M., Toivonen, H.: Interaction evaluation for human-computer co-creativity: a case study. In: ICCC, pp. 276–283 (2015)

KERIS: Workshop sourcebook of research school for smart education. Education and Research Information Service (2012)

Kim, Y., Lee, J.: A study on product design process for innovation based on iterative agile prototyping. J. Ind. Des. **13**(2), 61–71 (2019)

Korean Ministry of Education: National Science Curriculum, Korean Ministry of Education No. 2018-74, pp. 211–212 (2018)

Microsoft: Using holograms to train nurses: Pearson and Microsoft launch mixed-reality curriculum (2018). https://news.microsoft.com/en-gb/2018/01/22/using-holograms-train-nurses-pearson-microsoft-launch-mixed-reality-curriculum/

Tim, C.: The durability of consumer durables. Bus. Strategy Environ. **3**(1), 23–30 (1994)

Waller, A., Black, R., O'Mara, D.A., Pain, H., Ritchie, G., Manurung, R.: Evaluating the standup pun generating software with children with cerebral palsy. ACM Trans. Access. Comput. **1**(3), 16–27 (2009)

Wickens, C.D., et al.: An introduction to human factors engineering, p. 295 (1998)

Does Immersive VR Increase Learning Gain When Compared to a Non-immersive VR Learning Experience?

Khadija Mahmoud$^{(\boxtimes)}$ ⓘ, Isaac Harris$^{(\boxtimes)}$ ⓘ, Husam Yassin$^{(\boxtimes)}$ ⓘ,
Thomas J. Hurkxkens, Omar K. Matar, Nitesh Bhatia,
and Irene Kalkanis$^{(\boxtimes)}$ ⓘ

Imperial College London, London SW7 2AZ, UK
{Khadija.mahmoud17,
Husam.mogahid-taha-yassin17}@ic.ac.uk,
{Isaac.harris17,i.kalkanis}@imperial.ac.uk

Abstract. Currently, computer assisted learning and multimedia form a key part of teaching. Interactivity and feedback are valuable in promoting active as opposed to passive learning. The study is conducted as an assessment of the impact of immersive VR on learning gain compared with a non-immersive video capture of VR, with a primary research question focusing on exploring learning gain and a secondary question exploring user experience, whereby understanding this is paramount to recognizing how to achieve a complete and effective learning experience. The study found immersive VR to significantly increase learning gain whilst two key measures of reported experience; enjoyment and concentration, also appeared significantly higher for the immersive VR learners. The study suggests extensive avenues for further research in this growing field, recognizing the need to appeal to a variety of students' learning preferences. For educators, the relevance of self-directed and student-centered learning to enable active learning in the immersive tool is highlighted. Findings of such VR-based studies can be applied across several disciplines, including medical education; providing opportunity for users to learn without real-world consequences of error such as in surgical intervention.

Keywords: Virtual reality · Education · Medicine · Self-directed learning · Active learning

1 Introduction

1.1 Background

Virtual reality (VR) technology has a longer history than its recent popularity might suggest. The initial concept was formulated in the 1960s when Ivan Sutherland first described [1] "a display connected to a digital computer [which] gives us a chance to gain familiarity with concepts not realizable in the physical world. It is a looking glass into a mathematical wonderland." The term 'Virtual Reality', now widely understood in research and industry, was coined in 1989 by early VR pioneer Jaron Lanier [2].

© Springer Nature Switzerland AG 2020
P. Zaphiris and A. Ioannou (Eds.): HCII 2020, LNCS 12206, pp. 480–498, 2020.
https://doi.org/10.1007/978-3-030-50506-6_33

Today, VR describes a virtual environment generated by a computer that employs head and hand tracking systems to allow the user to move around and manipulate the environment in real time [3].

The earliest definitions do not differ widely from more modern definitions such as those provided by Fuchs and Bishop [4] who described VR as "real-time interactive graphics with 3D models, combined with a display technology that gives the user the immersion in the model world and direct manipulation". Despite slight differences in wording, three principles consistently feature in distinguishing the technology from others; presence, immersion and interactivity. Recently, advances in VR technology have led to its increasing similarity to the real world and thus potential for mass consumption. As computing power increases, VR shares an increased interconnectivity with it, allowing Human-Computer interfaces to form more better-adapted interactions with users.

Individual experiences of VR are often commercial, and most widely associated with gaming amongst other widely distributed media. Heavy investment from tech giants such as Facebook, who bought Oculus VR for two billion US dollars in 2014 [6], has helped convince smaller companies of the technology's potential. However, more recent reports suggest disappointing experiences for individuals stuck with cheaper smartphone-reliant headsets, whilst headsets such as Oculus Rift are too expensive for the average consumer; this indicates that the wait for the emergence of mass industry investment is set to continue [7].

1.2 Fields of Use

Despite commercial limitations, VR-based research is rapidly expanding into a range of fields outside individual commercial use. VR simulations have proved useful in laboratory and clinical studies which would previously have relied on direct, invasive interventions – relying on these methods is particularly limiting in clinical research [8]. Several studies demonstrate its application, where in one particular study [8], participants were immersed in virtual environments to recognize spatial deficits in Alzheimer's disease. The use of VR by scientists further reflects its value in understanding navigation and sensory systems. This is primarily a product of VR enabling researchers to exhaustively and clearly define their virtual world, thus, providing a high degree of control over user experience and thus, their experiment [9].

VR Classification. As the community of VR users grows, the range of its applications is expected to continue to grow. A systematic literature review investigating the uses of VR [10] exposed three main categories; 'exploration', 'health' and 'presentation entertainment', where 'exploration' involved VR uses in heritage projects and tourism, whereas 'presentation and entertainment' contained various applications, mostly focusing on the digitalization of the real world from engineering to the development of entertainment. The use of VR in education may occur in any one of these categories. This forms classification by system functions, adapted from Zhao [11], who also suggested a classification by immersion experience. In this case, VR can be divided into non-interactive and interactive where interactive experiences refer to either human-virtual environment or group-virtual environment by immersion.

In a non-interactive experience, the content is entirely planned and thus, the users' experience of virtual environment is completely passive, e.g. no scenic wandering. However, a human-virtual environmental interactive experience would involve users interacting with virtual environment through equipment, e.g. digital scalpels, with scenes responding to the interaction in time. Accordingly, users are able to feel a change in virtual environment and experience corresponding real world. The group virtual environmental interactive experience system is identical to this in terms of immersion but additionally involves multiple users sharing one virtual environment and interacting with it through user avatars for instance. Other similar classifications exist as highlighted by the literature [3], including categorization into; non-immersive VR, also known as 'desktop VR', semi-immersive VR, supporting head movement but not sensory output, and immersive VR; the ultimate system which supports total immersion according to the user's position and orientation and may be enhanced by sensory, audio and haptic interfaces.

Fields of study aim to develop VR systems for users; exploring user experience to understand how to complete the achievement of an immersive and effective experience. Thus, creating an application that is immersive and natural to the user is universally paramount.

1.3   Related Work

Technology-enhanced learning is gaining momentum as exemplified by e-learning, using media such as videos, which has recently formed a promising alternative to traditional learning (textbook and lecture-based tools); moving society towards achieving a vision of on-demand, lifelong learning [12]. However, whilst visualization likens VR to video-based learning, videos form passive learning objects whereas VR allows a direct interaction with the environment. Interactivity and feedback are valuable in promoting active as opposed to passive learning [12].

Instructional methods in classrooms may be affected by the personal styles of individual teachers, rather than the cumulative knowledge derived from experimental analysis of the variables involved in learning [13]. Thus, more recent technology-based study designs better reveal functional relations between dependent, i.e. student learning gain, and independent, i.e. learning material, variables which forms a more reliable base for exploration as they are not influenced by personal teaching styles or forms of interaction [14].

Self-directed learning is considered an indicator of success in learning and is defined as the student's capacity to drive the mental process in learning [15]. In order to stimulate active, self-directed learning; a key feature of immersive VR systems that promotes interactivity, is needed [16]. VR's provision of an active learning environment provides students with freedom in decision-making as part of the learning process.

Engagement remains a key factor behind the success of many e-learning activities [17], particularly in those that, more recently, use immersive, 3D virtual worlds to enhance the visualization of learning material. Immersive VR is dependent on the user's position and orientation and may be enhanced by sensory, audio and haptic interfaces; all features which may prove useful for education and training purposes.

Consideration of the forms in which learner engagement fits the wider picture of immersive technologies, alongside the factors that influence engaging experiences virtually, is a core consideration for studies, such as this one, proposing the use of such technologies. DELVE project [18] explores the relationships between engagement and immersion in VR where immersion forms a sense of presence and can thus be a notion of engagement. When considering engagement, the project's findings propose considering both the engagement level as a result of interactions and feedback from the VR as well as the level of engagement promoted by the learning activity featured in the VR with which the user is engaged. Thus, this study may be distinguished from others in focusing on the dimensions of deep levels of engagement as opposed to the existing large focus on multi-sensory experiences common in the VR literature. This study primarily focuses on learning gain, exploring the general dimensions of engagement by recognizing a person's motivation to engage, e.g. completion of the post-VR quiz, as well as relationship building through applying their knowledge to different scenarios. According to Yee's taxonomy [19], the three key motivational components are; immersion, social and achievement, where immersion is recognized as a key component in VR-user motivations. This study aims to explore these further, comparing quiz performance with secondary outcome measures such as enjoyment and comfortability in the VR.

The usefulness of VR in education might also depend on the type of learning. The visual–auditory–kinesthetic learning styles model [20] identifies three types of styles; auditory, visual and kinesthetic learning; all of which VR allows in a single application. Thus, studies have appreciated that VR encompasses multiple learning styles which enables it to benefit a wider range of individuals. However, findings are critical of learning styles theories [21], and point towards little empirical evidence. Accordingly, this study deviates from focusing on variations in sensory modalities which may affect learning approach within VR. Instead, one application is set for both groups to explore, thus, reducing the effects of varying learning styles.

A previous study [22] used simple online interactive simulations to mimic real experiments, publishing results that revealed 86% of the study's subjects found these simulations helpful alongside a reported increased willingness to answer questions. Furthermore, previous investigations [23] of VR as a learning resource have compared it directly to traditional learning, including one comparing lecture-based teaching to immersive VR-based teaching. Results highlight an improvement of 15% in favor of VR and generally similar findings exist within the literature. With vast amounts of existing evidence in favor of VR-based learning in education compared to traditional methods, there remains a need to explore the tool itself in an attempt to utilize its maximum potential. Consequently, this study focuses instead on exploring how different degrees of immersion in VR can lead to differences in learning gain, amongst other outcomes, which would support institutions already invested in using VR within curricula and would find interest in understanding how to enhance student engagement with this new tool. Three challenges have been identified; cost, usability and fear of technology [24], to explain why some educators may be reluctant to invest in its use and so evidence from this study aims to further identify whether the application is worth pursuing.

1.4   Aims of the Study

Based on previously highlighted classifications and definitions of degrees of immersion, this study is based on a system of human-virtual environmental interaction, also described as immersive experience, in comparison to a non-interactive, also classified as non-immersive, experience.

The study is conducted as an objective assessment of the impact of immersive virtual reality on learning gain compared with a non-immersive video capture of the VR application. Despite video capture fitting the earlier recognized classifications, the tool may not be perceived as a VR application as it fails to fit two of the basic characteristics of VR [25]; the three I's, known as interaction, immersion and imagination. However, studies have proven video to be a more effective medium than text for enhancing motivation during the learning process [26, 27], allowing video capture to form some other characteristics of VR including simulation. Furthermore, this video capture cannot be classed as "video-based" learning as instructional videos must allow students to interact with it to enhance learner engagement yet this study did not enable that. Similarly, a distinct media attribute of video includes random access to content; where users can select segments, another criterion that video capture does not fit. Thus, in its comparison to immersive VR, it is reasonably identified as non-immersive VR.

Learning gain is defined as the difference in skill, content knowledge and competency between two time points [28]. The study also aims to break down the multifaceted task of identifying differences in reported user experience into its constituent elements and then to evaluate each of these elements individually, thus measuring this as a secondary outcome; assessing variables such as enjoyment, concentration and immersion, supports this. Furthermore, understanding user experience is paramount in recognizing an effective experience for learning and serves to highlight students as active contributors rather than passive recipients in learning. While the primary research question focuses on learning gain, and existing studies have found evidence to identify VR as an interesting and enjoyable learning experience for students [29], our research aims to compare enjoyment to learning gain and identify potential correlations between the two.

The primary research question can be described by the hypothesis that improvements in learning gain would be higher when students used immersive VR. This hypothesis is based on the constructivist model which argues that tools which engage and motivate learning through interactivity, where learners play active roles, increase learning gain.

The secondary research question can be described by the hypothesis that reported enjoyment and engagement would be higher in students who use the immersive VR as this new environment reshapes the process of learning material delivery and thus is expected to be more attractive for students. Results from the study would consequently challenge existing problems with engagement in sessions that are meant to be practical but struggle with student enjoyment and thus utilize strict policies such as attendance monitoring to encourage participation.

1.5   Study Overview and Applications

The VR learning tool used in this study was a fluid dynamics app adapted from Matar Fluids Group's development for Imperial College London's chemical engineering department [30]. The app was primarily designed as an immersive VR tool to enable students to experience a liquid flow with real-time feedback through touch and sound. This could be applied to blood flow in vessels and identifying related pathology and thus, used for teaching across several disciplines, including medical education, to provide opportunity for users to learn without real-world consequences of medical error such as in surgical intervention. Additionally, surgical competence level can be determined before operating on live patients [31]. Despite medical knowledge known to be of contemporary nature, a significant proportion of approaches used to deliver this knowledge to students remain traditional. Accordingly, it is becoming increasingly challenging to incorporate the diversity and complexity of medicine into traditional learning systems [32]. Thus far, medical education has taken lead in demonstrating interest in the use of 3D computer applications, as proven by a study evaluating 3D model use in human anatomy; showcasing the technology's positive impact on students [33]. Other experiments exist to highlight the need for teaching safety procedures without involving the safety of a real patient [34, 35].

In summary, this study focuses on the effectiveness of immersive VR on learning, proposing how virtual tools should be designed to maximize this potential, with a large consideration of differences in immersion.

2   Method

2.1   Participants

The participants were 36 medical students recruited from a subject pool at Imperial College London. Of these 36 were 17 women and 19 men with ages ranging from 18–21 (M = 20, SD = 0.587). Participants were aware that this study would have no effect on their performance in their own degree as content explored was not to be directly relevant to them. Subjects were recruited using the exclusion criteria that a) they did not possess extensive VR use and b) did not have extensive fluid mechanics knowledge. 18 participants were randomly assigned to the immersive VR experience (VR group) and 18 were assigned to the video capture experience (non-immersive VR group).

2.2   Materials

Electronic Materials. The educational material consisted of a VR experience which was a 3D render of a pipe created by the Matter Fluids Groups [30] at Imperial College London and a PowerPoint designed by the study to explain the VR controls to participants. The software allowed participants to simulate fluid flow through a pipe whereby the effects of particle flow were shown in these simulations. Participants were able to move around the pipe or rotate it to appreciate different perspectives. In addition to visual cues, participants were able to hear the particles, as a high-pitched sound would play at high-pressure points and a low-pitched sound where the pressure was lowest. Similarly, vibrations from the controllers allowed participants to feel the particles. The simulation enabled them to generate particles themselves; allowing participants to compare two or more particles at multiple areas of the pipe. Both experiences were 10 min in duration and participants could leave and reenter the simulations at any point within the designated time frame. Students could ask questions about the controls of the immersive VR experience however to standardize responses across all participants, they were referred to a printed, annotated version of the PowerPoint they were originally shown explaining how best to use the experience. Screenshots of both the VR experience and the PowerPoint are shown in Figs. 1a and 1b respectively.

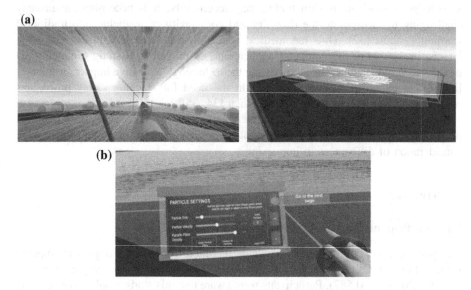

Fig. 1. (a) Screenshot from the VR simulation showing inside the pipe on the left and on the right, showing particles flowing through the pipe from a wide angle, (b) Screenshot from the VR simulation used in the PowerPoint presentation to explain the controls, including how to fire a variety of particles

The non-immersive VR group were also shown the PowerPoint which explained the controls of the VR experience. Following this they were shown an 8:36 min screen capture of the VR experience. The screen capture was based on a small pilot study which explored each of the possible features of the simulation multiple times and from different perspectives, based on how the typical participant would theoretically utilize the software. The video also had sound but failed to record controller vibrations for obvious reasons.

Paper Materials. The paper-based materials consisted of a pre-questionnaire, post-questionnaire and post-test. The pre-questionnaire solicited general demographic information such as age and gender and asked participants about their year and subject of study, particularly in relation to their understanding of physics. Following this, the participants were then asked to either "strongly agree," "agree," "neutral," "disagree," or "strongly disagree," with different statements such as "I can recall the basic principles of fluid mechanics," or "I can recall the factors affecting blood flow." The prequestionnaire was used to control for any preexisting differences in knowledge between both groups. As to not prime the learners, the study used a self-reported background knowledge questionnaire as opposed to a pre-test that mirrors the posttest [36].

The post-questionnaire asked students to make self-ratings in 8 different themes; nausea, comfortability, enjoyment, the controls, concentration, immersion, knowledge and time in experience. In each theme different statements corresponded to number where participants selected one that applies to them. For instance, the nausea theme asked students to select from; "N5 – I felt nauseous for a significant portion of the experience and this had a significant effect on my enjoyment," "N4 - I felt nauseous for a significant portion of the experience, but this didn't affect my enjoyment," "N3 – I felt nauseous briefly it passed but had a lasting effect on my enjoyment," "N2 – I felt nauseous briefly, but it passed and had no lasting effect on my enjoyment," "N1 – At no point during the experience did I feel nauseous." The postquestionnaire also included an open-ended question asking the participants for any additional comments.

Finally, the post-test consisted of eight questions designed based on the educational material provided. This included a multiple-choice question, a question which involved the participants drawing a velocity profile and six short answer questions to examine the learning gain of students. The questions ranged from simple factual recall such as "where was the velocity fastest?" to questions which demanded an application of what students had learned from the simulation or video to a real-life scenario relevant to them such as "A probe detects the arrival of two red blood cells – one at the center of the vessel and one near the wall. Assuming both are released from one end of a vessel at the same time, which will be first detected by the probe at the other end of the vessel?" This scenario was chosen as all the participants were from the medical faculty. The questions were then marked, with individual scores recorded. The post-test was given to the participants just before they entered the experience and were allowed to answer the questions at any point within the duration of ten minutes, including simulation time. For the participants, the term 'post-quiz' as opposed to post-test was used in order to avoid priming them for an assessment.

Apparatus. The VR lesson was presented via Steam Software using an Oculus Rift VR. The Oculus Rift VR is a virtual reality system which included two wireless controllers used to navigate the simulation, in addition to a head mounted display and headphones. The controllers provided some haptic feedback (i.e. vibrations) for certain parts of the simulation as mentioned above. The virtual reality system also included a pair of sensors which were constantly tracking the participants and mapped the space in which the user was free to move and explore. The video was presented on via a projector. The immersive VR system's controllers and sensors are shown in Fig. 2.

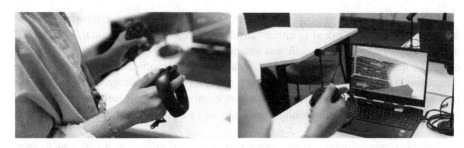

Fig. 2. A participant using the immersive VR system's controls

2.3 Procedure

Participants were signed up for the experiment by opportunistic methods. The participants were assigned to the immersive VR and non-immersive VR groups depending on which time slot they selected; this was not made aware to them before they selected a time slot. Multiple immersive VR participants were set up at once, with a maximum of 4 at one time, in an empty group study room with large space to facilitate the use of all VR features and enable walking around in the simulation. The non-immersive VR group were tested in a small group study room with up to 4 people watching the video at once. Participants were not allowed to interact with each other during the non-immersive experience to allow a fair comparison. A pre-questionnaire was completed before the VR controls were explained and the post-test was distributed. For the non-immersive VR group, the video was then started while the immersive VR group put the headsets on and began their experience. The post-test was to be completed at any point during both experiences. Following this, the post-questionnaire was completed with no time limit and participants were thanked and dismissed (Fig. 3).

Fig. 3. A participant during the immersive VR system simulation

A Shapiro-Wilks test justified the use of a Mann Whitney U test for analyzing the posttest data as well as the post-questionnaire data whilst a Wilcoxon signed rank test was justified in comparing pre-questionnaire data to post-test data.

3 Results

Initially, a Shapiro-Wilk test was performed on all data sets to test for normality; which proved non-normal distribution across the board [37]. Subsequently, data from the post-test scores was subjected to a Mann-Whitney U-test, which was used to test for significant differences between two independent sets of data which show non-normal distribution [38]. The immersive VR group scored a higher average post-test score than the non-immersive VR group (Fig. 4a). This was a significant result as confirmed by a Mann-Whitney U-test (p = 0.0385).

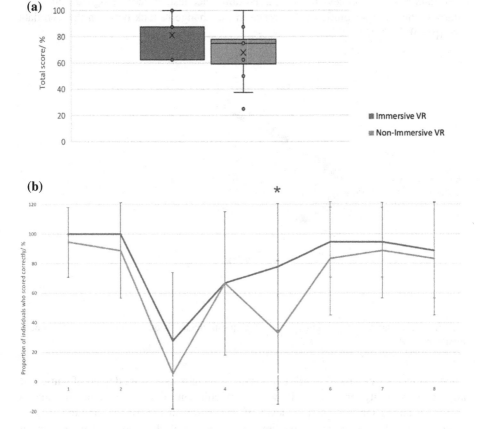

Fig. 4. (a) A comparison of total quiz score between immersive VR and non-immersive VR. (b) A comparison of posttest score per question between immersive VR and non-immersive VR groups. Note: statistically significant marked with asterisk (p < 0.05).

On average the VR group performed better than the non-VR group in all but one of the quiz questions; question 4. Question 5, which required students to draw a velocity profile, displayed a statistically significant difference according to a Mann-Whitney U-test (p = 0.0238) (Fig. 4b).

The pre-questionnaire was scored according to a predetermined mark scheme whereby higher scores were assigned to higher background knowledge prior to undertaking the experience. The subjects were then ranked according to these scores, with those of higher scores expected to perform best in post-test. After the post-test was performed, all subjects were ranked according to post-test scores. The changes in each ranking were compared per subject, to their performance in the pre-questionnaire. Following a calculation of rank change per individual, the findings were then split into the comparison groups; immersive VR and non-immersive VR and the average change in rank was registered and depicted in Fig. 5. The results show an improvement in the immersive VR group by an average of 5 ranks from pre-questionnaire rank to post-test rank. Contrastingly, the non-immersive VR group declined by an average of 5 ranks. Both rankings were processed via a paired difference test; Wilcoxon signed ranks test, which highlighted a significant difference in the change in rank between the two data sets (p = 0.01778).

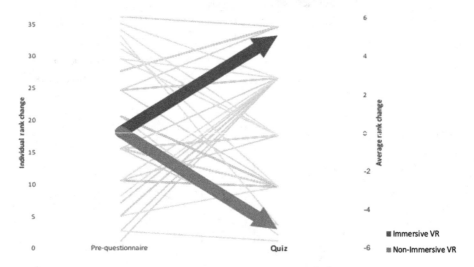

Fig. 5. A comparison of rank change from pre-questionnaire to quiz – immersive VR vs non-immersive VR.

All subjects were asked to fill in a postquestionnaire assessing; degree of nausea (if any), comfortability, enjoyment, how easy/difficult controls were, amount of concentration sustained throughout task, level of immersion in experience, amount of perceived knowledge gained from task, level of content with the amount of time spent in the task. The subjects then answered questions ranking these components on a scale of 1–5. Enjoyment and concentration were statistically significant (Table 1).

Table 1. Post-questionnaire results for the immersive VR group.

Post-Questionnaire Item	VR group (N=19) Mean SD	P-Value
Nausea	**1.56**	0.0561
"N2 – I felt nauseous briefly, but it passed and had no lasting effect on my enjoyment"	0.71	
Comfortability	**2.56**	0.6672
"C3 – throughout the experience I didn't feel uncomfortable once"	0.72	
Enjoyment *	**4.44**	**0.0074**
"E4 – I thoroughly enjoyed the experience but wouldn't want to do it again"	1.00	
The controls	**4.78**	0.7114
"O5 – I found the controls took a short time to understand but I had no problem using them once I understood them"	0.90	
Concentration *	**4.39**	**0.0001**
"CO4 – The experience kept my concentration for a majority of the time"	0.82	
Immersion	**4.67**	0.7039
"I5 - I temporarily forget worries about everyday life while in the experience"	1.76	
Knowledge	**3.44**	0.4473
"K3 – I try to apply the knowledge in the experience"	1.23	
Time in	**4.17**	0.0751
"T4 - The time spent in the experience was good but I would have preferred more or less time"	0.86	

Note: statistically significant marked with asterisk (p<0.01).

Figure 6 illustrates a comparison of the levels of perceived enjoyment and concentration between the immersive VR and non-immersive VR groups. The results show that the immersive VR group demonstrated higher average levels of enjoyment and concentration than the non-immersive VR group. The immersive VR group's data also reflected a smaller range of results and thus less variation; indicating a more consistent set of responses, as reinforced by a significant Mann-Whitney U-test p = 0.0074 (enjoyment) and p = 0.0001 (concentration).

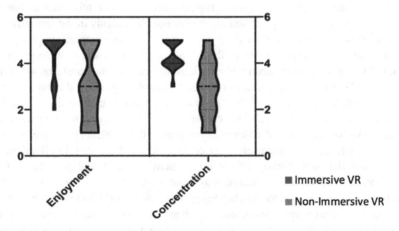

Fig. 6. Comparison between immersive VR and non-immersive VR - perceived enjoyment and concentration.

4 Discussion

4.1 Summary

Overall, data from the study recognized immersive VR to be significantly more effective in increasing learning gain whilst two key measures of reported experience; enjoyment and concentration also appeared significantly higher for the immersive VR learners. Students who used the non-immersive VR tool not only scored lower in the posttest, but also performed worse than expected based on calculated rank changes whilst the opposite was true for the comparison group. Reported experience results were also lower across the different variables assessing this and although differences were not wholly significant, it is reasonable to conclude that overall reported user experience was higher for immersive VR users.

4.2 Evaluation

A closer look at the post-test scores proved maximum scores to be equal for both groups, indicating that students experienced a large increase in their learning gain, regardless of the learning tool used. This suggests that immersion may not be a significant factor in improving performance academically. Important considerations of other factors include some highlighted by a study [39], which explored student engagement through virtual interactions but used alternative methodology to achieve this; observing student behavior as opposed to direct assessments of learning gain. The research revealed the effects of orientation on engagement and interactions. Despite the use of different methodology, the study recognized that students who did not orient themselves properly were observed to struggle with the virtual tools and assignment. This may thus provide an explanation as to why not all students in the immersive VR were able to achieve higher than their counterparts in the comparison group, as is affirmed by some of the qualitative feedback statements: "It took a while to understand the rules of using the console and maybe background info for the questions would have been useful". Orientation was bound to be more difficult to grasp in the immersive VR as they were made to make use of the tool in order to explore the learning elements, as opposed to those who watched a video capture of the virtual world to understand more about fluid mechanics. The self-efficacy theory argues that students put more effort into their work when they see themselves as competent for the task [40]. Bandura [41] further argued that self-efficacy affects the amount of effort and persistence that a person devotes to a task. Orientation may limit students' persistence if they deem themselves incompetent due to the challenges of the new world and thus it may hinder learning gain. Further investigations could perhaps focus on giving students more time for orientation and identify how much of a limiting factor orientation may be in preventing some students from acquiring maximum scoring.

Furthermore, an additional supporting explanation for such differences may be found in the cognitive theory of multimedia learning [42], and cognitive load theory [43], which identify that the addition of features such as visual effects, can create extraneous processing in the student, which describes cognitive processing that is not relevant to the instructional tasks. Learners have limited cognitive processing capacity, and thus if much of that capacity is dedicated to extraneous processing, less remains to engage with the material and make sense of it. This furthers arguments of orientation issues when using 'new' technology such as immersive VR.

Nonetheless, dispersion within the post-quiz scores for the non-immersive group was greater, indicating that there are more definitive factors responsible for differences in learning gain. These include consideration of variation in individual learning approaches. Considering that not all the immersive VR group were able to achieve this maximum score and thus due to dispersion in post-quiz scores within that group itself, differences observed with reduced confounding factors within each group are bound to be due to variations in the students themselves and their learning preferences. Creating a virtual world that is immersive may be preferable for some, but not all; suggesting that immersion is not the cause of increased learning gain as it may in fact decrease learning gain for some students, as proven by some students attaining maximum scores using non-immersive VR whilst others using immersive VR were not able to. Appreciating that learning material does not always complement the preferences and personality of learners allows recognition of the existence of variation within student learning preferences. However, whilst this variation is important to appreciate, results from this study suggest that overall, there was a distinct increase in learning gain in favor of the immersive tool. This is as results highlight that on average the immersive VR group improved in ranking by 5 ranks, while the non-immersive group declined by 5 ranks significantly, where ranking compared knowledge on topic areas, as expressed in pre-questionnaire, and thus determined an expectation for learning gain per individual. This proves that the immersive VR group performed significantly better than expected whilst the opposite was true for other group, enabling a conclusion that the differences within the tools themselves were responsible for this and that individual learning preferences had minor effects in this case.

Moreover, reported experience recognized significant gains in enjoyment as well as concentration, as students possibly demonstrated that breaking routine to use something different or new, made the learning more enjoyable and thus engaging. This argues against the cognitive load theory and in favor of students interacting with new technology. This is supported by findings that suggest that on average, immersive VR group performed better on all questions apart from question 4 where both groups performed the same on average. This was a simple recall question whereas question 5 was largely based on students applying their knowledge; demanding higher levels of engagement to enable better understanding. Results showed that the immersive VR group performed significantly better in this question whereby it was most reliant on exploration in requiring a velocity profile of particle flow. Explanation for this increased engagement is highly likely to be due to the immersion of the technology as the non-immersive group watched particles repeatedly firing in the walls compared to the center whilst immersive VR allowed individuals to explore outside of a fixed learning frame, i.e. they were able to fire particles in between. This is evidence to support that the difference between both groups is due to the immersive aspect of the VR that facilitated an explorative aspect which enabled active learning that was also self-directed.

Explanation of the importance of immersion as a factor contributing to learning gain is as highlighted earlier in this paper; the constructivist learning theory, where individuals are assumed to learn better by discovering by themselves and remaining in control of their learning pace, as highlighted by theoretically exploring the use of VR in road safety education [44]. The theory's explanations are in common with the findings from a study [29], which recognized the self-direction in immersive VR as an active experience. Additionally, research has proven evidence for principles when designing multimedia educational tools [45]. Amongst them is the segmenting principle that claims individuals learn better when lessons are presented in user-directed segments. This principle manages essential processing by allowing the learner to decide when to add more incoming information. The immersive features enable the user to feel a sense of exploration and involvement in the VR; incorporating active learning as the user is so involved, this also makes them more concentrated. This counters the cognitive load theory claims that suggest extraneous factors can inhibit performance when overloaded.

Student motivation plays a large role in learning, as those who are more motivated are more likely to engage and demonstrate resilience when overcoming obstacles in understanding [46]. This motivation enables the student to stay focused throughout continuous lessons and invest more energy in assigning cognitive tools to more difficult learning tasks. This provides further explanation for the higher learning gain results in immersive VR; based on interest theory and self-efficacy theory. According to interest theory, students are more engaged when they value learning material, either intrinsically (individual interest) or by the situation (situational interest) [47]. Since individual interest is not guaranteed (as explained by this study's results which noted variation in individual learning styles), immersive VR offers situational interest to account for this as a novel technology could prime a learner's situational interest more than traditional learning tools. Thus, students are more inclined to pay attention, actively interact and persist; fostering generative processing and deeper learning. Furthermore, the immersive aspect of VR enables a feedback system through facilitating user interaction. Specifically, when the user fired particles for instance, they were able to follow that particle's movement; enabling immediate and adaptive feedback to the students from the immersive tool. This feedback serves to boost the student's self-efficacy, which would in turn enhance their motivations to continue using the tool.

Outside of learning gain, the benefits of immersion to student experience retain their value as scores from reported experience were significantly higher for the immersive VR students, in addition to large variations in perceived enjoyment and concentration levels for those experiencing a non-immersive VR. Such findings imply that individual preferences, which may contribute to differences in learning styles, cause greater variation within the non-immersive VR tool as opposed to the immersive technology. Whilst it's important to consider individual experiences for students, educational institutions must consider tools that are generally more favorable for students and this is best demonstrated in the interactions students experience in the immersive VR group as a bigger proportion with less variation. Nonetheless, educators may account for individual learning styles by not restricting time spent on the learning tools as students across both groups stated that the time spent in the experience was "good" but they would've preferred more/less time; emphasizing the role of self-directed learning across all platforms.

4.3   Limitations and Further Research

The study presented a number of limitations that can be of important note to further research. Due to the set-up of the experiment, all participants were students from the same institution, yet, this population is sufficiently generic to allow certain generalizations to other institutions. Additionally, this study is exploratory in nature in basing some results on students' subjective views through self-reporting. Yet this was useful as qualitative feedback did reiterate other findings linking immersion to engagement, which was certainly well-demonstrated through learning gain, as students described how they "temporarily forget worries about everyday life in the experience" for immersive VR users. However, while the importance of self-reports should not be underestimated, such evaluations remain subjective and hence, they cannot completely reflect learning outcomes and so further studies should consider more objective measures of user experience.

Moreover, further investigations could explore allowing more time for orientation until learners have reached a satisfactory level before commencing on the tasks in the virtual world. Studies should also investigate the effects of long-term immersive VR use to identify differences in student engagement when the technology is no longer new or novel to learners. This is as this study raises questions as to whether students will still find the experience exciting and engaging, thus will reported experience still be in favor of using immersive VR? Further investigation can also explore whether a combination of tools may be more beneficial in comparison to each alone to help combat the potential loss in learning tools' novelty which could result in lower engagement in students. A more longitudinal study could also display long-term study effects and their impact on memory although this is notably difficult as it would require a replication in students of established curricula; introducing ethical barriers in randomizing students to different teaching methods.

Existing research has recognized that group work skills form invaluable teaching tools that support students in increasing learning and retention whilst simultaneously preparing them for working effectively in a professional environment [48]. Thus, future research could compare immersive VR to the other categorizations involving immersive group-VR whereby the tool allows simultaneous, real time access by multiple students and potentially educators themselves. Across all further research, a need remains for more rigorous methodologies and larger sample sizes to propel the value of existing explorative research; an aim that should be central to future studies.

5   Conclusion

The main contribution of this study is in examining the impact on learning gain; measuring student engagement through this, in addition to reported experiences. In research, replication is the essence of believability and as such, findings from this study come in agreement with the few others which focus on student engagement but employ different methodologies. The study thus adds to the small pool of evidence but suggests extensive avenues for further research in this growing and new field, recognizing the need for using the existing immersive technology to appeal to a variety of students' learning preferences by perhaps designing them to feature multiple learning techniques. This enables choice in engagement with the learning methods in a manner that interests students the most; enabling motivation due to individual interest in addition to the existing situational interest. This is particularly important as the novelty of this new tool may wear off and consequently decrease the effects of situational interest; a crucial consideration that future studies should explore.

Nonetheless, for educators, the important outcomes of learning focus on methods that facilitate more self-directed and student-centered learning to enable active learning, and this study recognizes the increasing need for the role of teachers or educators to be instructional designers or supporters of activities that aim to engage students [39]; allowing reasonable reliance on this new emerging tool. Educators' roles should now be adapted to "teach" students how to make the most of the content developed; allowing students to be supported in orienting and familiarizing themselves with the virtual world's tools and then independently exploring its potentials. Future studies may explore the addition of other users to enable teamwork and more social skills to be developed and applied to investigate whether this would boost the incentives for more intense interactions and consequently higher engagement levels.

Acknowledgements. The authors wish to acknowledge and thank the students who participated in the research experience. A special thanks to our supervisors Irene Kalkanis, Thomas Hurkxkens, Nitesh Bhatia and their colleagues in the Digital Learning Hub for their support and guidance throughout the project in addition to the Matar Fluid Group for their development of the learning tools used.

References

1. Sutherland, I.: Sketchpad a man-machine graphical communication system. Simulation **2**(5), R-3–R-20 (1964)
2. Lanier, J., Biocca, F.: An insider's view of the future of virtual reality. J. Commun. **42**(4), 150–172 (1992)
3. Mandal, S.: Brief introduction of virtual reality & its challenges. Int. J. Sci. Eng. Res. **4**(4) (2013). https://www.ijser.org/researchpaper/Brief-Introduction-of-Virtual-Reality-its-Challenges.pdf. Accessed 21 Dec 2019
4. Fuchs, H., Bishop, G.: Research Directions in Virtual Environments. University of North Carolina at Chapel Hill, Chapel Hill, NC (1992)
5. Suh, L.: The effects of virtual reality on consumer learning: an empirical investigation. MIS Q. **29**(4), 673 (2005)
6. Kovach, S.: Facebook Buys Oculus VR For $2 Billion. Business Insider. https://www.businessinsider.com/facebook-to-buy-oculus-rift-for-2-billion-2014-3?r=US&IR=T. Accessed 21 Dec 2019
7. Moore, M.: Reality check for VR as projects scrapped. https://www.thetimes.co.uk/article/reality-check-for-vr-as-projects-scrapped-frsqktxcw. Accessed 21 Dec 2019
8. Serino, S., Cipresso, P., Morganti, F., Riva, G.: The role of egocentric and allocentric abilities in Alzheimer's disease: a systematic review. Ageing Res. Rev. **16**, 32–44 (2014)
9. Bohil, C., Alicea, B., Biocca, F.: Virtual reality in neuroscience research and therapy. Nat. Rev. Neurosci. **12**(12), 752–762 (2011)

10. Berntsen, K., Palacios, R., Herranz, E.: Virtual reality and its uses. In: Proceedings of the Fourth International Conference on Technological Ecosystems for Enhancing Multicultur-ality - TEEM 2016 (2016)
11. Zhao, Q.: A survey on virtual reality. Sci. China Ser. F: Inf. Sci. **52**(3), 348–400 (2009)
12. Zhang, D., Zhou, L., Briggs, R., Nunamaker, J.: Instructional video in e-learning: assessing the impact of interactive video on learning effectiveness. Inf. Manag. **43**(1), 15–27 (2006)
13. Cooper, J., Heron, T., Heward, W.: Applied Behavior Analysis. Pearson/Merrill-Prentice Hall, Upper Saddle River (2008)
14. Nikopoulou-Smyrni, P., Nikopoulos, C.: Evaluating the impact of video-based versus traditional lectures on student learning (2010). http://internationalresearchjournals.org/full-articles/evaluating-the-impact-of-video-based-versus-traditional-lectures-on-student-learning.pdf?view=inline. Accessed 21 Dec 2019
15. Abdullah, J., Mohd-Isa, W., Samsudin, M.: Virtual reality to improve group work skill and self-directed learning in problem-based learning narratives. Virtual Real. **23**(4), 461–471 (2019)
16. Zimmerman, B., Schunk, D.: Self-regulated Learning and Academic Achievement: Theoretical Perspectives, 2nd edn. Routledge, New York (2001)
17. Keller, J., Suzuki, K.: Learner motivation and E-learning design: a multinationaly validated process. J. Educ. Media **29**(3), 229–239 (2004)
18. Mount, N., Chambers, C., Weaver, D., Priestnall, G.: Learner immersion engagement in the 3D virtual world: principles emerging from the DELVE project. Innov. Teach. Learn. Inf. Comput. Sci. **8**(3), 40–55 (2009)
19. Yee, N.: Motivations for play in online games. CyberPsychol. Behav. **9**(6), 772–775 (2006)
20. Barbe, W., Milone, M., Swassing, R.: Teaching Through Modality Strengths. ZanerBloser, Columbus, OH (1988)
21. Riener, C., Willingham, D.: The myth of learning styles. Change: Mag. High. Learn. **42**(5), 32–35 (2010)
22. Bellamy, M., Warren, A.: Using Online Practicals to Support Lab Sessions (2011). http://edshare.soton.ac.uk/id/document/243301. Accessed 21 Dec 2019
23. Webster, R.: Declarative knowledge acquisition in immersive virtual learning environments. Interact. Learn. Environ. **24**(6), 1319–1333 (2015)
24. Bricken, M.: Virtual reality learning environments: potentials and challenges. ACM SIGGRAPH Comput. Graph. **25**(3), 178–184 (1991)
25. Burdea, G., Coiffet, P.: Virtual reality technology. Wiley, New York (1994)
26. Choi, H., Johnson, S.: The effect of context-based video instruction on learning and motivation in online courses. Am. J. Distance Educ. **19**(4), 215–227 (2005)
27. Shyu, H.: Using video-based anchored instruction to enhance learning: Taiwan's experience. Br. J. Educ. Technol. **31**(1), 57–69 (2000)
28. McGrath, C., Guerin, B., Harte, E., Frearson, M., Manville, C.: Learning gain in higher education. Santa Monica, California and Cambridge UK: RAND (2015). https://www.rand.org/content/dam/rand/pubs/research_reports/RR900/RR996/RAND_RR996.pdf. Accessed 21 Dec 2019
29. Hussein, M., Natterdal, C.: The benefits of virtual reality in education a comparison study. Department of Computer Science and Engineering Chalmers University of Technology University of Gothenburg (2015). https://pdfs.semanticscholar.org/5310/aa72c3946d29ff1c538e82f89425c7f78d8f.pdf?_ga=2.249113359.98483112.1576846678-911970774.1576846678. Accessed 21 Dec 2019
30. West, S.: Innovative virtual reality software developed to enhance fluid dynamics lectures. Imperial College London News. https://www.imperial.ac.uk/news/189866/innovative-virtual-reality-software-developed-enhance/. Accessed 21 Dec 2019

31. Ota, D., Loftin, B., Saito, T., Lea, R., Keller, J.: Virtual reality in surgical education. Comput. Biol. Med. **25**(2), 127–137 (1995)
32. Alfalah, S., Falah, J., Alfalah, T., Elfalah, M., Muhaidat, N., Falah, O.: A comparative study between a virtual reality heart anatomy system and traditional medical teaching modalities. Virtual Real. **23**(3), 229–234 (2018)
33. Nicholson, D., Chalk, C., Funnell, W., Daniel, S.: Can virtual reality improve anatomy education? A randomised controlled study of a computer-generated three-dimensional anatomical ear model. Med. Educ. **40**(11), 1081–1087 (2006)
34. Shim, K., Park, J., Kim, H., Kim, J., Park, Y., Ryu, H.: Application of virtual reality technology in biology education. J. Biol. Educ. **37**(2), 71–74 (2003)
35. Huang, H., Liaw, S., Lai, C.: Exploring learner acceptance of the use of virtual reality in medical education: a case study of desktop and projection-based display systems. Interact. Learn. Environ. **24**(1), 3–19 (2013)
36. Fiorella, L., Mayer, R.E.: Learning as a Generative Activity: Eight Learning Strategies that Promote Understanding. Cambridge University Press, New York (2015). http://dx.doi.org/10.1017/CBO9781107707085. Accessed 21 Dec 2019
37. Ghasemi, A., Zahediasl, S.: Normality tests for statistical analysis: a guide for non-statisticians. Int. J. Endocrinol. Metab. **10**(2), 486–489 (2012). https://doi.org/10.5812/ijem.3505,lastaccessed2019/12/21
38. McKnight, P.E., Najab, J.: Mann-Whitney U Test- The Corsini Encyclopedia of Psychology. Wiley, Hoboken (2010). https://onlinelibrary.wiley.com/doi/abs/10.1002/9780470479216.corpsy0524. Accessed 21 Dec 2019
39. Christopoulos, A., Conrad, M., Shukla, M.: Increasing student engagement through virtual interactions: how? Virtual Real. **22**(4), 353–369 (2018)
40. Schunk, D., DiBenedetto, M.: Self-Efficacy: Education Aspects. Int. Encyclopedia Soc. Behav. Sci. 515–521 (2015)
41. Bandura, A.: Self-efficacy: toward a unifying theory of behavioral change. Psychol. Rev. **84**(2), 191–215 (1997)
42. Mayer, R.: Cognitive Theory of Multimedia Learning. The Cambridge Handbook of Multimedia Learning, pp. 43–71 (2014)
43. Sweller, J., Ayres, P., Kalyuga, S.: Cognitive Load Theory. Springer, New York (2011). https://doi.org/10.1007/978-1-4419-8126-4
44. Fokides, E., Tsolakidis, C.: Virtual reality in education: a theoretical approach for road safety training to students. Eur. J. Open Distance Learn. (EURODL) II (2008). http://www.eurodl.org/materials/contrib/2008/Fokides_Tsolakidis.htm. Accessed 21 Dec 2019
45. Mayer, R.E.: Multimedia Learning. Cambridge University Press, New York (2009). http://dx.doi.org/10.1017/CBO9780511811678. Accessed 21 Dec 2019
46. Mayer, R., Griffith, E., Jurkowitz, I., Rothman, D.: Increased interestingness of extraneous details in a multimedia science presentation leads to decreased learning. J. Exper. Psychol.: Appl. **14**(4), 329–339 (2008)
47. Schiefele, U.: Situational and individual interest. In: Wentzel, K.R., Wigfield, A. (eds.) Handbook of Motivation in School, 1st edn. Taylor and Francis, New York (2009)
48. Abdelkhalek, N., Hussein, A., Gibbs, T., Hamdy, H.: Using team-based learning to prepare medical students for future problem-based learning. Med. Teach. **32**(2), 123–129 (2010)

Fabric Robotics - Lessons Learned Introducing Soft Robotics in a Computational Thinking Course for Children

Bjarke Kristian Maigaard Kjær Pedersen[1][(✉)] ⓘ,
Emanuela Marchetti[2] ⓘ, Andrea Valente[1] ⓘ, and Jacob Nielsen[1] ⓘ

[1] Section of Game Development and Learning Technology,
Maersk Mc-Kinney Moller Institute, Odense, Denmark
bkp@mmmi.sdu.dk
[2] Section of Media Studies, Department for the Study of Culture,
University of Southern Denmark, 5230 Odense M, Denmark

Abstract. In this paper we present findings from the current and last year's season of a CT course: we investigated how soft materials enriched learning of CT in relation to embedded systems and creative thinking practices. We also addressed gender biases in the course, as we observed how boys and the few girls in the course responded to the practices related to fabric prototyping and sewing, when moving from LEGO Mindstorms to wearable devices and soft robotics. Data gathering was conducted following a qualitative approach, based on ethnography combining note taking, observations, pictures of the children artifacts and live drawings of the children in action. We observed changes that occurred in creativity, project context, in the hardware and debugging, flexibility and reusability, in addition to the gender balance. We also analyze the play moods observed in the children. The main contribution of the paper is to detail our approach, the methods used in the observations and analysis, and our findings, for the benefit of other institutions and groups striving to design CT curricula.

Keywords: Soft robotics · Educational robotics · Computational Thinking · CT · K-12 · Curriculum design · Gender · Microcontroller platforms · Circuit Playground Express · LEGO mindstorms EV3

1 Introduction

Computational Thinking [1] (CT for short) is currently being adopted in more and more teaching institutions as a way to introduce technical skills to learners. Having studied and followed the evolution of CT in Denmark as well as more globally, we are aware of the efforts and complexities of designing and deploying CT curricula at the different levels of education. In particular we observed two major trends: percolation from university courses downwards towards secondary and eventually primary school (a rather top-down process), and proliferation of extra-scholastic, hands-on courses and activities, often leveraging on volunteering experts (representing a less institutionalized, and less formalized, grassroot phenomenon). From our research and international

© Springer Nature Switzerland AG 2020
P. Zaphiris and A. Ioannou (Eds.): HCII 2020, LNCS 12206, pp. 499–519, 2020.
https://doi.org/10.1007/978-3-030-50506-6_34

networks, we know that these two trends are present in Denmark as well as internationally: for example Japan, Taiwan, and USA have institutional top-down efforts as well as a growing network of private programming clubs and courses. Since both efforts exist simultaneously, each with their own advantages and challenges, we propose to describe and analyze our experience with a novel approach to CT we recently attempted, within the context of a course at Teknologiskolen [2]. The goal with this paper is to present our approach, methodological reflections, and findings, for the benefit of other institutions and groups, striving to design working CT curricula; in particular we will consider gender balance, creativity and learning styles in young CT learners.

Teknologiskolen (literally "technology school", TS for short) is a volunteer association offering a series of weekly, spare time courses for children, centered on robotics and programming. Most of the activities in TS fall under the umbrella of Computational Thinking [1]. The school has been running for almost five years at the University of Southern Denmark (SDU) in Odense; the lectures last for 2 h over a period of approximately 27 weeks, from September to April. They are run by volunteers, primarily from SDU, often engineering students and teachers. Teaching is conducted through a learning-by-doing approach, encouraging children in engaging in individual and shared projects, typically involving LEGO robots, microcontroller circuits and visual programming, as means to introduce CT through fun and largely self-directed activities. Although the activities are self-directed, the children are also supervised on a 1 to 5 ratio (i.e. 1 voluntary supervisor per 5 learners). This ratio, which is much larger than what is found in normal school teaching in Denmark, informs a loose and facilitation-oriented style of teaching; hence, TS classes usually rely on on-demand, here-and-now guidance to support children when they get stuck in their technical endeavours.

After having run TS for many years with good results, with happy and returning participants, still fewer girls attend courses than boys. Especially when the kids reach age 10 and above, we see a drastic drop in the number of female participants.

We decided to focus on the course called RobotSpirerne (in English "Robot-Sprouts", RS for short) targeted at children from 10 to 12 years of age; we designed and ran a new activity called fabric robotics, an umbrella term we use to refer to soft robots, cardboard and fabric prototypes, as well as wearable artifacts augmented with microcontroller platforms - such as Adafruit Circuit Playground Express (CPX for short) [3]. The average RS classes have 15 to 20 children participants, and the course runs from September to April. The fabric robotics activity ran as part of the last season of TS, from September 2018 to April 2019, with a class of 18 children. After announcing the introduction of fabric robotics two girls signed up, and we currently have three girls attending, one of which has continued from the previous year.

In the rest of this paper we discuss findings from the current and last year's edition of the course, as we investigated how soft materials enriched learning of CT in relation to embedded systems and creative thinking practices. We also addressed gender biases in the course, as we observed how boys and the few girls in the course responded to the practices related to fabric prototyping and sewing, when moving from LEGO Mindstorms EV3 [4] to wearable devices and soft robotics.

The paper presents related work and our methodological approach (Sect. 2), followed by an overview of the fabric robotics activity organization (Sect. 3). Observations and discussion are in Sect. 4, followed by reflections and conclusion (Sects. 5 and 6).

2 Related Work and Method

CT has become a popular taught subject in formal and informal education settings, as a way to initiate children and teenagers to programming and electronics. In general CT has been defined as a set of skills from engineering and computer sciences, however, there is no unified definition of what CT is and the related learning goals. A commonly accepted definition comes from Wing [1], who has defined CT as a set of abilities belonging to the "mindset" of computer scientists, but which would be recommended to anybody in contemporary digitized society. According to Wing, CT includes problem solving, design thinking and knowledge of human behavior. In this definition, however, abilities regarding the conception and making of hardware and software are excluded. As a result, CT appears limited towards a subset of skills from the domain of design and management, as design thinking and knowing about human behavior are not hardcore skills of programmers or engineers. In our study, we aim at initiating children and teenagers to acquire knowledge and skills in the conception and making of hardware and software. In this respect other definitions of CT appear more relevant to our study, such as van de Oudeweetering and Voogt [5] who also define CT in terms of innovation, creativity, critical thinking, communication and collaboration, which could match Wing's reference to knowledge on human behavior. However, Oudeweetering and Voogt [5] also add the notion of "digital literacy" and digital citizenship, referring to a basic understanding of how digital technologies work and awareness on what it means to be a member of a digitized society, rights and duties. Jacob and Warschauer [6] define CT as including: algorithmic thinking, problem solving in terms of splitting large problems into smaller subproblems, relating to different levels of abstraction, and data science in relation to representing data through models. Other researchers, like Jansen et al. [7] have defined CT as "well-structured problem solving", taking place through the employment of tools and methods from computer science. A similar perspective is adopted by Weng [8] in defining CT as a skill in problem solving "rooted" in computer science. However, Jansen et al. [7] argue that even though there have been meaningful outcomes in relation to specific intervention in teaching CT, the notion of CT still lacks clarity. A similar argument is proposed by Tedre and Denning [9], who argue that CT is still under definition and have criticized the current proliferation of definitions of CT for creating an even larger lack of clarity. As a consequence, each study has to come up with an operative definition of CT, depending on the approach adopted in the study and the researcher's goal, hence leading to partial results. In order to overcome this issue, we ground our definition of CT on current research, while also clarifying that our goal is to initiate children in conceiving and crafting hardware and software, through the making of artefacts decided upon by the children. In this sense, we distinguish between digital skills and competences [10], where we see skills as practical abilities from the engineering and computer science domain, regarding assembling electronic components and creating simple functioning software. On the other hand, we see competences as higher level abilities, integrating digital skills with those derived from the management and design domain in Wing's definition [1] such as: problem solving, design, and planning. Hence, we define competences as metalevel abilities of children to apply the targeted digital skills on problem solving, in relation to the making of digital artefacts. Competences deal for instance with decision making and planning the making of a digital artefact, regarding selection of design materials (digital and analogue) such as: fabrics or LEGO bricks, electronic components, and the coding process.

Moreover, our study deals specifically with experimenting with different materials, such as fabrics and LEGO, with the goal of fostering different forms of creativity and learning, and to capture the interest of girls. In this respect, other studies confirm that boys tend to participate in larger numbers in informal courses in CT [8]. Interestingly participation in informal learning settings is volunteer, so participation is genuinely motivated by individual interest, in contrast to formal activities run by schools. Moreover, an experiment conducted within a CT module using Game Maker [11], shows that boys and girls express different attitudes towards CT activities, where boys demonstrate more confidence and performance in programming tasks. In the same study, a correlation was also found regarding level of confidence with time spent playing digital games, where boys seem to spend more time playing, however, girls were found more confident in troubleshooting computer problems [11]. However, at the end of the module, both boys and girls described the activity as "fun" and "exciting", giving them the opportunity to try something new [11]. A literature review on the spreading field of CT [12], argues that regardless of documented gender differences, boys and girls were reported to achieve improvements in their understanding of technologies and programming skills. Hence, gender differences were over all found to be of little significance regarding learning. On the other hand, a Korean survey with 86 elementary schools found that girls had more interest for the creative aspect of CT, while boys had more interest in the academic aspect.

Building on these insights, our study investigates how different materials might affect children in engaging with coding and hardware making, enabling them to express their creativity. In this sense, our assumption is that creativity might foster a more positive attitude of girls regarding digital technologies and CT.

2.1 Observation Analysis

In our study we focused on observing how the children were familiarized with the provided technology, making sense of it and creating new things for themselves. Our analysis leverages the theory of play moods [13, 14], which enabled us to detect connections between self-expression in the children's play and their understanding of the technology. During our observations, we noticed that as the children became proficient in coding and assembling the components the more their play became lively and louder.

The theory of play moods is grounded on Heidegger's philosophy [14] and his notion of being in the world, according to which our being in the world is always associated with being in a mood and our mood will determine our relationship with the world. Being in a mood does not require any conscious reflection, but at the same time it drives our interactions with others and with our surroundings. Building on Heidegger, Karoff [13] proposes an analytical framework to study children play, in which children's play is always associated with a specific play mood and play practice. Karoff's [13] framework includes four main play practices, defined by an increasing rhythm of action. The first practice is called sliding and it is linked to the mood called devotion, in which players tend to repeat what they were already doing. The second play practice is called shifting and it is linked to the intensity mood, in which players still adopt repetitive rhythm, but try now and then to surprise each other, introducing variation to the rhythm. The third practice is called displaying and it is linked to the mood tension, it is characterized by constant change and it typically involves forms of performing like dancing or singing as the players show off for each other. The last and fourth mood is called exceeding and it is linked to the mood called euphoria, these represent the opposite of sliding and devotion, as the players are embracing a chaotic rhythm in their play, expressing loud laughs and silly behavior.

2.2   Data Gathering

Given the informal setting of our courses, we found ethnography to be the most suited method for data gathering, as we could associate our supervision activity with observations and note taking. Hence we conducted a form of participant observations [15], as we set framing to the children's activities, for instance introducing the CPX, the sewing material, and different fabrics, which suggested different perceived affordances [16] for the children's design. By affordances we mean specific features in the provided materials (fabrics and electronic components), which inspired the children specific future scenarios regarding what they could make with those specific material. For instance, the furry fabric inspired the children to create animal-like creatures, while wool gloves inspired different wearables, to be worn on hands or wrists.

During the activities, we observed the children as part of our role as supervisors, to see how they were managing and help them when in need. In such cases we actively intervened to help with the tasks that were new or hard for them. Help was generally requested in connection to designing and constructing their fabric robots, for instance in:

- Deciding on which components to use and how to assemble them.
- Planning what the software should do and start coding.
- Deciding how much fabric is needed, cutting and sewing.

As soon as the children were able to continue without help, we gave the lead back to them, so that they could experiment and enjoy the activity on their own.

In our setting, we had limited opportunities for data gathering, since we did not have permission to take pictures of the children and since we were subjected to the new data protection law. For these reasons, we relied upon alternative data collection methods, hence we took pictures of the artefacts made by the children, which we analyzed in relation to how the children explored the possibilities offered by the Adafruit unit and its components. Moreover, we relied upon drawing as an ethnographic method [17] in situ. More specifically we took quick live sketches of the children, while they were engaged in their activities, alone and with others. Our drawing practice was aimed at data gathering, sense-making, and documenting our observations regarding the children's interactions. It forced us to "see more" than we could see [17] when using automatic methods of data gathering like video recordings, which is a reliable method enabling the researchers to store data to be analyzed later. Hence video recording can have the side effect to enable the researchers focus less on the subject during observations, since the researchers know that they will be able to access the data anytime. Instead, having to draw the children while engaged in their interactions, fostered a feeling of urgency, which lead us to observe the children more accurately and to analyze the children's mood and engagement with the situation. Since the children were mostly sitting, it was not hard to capture the essence of their inter-actions, focusing on posture and visible gestures, however, when they were sewing, cutting and assembling small parts, it was hard to capture the fine movements which might have revealed security or doubts, in dealing with the components or with the code. Therefore, in our data collection we focused on capturing the children while focused on their creations and visible occurrences, like when the children were expressing frustration when things did not work or go as expected or showing off when successful. A main challenge occurred as we were supervising the children while drawing them at the same time, therefore, our data collection was partial as we had to be careful in balancing the two activities.

The drawings were initially made with black or blue markers on a notebook and later remade digitally, to be clearer and more defined (Fig. 1). Color was added to the upper body and hands of the children, and to their artefacts, to attract attention to their attitude and posture as a resource to interpret the depicted interactions.

Fig. 1. A boy playing with his glove during class. On the left original sketch made during observations, on the right, a digital version of the same drawing for documentation purposes.

Drawing also enabled us to document our research in an ethical way, as the resulting drawings can provide meaningful visual documentation for our publications, without violating the privacy of the children. An advantage of drawings is also that, no matter how defined they need to be to show an interaction, the authors can still reveal aspects related to gender, age and identity or facial expression without adding specific details that will make the participants recognizable. However, since drawings can be made and edited freely by the authors, which nowadays is possible also with video footage, they might seem weak as scientific documentations as lacking an objective counterpart. **Nonetheless**, drawing provides the advantage to enable researchers to capture meaningful moments unobtrusively and without endangering the privacy of the participants. Moreover, to better document our drawings we transcribed the conversation that accompanied a specific occurrence, but to be sure not to spread personal data in our notes, we avoided writing the full names of the children only annotating the first letter of their names.

3   Organization of the Course

In the fabric robotics course activity, "soft robots" are seen as artefacts at the intersection of three areas: programming, hardware and physical materials (as depicted in Fig. 2).

The activity was organized according to a spiral pedagogical pattern [18] and informed by *use-modify-create* [19]. We would start with tasks based on provided material: the code, the hardware setup, and the instructions for physical models, with minimal space for customization.

The scope was then enlarged in further lectures; the coding and hardware side were expanded to cover more features of the programming language (such as conditionals, loops, events and control of the CPX's I/O ports) and more advanced electronic components were introduced, explained and used. Also, the physical part of the soft robots was expanded, to include stitching, use of different kinds of fabric and other materials and tools (e.g. cardboard and glue guns).

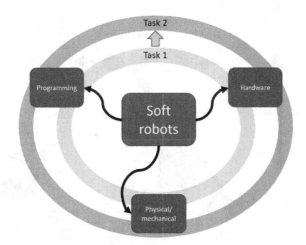

Fig. 2. Soft robotics/fabric robotics, seen as a subject at the intersection of three areas. Tasks were organized according to a spiral pedagogical pattern.

We had 4 months of lectures, once a week, from November 2018 to the Easter-break of 2019, excluding half of December 2018 and the first week of January 2019.

Each evening lecture is 2 h long, with a ten minutes break half-way; the participants are primary school pupils, and the mood is usually playful and the participants are energetic and curious, but often tired from their school activities and possibly from other free-time activities too. Frontal lecturing is usually avoided (or at least minimized) in this context, preferring a more indirect, supportive style of tutoring.

As the schema in Fig. 3 shows, we start each lecture of the fabric robotics activity, providing a few motivating links (possibly videos or short articles) to establish a domain of interest for the current lecture, followed sometimes by definitions and exemplars of systems, to establish ontologies or terminology necessary to formulate tasks in the given domain. A task related to soft robotics is then assigned, with DIY-style instructions, and the rest of the lecture revolves around supervision and realization of the robot (or wearable device). The schema in Fig. 3 exemplifies the visual layout, the balance between text and media (images, text and block-code diagrams), and the way we cover all three areas in every lecture: programming, hardware and physical materials. The slides are in Danish.

Moreover, from the first lecture we introduce the design cycle, which in our context has the following phases: design, sew or assemble the materials, program and build the hardware setup, deploy, test, and repeat until satisfied.

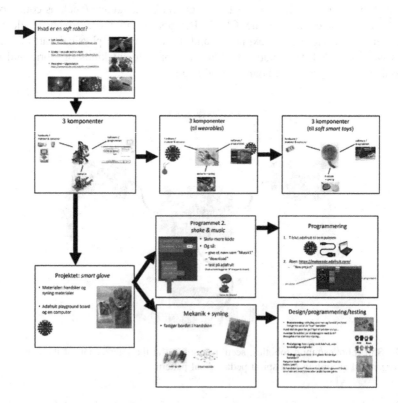

Fig. 3. Typical structure of a lecture.

The first task (introduced in lecture 1 and continued in lecture 2 and 3) was to create a "smart glove": a simple glove with a microcontroller attached. The goal was for the children to be able to quickly program simple behaviors and interact with the microcontroller physically. An example could be: when you shake your hand, the sensors pick up the motion and you can program the microcontroller to beep a specific note. We used this task to walk the children through the basic capabilities of the CPX and how to program interactive behavior in the MakeCode blockly-based editor.

The second task was to create a fabric monster and program its behavior. This task was introduced in lecture 4, and it was possible to iterate it in the rest of the course, customizing hardware, software and the design of the monster. Figure 4 shows the fabric pattern we provided for the participants; together with that, we also prepared a hardware setup with a battery pack, and two programs that the participants could try out: a heartbeat program, that made a sound at regular intervals using timers, and a "poke it until angry" code, that used a counter to remember how often a specific I/O port or button on the CPX was being touched or pressed. If the user made an input more than 10 times within a few seconds, then the monster would become "mad" and blink red lights for a while. The counter would however decrease automatically over time, so if the monster was left alone, it would go back to its usual "relaxed" state. A group of participants decided to reverse the behavior of this program and turned it into a "tickle me constantly or I get angry" behavior.

After the first 4 lectures, the participants were asked to define a project and work on that for the rest of the soft robotics course. Some participants decided to iterate and personalize the monster task, others focused on variations of the glove, and a few opted for a fastelavns costume (the Danish *Mardi Gras* period) augmented with special hardware and physical materials.

The role of the instructors also changed during the course activity. Initially there was minimal lecturing with step-by-step groupwise support. The second half of the fabric robotics course was based instead on self-defined projects (performed individually or in small groups of 2 to 3), and the role of the instructors changed to facilitation.

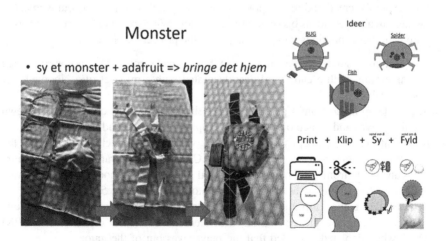

Fig. 4. The pattern and instruction to sew a fabric monster.

In our lectures, we tried to create a playful framework for the children, as we aimed at enabling them to learn how to assemble components and code the CPX, in an informal setting and let them engage in free explorations of possible use scenarios for their artefacts. In addition to the CPX, the children were presented with different materials including fabric, filling for making soft objects or puppets, various buttons, LEDs, motors, threads and needles. These were proposed as design materials which could be turned into toys or accessories of any kind. In this sense, we tried to set a frame for mediated play in which any objects could become a toy and foster playful interactions [20] and playful play [21], in which children play by creating new toys and future playful situations for themselves and their friends.

4 Observations, Findings and Discussion

The introduction of fabric robotics into our course proved to have a significant effect, especially in light of the previous seasons and their more traditional teaching materials. In particular, we observed changes that occurred in relation to previous seasons: in creativity, project context, in the hardware and debugging, flexibility and reusability as well as the gender balance. Finally, we analyze the play moods observed in the children, during the fabric robotics activity.

4.1 Creativity and Context

During previous seasons, children worked mainly with the LEGO Mindstorms EV3 platform. In our experience, when working with EV3 it was often a challenge getting the pupils to invent and define their own project ideas, and as a result, this initial part of the project was typically done by an instructor.

Also during the past season, after having received the first few lectures on fabric robotics, the pupils were challenged with reflecting on the presented thematics and starting from these, form concrete project ideas of their own. However, we observed a fundamental shift in the pupils' creative thinking practice, with the pupils requiring encouragement to define their own project ideas becoming the exception. We also found the project ideas to be more varied than previously observed; among the project ideas were:

- A fastelavns costume with a rotating saw blade, made from a DC-motor controlled by a transistor, with a cardboard disc decorated with a printout of a bloodied saw blade, see Fig. 5.
- A night lamp made from a painting of the Eiffel Tower, with colorful LEDs sewn into the canvas and turned on/off by the clapping of hands (loud noises), see Fig. 5.
- An Infinity Gauntlet [22] as know from Marvel Comics, which could pick up the Infinity Stones one by one, from a separate CPX through infrared communication.
- Toy guns made from cardboard, which could play different shooting sounds, based on their settings (single shot, burst, fully automatic), see Fig. 5.
- A laser tag game (infrared communication), where players could shoot one another's glove; the gloves had an integrated life bar (LED circle on the CPX) which when depleted, signaled that the player was out of the game.

- A light-up flower decoration for a bicycle basket, which can shift between two colors as well as blink, depending on which transistor is turned on/off, based on external inputs such as surrounding light-level, noise and button presses.
- A plushie which can move its arms (via DC motors) and legs (via servo motors), as well as turn its head around (also via a servo motor) and light up its eyes (a pair of red LEDs) when the surrounding light-level fades.
- A plushie of a made-up Pokémon [23], which can wiggle like a fish (using two servo-motors); the interfacing is still a work in progress.

The previous projects with the EV3 platform that often originated from instructors, had for the most part revolved around a theoretical context such as: imitating a warehouse robot, by navigating a grid of black lines on the floor, while moving boxes around among locations. In contrast, when analyzing the new fabric robotics project ideas, we found that they were for the most part set in a context in which they would be integrated into the pupils' private life outside of TS. We consider this a sign of appropriation by the children: the focus shifted away from the project context revolving around a theoretical framing, towards developing artefacts intended for actual real-life appliances, while keeping the internal logics of TS's learning-by-doing approach intact.

Another change is in the affordances offered by soft materials and fabric robots, when compared with the LEGO platform. For instance, since LEGO allows for easy reconfiguring and reconstructing of prototypes, the children had in previous seasons often started out by building their idea and add new functionalities or perform revisions to existing ones as they went along. This approach was no longer viable for them with fabric robots, and instead we have observed a need for pupils drawing models of their projects and more systematically work from there, detailing the desired functionalities and possible circuits before beginning the construction of their prototypes.

Soft materials also seem to present another downside compared to the LEGO platform: we have observed how difficult it can sometimes be for the pupils to work out mechanical solutions. In fact, most projects were very limited in their mechanical actuation; to make up for this we have therefore begun working with integrating the LEGO platform as a means for mechanical constructions, into the fabric robotics activity.

Fig. 5. On the left, a fastelavns costume with a rotating saw blade (cardboard), and on the right, an Eiffel Tower night lamp (LEDs sewn into the canvas) and Toy guns (cardboard).

4.2   Hardware and Debugging

The hardware side of the projects quickly became more and more complex when compared to the EV3 platform. The logic reason for this is that where the hardware components of the EV3 platform are all, without exception, encapsulated into ready-made plug and play devices; this is not the case when working with microcontroller platforms like the CPX, where working with low-level hardware, is often a necessity. An advantage of working with low-level hardware, is that it has afforded a natural way of introducing the teaching of basic electrical principles into the curriculum. The downside of the added complexity in the hardware is, that it also makes it less accessible, to some degree limiting the children's freedom, and as a result they might require additional supervision.

Debugging the systems has likewise become increasingly complex. With EV3 debugging, the children were mainly focused on the code and mechanical constructions. With fabric robots, the debugging now also includes wrong or lose connections and wrong or faulty components inside a circuit. On a technical note, the debugging of the code for the CPX is more difficult than with the EV3 programming environment, since the CPX does not afford for reading serial data in MakeCode, which could simplify common operations like reading the sensor values.

During the deployment of the course, we (the instructors) have also gained some practical experience in working with the CPX platform. For instance, we would initially build low-fidelity prototypes by using alligator-clips attached to the microcontrollers I/O ports. However, these would often fall off or slide to the side and touch one another, creating short-circuits: all very undesirable situations. Later on, when constructing the high-fidelity prototypes, we would use conductive-thread, to attach the electrical components, to the ports, by sewing the circuits into the fabric. A downside to this method was, that both the components and the microcontroller, were now permanently attached to the fabric, which made revisions highly difficult and time consuming. As a proposed solution for this, we have had good results with sewing a strip of velcro into the fabric, and gluing the other side of it, onto selected components and the CPX. For the connections between them, we are soldering snap-buttons onto the ports of the CPX and the cords. As a result, we can now attach and detach both, as desired, when doing revisions to both the low- and high-fidelity prototypes; as an added bonus this technique also makes the artefacts washable (see Fig. 6).

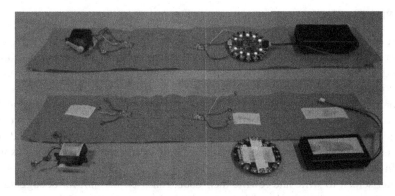

Fig. 6. A demonstration setup, of how using snap-buttons enables the attachment and de-attachment of electrical components.

4.3   Flexibility and Reusability

A major difference which we observed after the introduction of fabric robotics, was that pupils started working on their projects at home, or bring materials from their school or from home to use as parts of TS projects. As an example, one of the pupils had painted a painting of the Eiffel Tower at her primary school; she brought it to the TS in order to augment it with LEDs. She then made the CPX control the switching on and off of the LEDs by the clapping of her hands (using the built-in microphone), in order to use the painting as a night lamp.

Other examples include: integrating the CPX into Christmas ornaments, after which we could let the pupils borrow the CPX to bring back home, and when working with fastelavns costumes, the pupils have been able to borrow the CPX to bring it to school and show it of during the traditional festivities.

These are situations made possible by the low cost of the CPX, as well as the new range of cheap and versatile materials used for the projects. The EV3 platform was both too expensive and possibly too specialized for this. Interestingly however, the EV3 platform allows for full reusability of the involved materials, while the same is not true with our fabric robots. While it is normally possible to retrieve the electrical components and the CPX, the construction materials have most often been damaged beyond further use, by being cut to pieces, sewn and glued together.

Adopting cheap and versatile, expendable materials often seem to be at odds with the need for institutions to reuse and avoid having to re-order large quantities of supplies. Perhaps for the children to be able to appropriate their project and artifacts, disposable fabric robots work better than reusable kits. It is a fact that we have observed the pupils putting extra effort and time into carefully gluing or sewing the stitches, to make their fabric robots as pretty as possible; it seemed a waste to have to tear their artifacts apart, when we started preparing the materials for the next season of the course.

4.4   Play Moods

As part of our analysis, we decided to also adopt the approach proposed by Karoff [13] and her framework of play moods, in order to analyze how differently the children engaged in playful interactions with each other and the provided materials, in relation to how in control they were of the technology. The more chaotic and lively their play, the more in control they were of the technology. In this sense, we are looking into how childrens play, relate to their understanding, in order to evaluate their learning progress.

During our observations, the children tended to stick to a devotional mood when they were struggling to understand the code or how to connect new components to the unit. In such cases, the children were going back and forth from the unit to the computer screen to write and rewrite their code, run it on the unit for debugging, and recheck the screen for mistakes. Their faces looked concentrated and focused, at times addressing other children sitting close to them for help, but generally they will focus their attention on the unit and the computer. We interpreted this behavior as a sign that the children needed our support to solve an issue. It might be questioned if children displaying this interaction pattern were playing at all, while in fact they might be simply engaged in sense making. However, their artefacts showed that the children interpreted the activity as a form of playful play [21], as they were creating grotesque monsters or creatures, puppets and weapons. In doing so, the children engaged in imagining new toys and future playful scenarios for themselves and the reactions they would elicit from their friends.

On the other hand, shifts in play moods and practices, towards intensity and tension, were shown by the children when they achieved control of the unit. Moreover, when the children managed to fix their code or had overcome the difficulty of setting up their components, they shifted towards an intensive or pensive mood playing with their artefacts and the other children, at times also with us instructors. Their facial expression typically changed from focused to playful, displaying a mood matching the purpose embodied by the artefacts they were creating. For instance, two boys were creating a pair of fighting gloves to play with each other and as soon as they managed to make part of the code work, they started playing, pretending to attack each other, making faces and noises as if they were shooting. Afterwards they went back to the next step in their design. In one case two boys acted a bit wild, while one was showing off his interactive weapon/glove and another was taking a picture of his pose, while a third boy in the middle was trying to concentrate on the code (Fig. 7).

Fig. 7. Two boys playing while another boy in the middle is focusing on his computer to check his code.

The glove being a wearable object inspired the children to pose and show off their glove, while wearing it, for instance we saw boys and girls playing around with their interactive gloves and assuming cool poses to them show off before each other and us. A boy was posing, wearing his glove, while pretending to be natural so that everybody could see he was wearing his glove and afterwards laughed with the boy sitting close to him (Fig. 1). Likewise, a girl played, inserting both her hands inside her glove giggling (Fig. 8). In this way, both boys and girls shifted from moments of seriousness, being focused on the code and the construction of their artefacts to moments of silliness, playing around with their artefacts and giggling at each other and at us.

In other cases, the children made puppets or little monsters and took breaks to play with them as if they were pets or fantasy creatures. In this respect, design materials to make distinct puppets with buttons shaped like eyes and with furry fabric were most popular (Fig. 9). They were petting them, grabbing them and waving them around or even throwing them in the air, as it was done by a girl with her furry creature (Fig. 8).

Looking at the children's behavior, we noticed that the more satisfied the children were with their work, the more chaotic their behavior became when they were playing with their artefacts, acting in between an intensive and pensive mood, as they were experimenting how to attract the attention of the other children on themselves, making them laugh and keep them interested in their success. It was interesting to notice that the few girls in the group, acted mostly in a devoted mood during the LEGO Mindstorms module, but started to show intensive and pensive moods after the fabric robotics module started. They generally became noisier in class and were glad to display their sewing skills to the boys. In this sense, the girls seemed to have started playing more during the fabric robotic module than before, as they seemed more in control and more interested in the material. However, all the children had practiced sewing at school, so they mostly needed help to start for instance in planning the construction of their artefacts, deciding on the size of the pieces of cloth and on how to sew them and turn them inside out when completing their artefacts, and eventually when to add the filling inside to make a puppet.

Fig. 8. On the left, a girl giggling while inserting both her hands inside a single glove, and on the right, a girl throwing her little creature in the air.

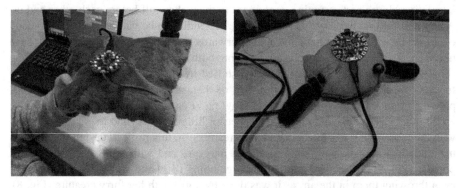

Fig. 9. On the left, a boy showing us a furry creature in the making with the Ada unit on top, and on the right, a creature in the making with animal features black buttons used as eyes and two limbs.

4.5   Gender Balance

Overall the introduction of fabric robotics has had a positive impact on the gender balance, and in our analysis we have identified two aspects as being the largest contributors to this: the development platform and the project context.

While we have observed that the male pupils, with a few exceptions, have been very happy working with the EV3 platform, the same cannot be said for the female pupils. They have often been nearly impossible to motivate, and when asked about their problems they have often replied "Because I can't" or "Because I'm not good enough". We know (from inquiries in our TS classes) that few girls in our courses play with LEGO at home, and of these almost none use LEGO Technic. Furthermore, the girls have tended to consider LEGO Technic very "boyish". As a result, we have often ended up building functional units for the girls in the class, in order for them to focus on the programming part; of course this did not solve the lack of engagement in the girls, nor did it help them feel in control of their projects.

This is in stark contrast to the male pupils, who typically love getting the robots to move and run. They engage in optimizing the sensors positioning and speed of the motors to make the robots deliver the boxes faster, etc. In other words, most of the male pupils simply seem satisfied working with the robots, for the sole reason of building, programming and playing with them afterwards.

With the introduction of fabric robotics, the situation for our female pupils has completely been turned around. They no longer feel inadequate at working with the materials, which they are often better at than their male colleagues. As a result, they have even been observed proudly showing off their prototypes and are now sincerely happy with working with the projects. This change is not only the result of the change in materials, but also of context, and it is now evident that the female participants have had a much higher need for working with something, which was not only theoretical relevant, but relevant for them personally and or others around them. This suggests that perhaps finding ways to balance the curricula towards inclusion of girls, might at the same time shed light on the much more complex problem of attracting non-technically minded students to CT courses.

We had initially expected that a few of the male pupils might not respond too well to the introduction of fabric robotics, partly due to the sewing practice; instead that turned out not to be the case. The large acceptance among the male pupils of this new activity, might however have less to do with their liking of fabric robotics, and more with our general observation that most of them are just happy working with robotics, regardless of platform or context. Another observation strengthening this notion, is that the projects not having an intended use outside the TS, have all been invented and carried out by male pupils.

The positive results from introducing fabric robotics, also means that for the first time ever, we now have a female pupil who has decided to continue another season. However, with her requiring that she could skip the EV3 projects and instead work with fabric robotics for the entire season, which she of course was allowed to do.

5   Reflections, Limitations and Future Work

We believe that our results show that working with fabric robotics enriches the learning of CT in different ways, compared to our previous work with the EV3 platform.

According to our analysis the new projects invented by the pupils, have a larger emphasis on being integrated into their world compared to the projects from previous seasons. We find that rethinking how technology can assist our participants or exist alongside them in more real-life scenarios, is an important feature of learning CT.

Our observations also show that the pupils feel more in control and are more skilled when working with fabric robotics materials, than when working with the LEGO platform. This is in tune with previous research which likewise shows that participants are more prone to feeling inadequate when working with the LEGO platforms in comparison to working with craft work for creating collages [24]. We believe that a large part of the observed boost in creativity, can be attributed to the wider selection of materials at their disposal; moreover, we designed the fabric robotics activity so that the materials used would be common, recognizable by the children: they are the same materials that make up their clothes, toys and everyday objects.

The necessity of more thorough planning and design required in a fabric robotics project, including sketching the functionalities, paper prototyping, and iterative testing, was due to the limitations and difficulties in performing late revisions to the fabric robot prototypes. However, we propose to consider these problems as an enriching factor of the CT learning, since it made the design cycle and its usefulness more practically evident to the pupils. With this more iterative nature of the projects, the role of and need for debugging have become more visible to the participants, who more often than in previous seasons found themselves having to think the entire system through and work more systematically in order to find the errors.

We noticed that for the fabric robotics activity, the hardware tended to become increasingly more complex in comparison with projects based on the EV3 platform; and this might in turn require more of the instructor, which has to be addressed when planning a similar course in other institutions. We also acknowledge that the EV3 platform has its own very valid and important qualities, and it is for this reason that we do not propose to replace LEGO technic or EV3 with fabric robots, and we are instead working on deeper integration of the two.

From the point of view of programming, our data suggest that there is a need to introduce state machines, since many of the children attempted to implement complex behaviors in their artifacts that would be classified as reactive systems [25, 26].

Finally, we have shown that with a different combination between development platform and context, the female pupils have become just as engaged as the male pupils and with a general need for more engineers on a world wide scale and with fewer females within the field [27], we argue that there is a need to bring in more. We feel that the situation of the TS is not unique, and that our recipe for including and empowering girls at a young age, as well as keeping boys and learning in focus too, can be easily adopted in a whole range of courses, possibly outside the CT domain.

5.1 Implications for the Next Season

Research has shown that keeping a project journal is helpful in order for pupils to get a better overview of their project, possible problems and solutions [28], in combination with our own findings of the need for drawing models of the artefacts functionalities, circuits and mechanics, we wish to provide the pupils with a project journal book for this purpose, starting this season.

The last two seasons we have started out the RobotSpirerne course working with the EV3 platform and later switched over to fabric robotics. However, in order to accommodate for a better gender balance, we will start out the following season with fabric robotics, and make it voluntarily to make the switch to EV3 later on. When the option for working with the EV3 platform will be presented, we will likewise work on offering ready made projects, with solid and relatable contexts.

Since we have found that the work with fabric robotics allows for asymmetrical project work, we wish to strengthen this. Therefore, beginning with the following season we will provide each pupil with a microcontroller kit of their own, including a selection of relevant sensors and motors, which they can keep also after the end of the course. At the same time, we want to try out with building up a culture, in which the pupils will take their project home every week together with the necessary materials, to continue working on it there. Hopefully this can also lead to reallocating the time needed for sewing, painting, etc. at home, instead of using only the limited time available at TS. Of course, it will be up to the individual pupil to decide how much time they desire to allocate for their projects at home or at school.

6 Conclusion

This paper reports on the success and pitfalls of our new learning activity, called fabric robotics, that we designed and deployed in the context of the Computational Thinking courses offered at Teknologiskolen. More specifically we wanted to alter the learning contents and curriculum of the course called RobotSpirerne (in English "Robot-Sprouts") aimed at children from 10 to 12 years of age, and move away from the traditional LEGO robotics building and programming tasks that have been used in these courses from its beginnings, five years ago, to foster girls' interest in the course.

We designed the new activity to be run as part of last year's season of the RobotSpirerne course, and we wanted to investigate how soft materials could enrich learning of CT, in relation to embedded systems and creative thinking practices; we also wanted to address gender biases in the course.

Regarding data gathering, we decided for ethnography, combining note taking, observations, pictures of the children's artifacts, and live drawings of the children in action [17]. This method, which we consider one of the contributions of this paper, was chosen as it fits well with the lose framework of Teknologiskolen, where the children are not formally evaluated and are free to decide on their projects, while receiving supervision. At the same time, this method also fitted the current, rather restrictive laws regarding privacy issues when filming children.

The activity itself has proven a success, much beyond the original goal of providing better support for the female participants to the course. Among other findings, we can definitely state that the introduction of fabric robotics elicited a general boost in creativity, suggesting new possibilities and affordances, with a larger acceptance of sewing practice found among boys than expected, and better gender balance in the participation and engagement, as the girls appeared more eager to take initiative and show off, then when interacting with the traditional LEGO platform. A major difference we observed was that children kept working on their prototypes and projects at home or brought school projects to the Teknologiskolen in order to enhance these. In this sense, the new activity was effective in bridging between children's daily life and our course.

Since we have only ran the fabric robotics activity twice, in two consecutive seasons of the TS, we are aware of the limitations resulting by the limited number of participants we could observe. Although we so far have only worked with data from the two girls who participated in the original run of the activity, and the three from the current one. However, we are confident on the validity of our analysis and findings, thanks to our choice of qualitative, ethnographic methods which are well suited to gather rich data from small groups.

As instructors, we also felt we learned much during the past season of the course, in particular on the pitfalls of switching to fabric robotics from the previous more mechanically-orientated LEGO platform. We do not propose abandoning the LEGO platform, which has proven very good to cover more traditional mechanical/robotic projects and to introduce programming in an embodied way; instead our analysis suggests that the course could be reorganized and start from the fabric robotics activity, and that children can later switch to LEGO or define their own projects. Hybridization and a better integration between fabric robotics and the EV3 LEGO platform would also provide an even larger design space for the children to experiment across the materials.

To conclude, in our opinion addressing gender balance, playing with different learning styles, and motivating through new problem domains and learning contexts, are essential factors when designing and deploying engaging CT courses to children.

References

1. Wing, J.M.: Computational thinking. Commun. ACM **49**(3), 33–35 (2006)
2. Teknologiskolen. http://www.teknologiskolen.dk/. Accessed 24 Feb 2020
3. Adafruit – CPX. https://www.adafruit.com/product/3333. Accessed 24 Feb 2020
4. LEGO Mindstorms EV3. https://www.lego.com/en-us/product/lego-mindstorms-ev3-31313. Accessed 24 Feb 2020
5. Oudeweetering, K., Voogt, J.: Teachers' conceptualization and enactment of twenty-first century competences: exploring dimensions for new curricula. Curriculum J. **29**(1), 116–133 (2018)
6. Jacob, S., Warschauer, M.: Computational thinking and literacy. J. Comput. Sci. Integr. **1**(1) (2018)
7. Jansen, M., Kohen-Vacs, D., Otero, N., Milrad, M.: A complementary view for better understanding the term computational thinking. In: International Conference on Computational Thinking Education, 14–16 June 2018, Hong Kong (2018)
8. Weng, X.: Students' attitude changes through integrating computational thinking into English dialogue learning. In: CTE 2018, International Conference on Computational Thinking Education 2018, pp. 50–56 (2018)
9. Tedre, M., Denning, P.J.: The long quest for computational thinking. In: Proceedings of the 16th Koli Calling Conference on Computing Education Research, 24–27 November 2016, Koli, Finland, pp. 120–129 (2016)
10. Iordache, C., Mariën, I., Baelden, D.: Developing digital skills and competences: a quick-scan analysis of 13 digital literacy models. Italian J. Sociol. Educ. **9**(1) (2017)
11. Jenson, J., Droumeva, M.: Exploring media literacy and computational thinking: a game maker curriculum study. Electron. J. e-Learning **14**(2), 111–121 (2016)
12. Shute, V., Sun, C., Asbell-Clarke, J.: Demystifying computational thinking. Educ. Res. Rev. **22**, 142–158 (2017)
13. Karoff, H.: Play practices and play moods. Int. J. Play **2**(2), 76–86 (2013)
14. Heidegger, M.: Being and Time. Blackwell (1962)

15. Preece, J., Rogers, Y., Sharp, E.: Interaction Design. Beyond Human-Computer Interaction. Wiley, Hoboken (2019)
16. Norman, D.: Emotional Design. Why We Love (or Hate) Everyday Things. Basic Books, New York (2003)
17. Causey, A.: Drawn to See: Drawing as an Ethnographic Method. University of Toronto Press (2017)
18. Bergin, J.: Fourteen pedagogical patterns. In: EuroPLoP, pp. 1–49, July 2000
19. Lytle, N., et al.: Use, modify, create: comparing computational thinking lesson progressions for STEM classes. In: Proceedings of the 2019 ACM Conference on Innovation and Technology in Computer Science Education, pp. 395–401, July 2019
20. Vygotsky, L.: Mind in Society. The Development of Higher Psychological Processes. Harvard University Press, Cambridge (1978)
21. Sutton-Smith, B.: The Ambiguity of Play. Harvard University Press, Cambridge (1997)
22. Marvel - Infinity Gauntlet. https://en.wikipedia.org/wiki/The_Infinity_Gauntlet. Accessed 24 Feb 2020
23. Pokémon. https://www.pokemon.com/dk/. Accessed 24 Feb 2020
24. Borum, N., Kristensen, K., Petersson Brooks, E., Brooks, A.L.: Medium for children's creativity: a case study of artifact's influence. In: Stephanidis, C., Antona, M. (eds.) UAHCI 2014. LNCS, vol. 8514, pp. 233–244. Springer, Cham (2014). https://doi.org/10.1007/978-3-319-07440-5_22
25. Berry, G., Gonthier, G.: The Esterel synchronous programming language: design, semantics, implementation. Sci. Comput. Program. **19**(2), 87–152 (1992)
26. Erik, M.: Reactive extensions (Rx): curing your asynchronous programming blues. In: ACM SIGPLAN Commercial Users of Functional Programming (CUFP 2010). Association for Computing Machinery, New York, Article 11, 1 (2010)
27. Hill, C., Corbett, C., St. Rose, A.: Why so few? Washington, D.C. (2010)
28. Lin, C.H., Liu, E.Z.F.: The effect of reflective strategies on students' problem solving in robotics learning. In: The 4th International Conference on Digital Game and Intelligent Toy Enhanced Learning, Takamatsu, Japan, pp. 254–257 (2012)

Preschool Safety Education with Digital Media-Based Learning Application – Kinder

Cheng-Feng Sun[1], Yao-Cheng Chan[2], Shih-Yi Chien[2(✉)],
Yi-Ling Lin[2], and I-Han Hsiao[3]

[1] University of Washington, Seattle, WA 98195, USA
ennovysun0629@gmail.com
[2] National Chengchi University, Taipei 11605, Taiwan
n810098@gmail.com, {sychien,yl_lin}@nccu.edu.tw
[3] Arizona State University, Tempe, AZ 85281, USA
Sharon.Hsiao@asu.edu

Abstract. While unintentional injuries are the leading cause of morbidity and mortality among children, reports have shown that unintentional injuries mostly take place at home or school environments with injuries like falls, contact with stationary objects and being caught in hinge side of doors reported frequently. Safety education targeting children is seen as an important intervention of children injury prevention for its direct affect. As there has been a rising usage of digital media devices among children, digital media-based learning has been discussed and researched in recent years. However, few has investigated the value of deploying digital devices in children environment safety education. We developed Kinder, a mobile application using Augmented Reality (AR) and object recognition technology, to support preschool children in identifying potentially dangerous objects in different environments. The ultimate goal of Kinder is to provide an interactive and encouraging learning experience for preschool children to foster their learning motivation and enhance their safety knowledge. Our main focus is to assess the usability and prospects of the application. In this paper, we present the methodology, setup, implementation and results of our preliminary assessment of Kinder. From questionnaire and interviews, the preliminary results have shown valid value of AR with object recognition technology in children safety knowledge learning in home and school environment. The present study also provides useful information for practical design in children learning applications.

Keywords: Digital media learning · Children safety education · Augmented reality · Object recognition

1 Introduction

Reports have shown that unintentional injury, any injuries that are caused by an accident, is one of the most prevalent child health problems of our time [1]. Unintentional injuries are reported as the leading cause of death and disability for US children less then 19 years old at a 44% [1]. Among them, preschool children (3 to 6 years old), tend to have a higher percentage of injury rate as they have lower awareness

© Springer Nature Switzerland AG 2020
P. Zaphiris and A. Ioannou (Eds.): HCII 2020, LNCS 12206, pp. 520–529, 2020.
https://doi.org/10.1007/978-3-030-50506-6_35

and less safety knowledge. As the cognitive developmental level reaches mature at the average age of 18, children aged 0–18 years have less awareness of danger, ability to foresee and respond to danger. Reports also shown that the predominant location of injury is the home [2]. Injuries including burns, scalds and various trauma are mostly caused by falsely using appliances. Thus, injury prevention is a major focus among advocates of children's health.

In the past, the most used methods for preventing children from home injuries are preschool teaching, parental supervision and access intervention. However, constant supervision and teaching is not possible. As a growing variety of media options has offered children broad learning opportunities, numerous electronic devices have been widely developed in the market with computer-based capabilities such as interactive story books, tag reading systems, electronic keyboards and music-makers, dolls and robots, electronic toys, dance pads and sports equipment. The advent of mobile application has stimulated a new aspect in the education domain. Several mobile applications have been developed for children in this age group such as ABC Memory Match, Peekaboo Barn, Mickey Mini Golf etc.

Active learning has been demonstrated as an important way to involve in learning [3]. Effective learning often takes place when children experience what is going on in their own heads [4]. Through physical engagement, involvement and activeness in learning can provoke children to reflect [5]. Digital augmentation allows children to interact with the physical world in a various of ways. While past studies have investigated the value of Augment Reality (AR) in children learning [6–8], few have paid attention to the potential of AR in home injury prevention.

Our study aims to explore the efficacy and possibilities of implementing smart devices into preschool safety education for its interacting features with real world settings. Therefore, we developed Kinder, an AR mobile application focusing on child safety education for this study. Because the most common environments where preschool children normally stay are schools and home, we focused on interviewing parents and preschool teachers. To understand how an AR application can be deployed in the context of safety education for preschool children, we focused on three research questions:

RQ1: How are digital devices used in families and in preschools?
RQ2: How are the safety educational measurement conducted in family and in preschool?
RQ3: How willing are parents and teacher to deploy the Kinder application?

2 Related Work

2.1 Digital Media-Based Learning

From the past decade, usage of traditional media for education and entertainment has shifted towards newer media such as physical objects or toys with computational features, physical activity equipment and smart devices [9–11]. Based on this trend, a spread of computer-based interactive products has been developed and a branch has been focusing on building applications that are tailored for young children. Studies in this field mainly focused on investigating the influence of such application on pre-school education. For instance, Yelland [12] found that digital media-based activities can engage children to learn and improve their abilities that were considered too advanced for such young children, including collaborative learning, reasoning, and problem solving [13]. In mobile device context, the accessibility of these devices provide more opportunity for children to use them repeatedly and ubiquitously [14] and such behavior may increase children's engagement with the applications. Education applications can apply this advantage and allow children to be more engaged in the education materials. Along with these benefits, since most preschool children do not own mobile devices, they usually borrow from their parents, therefore, studies have also investigated the parent-child relationship in the context of mobile devices usage behavior and parents' thoughts about this phenomenon [15, 16]. Even though using digital-based media for learning does provide promising results and show several benefits, there are still a few concerns about letting young children use these devices [17]. Several other benefits and drawbacks of digital media for young children can be found in the literatures [12, 18, 19].

2.2 Augmented Reality

Augmented Reality technology can offer great potential to engage learners [20] and to enhance the process of knowledge building [21]. We chose to apply AR technology because of the value of AR to bridge the learning gap between abstract descriptions and the real-world phenomena [22]. The potential of AR to enhance the presentations of real-world settings and the creation of engaging ways of interacting with simulations would motivate children to learn. There is also evidence that specific skills can be improved, and the technology offers many opportunities for collaboration [23, 24]. In present study we discussed an extensive evaluation of AR technology in the context of home and school safety education for preschool children.

Since children's level of safety knowledge cannot predict the their possibility of getting injured, the best predictors were children's compliance with home safety rules and the extent of parental supervision [25]. According to the over-learning effect, the learner's understanding of a certain message increases as the number of times the message appears [26]. Over-learning effect enables learners to comprehend the knowledge from low-level skills and apply it to a higher level. Repeated behaviors can also give children a sense of familiarity. By touching the same toys, reading the same storybooks, and playing the same games over and over again, children can get a familiar sense of safe behavior, along with pleasure and accomplishment. In the process of repeated operations, children can learn the structure, predictability and causality of things. For example, how to catch a throwing ball. Learning from such a repeated pattern can also establish its reasoning ability. As a result, this study focuses on developing an application that children are able to learn from repeated patterns of home safety knowledge.

3   System Design

3.1   Analysis and Requirements Specification

Prior to designing the application, we visited a few families with preschool children to gain a rough understanding of the items that should first be recognized in Kinder as potentially dangerous objects. Concluded from short interviews with the parents, *plugs*, *wires*, *stationaries*, *fans*, and *glasses* were the most commonly contacted dangerous objects at home. Parents expressed their need to supervise their children's behavior at all times and constantly warn their children not to touch these items. Therefore, the two objects we implemented as the "potentially dangerous objects" in the application are *plugs* and *scissors* for they have more features and are easier to be recognized. We used Unity for the application development and Vuforia with Unity to develop the AR features. We developed the application on Android studio in accordance with the industry standards and guidelines. To avoid introducing any additional user interface complexity, we used bigger fonts and buttons for readability and easier usage. The application was in Chinese and can be purchased for free through the mobile application store.

3.2   Application Design and Features

The benefits of learning through game playing (in a pedagogical perspective) has been widely acknowledged [27–30]. Many researches in the last decades have also shown that games which designed for mobile devices have potential to encourage learning [8, 31, 32]. Hence, we designed the Kinder as a game-based application that implemented quizzes for pedagogical purposes.

The application aimed to build exploring experiences. Once a child starts playing, there will be an anime character to interact with the child throughout the whole process. The anime character will move around the environment as the child scans around the room. When Kinder identifies a potentially dangerous object, the character would interact with the child either by having short informative conversations, playing videos showing how to correctly use the object or having the child take a few quizzes regarding the object. The child can earn points as he or she successfully selects the right answer. Getting the answers wrong over three times would end the game and provide options to start over.

Parents and teachers (or any kind of supervisors) play as "adults" in the Kinder application and act as an application manager for the children. Since different households can have very different furniture and objects in their homes, objects may not be recognizable due to unique shape or that they were undocumented in the database. In this case, adults can upload pictures of the objects that were not set in the system. After the objects are reviewed by the developers, the objects will be added to the database and will later be recognizable in the application. In addition to adding new objects to the "potentially dangerous object list", adults can also set a timer for each round of game play and set password to access the adult settings. The focus of Kinder is to let preschool children have fun when identifying potentially dangerous objects/scenarios through repetitive learning in games and, at the same time, engaging parents or teachers to participate the experience.

4   Research Methodology

The goal of Kinder is to enable children to learn from a real environment combining AR and object recognition. This study sought to determine if such technology would be beneficial and suitable for children to use. According to TAM, factors such as usability and ease of use strongly affects the level of acceptance towards an information system. Other elements that could influence the acceptance and frequency of usage should also be considered, such as the habits and the environment of using smart devices. To investigate these factors, an in-dept interview and a questionnaire were taken to gain a deeper understanding of each factor. We focused more on the qualitative analyses to learn the insights related to children's digital device using habits, safety education measurements of each family and preschool, and the overall feedback of the Kinder application. Through a mixed-method approach, the results can support and yield more decisive findings [33–35]. Our user target is people who interacts with preschool children on a daily basis and deals with safety rules and education, mainly parents and preschool teachers. There was little ethnic diversity in the sample of both methods as all of them were Asian. The participants and procedure of each method are presented below.

4.1   In-Depth Interview

The sample included 6 participants, 4 parents and 2 preschool teachers, recruited through local universities and kindergartens. The children in the parents' group includes 3 girls (2 four-year-old and one three-year-old) and 2 boys (four-year-old and six-year old). Children in the kindergarten group were between 3–6 years old. Before the interview, participants were first given the introduction video of Kinder to help them grasp a rough idea of the application. The interview was divided into three sections. Firstly, we asked questions about how digital devices were used in homes and preschools, such as how often the children use them and how familiar they were with the devices. The second part was how they conduct safety education in homes and schools, what were their approaches and what they found effective. Lastly was the Kinder application user experience feedback, where we discussed more on the application details and asked the participants to give feedback. There were a few common questions that every participant was asked to answer, but questions regarding details were directed towards each case. For example, we asked preschool teachers questions about teaching experience in classrooms and asked parents about parent-child interactions at homes.

4.2   Questionnaires

In total, we collected 23 responses from parents and preschool teachers, one of them was male and 22 of them were female, 4 of them were between 21–30 years old, 11 of them were between 31–40 years old and 8 of them were between 41–50 years old. In terms of character, 12 of the participants were mothers, 10 of them were preschool teachers and 1 of them was father. All respondents completed the questionnaire with 21 questions. The participants were first asked about the age of his/her children and gender. According to the suggestions from the professors of the department of education, we divided the preschool children into two groups, 3–4 and 5–6, based on their cognitive level. In the group of 3–4 years old, there were 11 boys and 10 girls. In the 5–6 years old group, there were 12 boys and 15 girls. If the participants have more than one child in the same age group (for example if a parent have a 3-year-old boy and a 4-year-old girl), they were asked to give an average answer (3.5 in this case). After the basic demographic information, an introduction video of Kinder was shown to them with the features of the application and using scenarios. The video was followed by series of questions regarding the usability of Kinder. Because the main purpose of this study was to explore possible benefits of Kinder, the questionnaire focused more on getting feedback from the participants.

5 Results

In this section, we first report results from the interview with parents and preschool teachers, then followed by the results from the questionnaire.

5.1 Digital Devices Using Habits

In terms of child use habits of digital devices, parents have more experience on this topic. The parents reported that their children were familiar with basic functions of smart devices, such as unlocking, swiping and camera. Even though the children were allowed to use smart devices on their own, they only use specific applications, mostly watch videos on YouTube. In addition, the parents would limit the length of time of using smart devices to prevent their children from staring at the devices for too long and cause vision damage. Preschool teachers have less experience of children using smart devices since in most kindergarten classes, smart devices are not used. The only cases where the devices are used are when the teachers use videos as tools to support learning. For example, showing pictures or videos of trees are effective to help children build knowledge of tree species. Another example that the preschool teachers provided was dance classes using videos.

5.2 Child Safety

In the context of home security education, most parents educate their children by repeated oral reminder and some of them use education videos, preschool teachers also agree that videos are good materials for security education. In addition to videos, most parents used tools or hardware such as safety plugs and drawer blocks to block children from accessing dangerous areas. However, both parents and teachers believed that security education must be personality-dependent. One point worth notice was that two out of the three parents reported that their children watched the same cartoon character repeatedly, the children gained deep impression of the behaviors of the character, and the parents would purchase the same series of education material.

5.3   Kinder Feedback

The last part of the interview is the user experience of Kinder. Overall, participants were positive about Kinder. They were willing and excited to use Kinder for child safety education. They reported that the game-based aspect of Kinder is an interesting idea and that it is very likely to attract children. Several other benefits of Kinder were also reported, including potential to improve literacy, problem solving skills and concentration. However, there were a few concerns that the participants reported. For instance, for children to start using smart devices at such young age, they must be accompanied by their parents, and the children may damage their vision if play time is not properly controlled. The participants also provided some suggestions, including adding more games or stories to enrich the application and prevent the children from getting bored easily, another one is to add an alert function that will send notification to parents if their child accidently interact with dangerous objects.

6   Discussion

Given the potential benefits of learning through digital media devices, we developed Kinder to support preschool children in identifying potentially dangerous objects in different real-world environments. As a pilot study, we focused firstly on parents and kindergarten teachers, who are the most experienced individuals in interacting with preschool children. Three aspects were closely studied to evaluate the possibilities of implementing Kinder: digital devices use habits of preschool children, safety education in families and schools, parents and preschool teachers' willingness to apply Kinder. Although at this stage our work cannot be conclusive, the preliminary results show promising prospects of digital media-based learning in safety education.

Amongst the responses to the various questions in the interview and questionnaire, there were several indications that supported the potential of the AR approach for promoting learning and motivating children to engage with learning activities. Most parents and teachers indicated that the application would be beneficial for children by supporting them to memorize the location of dangerous objects and the correct ways of using the objects. Both parents and teachers believed that children would have confidence in using Kinder. The results from the interview and questionnaire indicated that AR application can support in safety education to some degree. Some active parents and teachers were willing to cooperate to improve the development of Kinder.

Even though game-based learning through digital media devices have been proved to be beneficial [28, 31, 32, 36–38], there are still factors to consider in designing the application in the future. In Freitas's review of game-based learning, one of the key findings was that motivation was a vital factor of effective learning [39, 40]. Motivation needs to be sustained through feedback responses, reflection and active involvement. Although there is potential to implement AR and object recognition in home safety education, developers still have to create applications that ffer necessary learner control, challenging interactivity and motivating experience. Therefore, the main challenge for effective learning with games is for the learner to be engaged, motivated, supported and interested. In addition, the content and support materials need to be differentiated for school and home use in order to respect the differing needs of teachers and parents, and meanwhile maintaining the opportunity for coherent multi-location learning experiences.

We intent to further present study by adding more features based on the results, including designing functions that would induce motivation and construct more objects that children can interact with. Furthermore, we plan to conduct more user study to gain a deeper understanding of the effectiveness of Kinder.

7 Limitations

In this study, we used markerless AR to develop Kinder because the technology requires no prior knowledge of the user's environment to overlay 3D content into a scene and hold it to a fixed point in space. However, markerless AR is dependent on the number of angles of objects. There are three major object recognition limitations in the development process. First, for circular objects, the lack of angle may lower the reading ability due to its low score in Vuforia target manager. Second, complex patterns of objects could hamper the effectiveness of identifying the objects. Third, brightness in the environment would influence the rendering of objects. Even though Kinder can be used in various environment, currently it can only work in outdoor environment.

References

1. Borse, N., Sleet, D.A.: CDC Childhood Injury Report (2009)
2. Phelan, K.J., Khoury, J., Kalkwarf, H., Lanphear, B.: Residential injuries in US children and adolescents (2005)
3. Papert, S.: Mindstonns, p. 607. Basic Rooks, New York (1980)
4. Bruner, J.S.: Organization of early skilled action. Child Dev. 1–11 (1973)
5. Price, S., Rogers, Y.: Let's get physical: the learning benefits of interacting in digitally augmented physical spaces. Comput. Educ. 43, 137–151 (2004)
6. Luckin, R., Fraser, D.S.: Limitless or pointless? An evaluation of augmented reality technology in the school and home. Int. J. Technol. Enhanc. Learn. 3, 510 (2011)
7. Rogers, Y., Price, S., Randell, C., Fraser, D.S., Weal, M., Fitzpatrick, G.: Ubi-learning integrates indoor and outdoor experiences. Commun. ACM 48, 55–59 (2005)
8. Facer, K., Joiner, R., Stanton, D., Reid, J., Hull, R., Kirk, D.: Savannah: mobile gaming and learning? J. Comput. Assist. Learn. 20, 399–409 (2004)
9. Anand, S., Krosnick, J.A.: Demographic predictors of media use among infants, toddlers, and preschoolers. Am. Behav. Sci. 48, 539–561 (2005)
10. Plowman, L., McPake, J., Stephen, C.: The technologisation of childhood? Young children and technology in the home. Child. Soc. 24, 63–74 (2010)
11. Vandewater, E.A., Rideout, V.J., Wartella, E.A., Huang, X., Lee, J.H., Shim, M.: Digital childhood: electronic media and technology use among infants, toddlers, and preschoolers. Pediatrics 119, e1006 LP–e1015 (2007)

12. Yelland, N.: Critical Issues in Early Childhood Education. McGraw-Hill Education, New York (2005)
13. Resnick, M.: Technologies for lifelong kindergarten. Educ. Technol. Res. Dev. **46**, 43–55 (1998)
14. Arnold, B.A.: The seven traits of a learning environment: a framework for evaluating mobile learning engagement. Int. J. E-Education, e-Business, e-Management e-Learning **9**, 54–60 (2019)
15. Fox, A.K., Hoy, M.G.: Smart devices, smart decisions? Implications of parents' sharenting for children's online privacy: an investigation of mothers. J. Public Policy Mark. **38**, 414–432 (2019)
16. Erdogan, N.I., Johnson, J.E., Dong, P.I., Qiu, Z.: Do parents prefer digital play? Examination of parental preferences and beliefs in four nations. Early Child. Educ. J. **47**, 131–142 (2019)
17. Prasad, A., Ruiz, R., Stablein, T.: Understanding parents' concerns with smart device usage in the home. In: Moallem, A. (ed.) HCII 2019. LNCS, vol. 11594, pp. 176–190. Springer, Cham (2019). https://doi.org/10.1007/978-3-030-22351-9_12
18. McCarrick, K., Li, X.: Buried treasure: the impact of computer use on young children's social, cognitive, language development and motivation. AACE J. **15**, 73–95 (2007)
19. Thai, A.M., Lowenstein, D., Ching, D., Rejeski, D.: Game changer: investing in digital play to advance children's learning and health. Joan Ganz Cooney Center. Retrieved. **8**, 9 (2009)
20. Vretos, N., et al.: Exploiting sensing devices availability in AR/VR deployments to foster engagement. Virtual Real. **23**, 399–410 (2019)
21. Li, X., Yi, W., Chi, H.-L., Wang, X., Chan, A.P.C.: A critical review of virtual and augmented reality (VR/AR) applications in construction safety. Autom. Constr. **86**, 150–162 (2018)
22. Cai, S., Liu, E., Yang, Y., Liang, J.: Tablet-based AR technology: impacts on students' conceptions and approaches to learning mathematics according to their self-efficacy. Br. J. Educ. Technol. **50**, 248–263 (2019)
23. Piumsomboon, T., Lee, Y., Lee, G., Billinghurst, M.: CoVAR: a collaborative virtual and augmented reality system for remote collaboration. In: SIGGRAPH Asia 2017 Emerging Technology, pp. 1–2 (2017)
24. Liu, H., Wang, L.: An AR-based worker support system for human-robot collaboration. Procedia Manuf. **11**, 22–30 (2017)
25. Morrongiello, B.A., Midgett, C., Shields, R.: Don't run with scissors: young children's knowledge of home safety rules. J. Pediatr. Psychol. **26**, 105–115 (2001)
26. Tang, J., et al.: Association between non-suicidal self-injuries and suicide attempts in Chinese adolescents and college students: a cross-section study. PLoS One 6 (2011)
27. Bruer, J.T.: Schools for Thought: A Science of Learning in the Classroom. MIT Press, Cambridge (1994)
28. Prensky, M.: Digital game-based learning. **1**, 1–4 (2003)
29. Gee, J.P.: What video games have to teach us about learning and literacy. Comput. Entertain. **1**, 20 (2003)
30. Papert, S.: Does easy do it? Children, games, and learning. Game Dev. **5**, 88 (1988)
31. Chiong, C., Shuler, C.: Learning: is there an app for that? Investigations of young children's usage and learning with mobile devices and apps. In: New York Joan Ganz Cooney Cent. Sesame Workshop (2010)
32. Skiada, R., Soroniati, E., Gardeli, A., Zissis, D.: EasyLexia: a mobile application for children with learning difficulties. Procedia Comput. Sci. **27**, 218–228 (2013)
33. Creswell, J.W., Clark, V.L.P.: Designing and Conducting Mixed Methods Research. Sage Publications (2017)

34. Frechtling, J.A., Sharp, L.M.: User-Friendly Handbook for Mixed Method Evaluations. Diane Publications (1997)
35. Bebell, D., Russell, M., O'Dwyer, L.: Measuring teachers' technology uses: why multiple-measures are more revealing. J. Res. Technol. Educ. **37**, 45–63 (2004)
36. De Freitas, S.: Learning in Immersive worlds: a review of game-based learning (2006)
37. Hsiao, H.S., Chen, J.C.: Using a gesture interactive game-based learning approach to improve preschool children's learning performance and motor skills. Comput. Educ. **95**, 151–162 (2016)
38. Plowman, L., Stevenson, O., Stephen, C., McPake, J.: Preschool children's learning with technology at home. Comput. Educ. **59**, 30–37 (2012)
39. Daumiller, M., Dresel, M.: Supporting self-regulated learning with digital media using motivational regulation and metacognitive prompts. J. Exp. Educ. **87**, 161–176 (2019)
40. Jeno, L.M., Adachi, P.J.C., Grytnes, J., Vandvik, V., Deci, E.L.: The effects of m-learning on motivation, achievement and well-being: a Self-Determination Theory approach. Br. J. Educ. Technol. **50**, 669–683 (2019)

Let's Learn! An Initial Guide on Using Drones to Teach STEM for Children

Dante Tezza(✉), Sarah Garcia, and Marvin Andujar

University of South Florida, Tampa, FL 33620, USA
{dtezza,sarahgarcia}@mail.usf.edu, andujar1@usf.edu

Abstract. Although the number of careers calling for training and knowledge of STEM topics continue to grow, the presence of STEM education in K-12 is lacking. Therefore, there is a need to broaden the presence of STEM in current curricula. There is also a need for tools and guidelines to help educators in teaching STEM courses. Such tools should engage students in the subject and encourage them to pursue further education and careers in the field. In this paper, we support the use of drones as STEM teaching tools. Drones naturally spark students' interest, making it easier to engage them in the classroom. Additionally, they can be used to teach a broad spectrum of STEM courses and they allow students to get both hardware and software experience. Our contributions in this paper include (1) a discussion on how drones can be integrated in education, (2) a series of guidelines for educators on how to use drones in their classroom, (3) a detailed description of a five session (15-h) course designed to introduce young students to drones while motivating them to pursue further education in STEM.

Keywords: Drones · Education · Outreach · STEM · Summer camp · Unmanned aerial vehicles

1 Introduction

An education program focusing on Science, Technology, Engineering, and Mathematics (STEM) can lead students to become better problem solvers, innovators, and logical thinkers [24]. Additionally, strengthening STEM education is critical to maintain a high quality of life of citizens, and to ensure that a nation remains competitive in international science and technology [31]. A solid STEM education should teach students how the world around them works and improve their use of technologies [7]. Although research has shown a strong correlation between student engagement in the classroom and overall student success [10,20], engaging students is not an easy task [21], especially in STEM subjects. We believe drones naturally spark students' interest and can help educators increase their engagement. Therefore, in this paper, we suggest the use of drones to teach STEM-related courses and motivate students to pursue higher education in STEM fields.

P. Zaphiris and A. Ioannou (Eds.): HCII 2020, LNCS 12206, pp. 530–543, 2020.
https://doi.org/10.1007/978-3-030-50506-6_36

Drones have grown in popularity and their use is expected to continue to increase [30]. Nowadays, these flying robots are widely used in various applications (e.g. racing, film-making, precision agriculture), and have been a topic of focus for many researchers. An emerging trend is the use of drones in the education realm to teach STEM for young students (e.g. K-12). General robotics has been integrated in classrooms to spark students interest in STEM, starting in kindergarten [5], and elementary school [2]. Similarly to other robots, drones are highly engaging, and they inspire students to perform critical thinking and become problem solvers [8]. STEM education integrates knowledge from various study fields [11]. As drones also require knowledge from many areas, they can be used to teach a variety of courses. Also, drones are becoming more adapted to different domains within society, and some universities have programs dedicated to drone technologies. Therefore, it can be beneficial to introduce the field to students early on during their education.

Our purpose in writing this paper is to encourage drone usage in the education realm and to guide STEM teachers on how to integrate drones in their lectures. Our main contributions are (1) a discussion on how these systems can be used to teach STEM, (2) a series of guidelines and special considerations necessary when using drones as teaching tools, and (3) a detailed curriculum for a five session (15-h) course designed to introduce students to drone technologies and increase their interest in further studying STEM. Our proposed guidelines and considerations are meant to guide teachers in designing curriculum's and utilizing drones in their lectures. Our goal when designing the guidelines was to enforce and enhance (1) students' engagement, (2) knowledge retention, and (3) students' safety.

We suggest this curriculum for both middle and high school teachers to introduce students to drones and raise their interest in further studying STEM. In this paper, we provide a description of what should be covered during each session, the technologies involved (both hardware and software), the reasoning behind it, and how students can learn while interacting with the drones. During each session, students attended a one hour lecture followed by a two-hour hands-on experience in a lab environment. We successfully employed this curriculum with a class of fifteen middle-school students, and another class of fifteen high-school students. From our observations, the curriculum provided an effective and easy-to-follow path to teach students, who were highly engaged throughout the camp.

2 Literature Review

2.1 STEM Education

Studies have shown that teaching STEM for young students provides several benefits, such as increasing their ability to solve problems, innovate, and perform logical thinking [24]. Additionally, introducing STEM at an early age can motivate students to pursue a career in STEM-related fields [29], and help avoid stereotypes and other impediments to becoming innovators later on [22]. Studies have also shown that teaching math and science improves students' attitude and interest in school [4], and motivates their learning experience [12]. Mathematics and sciences are integrated into the K-12 curriculum, and although engineering has some presence as well, its' extent is not consistent to the extent of engineering careers and contributions to society [6]. Integrating engineering in K-12 also provides specific benefits, such as the ones listed by the National Research Council: (1) improved achievement in mathematics and science, (2) increased awareness of engineering, (3) understanding and being able to do engineering design, (4) and increased technological literacy [18].

The National Science Board (NSB) states that to effectively teach STEM education for the K-12 audience, it is important to attract, prepare, and retain well-qualified, committed and highly effective teachers [31]. In [29], the authors provide recommendations on how educators can be effective in lecturing STEM. They present the "s.t.e.m." model, standing for Support, Teaching, Efficacy, and Materials. This model was developed through a year-long collaboration with a middle school and can be used as a starting point for teachers to improve their STEM lecturing. Additionally, previous studies have elicited best-practices for science and mathematics education, which also provides insights into the broader STEM realm. For instance, the following are 10 well-known best-practices that teachers can use to guide their teaching methodology [33].

1. use manipulative and hands-on learning;
2. cooperative learning;
3. discussion and inquiry;
4. questioning and conjectures
5. use justification of thinking
6. writing for reflection and problem solving
7. use a problem solving approach
8. integrate technology
9. teacher as a facilitator
10. use assessment as a part of instruction

2.2 Robotics and Drones in Education

Robotics are powerful teaching tools for non-technical subjects (e.g. language and music [13,14,16]), technical fields (e.g. robotics and programming [1,25]), and general STEM related topics [23]. In fact, robot-based learning has been explored since 1980 [26]. It has been shown that its use can improve critical thinking and problem solving skills [27,28,32], as well as improving students motivation, engagement, and attitude [17,28]. In the STEM education realm, robotic-based learning provides at least five advantages over a traditional approach: (1) in integrates STEM topics in a multidisciplinary fashion, (2) it transforms abstract concepts into concrete learning, (3) it combines STEM theory with practice, (4) it provides a hands-on experience that it is active and engaging, (5) it provides a enjoyable and motivating learning environment [9]. A challenge in using robotics for learning is the need for new technologies that are affordable and designed specifically developed for young learners [3]. In [23], the authors describe a project in which they partnered with a robotics company (iRobot) and Microsoft Research to develop a workbook on robot programming. This workbook is freely distributed, and educators can use it to teach robotics programming to a K-12 audience. The authors, also provide a detailed description of the accompanying hardware and software related to the project. A review of robotics hardware for education can also be found in [17], including brick-based robot kits, modular robots, and pre-assembled robots.

The use of drones in education benefits from the same aforementioned benefits of robot-based learning. Their use in the classroom is an emerging trend in education [8]. In [19], the authors present the results of a one-week long summer camp designed to impact middle-school students' attitudes towards STEM. In this pre-post within-subject study, 20 underrepresented students from a rural area learned how to program ground robots (Ozobots) and drones (Parrot Mamba). A block-based programming language was used to teach the students. Results indicated that students enjoyed their experience, developed an appreciation of the importance of planning in problem-solving. The post-survey data showed an increase in the attitude towards STEM, but few statistically significant changes were noticed, most likely due to the small sample size. Another drone summer camp, designed to impact high-school students' decision to choose STEM-related careers is held yearly at Old Dominion University [15]. This program was created through a collaboration among a funding agency, the Virginia Space Grant Consortium, and three state universities. It consists of a three-day program, containing hands-on, intensive workshops, where students have the opportunity to build a drone themselves. Additionally, as this is a residential program, students spend 3 days on the university, sleeping in dorms and eating in the dining halls, essentially experiencing the life of an on-campus undergraduate student.

3   Use Cases for Drones in Teaching

Integrating drones in the classroom allows students to apply science concepts from various fields in a hands-on fashion, during a fun and engaging activity [11]. In this section, we list and discuss some examples of courses in which drones can be applied.

Mechanical Drawing and Design. The mechanical aspects of the drone structure can be explored to teach students about mechanical design, material science, and the strength of materials. Additionally, Computer-Aided Design (CAD) can be combined with 3D-printing of drone parts to teach students how to design and test their 3D models. For instance, a class activity could consist of students designing a drone frame using mechanical concepts learned in class, printing the design using a 3D printer, and testing the frame in flight.

Software. Drones can also be used to teach the fundamentals of programming, providing the benefit that students can see their code controlling an actual physical system. For instance, a beginner programming student is more likely to be impressed and engaged in the activity when a drone taking-off and landing rather than simply seeing a print statement on the screen (e.g. hello world code). Currently, there is a wide availability of commercial-off-the-shelf drones providing ready-to-use software interfaces using a variety of languages. The teacher must decide which language is the most appropriate for his students. We first recommend block-based programming (e.g. Scratch) to teach the younger students (middle school), and as they learn the concepts they can shift to code-based programming (e.g. Python, C, Java). High-school students can either start with a block-based or a code-based language, depending on their previous experience.

Electricity and Electronics. Drones can also be used to illustrate how electricity and electronic systems work. They can be used to explain concepts such as voltage, current, signals, and fundamentals of electrical circuits. They allow teachers to explain such concepts using a hands-on approach by building a drone in front of the class and involving students in the process. This approach allows students to learn how to build electrical circuits, connect and solder electronic components.

Motion and Kinematics. Drones can also be used to demonstrate the sciences related to motion and kinematics. Teachers can use drones applications to discuss the concepts, challenge students to solve exercises, and demonstrate how such concepts work during flights. For instance, a professor can use the drone's characteristics (e.g. thrust, weight) and physics concept (e.g. gravity) to create exercises that can be solved theoretically and validated with flight. Students can be asked questions such as "A quad-copter weights 750 g and is capable of generating 500 g of thrust per propeller. Calculate the thrust to weight ratio of this drone, and the required throttle position (0–100%) required to hover the drone?"

4   Guidelines

In this section, we present a series of 10 guidelines designed to help teachers in using drones during their lectures. We elicited these guidelines by analyzing the existing literature on the topic (see Sect. 2), and from our experience teaching children using drones. The guidelines are meant to enforce and enhance (1) students' engagement, (2) knowledge retention, and (3) students' safety.

1. Increase students' engagement through the addition of fun activities. For instance, incorporating exercises and activities that involve flying can increase students' interest in the lecture.

2. Utilize a problem-solving approach, encouraging students to perform critical thinking. This will teach students good habits that will not only benefit in the lecture itself but also various aspects of their life.
3. When developing a drone or using it to solve a problem, students should justify their thinking. Teach them how to perform an informed design process, predicting their outcome before implementation instead of a trial and error approach. This will teach students an approach consistent with what they would find outside the classroom (e.g. industry development).
4. Teachers should be aware of hazards related to drones and ensure students' safety during classes. The fast-spinning propellers can cause lacerations and should be removed from the motors while students are working on the drone inside the classroom. Lithium-polymer batteries (commonly used in drones) are highly inflammable, therefore battery handling (charging, balancing, discharging) should be done in fire-proof bags. Also, flying should be done in designated areas and under teacher supervision.
5. Spark students' interest by demonstrating drones' capabilities. For instance, a fully-autonomous flight or a racing drone can impress students and raise curiosity about the field.
6. Teachers should be knowledgeable and up to date in drone technologies, laws and regulations. Schools should provide teachers adequate training and materials. One approach to mitigate this step is to create collaborations with local universities and drone companies.
7. Provide the underlying theory and concepts that will enable students to understand how the subject being taught works.
8. Reinforce the theory and concepts taught by applying it during a hands-on lecture using drones.
9. Encourage cooperative learning and open discussions among students.
10. Assess students' learning experience by challenging them to apply the knowledge learned in hands-on exercises.

5   Introduction to Drones - Course Curriculum

In this section, we present a 5-session intensive course designed to introduce new students to drone technologies and motivate them to pursue further education in the STEM field. A summary of our proposed curriculum can be seen in Table 1. As this is a relatively short course, totaling 15 hours, the amount of knowledge that can be taught is limited. Therefore, our goal is to spark students' interest in the field and provide a solid foundation that will allow them to further study drone technologies in the future. Nonetheless, by the end of this course, students were able to not only pilot a drone but also to understand the underlying fundamentals of the technology. Students will be familiar with the types and characteristics of drones, legislation, identification of parts and assembly of a multi-rotor drone, the basics of programming autonomous drones, as well as discuss applications and careers related to drones. We tested this curriculum with a class of 15 middle-school students and another class of 15 high-school students. From our observations, students were highly engaged throughout the course and successfully learned the fundamentals of drones, further results are presented in Sect. 5.2.

Table 1. Curriculum designed to introduce students to drone technologies and STEM.

	Goal
Session 1	• Spark interest • Introduce drone concepts • Introduce drone hardware
Session 2	• Encourage and teach legal and safe use of drones • Drone design and implementation
Session 3	• Overview of drone applications and careers • Introduction to drone piloting
Session 4	• Provide an overview of the future of drones • Introduction to drone programming
Session 5	• Course recap • Assess knowledge through a mini-hackathon challenge

This course can be used by both middle and high school teachers as a fast and relatively low-cost approach to inspire students to study STEM. We recommend this course to be lectured over a short period of time. For instance, this course can be taught during a week summer-camp, or over a period of two weeks during the school year (after-school or weekend programs). The curriculum consists of 5 sessions, each lasting 3 h. Each session is divided into first a class theory portion (approximately 1 h) followed by a hands-on portion (approximately 2 h). During the hands-on section, the course is taught either in a lab environment (when building or programming drones) or in a flying area (e.g. basketball course, football field).

As drone technologies rapidly evolve over time, a paper covering the current body of knowledge can become obsolete in a short period of time. Additionally, drone laws and regulations are highly dependent on the localization where the course is taught, as cities, states and countries legislate drones differently. Therefore, in this curriculum, we focus on providing a framework containing the high-level concepts that should be taught to students instead of the specific content. We provide a path-road for teachers to follow, but, they should be up-to-date with drone technologies and knowledgeable on the specifics covered during the course. Additionally, our curriculum can serve as a starting point for teachers, as they can tailor it to better fulfill their specific requirements and resources (i.e. financial, time, space). A detailed description of the content and material for each day are further discussed on the subsections below.

5.1 Curriculum

Session 1. The first session is designed to spark students' interest in drones, and introduce them to the field. During the first hour, the teacher provides a theory lecture covering the following topics:

- Drone terminology
- Drone use-cases and applications
- Benefits and limitations of drones
- Categories based on their implementation (e.g. fixed-wing vs multi-rotor)
- Categories based on autonomy (e.g. manual control vs. fully autonomous)

The following 2 h are dedicated to teaching the functionality of each hardware component, and how to assemble a multi-rotor drone. To do this, the class assembles a single multi-rotor drone while learning about its hardware. The teacher explains the purpose of each hardware component and how it should be connected, including the flight controller (FC), electronic speed controller (ESC), motor, propeller, battery, radio receiver, flight sensors (GPS, accelerate, gyroscope), and frame. As each component is explained, a student is asked to assemble that specific hardware in the aircraft under the teachers' supervision. We recommend the drone to be at least a 450 mm size drone for visibility purposes. The drone built during this session can be seen in Fig. 1. Additionally, due to time constraints, parts that require soldering should be prepared before the class (e.g. make use of bullet connectors). However, one device (e.g. a single motor) can be soldered during the class to teach students the process of soldering electronics. At the end of the session, a flying demonstration should be conducted as it can further raise students' interest in the following session. During this demonstration, the teacher can fly the drone built during the class to create excitement among students, as they watch the drone they helped build now fly.

Session 2. The second day has two main goals: (1) teach safety and legislation related to drones, and (2) provide a deeper understanding of drones' hardware and implementation by allowing students to build a drone. Safety discussion should include topics such as accident hazards due to fast-spinning propellers, fire hazards related to the use of lithium-polymer batteries, and crashes against property, individuals and manned aircraft. Additionally, the teacher should present the drone legislation accordingly to the country where the course is being taught. For instance, in the USA (where we first tested this curriculum) drones that weight 250 g or more are required to be registered with the Federal Aviation Administration (FAA). Following, students should be divided into groups, and each is handled parts to build their multi-rotor drone, in contrast to the first day where a single drone was built by the whole class. Small groups of 2 to 3 students are preferred so that every student has the opportunity to have hands-on experience in assembling the drone. This step builds upon the knowledge acquired during the first day. We recommend that students build a micro racing drone, such as the one displayed in Fig. 2.

Fig. 1. Drone built during session 1.

Fig. 2. Drone built during session 2.

Session 3. During the third session, we further discuss real-world applications where drones are currently employed. Furthermore, we present students' possible career paths involving drones, both in the development (e.g. engineering) and application (e.g. cinematography pilot) realms. Following, we teach students how to fly and safely operate drones and allowed them to get hands-on experience in flying. They first piloted a Ryze Tello drone (displayed in Fig. 3, which is an easy-to-fly drone indicated for beginners. Following, each student controlled the micro-racing drone they built during session 2.

Session 4. The fourth session is designed to teach students (1) future of drones, (2) an overview on how to further pursue an education related to drones, and (3) an introduction to drone programming. We provided insights on the future of drones by discussing state-of-the-art research in the field, as well as future use cases. For instance, we discussed novelty control modalities and conducted a demonstration of brain-controlled drones using a brain-computer interface, where EEG brain signals from the user are used to control the drone in flight. We also recommend the use of videos to show scenarios of how drones may be used in the future, as they can be easier for students to understand. Also, we introduced students to universities' STEM degrees and how they relate to drones, providing insights for students that would like to pursue higher education in the field. Lastly, on this day we taught students basic software programming concepts and an introduction to drone programming. Students were divided into small groups (2 to 3 students) to learn how to program small tasks (e.g. take-off, fly forward, land). Each group received a Tello drone (displayed in Fig. 3 to test their code. We recommend the use of the Tello drone, or a similar low cost model that also provides software interfaces for different programming languages. For middle school students, we used block-based programming (e.g. Scratch), and for high-school students, we taught code-based programming (e.g. Python).

Session 5. In session 5, we provide a recap of the course, while answering the remaining questions that the students had about the content delivered. Following, we concluded the course by holding an autonomous drone programming challenge (similar to a hackathon). Students were divided into small groups once more, each group receiving a Tello drone to program. Additionally, each group received a list of 5 tasks they had to program the Tello drone to complete autonomously. The tasks were of increasing difficulty, each testing different concepts related to drones and programming:

- **Task 1** The drone should take of, fly around a square track, and land in the same position.
- **Task 2** The drone should take of, fly around a more complex race track, including curves, altitude changes, and going through gates. At the end of the lap the drone should land on the same spot.
- **Task 3** The drone should continuously fly laps around a race track shaped like a figure 8 (a loop must be used). Once the user presses a key the drone will land at the end of that lap.

– **Task 4** The drone should fly laps around a track shaped like a figure 8. At
the end of each lap, the software prompts the user if the drone should land,
continue flying, reverse direction.
– **Task 5** The drone should be fully controllable by pressing keyboard keys.
Including keys to: take-of, land, fly forward, left, right, back, rotate left, right,
increase and decrease altitude.

Fig. 3. Tello drone.

5.2 Course Results

We implemented the proposed curriculum during a Summer Camp at a middle
and a high school in Texas, USA with underrepresented students from low-
income families. From our observations, the camp was successful at both teaching
the fundamentals of drones and increasing students' interest in STEM education
and careers. For instance, at the beginning of the course, 5 out of 30 students
(across the two classes) raised their hands when asked if they were planning to
pursue a career with drones or STEM. In contrast, all 30 students raised their
hands when the same question was asked at the end of the summer camp. As the
majority of these students were from minority groups, this implies that drones
can be an effective tool to increase interest in STEM for groups that are currently
underrepresented. This curriculum can be used to increase diversity in computing
fields. Additionally, students provided positive feedback about their experience.
Various students confirmed that the hands-on approach was successful in keeping
the lectures engaging, especially when building, programming, and flying drones.
Following are some quotes examples received at the end of the camp that support
the success of the curriculum:

- "It was fun and a great experience for me. I wish to continue using drones throughout my life."
- "I really enjoyed this class. I loved flying the drones, building them, and learning how to code. Everything we did this week was really informative and fun."
- "I really like all the hand on activities with the drones"
- "What I liked most is that we got to make a drone from scratch."
- "Building drones was so fun, after I finished it felt amazing. The programming was also really fun."
- "I really liked programming drones. I want to learn more about it."
- "One thing I liked the most was programming drones."
- "During the drone camp, my favorite thing was programming"
- "I liked programming the drone because you could experiment it in different ways."
- "I really like how the teacher interacted with us. He made everything fun and not boring. Flying drones was fun."
- "I liked flying the drones, it was really fun."

6   Conclusion

Integrating STEM into the curriculum for young students is of crucial importance. Nonetheless, there is a need to increase the extent in which STEM is present in current curriculum's, and a need for tools that aid educators in the classroom. We believe that drones can assist STEM teachers, and motivate students to further pursue STEM education. Drones are powerful teaching tools because (1) they embody a broad spectrum of STEM knowledge, and (2) they naturally spark students' interest. In this paper, we discussed how drones can be used for teaching STEM courses and broadening participating from underrepresented groups. We also provided a series of guidelines and considerations to help future teachers in integrating drones in their lectures. We provided a detailed description of a 15 h course (5 sessions) designed to introduce students to drone technologies and encourage them to pursue further education in STEM fields. We used this curriculum with two classes of middle and high school students (15 students in each). We found the curriculum to be easy to follow and effective in keeping students interested and engaged throughout the course. Additionally, the course increased students interest in pursuing an education and career with drones or STEM.

References

1. Alimisis, D.: Educational robotics: open questions and new challenges. Themes Sci. Technol. Educ. **6**(1), 63–71 (2013)
2. Atmatzidou, S., Demetriadis, S.: Advancing students' computational thinking skills through educational robotics: a study on age and gender relevant differences. Robot. Auton. Syst. **75**, 661–670 (2016)

3. Bers, M., Seddighin, S., Sullivan, A.: Ready for robotics: bringing together the T and E of STEM in early childhood teacher education. J. Technol. Teach. Educ. **21**(3), 355–377 (2013)
4. Bragaw, D., Bragaw, K.A., Smith, E.: Back to the future: toward curriculum integration. Middle Sch. J. **27**(2), 39–46 (1995)
5. Brophy, S., Klein, S., Portsmore, M., Rogers, C.: Advancing engineering education in P-12 classrooms. J. Eng. Educ. **97**(3), 369–387 (2008)
6. Bybee, R.W.: Advancing STEM education: a 2020 vision. Technol. Eng. Teach. **70**(1), 30 (2010)
7. Bybee, R.W.: What is STEM education? (2010)
8. Carnahan, C., Crowley, K., Hummel, L., Sheehy, L.: New perspectives on education: drones in the classroom. In: Society for Information Technology & Teacher Education International Conference, pp. 1920–1924. Association for the Advancement of Computing in Education (AACE) (2016)
9. Chung, C.C., Cartwright, C., Cole, M.: Assessing the impact of an autonomous robotics competition for STEM education. J. STEM Educ. Innov. Res. **15**(2), 24 (2014)
10. Fredricks, J.A., Blumenfeld, P.C., Paris, A.H.: School engagement: potential of the concept, state of the evidence. Rev. Educ. Res. **74**(1), 59–109 (2004)
11. Grubbs, M.: Robotics intrigue middle school students and build STEM skills. Technol. Eng. Teach. **72**(6), 12 (2013)
12. Guthrie, J.T., Wigfield, A., VonSecker, C.: Effects of integrated instruction on motivation and strategy use in reading. J. Educ. Psychol. **92**(2), 331 (2000)
13. Han, J.H., Kim, D.H., Kim, J.W.: Physical learning activities with a teaching assistant robot in elementary school music class. In: 2009 Fifth International Joint Conference on INC, IMS and IDC, pp. 1406–1410. IEEE (2009)
14. Han, J., Kim, D.: R-learning services for elementary school students with a teaching assistant robot. In: 2009 4th ACM/IEEE International Conference on Human-Robot Interaction (HRI), pp. 255–256. IEEE (2009)
15. Jovanović, V.M., et al.: Exposing students to STEM careers through hands-on activities with drones and robots (2019)
16. Kanda, T., Hirano, T., Eaton, D., Ishiguro, H.: Interactive robots as social partners and peer tutors for children: a field trial. Hum.-Comput. Interact. **19**(1–2), 61–84 (2004)
17. Karim, M.E., Lemaignan, S., Mondada, F.: A review: can robots reshape K-12 STEM education? In: 2015 IEEE International Workshop on Advanced Robotics and its Social Impacts (ARSO), pp. 1–8. IEEE (2015)
18. Katehi, L., Pearson, G., Feder, M.: National academy of engineering and national research council report: engineering in K-12 education (2009)
19. Khan, M.J.: Impact of programming robots and drones on STEM attitudes (2017)
20. Klem, A.M., Connell, J.P.: Relationships matter: linking teacher support to student engagement and achievement. J. Sch. Health **74**(7), 262–273 (2004)
21. Leamnson, R.: Learning as biological brain change. Change Mag. High. Learn. **32**(6), 34–40 (2000)
22. Markert, L.R.: Gender related to success in science and technology. J. Technol. Stud. **22**(2), 21–29 (1996)
23. Mataric, M.J., Koenig, N.P., Feil-Seifer, D.: Materials for enabling hands-on robotics and STEM education. In: AAAI Spring Symposium: Semantic Scientific Knowledge Integration, pp. 99–102 (2007)
24. Morrison, J.: TIES STEM education monograph series, attributes of STEM education (2006)

25. Mubin, O., Stevens, C.J., Shahid, S., Al Mahmud, A., Dong, J.J.: A review of the applicability of robots in education. J. Technol. Educ. Learn. 1(209–0015), 13 (2013)
26. Papert, S.: Mindstorms: Children, Computers, and Powerful Ideas. Basic Books Inc., New York (1980)
27. Ricca, B., Lulis, E., Bade, D.: Lego Mindstorms and the growth of critical thinking. In: Intelligent Tutoring Systems Workshop on Teaching with Robots, Agents, and NLP. Citeseer (2006)
28. Robinson, M.: Robotics-driven activities: can they improve middle school science learning? Bull. Sci. Technol. Soc. 25(1), 73–84 (2005)
29. Stohlmann, M., Moore, T.J., Roehrig, G.H.: Considerations for teaching integrated STEM education. J. Pre-Coll. Eng. Educ. Res. (J-PEER) 2(1), 4 (2012)
30. Tezza, D., Andujar, M.: The state-of-the-art of human-drone interaction: a survey. IEEE Access 7, 167438–167454 (2019)
31. National Science Foundation (US): A national action plan for addressing the critical needs of the US science, technology, engineering, and mathematics education system. National Science Foundation (2007)
32. Wagner, S.P.: Robotics and children: science achievement and problem solving. J. Comput. Child. Educ. 9(2), 149–92 (1998)
33. Zemelman, S., Daniels, H., Hyde, A.A., Varner, W.: Best Practice: New Standards for Teaching and Learning in America's Schools. Heinemann Educational Publishers, Portsmouth (1998)

Using Arduino in Service Learning to Engage Pre-service STEM Teachers into Collaborative Learning

Yu-Liang Ting[1], Yu-Chen Lin[2], Shin-Ping Tsai[3(✉)], and Yaming Tai[4]

[1] Department of Technology Application and Human Resource Development,
National Taiwan Normal University, Taipei, Taiwan
[2] Department of Computer Science and Information Engineering,
National Taiwan Normal University, Taipei, Taiwan
[3] Department of Special Education, National Taipei University of Education,
Taipei, Taiwan
sptsai@tea.ntue.edu.tw
[4] Department of Children English Education,
National Taipei University of Education, Taipei, Taiwan

Abstract. Engineers must be able to collaborate with colleagues to successfully respond to the complex challenges in a contemporary workplace. The related training and research is limited, especially in curriculum design. Service learning integrates community service to provide students with field experiences, situating course concepts and objectives in the context of authentic situations and making links to their academic learning. In a teacher education program, service learning has the potential to help pre-service teachers realize the challenges that they are going to face, and aid them in becoming reflective practitioners. This issue is more challenging for STEM education, in which pre-service teachers are trained to teach students how to integrate Science, Technology, Engineering, and Mathematics knowledge and build up real-world problem-solving skills. This study adopted Arduino as a technology tool for pre-service teachers to create teaching artifacts for elementary school technology education. The participants of this study were fourteen pre-service teachers. To examine the learning benefits, this study adopted diary methods, participant interviews, documents such as photos of making Arduino-supported artifacts, an intrinsic motivation inventory and reflection worksheets. The results showed participants had gained better understanding of STEM and positive attitude toward the collaborative service learning. Participants appreciated the opportunity in gaining different views of what they had learned in classrooms and how a STEM curriculum could be implemented in an elementary school. The results supported the proposed use of Arduino in service learning for pre-service teachers in teaching children STEM knowledge. This study hopes to broaden the spectrum of service learning, STEM education, and teacher education.

Keywords: Service learning · STEM · Collaborative learning · Boundary object · Technology education

© Springer Nature Switzerland AG 2020
P. Zaphiris and A. Ioannou (Eds.): HCII 2020, LNCS 12206, pp. 544–559, 2020.
https://doi.org/10.1007/978-3-030-50506-6_37

1   Introduction

Engineers must be able to collaborate with colleagues to successfully respond to the complex challenges in a contemporary workplace. The related training and research on motivating and engaging engineering students in schools is limited, especially in the curriculum design [1]. In addition, service learning uses community service to provide students with field experiences, situating course concepts and objectives in the context of authentic situations and making links to their academic learning, so that both the students and the community can benefit [2]. A growing body of research indicates that when service learning is embedded in the context of learning and connected to a specific course, it can contribute positively to students' content knowledge and professional growth [3, 4] and help students improve self-efficacy and acquire the ability of critical thinking [4].

In teacher education programs, service learning requires pre-service teachers to apply their pedagogical content knowledge in real life contexts and put relevant theoretical concepts, pedagogical techniques, and methodology into practice. Service learning has the potential to help pre-service teachers realize the challenges of school work that they are going to face, and aids them in becoming reflective practitioners, problem solvers, and partners in the school/community collaborative relationships [4]. This issue is even more challenging for STEM education, in which pre-service teachers are trained to teach students how to integrate Science, Technology, Engineering, and Mathematics knowledge and build up real-world problem-solving skills.

This study adopted Arduino as a technology tool for pre-service teachers to create teaching artifacts for elementary school technology education. Arduino has features of a "low floor" (easy to get started) and a "high ceiling" (opportunities to create increasingly complex projects over time) [5–7]. Resnick *et al.* [7] proposed one additional feature of "wide walls", supporting different types of projects so users with different interests and backgrounds can all become engaged. From the aspect of STEM, Arduino supports a large number of science sensors, such as accelerometers and distance and light detectors. Arduino also supports actuators for the purpose of control. It allows students to perform multiple science measurements. Arduino is also programmable with mathematics equations based on science laws and performs engineering functions, for example, detecting the approaching of an object by calculating the distance and signaling the servo motor to rotate leverage. These technical features are asserted to supporting pre-service teachers' adoption and implementation of technology and engineering education activities in the community service. This study aimed to examine the pre-service STEM teachers' collaborative learning and reflection from the aspect of service learning.

2   Literature Review

Academic service learning as a credit-bearing educational activity in which students participate in an organized community service that meets identified community needs. That is, service learning combines service with community needs and academic applications. Hence service learning is a form of experiential learning that combines academic coursework with voluntary service in the community. Unlike extracurricular voluntary service, service learning is a course-based service experience that service activities are related to course materials through reflection activities such as self-directed writings, group discussions, and class presentations [8]. Service learning aims to benefit both students and the community they serve. The fundamental requirements of service learning include that the community service is connected with the academic coursework and through critical reflection students make the connections between their service experiences and the knowledge and skills acquired in the courses [9].

Through serve learning courses, students are trained to reflect on the service activity to gain further understanding of academic course content, appreciation of the discipline, and sense of social responsibility [8]. Service learning enhances students' academic growth as well as encourages community awareness and social action skill development [10, 11]. Service learning combines the cognitive with the affective aspects and contributes to students' personal development [9, 12, 13]. Service learning may help students gain personal confidence and increase social awareness [9, 14]. Service-learning is conducive to increasing students' self-esteem and personal confidence and developing their interpersonal skills and collaborative group work [9, 15].

Academic service learning is not the addition of a community service option to an academic course, but rather the integration of service with learning [16]. Rather than serving as a parallel activity, the community service activities in academic service learning function as a critical learning complement to the academic goals of the school courses [16]. The academic course objectives and the service learning must be aligned to benefit both the students and the community [17]. Eyler and Giles [18] recommend balanced programs with meaningful services coupled with learning goals and reflection. Student learning and community benefits should be simultaneous and reciprocally related; the service experiences inform and transform the academic learning, and the academic learning informs and transforms the service experience [16, 19]. Geleta and Gilliam [20] state that "a well-planned service learning project allows students to learn and develop through active participation in a carefully planned service that is specifically developed to meet and address real community needs" (p. 10).

From the aspect of teaching, service learning has been described in various terms as a pedagogy, a philosophy, a program and an experience [9, 21]. A typical service learning program includes classroom sessions to prepare and situate a service experience, participation in a service activity, and a reflection that links the field experience and the academic course content [17]. Howard [16] expressed that "academic service learning is a pedagogical model that intentionally integrates academic learning and relevant community service. Integrating service with academic learning, however, catalyzes a complexity to the teaching-learning process." Howard [16] further listed four features to clarify this definition, and they are: a *pedagogical model; intentional effort* made to bridge community service with academic learning; an *integration* of the experiential service learning and academic learning; and *relevance* of community service experiences to the academic course content of study [22]. All four components are necessary in the enactment of academic service learning.

There is a dearth of critical analysis of the service-learning, especial regarding 1) how intellectual and personal development may be facilitated through service-learning, and 2) the links between theory and practice, in which students can relate the academic part to their service learning experience that makes them learn [9].

2.1 Kolb's Learning Cycle and Reflective Learning

Service learning, as an experiential learning technique, provides an authentic platform for rich educational experiences that optimize the potential for transfer [17]. The purpose of service learning in this study is to encourage students to experience engineering with hands-on activities as a practical application of mathematics and science knowledge. The required hand-on activities and exercises of knowledge and skills are designed to be aligned with the Kolb's [23] experiential learning cycle (Fig. 1). The experiential learning cycle guides the development of service learning activities (creation or tinkering with engineering artifacts) that integrate different phases and allow for a fluent transition among different types of learning activities. In Kolb's learning cycles, there are four phases: concrete experience, reflection, abstract conceptualization, and active experimentation. When students work on a hand-on activity in service learning, they first establish the observational experience in the physical world. While the students move to the phase of reflection, they deliberate their thinking about a learning experience and integrate their knowledge. Through reflective thinking, students conceptualize phenomenological experience and construct the knowledge. In the abstract conceptualization stage, learners use their practice, observation and reflection to link practice to theory and conceptualize what they have learned from a new aspect. If the tentative resulting experience and conclusion do not fit the conceptualizations, students are adapted and tested with new conceptions [24]. In the fourth phase, active experimentation, students actively construct their conceptual schemes and revise them with more experiences to renew the knowledge with fidelity. Finally, students can apply their newly acquired knowledge in the service learning again.

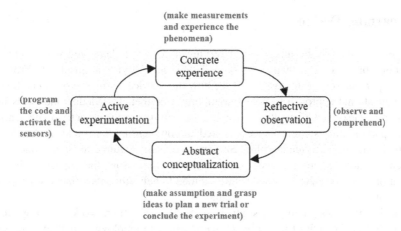

Fig. 1. Modified Kolb's experiential learning model for the hands-on work [28]

Kolb argued that learning from experience is an appropriate way to acquire knowledge: *"Learning is the process whereby knowledge is created through the transformation of experience"* [24, 25]. His experiential learning cycle illustrates how learners construct and refine their knowledge through experimentation, development of STEM teaching artifacts for the community service. After having a concrete experience, one can reflect on observations, conceptualize abstractly how it might work, and test these newly formed concepts through active experimentation. The proposed task of service learning is to tackle one general concern about hands-on activities, in which students do not learn how the knowledge, both previously acquired in classroom and to-be-learned in service learning, can be applied and delivered in service learning [26, 27].

In Kolb's [23] experiential learning cycle, reflection is deliberate thinking about a learning experience and help integrate knowledge [29]. Reflective learning is an important element emerging from the process of service learning. However, students often have difficulty engaging in reflective thinking and fail to reflect thoughtfully on what they did or learned and how they can improve [30]. It is important to provide reflection support through the process of service learning to help students see what they should reflect on and articulate throughout their hands-on work in preparing and carrying out the community service. It allows students to make connections between theory and practice and allows them to apply the theories and principles learned in a classroom elsewhere. Boyd and Fales [31] describe reflective learning as "the process of internally examining and exploring an issue of concern, triggered by an experience, which creates and clarifies meaning in terms of self, and which results in a changed conceptual perspective." Boyd and Fales [31] suggest that this process is central to understanding the service learning, an experiential learning process. Reflective learning may facilitate personal change and development expected in service learning, and may include guided discussion and reflective writing.

3 Learning Design

College students may be interested in serving minority students and witnessing how their contributions help them gain knowledge on a joyful atmosphere. From the teaching perspective, professors could see how this service learning project can be used as an educational approach to help students practice their knowledge and skills in an authentic context and view their own learning from a new aspect. In the learning design, participating students were required to complete midterm and final reflection reports during their service learning. Students were also required to fill out one survey of their attitude toward the proposed service learning from the aspect of intrinsic motivation. The worksheets and inventory aimed to help students reflect on the service learning in a structured and critical manner.

The learning design in this study is referred to the frameworks of constructing socio-technical creativity to aid pre-service teachers in employing their existing engineering knowledge to collaboratively develop and practice STEM curriculum. The educational artifacts created by Arduino serve as the role of a boundary object in

Fig. 2. Process of developing Arduino-supported STEM learning tools by pre-service teachers (top: assembling the wood plates; middle: programming Arduino; bottom: trying out the tool with kids)

collaborative learning for the STEM pre-service teachers to express, communicate, and coordinate their perspectives, knowledge and practice [1].

Fig. 3. Pre-service teachers collaboratively instructed students to play the game in the school carnival

Tai and Ting [1] commented that "*Social creativity in collaborative activities means that people have unique ideas or apply existing ideas to new contexts. Moreover, these ideas must be expressed to enable evaluations wherein other people from different perspectives can understand, reflect, and improve [32, 33]. In an engineering course, sharing creative ideas requires appropriate socio-technical settings fostering a shared understanding and help group members use others' knowledge or imagination [32, 34]. For supporting social creativity, the so-called boundary object [35] helps participants externalize tacit knowledge and promote distributed cognition [32]. Boundary objects communicate and coordinate the perspectives of various constituencies; each constituency has only partial knowledge and partial control over the interpretation of the object [32, 36, 37]. Thus, collaborators are grouped around an object with different meanings for each participant but sufficient shared understanding to proceed. In school the boundary objects could be designed and created by students to help them externalize their creativity and intuition, and the boundary object should (1) cause students to move from a vague mental conceptualization of an idea to a more concrete representation of it; (2) create situational balk-talk and make thoughts and intentions more accessible for students to reflect on; (3) be a record of students' mental efforts, one that is external rather than in memory; (4) provide a means for students to interact with, react to, negotiate around, and build upon an idea; and (5) contribute to a common language of understanding among participants in a cross-disciplinary collaboration [32].*"

Figure 2 illustrates the process of students' assembling the wood plates; programming Arduino; and trying out the tool with kids, and demonstrated a process of participants' collaborative work in creating the Arduino-technology artifacts. It is believed that the artifacts not only helped participants co-work in a step-by-step manner but also enabled them to collaboratively discuss how to realize the goals of community service.

Figure 3 shows how the participating pre-service teachers collaboratively instructed elementary school students to operate the Arduino-supported robotics arm to pick up the wooden ring in the school carnival.

4 Method

The participants of this study were fourteen pre-service teachers, who had learned Arduino in prior university courses. Participants formed into five groups on their own. Each group needed to use Arduino to create STEM learning for elementary 5th and 6th graders for a half-day school carnival. The entire design of service learning was original and different from traditional classroom teaching so there is little value to carry out a comparative study of learning outcomes [38]. In fact, the current objective for K12 STEM education is not to assess students' learning performance gains, nor to compare the proposed learning and science or mathematics learning, but rather to promote the learning of STEM and build up learners' positive attitude toward STEM. On the other hand, for pre-service teacher training the goal is to explore and document the process of developing pre-service teachers' collaborative and reflective learning in technology teacher education. Nonetheless a more in depth question in this study aimed to develop a better understanding of the process each participant went through. Hence, instead of assessing how students learned through the proposed activity, the evaluation focused on examining their responses toward this type of learning, and more importantly, their perception and reflection on the combination of service learning with their academic subject content.

Multiple methods and data sources [39] were used to produce more reliable evidence for identifying the assumed learning benefits in this study. This study adopted diary methods, thematic participants' interviews, documents such as photos of making Arduino-supported artifacts and school carnival, an intrinsic motivation inventory and reflection worksheets. The intrinsic motivation inventory (IMI) assessed participants' interest/enjoyment, perceived competence, effort/importance, and value/usefulness [40]. The reflection worksheets were created to aid students reflect on their collaborative work, which included three dimensions of content, inspiration, and new perspective of learning. The questions included the work they were responsible for, the inspiration brought to them, the new perspective of university education, and how it may affect their further learning.

4.1 The Questions in the Mid-term Reflection Worksheet

1. Service content: What are the work contents you participated in during the implementation of the service? Please describe and classify them one by one.
2. Learning inspiration: What references do you see and hear during the service process? Do they give you any inspiration toward, for example, schoolwork, attitudes on life, outlook on life, or future employment?
3. New direction of learning: What is the experience of service learning that gives you a new perspective on university education? How will it affect your future learning?

4.2 The Questions in the Semester-End Reflection Report

1. What is your overall opinion or feeling about this service learning study?

2. What do you think can be improved for this service learning? (For example, the combination and application of the activity content with the previously learned professional knowledge)
3. What do you think of college students can relate the schoolwork to service learning and relevant regulations and methods?
4. After this course, what learning outcomes did you achieve in terms of general competence? (For example, improvement of communication skills, understanding of the connotation of services, establishment of a correct service concept, improvement of service skills, etc. Please provide examples.)
5. What learning outcomes did you gain in terms of professional competence through this course? (For example, the use of electronic circuit knowledge or computer multimedia technology for teaching aid production, event design and explanation, etc. Please provide examples.)

4.3   The Intrinsic Motivation Inventory (IMI)

The evaluation surveyed whether the proposed learning makes students adopt a positive attitude toward service learning, and focused on examining students' perception of the proposed learning practice in terms of their intrinsic motivation, including the four dimensions of interest/enjoyment, perceived competence, effort/importance, and value/usefulness [40, 41]. The original inventory has twenty-five items from the seven-point Likert scale [40] and revised as three items for each dimension with a total of 12 items. The intrinsic motivation inventory (IMI) was held in a pre- and post-survey format to gauge the difference of students' general responses and this proposed learning. Items in the intrinsic motivation inventory (IMI) refer to Table 1.

Table 1. Summary of pre-service students' intrinsic motivation toward using Arduino in service learning (N = 14)

	Mean (SD)	Strongly disagree	Disagree	Slightly disagree	Neutral	Slightly agree	Agree	Strongly agree
Interest/enjoyment								
1. I enjoyed doing this scientific activity very much	6.36 (0.60)	0%	0%	0%	0%	7.14%	50%	42.86%
2. This scientific activity was fun to do	6.29 (0.85)	0%	0%	0%	7.14%	7.14%	35.71%	50%
3. While I was doing this scientific activity, I was thinking about how	6.07 (1.03)	0%	0%	0%	7.14%	28.57%	14.29%	50%

(*continued*)

Table 1. (*continued*)

	Mean (SD)	Strongly disagree	Disagree	Slightly disagree	Neutral	Slightly agree	Agree	Strongly agree
much I enjoyed it								
Perceived competence								
4. I think I am pretty good at this scientific activity	5.93 (0.88)	0%	0%	0%	7.14%	21.43%	42.86%	28.57%
5. I think I did pretty well at this scientific activity, compared to other students	6.00 (1.13)	0%	0%	7.14%	7.14%	0%	50%	35.71%
6. I was pretty skilled at this scientific activity	5.86 (1.06)	0%	0%	0%	14.29%	21.43%	28.57%	35.71%
Effort/importance								
7. I tried very hard to do well at this scientific activity	6.21 (1.08)	0%	0%	0%	14.29%	7.14%	21.43%	57.14%
8. I put a lot of effort into this scientific activity	6.07 (1.16)	0%	0%	7.14%	7.14%	0%	42.86%	42.86%
9. It was important to me to do well at this scientific activity	6.29 (0.88)	0%	0%	0%	0%	28.57%	14.29%	57.14%

(*continued*)

Table 1. (*continued*)

	Mean (SD)	Strongly disagree	Disagree	Slightly disagree	Neutral	Slightly agree	Agree	Strongly agree
Value/usefulness								
10. I believe this scientific activity could be of value to me	6.43 (0.90)	0%	0%	0%	7.14%	7.14%	21.43%	64.29%
11. I believe doing this scientific activity could be beneficial to me	6.36 (0.90)	0%	0%	0%	7.14%	7.14%	28.57%	57.14%
12. I think this is an important scientific activity	6.43 (0.82)	0%	0%	0%	0%	21.43%	14.29%	64.29%
Total score	**6.19 (0.94)**							

5 Results and Discussions

In this study, participants used the technology tools to facilitate their collaborative work. Especially, the use of internet tools in service learning had been evident in that students adopted communication tools, for example, one student commented that "I notified the course information in the LINE group (an instant message mobile internet tool), and passed my materials to peers through Gmail, as real-time communication." Regarding how to improve the service learning, some participants showed their worries about elementary school students' difficulties to absorb the knowledge and started to think about how to design and teach in the most appropriate way and how to guide elementary school students in an easy-to-understand way. In addition, some participants also commented about ideas for the design of the activity and teaching aids, including the conversion of single-person operation to peers and parent-child interactions. In this service activity, participating pre-service teachers were concerned about the instruction, especial about "how to teach", and also were inspired by the design of teaching materials and activities. During experiential learning, reflection and thinking are critical. The results showed that participating pre-service teachers could think about how to meet the needs of primary school students. This also indicated the beginning of students' cognitive act in linking theory with practice.

One participating pre-service teachers commented that "Even though it is so hard and tiring in the teaching process, I found that the children can learn happily and operate the teaching aids we made, and then I realized the real purpose of service learning." This implied that an engaging service learning project has been created and participants were willing to work hard and devoted into the community service. Moreover, one student reported that "In this service process, experiential learning is used, which is a learning method through practice, including participating in activities to gain experiences and emotions, and then reflecting on them. The main features are "input experience", "experience with a unique personal meaning", etc. In the practice of the activity, each student creates a unique meaning, and obtains emotions, experiences and sense of accomplishment to understand the requirements of the "service learning" activity formulated by the university and the real intention conveyed accordingly." This comment was made by one of the group leaders in this course, and seemed to indicate that he can reflect on what he has done and express what the service learning intended to deliver. This indicates that the proposed service learning is able to fulfill the preliminary requirement expected by the research community.

Regarding the mapping between academic courses and service learning, one student commented that "The courses "Electronic Circuits", "Basic Design" and "Computer Image Processing" provided in the first year of the academic department had helped me achieve great effectiveness in this community service activity. Thus, it is recommended to plan the service learning activities in the second or third year of study in the future, and even carry out these activities as a course. It is also suggested to plan two courses to jointly organize activities, courses, etc., to help students of science and technology departments think and work across different disciplinary fields. This is advocated by STEM education, encouraging students to think about the four different areas with different ideas. Moreover, results of reflection sheets indicated that participants appreciated the opportunity in gaining different views of how a STEM curriculum could be implemented in an elementary school. One participant mentioned that he had gained better understanding of STEM when he was required to integrate pedagogy with content knowledge of Arduino and science and mathematics to teach children about STEM. Photos of the school carnival showed teachers' and children's engagement in carrying out the service learning and engaging in the educational activities respectively. The results supported the proposed use of Arduino as a boundary object in service learning to help pre-service teachers teach kids for STEM education. These comments also indicated that students could apply the knowledge and skills acquired in school and exercise them in the service learning, which supports the assertion that the proposed learning fulfilled the goal of service learning in helping pre-service teachers link theory with practice and have a new aspect of what they have learned.

An intrinsic motivation inventory (IMI) assessing pre-service teachers' perceptions on using Arduino in service learning was implemented after the learning activities. The IMI includes four components, including Interest/Enjoyment, Perceived Competence, Effort/Importance, and Value/Usefulness. There are three items in each component resulting in a total of 12 items. For each of the 12 items in the IMI, the score ranges from 1 to 7 (1 = strongly disagree; 2 = disagree; 3 = slightly disagree; 4 = neutral; 5 = slightly agree; 6 = agree; 7 = strongly agree). Table 1 presents the percentage of each score, mean, and standard deviation for each item.

An examination of the percentages of each score showed that for the items in the four components of Interest/Enjoyment (Items 1–3), Perceived Competence (Items 4-

6), Effort/Importance (Items 7–9), and Value/Usefulness (Items 10–12), 85.71%–100% of the participants' responses fell into the "slightly agree," "agree" and "strongly agree" categories (equal or above 5). The components with the highest percentages of participants who showed agreement were Interest/Enjoyment ($M = 95.24\%$) and Value/Usefulness ($M = 95.24\%$), while the component with the lowest percentage was the Perceived Competence ($M = 88.09\%$).

The mean score across the 12 items in the survey was 6.19 ($SD = 0.94$), which indicated that pre-service teachers positively agreed that using Arduino in service learning made them maintain a high level of motivation. When breaking down the scale into the four components, the mean scores were 6.07–6.36 ($SD = 0.60$–1.03) for Interest/Enjoyment, 5.86–6.0 ($SD = 0.88$–1.13) for Perceived Competence, 6.07–6.29 ($SD = 0.88$–1.16) for Effort/Importance, and 6.36–6.43 ($SD = 0.82$–0.90) for Value/Usefulness. Among the 12 items, Items 1, 2, 7, 9, 10, 11, and 12 had an average score above the grand mean ($M = 6.19$), indicating that pre-service teachers showed higher agreement on the "I enjoyed doing this learning activity very much ($M = 6.36$)", "the learning activity was fun to do ($M = 6.29$)", "I tried very hard to do well at this learning activity ($M = 6.21$)", "it was important to me to do well at this scientific activities ($M = 6.29$)", "I believe this learning activity could be of value to me ($M = 6.43$)", "I believe doing this learning activity could be beneficial to me ($M = 6.36$)", and "I think this is an important learning activity ($M = 6.43$)."

In summary, the results above indicated that after the service learning, pre-service teachers showed strong interest and enjoyment in applying Arduino in service learning, perceived relatively competent at this activity, thought this activity was important to them, and strongly believed this activity was valuable and useful.

These results revealed that participants felt competent in their service learning and gave them a more assured sense of confidence. They can see the linkage of knowledge with the practice in the community service and value what they have learned in classroom. Many aspects of positive learning benefits were evident and echoed Deeley [9] in that service learning constitutes a variety of components contributing to effective learning. It is acknowledged by participants that the success of service learning depends on how it was held and the context of practices. In this study, critical reflection served to not only aid participants to enhance intellectual development, but also contribute to personal growth. Moreover, small-group work and Arduino tools seemed to encourage participants to engage intellectually with the community service. Within these groups, participants also gained emotional support from each other as evident from the response and activity photos. The results supported the proposed use of Arduino as a boundary object in a service learning to make pre-service teachers teach kids for STEM education. It hopes to not only broaden the spectrum of service learning, STEM education, and teacher education, but also positively affect students intellectually and emotionally, to the extent of transformation. As Mezirow [42] claims, 'there is no higher priority for adult education than to develop its potentialities for **perspective transformation,** or **'transformative pedagogy'** [43]. From the aspect of learning transfer, the proposed service learning intentionally leverages experiential learning techniques for transfer, for example, "engaging students in deep, active learning activities; providing time for reflection; allowing for instructor feedback and role modeling; including a highlight or culminating event; and using real-world, contextualized problems to simulate, establish, or enhance relevancy [17]." However, "There is little agreement in the scholarly community about the nature of transfer, the extent to which it occurs, and the nature of its underlying mechanisms" [17] (p. 612). Nonetheless, if deeper and more conceptual learning forms the foundation of transferable learning, then experiential learning techniques are well situated to increase transfer [17]. These techniques provide an authentic platform for rich educational experiences that optimize the potential for transfer [17]. As to this study, it is the service learning fitting well with the needs of adult learners and the educational content into an immediately relevant context.

6 Conclusions and the Further Study

Howard [16] describes the service learning with an overarching goal of leading the relationship between students' school learning and their social responsibility. That is, "it is absolutely necessary to deprogram or desocialize students and instructors away from traditional classroom roles, relationships, and norms, and then resocialize them around a new set of classroom behaviors." He further commented that "To accomplish the desocialization and resocialization processes requires that the instructor and the students *travel together* on a journey to remake the classroom." These comments echo the purpose of this study in using Arduino technology tools to support pre-service teachers' collaborative work of service learning and transform their academic learning.

The learning benefits of this proposed service learning have been evidenced by the multiple source data. Although the sample of pre-service teachers was too small for this element of quantitative data to be significant, it offered valuable insight into some of the effects of the course. As the sample size was small, the findings may not necessarily be generalizable. In addition, there was a risk that the findings and their interpretation could be biased because the author was also the instructor of the service learning. A halo or Hawthorn effect [44] may be induced, whereby enthusiasm may have impacted on the effects of the proposed practice. Further qualitative research would be beneficial to good practice in the pedagogy of service-learning.

References

1. Tai, Y., Ting, Y.-L.: English-learning mobile app designing for engineering students' cross-disciplinary learning and collaboration: a sample practice and preliminary evaluation. Australas. J. Educ. Technol. **36**(2), 120–136 (2020). https://doi.org/10.14742/ajet.4999
2. Ryan, L.B., Callahan, J.: Making connections: service-learning competencies and beginning teacher standards. Teach. Educ. **38**(2), 126–140 (2002). https://doi.org/10.1080/08878732029555312
3. Conrad, D., Hedin, D.: School-based community service: What we know from research and theory. Phi Delta Kappan **72**(10), 743–749 (1991)
4. Bernadowski, C., Perry, R., Del Greco, R.: Improving preservice teachers' self-efficacy through service learning: lessons learned. Int. J. Instr. **6**(2), 67–86 (2013)

5. Lye, S.Y., Koh, J.H.L.: Review on teaching and learning of computational thinking through programming: what is next for K-12? Comput. Hum. Behav. **41**, 51–61 (2014). https://doi.org/10.1016/j.chb.2014.09.012

6. Papert, S.: Mindstorms: Children, Computers, and Powerful Ideas. Basic Books, New York (1980)

7. Resnick, M., et al.: Scratch: programming for all. Commun. ACM **52**, 60–67 (2009). https://doi.org/10.1145/1592761.1592779

8. Bringle, R.G., Hatcher, J.A.: Implementing service learning in higher education. J. High. Educ. **67**(2), 221–239 (1996)

9. Deeley, S.J.: Service-learning: thinking outside the box. Act. Learn. High Educ. **11**(1), 43–53 (2010). https://doi.org/10.1177/1469787409355870

10. Moore, K.P., Sandholtz, J.H.: Designing successful service learning projects for urban schools. Urban Educ. **34**(4) (1999). https://doi.org/10.1177/0042085999344004

11. Stenhouse, V.L., Jarrett, O.S.: In the service of learning and activism: service learning, critical pedagogy, and the problem solution project. Teach. Educ. Q. **39**(1), 51–76 (2012)

12. Butin, D.W.: Preface: disturbing normalizations of service-learning. In: Butin, D.W. (ed.) Service-Learning in Higher Education: Critical Issues and Directions, pp. vii–xx. Palgrave Macmillan, Basingstoke (2005)

13. Kearney, K.R.: Students' self-assessment of learning through service-learning. Am. J. Pharm. Educ. **68**(1), 1–13 (2004)

14. Batchelder, T.H., Root, S.: Effects of an undergraduate program to integrate academic learning and service: cognitive, prosocial cognitive, and identity outcomes. J. Adolesc. **17**(4), 341–355 (1994). https://doi.org/10.1006/jado.1994.1031

15. Lisman, C.D.: Toward a Civil Society. Bergin & Garvey, Westport (1998)

16. Howard, J.P.: Academic service learning: a counternormative pedagogy. New Dir. Teach. Learn. **73**, 21–29 (1998)

17. Furman, N., Sibthorp, J.: Leveraging experiential learning techniques for transfer. New Dir. Adult Continuing Educ. **2013**(137), 17–26 (2013). https://doi.org/10.1002/ace.20041

18. Eyler, J., Giles Jr., D.E.: Where's the Learning in Service Learning?. Jossey-Bass, San Francisco (1999)

19. Honnet, E.P., Poulsen, S.J.: Principles of good practice in combining service and learning. Wingspread special report. The Johnson Foundation, Racine (1989)

20. Geleta, N.E., Gilliam, J.: An introduction to service-learning. In: Teacher Education Consortium in Service-Learning, Learning to Serve, Serving to Learn: A View from Higher Education, pp. 10–13. Salisbury University, Salisbury (2003)

21. Kenworthy-U'Ren, A.: Service-learning and negotiation: engaging students in real-world projects that make a difference. Negot. J. **19**(1), 51–63 (2003). https://doi.org/10.1111/j.1571-9979.2003.tb00279.x

22. Howard, J.: Community service learning in the curriculum. In: Howard, J. (ed.) Praxis I: A Faculty Casebook on Community Service Learning. OCSL Press, Ann Arbor (1993)

23. Kolb, D.: Experiential Learning: Experience as the Source of Learning and Development. Prentice-Hall, Upper Saddle River (1984)

24. Conradi, B., Lerch, V., Hommer, M., Kowalski, R., Vletsou, I., Hussmann, H.: Flow of electrons: an augmented workspace for learning physical computing experientially. In: Proceedings of the ACM International Conference on Interactive Tabletops and Surfaces, pp. 182–191. ACM, New York (2011)

25. Kolb, D., Boyatzis, R.E., Mainemelis, C.: Experiential learning theory: previous research and new directions. In: Sternberg, R.J., Zhang, L.F. (eds.) Perspectives on Cognitive, Learning, and Thinking Styles, pp. 227–247. Lawrence Erlbaum (2000)

26. Apedoe, X.S., Reynolds, B., Ellefson, M.R., Schunn, C.D.: Bringing engineering design into high school science classrooms: the heating/cooling unit. J. Sci. Educ. Technol. **17**(5), 454–465 (2008). https://doi.org/10.1007/s10956-008-9114-6

27. Kirschner, P.A., Sweller, J., Clark, R.E.: Why minimal guidance during instruction does not work: an analysis of the failure of constructivist, discovery, problem-based, experiential, and inquiry-based teaching. Educ. Psychol. **41**(2), 75–86 (2006). https://doi.org/10.1207/s15326985ep4102_1

28. Ting, Y.L.: Engineering design explores STEM and hands-on education. T & D Fashion, National Civil Academy, no. 258 (2019)

29. Davis, E.A.: Prompting middle school science students for productive reflection: generic and directed prompts. J. Learn. Sci. **12**, 91–142 (2003). https://doi.org/10.1207/S15327809JLS1201_4

30. Woodward, H.: Reflective journals and portfolios: learning through assessment. Assess. Eval. High. Educ. **23**, 415–426 (1998). https://doi.org/10.1080/0260293980230408

31. Boyd, E.M., Fales, A.M.: Reflective learning: key to learning from experience. J. Humanistic Psychol. **23**(2), 99–117 (1983). https://doi.org/10.1177/0022167883232011

32. Fischer, G., Giaccardi, E., Eden, H., Sugimoto, M., Ye, Y.: Beyond binary choices: Integrating individual and social creativity. Int. J. Hum.-Comput. Stud. **63**(4), 482–512 (2005). https://doi.org/10.1016/j.ijhcs.2005.04.014

33. Harrington, D.: The ecology of human creativity: a psychological perspective. In: Runco, M. A., Albert, R.S. (eds.) Theories of Creativity, pp. 143–169. Sage, Riverside (1990)

34. Kim, H.J., Park, J.H., Yoo, S., Kim, H.: Fostering creativity in tablet-based interactive classrooms. Educ. Technol. Soc. **19**(3), 207–221 (2016)

35. Star, L.S., Griesemer, J.R.: Institutional ecology, "translations" and boundary objects: amateurs and professionals in Berkeley's Museum of Vertebrate Zoology, 1907–39. Soc. Stud. Sci. **19**(3), 387–420 (1989)

36. Arias, E., Fischer, G.: Boundary objects: their role in articulating the task at hand and making information relevant to it. In: International ICSC Symposium on Interactive & Collaborative Computing (ICC'2000), University of Wollongong, Australia, pp. 567–574. ICSC Academic Press, Wetaskiwin (2000)

37. Bowker, G.C., Star, S.L.: Sorting Things Out—Classification and Its Consequences. MIT Press, Cambridge (2000)

38. Sharples, M.: Methods for evaluating mobile learning. In: Vavoula, G.N., Pachler, N., Kukulska-Hulme, A. (eds.) Researching Mobile Learning: Frameworks Tools and Research Designs, pp. 17–39. Peter Lang, Pieterlen and Bern (2009)

39. Mathison, S.: Why triangulate? Educ. Res. **17**(2), 13–17 (1988). https://doi.org/10.3102/0013189X017002013

40. Bertacchini, F., Bilotta, E., Pantano, P., Tavernise, A.: Motivating the learning of science topics in secondary school: a constructivist edutainment setting for studying Chaos. Comput. Educ. **59**, 1377–1386 (2012). https://doi.org/10.1016/j.compedu.2012.05.001

41. Tseng, T.H., Tai, Y., Tsai, S.P., Ting, Y.L.: Students' self-authoring mobile App for integrative learning of STEM. Int. J. Electr. Eng. Educ. (2018). https://doi.org/10.1177/0020720918800438

42. Mezirow, J.: Perspective transformation. Adult Educ. **28**(2), 100–110 (1978)

43. Hooks, B.: Teaching to Transgress: Education as the Practice of Freedom. Routledge, London (1994)

44. Kember, D.: To control or not to control: the question of whether experimental designs are appropriate for evaluating teaching innovations in higher education. Assess. Eval. High. Educ. **28**(1), 89–101 (2003). https://doi.org/10.1080/02602930301684

Teaching STEM Competencies Through an Educational Mobile Robot

José Varela-Aldás[1]([⊠]) [iD], Jorge Buele[1] [iD], Janio Jadan-Guerrero[2] [iD],
and Víctor H. Andaluz[3] [iD]

[1] SISAu Research Group, Universidad Tecnológica Indoamérica,
180103 Ambato, Ecuador
{josevarela, jorgebuele}@uti.edu.ec
[2] Research Center of Mechatronics and Interactive Systems,
Universidad Tecnológica Indoamérica, 180103 Ambato, Ecuador
janiojadan@uti.edu.ec
[3] Departamento de Eléctrica y Electrónica, Universidad de las Fuerzas
Armadas – ESPE, 171103 Sangolquí, Ecuador
vhandaluz1@espe.edu.ec

Abstract. The STEM (Science-Technology-Engineering-Mathematics) competences have taken the classroom of new generations, due to the need to instill interest in technical sciences and promote the careers of the future. In underdeveloped countries, free access to technology is limited by the scarcity of economic resources, for this it is required low-cost tools that facilitate better multidisciplinary learning. This work presents the implementation of an educational mobile robot to teach STEM competencies; the physical structure has been designed using 3D modeling and printing in PLA. The electronic system presented in this work is based on the Arduino embedded card that connects distance, weight, temperature and color sensors, two DC motors, and an LCD screen. In addition, the mobile robot has Bluetooth communication to connect it to external devices. The interaction with the user (student) is done through a mobile application and an HMI that is displayed on a personal computer. The robot's features allow the measurement of physical variables, conversion of magnitudes, analysis of the operation of sensors and actuators, and the use of control interfaces. Experimental performance tests are carried out by individuals with an average age of 12 years (K-12), who are subjected to a learning test before and after applying this proposal. Finally, usability tests are carried out on teachers to validate the system developed.

Keywords: STEM competencies · Mobile robot · Sensors · App

1 Introduction

The constant development of technology has allowed a greater distribution of information, interconnection and unimaginable cultural and social progress [1, 2]. Notably in this century, science, technology, engineering, and mathematics are present in almost all aspects of people's lives, since their academic training [3, 4]. The impact produced by this accelerated technological innovation has led to social and economic changes

P. Zaphiris and A. Ioannou (Eds.): HCII 2020, LNCS 12206, pp. 560–573, 2020.
https://doi.org/10.1007/978-3-030-50506-6_38

[5]. In particular, the incursion in the field of process automation and robotics has caused certain trades to be replaced by machines, producing a "technological unemployment" [6]. With this, work done generationally by human beings could be replaced by automatons that incorporate artificial intelligence algorithms [7]. This encourages government institutions in developing countries to train engineers and scientists of the future and improve society's literacy in these fields. The application of new techniques to generate an education of excellence will improve the intellectual capital that interacts with smart cities, despite a marked social inequity and deep environmental problems. In this context, the STEMs are created, subjects for a prosperous economy and for a safe and healthy society [8, 9]. STEM education is an interdisciplinary approach to learning that removes the traditional barriers of these four disciplines and integrates them into the real world with rigorous and relevant experiences for students.

In developed countries, the vast majority of institutions focus on teaching "S" sciences and "M" math, paying very little attention to "T" technology that reflects the products and systems that most human beings need and less to the "E" engineering that reflects the design and innovation process of each system [8]. The integration of these 4 subjects is not achieved properly and the sciences and mathematics are still taught in an isolated and preponderant way to the remaining [10]. An appropriate definition is presented in [11], where it is described that STEM education contemplates the resolution of problems based on concepts and procedures of science and mathematics by incorporating work methodologies, in addition, engineering designs and the use of appropriate technology. In this way, STEM competences have become the center of global attention in the educational field, since having these skills is increasingly demanded in certain specific professions [12]. STEM education is considered of paramount importance in many nations, as it promotes innovation, productivity, and general economic growth. Addressing the range of possible directions that STEM education can take in primary-level educational institutions or suggesting new approaches is complicated and challenging, since the topics to be dealt with in the curriculum are broad [13].

Despite the promotion made by doctors, employers, politicians, and businessmen in the last decade, STEM education in the classroom is not adequate [14]. This has caused the students' interest in pursuing technical careers to decrease, resulting in a lack of well-trained engineers, technicians, and researchers. Although it is recommended to increase the presence of engineering in the elementary and secondary grades, assigning equal time to the other disciplines does not seem feasible in many already saturated curricula. However, given the significant contributions of design and engineering processes to society, this discipline visibly supports its importance within the curriculum; avoiding dulling its potential to enrich other disciplines and foster an early interest in learning STEM [15, 16]. Unlike engineering as a lagged member, technology is experiencing greater interest with the gradual implementation of new tools and computerized systems. With the growing popularity of basic programming in software developed for school environments and the expansion of associated computational thinking skills, the educational landscape is changing rapidly [17].

Emphasis should be placed on providing adequate training to teachers, as they are responsible for guiding the student in STEM education [18]. Teachers' professional development programs should provide learning opportunities for teachers themselves, to deepen their conceptual understanding and participation in scientific and/ or engineering practices. In addition, to appreciate science as a form of knowledge, in a community of knowledge builders and know how to interrelate it with other disciplines. Since, as is public knowledge, these are dictated separately or in blocks.

2 Related Works

It is often claimed that the dominant approaches to STEM education used in schools do not reflect the natural way in which disciplines are connected in the real world. School subjects tend to be taught in isolation, in a society where students must acquire knowledge and skills from multiple disciplines to provide solutions to political, economic, and social challenges. Although the views vary, the teaching should be inclusive as it is presented in [19], because it is a continuous and dynamic process, where the student represents the central axis. The real challenge for educators lies in how disciplines can be integrated effectively and at the same time guarantee the integrity of each one. The need to prepare students with 21st century skills through STEM-related teaching is growing, especially at the primary level, as described in [20]; this work theoretically justifies the implementation of workshops and robotics classes to increase mathematical literacy, scientific-technical information, and social skills. A survey is applied to teachers and future teachers, obtaining positive results that support this research; evidencing the need to introduce these activities at the primary level, to develop appropriate knowledge, skills and aptitudes for the current labor demand. Similarly, in the study of [21] issues related to STEM education are analyzed; this includes: previous experiences, research, publications and a review of examples of the implementation of robotics, programming and associated educational activities in primary school. There were 91 primary school teachers and future teachers from Poland and Ukraine, and a 15-question survey was conducted to validate the results, as part of the "Robotics and children" pedagogical research. The study was carried out to determine the needs of modern education, and to introduce the basic concepts of robotics in the elementary school educational process, hoping that in the coming years it can be carried out in secondary schools and VET (Vocational Education and Training).

Although the idea of using robotics elements in the learning process is no longer new and innovative, results can still be checked based on the implementation of new tools with higher performance. The application of activities and modules completely oriented to the teaching of robotics, guarantee a better cognitive development and increase motivation in the student, as shown in [22]. This study provides a research model and five tools (different questionnaires before and after research, applied to students and teachers) to evaluate the results of organized robotics activities outside the school day. This model was tested with students who run the risk of leaving school early and students participating in robotics activities to develop their computational thinking. One technique used for greater interaction between children and robotics is their participation in events such as the "FIRST® LEGO® League" championship and then spread their experiences [23]. This manuscript provides objective data obtained from the opinions of teachers and students who participated in this championship. A globalizing approach is applied to the different areas of the curriculum and the impact of STEM competencies in the secondary education learning process is analyzed. The execution of surveys allows us to conclude that both teachers and students agree that this type of event promotes interest and scientific curiosity, as well as social skills through teamwork.

As it has been shown both in theory and in practice, the implementation of teaching tools and modules that involve robotics, contribute positively to the student's learning process. In this context, this study presents a prototype educational mobile robot built with materials and low-cost devices that contribute to the teaching-learning process of STEM skills. To make a greater interaction with the robot, the user is allowed to observe the operation of sensors and actuators, to understand how physical magnitudes vary in the real world. Experimental tests with the assembled mobile robot and the results obtained from the learning and usability tests performed on users allow this proposal to be approved.

This document is divided into five sections, including the introduction in Sect. 1 and the related works in Sect. 2. Section 3 presents the materials and methods used and Sect. 4 describes the results obtained. Finally, discussions and conclusions are presented in Sect. 5.

3   Materials and Methods

The purpose of the educational robot is to provide the teacher with technological tools to instruct users (school students between 11 and 13 years old) in STEM competitions. For this, a mobile robot with several sensors and actuators is proposed that allow the analysis of physical variables, incorporating connectivity means that use known technological resources, and that allow interaction with the mobile robot. In addition, it is important to use low-cost devices that allow replicating the proposal with few resources in similar projects, using easily accessible equipment and with flexibility of use.

Figure 1 shows the components of the proposed robot, where the Arduino card is used as a system information processor. The system inputs are distance, weight, temperature, humidity, and color sensors to analyze physical measurements and states in the classroom, data that can be displayed on the liquid crystal display (LCD). Robot mobility is generated by two direct current motors arranged in the form of a unicycle mobile robot to control linear and angular movements. In addition, it has a Bluetooth module that allows the robot to be connected to an external device (computer or smartphone).

3.1   Hardware

The external structure of the mobile robot is carried out with an aesthetic and colorful criterion to capture the attention of students and of little weight to facilitate the manipulation of the prototype. In this way, all components are designed using computational assistance, as 3D solids. Figure 2 shows the robot made in AutoCAD; in the front part, the spaces to locate the distance sensor and the LCD are observed, in the

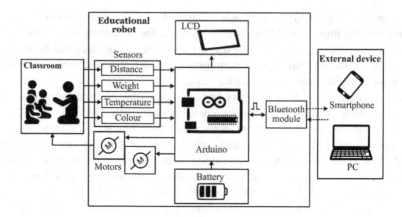

Fig. 1. General diagram of the educational mobile robot.

Fig. 2. 3D design of mobile robot.

upper part an area for the color sensor is established and a plate for the operation of the balance is mounted, in the rear part are the circuit and the temperature sensor, and at the bottom are the driving wheels and the crazy wheel. All these components are generated by 3D printing with polylactic acid (PLA).

Another physical subsystem of the mobile robot is the electronic circuit; this is developed using low-cost components. In Fig. 3 it can be seen the proposed circuit designed in the Fritzing software, where Arduino UNO is presented as the main control device, connected to several complementary elements. These are described below: a 9 V battery that provides the power for the operation of the sensors, actuators, controllers and LCD; two DC motors that operate with a TB6612NG driver that allows you to control the speed and direction of rotation; an LCD that has an I2C adapter that reduces connections to two communication cables. In addition, a 5Kgr load cell is placed that has an HX711 adapter and allows I2C communication; Color (TCS3200), distance (HC-SR04) and temperature (DHT) sensors use digital pins for reading data. The Bluetooth module connects to the serial communication pins of the Arduino.

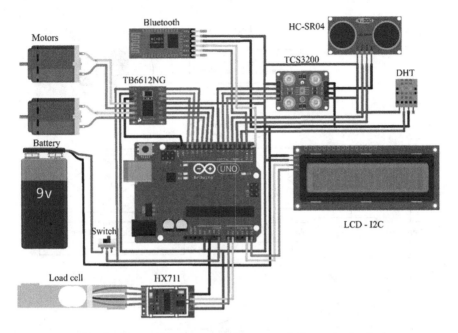

Fig. 3. Connection diagram of the proposed electronic circuit.

3.2   Software

As part of the software design a main program installed in the Arduino is developed, and two user interface applications for computer and mobile device respectively. Figure 4 shows the flow chart with which the main control program operates. In the first instance, all the input and output devices connected to the Arduino are configured and the operating mode is selected, which can be chosen from the phone or the computer. When choosing the sensor mode, the data of any of the sensors (distance, temperature, humidity, weight and color) can be displayed, this information is displayed on the LCD and sent via Bluetooth. In the case of choosing the movement mode, the prototype can be controlled by phone or computer. This cycle is repeated simultaneously the times that the user requires or otherwise the programming comes to an end.

The user interface of the phone is developed in App Inventor and is compatible with devices that have an Android operating system. Figure 5 shows the screens designed for the mobile application. The main window has the connection buttons of the device via Bluetooth (blue), of the sensors for reading data (red), and of the robot control (green). The sensor screens have illustrative images that present the data of the measured variables and the motion control interface allows to command the linear and angular displacements of the mobile robot.

The computer user interface is implemented in the MATLAB software, using the coding tools (*uicontrol*), the two windows for interaction with the robot are shown in Fig. 6. The start window allows wireless communication to start with the Bluetooth

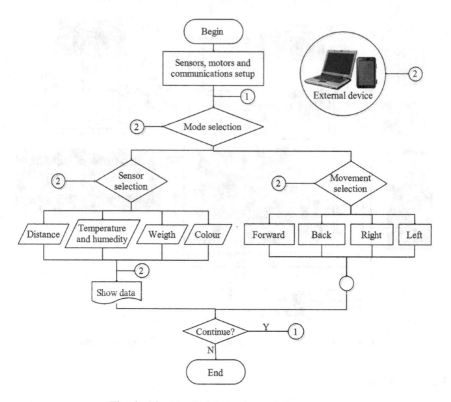

Fig. 4. Flowchart of the main control program.

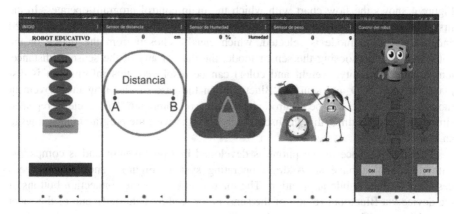

Fig. 5. Screens that make up the mobile user interface.

device selected. Next, the main window presents the data of all the sensors in the robot, including a box that shows the color measured by the TCS320 module, also has the buttons to control the movements of the mobile robot.

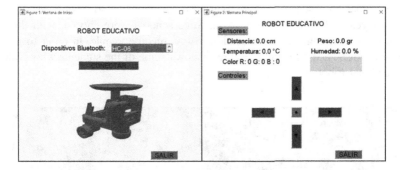

Fig. 6. Screens that make up the user interface for PC.

4 Experimental Results

The respective performance tests of the implemented system are performed, reviewing the correct functioning of all its elements. As can be seen in Fig. 7, the robot is in full operation, where all the components of the system work within the ranges established in its design and the external applications present a satisfactory communication.

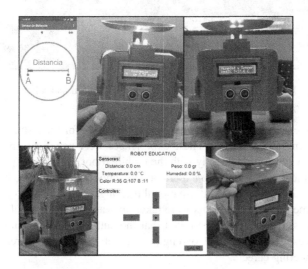

Fig. 7. Tests carried out with the educational mobile robot.

4.1 Participants

Two schools in Ambato (Ecuador), all non-private (state and free) participated in this study; where 45 students of eighth level of basic training, 24 boys and 21 girls, with an average age of 12 years (K-12) were selected. Considering that the participants' mother tongue is Spanish, all activities (orally and in writing) were based on that language.

Engineering design processes require long-term development, so it is necessary to start in the first years of secondary education. State schools were chosen, with the commitment to present engineering education to low-income people, in order to increase their interest in STEM education. Figure 8 shows some of the students who evaluated the educational robot.

Fig. 8. Participants interacting with the educational robot.

All schools expressed their enthusiasm and openness for their students to participate in new learning experiences. These experiences were new for some teachers and their students, by interacting directly with the mobile robot. 17 teachers participated (10 men and 7 women) with extensive experience in school education. Both teachers and students participated in eventual informational meetings, before and after the execution of each experiment. Your comments were taken into account, as part of the respective feedback process. It should also be noted that the authors of this document provided their experiences within the field of engineering in order to be a real example of pursuing engineering careers.

4.2   Learning Test

The purpose of this proposal is to instruct school students in STEM competitions, so a learning test is designed based on the skills, knowledge and work activities provided by the educational mobile robot [8]. Table 1 presents the questions posed in the learning test, each affirmative answer question is equivalent to one point in the total score.

Regarding the questions formulated in the learning test, a simple writing has been carried out, avoiding technicalities and that allows to determine in a statistical way the

Table 1. Learning test questions.

Domain	Competencies	Question	Robot feature
Skill	Monitoring	1. Have you monitored the ambient temperature?	Sensors
	Active learning	2. Have you learned playing?	Mobile robot
	Systems analysis	3. Have you reviewed the characteristics of the classroom elements?	Sensors
Knowledge	Mathematics	4. Do you know the units of measure?	Sensors
	Computers and electronics	5. Do you know the sensors and actuators?	Sensors y motors
	Engineering and technology	6. Do you know the characteristics of a robot?	Mobile robot
Work activities	Getting information	7. Have you read data using sensors?	Sensors
	Interacting with computers	8. Have you used remote user interfaces?	Connectivity

knowledge acquired by the student during the development of this experiment. Next, a contextual justification of the content of each question is briefly described, so in questions 1 and 3 a real application of the use of temperature and humidity sensors is presented; and weight, color and distance sensors respectively. Question 2 demonstrates its interaction with technological tools that improve conventional learning and 4 allows you to evaluate your knowledge about units of measure and perform conversions. In the fifth question you can evaluate its conception about the sensors and actuators that make up the robot, and in the sixth question identify the general characteristics of the robot. Questions 7 and 8 have a certain technical criterion, which allows to determine their interaction with computer systems when talking about the use of sensors to obtain data and the use of mobile and computer applications respectively.

The learning test is applied before and after the training process with the mobile robot in the 45 students selected and Fig. 9 shows the results of the learning test. In the pretest, low scores are observed, except in question 3, where 31 students indicated knowing about units of measurement, in the other questions not even half of the total score is reached. In the posttest all students answered affirmatively to questions 1, 4 and 8, and in the rest of the questions there was also a considerable improvement in the scores regarding the pretest.

4.3   Usability Test

At the end of the activities, the level of satisfaction that teachers perceive with the interfaces presented during the experiments developed is evaluated. It should be emphasized that this test requires the participation of people with trained criteria and that it is the teachers who will benefit from this technological tool to improve learning. For this stage, a questionnaire based on the SEQ usability test developed by Gil-Gómez

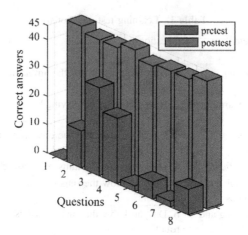

Fig. 9. Learning test results.

et al. [24] with a certain variant oriented to this proposal. There are 13 questions that are assessed with a score of 1 to 5 points according to the following scheme: the first seven questions (Q1 - Q7) are related to the level of acceptance. The following four questions (Q8 - Q11) are related to the effects and discomforts that the system can cause, such as: nausea, disorientation or eye discomfort, as well as its contribution to the teaching process. The next two questions are related to the difficulty of performing the tests. If the result obtained is in the range of 40-65, the implemented system is

Table 2. Results of the questionnaire implemented based on the SEQ test.

Question	Result (N = 17)	
	Mean	SD
1. How much did you enjoy your experience with the system?	4,85	0,36
2. How much did you sense to be in the environment of the system?	4,38	0,49
3. How successful were you in the system?	4,77	0,42
4. To what extent were you able to control the system?	4,08	0,62
5. How real is the virtual environment of the system?	3,85	0,66
6. Is the information provided by the system clear?	4,92	0,27
7. Did you feel discomfort during your experience with the system?	1,15	0,36
8. Did you experience dizziness or nausea during your practice with the system?	1,00	0
9. Did you experience eye discomfort during your practice with system?	1,00	0
10. Did you feel confused or disoriented during your experience with the system?	1,08	0,27
11. Do you think that this system will be helpful for your teaching?	4,46	0,63
12. Did you find the task difficult?	1,08	0.27
13. Did you find the devices of the system difficult to use?	1,31	0,46
Global score (total)	59,1	0,20

considered acceptable. The questions asked to the teachers about the proposal when applying the SEQ questionnaire are shown in Table 2. As can be see there is a positive result that allows validating the system proposed for the students and the comments were collected to improve the system later.

5   Discussions and Conclusions

Although in the traditional education model the subjects are taught separately, a new challenge of STEM competencies is to integrate them to ensure the transmission of knowledge in a more efficient way, responding to current professional requirements. Thus, school-age children who receive this special training can acquire greater skills and aptitudes, necessary to improve their learning process. In the presented literature it can be seen that in several parts of the world it is intended to implement engineering education in schools, characteristically of robotics. In particular, in this proposal a prototype educational robot has been designed and built that gathers other complementary knowledge from mathematics and engineering, in order to provide better results. Innovation and interest that an automaton arouses in a child is encouraged, to allow him to learn while having fun and experiencing an unconventional activity within the classroom.

In this way, teachers are provided with a technological tool that facilitates their work by promoting the full learning of STEM skills, i.e. the use of technology and automation in young students. The mobile robot implemented in this work shows the student how physical quantities are present in their environment and how they can be converted into digital variables. All this thanks to the use of sensors and actuators found in automatic, domotic and industrial systems, learning in a fun way and creating a context that allows you to have a professional inclination in the future towards a certain branch of science.

This work is carried out using low-cost devices that allow the proposal to be replicated with a reduced economic investment. In addition, the robot has wireless connectivity via Bluetooth that allows remote operation and easier interaction between student and teacher. The proposal is evaluated in the classroom with 45 students with an average age of 12 years, with the supervision of experienced teachers. The results indicate an increase in students' knowledge in the learning test questions, instructing users in STEM competitions. A usability test is also applied to teachers in charge, obtaining an acceptable usability score (59.1 ± 0.20), which demonstrates the satisfaction obtained with the system presented.

Acknowledgment. The authors would like to express their gratitude to the Universidad Tecnológica Indoamérica, to the project of linkage with society "Mejoramiento del aprendizaje de competencias STEM mediante el uso de un kit robótico educativo" for the support of the students linked to the project.

References

1. McCarthy, J.D.: Pro-life and pro-choice mobilization: Infrastructure deficits and new technologies. In: Social Movements in an Organizational Society: Collected Essays (2017). https://doi.org/10.4324/9781315129648
2. Dutfield, G.: Intellectual Property Rights and the Life Science Industries (2017). https://doi.org/10.4324/9781315252131
3. Proaño, L., et al.: Adaptation of the bioloid humanoid as an auxiliary in the treatment of autistic children. In: Kim, Kuinam J., Kim, H., Baek, N. (eds.) ICITS 2017. LNEE, vol. 449, pp. 256–266. Springer, Singapore (2018). https://doi.org/10.1007/978-981-10-6451-7_31
4. Buele, J., et al.: Interactive system to improve the skills of children with dyslexia: a preliminary study. In: Rocha, Á., Pereira, R.P. (eds.) Developments and Advances in Defense and Security. SIST, vol. 152, pp. 439–449. Springer, Singapore (2020). https://doi.org/10.1007/978-981-13-9155-2_35
5. Majumdar, S., Guha, S., Marakkath, N. (eds.): Technology and Innovation for Social Change. Springer, New Delhi (2015). https://doi.org/10.1007/978-81-322-2071-8
6. Walker, M., Walker, M.: Peace, Robots, and Technological Unemployment. In: Free Money for All (2016). https://doi.org/10.1057/9781137471338_5
7. Ford, M., Martin, R.: The Rise of the Robots: Technology and the Threat of Mass Unemployment. 1st edn. Oneworld Publ., London (2015)
8. Jang, H.: Identifying 21st century STEM competencies using workplace data. J. Sci. Educ. Technol. 25(2), 284–301 (2016). https://doi.org/10.1007/s10956-015-9593-1
9. McDonald, C.: STEM education: a review of the contribution of the disciplines of science, technology, engineering and mathematics. Sci. Educ. Int. 27(4), 530–569 (2016)
10. Sánchez Carracedo, F., et al.: Competency Maps: an effective model to integrate professional competencies across a STEM curriculum. J. Sci. Educ. Technol. 27, 448–468 (2018). https://doi.org/10.1007/s10956-018-9735-3
11. Shaughnessy, J.M.: Mathematics in a STEM context. Math. Teach. Middle Sch. 18(6), 324–327 (2013). https://doi.org/10.5951/mathteacmiddscho.18.6.0324
12. Noonan, R.: STEM Jobs: 2017 Update (ESA Issue Brief # 02-17). Office of the Chief Economist.. Economics and Statistics Administration. US Department of Commerce, March 30, 2017
13. English, L.D.: Advancing elementary and middle school STEM Education. Int. J. Sci. Math. Educ. 15, 5–24 (2017). https://doi.org/10.1007/s10763-017-9802-x
14. Hsu, Y.S., Lin, Y.H., Yang, B.: Impact of augmented reality lessons on students' STEM interest. Res. Pract. Technol. Enhanc. Learn. 12(2), 1–14 (2017). https://doi.org/10.1186/s41039-016-0039-z
15. English, L.D., King, D.T.: STEM learning through engineering design: fourth-grade students' investigations in aerospace. Int. J. STEM Educ. 2(14), 1–18 (2015). https://doi.org/10.1186/s40594-015-0027-7
16. Varela-Aldás, J., Miranda-Quintana, O., Guevara, C., Castillo, F., Palacios-Navarro, G.: Educational robot using lego mindstorms and mobile device. In: Nummenmaa, J., Pérez-González, F., Domenech-Lega, B., Vaunat, J., Oscar Fernández-Peña, F. (eds.) CSEI 2019. AISC, vol. 1078, pp. 71–82. Springer, Cham (2020). https://doi.org/10.1007/978-3-030-33614-1_5
17. Andaluz, V.H., et al.: Multi-user Industrial Training and Education Environment. In: De Paolis, L.T., Bourdot, P. (eds.) AVR 2018. LNCS, vol. 10851, pp. 533–546. Springer, Cham (2018). https://doi.org/10.1007/978-3-319-95282-6_38

18. Bozkurt Altan, E., Ercan, S.: STEM education program for science teachers: Perceptions and competencies. J. Turkish Sci. Educ. (2016). https://doi.org/10.12973/tused.10174a
19. Wells, J.G.: Integrative STEM education at Virginia Tech: graduate preparation for tomorrow's leaders. Technol. Eng. Teach. **72**, 28–35 (2013)
20. Smyrnova-trybulska, E., Morze, N., Kommers, P., Zuziak, W., Gladun, M.: Educational robots in primary school teachers' and students' opinion about STEM education for young learners. In: Proceedings of the International Conference on Internet Technologies & Society (ITS), Education Technologies, ICEduTech STE 2016 (2016)
21. Smyrnova-Trybulska, E., Morze, N., Kommers, P., Zuziak, W., Gladun, M.: Selected aspects and conditions of the use of robots in STEM education for young learners as viewed by teachers and students. Interact. Technol. Smart Educ. (2017). https://doi.org/10.1108/ITSE-04-2017-0024
22. Daniela, L., Strods, R., France, I.: Activities with educational robotics: research model and tools for evaluation of progress. In: Daniela, L. (ed.) Smart Learning with Educational Robotics, pp. 251–266. Springer, Cham (2019). https://doi.org/10.1007/978-3-030-19913-5_10
23. Arís, N., Orcos, L.: Educational robotics in the stage of secondary education: empirical study on motivation and STEM skills. Educ. Sci. **9**, 73 (2019). https://doi.org/10.3390/educsci9020073
24. Gil-Gomez, J.A., Gil-Gomez, H., Lozano-Quilis, J.A., Manzano-Hernandez, P., Albiol-Perez, S., Aula-Valero, C.: SEQ: suitability evaluation questionnaire for virtual rehabilitation systems. Application in a virtual rehabilitation system for balance rehabilitation. In: Proceedings of the 2013 7th International Conference on Pervasive Computing Technologies for Healthcare and Workshops, PervasiveHealth 2013 (2013). https://doi.org/10.4108/icst.pervasivehealth.2013.252216

The Use of Augmented Reality for Solving Arithmetic Problems for Preschool Children

Siyuan Zhou⬤, Xu Sun⁽⊠⁾⬤, Zhiyu Shi, and Yanyi Lu

University of Nottingham Ningbo China, 199 Taikang East Road,
Ningbo 315100, China
{siyuan.zhou,xu.sun}@nottingham.edu.cn,
{zyl8438,zyl9436}@alumni.nottingham.edu.cn

Abstract. Preschool children are required to acquire problem-solving ability and related time and sequence concepts to solve mathematical story problems. The maturation and pervasion of disruptive technologies, such as augmented reality (AR), may help preschool children to better acquire this knowledge and skills. However, it is still unknown how preschoolers would make use of AR as a learning tool for tackling arithmetic story problems with the involvement of the concepts of time and sequence. Consequently, the present study attempted to employ direct observation and interview methods to compare and gain insights into young children's learning behaviors under traditional 2D pictorial and AR contexts. In line with the early development trajectories of a normal child aged 4–6 years old, a series of planned arithmetic problems which primarily comprised seriation (e.g. first, second, third) and scheduling (e.g. arriving, leaving) concepts were structured in scenario-based stories and designed specifically for preschool children. The findings of the current study reveal that AR intervention may well develop the problem-solving and independent mathematical thinking ability for preschool children by encouraging them to consider all information involved in the story problems, rather than simply guessing the answer from a 2D pictorial mode. Finally, based on the fact that the majority of preschool children still rely on a concrete counting method, the recommendation is to integrate AR technology into the traditional pictorial scenarios for the purpose of supporting the development of children's ability to solve arithmetic story problems.

Keywords: Augmented reality · Preschool children · Problem solving · Time and sequence

1 Introduction

Problem solving is an essential mathematical ability for preschool-aged children to achieve school readiness and later academic success [1, 2]. It comprises primarily the synthesis of already acquired knowledge in "representing a situation mathematically, devising a strategy to solve the problem, carrying out the solution, and reflecting on the answer" (p. 153) [3]. As suggested by several researchers, the inclusion of arithmetic story problems within the kindergarten curriculum can encourage young children to establish connections between conceptual and mathematical knowledge [4], as well as

© Springer Nature Switzerland AG 2020
P. Zaphiris and A. Ioannou (Eds.): HCII 2020, LNCS 12206, pp. 574–584, 2020.
https://doi.org/10.1007/978-3-030-50506-6_39

integrating these practices into real-life scenarios [3, 4]. In addition to regular classes, preschool children are also often exposed to natural mathematics learning contexts informally in daily routines, such as by participating in various pedagogic activities, as instructed by their family [5].

As one vital constituent element, the concepts of time and sequence typically provide a chronological structure for problem-solving [2, 6]. Such knowledge starts to develop at a young age [2] and often serves as a foundation for preschoolers to solve more complicated story problems and cultivate higher-order mathematical thinking [1]. Nunes and Moreno [7] have highlighted how poor problem-solving performance by preschool-aged children is closely associated with weaknesses in their learning and understanding of time and sequence. These concepts are abstract and lack any tangible references, thus making them more difficult for preschoolers to process than concrete concepts, such as colors and shapes [8]. The study by Ponari et al. [9] provided evidence that abstract words acquired by four-year-old children accounted for less than 10% of their total vocabulary, rising to approximately 20% by the age of six. Moreover, Gleitman et al. [10] also proposed a further explanation for the difficulty of abstract word acquisition, indicating that the lexical formatives of children are largely based on their perception of the surrounding environment so that sufficient linguistic experience was demanded for preschoolers prior to their understanding of abstract concepts.

On this basis, the maturation and pervasion of disruptive technologies in the current era, such as virtual reality (VR) and augmented reality (AR), are likely to help preschool children to better acquire the knowledge and problem-solving skills mentioned above. A previous research by Eden [11] demonstrated the huge potential for applying VR technology to improve the sequential time perception of normal young children. It was found that immersion in multi-sensory learning contexts would facilitate the conversion of abstract concepts into something more concrete, thus helping preschoolers to better understand abstract words. Based on the fact that, for safety reasons, commercial VR headsets are not usually recommended to be used by children under the age of 13 years [12], AR is regarded as an effective and safe alternative for early childhood education. According to Azuma et al. [13], an AR system "supplements the real world with virtual (computer-generated) objects that appear to coexist in the same place as the real world" (p.34). Unlike VR, which provides a completely virtual world as its backdrop and main content, the dominant perception of AR users is still located within a realistic environment but blended with virtual content [14]. Although in theory the main features of VR, including interactivity, immersion and sensitivity of information, can be similarly achieved in AR [14], it is reasonable to assume that the objectively existing differences between AR and VR, such as varying degrees of immersion, may present different impacts on the learning performance of young children. As a consequence, it is necessary to investigate whether AR technology would contribute to the acquisition of time and sequence concepts for preschoolers in similar patterns within the frame of arithmetic story problems.

Meanwhile, recent studies have explored AR and its influence on mathematics education in early childhood, including the learning of subitizing and equipartitioning [15] and geometry [16]. The main purpose of these studies was to examine whether it was possible to improve the relative mathematical skills of children through the use of

AR technology. For instance, Gecu-Parmaksiz and Delialioglu [16] compared the traditional method (i.e. physical manipulatives) to AR based virtual manipulatives in teaching geometry for preschool-aged children. The findings of their research revealed that AR intervention was more effective than physical manipulatives in supporting target groups to understand geometric shapes. Nevertheless, in the field of early childhood mathematics education, the effect of AR on helping preschoolers to solve arithmetic story problems still remain unknown and deserve to be further investigated. Consequently, this study attempted to employ direct observation and interview techniques to compare and gain insights into preschoolers' learning behaviors under traditional 2D pictorial and AR contexts when tackling mathematical story problems with the involvement of essential time and sequence concepts.

2   Methods

2.1   Participants

The participants in this study were 33 preschool children (16 males, 17 females, with ages ranging from 58 months to 77 months, M = 64.12; SD = 3.89) who had been invited from a public kindergarten in Ningbo, China. They all received formal kindergarten education systematically and were randomly chosen to prevent uncontrolled factors from influencing the results.

2.2   Intervention Design

Arithmetic Story Problems. Owing to the age characteristics of the participants, the mathematical problems that young children are able to solve are limited [4]. Therefore, the difficulty level of the arithmetic story problems featured in this study complies with the early development trajectories of a normal child aged 4–6 years old [2]. With regard to problem-solving skills, a preschool-aged child progresses from identifying sums up to five and their subtraction counterparts with objects mentally (4-year-old level), to solving relatively simple mathematical story problems with concrete counting methods (5-year-old level), to tackling repeated addition problems with more sophisticated strategies (6-year-old level). Furthermore, based on early childhood conceptual standards [6], it was highlighted by Schafer [17] that the following four sub-domains in the category of time/sequence could be difficult for preschool-aged children to understand: temporal absolutes (e.g. never, always); scheduling (e.g. arriving, leaving, early, late); temporal nuances (e.g. young, old) and seriation (e.g. first, second, third).

As shown in Table 1, a series of planned problem-solving tasks, which include principally scheduling and seriation concepts with two different levels of complexity, were structured for preschool children exclusively. This should help to assess participants with varying degrees of mathematical ability, and help to avoid certain coincidental occasions, such as the correct answer being guessed. Within this framework of mathematical story problems, we attempted to examine the effects of AR intervention by comparing it with traditional 2D pictorial representation and then evaluating the performance of preschoolers before and after the exposure to the AR-based learning environment. Since Perihan [4] suggested that children can respond more easily to mathematical problems in word format rather than using symbols (e.g. plus and minus signs), only pictures and animations excluding symbols and text were presented to the participants. All of the story problems were delivered verbally by the researchers.

Table 1. Structure of arithmetic story problems.

Task groups	Problem types and story scripts (English version)
Task 1 Seriation concepts: First, second	1.1 Separate problem (result unknown) with a single-step calculation (easy): There were 7 carrots in the ground. First, the rabbit took 2 carrots. How many carrots are left in the ground now?
	1.2 Separate problem (result unknown) with a two-step calculation (complex): There were 9 candies in the jar. First, the piglet took 3 candies. Second, the kitty took another 2 candies. How many candies are left now?
Task 2 Scheduling concepts: Arriving, leaving	2.1 Join problem (result unknown) with a single-step calculation (easy): There were 2 cars on the road. Then 4 more cars arrived. How many cars are there on the road now?
	2.2 Separate-Join problem (result unknown) with a two-step calculation (complex): There were 7 planes in the sky. 4 planes left, and then 3 more planes arrived. How many planes are there in the sky now?
Task 3 Scheduling concepts: Early, late	3.1 Compare problem (later unknown) with a single-step calculation: Two people departed from the same place at the same time by car and bicycle, respectively. The car driver spent 2 units of time to reach the destination. The cyclist arrived 3 units of time later than the car driver. How many units of time did it take the cyclist to reach the destination?

Moreover, according to Perihan [4], word problems can be divided into four groups as follows: joining, separating, comparing and part-part-whole. In this case, only the first three types of word problems were included. In a join problem (i.e. using an addition operation), there are three fundamental elements: the initial, the change (the part being added) and the result (the largest amount). In a separate problem (i.e. using a subtraction operation), the initial amount is normally the whole while the change refers to the difference in a quantity from the initial quantity. Furthermore, in a compare problem, it often consists of the comparison of two amounts. The third element is the difference between these two already-given quantities. On this basis, one of the elements (e.g. the result) can be the unknown part in the various types of story problems.

Pictorial Mode of Representation. Five pictorial scenarios were designed, corresponding to the tasks listed above. Each scenario comprised several 2D still pictures forming an arithmetic story problem with relative time and sequencing concepts. For example, the script for task 1.1 was divided into two episodes as presented in Fig. 1. The first episode illustrated 7 carrots in the field while the second depicted 2 carrots being taken away by a rabbit. The remaining number of carrots in the ground was blurred in the second episode in order to prevent the participants from counting directly to obtain the answer without clearly understanding the problem itself.

Fig. 1. Images for the pictorial mode (Task 1.1)

AR Mode of Representation. With regard to the design of AR intervention, 2D and 3D animation were the two most common methods employed to generate the initial scenarios (i.e. what is known as content). As suggested by Kataja [18], the flat 2D animations were considered to be less immersive and attractive than the 3D models, but they have significant advantages in terms of budgets and time consumption. 2D animation may be preferable if viewing a character (or model) at different angles does not add any distinct value, particularly in the early exploration stage. Therefore, this project began with 2D animation for the building of scenarios as guided by the above scripts (see Table 1). The animations were then exported in a video file format, in preparation for being integrated into augmented reality apps. There are several such apps available on the market which allow for the achievement of AR functions, such as Google Glass, Unity, Aris and Aurasma. This technology is delivered via two practices: (1) scanning with a camera on a mobile device; (2) equipping with a head mounted display (HMD). The research by Parton [19] indicated that there were no real learning differences between two groups of children who used a mobile device (i.e. an iPad) and a HMD (i.e. Google Glass) respectively. As a consequence, when taking the cost and accessibility of equipment into account, a mobile device featuring an interactive AR app generated by Unity was utilized in this project. The video file for each scenario was then positioned over an image target (i.e. the first episode) through the Unity platform. The new AR app created by Unity was dependent on image recognition technology. By scanning the image target via a mobile device, the participants were able to see the AR content of 2D animation merged with the surroundings on the display screen (Fig. 2).

Fig. 2. Images for the AR mode (Task 2.1)

Moreover, the main characters in each AR scenario were altered to provide the participants with a fresh story background. Other variables, including the problem types and their related algorithms, remained the same. For example, the scenario of task 2.1 changed from featuring cars to featuring birds. Based on the above script (see Table 1), the first episode presented two birds in the tree, while the second depicted another four birds arriving. The participants were required to calculate the total number of birds in the tree ultimately. Similarly, only the process of birds moving, rather than direct results, were presented to the participating children.

2.3 Procedure

After gaining approval from the research ethics committee at the University of Nottingham Ningbo China, as well as the consent of kindergarten teachers, 33 Chinese preschool children aged 4–6 years were recruited. Each participant followed the same six-step activity structure shown below.

Step 1. For task 1, prior to being exposed to the pictorial mode of representation, each child was first assessed to check whether s/he had acquired the seriation concepts or not. For example, the researcher would ask each participant which character had obtained the candy first, second and third, by showing him/her the storyboard (see Fig. 3) and verbally narrating the story. The answer was recorded as true or false.

Fig. 3. Storyboard to assess the concept acquisition level of the participants

Step 2. In the pictorial scenario of task 1.1, the researcher first placed two images (see Fig. 1) in front of the child and then described the mathematical story problem. Each participant was required to calculate the number of carrots remaining in the field.

As the principal criteria for evaluating the problem-solving skills of the children, their answers and response times were recorded. In addition, the question "who was the first to take away a carrot?" was asked to ascertain the child's understanding of related sequential concepts.

Step 3. In the AR scenarios, the still images with altered story backgrounds, as well as the AR content containing 2D animation on a mobile phone, were both provided to the participants. Similar to step 2, responses to the problem and the seriation concept were all recorded.

Step 4. Repeat steps 2–3 for task 1.2.

Step 5. Repeat steps 1–4 for tasks 2 and 3.

Step 6. At the end of activity, the researcher was able to gather each child's subjective opinions with regard to their preferred mode of representation. The recorded interview results were later analyzed via NVivo software in order to identify key insights from their answers.

3   Results

The results of the observations reveal that the majority of participating children did not fully understand the story problems or concepts in the 2D pictorial mode. They tended to seek answers directly from the pictures in the final episode of each scenario, and neglected the other information provided beforehand. For example, with regard to task 2.1, the initial two cars staying in front of a house were blurred and only the four additional cars were depicted arriving at that house in the second episode. Although the researchers had explained the story problem unambiguously to the respondents, some still thought that there would ultimately be four cars (the correct answer was six) in total in front of the house, simply based on what they had seen in the final episode. In contrast, under the AR mode, the participants exhibited better acquisition of the concepts of time and sequence, and they were more likely to take into account all the information involved in the narrative to solve the problems. In addition, it was noticeable that some of the children still relied heavily on a concrete counting strategy and were inclined to look again at the pictures to answer the questions after watching the AR content. For instance, once the children knew the process of birds arriving at the roost, they were accustomed to counting the number of birds on the still pictures to obtain the answer.

With regard to the results of the brief post-experiment interviews, 45.5% of participants (n = 15) were in favor of the 2D pictorial mode, while the remainder (n = 18) preferred the AR mode. Tables 2 and 3 summarize several key factors affecting the choices of the children regarding their preferred mode of representation. Due to age limitations, the children could only provide brief (or no) responses to this issue. It was, therefore, interesting to find that 2D still pictures were more intuitive for certain children, such as for those who relied largely on concrete counting strategies when solving the problems. As pointed out by two of the children:

Table 2. Reasons for choosing the 2D pictorial mode.

	2D Pictorial Mode	Mentioned by (No.)
1	It was intuitive and quick to get the answer.	4
2	It was good for my eyesight.	1

"The picture did not move, so I could count the number on it directly." [P24]

"It was quicker for me to get the answer by looking at the 2D still pictures." [P14]

To our surprise, one participant also considered the potential threat to their eyesight caused by digital devices when determining their preference between the two modes.

"The pictorial mode was more beneficial for maintaining good eyesight." [P13]

By contrast, AR intervention was found to enable the interpretation of the contexts of the story problems and the abstract concepts more clearly in an animated style, thus promoting the understanding and motivation of the target user group. As stated by three respondents:

"AR was more interesting, and I enjoyed seeing the animation." [P03]

"The objects will move." [P09]

"It was easier for me to understand." [P24]

Moreover, it is noteworthy that the current AR intervention may be less attractive and useful for some preschoolers who had relatively good mathematical ability. They mentioned that there was no necessity to see the full AR animation prior to answering the question.

"The AR mode was time-consuming and meaningless for me." [P07]

Table 3. Reasons for selecting the AR mode.

	AR Mode	Mentioned by (No.)
1	The AR animation was interesting.	2
2	The objects created in the animation will move.	2
3	It was easy to understand.	3

4 Discussion

By comparing the learning behaviors of preschool children under traditional 2D pictorial and AR scenarios, this study has revealed that AR intervention can, to some extent, help preschoolers to improve their acquisition of time and sequence concepts and further to enhance their ability to solve arithmetic story problems.

The first possible explanation for this relates to the capacity of AR to concretize abstract concepts. By integrating digital 2D animations into a user's physical world seamlessly and simultaneously, AR technology is capable of presenting and visualizing the essential time and sequence concepts (e.g. arriving and leaving) in an animated and concrete way to the target user. Therefore, young children can probably perceive these abstract concepts more clearly and easily in the AR mode. This is consistent with previous researches (e.g. [20]) on the application of AR in the field of education. The acquisition of these concepts can further help preschool children to better understand the problems presented in stories.

Secondly, it is evident that AR technology is able to encourage preschoolers to think in a deep and comprehensive way when they use a problem-solving approach to tackle arithmetic problems. The evidence in our study indicates that, in comparison with the 2D pictorial mode, the participating children were more inclined to take into account all the processes needed to respond to the problems under the AR mode, rather than merely focusing on seeking the correct answer from the picture in the last episode of a story sequence.

The third contributing factor may be that as a novel teaching tool, AR intervention can also improve the enthusiasm for learning, and the levels of attention and motivation of preschool children. The post-experiment interviews suggest that, although all participants showed their willingness to take part in both intervention programs, some preschoolers were more motivated by and interested in using AR technology. It is possible that interventions such as this can motivate young children owing to their novelty value. This finding is in accordance with previous studies (e.g. [8, 16]) showing that there are high levels of motivation among young children when they are first exposed to AR technology.

However, it should also be noted that because of the differences in their mathematical ability, a number of the children preferred to choose a concrete counting strategy when solving the arithmetic problems. In fact, this is consistent with the early development trajectories of normal children aged 4–6 years old [2]. Hence, a brief animation shown on a mobile device may hinder their learning process. The physical learning materials still appear to exert an essential role in the problem-solving processes of this type of end users.

5 Conclusion and Limitations

In conclusion, AR intervention may well develop independent mathematical thinking ability for preschool children by encouraging them to consider all information involved in a problem, rather than simply guessing the answer from a 2D pictorial mode. One of the most significant features of AR is that it enables the conversion of abstract sequential concepts to those which are more concrete, thus helping young children to better understand such vocabulary within the frame of a mathematical story problem, and thereby further enhancing their problem-solving skills in an engaging way. Finally, based on the fact that the majority of preschool children continue to rely on a concrete counting method, the recommendation is to integrate AR technology into traditional pictorial scenarios to support the development of children's ability to solve arithmetic problems.

With regard to the limitations, only 2D animation was used for the AR content in this pilot study, in line with the time and budgetary constraints. The AR mode can be further developed, for instance, by importing 3D models or characters to enhance the immersion and interactivity between an AR-based mobile device and preschool children. Consequently, the effects of AR technology on facilitating preschoolers' ability to solve arithmetic story problems can be further explored in the future research.

References

1. Harrington, M., Desjardin, J.L., Shea, L.C.: Relationships between early child factors and school readiness skills in young children with hearing loss. Commun. Disord. Q. **32**(1), 50–62 (2010)
2. Pagliaro, C.M., Kritzer, K.L.: The math gap: A description of the mathematics performance of preschool-aged deaf/hard-of-hearing children. J. Deaf Stud. Deaf Educ. **18**(2), 139–160 (2013)
3. Ansell, E., Pagliaro, C.M.: The relative difficulty of signed arithmetic story problems for primary level deaf and hard-of-hearing students. J. Deaf Stud. Deaf Educ. **11**(2), 153–170 (2005)
4. Perihan, D.A.: Preschool children skills in solving mathematical word problems. Educ. Res. Rev. **10**(18), 2539–2549 (2015)
5. Kritzer, K.L.: Families with young deaf children and the mediation of mathematically based concepts within a naturalistic environment. Am. Ann. Deaf **153**(5), 474–483 (2008)

6. Bracken, B.A., Crawford, E.: Basic concepts in early childhood educational standards: a 50-state review. Early Childhood Educ. J. **37**(5), 421–430 (2010)
7. Nunes, T., Moreno, C.: An intervention program for promoting deaf pupils' achievement in mathematics. J. Deaf Stud. Deaf Educ. **7**(2), 120–133 (2002)
8. Eden, S., Ingber, S.: Virtual environments as a tool for improving sequence ability of deaf and hard of hearing children. Am. Ann. Deaf **159**(3), 284–295 (2014)
9. Ponari, M., Norbury, C.F., Vigliocco, G.: Acquisition of abstract concepts is influenced by emotional valence. Dev. Sci. **21**(2), e12549 (2018)
10. Gleitman, L.R., Cassidy, K., Nappa, R., Papafragou, A., Trueswell, J.C.: Hard words. Lang. Learn. Dev. **1**(1), 23–64 (2005)
11. Eden, S.: Enhancing children with hearing impairment with virtual reality (2010). http://homepage.divms.uiowa.edu/~hourcade/idc2012-specialneeds/eden.pdf. Accessed 23 July 2019
12. Digital Trends. https://www.digitaltrends.com/virtual-reality/is-vr-safe-for-kids-we-asked-the-experts/. Accessed 27 July 2019
13. Azuma, R., Baillot, Y., Behringer, R., Feiner, S., Julier, S., Macintyre, B.: Recent advances in augmented reality. IEEE Comput. Graphics Appl. **21**(6), 34–47 (2001)
14. Yuen, S.C.Y., Yaoyuneyong, G., Johnson, E.: Augmented reality: an overview and five directions for AR in education. J. Educ. Technol. Dev. Exchange **4**(1), 119–140 (2011)
15. Zanchi, C., Presser, A.L., Vahey, P.: Next generation preschool math demo: tablet games for preschool classrooms. In: Proceedings of the 12th International Conference on Interaction Design and Children, pp. 527–530. ACM Press, New York (2013)
16. Gecu-Parmaksiz, Z., Delialioglu, O.: Augmented reality-based virtual manipulatives versus physical manipulatives for teaching geometric shape to preschool children. Br. J. Edu. Technol. **50**(6), 3376–3390 (2019)
17. Schafer, L.: Knowledge of basic concepts in deaf/hard of hearing children (2012). https://digitalcommons.wustl.edu/cgi/viewcontent.cgi?article=1653&context=pacs_capstones. Accessed 25 April 2019
18. Kataja, T.: 2D animation in the world of augmented reality (2019). https://www.theseus.fi/bitstream/handle/10024/172563/Kataja_Terhikki.pdf?sequence=2&isAllowed=y. Accessed 25 July 2019
19. Parton, B.S.: Glass vision 3D: digital discovery for the deaf. TechTrends **61**(2), 141–146 (2017)
20. Ozdemir, M., Sahin, C., Arcagok, S., Demir, M.K.: The effect of augmented reality applications in the learning process: a meta-analysis study. Eurasian J. Educ. Res. **18**, 1–22 (2018)

Collaboration Technology and Collaborative Learning

Towards an Information Security Awareness Maturity Model

Tobias Fertig[(✉)], Andreas E. Schütz, Kristin Weber, and Nicholas H. Müller

Faculty of Computer Science and Business Information Systems,
University of Applied Sciences Würzburg-Schweinfurt, Sanderheinrichsleitenweg 20,
97074 Würzburg, Germany
{tobias.fertig,andreas.schuetz,kristin.weber,nicholas.mueller}@fhws.de

Abstract. In order to achieve continuous improvement Maturity Models (MM) are often used to assess the abilities of employees. Moreover, the continuous improvement is also required in the field of Information Security Awareness (ISA). This is due to the fact, that ISA trainings have to be repeated frequently in order to keep the level of awareness of the employees up and to stay in their mind. Within our research project, we are using the Integrated Behavorial Model (IBM) as definition of ISA. The IBM includes many different aspects like knowledge, attitude, and habit. We carried out a systematic literature review to determine if a MM based on the IBM can be defined to assess the maturity of ISA. Since the IBM covers aspects of psychology, we did not only search for MM for information security, since the human factor is often neglected. Moreover, the awareness is often only assessed via the knowledge of employees. However, knowledge is only one aspect of the IBM. At the end, none of the uncovered MMs considers all aspects of the IBM. In contrast to MM for information security, MM of other fields of research are considering psychological aspects if they are dealing with human factors. Therefore, it is possible to create a MM based on the IBM for ISA. Moreover, we can easily derive some of the used assessments for our MM.

Keywords: Information Security Awareness · Measuring · Maturity Models · Metrics · Automated measuring

1 Introduction

Maturity Models (MM) can help to assess the abilities of employees for a given field. Moreover, the process and ability of continuous improvement of organizations can be evaluated and tracked via MMs. The continuous improvement is also required in the field of Information Security Awareness (ISA). This is due to the fact, that ISA trainings have to be repeated frequently in order to keep the level of awareness of the employees up and to stay in their mind [16]. An MM would allow to frequently assess the ISA level of the employees. However, there is no sufficient MM for ISA, yet.

© Springer Nature Switzerland AG 2020
P. Zaphiris and A. Ioannou (Eds.): HCII 2020, LNCS 12206, pp. 587–599, 2020.
https://doi.org/10.1007/978-3-030-50506-6_40

Within our research project, we are using the Integrated Behavorial Model (IBM) to help to explain the aspects that influence human behavior. The IBM includes many different aspects like knowledge, compliant behavior, and organizational constraints. In contrast to other definitions of ISA, the IBM is derived from the model of [34] and considers psychological aspects of humans. There are already different MMs for some of the aspects of the IBM. The Capability Maturity Model assesses the processes of an organization [37]. Whereas, the E-Learning Maturity Model focuses on the success of e-learnings [31]. Since the IBM is a combination of different aspects, it should be possible to create a MM to assess the level of ISA of employees.

As we discovered in our previous research, organizations need sufficient measurings and metrics for ISA [14]. Moreover, they would prefer if the measuring could be automated. The companies require metrics in order to justify their budget and efforts for ISA trainings. However, the challenge within the definition of metrics is to quantify human behavior. Furthermore, making assumptions about the ISA based on a single metric is not recommended. This is why multiple metrics should be considered in order to assess the level of ISA. A MM for ISA would consider multiple metrics and thus, allow an assumption. Moreover, a MM for the assessment of ISA would allow repeated measuring of ISA.

We did a systematic literature review about MM. We determined, whether MM for ISA already exists and what definition of ISA they are based on. Afterwards, we anaylized the strengths and weaknesses. Moreover, we were looking for MM for human behavior in other fields of research, to determine if some of those MM could be derived for ISA.

At the end, a MM for ISA can improve the overall security within an organization since humans play a central role in information security. The behavior of workers at their workplace and at their home affects the confidentiality, integrity, and availability of sensitive corporate information. To make employees aware of their important role, companies typically carry out security awareness campaigns [19,45]. In order to determine the success of those campaigns, sufficient metrics as well as a MM is needed.

At the beginning, we summarize the theoretical background. We cover different definitions for ISA as well as the IBM. Afterwards, we define our four research questions that we will answer within this paper. In Section "Research Approach", we describe our approach for this systematic literature review. In Section "Used Data Sources", we present the journals, the digital libraries as well as the conference proceedings we covered within our search. Afterwards, we gather the research results in Section "Research Results". The results are discussed in Section "Results Discussion" and we will answer our research questions. Finally, we will give a short summary of the paper and will conclude with an outlook and future work.

2   Theoretical Background

The research area ISA targets the "human factor" and how IT users can be trained to an information security-compliant behavior. Users need to be

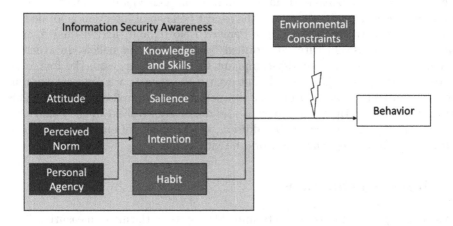

Fig. 1. Aspects of ISA according to the IBM [42]

motivated to use their theoretical knowledge about information security in practice [3]. Moreover, they need to be convinced of the importance of their actions. Three possible perspectives of ISA are described in the following [17]:

1. Employees know, which threats exist and recognize them ("perception").
2. Employees further know, how to protect themselves against threats ("protection").
3. Employees know what a threat is, what they can do about it and that they behave accordingly ("behavior").

An actual increase of information security within an organization can only be achieved by employees that are behaving compliantly. ISA defines that employees know how to behave in compliance with information security and how to apply this knowledge in critical situations. Moreover, employees know the consequences arising out of non-compliant behavior.

The organization is named as an additional aspect of ISA by [19]. The organization ensures that employees in the company are able to behave in compliance with information security. This denotes that no barriers exist, which are in conflict with compliant behavior. For example, a barrier can be a password reset link which is hidden in the depths of the organization's intranet. At the same time, organizational measures, such as increasing usability of applications, can support information security.

The IBM from health psychology helps to explain human behavior [34]. The IBM was already interpreted in the context of ISA and used to explain the mental construct Security Awareness [41]. As shown in Fig. 1 the ISA of a person is the sum of the four aspects knowledge and skills ("I know how the behavior is performed"), habit ("I'm used to perform the behavior"), salience ("The performance of the behavior is in my mind"), and behavioral intent ("I want to perform the behavior"). Especially the aspect behavioral intention is formed by the mental constructs Attitude, the Perceived Norm, and the Personal Agency of a person. These, in turn, are formed by emotions and beliefs. In order to achieve an information security-compliant behavior of a person, the four indicated aspects must be influenced. But even if the aspects are distinct, environmental constraints can still prevent the person from compliant behavior. This clearly shows that the environment is also decisively involved in the behavioral formation of a human being. In addition, the influence of environmental constraints can also affect the behavioral intention [34].

3   Research Questions

Within our previous work, we determined the state of the art of measuring ISA. Therefore, we interviewed companies and carried out a structured literature review. Both, theory and practice, revealed that the quantification of human behavior is a challenging task. Nevertheless, metrics for ISA and automated measuring was considered as highly appreciated. Since a single metric cannot be used to determine the level of ISA of employees, we are aiming at the creation of an MM for ISA.

There are already some MMs for information security in general. Therefore, we will analyze them if we can reuse some aspects for ISA. However, maybe we can uncover an existing MM that already fulfills all aspects of the IBM. Moreover, we want to uncover all existing MMs that are focusing solely on ISA and see if they are covering all aspects of the IBM.

Since there are already many different MMs focusing on different fields, we will examine if the existing MMs are already quantifying human behavior. If they do, we will determine if we can reuse or derive some metrics or approaches from them to the field of ISA. However, since the interviewees from our previous work would prefer an automated way of measuring, we will examine if the assessment of maturity can be automated. This is why the research questions for this structured literature review are the following:

Q1) Is ISA considered within current MM for information security?
Q2) Are there any MM focusing solely on ISA?
Q3) Can we reuse MMs that are focusing on single aspects of ISA according to the IBM?
Q4) Can the assessment of maturity be automated?

4   Research Approach

In this section, we describe the approach for this structured literature review. We describe the identification and selection of relevant references. Therefore, we define the keywords for the search process and describe the coding used to filter the findings.

We used the proposed approach of Webster and Watson for the identification of relevant references [46]. The structured approach improves the search process, and the search process is fundamental for the quality of this literature review [6]. A thorough literature research must be valid and reliable according to Brocke et al. [6]. A valid literature research has to accurately uncover the sources the reviewer wants to collect [6,28]. A reliable literature research has to be repeatable in order to allow other researchers to collect the same sources [6]. Therefore, we documented our research process:

Table 1. Each keyword was AND concatenated with maturity model.

Information Security Awareness	Information Security
IT Security	Salience
Knowledge	Compliant behavior
Attitude	Perceived norm
Personal agency	Intention
Organization	Habit

According to Webster and Watson we started our search process by a keyword search using the pre-defined keywords shown in Table 1 [46]. The keywords were defined based on the different aspects of the IBM. Moreover, we included the keyword 'Information Security Awareness' as well as 'Information Security' and 'IT Security' to uncover related MMs in our field. All keywords were AND concatenated with the term 'Maturity Model'. We limited our search to publications written in English. Moreover, we did not limit our results based on the publication date. Many maturity models have been proposed way before 2000. However, our research could profit from every maturity model no matter when it was initially published. In order to filter publications that are not relevant for our research questions, we did a manual screening of all titles, abstracts and if necessary of the full text. Afterwards, a backward as well as a forward search was carried out. Both searches were carried out manually.

5 Used Data Sources

In this section we describe the used data sources and the papers found during the literature review. Based on our keyword search defined in Sect. 4 we found a total of 36 papers after removing the duplicates. Table 2 shows all used data sources and the number of hits during the search. Moreover, Table 2 shows how many papers were included and retrieved by forward and backward search. Table 2 is ordered by the order of searching the data sources. The numbers of included papers are without duplicates. Many of the digital libraries revealed the same papers. Therefore, the number of included papers was only increased if the data source revealed a new paper.

Table 2. Number of search hits and included papers per data source

Data source	Hits	Included	FW/BW
IEEE Xplore Digital Library	1261	13	1
ACM Digital Library	1035	2	0
ScienceDirect	252	5	0
Scitepress Digital Library	8	1	1
Springer Link	176	4	0
Review of Business Information Systems	1	0	0
Computers & Security	0	0	0
Computers & Education	2	0	0
MIS Quarterly	0	0	0
Information Systems Research	1	0	0
Management Science	2	0	0
Computer Fraud & Security	2	0	0
AIS eLibrary	91	1	0
Semantic Scholar	246	3	2
Google Scholar	178	2	0
WISO-net	22	1	0
Total without duplicates		**36**	

Since we started with IEEE Xplore Digital Library, we discovered the most relevant findings within the 1261 hits: 18 papers. The forward and backward search revealed one additional paper matching the inclusion criteria. The ACM Digital Library was searched afterwards and had 1035 hits within the *ACM Full-Text Collection*. However, we could include two additional papers from the results. The keyword based search on ScienceDirect revealed 252 hits within the selected article types: "Review articles", "Research articles", "Book chapters", and "Case reports". Based on the inclusion criteria we could include five of those papers. Searching the Scitepress Digital Library revealed eight hits and one paper could be included. The forward and backward search on this paper revealed another one. Moreover, Springer Link had 176 hits which led to 4 additional papers.

After searching the digital libraries, we continued with manual searches within journals. Therefore, we chose journals, we already had papers included from. Unfortunately, we could not uncover any additional paper. Two of the journals did not reveal a hit based on our search query.

In addition to the journals we searched the conference proceedings of AIS conferences. Therefore, we used the AIS eLibrary. The AIS eLibrary had 91 hits and one additional paper was included after removing the duplicates.

Afterwards, we used Semantic Scholar to uncover other sources as well. The keyword search result had 246 hits and three papers matched our inclusion criteria. Those three papers uncovered two additional papers during the forward and backward search. Google Scholar revealed 178 hits. However, many of the hits have been duplicates to our previous sources. Nevertheless, we could include two additional papers. Last but not least we checked the WISO-net. WISO-net is a database for socio-psychological papers. We had 22 hits and could include one additional paper.

6   Research Results

Table 3 shows the different categories we retrieved from literature. A paper can be in more than one category, if multiple categories are included within a MM. The first three categories are focusing on the aspect of knowledge. However, some MM only focus on the amount of trainings not on the knowledge of each employee itself. Therefore, we splitted the knowledge category.

Table 3. Categorization of found literature

Category	Found papers
Knowledge	[4, 13, 18, 20, 21, 25, 39, 44]
Awareness trainings	[2, 4, 7–9, 12, 15, 23, 24, 36, 39, 43, 48, 50]
Education	[4, 30, 43]
Attitude	[1, 5, 20–22, 25, 26, 48]
Perceived norm	[11, 47, 49, 50]
Habit	[10]
Behavior	[44]
Awareness and human factor unconsidered	[27, 29, 32, 33, 35, 38, 40]

The category "Knowledge" includes 8 papers in total. 2 papers are also within the category "Awareness Trainings" which includes 14 papers in total. 3 papers are focusing on education instead of only awareness trainings. Some papers are evaluating the knowledge of employees via online tests whereas some papers are only tracking the amount of awareness training days for example.

Another aspect of the IBM is the represented by the category "Attitude". All 8 MM in those papers were not designed for information security or ISA. However, the MMs are covering the attitude of employees towards the topic the MM wants to assess. The motivation to participate is also considered within those MMs. The category "Perceived Norm" represents one subaspect of attitude. 3 out of 4 papers propose MMs that were designed for information security. All of them assess the vision and philosophy of the management. Moreover, 2 of the MMs are assessing the level of promotion of ISA by the management.

The category "Habit" includes only 1 paper. The proposed MM is not focusing on information security or ISA at all. However, the MM for hospital information systems assesses the amount of compliant behavior that is done due to habits of the employees.

Only one of the MMs includes the actual behavior. The MM is also focusing on ISA and knowledge of the employees. However, the MM assesses how regular reporting is done by the employees and includes this metric within the decision about maturity.

The last category includes all papers that propose MM for information security but are not considering the awareness or human factor at all. We could identify 7 papers for this category. The MM are only assessing the technology or quality of software. Some of them are considering the process quality of the organizations. However, not a single aspect of the IBM is considered.

7   Results Discussion

The results of the systematic literature review are used to answer our research questions proposed in Sect. 3. To answer Q1, we take a look at Table 3. ISA is already considered within 73% of current MM for information security. Therefore, ISA is considered as important aspect for the maturity of information security. Moreover, ISA was already considered within the oldest MMs we uncovered during the structured literate review [9,43]. However, 27% of the proposed MM do not consider ISA or the human factor at all.

Regarding Q2, we could not uncover any MM focusing solely on ISA. ISA was only considered within MM for information security. Therefore, ISA is often assessed by the amount of trainings the employees have received within one year for example. Since it is a challenging task to quantify human behavior there are not many measuring methods for ISA [14]. According to the interviewees of some small- and medium-sized companies the measuring of ISA is strongly appreciated but their is a lack of metrics [14]. Therefore, ISA is often only assessed via the amount of trainings received.

We had to analyze all MMs if they are assessing any aspect of the IBM in order to answer Q3. Therefore, we checked all MMs for the following aspects mentioned in Sect. 2: attitued, perceived norm, personal agency, intention, salience, habit, and knowledge and skills. All aspected are leading to compliant behavior of the employees which is the goal of our research project. Therefore, MMs should consider the behavior of employees to determine the maturity of an organization. However, only one MM has mentioned the behavior of employees [44]. Nevertheless, measuring how regular incidents are reported is not sufficient for conclusions about the behavior.

The goal of our MM is to consider all aspects of the IBM in order to assess the maturity of ISA. Regarding the aspects of salience and personal agency we could not uncover any MM within this systematic literature review. Therefore, we have to consider new approaches in future research. All other aspects have been covered in MMs of different fields of research. The aspect of habit was covered within a MM for hospital information systems [10]. However, we could derive the assessments from this MM. The authors are checking the employees that are behaving compliant due to habits rather than knowledge or awareness. All MMs that are considering the attitude of employees are not designed for information security. Nevertheless, the assessment of attitude can easily be derived for ISA. Therefore, our MM has to assess the motivation, the willingness to cooperate as well as the general attitude towards ISA. The assessment of perceived norm is already included within MM for information security. Therefore, we can easily reuse their approaches [47,49,50]. Since knowledge and skills are not only assessed by MMs for information security, but also within MMs for education and elearning platforms, we have plenty of approaches to reuse. However, since knowledge does not lead to compliant behavior by itself, the MM should not reuse to much knowledge assessments.

To sum up, none of the uncovered MMs considers all aspects of the IBM. MM for information security are often relying on the aspect of knowledge to assess the ISA without considering psychological aspects. In contrast, MM of other fields of research are considering psychological aspects if they are dealing with human factors. Therefore, it is possible to create a MM based on the IBM. Moreover, we can easily derive some of the used assessments for our MM.

To answer Q4, further investigations are required. Most of the proposed MM do not reveal the used measuring methods. Therefore, we cannot make assumptions about whether assessments of maturity can be automated. However, some MM are using online tests to assess the knowledge. Those tests can be designed in a way to enable automation. Since the quantification of human behavior based on metrics is a challenging task, the other methods mentioned are interviews, surveys, and questionnaires. Therefore, additional measuring methods are required to enable automation.

8   Conclusion

We carried out a systematic literature review to determine if a MM based on the IBM can be defined to assess the maturity of ISA. Since the IBM covers aspects of psychology, we did not only search for MM for information security, since the human factor is often neglected. Moreover, within the field of information security, the awareness is often assessed via the knowledge of employees. However, knowledge is only one aspect of the IBM. Therefore, we expanded our search into other fields of research.

We uncovered several MM that are assessing single aspects of the IBM, but we could not find any MM covering all those aspects. Therefore, we examined if we can reuse some parts of the MMs to derive a new MM for ISA. Within our discussion we described for each aspect if we can reuse existing approaches.

In our future work we have to examine how the aspects salience and personal agency can be assessed within a MM. Therefore, we will run some experiments to check whether salience can be measured if we put pressure on employees during the experiment.

Furthermore, we have to define metrics to quantify human behavior in order to assess the compliant behavior. Moreover, we need additional metrics for all aspects of the IBM. Finally, we will use those metrics and check if we can automate the collection of data for the defined metrics.

Acknowledgements. Tobias Fertig and Andreas E. Schütz were supported by the BayWISS Consortium Digitization.

References

1. Aggestam, L.: Towards a maturity model for learning organizations - the role of knowledge management. In: 17th International Workshop on Database and Expert Systems Applications (DEXA 2006), pp. 141–145, September 2006. https://doi.org/10.1109/DEXA.2006.138. ISSN: 2378-3915
2. Almuhammadi, S., Alsaleh, M.: Information security maturity model for Nist cyber security framework. In: ICIT 2017 (2017). https://doi.org/10.5121/csit.2017.70305
3. Bada, M., Sasse, A.M., Nurse, J.R.: Cyber security awareness campaigns: why do they fail to change behaviour? Global Cyber Security Capacity Centre: Draft Working Paper, pp. 188–131 (2014)
4. Barclay, C.: Sustainable security advantage in a changing environment: the cyber-security capability maturity model (CM2). In: Proceedings of the 2014 ITU Kaleidoscope Academic Conference: Living in a Converged World - Impossible Without Standards? pp. 275–282, June 2014. https://doi.org/10.1109/Kaleidoscope.2014.6858466. ISSN: null
5. Boughzala, I., Vreede, T.D., Nguyen, C., Vreede, G.J.D.: Towards a maturity model for the assessment of ideation in crowdsourcing projects. In: 2014 47th Hawaii International Conference on System Sciences, pp. 483–490, January 2014. https://doi.org/10.1109/HICSS.2014.67. ISSN: 1530-1605
6. Brocke, J.V., Simons, A., Niehaves, B., Riemer, K., Plattfaut, R., Cleven, A.: Reconstructing the giant: on the importance of rigour in documenting the literature search process. In: ECIS (2009)
7. de Bruin, R., von Solms, S.H.: Modelling cyber security governance maturity. In: 2015 IEEE International Symposium on Technology and Society (ISTAS), pp. 1–8, November 2015. https://doi.org/10.1109/ISTAS.2015.7439415. ISSN: 2158-3412
8. de Bruin, R., von Solms, S.H.: Cybersecurity governance: how can we measure it? In: 2016 IST-Africa Week Conference, pp. 1–9, May 2016. https://doi.org/10.1109/ISTAFRICA.2016.7530578. ISSN: null
9. Canal, V.A.: ISM3 1.0. Information security management maturity model. Institute for Security and Open Methodologies (2004)
10. Carvalho, J.V., Rocha, A., van de Wetering, R., Abreu, A.: A maturity model for hospital information systems. J. Bus. Res. **94**, 388–399 (2019). https://doi.org/10.1016/j.jbusres.2017.12.012. http://www.sciencedirect.com/science/article/pii/S0148296317305076
11. Cornu, C., Chapurlat, V., Quiot, J.M., Irigoin, F.: A maturity model for the deployment of Systems Engineering processes. In: 2012 IEEE International Systems Conference SysCon 2012, pp. 1–6, March 2012. https://doi.org/10.1109/SysCon.2012.6189535. ISSN: null
12. Da Veiga, A., Martins, N.: Information security culture and information protection culture: a validated assessment instrument. Comput. Law Secur. Rev. **31**(2), 243–256 (2015). https://doi.org/10.1016/j.clsr.2015.01.005. http://www.sciencedirect.com/science/article/pii/S0267364915000060
13. Dzazali, S., Sulaiman, A., Zolait, A.H.: Information security landscape and maturity level: case study of Malaysian public service (MPS) organizations. Gov. Inf. Q. **26**(4), 584–593 (2009). https://doi.org/10.1016/j.giq.2009.04.004. http://www.sciencedirect.com/science/article/pii/S0740624X09000859

14. Fertig, T., Schütz, A.: About the measuring of information security awareness: a systematic literature review. In: 53rd Hawaii International Conference on System Sciences, January 2020. http://scholarspace.manoa.hawaii.edu/handle/10125/64540
15. Ghaffari, F., Arabsorkhi, A.: A new adaptive cyber-security capability maturity model. In: 2018 9th International Symposium on Telecommunications (IST), pp. 298–304, December 2018. https://doi.org/10.1109/IS.2018.8661018. ISSN: null
16. Gundu, T., Flowerday, S., Renaud, K.: Deliver security awareness training, then repeat: deliver; measure efficacy. In: 2019 Conference on Information Communications Technology and Society (ICTAS), pp. 1–6, March 2019. https://doi.org/10.1109/ICTAS.2019.8703523
17. Hänsch, N., Benenson, Z.: Specifying IT security awareness. In: 2014 25th International Workshop on Database and Expert Systems Applications, pp. 326–330, September 2014. https://doi.org/10.1109/DEXA.2014.71
18. Harigopal, U., Satyadas, A.: Cognizant enterprise maturity model (CEMM). IEEE Trans. Syst. Man Cybern. Part C (Appl. Rev.) **31**(4), 449–459 (2001). https://doi.org/10.1109/5326.983928
19. Helisch, M., Pokoyski, D.: Security awareness: Neue Wege zur erfolgreichen Mitarbeiter-Sensibilisierung. Vieweg+Teubner Verlag/GWV Fachverlage GmbH Wiesbaden, Wiesbaden (2009). https://doi.org/10.1007/978-3-8348-9594-3
20. Ifenthaler, D., Egloffstein, M.: Development and implementation of a maturity model of digital transformation. TechTrends **64**, 302–309 (2019). https://doi.org/10.1007/s11528-019-00457-4
21. Jacob, A., Teuteberg, F.: Development of a social media maturity model for logistics service providers. In: Abramowicz, W., Corchuelo, R. (eds.) BIS 2019. LNBIP, vol. 354, pp. 96–108. Springer, Cham (2019). https://doi.org/10.1007/978-3-030-20482-2_9
22. Jørgensen, F., Boer, H., Laugen, B.T.: CI implementation: an empirical test of the CI maturity model. Creat. Innov. Manag. **15**(4), 328–337 (2006). https://doi.org/10.1111/j.1467-8691.2006.00404.x. https://onlinelibrary.wiley.com/doi/abs/10.1111/j.1467-8691.2006.00404.x
23. Karokola, G., Kowalski, S., Yngström, L.: Secure e-government services: towards a framework for integrating it security services into e-government maturity models. In: 2011 Information Security for South Africa, pp. 1–9, August 2011. https://doi.org/10.1109/ISSA.2011.6027525. ISSN: 2330-9881
24. Karokola, G., Kowalski, S., Yngström, L.: Towards an information security maturity model for secure e-government services: a stakeholders view. In: HAISA (2011)
25. Klötzer, C., Pflaum, A.: Toward the development of a maturity model for digitalization within the manufacturing industry's supply chain. In: Hawaii International Conference on System Sciences 2017 (HICSS-50), January 2017. https://aisel.aisnet.org/hicss-50/in/digital_supply_chain/5
26. Lasrado, F.: "How are we doing?" using a maturity model assessment. Fostering Creativity and Innovation, pp. 89–126. Springer, Cham (2019). https://doi.org/10.1007/978-3-319-99121-4_4
27. Le, N.T., Hoang, D.B.: Can maturity models support cyber security? In: 2016 IEEE 35th International Performance Computing and Communications Conference (IPCCC), pp. 1–7, December 2016. https://doi.org/10.1109/PCCC.2016.7820663. ISSN: 2374-9628

28. Lebek, B., Uffen, J., Breitner, M.H., Neumann, M., Hohler, B.: Employees' information security awareness and behavior: a literature review. In: 2013 46th Hawaii International Conference on System Sciences, pp. 2978–2987, January 2013. https://doi.org/10.1109/HICSS.2013.192

29. Lima, M.V.M., Lima, R.M.F., Lins, F.A.A.: A multi-perspective methodology for evaluating the security maturity of data centers. In: 2017 IEEE International Conference on Systems, Man, and Cybernetics (SMC), pp. 1196–1201, October 2017. https://doi.org/10.1109/SMC.2017.8122775. ISSN: null

30. Lutteroth, C., Luxton-Reilly, A., Dobbie, G., Hamer, J.: A maturity model for computing education. In: Proceedings of the Ninth Australasian Conference on Computing Education, ACE 2007, vol. 66. pp. 107–114. Australian Computer Society Inc., Ballarat, January 2007

31. Marshall, S., Mitchell, G.: Applying spice to e-learning: an e-learning maturity model? In: Proceedings of the Sixth Australasian Conference on Computing Education, ACE 2004, vol. 30. pp. 185–191. Australian Computer Society Inc., Australia (2004)

32. Matrane, O., Talea, M.: A maturity model for information security management in small and medium-sized Moroccan enterprises: an empirical investigation. Int. J. Adv. Res. Comput. Sci. **5**(6), 61–69 (2014)

33. Matrane, O., Talea, M., Okar, C.: Towards a new maturity model for information security management. Int. J. Adv. Res. Comput. Sci. Softw. Eng. **4**(6), 268–275 (2014)

34. Montaño, D.E., Kasprzyk, D.: Theory of reasoned action, theory of planned behavior, and the integrated behavior model. In: Glanz, K., Rimer, B.K., Viswanath, K. (eds.) Health Behavior and Health Education, pp. 67–96. APA PsycNet (2008)

35. Muthukrishnan, S.M., Palaniappan, S.: Security metrics maturity model for operational security. In: 2016 IEEE Symposium on Computer Applications Industrial Electronics (ISCAIE), pp. 101–106, May 2016. https://doi.org/10.1109/ISCAIE.2016.7575045. ISSN: null

36. Park, J.O., Kim, S.G., Choi, B.H., Jun, M.S.: The study on the maturity measurement method of security management for ITSM. In: 2008 International Conference on Convergence and Hybrid Information Technology, pp. 826–830, August 2008. https://doi.org/10.1109/ICHIT.2008.251. ISSN: null

37. Paulk, M.C., Curtis, B., Chrissis, M.B., Weber, C.: Capability maturity model for software (Version 1.1). Technical report CMU/SEI-93-TR-024, Carnegie Mellon University (1993). https://resources.sei.cmu.edu/library/asset-view.cfm?assetid=11955

38. Rojas, R., Muedas, A., Mauricio, D.: Security maturity model of web applications for cyber attacks. In: Proceedings of the 3rd International Conference on Cryptography, Security and Privacy, ICCSP 2019, pp. 130–137. Association for Computing Machinery, Kuala Lumpur, January 2019. https://doi.org/10.1145/3309074.3309096

39. Saleh, M.F.: Information security maturity model. Int. J. Comput. Sci. Secur. **5**(3), 316–337 (2011). https://www.cscjournals.org/library/manuscriptinfo.php?mc=IJCSS-497

40. Sánchez, L.E., Villafranca, D., Fernández-Medina, E., Piattini, M.: Developing a maturity model for information system security management within small and medium size enterprises. In: Proceedings of the 4th International Workshop on Security in Information Systems, pp. 256–266 (2006). https://www.scitepress.org/PublicationsDetail.aspx?ID=HU/Pb1mEyuY=&t=1

41. Schütz, A.E.: Information security awareness: it's time to change minds! In: Proceedings of International Conference on Applied Informatics Imagination, Creativity, Design, Development - ICDD 2018, Sibiu, Romania (2018)
42. Schütz, A.E., Weber, K., Fertig, T.: Analyze before you sensitize: preparation of a targeted ISA training. In: 53rd Hawaii International Conference on System Sciences (2020)
43. Thomson, K.L., von Solms, R.: Towards an information security competence maturity model. Comput. Fraud Secur. **2006**(5), 11–15 (2006). https://doi.org/ 10.1016/S1361-3723(06)70356-6. http://www.sciencedirect.com/science/article/ pii/S1361372306703566
44. Wahlgren, G., Kowalski, S.: A maturity model for IT-related security incident management. In: Abramowicz, W., Corchuelo, R. (eds.) BIS 2019. LNBIP, vol. 353, pp. 203–217. Springer, Cham (2019). https://doi.org/10.1007/978-3-030-20485-3_16
45. Weber, K., Schütz, A.E.: ISIS12-Hack: Mitarbeitersensibilisierenstatt informieren. In: Drews, P., Funk, B., Niemeyer, P., Xie, L. (eds.) Multikonferenz Wirtschsinformatik 2018, vol. IV, pp. 1737–1748. Lüneburg, Germany (2018)
46. Webster, J., Watson, R.T.: Analyzing the past to prepare for the future: writing a literature review. MIS Q. **26**(2), xiii–xxiii (2002). https://www.jstor.org/stable/ 4132319
47. White, G.B.: The community cyber security maturity model. In: 2011 IEEE International Conference on Technologies for Homeland Security (HST), pp. 173–178, November 2011. https://doi.org/10.1109/THS.2011.6107866. ISSN: null
48. Woodhouse, S.: An ISMS (Im)-maturity capability model. In: 2008 IEEE 8th International Conference on Computer and Information Technology Workshops, pp. 242–247, July 2008. https://doi.org/10.1109/CIT.2008.Workshops.46
49. Xiao-yan, G., Yu-qing, Y., Li-lei, L.: An information security maturity evaluation mode. Procedia Eng. **24**, 335–339 (2011). https://doi.org/10.1016/j.proeng.2011. 11.2652. http://www.sciencedirect.com/science/article/pii/S1877705811055044
50. Yulianto, S., Lim, C., Soewito, B.: Information security maturity model: a best practice driven approach to PCI DSS compliance. In: 2016 IEEE Region 10 Symposium (TENSYMP), pp. 65–70, May 2016. https://doi.org/10.1109/ TENCONSpring.2016.7519379. ISSN: null

Who Knows What in My Team? – An Interactive Visualization-Based Instrument for Developing Transactive Memory Systems in Teams

Josef H. Gammel[1(✉)], Dorothea Pantfoerder[2], Timon Schulze[2], Katharina G. Kugler[1], and Felix C. Brodbeck[1]

[1] Ludwig-Maximilians-Universitaet Muenchen, 80539 Munich, Germany
{josef.gammel,katharina.kugler,brodbeck}@psy.lmu.de
[2] Technical University of Munich, 80333 Munich, Germany
{pantfoerder,timon.schulze}@tum.de

Abstract. To be successful, a team must effectively use the individual knowledge that is distributed among its members. The theory of the transactive memory system (TMS) explains how such distributed knowledge is socially organized and exploited to the benefit of the whole team. In this paper, we focus on the concept and design of a visualization-based instrument for TMS development in teams that is grounded in TMS theory. More specifically, we develop a theoretical framework and concept for computer-supported TMS development on the basis of visualization and present a web-based interactive TMS visualization system and instrument for developing TMSs in small teams. The instrument consists of a step-by-step diagnosis, intervention, and evaluation of a TMS and helps teams to strengthen their TMS structure (i.e., knowing who knows what) and TMS processes (i.e., communication to update, encode, and retrieve knowledge). We explain how practitioners can use the here presented instrument for the assessment and development of TMSs and make suggestions for future research.

Keywords: Transactive memory system · Network visualization · Computer-supported team development

1 Introduction

In times of increasing knowledge work and specialization, organizations and their teams must successfully manage and exploit their knowledge resources to perform well (Faraj and Sproull 2000; Spender and Grant 1996). To bring diverse knowledge from different persons together and thus, better exploit the existing knowledge, organizations often rely on teams (Devine et al. 1999; Galbraith 1994). Therefore, it is crucial for researchers and practitioners to understand how knowledge is organized within teams and how teams can be supported to exploit their existing knowledge.

© Springer Nature Switzerland AG 2020
P. Zaphiris and A. Ioannou (Eds.): HCII 2020, LNCS 12206, pp. 600–614, 2020.
https://doi.org/10.1007/978-3-030-50506-6_41

The theory of the *transactive memory system* (TMS; Wegner et al. 1985; Wegner 1986) offers a social psychological explanation of how individual knowledge is socially organized by memory structures and communication processes within teams. A TMS is commonly defined as a collective system for encoding, storing, and retrieving information (Bachrach et al. 2018; Ren and Argote 2011), which facilitates fast access to team members' knowledge and helps whole teams to perform better (for reviews, see: Lewis and Herndon 2011; Ren and Argote 2011). TMSs generally develop when team members communicate with each other, learn about what other team members' know, and start dividing the labor for learning, remembering, and communicating knowledge (Wegner 1986; Wegner et al. 1991). Accordingly, technologies that provide knowledge about team member's knowledge (e.g., Schreiber and Engelmann 2010) and that influence respective communication processes (e.g., Choi et al. 2010) have been developed and shown to relate to TMS development positively. However, to the best of our knowledge, there is no practical instrument for team development that captures structural (i.e., knowledge in the team including knowledge about who knows what) and processual (i.e., communication for encoding, storing, and retrieving relevant information) components of TMS.

In this paper, we addressed the question of how a team can be supported in capturing, understanding, and developing its TMS by using computer-supported visualization. Our goal was to design and implement a prototypical web-based application and instrument for TMS development that (a) is theoretically grounded (b) allows users to dynamically and independently reconstruct TMS structures and processes, and (c) is applicable in practice. We decided to use an interactive graph-based visualization approach, as visualization techniques (e.g., digital concept maps, interactive visualization) are useful for capturing knowledge and to visualize complex networks and relationships as they are also characteristic for TMSs (e.g., Engelmann and Hesse 2010; Schreiber and Engelmann 2010; Pantförder et al. 2019). The visualization is embedded in a psychological team TMS development instrument, comprising the diagnosis, visualization-based intervention, and evaluation of a TMS.

2   Theoretical Framework and Concept

2.1   Components of a TMS in Teams

A TMS is defined as a collective system for encoding, storing, and retrieving information (Bachrach et al. 2018; Ren and Argote 2011). It can be seen as a property of a team that influences what the team can remember as a whole and how information is collectively processed and integrated (Wegner et al. 1985; Wegner 1986). This system consists of two basic and interdependent components: The organized knowledge contained entirely in the team members' individual memories (*TMS structure*) and specific communication processes that occur among team members (*TMS processes*) (Wegner et al. 1985). Table 1 provides an overview of the key components of a team TMS.

The TMS structure comprises the knowledge existing in a group: The *team knowledge stock* and *transactive memory*–the knowledge of who knows what (see Ren and Argote 2011). The transactive memory links individual memories in a way that members can effectively use other members as memory storage. In other words, TMS structure includes not only the specific knowledge of team members that might be of interest to the others but also the knowledge about what other team members know. However, this knowledge might be more or less accurate and more or less shared between team members (Wegner 1986).

TMS processes comprise team member communication that links individual memories within the team. Three fundamental communication processes of TMS have been described in analogy to a computer metaphor: Directory updating, information allocation or transactive encoding, and information retrieval (Wegner 1995; Wegner et al. 1985). This taxonomical framework, which has been used to study TMS networks by other researchers (e.g., Contractor et al. 1998; Palazzolo 2005), is also used in the current paper.

Directory updating is the recognition of expertise, where team members learn about what other team members are likely to know. In other words, team members learn about the expertise or topics of other team members without learning the actual information themselves. This process creates 'expertise directories' that can be used by the team members for the allocation and retrieval of information within the team. This is an important maintenance mechanism of a TMS (see also Palazzolo 2005).

Transactive encoding describes the process when team members collectively organize the storage of new or incoming knowledge. In other words, incoming or new knowledge is encoded and assigned to the team member who seems to be qualified to store it. For example, team members discuss or negotiate who is responsible for a piece of knowledge, or forward incoming knowledge to the person who is seen as responsible (Wegner 1986; Wegner et al. 1985).

Information retrieval happens when team members try to locate and retrieve a piece of knowledge through communication when their own knowledge is not sufficient. This process might involve several communicative steps and require the combination of other knowledge pieces as well (Wegner et al. 1985).

In sum, a team needs efficient TMS structures and processes for the storage, retrieval, and coordination of knowledge to effectively manage and exploit the team's knowledge stock. The TMS structure and processes are dynamically interwoven and influence each other (Lewis and Herndon 2011). Here, the development of the transactive memory–the knowledge about who knows what–plays a central role and is both basis for and depending on TMS processes. We therefore conclude that both components must be taken into account to fully understand and support TMS development in teams.

Table 1. Components of a TMS in teams.

Component	Subcomponent	Description	Key Question
TMS structure	Knowledge stock	Individual team member knowledge, which might be shared or not shared	Which knowledge do the team members possess?
	Transactive memory	Knowledge about *other* team members' memories (e.g., who knows what, who gets knowledge from whom), which might be shared or not shared	What do team members know about each other's memories/knowledge?
TMS processes	Directory updating	Communication between team members through which team members learn about other's knowledge domains or update their 'expertise directory'	What are the team members' knowledge domains?
	Transactive encoding	Communication between team members to define how incoming, new knowledge is collectively stored; this can involve discussion and modification of knowledge	Who should store/be responsible for a specific piece of knowledge within this group?
	Information retrieval	Communication between team members to retrieve pieces of knowledge that is not stored in the person who is asking	Who asks which team member to retrieve specific knowledge?

To illustrate a TMS as a whole, Fig. 1 shows a very simplified conceptual team TMS. Network nodes represent team members who possess individual knowledge (in the following we call different pieces of individual knowledge *knowledge items*). Knowledge items available in the team form the team knowledge stock. Each knowledge item is characterized by a location (i.e., team member's memory) and a label (i.e., an abstract category for this piece of knowledge) (see also Wegner 1986). For example, item A1 is possessed only by team member A. Knowledge item BC1 is possessed by team member B and C–both team members know the same thing (Note that knowledge items existing in a team can be shared or unshared between team members and thus the TMS be rather undifferentiated or differentiated.). Italian letters indicate the transactive memory, i.e. which team members have accurate representations of where knowledge is stored without necessarily possessing the knowledge themselves. For example, all team members know that team member C possesses knowledge item C3, but only person B knows that he or she possesses knowledge item B3. Network edges represent TMS processes (directory updating, information allocation, information retrieval) that occur between the team members. These processes have the potential to link the team members' knowledge items and can be described in terms of their frequency (How often do these processes happen?), quality (Do the processes lead to intended output?), and immediateness (Is technology mediating the processes?).

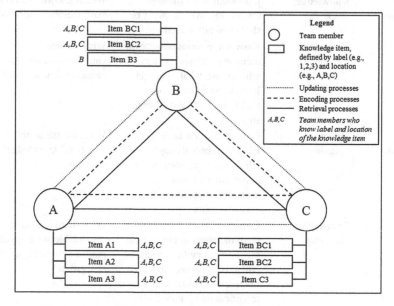

Fig. 1. A simplified conceptual TMS network of a 3-person team.

2.2   Computer-Supported TMS Development

How can computer technology help a team to understand and develop its TMS? A TMS naturally emerges when the members communicate with each other, gain knowledge about other team members' knowledge, and start dividing the labor for learning, remembering, and communicating relevant information (Wegner 1986). Accordingly, shared team experiences and intermediate communication between team members have been shown to be helpful to elaborate a transactive memory (for a review, see: Ren and Argote 2011). However, by solely interacting face-to-face, information exchange does not necessarily reveal all partner information (i.e., knowledge, belief, goals) that is useful for a given task (see also Engelmann et al. 2009). Further, providing additional written information on the knowledge of other team members has been also shown to be useful for TMS development (e.g., Moreland and Myaskovsky 2000). Thus, information technology may be especially helpful for team TMS development when providing detailed information about the team members' knowledge *and* helping to locate expertise within the team (Lewis and Herndon 2011).

In this regard, computer technologies have already been developed to investigate and influence TMS structure or specific TMS processes. For example, software systems that enhance group awareness–the consciousness and information of various aspects of the group and its members–should help to develop TMSs (Gross et al. 2005). Digital concept maps containing information about knowledge and underlying collaboration of partners help teams to initiate TMS processes and establish knowledge awareness among members in computer-supported collaborating ad-hoc teams (Engelmann et al. 2009; Engelmann and Hesse 2010; Schreiber and Engelmann 2010). Ren et al. (2006) developed a multiagent-system modeling approach to study transactive memory and found positive effects of transactive memory on team performance in an experimental group-simulation (Ren et al. 2006). Other researchers developed web-based knowledge mapping programs such as the Inquiring Knowledge Networks On the Web (IKNOW; Contractor et al. 1998), which automatically searches for knowledge structures on the web. Similarly, TMS retrieval processes between team members were studied in detail using network analytical techniques (e.g., Palazzolo 2005). Although these existing technologically-supported instruments are useful for researchers to analyze specific aspects of a TMS in detail, they were not designed to dynamically and independently capture real-life TMSs *as a whole*, require ressources and expertise, and are therefore not practical for team TMS development interventions in the field.

2.3   Principles for TMS Development Using Visualization Techniques

Information visualization has been generally shown to be capable of capturing complex information and relationships as they are inherent to social systems such as TMSs. For example, digital visualization techniques were used for developing shared mental models; mental model visualization helped persons to understand implicit knowledge and supported knowledge transfer (Novak 2007; Zhang et al. 2010). Novak (2007) used a collaborative visualization of knowledge to capture implicit structures of personal and community knowledge. Zhang et al. (2010) illustrated that knowledge visualization using concept maps, mind maps, and visual metaphors can improve learning. Further, graph-based visualizations were also used to support individuals to process complex information better, identify network relationships and explore inconsistent patterns within data (e.g., Feldmann et al. 2017; Pantförder et al. 2019). Thus, we assume that graphically reconstructing and visualizing TMS structure and processes should help teams to better understand and learn about their TMS and discover opportunities for improving the way they share and process knowledge as a team.

How can TMS visualization be effectively embedded in a computer-supported instrument for team TMS development? To answer this question, we developed three principles on the basis of TMS theory and team development practice. Effective team development approaches generally include the following steps: (1) The diagnosis or analysis of the system; (2) deciding, designing and executing the intervention; (3) planning of actions and follow-ups as well as evaluating the success of the intervention (see Dyer 1987). Following this logic, we suggest the following theoretical principles for the diagnosis, intervention, and evaluation of team TMS development:

(1) Diagnosing both TMS structure and processes through accumulating individual perceptions to visualize the system
(2) Interactive and social interventions based on the visualization to generate collective transactive memory updates and initiate TMS processes
(3) Pre- and post-evaluation of the intervention using validated TMS measures

Diagnosing TMS Structure and Processes. A team TMS as a whole can only be understood when both TMS structure and processes are assessed, because these components are dynamically interwoven and influence each other (Lewis and Herndon 2011). Further, only direct measures enable researchers to draw conclusions about the TMS as a whole (Lewis and Herndon 2011). To directly assess TMS structure and processes, all team members and supervisors of a given team must report their own individual knowledge as well as their perceptions (internal representations) of team TMS structure and processes. Thereby team members and supervisors collectively reconstruct the team-level TMS, which then can be brought together in a visual representation. To measure the knowledge stock, individuals can qualitatively report their knowledge items relevant to the team. To measure TMS processes and transactive memory using team members' individual perceptions, we developed items based on the initial theoretical descriptions of TMS processes and transactive memory (Wegner 1986; Wegner et al. 1991; Wegner et al. 1985).

Interactive and Social Intervention Using Visualization Techniques. TMS visualization should be especially useful when it enables team members to learn about each other's knowledge *actively* and when it supports new TMS processes. However, the pure existence of technology does not necessarily trigger social interaction (Kreijns et al. 2003). Thus, an overall psychological instrument for team TMS development must include opportunities for team members to update their shared transactive memory and actively engage in TMS processes. Recalling information about team member's own knowledge and assessing whether who knows what at the diagnosis stage already triggers the formation of new connections in individual memories and sets the stage for an update of the transactive memory. Here, a visualized TMS can then be further used for collective reflection and refinement of the team TMS. We assume that those team members who actively generate the TMS and then collectively reflect, discuss, and refine it have better chances to learn about and strengthen their TMS (see also Johnson and Raye 1981; Wegner et al. 1985). Thus, collectively developing and discussing a graphical visualization of TMS structure and processes provides feedback and insights into other team members' perceptions of the TMS and creates momentum for team learning.

Evaluation Using Validated TMS Measures. To validate that the intervention positively influences TMS development in teams, we suggest assessing team TMS existence before and after the intervention has taken place. For example, the behavioral indicators specialization, credibility, and coordination (Lewis 2003) may be used to indirectly assess the degree to which extend a TMS is existent in a team. This measure is frequently used in field settings (Lewis 2003; Lewis and Herndon 2011).

2.4 Concept of the Visualization-Based Team TMS Development Instrument

For the visualization-based diagnosis, intervention, and evaluation of team TMS development, we suggest a *web-based step-by-step procedure*, which requires that all supervisor(s) and team members participate. Before the intervention can be successfully conducted, the goal, application focus, involved persons, contextual influences, responsibilities, as well as data security and privacy must be clarified. Information and instructions addressing these topics must be provided. We note that the application of the instrument might be supervised by researchers, team leaders, HR professionals, or other persons who are responsible for the teams' development.

Step I: Define Team Characteristics. Initially, the person who is responsible for the intervention (hereinafter referred to as supervisor) creates an on-line account by following the instructions on a web page. The supervisor must enter his name, key task, and password to create an account. To create a team, a short description of the team's overall goal, as well as the names and responsibilities of each of the team members, must be added.

Step II: Assess Individual Knowledge Stock. After the team is characterized, the diagnosis of the actual TMS begins. First, team knowledge stock is assessed. For this, team members independently visit the web page and enter their concrete key knowledge areas or domains (following referred to as knowledge items) using meaningful terms. For example, a software developer from a start-up team who is responsible for developing a product software might enter "programming language Python" as a knowledge item, because he or she knows the programming language, which might be relevant for the given team.

To reduce complexity, we recommend focusing on knowledge items that are or might be related to the team goal and the team member's tasks, roles, or responsibilities (as noted earlier, the scope of the analysis should be defined and discussed in advance). However, the individual knowledge items entered should capture *all* individual knowledge that is potentially relevant to the whole team. Further, the knowledge items should be formulated on a similar and concrete level of abstraction. For example, entering a knowledge item called "software development" is probably not detailed enough to be helpful in a software development project.

Step III: Assess TMS Processes. After all individual knowledge items are entered, TMS processes are assessed on the web page. The team members are asked to individually rate their communication with each of the other team members by answering items on a 5-point Likert scale (1: not at all; 3: to some extent; 5: totally). The three items are: "To which degree could you learn about the team member's knowledge?"; "to which degree do you make this team member responsible for specific topics (e.g., forwarding incoming tasks or information)?"; "to which degree do you retrieve knowledge from this team member?". These items reflect the quality of the TMS processes.

After all team members rated the TMS processes individually, the information is represented within a visualization. Figures 3 and 4 show screenshots of an exemplary TMS visualization. By clicking on the team members, individual knowledge items and individual rating results of TMS processes are shown.

Step IV: Assess Quality of the Transactive Memory. Finally, to assess the quality of the team members transactive memory, all team members are individually asked to look thoroughly at the interactive graph-based visualization, explore the team's knowledge stock, and then individually rate the degree to which they knew about each of the other team member's knowledge and communication by answering an item on a 5-point Likert scale again (1: not at all; 3: to some extent; 5: totally). The items are: "To which degree are you currently aware of the knowledge (items) of this team member?";

"To which extent did you know about the person's communication (updating, encoding, retrieval)?

Step V: Integrate Results and Plan Team Action. In the final step, the team may print and use the results as a basis for discussion, integration, and planning further action to improve the TMS. The visualized TMS and statistical outputs provide insights into the current status of the TMS. The team as a whole can use this information to collectively identify knowledge and communication gaps and integrate the results by answering questions such as: What is surprising? Who talks to whom, and why? Which knowledge items are relevant for whom? How can we improve the way we share our knowledge? How can we make sure that everyone gets access to all knowledge items relevant to his or her tasks and responsibilities? By answering these questions, TMS processes and updates of the transactive memory are triggered.

After the intervention is completed, it should be finally evaluated using validated measures for TMS (e.g., Lewis 2003) again. Table 2 provides a summary of the overall procedure.

Table 2. Step-by-step procedure of the visualization-based TMS development

Step		Description
Pre	Preparation and pre-evaluation	Goal, context, involved persons, responsibilities, data protection, and privacy issues must be clarified in advance. A pre-evaluation of the team TMS using validated scales for TMS measurement is highly recommended
I	Define team characteristics	The supervisor creates an account and enters the team's overall goal, team member names, and team member key responsibilities/tasks/roles
II	Assess individual knowledge stock	Each team member can individually log in and enter his or her concrete individual knowledge areas (knowledge items) related to the team's goal via a separate web page
III	Assess TMS processes	Each team member individually answers a set of questions on the web page that address individual perceptions of their communication with each of the other team members
IV	Assess quality of transactive memory	After step II and III are completed by each team member, the TMS is fully visualized. Team members look at the interactive graph and answer questions about their knowledge about who knows what (transactive memory) and others' communication
V	Integrate results and plan team action	The team uses the results report for discussion and improvement of the team's understanding of it's TMS. The team should also plan further actions to improve the effectiveness of their TMS
Post	Post-evaluation	To evaluate the success of the intervention, a post-evaluation of the team's TMS using validated TMS measures is highly recommended

3 Implementation and Evaluation of the Web-Based TMS Visualization System

For the implementation of the visualization system, we decided on a web-based approach, which allows users to reconstruct a TMS independently and dynamically and without any restriction by different platforms or proprietary tools. Details about the technical implementation and a first qualitative evaluation are presented in the following section.

3.1 Technical Implementation

Figure 2 shows the general implementation concept of the TMS visualization system. For the visualization of a TMS, quantitative and qualitative information on the team and its TMS is collected in order to make it available to a computer-supported visualization system. As explained above, general data on the team (i.e., team goal, team members, etc.) is entered by a supervisor on a web page. The data reflecting TMS structure and processes are entered by team members independently on a different web page.

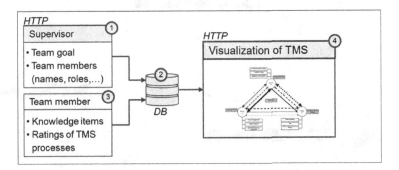

Fig. 2. Concept of the TMS visualization system architecture.

General information about the team – as entered by the supervisor in a first step (Fig. 2, (1)) – is transferred via a PHP-script into a server-sided MySQL database (Fig. 2, (2)). On a second web page (Fig. 2, (3)), team members independently enter data representing the TMS knowledge stock (knowledge items) and also rate TMS processes with each of the other team members in a predefined quantitative questionnaire. These relationships are stored in the database with an indication of the source (ID of the entering team member) and target (ID of the other team member) and their weight (Likert scale rating). Subsequently, this information is read from the database and transferred to the visualization system (Fig. 2, (4)).

For the visualization of the collected data, we have chosen an *interactive graph visualization*, as it is suitable to show the different team members, the TMS processes between them, and individual as well as shared knowledge items. Graphs generally provide an easy way to display objects, respective the team members, and their directed or undirected relationships (TMS processes between the team members). Within the visualization, undirected relations for the mean value of the rated TMS processes from the involved team members as well as directed relation for the individual rated TMS processes from one team member to each other team member are captured. To be independent of proprietary software, we have chosen a web-based solution here as well. The graph visualization was implemented with the help of the javascript library D3.js (https://d3js.org/). The library allows the representation of different visualization forms within a web browser with the help of HTML, SVG, and CSS without using proprietary frameworks. Figure 3 shows a screenshot of an exemplary TMS visualization for a three-person team with the respective key tasks and a dropdown-list with the individual knowledge items. Since none of the team members are selected, the TMS graph is visualized as an undirected graph, and the relations reflect the mean value of communication between the team members. In contrast, Fig. 4 shows a screenshot of the TMS graph where person B is selected by clicking on the node. Now the TMS graph is a directed graph and shows person C's knowledge items and how the person has rated their TMS communication processes.

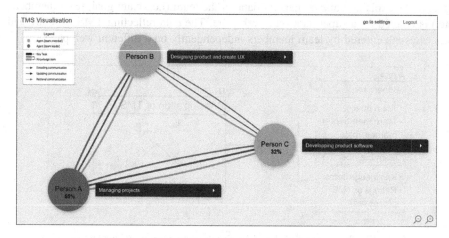

Fig. 3. Visualization of an exemplary TMS in a 3-person team.

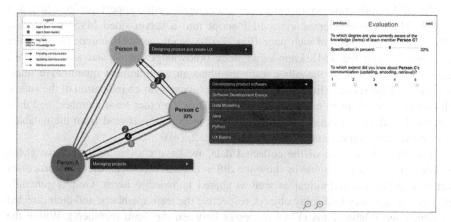

Fig. 4. Visualization of a team member's individual perception of TMS processes in a 3-person team

3.2 Qualitative Evaluation

The system prototype was tested by several persons and teams from the collaborative research center CRC 768 (SFB 768) funded by the German research foundation (DFG). After the system was implemented, we conducted an evaluation workshop with practitioners and researchers in the context of a knowledge management seminar (https://www.innovation360grad.de/) The practitioners and researchers received an introduction on the web-based instrument and procedure and were asked to critically test and discuss its relevance, usefulness, and practicability. The discussion provided initial support for the validity of the concept and implementation: Participants found that the instrument is potentially helpful to develop and strengthen specific TMSs in working teams. Teams that socially reconstruct, visualize, and discuss all components of their TMS by using the application can strengthen their transactive memory and also increase efficient communication and specialization. However, further tests and validation studies for the system are necessary and planned. We note that we permanently improve and further develop the web application and instrument. Please contact the corresponding authors for the web page address and further details.

4 Discussion

In this exploratory paper, we focus on the development of a team intervention instrument for fostering team TMS development. More specifically, we developed a computer-supported, web-based interactive information visualization instrument that helps small teams to strengthen their TMS structure (i.e., knowing who knows what) and TMS processes (i.e., communication to update, encode, and retrieve knowledge). The visualization system is embedded in an overall team development approach that consists of a step-by-step diagnosis, intervention, and evaluation of the team TMS. The procedure is applicable for all kinds of small teams in the field of knowledge-intense work (e.g., project teams, ad-hoc teams, R&D teams, research teams).

Through the social reconstruction and visualization of the TMS, teams get visual and quantitative feedback on the status of their TMS, which strengthens the TMS and provides the basis for further action. The approach is useful for different types of teams in knowledge-intense contexts. We note that learning about other team members' knowledge seems to be positive for TMS development in the early stages of group activity (Ren and Argote 2011). Thus, newly formed teams and ad-hoc teams may benefit from the intervention in particular.

We hypothesize that the instrument helps researchers and practitioners to analyze team TMSs and supports teams to develop their TMSs further. This is important because elaborated TMSs have been shown to constantly predict different types of team performance (for reviews, see: Lewis and Herndon 2011; Ren and Argote 2011). However, the instrument presented in this exploratory paper is at an early developmental stage and requires further testing and validation. We thus suggest using the instrument in future experimental and field studies to evaluate its predictive and practical value.

Another limitation is of a theoretical nature. The instrument relies on the social reconstruction and visualization of the TMS based on individual self-reports. It does not objectively capture TMS structure and processes. However, the fact that the approach includes all team members of a team, individual perceptions can be integrated into a more coherent and complete picture of a team's TMS.

Although the instrument is grounded in TMS theory, further theory-based extensions may increase its value. Key antecedents and moderating variables of TMS development (see Bachrach et al. 2018; Ren and Argote 2011) may be included to help teams better understand their TMS. For example, team members are likely to develop a stronger TMS when they have to interact with each other because of a shared team goal and team member interdependencies (e.g., Zhang et al. 2007). Thus, capturing and visualizing detailed goal structures and team member interdependencies could also help a team to better understand the development of their TMS in the past and future.

Considering further context variables such as team and multiteam leadership (see Seeholzer and Gammel 2018) could also help a team to better understand factors influencing their TMS. Other extensions of the instrument might be useful as well. Besides the three main types of TMS processes, other transactive phenomena might also naturally occur in a team–such as the modification or integration of information and generation of new knowledge (Wegner 1986). Thus, such processes could be included in the analysis as well. This would help the team to get further insights in their social organization of knowledge.

The visualization presented in this paper does also not capture content-specific communication between team members. However, depicting content-specific communication paths between team members requires a rather complex and qualitative in-depth analysis of the TMS, which makes it less practicable. Such extensions are likely to reduce the practicability of the intervention.

We finally argue that the instrument should be not restricted to single teams, but also conceptually extended to other team and not-team based social networks. For example, extending the approach to the level of multiteam-systems (Mathieu et al. 2001, 2002) appears to be beneficial, as teams usually operate in bigger team networks and profit from the communication and knowledge exchange across teams to be innovative (Hülsheger et al. 2009).

Acknowledgments. This work was supported by the German Research Foundation (Deutsche Forschungsgemeinschaft, DFG) as a part of the collaborative research center Sonder-forschungsbereich SFB 768 – Managing cycles in innovation processes – Integrated development of product-service-systems based on technical products.

References

Bachrach, D.G., Lewis, K., Kim, Y., Patel, P.C., Campion, M.C., Thatcher, S.M.B.: Transactive memory systems in context: A meta-analytic examination of contextual factors in transactive memory systems development and team performance. J. Appl. Psychol. **104**(3), 464–493 (2018). https://doi.org/10.1037/apl0000329

Choi, S.Y., Lee, H., Yoo, Y.: The impact of information technology and transactive memory systems on knowledge sharing, application, and team performance: a field study. MIS Q. **34** (4), 855–870 (2010). https://doi.org/10.2307/25750708

Contractor, N.S., Zink, D., Chan, M.: IKNOW: a tool to assist and study the creation, maintenance, and dissolution of knowledge networks. In: Ishida, T. (ed.) Community Computing and Support Systems: Social Interaction in Networked Communities, pp. 201–217. Springer, Heidelberg (1998)

Devine, D.J., Clayton, L.D., Philips, J.L., Dunford, B.B., Melner, S.B.: Teams in organizations: prevalence, characteristics, and effectiveness. Small Group Res. **30**(6), 678–711 (1999). https://doi.org/10.1177/104649649903000602

Dyer, W.G.: Team Building: Issue and Alternatives, 2nd edn. Addison-Wesley, Reading (1987)

Engelmann, T., Dehler, J., Bodemer, D., Buder, J.: Knowledge awareness in CSCL: a psychological perspective. Comput. Hum. Behav. **25**(4), 949–960 (2009). https://doi.org/10.1016/j.chb.2009.04.004

Engelmann, T., Hesse, F.W.: How digital concept maps about the collaborators' knowledge and information influence computer-supported collaborative problem solving. Int. J. Comput.-Support. Collaborative Learn. **5**(3), 299–319 (2010). https://doi.org/10.1007/s11412-010-9089-1

Faraj, S., Sproull, L.: Coordinating expertise in software development teams. Manage. Sci. **46** (12), 1513–1641 (2000). https://doi.org/10.1287/mnsc.46.12.1554.12072

Feldmann, S., Hauer, F., Pantförder, D., Pankratz, F., Klinker, G., Vogel-Heuser, B.: Management of inconsistencies in domain-spanning models – an interactive visualization approach. Paper presented at the Human Interface and the Management of Information: Information, Knowledge and Interaction Design, Cham, May 2017

Galbraith, J.R.: Competing with flexible lateral organizations, 2nd edn. Addison-Wesley, Menlo Park (1994)

Gross, T., Stary, C., Totter, A.: User-centered awareness in computer-supported cooperative work-systems: structured embedding of findings from social sciences. Int. J. Hum.-Comput. Interact. **18**(3), 323–350 (2005). https://doi.org/10.1207/s15327590ijhc1803_5

Hülsheger, U.R., Anderson, N., Salgado, J.F.: Team-level predictors of innovation at work: a comprehensive meta-analysis spanning three decades of research. J. Appl. Psychol. **94**(5), 1128–1145 (2009). https://doi.org/10.1037/a0015978

Johnson, M.K., Raye, C.L.: Reality monitoring. Psychol. Rev. **88**(1), 67–85 (1981). https://doi.org/10.1037/0033-295X.88.1.67

Kreijns, K., Kirschner, P.A., Jochems, W.: Identifying the pitfalls for social interaction in computer-supported collaborative learning environments. a review of the research. Comput. Hum. Behav. **19**(3), 335–353 (2003)

Lewis, K.: Measuring transactive memory systems in the field: scale development and validation. J. Appl. Psychol. **88**(4), 587–604 (2003). https://doi.org/10.1037/0021-9010.88.4.587

Lewis, K., Herndon, B.: Transactive memory systems: current issues and future research directions. Organ. Sci. **22**(5), 1254–1265 (2011). https://doi.org/10.1287/orsc.1110.0647

Mathieu, J.E., Marks, M.A., Zaccaro, S.J.: Multi-team systems. In: Anderson, N., Ones, D., Sinangil, H.K., Viswesvaran, C. (eds.) International Handbook of Work and Organizational Psychology, pp. 289–313. Sage, London (2001)

Mathieu, J.E., Marks, M.A., Zaccaro, S.J.: Multiteam Systems. In: Anderson, N., et al. (eds.) Handbook of Industrial, Work and Organizational Psychology, vol. 2, pp. 289–313. Sage Publications, Thousand Oaks (2002)

Moreland, R.L., Myaskovsky, L.: Exploring the performance benefits of group training: transactive memory or improved communication? Organ. Behav. Hum. Decis. Process. **82**(1), 117–133 (2000). https://doi.org/10.1006/obhd.2000.2891

Novak, J.: Helping knowledge cross boundaries: Using knowledge visualization to support cross-community sensemaking. Paper presented at the 40th Annual Hawaii International Conference on System Sciences, Waikoloa, HI, USA, January 2007

Palazzolo, E.T.: Organizing for information retrieval in transactive memory systems. Commun. Res. **32**(6), 726–761 (2005). https://doi.org/10.1177/0093650205281056

Pantförder, D., Vollenweider, E., Leitner, F.: Interactive visualization of model dependencies in a transdisciplinary environment. In: 14th IFAC/IFIP/IFORS/IEA Symposium on Analysis, Design, and Evaluation of Human-Machine Systems (HMS), IFAC, p. 6 (2019)

Ren, Y., Argote, L.: Transactive memory systems 1985-2010: an integrative framework of key dimensions, antecedents, and consequences. Acad. Manag. Ann. **5**(1), 189–229 (2011). https://doi.org/10.1080/19416520.2011.590300

Ren, Y., Carley, K.M., Argote, L.: The contingent effects of transactive memory: when is it more beneficial to know what others know? Manage. Sci. **52**(5), 671–682 (2006). https://doi.org/10.1287/mnsc.1050.0496

Schreiber, M., Engelmann, T.: Knowledge and information awareness for initiating transactive memory system processes of computer-supported collaborating ad hoc groups. Comput. Hum. Behav. **26**(6), 1701–1709 (2010). https://doi.org/10.1016/j.chb.2010.06.019

Seeholzer, S., Gammel, J.H.: Wie beeinflusst Führung die Entwicklung transaktiver Wissenssysteme in Multiteam Systemen? Eine explorative Interviewstudie. Poster presented at the 51st Congress of the German Psychological Society (DGPs), Frankfurt/Main, Germany, September 2018

Spender, J.C., Grant, R.M.: Knowledge and the firm: overview. Strateg. Manag. J. **17**(S2), 5–9 (1996). https://doi.org/10.1002/smj.4250171103

Wegner, D.M.: Transactive memory: a contemporary analysis of the group mind. In: Mullen, B., Goethals, G.R. (eds.) Theories of Group Behavior, pp. 185–208. Springer-Verlag, New York (1986)

Wegner, D.M.: A computer network model of human transactive memory. Soc. Cogn. **13**(3), 319–339 (1995). https://doi.org/10.1521/soco.1995.13.3.319

Wegner, D.M., Erber, R., Raymond, P.: Transactive memory in close relationships. J. Pers. Soc. Psychol. **61**(6), 923–929 (1991). https://doi.org/10.1037/0022-3514.61.6.923

Wegner, D.M., Giuliano, T., Hertel, P.T.: Cognitive interdependence in close relationships. In: Ickes, W. (ed.) Compatible and Incompatible Relationships, pp. 253–276. Springer, New York (1985)

Zhang, J., Zhong, D., Zhang, J.: Knowledge visualization: an effective way of improving learning. Paper presented at the 2010 Second International Workshop on Education Technology and Computer Science, Wuhan, China, 6–7 March 2010

Zhang, Z.-X., Hempel, P.S., Han, Y.-L., Tjosvold, D.: Transactive memory system links work team characteristics and performance. J. Appl. Psychol. **92**(6), 1722–1730 (2007). https://doi.org/10.1037/0021-9010.92.6.1722

Proactive Smart City Interactions

Madlen Müller-Wuttke[1], Andreas E. Schütz[2], Felix Franz[2],
and Nicholas H. Müller[2(✉)]

[1] LohrOnPlan, Schlossplatz 3, 97816 Lohr a.Main, Germany
[2] Socio-Informatics and Societal Aspects of Digitalization,
Faculty of Computer Science and Business Information Systems,
University of Applied Sciences Würzburg-Schweinfurt, Bavaria, Germany
nicholas.mueller@fhws.de

Abstract. The following paper describes how an application for a Smart City Interaction is being developed at the small city of Lohr a.Main in Bavaria Germany. The project is ongoing, but a first prototype has been developed and was introduced to the local community. Results of those first interaction tests are being presented and implications for the project are being discussed.

Keywords: Smart city · Proactivity · Digitalization

1 Introduction

Smart City functions are topics being widely discussed in current literature. It is a topic of great interest in the scientific communities as well as within the popular sciences and within political and societal discourse. The Alphabet group for example even proposed to establish a fully digitalized city district in Toronto, Canada. All those concepts attempt to deliver a more comfortable way of living for citizens by thinking ahead of the inhabitants. As we were able to show [1–3], proactive system components are quite a useful tool when trying to establish a more natural form of human computer interaction. Especially the addition of a smart and user centered electronic educational instance (EEI) [2] is a rather easy and readily available component to add to any other HCI system.

Therefore, within the 'Lohr Online Planning' project, we are discussing the addition of said EEI in order to incorporate attention as well as taking distracting elements into account. The project itself is a joined effort of the small city Lohr a.Main (Lohr at Main) and the University of Applied Sciences Würzburg-Schweinfurt. The goal is to allow for the citizens of Lohr a.Main to use an online platform for various tasks.

Local businesses, service providers, shops and the food service industry will share an online presence with the municipality as well as with registered associations. Each will be able to present themselves on this site, share goods, services or simply offer a way of reserving a table at a local restaurant. Furthermore, the platform will display information about the town and about local events.

© Springer Nature Switzerland AG 2020
P. Zaphiris and A. Ioannou (Eds.): HCII 2020, LNCS 12206, pp. 615–624, 2020.
https://doi.org/10.1007/978-3-030-50506-6_42

Citizens of Lohr a.Main will then be able to interact with the vendors, the city administration or medical professionals and plan their tasks accordingly. For example, if a certain book is available in an online shop, then the platform could be used to check for the availability at the local bookstore. If it is available there, then the customer could pick it up during his or her scheduled trip downtown and start reading in the evening, instead of having to wait for the book delivery on the next day.

But especially in cases of physiotherapy or other health related appointments, the EEI, as a system-add-on with an open sensory data input, can be utilized to proactively suggest events for the personalized LOHR ONLINE PLAN. For example, by analyzing activity levels from fitness trackers, smart watches or cell phones, the system might suggest a corresponding workout event, like Yoga, running classes or strength training. By being able to take individualized information into account, this would allow for the system to make accurate suggestions suited for each user and leading to a very specific chain of planned events.

Furthermore, due to the established Media Equation Theory by Reeves and Nass [4], as well as the persona effect by Lester et al. [5] the beneficial aspects of an on-screen agent will have to be discussed. Some form of a town mascot or something similar might be a suitable way of opening up the platform to a more willing audience or, at a later stage, might be appropriate to take the planning needs of children and adolescents into account. Thereby offering school-related planning as well as weekend and holiday related extracurricular activities in Lohr a.Main.

But since our EEI related research regarding pedagogical agents [6] was not able to show conclusively that there is a truly advantageous aspect of an on-screen agent while learning, the usefulness of a helping agent system for the platform has to be examined. We are going to use a Tobii Eye-tracker to check for gaze patterns while using the platform to plan various tasks. In addition, we are going to record the pupil dilations to get an insight into cognitive load levels [7]. In theory, this in combination with our proactive system would allow for the system to react adequately to any confusion or misleading parts of the user interface. Due to human computer interfaces still relying mainly on the inputs of a keyboard or mouse movements, the development of a more natural form of Human Computer Interaction, taking those nonverbal input methods into account. Regarding persuasion of technologically unsavvy users to actually use the proposed system, those forms of interaction and nonverbal feedback might be key in establishing a broad and sustainable user base both on the side of the customers as well as with the vendors.

2 Lohr a.Main

The city of Lohr a.Main is a medium-sized city with around 15,000 inhabitants in the district of Main-Spessart, Bavaria, with a high degree of centrality in relevant indicators such as the number of employees, the availability of health care facilities, educational, cultural and leisure facilities as well as ensuring the basic supply of goods, services and additional infrastructure.

The Lohrer population is divided into nine districts with great spatial distance to the old town and urban supply facilities. Around 40,000 people live in the rural catchment area of Lohr a.Main. As a focus point in a rural area, Lohr a.Main acts as an important driver of regional development. Lohr a.Main is the economically most important location in the Main-Spessart district. Of the approximately 13,500 employees, only around 4,200 live in Lohr. The larger number, around 9,300 employees, commute to Lohr every day. Numerous schools and kindergartens as well as an extensive range of cultural and leisure activities make up a high standard of living.

However, the current weakening of local trade and thus regional local shops, due to the increasing demand coverage of the rural population via online trade, endangers the urban supply function and consequently will lead to the loss of jobs and will have a strong impact on the entire district.

In this context, the impact on the structural infrastructure of Lohr's old town should not be neglected. A loss of local shops and the associated lack of fulfillment of the supply purpose has a direct impact on the maintenance and renovation of the existing buildings in the old town of Lohr, as well as the securing of the structural infrastructure.

Local retail in particular, but also all economic and municipal service providers (medical care, culture and leisure activities) need modern perspectives in order to meet the challenges of increasing digitization and to keep the city of Lohr attractive for older people, families, workers and the entire rural population.

With the project LohrOnPlan (Lohr Online Planning), the city of Lohr will create a digital platform on which citizens, traders, service providers, r and the city administration can interact with each other. These interactions expand the extensive range of Lohr's city center into the digital space and shorten the distances from the peripheral rooms to the Lohr center through a "smart" application, strengthen the position of the retail trade in relation to online competition and improve the attractiveness of the city center.

3 The Prototype

In order to reach a broad user-base, the prototype is being developed for desktop-systems as well as Android and iOS devices (Fig. 1).

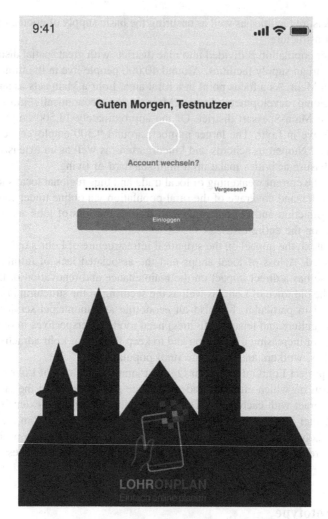

Fig. 1. The login screen of the application (in German)

Currently, the range of functions of the application is to provide information about six areas of interest: services and appointments, shopping, reservations, events and municipal administration. But before we are going to have more detailed look at the features, the challenges of digitalization have to be discussed.

Within our project, one of the main challenges remains to have small shops adapt to a basic level of digitalization. Various service industries are common even in the smallest cities. But one of the main challenges remains to get small shops, who have relied on walking-in-customers or appointments by phone for decades, to implement some form of digitalization. It is not realistic to attempt to change date-planners and appointment-books over to a fully digital solution. Neither would it be possible to simply hand out tablets, computers and internet landlines into every shop as part of our project budget. In order to have those small shops being able to participate and, furthermore, to have their services and goods available for the inhabitants of the city, we had to compromise. The infrastructure of the app allows for varying degrees of digital proficiency. In cases of high competence, APIs are available to facilitate a service. In cases of low competence, the application can work as a relatively simple messaging tool. For example, before getting a haircut the appointment process is to either walk into the store or call it and negotiate a date. Obviously, the application could provide users with a phone number. But instead, we rely on a system which allows for an asynchronous exchange between service- or goods-provider and customer. So, when an appointment has to be negotiated, the customer can request one via the in-app-messaging system and include a couple of slots when he or she would be available. The shop owner on the other hand is then able to check the offline-paper-datebook and pencil one of the requested dates – or suggest an alternative (Fig. 2).

Fig. 2. Product being reserved for pickup

The same is true for goods instead of services. The goal is not to get every small clothing shop online – rather to enable them to have a couple of highlighted products on the application, an appointment system for services like style-recommendations and for customers to reserve a certain product for pickup. Due to this approach, the level of entry to participate is much lower than in other digitalization-transformation-applications.

In addition to enable people to have a better shopping experience, the application also provides information regarding events and the possibility of registering interest in those events. Allowing for the organizers to have a much better knowledge about how many people are going to attend. Furthermore, the administrative bodies of the city of Lohr a.Main have their own area, where they can inform about municipal requirements, services like pensions and benefits as well as appointments at the local residents' registration office.

4   Prototype Evaluation

In order to get a better insight into the citizen's opinion on digitalization and to test the planned features of the application, we prototyped the main workflow. Then, we inquired about the application during the Christmas fair at Lohr. Participants had to conduct certain tasks within the application, like reserving a product for pickup, check for messages, make an appointment, register for an event and to place a reservation at the local coffee shop (Fig. 3).

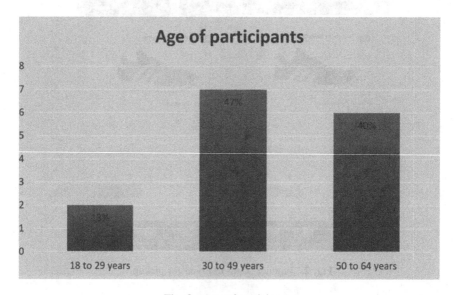

Fig. 3. Age of participants

We asked N = 15 people (m = 9, f = 6) ranging from 18 to 64 years of age. One of the main points of interest was to inquire about the technical devices at home. Almost all of them owned a Smartphone, which was to be expected. Only two thirds however used a computer or a tablet (Fig. 4).

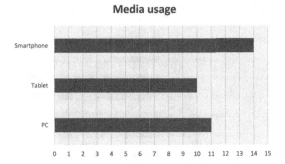

Fig. 4. Usage of media

When asking how often those devices are being used, all of them use their Smartphones on a daily basis. One third is never using a tablet device and half of them using the computer less than twice per week (Fig. 5).

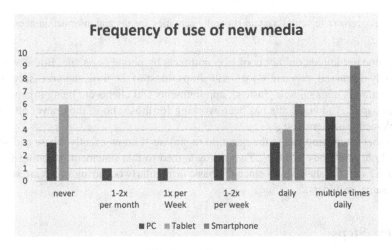

Fig. 5. Media usage

These numbers clearly show that the focus of development, at least pertaining to this demographic, has to be focused on being available on a Smartphone. And when asking the participants about their agreement to certain statements like appointments or buying books online, appointments seem to be an area where digitalization could be used very effectively (Fig. 6).

Agreement

Fig. 6. Agreement regarding certain shopping activities, events and information about Lohr

Just one participant did not book appointments by phone or on site. But as we have previously discussed, especially for small shops, most of the time, the necessary digital infrastructure is not available. Instead, appointments and clients are being organized by pen and paper. And since this has been working for those shops, they never attempted to implement an alternative.

Another interesting fact is the question regarding 'I know exactly where and what I find in Lohr and I buy it there'. Two thirds agreed to this statement, meaning there is not much room for alternatives since the basic or regularly occurring needs are supplied by the same providers.

5   Next Steps

Building on top of the first prototype evaluation, we are now in the middle of applying these information's towards our application. Through the intelligent use and networking of existing infrastructure and actors, with the involvement of specific users on site, the diverse supply functions of Lohr a.Main for the city and the surrounding area should be sustainably secured. By bringing local shops and local people together, the project starts where the online trade simply cannot provide an adequate alternative: by providing a diverse set of different services and goods as well as by linking online and offline content, like with small shops and their datebooks.

The project relies on merging the diverse functions of a city in a needs-oriented and conveniently plannable way to create a successful city experience. This also counteracts job losses through the strengthening of local companies and the opportunities of digitization for the city of Lohr are used in a targeted manner.

Furthermore, at this stage, the earlier mentioned EEI could be implemented in the form of a proactive shopping assistance (Fig. 7).

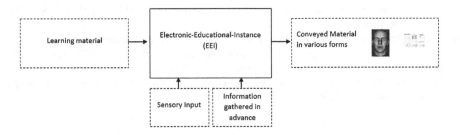

Fig. 7. The electronic educational instance (EEI) [2, 3]

By accessing the calendar function, the EEI would be able to learn about recurring events like haircuts, cosmetics or even food products. This would allow for the system to automatically recommend a specific date or time for an appointment. It could furthermore be linked to other databases and, for example, recommend locally and seasonally grown fruits and vegetables.

6 Conclusion

We presented the project LohrOnPlan and the current empirical questionnaire regarding the status of the project. Current Smart City projects were discussed and an ambitious proactive element regarding the implementation of smart trackers. The current prototype was shown and the evaluation at the Christmas market of Lohr a.Main was discussed, including the next steps of the project.

Acknowledgments. The project is supported by funds of the Federal Ministry of Food and Agriculture (BMEL) based on a decision of the Parliament of the Federal Republic of Germany via the Federal Office for Agriculture and Food (BLE) under the innovation support programme.

References

1. Wuttke, M., Heidt, M., Rosenthal, P., Ohler, P., Müller, N.H.: Proactive functions of a pedagogical agent – steps for implementing a social catalyst function. In: Zaphiris, P., Ioannou, A. (eds.) LCT 2016. LNCS, vol. 9753, pp. 573–580. Springer, Cham (2016). https://doi.org/10.1007/978-3-319-39483-1_52
2. Wuttke, M.: Pro-active pedagogical agents. In: Fakultät für Informatik (Ed.) Proceedings of International Summer Workshop Computer Science, July 2013, pp. 59–62 (2013)
3. Wuttke, M., Heidt, M.: Beyond presentation - employing proactive intelligent agents as social catalysts. In: Kurosu, M. (ed.) HCI 2014. LNCS, vol. 8511, pp. 182–190. Springer, Cham (2014). https://doi.org/10.1007/978-3-319-07230-2_18

4. Reeves, B., Nass, C.: The Media Equation: How People Treat Computers, Televisions, and New Media like Real People and Places. Cambridge University Press, New York (1996)
5. Lester, J.C., Converse, S.A., Kahler, S.E., Barlow, S.T., Stone, B.A., Bhogal, R.S.: The persona effect: Affective impact of animated pedagogical agents. In: Pemberton, S. (ed.) Human Factors in Computing Systems: CHI'97 Conference Proceedings, pp. 359–366. ACM Press, New York (1997)
6. Müller-Wuttke, M., Müller, N.H.: Cognitive load levels while learning with or without a pedagogical agent. In: Zaphiris, P., Ioannou, A. (eds.) HCII 2019. LNCS, vol. 11590, pp. 266–276. Springer, Cham (2019). https://doi.org/10.1007/978-3-030-21814-0_20
7. Rosch, J.L., Vogel-Walcutt, J.J.: A review of eye-tracking applications as tools for training. Cogn. Technol. Work. 15(3), 313–327 (2012)

An Authoring Platform for CSCL Script Definition

Andreas Papasalouros[(⊠)] and George Chatzimichalis

University of the Aegean, 83200 Karlovassi, Greece
{andpapas,hatzimih}@aegean.gr

Abstract. Computer Supported Collaborative Learning scripts define pedagogically effective practices for organizing collaborative activities. This paper presents a novel platform for defining CSCL scripts. This platform is composed of the following components: a) a formal language named COSTLy for the specification of CSCL scripts based on logic and constraints, b) a visual environment that facilitates the authoring of scripts, based on the formal language, and c) a mechanism that translates the abstract definitions of scripts into constraint logic programs, thus implementing group formation and task distribution of actual scenario instances. The expressiveness of the proposed language was evaluated. Also the results of a usability evaluation of the proposed platform are reported in the paper. It was shown that university students were able to use the platform in order to describe CSCL scripts of high complexity.

Keywords: Authoring platform · Learning activity representation · CSCL scripts · Constraint logic programming

1 Introduction

In the context of Computer Supported Collaborative Learning (CSCL), unguided/unsupported collaboration delivers less than optimal educational benefits [15]. To alleviate this problem, CSCL scripts describe pedagogically effective practices for organizing the experiences of individuals when engaged in collaborative activities. They consist of proper specifications of educational scenarios defined by teachers or instructional designers. These specifications comprise a number of components, that is, participants, activities, roles, groups and resources, as well as certain mechanisms, i.e. task distribution, group formation and sequencing [7].

In this paper we present a logic-based formalism for describing scripts. That is, we describe a language named COSTLy that can express the logical conditions that define certain formations of groups. This language is expressive enough so that it can formally describe various CSCL scripts that exist in the literature. An initial version of COSTLy language is presented in [10]. Based on the language above, we have developed a platform that allows the authoring of scripts through a visual environment. Also, this platform supports the automatic translation of

© Springer Nature Switzerland AG 2020
P. Zaphiris and A. Ioannou (Eds.): HCII 2020, LNCS 12206, pp. 625–640, 2020.
https://doi.org/10.1007/978-3-030-50506-6_43

script descriptions into constraint logic programs. By running these programs with a constraint solver, we provide a reasoning mechanism for performing group formation in actual educational settings.

The structure of this paper is as follows: In Sect. 2 related literature is presented. The following Sect. 3 provides an informal and formal presentation of the proposed language for CSCL script descriptions. The implementation of the platform is presented in Sect. 4, followed by the evaluation Sect. 5. The paper ends with conclusions and directions for future work.

2 Related Work

The automation of group formation in collaborative scripts is currently an active field of research [2,3,9,13]. A number of works approach the problem of automatic group formation in CSCL settings as an optimization problem concerning the minimization or maximization of a metric referring to the participant characteristics and/or preferences. Thus, the proposed solutions are based on probabilistic, clustering, Bayesian or multi-agent algorithms [1,4,12].

Ounnas et al. [8,9] have found that if the allocation of students to groups follow certain criteria and constraints, for example certain roles in each group, constraints of characteristics of members of the groups, this has an effect in student satisfaction after collaboration. Thus, they have addressed the problem of automatic group formation as a Constraint Satisfaction Problem. They proposed a semantic group formation framework that utilizes semantic descriptions and logical constraints as means of automatic group formation in CSCL settings. They have implemented a system of constraints based on ontologies and the Datalog system, that supports constraint satisfaction with priorities. A user interface is given to teachers for the selection of predefined constraints, defined as appropriate Datalog expressions.

Amarasinghe et al. [2] describe a method for expressing the specific phases of the Jigsaw Collaborative Learning script [7] in the form of optimization constraint expressions. Further, they use a specific optimization software in order to actually solve certain instances of group formation problems.

In [13] a method for group formation is described, building on [9]. Based on Constraint Logic Programming, it aims to satisfy constraints pertaining to, among others, student preferences, individual proficiency and learning styles. Balmaceda et al. [3] also perform group formation based on certain team roles, psychological styles, and social relationships.

The above methods are mostly addressing the problem of automatic, criteria-based group formation, given that this kind of group formation has been demonstrated to be preferable to random assignment into groups [12]. Only [2] is dealing with other mechanisms of CSCL scripts such as task distribution or with the description of various script phases. Conversely, our work aims at both group formation and task distribution, as mechanisms of CSCL scripts.

The above methods use fixed sets of constraints and/or pre-defined algorithms for group formation. These constraints are authored by using low level languages such as Prolog. A user interface is provided by [8] that allows parametrization of predefined constraints. The work presented in this paper aims at shifting the definition of scripts from the engineering [5] to the authoring level by proposing an specialized logic-based formalism, a visual representation and a supporting platform in order to facilitate the authoring and execution of CSCL scripts.

3   A Script Definition Language

The proposed platform is based on COSTLy, a specialized language for script definition which is described in this section. First, an informal presentation of the language is given, followed by a formal presentation.

3.1   Informal Description of the Language

In the proposed formalism, a script definition is a sequence of phase descriptions. In each phase a number of groups is formed, where students are allocated to specific tasks, possibly engaging in specific roles.

The allocation in groups is specified as a partition definition. A partition is a collection of non-empty groups of participants such that every participant belongs to only one group and the union of all partition groups adds to the initial set of participants. The definition of a partition in a specific phase, or for the whole script, is expressed as a constraint. In a partition definition, a logical predicate is provided that formally describes a constraint which must be satisfied by the partition for the particular phase. An instance of a phase definition is given in Example 1.

Example 1. An example phase definition.

```
1    phase EG: create-partition P for S,Tasks with |Tasks| groups .
2      forall T in Tasks exists! Gr in P
3        forall St in Gr
4          ASSERT(performs(St,T)).
```

This description for a partition, P, takes as parameters a set of participants, S, and an optional set of resources or $Tasks$. The number of groups in the partition must be defined. In the example, the number of groups in the partition is set to $|Tasks|$, that is, to the number or available tasks. The predicate for a partition can be a simple predicate, such as *reads(John, chapter1)*, a complex formula involving logical connectives (**and**, **or**, **not**) or, as in line 2 of Example 1, a quantifier expression: **forall** or **exists**. The latter provide universal and existential quantification, respectively, over the elements of a set.

A special quantifier named **exists!** appears in line 2 of Example 1. It syntactically follows, a universal quantifier (**forall**). This form defines a relation among the elements of the two quantified sets so that the elements of the second are evenly allocated to the elements of the first. Thus, in the expression in line 2, the elements of set P, that is, the groups of the partition P are evenly associated with the tasks in set $Tasks$. As an example, in a specific setting with sets $Tasks = \{a, b\}$ and $P = \{g_1, g_2, g_3, g_4\}$, the relation pairs $\{(a, g_1), (a, g_3), (b, g_2), (b, g_4)\}$, satisfy the condition in line 2.

The ASSERT, (meta-)predicate, used in logic programming, is a special form that asserts the truth of a certain fact, in the form of an atomic predicate that it takes as its argument. This is of particular importance since this predicate generates new relations during a certain phase of a script. Thus, in Example 1, it is designated that each participant, St in group Gr, (line 3) is assigned to perform a certain task, T (line 4). In the example, it is designated that for the particular phase, EG, the available tasks are evenly allocated to groups so that every participant in a group performs the same task. This is the expert phase of the jigsaw script, presented later in Sect. 5.

Predicates such as *performs* above are not part of the language and they can be arbitrarily defined by the designer of a certain script, allowing for group formation based on arbitrary binary relations. However, there is also a number of special, built-in predicates such as max, min and functions (sum, abs). Certain variants of a basic script can be defined by providing additional, extrinsic constraints [2], in the form of new logical conditions that are conjunctively connected with the constraint of the basic script.

A simple example of a minimization constraint is given in Example 2. In the example, the sum of grades for each *Student* in group G is minimal. Here, the grade of each student is represented as a function.

Example 2. Minimization of the sum of grades of the students in a group.

min(sum($grade(Student)$ for $Student$ in G))

3.2   Formal Definition of COSTLy Language

In the proposed language, a script is defined as a predicate that involves a sequence of phases. In BNF form, this is expressed as

⟨*script-definition*⟩ := 'define' 'script' ⟨*script-var*⟩: ⟨*predicate*⟩

⟨*phase-definition*⟩ := 'phase' ⟨*phase-var*⟩ ':' ⟨*predicate*⟩ '.'

⟨*phase-sequence*⟩ := ⟨*phase-definition*⟩*

In the above definition, ⟨*script-var*⟩ is the name of the script and ⟨*phase-var*⟩ is the name of a particular phase. The ⟨*predicate*⟩ element above defines the constraints, in the form of logical conditions that have to be satisfied in the particular partition definition. A ⟨*predicate*⟩ may have the following forms:

⟨*predicate*⟩ := ⟨*partition-pred*⟩
  | ⟨*phase-sequence*⟩
  | ⟨*atomic-predicate*⟩
  | ⟨*composite-predicate*⟩
  | ⟨*quantifier-form*⟩
  | ⟨*meta-predicate*⟩

A ⟨*partition-pred*⟩ is a proposition that defines the groups of participants in the particular phase, as explained below. A partition predicate is defined as

⟨*partition-pred*⟩ := 'create-partition' (⟨*partition-term*⟩
 | '('⟨*groups-list*⟩')') 'for' ⟨*participants*⟩ (',' ⟨*parameter*⟩)*
 ['with' ⟨*term*⟩ 'groups'] '.' ⟨*predicate*⟩ '.'

where ⟨*partition-term*⟩ is a variable denoting the set of groups defined in the partition which is to be arranged into groups. In the above, ⟨*participants*⟩ is a variable denoting the list of participants. The ⟨*parameter*⟩ sequence following is a list of optional parameters, such as the set of resources that are needed in case that task allocation is specified in the particular partition statement. From the above definitions it follows that a ⟨*partition-pred*⟩ can be applied at the phase or at the script level, that is, we can define a partition for a particular phase or for the whole script.

Other kinds of predicates are defined as follows:

⟨*atomic-predicate*⟩ := [⟨*phase-term*⟩] '.' ⟨*pred-symbol*⟩ '(' ⟨*term-list*⟩')'
 | ⟨*a-predicate*⟩

⟨*a-predicate*⟩ := ('min'
 | 'max') '(' ⟨*term*⟩ ')')
 | ⟨*term*⟩ ⟨*predicate-symbol*⟩ ⟨*term*⟩

⟨*composite-predicate*⟩ := 'not' ⟨*predicate*⟩
 | '(' ⟨*predicate*⟩ ⟨*connective*⟩ ⟨*predicate*⟩ ')'

⟨*connective*⟩ := 'and'
 | 'or'
 | ⇒ (implies)

⟨*meta-predicate*⟩ := 'ASSERT' '(' ⟨*atomic-predicate*⟩ ')'

⟨*predicate-symbol*⟩ := '=' (equals)
 | '\=' (different)
 | '<' (less)
 | '>' (more)

As seen in the above definition, a ⟨*predicate*⟩ constraint can be atomic, or it may be composed by using the usual logical connectives (and, or, implies). The ASSERT, meta-predicate takes as an argument a certain proposition (in the form of an ⟨*atomic-predicate*⟩) and asserts its truth value.

The quantified predicates provide quantification (e.g. forall, exists, and exists!, explained above) over sets of data, such as the set of participants or the set of members of a specific group.

$\langle quantifier \rangle := $ 'forall'
  | 'exists'
  | 'exists!'
$\langle quantifier\text{-}form \rangle := \langle quantifier \rangle \langle variable \rangle$ 'in' $\langle variable \rangle$
    $\langle predicate \rangle$

Predicates can be defined by the designer of a specific script. However, there are also defined a number of special, built-in predicates, such as max and <, with apparent meaning.

Finally, terms can be constants, variables, functions as well as more complex mathematical expressions with the usual algebraic syntax. The special function $|S|$ returns the number of elements in a specific set, S.

$\langle term \rangle := \langle constant \rangle$
  | $\langle variable \rangle$
  | $\langle math\text{-}expression \rangle$
  | '|' $\langle variable \rangle$ '|'

$\langle term\text{-}list \rangle := \langle term \rangle$ (',' $\langle term \rangle$)*

$\langle function\text{-}term \rangle := \langle function\text{-}symbol \rangle$ '(' $\langle term\text{-}list \rangle$ ')' | 'sum' '(' $\langle term \rangle$ ')'
    'for' $\langle variable \rangle$ 'in' $\langle variable\text{-}set \rangle$

The sum function either sums the values of its argument set over the elements of $\langle variable\text{-}set \rangle$ (as in Example 2). Other functions can be supported, either built-in or user-defined.

4   Implementation

A web based editor allows script designers to create, process, save, and print a script in a graphical manner by connecting language instructions' tiles together, as illustrated in Fig. 1. This editor has been developed using HTML5 and Google Blockly [6]. The users of the editor may export their script to the Java back-end subsystem after having instantiating it. Instantiation of a script includes steps like the loading of participants' names and resources from files during the group formation process.

The Java back-end subsystem is accessed thought a Java Servlet interface, passing it all the necessary information for the desired group formation, like script text code, names and attributes of the participants, available resources etc. Parsing of the script's text is accomplished by the ANTLR4 Java library [11], producing in this way the necessary lexing and parsing rules of the script. The syntax of the language has been defined within the context of the Java back-end subsystem as an ANTLR4 language description. Using the produced ANTLR4 parsing tree, an automated translation of the script to Prolog is being performed, in order the script specific Prolog clauses to pair the intrinsic Prolog clauses.

The whole set of Prolog rules is being utilized in the Prolog CLP(FD) Constraint Solver [14] to produce the partition table with information regarding the groups' configuration, according to the directives and the restrictions specified in

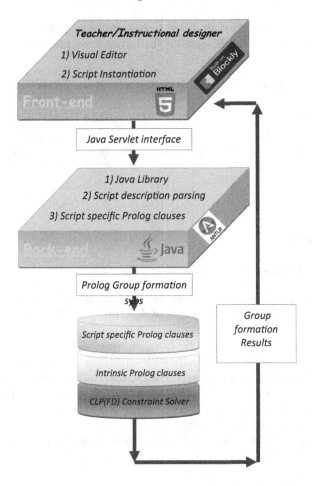

Fig. 1. The flow of transformation

the script by its creator. This table is being returned to the front-end to depict the results of partitioning in a user friendly manner.

As in previous works (e.g., [2]), the allocation of participants to groups is expressed as an integer constraint satisfaction problem. In the implementation presented here, a partition is represented as a table of binary elements where each element p_{ij} is 1 if participant i is allocated in group j and 0, otherwise. All M columns of this table have non zero sum, representing non-empty subsets of participants: $\sum_{i=1}^{N} p_{ij} > 0$, $\forall j \in \{1, \ldots, M\}$. Furthermore, each participant is considered to participate in only one group: $\sum_{j=1}^{M} p_{ij} = 1$ $\forall i \in \{1, \ldots, N\}$.

The descriptions of the proposed language are automatically transformed into appropriate Prolog expressions containing constraints, which are executed by using the constraint solver. These constraints are imposed on the table p_{ij} that represents the formation of groups. The transformation is based on certain rules, some of them depicted in Table 1. In this table, `pred'` is the generated Prolog clause head that corresponds of the initial `pred` predicate.

Table 1. Indicative constraint generation rules

Expression	Generated Prolog code
`forall A in Set: pred(Params, A)`	`maplist(pred'(Params),Set)`
`exists A in Set: pred(Params,A)`	`member(A,Set),pred'(Params,A)`

5   Evaluation

5.1   Expressiveness Evaluation

The main research question that is investigated in this subsection is the following: "Is the proposed language capable of describing CSCL scripts found in the related literature and used in educational practice?"

In order to answer the above question, we were based on the generic framework for CSCL script specification provided in [7]. This framework provides a set of components and mechanisms for script description, namely, participants, groups, activities, roles, group formation, task distribution, and sequencing. The above were exemplified by a set of scripts described in the paper: Jigsaw, Argue-Graph, Universante and MURDER.

For every one of the above scripts the proposed platform was used in order to perform the following:

- The set of phases was identified.
- The constraints for each script expressed in the visual notation for script description provided by the online editor.
- Each script definition was automatically translated into CLP(FD)/Prolog by the use of the platform.
- An indicative setting was provided as input, pertaining to a set of participants and a set of tasks and additional resources, as test cases for actually running and solving the constraints of each script.

Given the above, we examined the expressiveness and effectiveness of the presented language and platform. In order to determine expressiveness, we checked whether the proposed language can describe the phases of each script at the visual or the textual level. In order to determine effectiveness, we examined whether the platform was able to form groups and allocate students to tasks according to the constraints imposed, for concrete phases.

The Jigsaw Script. The Jigsaw script is extensively used and studied in the relative literature. The script comprises two distinct phases, related to group formation:

- In the first *Expert Group* (EG) phase, participants are divided in expert groups so that, given a set of tasks, all participants in an expert group are assigned to the same task.
- In the second *Jigsaw Group* (JG) phase, there should be at least one student for each task within each jigsaw group.

The textual definition for the, first, expert group phase has been already given in Example 1 while the definition of the second, jigsaw group phase, is given in Example 3 below.

Example 3. Textual definition of the jigsaw group phase of jigsaw script

```
1    phase JG: create-partition Pj for S,Tasks with |S|/|Tasks|
2    groups .
3      forall Gr in Pj
4        forall T in Tasks exists! St in Gr
5          EG.performs(St,T).
```

In the jigsaw phase presented above, the number of formed groups is the integer ratio of the number of participants, over the number of tasks, $|S|/|Tasks|$. The allocation of students to groups must satisfy the following constraint (lines 3–5 in Example 3): In each jigsaw group, Gr, in the new partition P_j (line 3), the students of the group must be evenly associated to each task (line 4) according the allocation of students to tasks in the previous, expert phase (*EG.performs(St,T)* in line 5).

Figure 2 illustrates the visual definition of the Jigsaw script, utilized by the web interface of the proposed platform. This definition corresponds to the textual definition in Examples 1 and 3. The platform automates the translation from visual to textual definition and also enables the translation of the script definition into to a numerical constraint satisfaction problem, as stated above.

Table 2 illustrates the allocation of students to groups in the two phases of the Jigsaw script, expert phase and jigsaw phase for a setting with 12 students and 3 tasks. In the expert (group) phase (EG) three groups are generated, each group corresponding to one of the three tasks in the script. All students are allocated to the same task for each group in this phase. In the following jigsaw group phase (JG), four groups are defined, each group containing one student from each group from the previous, expert phase. In each group, each student is allocated to a different task in this phase.

ArgueGraph Script. Initially, a questionnaire is given to all the participants. Their summarized opinion is plotted onto a graph. Participants with extremely contradictory opinions (point distance in the graph) are paired and a new copy

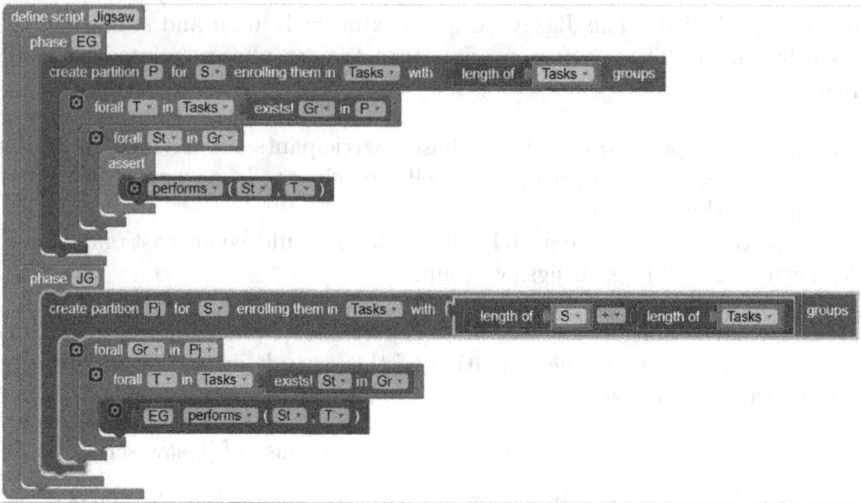

Fig. 2. The visual definition of the Jigsaw script

Table 2. Jigsaw partitioning with 12 students and 3 tasks

Student	1	2	3	4	5	7	7	8	9	10	11	12
Expert (EG) group	1	1	1	1	2	2	2	2	3	3	3	3
Jigsaw (JG) group	1	2	3	4	1	2	3	4	1	2	3	4

of the questionnaire is given to them. Within their group, participants should discuss on what arguments to point out for each item of the questionnaire. The teacher collects the results of the discussion and aids each group to review their arguments. The teacher then summarizes distinct arguments by item. Finally, an essay is assigned to the participants targeting to a synthesis of all the discussed arguments.

From the description above, we model two distinct phases: In the first phase, named $AG1$ here, the students are grouped in pairs. It is considered that before partitioning the students answer certain questions in a questionnaire giving positive or negative answers, semantically described with function $answer$ in Example 4 below. Then, partitioning is performed with the constraint of minimizing the absolute difference of grades (line 3) for all questions and student pairs.

Example 4. Maximizing the diversity of opinions in student pairs in Argue-Graph.

```
1  phase AG1: create-partition Groups:
2    for S, Questions with |S|/2 groups .
3    max(sum(sum(sum(sum(abs(answer(S1,Q)-answer(S2,Q))
4      for S1 in G)
5        for S2 in G)
```

```
6        for G in Groups)
7          for Q in Questions)).
```

The second phase of the ArgueGraph script involves only one group with all students involved. The items of discussion are equally distributed to students.

Example 5. Second phase of ArgueGraph script

```
1  phase AG2: create-partition Pj for S,Items with 1 groups .
2    forall G in Pj
3      forall I in Items exists! St in G
4        ASSERT(is_assigned_to(St,I)).
```

The UniverSante Script. Problem cases are discussed and solved by participants from different nations in mixed and rotating teams. Initially, mixed nations groups read and discuss cases. Results are then presented and analyzed in national teams in order to create a national fact sheet. In a later phase, teams of participants with similar cases, review these national fact sheets (mixed nations). Reviewing summaries, after being discussed among participants of the same country, are analyzed within the initial groups in order to investigate a case solution.

Example 6. Textual definition of UniverSante script

```
1  define script UniverSante:
2    phase MNT:
3      create-partition Un1 for S,Countries with |S|/|Countries|
4      groups .
5        forall Group in Un1
6          forall Nationality in Countries exists! P in Group
7            country(P,Nationality).
8
9    phase SNT:
10     create-partition Un2 for S,Countries with |Countries|
11     groups .
12       forall Nationality in Countries exists! Group in Un2
13         forall P in Group
14           country(P,Nationality).
```

In the MNT Group phase above, four groups are generated, each group containing members from a different country. In the following UniverSante Group phase (SNT) four groups are defined, each group consisting of students from the same country.

MURDER Script. MURDER is an acronym for Mood, Understanding, Recall, Detection, Elaboration, and Review. Pairs of participants are learning from a textbook, one being the summarizer and the other the listener. After the initial phase of preparing the studying mood, both participants in each group read a text passage for comprehension. The summarizer is trying to remember what has been read while the other participant (the listener) tries to detect mistakes, inaccuracies or omissions and gives feedback. Then, both cooperate on the read passage and repeat everything with swapped roles for the next passage of the assigned text. At the end, both participants should recall the read passages and assess what they have learned.

In this case, groups in the form of pairs of students are formed once at the begin at the script so that the same pairs of students exist in all phases. In each phase, the roles of particular students are interchanged, while the groups (pairs) remain unchanged. Thus, the `create-partition` form is applied at the script definition level (line 1 in Example 7), rather than the phase definition levels. There are three phases in the script description. In the first phase (lines 4–8), the two students are assigned two distinct roles, *summarizer* and *listener*, while in the second phase the roles are interchanged. In the *Final* phase every student in each pair asserts and reviews the same text.

Example 7. MURDER script definition with three phases.

```
1   define script MURDER: create-partition Groups for S
2     with |S|/2 groups .
3     forall G in Group
4       phase Ph1:
5         exists St1 in Group
6           exists St2 in Group
7             (S1 \= S2 and ASSERT(summarizer(St1))
8               and ASSERT(listener(St2))) .
9
10      phase Ph2:
11        exists St1 in Group (not Ph1.summarizer(St1) and
12          exists St2 in Group (not Ph1.listener(St2)
13            and ASSERT(summarizer(St1))
14              and ASSERT(listener(St2)))) .
15
16      phase Final:
17        forall St in Group
18          (ASSERT(reviews(St)) and ASSERT(reads(St))) .
```

In the current version of the language there is no distinct construct for roles in a script, so they are described as assertions in certain predicates as in the example above. For the sake of simplicity, in Example 7 no allocation to actual tasks is provided, although it is supported by the language.

Analysis of Expressiveness. From the above descriptions it has been demonstrated that the proposed language and platform can describe the various aspects of CSCL scripts. In all of the scripts, group formation was supported and adequately described. Groups are formed at the level of a particular phase, while in the MURDER script, where participants are allocated to the same pair for the whole script. The language/platform supports both kinds of group formation. Distribution of tasks to participants is also supported for all the scripts above, although not demonstrated in the MURDER script. As demonstrated in the MURDER script, the language/platform can also describe roles indirectly, through the appropriate use of predicates (e.g. "summarizer" and "listener"), although there is not a specific construct in the language for roles in its current version. Also, mechanisms such as role exchange are supported in an ad hoc manner, by utilizing certain predicates provided by the language/platform. Finally, sequencing of various phases of the scripts is also supported through the construct of phases, although composite patterns of sequencing such as repetitions and conditional executions of phases are not supported yet. From the above, the proposed language and platform has been shown to at least partially support the main mechanisms and components of CSCL scripts.

5.2   Usability Evaluation

In order to evaluate the usability of COSTLy as a language as well as the usability of the visual front end of the platform, a task-based evaluation protocol was applied, as described in this subsection. For this purpose, the results of an experiment with student participants from a course in Educational Technology are reported.

A number of $N = 31$ students participated in the evaluation, 14 males and 17 females. All students have attended a university semester course in Educational Technology in a Greek University, which is taught by one of the authors of this paper. The course has a theoretical part that covers, among other topics, CSCL and scripts. Also, the course has a laboratory part with three educational technology environments covered and three corresponding laboratory assignments. The COSTLy language and platform were covered in the third assignment that lasted for four weeks. All participants were Mathematics students, so they were assumed to be familiar with elements of first order logic such as variables, sets and quantifiers. Nevertheless, during the first week in the laboratory, an introduction to propositional and first order logic was given by the instructor, which constitute prerequisite knowledge for the proposed language, which is logic-based [10]. During the next two weeks, COSTLy language and the platform were presented to the students, together with appropriate examples and accompanying study material. At the end of the forth week, each student was orally interviewed by one of the authors in order to gain an insight of the students' understanding and attitude of the proposed language/platform.

The assignment consisted of nine exercises to be submitted atomically by each student. In each exercise the students had to translate a verbally described CSCL scenario into the COSTLy language. In order to author the scenarios, the visual environment could be used or, alternatively, the students could directly write the scripts in their textual form, as it is defined earlier in this paper.

The exercises are of increasing difficulty. That is, exercises 1 to 5 only demanded understanding of example scenarios already presented in the laboratory sessions and in the learning material, while exercises 6 to 9 are original and complex scenario descriptions. The students should have acquired a deep understanding of the mechanisms of the language and of the combination of various types of expressions in order to successfully accomplish all exercises, and especially exercises 6 to 9. For example, exercise 8 describes a variation of the Jigsaw script, a highly complicated script that involves more than one phases and an interdependence among these phases. During the assignment some students could ask questions about the exercises that were explained by the teacher of the course, that by no means provided hints for the answers.

The two authors evaluated independently the assignments of the students based on a five-grade scale from 1 to 5, with 1 corresponding to a totally inadequate answer and 5 corresponding to a perfect answer by each student. The inter-rater reliability was found to be substantial (squared-weighted Cohen's kappa $= 0.8$).

Table 3. Performance evaluation results

	Exercise								
	1	2	3	4	5	6	7	8	9
Average grade	4.82	4.66	4.65	4.34	3.92	2.82	3.42	2.89	2.35
Grade STD	0.60	0.64	0.72	1.36	1.23	1.41	1.64	1.54	1.36
# of students with grade > 4	29	26	25	24	20	6	14	7	3
% of students with grade > 4	93.5	83.9	80.6	77.4	64.5	19.4	45.2	22.6	9.7

The results of the performance evaluation of the nine exercises for all students based on the mean grades of the two evaluators are illustrated in Table 3. It is shown in the table that most students were able to complete the task of expressing the easiest of the assigned scripts (1–6). Even in the harder script no. 9, three students were able to achieve a grade above 4, meaning that they gave an almost perfect formal description of the script with the COSTLy language.

Thus, it was verified that in the above evaluation students were able to formally define CSCL scripts in the proposed language through the platform based on textual descriptions and examples of these scripts.

6   Conclusions and Future Work

This paper proposed a formal representation and a reasoning mechanism, in the form of a formal language that is executable by being translated into constraint logic programs. While other works exist in the literature that support group formation with various methods, including constraint satisfaction, this work proposes a specialized language and a supporting platform for representing CSCL scripts rather than a generic formalism, only accessible by technical experts.

It has been demonstrated that the proposed language and platform are able to both express and solve a set of well-known CSCL scripts found in the literature and also to support main components and mechanisms of scripts. Furthermore, we have found that university students were able to effectively use the proposed language and its visual front end in order to describe CSCL scripts of high complexity. Thus, the proposed platform is expected to enable instructional designers to design collaborative scripts in an open and usable manner.

As future work, we plan to incorporate the proposed platform into a collaborative learning management system such as moodle in order to further study its use in a real learning environment.

References

1. Alberola, J.M., Del Val, E., Sanchez-Anguix, V., Palomares, A., Teruel, M.D.: An artificial intelligence tool for heterogeneous team formation in the classroom. Knowl.-Based Syst. **101**, 1–14 (2016)
2. Amarasinghe, I., Hernández-Leo, D., Jonsson, A.: Intelligent group formation in computer supported collaborative learning scripts. In: 2017 IEEE 17th International Conference on Advanced Learning Technologies (ICALT), pp. 201–203. IEEE (2017)
3. Balmaceda, J.M., Schiaffino, S.N., Pace, J.A.D.: Using constraint satisfaction to aid group formation in CSCL. Inteligencia Artificial, Revista Iberoamericana de Inteligencia Artificial **17**(53), 35–45 (2014)
4. Cruz, W.M., Isotani, S.: Group formation algorithms in collaborative learning contexts: a systematic mapping of the literature. In: Baloian, N., Burstein, F., Ogata, H., Santoro, F., Zurita, G. (eds.) CRIWG 2014. LNCS, vol. 8658, pp. 199–214. Springer, Cham (2014). https://doi.org/10.1007/978-3-319-10166-8_18
5. Dillenbourg, P., Tchounikine, P.: Flexibility in macro-scripts for computer-supported collaborative learning. J. Comput. Assist. Learn. **23**(1), 1–13 (2007)
6. Google: Blockly - A library for visual programming editors. https://developers.google.com/blockly/. Accessed Jan 2020
7. Kobbe, L., et al.: Specifying computer-supported collaboration scripts. Int. J. Comput. Support. Collab. Learn. **2**(2), 211–224 (2007)
8. Ounnas, A., Davis, H., Millard, D.: A framework for semantic group formation. In: Eighth IEEE International Conference on Advanced Learning Technologies (ICALT2008), pp. 34–38. IEEE (2008)
9. Ounnas, A., Davis, H.C., Millard, D.E.: A framework for semantic group formation in education. J. Educ. Technol. Soc. **12**(4), 43–55 (2009)
10. Papasalouros, A.: Formalizing CSCL scripts with logic and constraints. In: Pammer-Schindler, V., Pérez-Sanagustín, M., Drachsler, H., Elferink, R., Scheffel, M. (eds.) EC-TEL 2018. LNCS, vol. 11082, pp. 660–663. Springer, Cham (2018). https://doi.org/10.1007/978-3-319-98572-5_68
11. Parr, T.: The Definitive ANTLR 4 Reference. 2nd edn. Pragmatic Bookshelf (2013)

12. Sanz-Martínez, L., Martínez-Monés, A., Bote-Lorenzo, M.L., Muñoz-Cristóbal, J.A., Dimitriadis, Y.: Automatic group formation in a MOOC based on students' activity criteria. In: Lavoué, É., Drachsler, H., Verbert, K., Broisin, J., Pérez-Sanagustín, M. (eds.) EC-TEL 2017. LNCS, vol. 10474, pp. 179–193. Springer, Cham (2017). https://doi.org/10.1007/978-3-319-66610-5_14
13. Tacadao, G., Toledo, R.P.: Forming student groups with student preferences using constraint logic programming. In: Dichev, C., Agre, G. (eds.) AIMSA 2016. LNCS (LNAI), vol. 9883, pp. 259–268. Springer, Cham (2016). https://doi.org/10.1007/978-3-319-44748-3_25
14. Triska, M.: The finite domain constraint solver of SWI-Prolog. In: Schrijvers, T., Thiemann, P. (eds.) FLOPS 2012. LNCS, vol. 7294, pp. 307–316. Springer, Heidelberg (2012). https://doi.org/10.1007/978-3-642-29822-6_24
15. Weinberger, A.: Scripts for computer-supported collaborative learning. Ph.D. thesis, LMU (2003)

Utilizing Context Effects of Banner Ads for Conversion Rate Optimization

Peter Silbermann[(⊠)], Tobias Fertig, Andreas E. Schütz, and Nicholas H. Müller

Faculty of Computer Science and Business Information Systems,
University of Applied Sciences Würzburg-Schweinfurt,
Sanderheinrichsleitenweg 20, 97074 Würzburg, Germany
peter.silbermann@student.fhws.de, {tobias.fertig,
andreas.schuetz,nicholas.mueller}@fhws.de

Abstract. The purpose of this paper is to seek answer to the questions how banner ads and their possible effects can be utilized for conversion rate optimization. Therefore, the concept of the alleged banner ad (ABA) was developed, which can be utilized in the context of the conversion optimization. The implementation of distracting elements is counter intuitive for conversion optimizers – especially in critical steps of the user journey like the product detail page. However, a very deliberate placement of an alleged banner ad could offer new potentials for conversion rate optimization. In contrast to the first intention of conversion optimizers, the user will not be distracted due to intentional leveraging of banner blindness. The use of this concept must be viewed very critically and must be implemented in a nuanced and individual manner. The risks for companies underly in its increased possibility that the user might consider ABAs as an attempt of manipulation. The concept of the ABA should be seen much more as a possibility to place conversion-promoting content in a targeted manner. This placed content in the product environment can be, nevertheless, thematically more distant from the product.

Keywords: Banner advertising · Context effects · Conversion rate optimization

1 Introduction

Online advertising is a way for website operators to monetize their digital assets. Nowadays, all website operators have the possibility to implement online advertising. However, this does not necessarily make sense for all websites from a financial and strategic point of view. It is uncommon that an online shop would implement third-party advertising content on its product detail pages for example. The fact, that the content of an advertising banner does not necessarily have to be in any meaningful connection with the product being advertised on the website, provides website operators with the fundamental possibility of placing any desired content on their web pages.

The placement of advertising in a critical step of the user journey, say, the product detail page, presents a high potential to distract the user from the intended conversion -

© Springer Nature Switzerland AG 2020
P. Zaphiris and A. Ioannou (Eds.): HCII 2020, LNCS 12206, pp. 641–649, 2020.
https://doi.org/10.1007/978-3-030-50506-6_44

in form of a product purchase. The implementation of distracting elements is counter intuitive for conversion optimizers. However, advertising in general is not presented in isolation, as advertisements are integrated into media. The environment in which advertising is integrated has an influence on the evaluation of the advertising itself (Kroeber-Riel and Gröppel-Klein 2013). The theoretical basis for this can be priming, because the advertising environment acts as prime for a later perception of the advertising itself (Kroeber-Riel and Gröppel-Klein 2013). Therefore, the content of an advertising banner can also act as a prime and influence the subsequent information processing of the advertising environment. A very deliberate placement of a fictitious advertising banner or an element that is specifically designed to be perceived like an advertising banner could offer new potentials for conversion rate optimization - without distracting the user as much as one might intuitively thought by intentionally leveraging the phenomenon called banner blindness.

The purpose of this paper is to seek answers to the following research questions:

Q1. How to utilize advertising banners and their possible effects for conversion rate optimization?
Q2. What are the potential risks for companies if they use these possible effects?

The structure of this paper is the following: At the beginning, Sect. 2, we summarize the theoretical background of banner blindness, the representations of knowledge in memory and the product evaluation. Afterwards, in Sect. 3 we introduce the concept of the alleged banner ad (ABA). In Sect. 4 and we will answer our research questions. Finally, we will give a short summary of the paper and will conclude with an outlook and future work.

2 Theoretical Background

2.1 Banner Blindness

In the context of this paper, the phenomenon of banner blindness must be highlighted. Benway (1998) named the phenomenon and describes that elements of a website which are especially highlighted by web designers to draw more attention to them tend to be ignored by the user paradoxically. The phenomenon also describes the tendency of users to ignore page elements whether they are correctly or mistakenly perceived as advertising. According to Hervet et al. (2011) research findings on banner blindness are mostly based on indirect evidence in the form of surveys. According to the authors, the participants in these surveys state that they do not consciously recall the content of the ad afterwards. Their eye-tracking study found that users fixates a textual banner ad at least once during a website visit despite the phenomenon of banner blindness. Thus, if banner blindness is considered as an absence of fixation, this is incorrect according to the authors of the study.

2.2   Representation of Knowledge in Memory

The representation of knowledge in memory consists to a large extent of standardized conceptions, which join together in a cognitive semantic network (Collins and Loftus 1975). These concepts include, inter alia, schemas, categories and prototypes:

Schema. A schema contains salient features of an object (Fiske and Taylor 1991), it is more or less abstract or concrete and also hierarchically organised (Kroeber-Riel and Gröppel-Klein 2013). If the "banner advertising" scheme is considered, the salient characteristics would be, for example, size and behaviour.

Category. Categories are defined for objects that are considered to be the same (Rosch et al. 1976). However, the difference between schemes and categories may not always be explicit (Zadeh 1965). For example, advertising banners could be allocated to the category "bold and within a frame". However, this description of the category is very vague and could also be a salient feature of the "online advertising" schema. Categories which do not have distinct boundaries to other categories are called "fuzzy sets" (Zadeh 1965).

Prototype. A prototype is considered as the most typical example of a category or schema (Rosch 1973), which has the least similarity to other categories as well as many features with the members of its own category or schema (Rosch and Mervis 1975). For example, according to subjective perception and standardized individual mental representation, a pop-up banner with the content "You have a computer problem. Please contact Microsoft [...]" could be used as a prototype for the category or scheme "fake banner". The salient feature in the behaviour, i.e. the sudden appearance of the banner in a separate browser window, would therefore be very similar to other participants in the "fake banners" scheme.

Priming. The idea of priming is the activation of a certain mental representation and the increased probability that this certain mental representation gets again activated subsequently i.e. is more accessible (Bargh and Chartrand 2014). Conceptual priming is the activation of a mental representation in a certain context or task so that this activation exerts a passive, unintentional and unconscious influence in a subsequent unrelated context or task (Bargh and Chartrand 2014).

2.3   Product Evaluation

Product evaluation is the perception of products (Kroeber-Riel and Gröppel-Klein 2013). Perception is not characterized by the mere projection of the environment in the form of light waves onto the retina of the human eye. Perception is characterized by subsequent analysis and processing taking place in the brain (Müssler 2017). Therefore, perception functions only by interpreting the raw data recorded by the eye, i.e. by information processing. Influencing factors on the process of product evaluation can be divided into currently presented information, stored information and programs for information processing (Kroeber-Riel and Gröppel-Klein 2013). Kroeber-Riel and Gröppel-Klein distinguish between current and stored information, product information and environmental information, as well as, between simple and complex programs for information processing (Fig. 1).

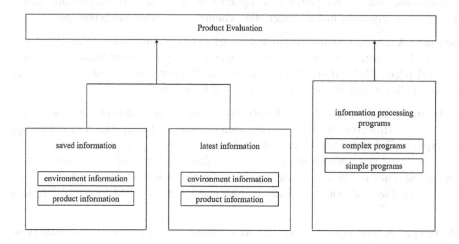

Fig. 1. Influencing factors on the product evaluation regarding Kroeber-Riel and Gröppel-Klein (2013, p. 372)

Current Product Environment Information. According to the authors, product environment information is the information that is perceived in the current product's offer situation, yet not initially related to the product but is included in the product evaluation process. Product environment information are regarded as interpretation cues of the product itself. Moreover, they are usually perceived and processed incidentally. This leads consumers to conclude from one impression to another in a cognitively simplified process (Kroeber-Riel and Gröppel-Klein 2013). This process can be observed for example when buying fashion offline. The interpretation of the quality of the textiles could also depend on the perception of the quality of the staff or the shop.

Current Product Information. Direct product information includes firstly the perceived features of the product, as well as other features of the entire product offering, such as the price or a guarantee. Within the scope of current direct product information, so called key information is also present. This information is of importance for the assessment of the product and substitutes for several different kinds of product information (Kroeber-Riel and Gröppel-Klein 2013).

Stored Product Information. During product evaluation, the perceived product information is compared with the product scheme, which is already memorized. Whether or not the presented stimuli can be used for product evaluation essentially depends on the product evaluation schemata of the consumers. Therefore, the presented product stimuli should either be tuned to the product evaluation schemes of the consumers or the product evaluation schemes of the consumers should be changed by influencing them (Kroeber-Riel and Gröppel-Klein 2013).

3 Concept of the Alleged Banner Ad (ABA)

Nielsen and Pernice (2010, p. 75) have described banner blindness as "[...] the tendency to ignore items that are bold and inside a border". As described in Sect. 2.1, banner blindness is also the tendency of users to ignore page elements whether they are correctly or mistakenly perceived as advertising. Based on this, the concept of ABA includes two variants. On the one hand, fictitious advertising banners implemented by website operators that seem to be from a third party (henceforth called "third-party ABA"). And on the other hand, elements which, due to an intended design, are mistakenly perceived by the user as advertising (henceforth called "first-party ABA").

The fact that ABAs do not have to be in any meaningful association with the product advertised on the website facilitates the theoretical placement of any content. When selecting the content for conversion optimization of the ABA, it is important to ensure that the content activates the mental representation that is advantageous for the evaluation of a product. Since humans perceive the environment subjectively, the personal world, i.e. the individual mental representations memorized, can deviate from those of others (Kroeber-Riel and Gröppel-Klein 2013). This inevitably raises the complex question of the content of the ABA respectively the choice of mental representation to be activated.

In general, ABAs offer the possibility to place conversion-promoting content in a targeted manner in the product environment that is nevertheless thematically more distant from the product. Although ABAs may seem intrusive and too prominently placed at first, they do not really distract the user due to the phenomenon of banner blindness. The following comparison with the offline world is intended to illustrate this connection (related to first-party ABAs): At Christmas time, a fashion shop puts a large attractively decorated Christmas tree in the entrance area of the shop. This tree can be seen from every position in the shop. One the one hand, due to the prominent and spacious positioning, it is impossible not to fixate the Christmas tree at least once during the "session". On the other hand, the Christmas tree is unlikely to disturb the customer while shopping. In fact, quite the contrary might be the case: The Christmas tree may enhance the user experience and eventually presents another sales incentive for the customers in the shop: buying Christmas presents.

3.1 Theoretical Foundation for ABA

Schema Activation on Banner Ad Fixation. If a fixation is measured during a gaze recording, it indicates the basic possibility that the stimulus respectively the visual information unit is transferred into the working memory of the user (Kroeber-Riel and Gröppel-Klein 2013, p. 343). If a website user fixes an ABA, this transfer of the information unit activates the associated schema in the working memory of the user. Thus, an ABA can act as a prime and influence subsequent information processing of the advertising environment. Priming effects due to inattentional blindness cannot be excluded (Mack and Rock 1998). Therefore, even if a user fixates an ABA, but the user's attention is focused on something else (i.e. condition of inattention), priming effects cannot be excluded.

ABAs as Product Environment Information. If an ABA is implemented on a product detail page, it would be classified as a product environment information in context of the product evaluation model of Kroeber-Riel and Gröppel-Klein (2013). Therefore, this ABA would be included as product environment information in the product assessment of a website user. Thus, it affects the assessment of the product itself.

3.2 Use Case: Applying a UVP to an ABA

On websites of online retailers or companies that offer an online service, the benefits of the offer or the purchase procedure itself are usually explicitly highlighted. A "value proposition" is the result of the user assessing the perceived benefits and expenses of the offer (Goward 2013). In this context the term "Unique Value Proposition" (UVP) must be described. UVPs refer to the unique value proposition of an offer from the customer's perspective and they are intended to communicate the benefits of an offer to website visitors in an brief manner (Laja 2019). When creating UVPs, a special focus is placed on the real benefit for the user or potential customer and not on a mere specification of product features (Morys 2011). In practice, UVPs are encountered, inter alia, in the form of enumerated lists or concatenations, whose textual elaboration is reduced and kept brief to the essential characteristics (Laja 2019).

Since UVPs are created especially from a customer's perspective and are the result of a consideration of the advantages and costs of an offer, UVPs classify as key information in the product evaluation model of Kroeber-Riel and Gröppel-Klein (2013). As described in Sect. 2.3, key information substitutes several different product information. If product information is regarded as a semantic network, UVPs form superordinate nodes that have been abstracted from individual product information. Under the premise that the product assessment schemata of the users are known to the website operators and that the key information of the product is reflected by the UVPs, a schema related to a single UVP or the prototype of the UVP itself can be used as content of the ABA. This increases the probability that the content of the ABA will be used in subsequent information processing if it had been fixated and therefore activated the corresponding schema before.

4 Discussion

To answer Q1 we will discuss the following possible effects: customers might consider an ABA as an attempt of manipulation, the fact advertisement in the product environment and the characteristics of banner ads on mobile devices.

Consideration as an Attempted Manipulation. Regarding context effects between the advertising environment and advertising banners, it is important to note that a website user is not a naive individual (Kroeber-Riel and Gröppel-Klein 2013). It is quite possible for the user to recognise an attempt to be influenced by advertising in general (Kroeber-Riel and Gröppel-Klein 2013). For example, users can recognize through previous experience when they are being persuaded (Kroeber-Riel and Gröppel-Klein 2013). If an ABA is deliberately implemented by website operators and if this is perceived by the website user as an attempt to influence them, this could have serious negative consequences for the website operators: Since users no longer feel comfortable on the website due to the detected attempt to influence them for example, they are less likely buy the product.

The Fact Advertisement. Not only the content of a third-party ABA, but also the fact that an advertisement is presented in a product environment must be addressed. The learned experiences – positive and/or negative - of the website user with the schema "advertising" influences which mental representations are activated during the exposure of an advertisement. This problem is further intensified by the fact that third-party advertising content in the direct product environment is a rather unusual case. However, this special case could have the advantage that a third-party ABA in the direct product environment receives more attention on a product detail page.

Mobile Devices. The context of use of mobile devices is a great example of shared attention: In comparison to a desktop system, the mobile device can be used in more situations than stationary devices (Kroeber-Riel and Gröppel-Klein 2013). The design aspects of banner advertising on mobile devices also differ fundamentally, as the screen sizes are smaller, and the context of use is different. The phenomenon of banner blindness has also been proven on mobile devices (Pernice 2018). The design aspects of ABAs should therefore be adapted for mobile devices. Since less information can be presented at once, it becomes more difficult to perceive elements that are distinct from the content of the website (Pernice 2018). However, since a large advertisement also takes up a large part of the screen of the mobile device, it is more difficult for users to avoid it (Pernice 2018). The probability that an advertisement is fixed can therefore be higher if users do not simply skip the advertising content by scrolling quickly (Pernice 2018). The possibility that advertising can be fixed on mobile devices and the possible priming effects that can result from this, given the special characteristics of design aspects for mobile advertising, do not exclude the effect of ABAs.

To answer Q2 we will discuss the following possible risks: linking the ABA and missing evidence.

Linking the ABA. Since it is a common campaign goal for online advertisements to generate traffic from external sources (Lammenett 2019), the question whether the ABAs should link somewhere has to be highlighted - even though users might avoid them after they had fixated them due to the phenomenon banner blindness. In the context of conversion optimization, the mere possibility of a decreased user experience due to missing feedback when clicking on the ABAs must be avoided. When implementing first-party ABAs a dedicated page could be created and linked to if not existing web pages can be used by website operators. Regarding the third-party ABAs, and their nature of trying to pretend to be from someone else than the website they are implemented in, a web page under the same domain would increase the possibility that users might consider it as an attempted manipulation.

Missing Evidence. The concept of ABAs must be viewed very critically. Just because a website user could theoretically include an ABA as product environment information in his product evaluation, it is not clear what effects these possibilities have on the product evaluation itself or whether priming effects occur at all during a website visit with only a few fixations on ABAs. Even though the theoretical basis for the effect exists, it is not yet known whether this is also the case in practice. This is a risk for companies because an experimental evaluation of the theoretical background of the concept of ABAs is still in progress to this point.

In addition to the research questions Q1 and Q2, we would like to express that we do not recommend using the third-party variation of the concept of ABA. The implementation of a third-party ABA provides a higher potential to be considered as an attempted manipulation by the user because of the "fact advertising" especially "third-party advertising in the product environment".

5   Conclusion

We developed the concept of the ABA and provided a use case where we applied a UVP to an ABA. Through the development of this concept we determined how advertising banners and their possible effects could be utilized for conversion rate optimization. We described the effect that customers might consider an ABA as an attempt of manipulation. Moreover, the fact advertisement in the product environment was another possible effect, and the characteristics of banner ads on mobile devices was also discussed.

Furthermore, we also determined what the potential risks for companies are, if they use the previous described possible effects. The risks for companies underly linking a third-party ABA and the fact advertising and therefore, its increased possibility that the user might consider the third-party ABA as an attempt of manipulation.

The concept of the ABA was developed, which can be utilized in the context of the conversion optimization. The concept of the ABA should be seen much more as a possibility to place conversion-promoting content in a targeted manner. This placed content in the product environment can be, nevertheless, thematically more distant from the product.

In future work, we will examine what effects the inclusion of the ABA as product environment information has on the product evaluation. We also have to examine whether a few fixations on an ABA is a stimulus that has the potential to be strong enough to obtain priming effects. Therefore, the next step is to develop test hypotheses for a conceptional priming experiment and working on an adequate experimental design.

References

Bargh, J.A., Chartrand, T.L.: The Mind in the Middle. Cambridge University Press, New York (2014)

Benway, J.P.: Banner blindness: the irony of attention grabbing on the world wide web. Proc. Hum. Factors Ergon. Soc. Annu. Meet. **42**(5), 463–467 (1998)

Collins, A., Loftus, E.: A spreading-activation theory of semantic processing. Psychol. Rev. **82**(6), 407–428 (1975)

Fiske, S.T., Taylor, S.E.: Social Cognition: MacGraw-Hill Series in Social Psychology. MacGraw-Hill, New York (1991)

Goward, C.: You Should Test That!: Conversion Optimization for More Leads, Sales and Profit or the Art and Science of Optimized Marketing. Wiley Sybex, Hoboken (2013)

Hervet, G., Guérard, K., Tremblay, S., Chtourou, M.S.: Is banner blindness genuine? Eye tracking internet text advertising. Appl. Cogn. Psychol. **25**(5), 708–716 (2011)

Kroeber-Riel, W., Gröppel-Klein, A.: Konsumentenverhalten: EBL-Schweitzer, 10th edn. (Online-ausg.). Franz Vahlen, Munich (2013)

Laja, P.: How to Create a Unique Value Proposition - with Examples. Accessed 30 Jan 2020 (2019). https://cxl.com/blog/value-proposition-examples-how-to-create/

Lammenett, E.: Praxiswissen Online-Marketing: Affiliate-, Influencer-, Content- und E-Mail-Marketing, Google Ads, SEO, Social Media, Online- inklusive Facebook-Werbung (7. Aufl. 2019). Springer Fachmedien Wiesbaden, Wiesbaden (2019)

Mack, A., Rock, I.: Inattentional Blindness: Bradford Books Series in Cognitive Psychology. MIT Press, Cambridge (1998)

Morys, A.: Conversion-Optimierung: Praxismethoden für mehr Markterfolg im Web. Entwickler Press, Frankfurt am Main (2011)

Müssler, J.: Visuelle Informationsverarbeitung. In: Müsseler, J., Rieger, M. (eds.) Allgemeine Psychologie, 3rd edn, pp. 13–49. Springer, Berlin, Heidelberg (2017)

Nielsen, J., Pernice, K.: Eyetracking Web Usability: Safari Tech Books Online. New Riders, Berkeley (2010)

Pernice, K.: Banner Blindness Revisited: Users Dodge Ads on Mobile and Desktop. https://www.nngroup.com/articles/banner-blindness-old-and-new-findings/ (2018). Nielsen Norman Group, Accessed 05 Aug 2019

Rosch, E., Mervis, C.B.: Family resemblances: Studies in the internal structure of categories. Cogn. Psychol. **7**(4), 573–605 (1975). http://www.sciencedirect.com/science/article/pii/0010028575900249

Rosch, E., Mervis, C.B., Gray, W.D., Johnson, D.M., Boyes-Braem, P.: Basic objects in natural categories. Cogn. Psychol. **8**(3), 382–439 (1976) http://www.sciencedirect.com/science/article/pii/001002857690013X

Rosch, E.H.: Natural categories. Cogn. Psychol. **4**(3), 328–350 (1973)

Zadeh, L.A.: Fuzzy sets. Inf. Control **8**(3), 338–353 (1965)

Exploiting the Human Factor: Social Engineering Attacks on Cryptocurrency Users

Kristin Weber, Andreas E. Schütz[✉], Tobias Fertig,
and Nicholas H. Müller

Faculty of Computer Science and Business Information Systems,
University of Applied Sciences Würzburg Schweinfurt,
Sanderheinrichsleitenweg 20, 97074 Würzburg, Germany
{kristin.weber,andreas.schuetz,tobias.fertig,
nicholas.mueller}@fhws.de

Abstract. Social engineering is one of the preferred methods used by criminals to gain unauthorized access to information and information systems. Social engineering targets especially the users of a system. It is increasingly being applied to cryptocurrency users. The paper looks at five cases of cryptocurrency frauds that left a lasting impression in the cryptocurrency community. The cases are systematically investigated using an ontological model for social engineering attacks. The paper analyses which psychological tricks or compliance principles have been used by the social engineers in these cases. With the exploitation of principles such as "Distraction", "Authority", and "Commitment, Reciprocation & Consistency" the attackers gained access to users' financial values, stored in cryptocurrencies, without undermining the security features of the blockchain itself. One reason for the attackers' success is a lack of knowledge about risks and security among cryptocurrency users. Efforts to increase the information security awareness of cryptocurrency and blockchain users is recommended to protect them.

Keywords: Social engineering · Cryptocurrencies · Blockchain

1 Introduction

Social engineering attacks are often used in cybercrime. With the subtle use of psychological tricks, criminals exploit the natural weaknesses of humans. The victims of social engineering attacks are unknowingly influenced in their actions and persuaded to reveal secret information. For example, the sender of a phishing e-mail pretends to be a financial institution and orders the recipient to disclose personal account data on a phishing website. Due to the use of persuasion principles such as authority, social proof, and reciprocity social engineering is quite successful.

Previous research describes and analyses compliance principles and their application in social engineering [e.g., 1–7]. The research of [8] defines a commonly accepted set of five persuasion principles (Authority; Social Proof; Liking, Similarity & Deception; Commitment, Reciprocation & Consistency; Distraction) and assesses their occurrence in phishing e-mails.

P. Zaphiris and A. Ioannou (Eds.): HCII 2020, LNCS 12206, pp. 650–668, 2020.
https://doi.org/10.1007/978-3-030-50506-6_45

Overall, blockchain applications, such as cryptocurrencies, are considered secure [9]. This security has been proven in the past, especially for the integrity and availability of stored data. The decentralized applications have many built-in protection mechanisms, such as cryptographic algorithms or redundant data storage. However, these technical security mechanisms are useless when cyber criminals target the "weakest link" in security – the user [1].

Recent cases of successful attacks on cryptocurrency users - resulting in losses of millions of dollars - make use of social engineering techniques and compliance principles. For example, in November 2017 several potential buyers of the Red Pulse Token responded to fake news spread by Twitter accounts and entered their access credentials into a phishing website. The lost tokens being worth more than $3 million.

Although the numbers show that there is a severe impact of social engineering attacks on cryptocurrency users, no research exists – to the best of our knowledge – that analyses the exploitation of human weaknesses in cryptocurrency frauds. Within this paper, we therefore describe five cases of cryptocurrency frauds. We analyze, based on the [8] set of compliance principles, which psychological tricks have been used by the social engineers to steal the users' cryptocurrencies. For the description of the cases, we use the ontological model for social engineering attacks proposed by [10].

With this paper we contribute to research by

- increasing the understanding of the users' role in information security with regards to a new technology (blockchain, cryptocurrency);
- adding a psychological perspective to the use of cryptocurrencies and blockchain technology;
- testing the compliance principles from [8] in a broader social engineering context (not only considering phishing e-mails);
- assessing the applicability of the ontological model of social engineering attacks in the context of cryptocurrency frauds;
- describing and analysing the impact of social engineering on cryptocurrency users; and
- deriving initial recommendations for protecting cryptocurrency users against exploitation from social engineers.

The rest of the paper is organized as follows. In the related work section, we give a quick introduction to the blockchain technology and cryptocurrencies. Further, we introduce the concept of social engineering and the psychological tricks used within. We then introduce and describe five cases on cryptocurrency fraud. Afterwards we explain the utilization of the compliance principles in the cases. In the discussion section we analyze the results, describe our contributions, and give recommendations. Finally, we summaries our findings and give an outlook to future research.

2 Related Work

2.1 Security Issues in Blockchain Technology and Cryptocurrencies

The blockchain technology has become very popular since the introduction of Bitcoin, especially due to Bitcoin's rapid price increase. A blockchain is a distributed ledger, with the fundamental property that once the data has been recorded, it becomes nearly impossible to change it [11]. A network of computers, known as nodes, verifies that the data added complies with the rules of the network, thus providing consensus among the participants. By using cryptographic techniques such as asymmetric cryptography or cryptographic hash functions, the blockchain helps building up trust between two or more parties, without relying on a trusted third party.

The blockchain was first described by [12] in the context of Bitcoin and was later adapted by numerous other cryptocurrencies, such as Litecoin or Ether. Cryptocurrencies are virtual currencies that are not hedged and managed by a central, administrative entity, but by cryptographic methods [13]. A cryptocurrency is called token if it has other uses in addition to the currency function. For example, such a token could be a right to vote or the digital representation of an asset.

The interaction of human users with cryptocurrencies is based on public-key encryption methods. A new participant in the network initially generates a private key, from which the public key and the user's address are calculated. With their private keys the users are able to authenticate themselves in the network. Anyone who is in the possession of the private key can digitally sign transactions and thus has access to the balance of the corresponding address. Private keys can be stored in so-called wallets. There are paper, hardware, software, and website wallets [14]. For paper wallets, the private key and public key are printed on paper. In hardware wallets, the private key is permanently stored in a hardware device that can be connected to a computer. Software and website wallets allow users to interact with the blockchain via a visually enhanced graphical user interface. Depending on the provider, website wallet users can view their balance and transaction history, send transactions, or use other services. To access their address, users enter their private key or upload a file that stores the key. This can be done in combination with a password or a hardware wallet.

Most researchers analyzing security and privacy issues of blockchain and cryptocurrencies focus on systems flaws, technical limitations, and network attacks, such as double spending, DDoS attacks, and man-in-the-middle attacks [e.g. 15–17].

Few studies take a different approach and analyze the risks a user faces when interacting with blockchain technology in general and cryptocurrencies specifically. [18] state that cryptocurrency users face some risk when using intermediaries such as currency exchanges, online wallets, mining pools, and investment services; because those operate as de facto centralized authorities. For example, if the intermediary becomes insolvent or it absconds with the users' deposits, users suffer a financial loss. Further, blockchain transactions are irreversible in contrast to other forms of financial transactions such as credit card payments or bank transfers. Therefore, cryptocurrency transactions are prone to abuse by cyber criminals. Their victims usually only identify fraud after the transaction took place and hence cannot reclaim their money.

As an additional risk for cryptocurrency users, [9] identified the usage of software and website wallets. Those wallets have become a target for cyber criminals, too. Having analyzed some successful cryptocurrency attacks, they name, among others, the exploitation of human weaknesses, neglect, and inexperience as success factors. They state that attackers often utilize social engineering techniques.

The role of the user in protecting the security and privacy in a cryptocurrency environment has been intensively studied by [19]. In their online survey participated nearly 1'000 Bitcoin users. They found evidence for the risks involved in using website wallets. Many survey participants used at least one website wallet, but many of them lack background knowledge: About a third of the participants were unaware whether their wallet was encrypted or backed up. Moreover, nearly one fourth of the participants had already lost Bitcoins or their private keys at least once. With nearly 45%, the main reason for those losses had been the user's own mistakes, such as formatting the hard drive or losing the physical device storing the private keys. Other reasons had been hardware and software failures. About 20% had been victims of hackers or malware.

2.2   Social Engineering

When securing information and information technology, it is not sufficient to rely on technical security controls such as firewalls and virus scanners. Including the user – or the "human factor" – in information security considerations is at least as much as important [20, 21]. The user is sometimes seen as the weakest link in information security [e.g., 22–24] – or as Kevin Mitnick poses: "… security is not a technology problem - it's a people and management problem." [1]. However, recent research shows that users are also an important line of defense [25].

Social Engineering is the art of manipulating human behavior without the victim being aware of it. The "target" takes an action that may not be in her best interest [4]. "Social Engineering uses influence and persuasion to deceive people by convincing them that the social engineer is someone he is not, or by manipulation. As a result, the social engineer is able to take advantage of people to obtain information with or without the use of technology." [1]. In the context of information security, social engineering is usually used in its malicious form. A social engineer may try to obtain login credentials by pretending to be an IT administrator and simply asking users over the phone about their password. This social engineering technique is called pretexting or impersonation [26, 27]. A typical example of the baiting technique is when the social engineer leaves an infected USB flash drive lying around with the intention of it being picked up by the curious target [10, 28]. The social engineer employs the information obtained or the inappropriate action taken by the user in the actual attack in order to reach the intended goal (e.g., getting access to confidential information, stealing money) [29].

The most prominent and successful social engineering technique is phishing [30]. Phishing is an attempt to get unauthorized access to sensible information [31]. A common approach for phishing attacks is to send e-mails to random e-mail addresses. The fraudulent e-mail contains links to a spoofed website and a text requiring the victims to follow the link and enter their personal data. As soon as the form on the website is submitted, all information entered is sent to the attackers. If the spoofed website is an exact copy of the original entity, the individual will not ever suspect that she was a victim of phishing [32]. Spear phishing is a more sophisticated phishing approach in which a specific user or group of users is targeted. The attacker incorporates personalized information, such as the salutation, in the e-mail to make it more believable [33].

The Social Engineering ontological model proposed by [10] allows for systematically describing and analyzing social engineering attacks: "A Social Engineering attack employs either direct communication or indirect communication, and has a social engineer, a target, a medium, a goal, one or more compliance principles and one or more techniques." Direct communication is when attacker and target directly communicate with each other, either bidirectional (e.g., in an (e-mail) conversation, over telephone) or unidirectional (one-way, usually from attacker to target, e.g., as in phishing). In an indirect communication, communication occurs through some third-party medium, e.g., a USB flash drive or a web page. Figure 1 shows the ontological model and gives some examples of media, goals, and techniques. Compliance principles will be discussed in the following section.

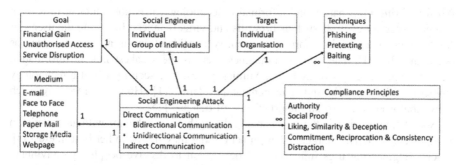

Fig. 1. Ontological model of a social engineering attack [in accordance with 10].

2.3   Compliance Principles

Social engineers are excellent psychologists exploiting typical human behavioral patterns as vulnerabilities, such as the desire to be helpful, the tendency to trust people and the fear of getting into trouble [7]. In their study, which investigated whether end users really plug in USB flash drives they eventually find, [28] found that at least 45% of their dropped drives indeed had been used. Their victims disclosed two reasons for picking up the USB flash drives: the altruistic intention of returning the USB drive to its owner, and curiosity.

Social engineers know how to influence and persuade their victims by linking their message to deep human motivations. Humans show recurring behavioral patterns that constitute inherent security vulnerabilities in any complex system [34]. One of those behavioral patterns is reciprocity, which refers to the feeling of being obliged to return a favor [35]. In a society it is expected behavior that people repay what another person has provided. For example, if we get a present from our colleague for birthday, we feel obliged to also make them a gift to their birthday. Reciprocity is also involved in a mutual exchange of information and knowledge. [7] demonstrate the power of reciprocity in their study on password disclosure. They conducted short interviews on IT behavior with more than 1'100 participants. During the interviews, participants were asked to disclose their passwords. In the total sample, 30% revealed their password. Nearly one third of participants were offered a piece of chocolate directly before the password question. Of those participants, even 48% revealed their password. Due to the reciprocity effect, the incentive given (a piece of chocolate) to the participants resulted in returning the favor by revealing some personal data (i.e., the password). As this study demonstrates, it is important to understand the psychological triggers or principles used in social engineering attacks in order to set up an effective defense strategy [2].

[8] analyzed work of [2, 34, 35] and proposed a reviewed list of persuasion principles used in social engineering. Their list contains the following five principles:

- Authority: People are trained to not question authorities, such as teachers, parents, policeman, doctors, or chief executives. They usually follow the requests or orders of someone they think is an authority. In a CEO fraud, this principle is used: an employee from the financial department receives a fake e-mail from a company executive and is convinced to transfer a large amount of money to a fraudulent account. Authority can be indicated by titles, clothes (especially uniforms), or trappings (e.g., jewellery, cars) [35].
- Social Proof: Especially in unfamiliar situations, people tend to mimic the behaviour of others. That way they limit the risk of showing inappropriate behaviour. Further, they feel not being held solely responsible for their actions. A social engineer can convince a person to comply with a request by informing the person that many other individuals, maybe friends or colleagues, already took the same action or behaviour [4].
- Liking, Similarity & Deception: People more willingly comply with requests from friends. This principle also works on people they know or like, as well as on people they are similar to or familiar with, as well as attracted to. If social engineers get their victims to like them, for example with compliments or shared interests, it is a much more likely that they will be successful in their requests.
- Commitment, Reciprocation & Consistency: Once committed to a specific action or decision, people tend to follow it through until the end. They comply with requests consistent with their position. People also feel socially obliged to repaying favours. Once a social engineer gets the victim to divulge some information, the victim remains consistent with further requests on disclosing information [4].
- Distraction: As people have limited ability of processing information, they focus on seemingly important facts or actions and automatically ignore other stimuli. Distraction can take several forms: information overload, surprise, needs and desires, time pressure, fear, greed, scarcity, or decreasing availability of goods or information. A social engineer that directs the attention of the victim in a desired direction, interferes with the victim's ability to think logically. A fake competition that offers prices to the fastest respondents makes use of that principle [1].

The psychological principles used or named by other researchers in social engineering [e.g., 1, 3–5, 36, 37] can be mapped onto those five principles. Therefore, we use this list as basis for our investigation on social engineering in cryptocurrency fraud.

3 Case Studies

Criminals are creative when manipulating cryptocurrency investors. This section describes five cases of successful cryptocurrency frauds. We will show that the selected cases can be classified as social engineering attacks. All cases took place within the last 36 months, when the public interest in cryptocurrencies attracted many unexperienced and non-IT-savvy people to invest in cryptocurrencies. The selected cases gained attention within the cryptocurrency community due to their heavy or lasting impact. It is not our intention to give a complete overview on cryptocurrency frauds. We selected the cases to demonstrate the impact of social engineering on cryptocurrency investors and to show several types of social engineering attacks.

We base our case descriptions on the ontological model proposed by [10]. In all cases, the goal of the social engineers was financial gain, therefore we do not include this item in the description. The social engineers convinced their victims to either transfer the cryptocurrencies to the attackers' addresses, or to disclose their private keys. With the private keys the attackers were able to steal the cryptocurrencies from the victims' address. In addition to the ontological model, we add some background information, a description of each attack and its impact to make the attacks more comprehensible. We explain and discuss our appraisal of used compliance principles (based on the list of [8]) in the subsequent chapter.

3.1 A) Red Pulse [38]

The project NEO is an open platform network for creating decentralized applications and is also known as the Chinese Ethereum [39]. Red Pulse, being the first Initial Coin Offering (ICO) on the NEO platform network, was sold out in one hour raising $15 million. Red Pulse is a market intelligence platform that covers China's financial and capital markets. The Red Pulse platform promises to deliver real-time information impacting Chinese companies, sectors and the overall economy for investors to make better informed decisions [40]. In November 2017, cyber criminals offered a fake airdrop for the newly launched Red Pulse Tokens (cf. Table 1). An airdrop is when a blockchain project decides to offer free tokens or coins to the community [41]. It is a common marketing method used by many companies to promote or to spread their tokens.

Attack Description. Criminals used a fake Twitter account (@RedPulseNEO) to lure victims to a phishing website (redpulsetoken.co), promising to offer an airdrop (free tokens) for a limited period of time. The attackers made the site look secure by using a real HTTPS certificate. The website offered a bonus calculator. Visitors were asked to enter the amount of their Red Pulse tokens into the calculator which then outputted the alleged bonus of 30%. To claim that bonus, the victims were asked to enter their private key of their NEO wallet. The description on top of this form stated that this was a secured process and every input would be encrypted. With the private keys the criminals stole the victims' funds.

Impact. 246 investors lost more than $3 million worth of tokens.

Table 1. Social engineering features of the Red Pulse attack

Communication Model and Medium	Technique
Indirect communication via Twitter and website	Phishing
Target	
Cryptocurrency investors, specifically NEO and Red Pulse token holders	
Social Engineer	
Unknown, probably experienced attackers that recreated the original website and spread it on social media	
Compliance Principles	
Authority; Commitment, Reciprocation & Consistency; Distraction	

3.2   B) Blockchain.Info [42]

The website www.blockchain.info offers free website wallets for users of the cryptocurrencies Bitcoin, Ether, and Bitcoin Cash. It allows users to easily generate a wallet in the required network, check their balance, do transactions, or buy and sell currencies. After signing up, users can log into their address by submitting their e-mail and password. In February 2017 a Google AdWords campaign lured users to a phishing site that appeared like the popular website wallet (cf. Table 2).

Attack Description. The criminals created a Google AdWords campaign. When victims searched for terms like "blockchain" or "bitcoin wallet", the targeted ads eventually showed up and lured them to URLs like www.blockchien.info or www. block-chain.info, showing a nearly perfect copy of the original www.blockchain.info. The websites had HTTPS certificates and were hosted by European companies. When victims tried to log in, their login credentials were submitted to the hacker group, allowing the hackers to steal the victims' funds.

Table 2. Social engineering features of the blockchain.info attack

Communication Model and Medium	Technique
Indirect communication via Google search engine and website	Phishing
Target	
Users of the platform www.blockchain.info	
Social Engineer	
Hacker group called COINHOARDER; invested time and money in the AdWords campaign	
Compliance Principles	
Authority; Commitment, Reciprocation & Consistency; Distraction	

Impact. Around $50 million of funds were stolen by the attackers. This type of attack was later expanded to other similar websites such as www.myetherwallet.com.

3.3   C) Bee Token [43, 44]

Bee Token is the currency of the decentralized Beenest platform. The project aims to develop a decentralized home sharing marketplace, which is similar in functionality to the Airbnb platform. Bee Tokens were sold in advance to investors in an ICO. Investors interested in the ICO took either part in the outsourced Know-Your-Customer (KYC) procedure or registered to a newsletter. The Bee Token team limited the contribution to all investors between 0.1 and 0.2 Ether (ETH). Many investors were complaining about this fact. On January 31, 2018 investors' e-mail addresses were leaked [44].

Attack Description. Attackers either stole customer data from the outsourced KYC procedure or from the newsletter module. Having heard about the complaints of strongly limited contributions, they sent e-mails to potential investors a few minutes before the ICO launch (cf. Table 3). They explained that they decided to increase the contribution limit up to 30 ETH and included their own addresses. Although Bee Token stated that the correct wallet address will only be announced through a YouTube video, many investors sent their contribution right into the attackers' wallets [43].

Table 3. Social engineering features of the Bee Token attack

Communication Model and Medium	Technique
Direct, unidirectional communication via e-mail	Pretexting, spear phishing
Target	
Individual investors that have subscribed to the Bee Token newsletter or participated in the KYC process	
Social Engineer	
Unknown, the experienced attackers that did not leave any tracks: either used vulnerabilities in the third-party code of the newsletter module or the KYC process	
Compliance Principles	
Authority; Commitment, Reciprocation & Consistency; Distraction	

Impact. With three of the fraudulent ICO addresses the criminals gathered about $1 million – half as much Ether as the real ICO collected. Many investors lost their trust in the Bee Token team and even the blockchain technology as a whole.

3.4   D) Fake Twitter Accounts [45]

Twitter is a popular social media platform within the cryptocurrency community when it comes to announcing news and share thoughts or ideas. All the important players of the blockchain and digital economy have a Twitter account. Scammers used the social network in early 2018 to trick users into a false competition using fake Twitter accounts impersonating these players (cf. Table 4).

Attack Description. The scammers copied the account of the famous entrepreneur and investor Elon Musk by choosing "Elon Musk" as display name and using his profile picture. As username they chose "@elonlmusk", similar to the original username "@elonmusk". The scammers gained attention of Twitter users by commenting a post of the original Elon Musk. In their comment they said that they gave away 5,000 ETH to Elon's followers. In order to participate, the followers should send 0.5-1 ETH to his address and would get 5-10 ETH back. The scammers also used other fake accounts, to seemingly verify the offer, by commenting that they received the offered ETH. Several followers transferred some of their ETH to the fake addresses.

Table 4. Social engineering features of the Fake Twitter Account attack

Communication Model and Medium	Technique
Indirect communication via Twitter	Pretexting
Target	
Twitter users interested in cryptocurrencies following the account of a blockchain celebrity	
Social Engineer	
Unknown; anyone could set up a fake account to impersonate a celebrity and wait for the right moment to comment on a Twitter post	
Compliance Principles	
Social Proof; Liking, Similarity & Deception; Commitment, Reciprocation & Consistency; Distraction	

Impact. The scammers were able to obtain about 172.57 ETH from 282 different wallets. Later, a lot of other fake accounts from Elon Musk or other people like Vitalik Buterin, co-founder of Ethereum, started to appear. Due the large amount of fake accounts, it is hard to estimate the total amount of lost ETH.

3.5   E) Minerium Token [46]

Minereum Token (MNE) is a project focusing on a self-mining smart contract approach on the Ethereum blockchain. It was released in April 2017 and used a custom implementation. Therefore, commonly used websites like Etherscan.io display wrong balances. In April 2018, scammers used some of those tokens in a honeypot like scam [47] (cf. Table 5).

Attack Description. In a crypto chat, criminals published the private key to their address containing 31,500 MNE ($5,000). Would-be thieves tried to withdraw those tokens. However, there was no ETH on that wallet, so the transaction fee for

Table 5. Social engineering features of the Minereum Token attack

Communication Model and Medium	Technique
Direct, probably bidirectional communication via chat	Baiting

Target
Users of several crypto chat channels that did not want to miss the opportunity to steal tokens

Social Engineer
Unknown owner (nickname GoldenBro) of one of the 4'268 MNE Genesis addresses; the attackers required fundamental knowledge about the Minereum implementation

Compliance Principles
Authority; Social Proof; Liking, Similarity & Deception; Commitment, Reciprocation & Consistency; Distraction

withdrawal could not be paid. The would-be thieves started to send ETH to the address in hope to be the first able to pay the transaction fee for the MNE withdrawal. The attackers prepared a script that sent all incoming ETH from the leaked wallet to another safe wallet.

Impact. 0.755 ETH were collected through 242 transactions. The attackers did this kind of attack multiple times, since their wallet shows incoming transaction from at least three different wallets filled with MNE [48].

4   Findings

In all of the above presented cases three or more compliance principles have been used by the social engineers. Based on our appraisal, examples for two of them can be found in all five cases: Commitment, Reciprocation & Consistency as well as Distraction. The Authority principle had been used in four cases. Two cases utilized the Liking, Similarity & Deception principle and the Social Proof principle. In the following we will give short explanations that should demonstrate our appraisal and the usage of the principles in the cases.

From the Commitment, Reciprocation & Consistency principle the social engineers make specifically use of commitment and consistency. What the social engineers utilized is the commitment of the investors to their previously taken actions and decisions [35]. And the investors want to appear consistent in their own behavior as well. Once the victims had decided to visit the website, i.e., clicked on a link, in both the Red Pulse case (case A) and the blockchain.info case (case B), they were trapped by their own commitment. In order to be consistent with their previous decision to visit the website, in order to obtain free tokens (A) or access their website wallet (B), the investors follow through with their initial intention and enter their private keys into the phishing sites. In the Bee Token Case (case C) commitment is quite strong. With taking part in the KYC process or registering at the website, the potential investors already claimed their interest in investing in the ICO. Once the offer came, they consistently took the chance.

Similar, in the fake Twitter account case (case D), the victims committed to be interested in ETH investments when they decided to follow Vitalik Buterin on Twitter. The would-be thieves in the Minereum case (case E), were committed to steal the MNE from the address once they happened to get access to it. When they found out, they first have to transfer ETH to the address in order to be able to withdraw the MNE, they consistently did so.

Reciprocation only plays a minor role in the cases. One could argue that the offer of 30% bonus tokens in case A is seen as a favor that the victims returned with entering their private keys into the phishing site. The valuable information that the maximum investment amount has risen to 30 ETH in case C is probably a stronger example of reciprocation [4]. The investors returned the favor when transferring their ETH to the social engineers' address.

Distraction takes many forms in the cases and is usually the main driver for the victims to comply with the social engineers' requests. Due to the distractions the victims are not able to evaluate facts or actions by logical reasoning [36]. In case A the victims get distracted in several ways. First, the airdrop offering arose their desire, if not to say greed, in receiving free token. Which was intensified by offering a bonus calculator at the website that showed them the expectable bonus. Second, the offer was only available for a limited time (scarcity [cf. 35]). And third, the social engineers made sure that their website was considered to be secure by using HTTPS certificates and other clues demonstrating its trustworthiness. The victims in case B were so focused on their task to access their own website wallets and therefore did not recognize slight differences in the websites' URL or appearance. The rush to make a quick decision distracted the victims from thinking logically in case C. The offer to invest more ETH than originally announced was valid for 24 h only. Furthermore, it seemed to be a scarce one – offered to selected individuals only. In case D the social engineers combined the victims' desire for free tokens with a fake competition, in which only the fastest respondents would be able to win. Greed was the main distraction in case E as well.

When using the Authority principle victims are less likely to question the validity of a request (or offer). In the cases, authority is established through pretending to be a valid and trustworthy entity using digital symbols of authority [cf. 8]. In cases A and B, the websites included security mechanisms and imitated the look and feel (B) or at least the names (A, B) of the true entities. Also, the social engineers in case C pretended to be the original Bee Token team in their e-mails by, e.g., using the correct logo [43]. The strongest effect did the authority principle show in the fake Twitter accounts (case D). The scammers copy the online appearance and name of a celebrity. They show a surprising but believable behavior when offering free Tokens to the community. Through imitating a celebrity at Twitter the attackers made themselves look trustworthy and credible with a significant chance that their victims would follow their offer [49].

With the Liking, Similarity & Deception principle the social engineers take advantage of the fact that their victims are more likely to respond to someone they like or is similar to them. In case D the victims follow the famous Elon Musk (and other celebrities) because they probably like or respect him. When getting the chance to receive free tokens from their idol, they took it of course. Investors of cryptocurrencies and participants of crypto chats surely share the same interests and have further similarities, too. For example, the participants in the [19] study were male (85%) and had an IT background ($\tilde{}$50%). So, the would-be thieves in case E were more willing to believe that a poor (similar to them) individuum by accident disclosed its private key on the crypto chat.

A strong evidence for the Social Proof principle can be found in case D. The social engineers not only faked the account of the celebrity but created additional fake Twitter accounts. Those fake Twitter accounts responded to the initial offer and "verified" that they indeed received some of the promised free tokens. According to the social proof principle this twist probably convinced several till then uncertain followers to mimic the behavior of the other followers. They transferred their ETH to the fake address. In case E, social proof worked in a criminal way. None of the crypto chat users alarmed the social engineers that they disclosed their private key. They either ignored or even tried to profit from this mistake. Obviously, this seemed to be the correct behavior in the situation. Otherwise, surely someone would have helped the "victim".[1]

5 Discussion

The five cases illustrate that social engineering attacks can be successful and profitable in the cryptocurrency environment. The social engineers succeeded with a combination of different communication strategies, techniques, media, and compliance principles. They either convinced their targets to transfer their funds directly to the attackers' addresses or they lured their targets into revealing their private keys.

We used the social engineering ontological model from [10] to describe the five cases. The model provides a valid and convenient way to structure and compare social engineering attacks. A description of the impact of the attacks could be considered as an additional class in the ontological model. The impact could indicate from the social engineers' point of view whether the attack was successful or not, i.e., whether they reached their intended goal. Further, it could specify the impact or damage caused by the attack from the victim's point of view, for example, the amount of the financial loss.

In all cases, the social engineers took advantage of several psychological triggers, persuasion or compliance principles. We found evidence for all five principles proposed by [8]. We demonstrated that the principles can be applied to the cryptocurrency context and that they are not only utilized in phishing e-mails but in other social engineering techniques as well.

When using compliance principles, the social engineers induce their victims to use automatic decision mechanisms rather than rational reasoning [36]. These mechanisms are also called heuristics or mental shortcuts. Humans automatically use these heuristics in most decisions taken every day in order to reduce cognitive load [6]. The heuristics are evolutionary beneficial, because people cannot fully analyze every decision.[2] The distraction principle can serve as an excellent example for intuitive decision making.

---

[1] Alarming evidence for the social phenomenon of bystander inaction can be found in [35, p. 128ff].

[2] Cognitive psychology distinguishes two systems for decision making [50]: System 1 uses intuitions and System 2 uses reasoning. Social engineers try to push their victims to rely on System 1.

Instead of having time to carefully consider an offer, the cryptocurrency investors were rushed by the social engineers to make quick (automated) decisions. In the case of the fake Twitter accounts (case D), the followers were offered a limited number of free tokens. They were distracted for at least three reasons: (1) the greed to get something valuable for free, (2) scarce availability of the tokens, and (3) time pressure due to many potential rivals (Elon Musk has more than 20 Mio. followers). If the victims would have taken some time to carefully consider the offer, they could have easily found out, that the Twitter account was fake due to the wrong account name.

The cryptocurrency cases indicate that, by cutting out the middlemen, there is one major shortcoming for blockchain users: there are no banks or other trusted third parties to protect unsuspecting users from malicious acts and frauds. Moreover, due to the structure of the blockchain, the damage is irreversible. As it is true for other information systems as well, the attackers target the human factor as the weakest link to fulfil their goals. Although, the attackers need technical skills in preparing and executing their attacks, they ultimately exploit human weaknesses. Compared to an attack on blockchain's technology, it is far easier to hack its users [1].

In addition to the exploitation of the compliance principles, another success factor might be the lack of knowledge of cryptocurrency investors about blockchain technology. A study shows that 80% of people who have heard of blockchain technology do not understand it [51]. However, understanding is essential for securely using a technology [52]. Users need at least basic knowledge of blockchain constructs, such as private keys, to prevent them from simply revealing it as shown in case A. The [19] study also revealed a lack of security knowledge amongst cryptocurrency users. Many users did not even apply basic security measures such as encryption and backups. On the other hand, when it comes to social engineering, users seem to be overconfident: they think it is not likely that they will be targeted by a social engineer and if so, they would be able to detect or resist such an attack [36, 53].

In order to decrease the possibility that cryptocurrency investors fall for social engineering attacks – as it is the case for all threats that exploit the human factor in information security – there is a need to increase their information security awareness [54, 55]. Several theoretical models express different views on what constitutes information security awareness. However, there is a common understanding about three aspects of information security: cognition (understanding of the problem and the knowledge to solve it), intention to act (willingness of the user to behave in accordance with the knowledge), and organization [56].

Therefore, users need to be informed about blockchain technology, public key cryptography, monetary systems and cryptocurrencies, and effective technical security mechanisms (e.g., for website wallets) [19]. Additionally, they need to know about social engineering attacks including compliance principles, the principles' effects, and possible counter strategies [2]. The intention to act or behavioral intention is a complex construct consisting of several factors, such as attitude to the specific behavior, the perceived norm of that behavior, and the assessment of the personal capacity to act [57]. In order to influence the behavioral intent, security awareness measures must address the users' feelings and beliefs [58]. As one specific consequence, users not only need to be informed about social engineering attacks, but effectively trained in detection and counter strategies, using for example serious gaming, role plays, experimental exercises, and repeated decisions trainings [2, 56]. The above mentioned overconfidence might be tackled by confronting users with examples of successful attacks [59]. The last aspect of information security awareness – organization – refers to the ability to behave according to knowledge and intention. The organizational setting should be designed in a way that it does not hinder but facilitate secure behavior. The whole research field of usable security or user-centered design of security mechanism addresses this aspect [e.g., 20, 21]. An improvement in the cryptocurrency context would be more intuitive user interfaces of website wallets or key management systems [19].

Programs for raising information security awareness of employees have a long tradition in public and private organizations [cf. 54]. The programs not always deliver the intended results, one reason being that the above-mentioned aspects of information security awareness and their implications in how to design effective programs have not yet been fully understood by most organizations [60, 61]. The importance for also addressing individual or home users with information security awareness programs is stressed by [e.g., 55, 62]. However, it is even more difficult to effectively address an uncoordinated group of inhomogeneous private cryptocurrency users. [60] demonstrate that awareness campaigns started by governmental organizations often fail. To conclude, future research is needed to propose methods that effectively increase information security awareness of individual users in general and of cryptocurrency users specifically. It should be in the interest of cryptocurrency service providers to educate their users about risks and threats. If the blockchain technology loses acceptance, their business model would suffer as well. The platform www.myetherwallet.com gives two examples of how to increase awareness. Upon entering the website, a popup informs visitors about important facts about website wallets: users' responsibility for security, services the platform offers and not offers, blockchain technology, the role and importance of private keys, threats such as phishing and scam, as well as protection mechanisms.

6   Conclusion and Outlook

The human nature of using mental shortcuts is being exploited successfully by social engineers. They take advantage of the five compliance principles Authority; Social Proof; Liking, Similarity & Deception; Commitment, Reciprocation & Consistency; and Distraction to make their targets fall for their attack [8]. Social engineering has been used in five recent cryptocurrency frauds, resulting in financial losses for the victims. The social engineers lured the targets either into transferring cryptocurrencies to the social engineers' addresses or into disclosing the targets' access credentials to their addresses.

To the best of our knowledge, this has been the first study that analyses social engineering attacks in the cryptocurrency (and blockchain) environment. As a limitation, we did not do a thorough, quantitative assessment of all known cryptocurrency frauds, and the selected cases are probably not representative for all types of frauds. However, it was our intention to generate some first substantial insights into the use of social engineering in blockchain applications. We showed that the above-mentioned compliance principles have been exploited by the social engineers in their attacks and we analyzed how the principles helped the social engineers to reach their goals. We described five cases of cryptocurrency frauds, structured according to the social engineering ontological model of [10], which proved to be a valid and helpful tool for this purpose. An additional purpose of our paper was to increase the awareness of cryptocurrency users for potential threats by presenting real world cases that resulted in severe financial losses.

We encourage future researchers to follow the path of analyzing social engineering attacks, the use of compliance principles, and information security awareness in the cryptocurrency and blockchain environment. So far, the social engineers targeted mainly individual users and profited financially from their attacks. But with the increasing adoption of blockchain technology in the business environment (e.g., in biomedical and health care [63]), criminals will draw their attention to companies and their employees. They will use similar tactics to gain access to the companies' information and information systems. In other blockchain use cases, stolen token may as well represent a suffrage or an identity proof [e.g., 64]. It is advisable to prepare for these new threats.

Acknowledgments. Andreas E. Schütz and Tobias Fertig were supported by the BayWISS Consortium Digitization.

References

1. Mitnick, K.D., Simon, W.L.: The Art of Deception: Controlling the Human Element of Security. Wiley, New York (2002)
2. Gragg, D.: A multi-level defense against social engineering. SANS Institute (2003)
3. Scheeres, J.W.: Establishing the Human Firewall: Reducing an Individual's Vulnerability to Social Engineering Attacks (2008). http://www.dtic.mil/dtic/tr/fulltext/u2/a487118.pdf
4. Hadnagy, C., Wilson, P.: Social Engineering: The Art of Human Hacking. Wiley, Hoboken (2011)
5. Schumacher, S.: Die psychologischen Grundlagen des Social-Engineerings. IWP **65**, 215 (2014). https://doi.org/10.1515/iwp-2014-0039
6. Uebelacker, S., Quiel, S.: The social engineering personality framework. In: 2014 Workshop on Socio-Technical Aspects in Security and Trust (STAST), pp. 24–30. IEEE (2014)
7. Happ, C., Melzer, A., Steffgen, G.: Trick with treat–reciprocity increases the willingness to communicate personal data. Comput. Hum. Behav. **61**, 372–377 (2016)
8. Ferreira, A., Coventry, L., Lenzini, G.: Principles of persuasion in social engineering and their use in phishing. In: Tryfonas, T., Askoxylakis, I. (eds.) HAS 2015. LNCS, vol. 9190, pp. 36–47. Springer, Cham (2015). https://doi.org/10.1007/978-3-319-20376-8_4
9. Zhao, Y., Duncan, B.: The impact of crypto-currency risks on the use of blockchain for cloud security and privacy. In: 2018 International Conference on High Performance Computing Simulation (HPCS), pp. 677–684 (2018). https://doi.org/10.1109/HPCS.2018.00111
10. Mouton, F., Leenen, L., Malan, M.M., Venter, H.S.: Towards an ontological model defining the social engineering domain. In: Kimppa, K., Whitehouse, D., Kuusela, T., Phahlamohlaka, J. (eds.) HCC 2014. IAICT, vol. 431, pp. 266–279. Springer, Heidelberg (2014). https://doi.org/10.1007/978-3-662-44208-1_22

11. Condos, J., Sorrell, W.H., Donegan, S.L.: Blockchain Technology: Opportunities and Risks. Vermont State House (2016)

12. Nakamoto, S.: Bitcoin: a peer-to-peer electronic cash system. Bitcoin (2008). https://bitcoin.org/bitcoin.pdf

13. Rennock, M., Cohn, A., Butcher, J.: Blockchain technology and regulatory investigations. Pract. Law Litigation **2018**, 35–44 (2018)

14. Liu, Y., et al.: An efficient method to enhance Bitcoin wallet security. In: 2017 11th IEEE International Conference on Anti-counterfeiting, Security, and Identification (ASID), pp. 26–29. IEEE, Xiamen (2017). https://doi.org/10.1109/ICASID.2017.8285737

15. Dai, F., Shi, Y., Meng, N., Wei, L., Ye, Z.: From Bitcoin to cybersecurity: a comparative study of blockchain application and security issues. In: 2017 4th International Conference on Systems and Informatics (ICSAI), pp. 975–979 (2017). https://doi.org/10.1109/ICSAI.2017.8248427

16. Tosh, D.K., et al.: Security implications of blockchain cloud with analysis of block withholding attack. In: 2017 17th IEEE/ACM International Symposium on Cluster, Cloud and Grid Computing (CCGRID), pp. 458–467 (2017). https://doi.org/10.1109/CCGRID.2017.111

17. Conti, M., Sandeep Kumar, E., Lal, C., Ruj, S.: A Survey on Security and Privacy Issues of Bitcoin. CoRR. abs/1706.00916 (2017)

18. Moore, T., Christin, N.: Beware the middleman: empirical analysis of Bitcoin-exchange risk. In: Sadeghi, A.-R. (ed.) FC 2013. LNCS, vol. 7859, pp. 25–33. Springer, Heidelberg (2013). https://doi.org/10.1007/978-3-642-39884-1_3

19. Krombholz, K., Judmayer, A., Gusenbauer, M., Weippl, E.: The other side of the coin: user experiences with Bitcoin security and privacy. In: Grossklags, J., Preneel, B. (eds.) Financial Cryptography and Data Security, pp. 555–580. Springer, Heidelberg (2017)

20. Adams, A., Sasse, M.A.: Users are not the enemy. Commun. ACM **42**, 40–46 (1999). https://doi.org/10.1145/322796.322806

21. Gonzalez, C., Ben-Asher, N., Oltramari, A., Lebiere, C.: Cognition and technology. In: Kott, A., Wang, C., Erbacher, R.F. (eds.) Cyber Defense and Situational Awareness. AIS, vol. 62, pp. 93–117. Springer, Cham (2014). https://doi.org/10.1007/978-3-319-11391-3_6

22. Solms, R., Warren, M.: Towards the human information security firewall. Int. J. Cyber Warfare Terrorism (IJCWT) **1**, 10–17 (2011). https://doi.org/10.4018/ijcwt.2011040102

23. Ifinedo, P.: Understanding information systems security policy compliance: an integration of the theory of planned behavior and the protection motivation theory. Comput. Secur. **31**, 83–95 (2012). https://doi.org/10.1016/j.cose.2011.10.007

24. da Veiga, A.: An information security training and awareness approach (ISTAAP) to instil an information security-positive culture. In: HAISA (2015)

25. Heartfield, R., Loukas, G.: Detecting semantic social engineering attacks with the weakest link: implementation and empirical evaluation of a human-as-a-security-sensor framework. Comput. Secur. **76**, 101–127 (2018)

26. Ivaturi, K., Janczewski, L.: A taxonomy for social engineering attacks. In: International Conference on Information Resources Management, pp. 1–12. Centre for Information Technology, Organizations, and People (2011)

27. Tetri, P., Vuorinen, J.: Dissecting social engineering. Behav. Inf. Technol. **32**, 1014–1023 (2013)

28. Tischer, M., et al.: Users really do plug in USB drives they find. In: 2016 IEEE Symposium on Security and Privacy (SP), pp. 306–319 (2016). https://doi.org/10.1109/SP.2016.26

29. Mouton, F., Malan, M.M., Leenen, L., Venter, H.S.: Social engineering attack framework. In: Information Security for South Africa (ISSA 2014), pp. 1–9. IEEE (2014)

30. Gupta, B.B., Arachchilage, N.A.G., Psannis, K.E.: Defending against phishing attacks: taxonomy of methods, current issues and future directions. Telecommun. Syst. **67**, 247–267 (2018). https://doi.org/10.1007/s11235-017-0334-z
31. Stavroulakis, P., Stamp, M.: Handbook of Information and Communication Security. Springer, Heidelberg (2010)
32. van der Merwe, A., Loock, M., Dabrowski, M.: Characteristics and responsibilities involved in a phishing attack. In: Proceedings of the 4th International Symposium on Information and Communication Technologies, pp. 249–254. Trinity College Dublin, Cape Town, South Africa (2005)
33. Jones, H.S., Towse, J.: Examinations of email fraud susceptibility: perspectives from academic research and industry practice. Psychol. Behav. Examinations Cyber Secur. (2018). https://doi.org/10.4018/978-1-5225-4053-3.ch005
34. Stajano, F., Wilson, P.: Understanding scam victims: seven principles for systems security. Commun. ACM **54**, 70 (2011). https://doi.org/10.1145/1897852.1897872
35. Cialdini, R.B.: Influence: The Psychology of Persuasion. Collins, New York (2007)
36. Schaab, P., Beckers, K., Pape, S.: Social engineering defence mechanisms and counteracting training strategies. Inf. Comput. Secur. **25**, 206–222 (2017)
37. Rajivan, P., Gonzalez, C.: Creative persuasion: a study on adversarial behaviors and strategies in phishing attacks. Front. Psychol. **9**, 135 (2018)
38. Jeffs, D.: Scam warning – There is no Red Pulse airdrop. https://neonewstoday.com/general/fake-red-pulse-airdrop/
39. NEO: NEO White Paper. http://docs.neo.org/en-us/. Accessed 23 Nov 2018
40. Ha, J., Chao, S.: Red Pulse RPX Whitepaper. https://coin.red-pulse.com/wp-content/uploads/redpulse-whitepaper-en.pdf
41. Bogart, S.: The Trend That Is Increasing The Urgency Of Owning Bitcoin And Ethereum. https://www.forbes.com/sites/spencerbogart/2017/10/08/the-trend-that-is-increasing-the-urgency-of-owning-bitcoin-and-ethereum/#4ce82dbd116b
42. O'Connor, J., Maynor, D.: COINHOARDER: Tracking a Ukrainian Bitcoin Phishing Ring DNS Style. http://blog.talosintelligence.com/2018/02/coinhoarder.html#more
43. Mix: Hackers breached BeeToken's email list and stole \$1 M worth of Ethereum. https://thenextweb.com/hardfork/2018/02/01/beetoken-ico-hacked-airbnb/
44. thebeetoken.com: The Bee Token - The Future of the Decentralized Sharing Economy. https://s3-us-west-2.amazonaws.com/beenest-public/whitepaper/bee_whitepaper_v3.pdf
45. Morse, J.: Fake Elon Musk successfully scams Twitter users out of cryptocurrency. https://mashable.com/2018/02/21/elon-musk-twitter-ethereum-scam/#jh7uCR66rSqb
46. Minereum: Minereum: The First Self Mining Smart Contract. http://files.minereum.com/minereumwhitepaper.pdf
47. Bruno: A Creative New Scam – Honeypot with a Private Key. https://bitfalls.com/2018/04/13/creative-new-scam-honeypot-private-key/
48. Etherscan: Wallet of False Victim Attack. https://etherscan.io/address/0x3f3eacb691462d3d067f031f88c9a8bc54fabc79
49. Jin, S.-A.A., Phua, J.: Following celebrities' tweets about brands: the impact of twitter-based electronic word-of-mouth on consumers' source credibility perception, buying intention, and social identification with celebrities. J. Advertising **43**, 181–195 (2014). https://doi.org/10.1080/00913367.2013.827606
50. Kahneman, D.: A perspective on judgment and choice: mapping bounded rationality. Am. Psychol. **58**, 697–720 (2003)
51. HSBC: Trust in Technology (2017)

52. Hänsch, N., Benenson, Z.: Specifying IT security awareness. In: 2014 25th International Workshop on Database and Expert Systems Applications, pp. 326–330 (2014). https://doi.org/10.1109/DEXA.2014.71

53. Quiel, S.: Social engineering in the context of Cialdini's psychology of persuasion and personality traits (2013)

54. Thomson, M.E., von Solms, R.: Information security awareness: educating your users effectively. Inf. Manage. Comput. Secur. 6, 167–173 (1998). https://doi.org/10.1108/09685229810227649

55. Siponen, M.: Five dimensions of information security awareness. SIGCAS Comput. Soc. 31, 24–29 (2001). https://doi.org/10.1145/503345.503348

56. Scholl, M.C., Fuhrmann, F., Scholl, L.R.: Scientific knowledge of the human side of information security as a basis for sustainable trainings in organizational practices. In: Proceedings of the 51st Hawaii International Conference on System Sciences, pp. 2235–2244 (2018)

57. Fishbein, M., Ajzen, I.: Belief, attitude, intention, and behavior: an introduction to theory and research. Addison-Wesley, Reading, Mass (1975)

58. Montaño, D.E., Kasprzyk, D.: Theory of reasoned action, theory of planned behavior, and the integrated behavior model. In: Glanz, K., Rimer, B.K., Viswanath, K. (eds.) Health Behavior and Health Education. pp. 67–96. APA PsycNet (2008)

59. Jaeger, L., Ament, C., Eckhardt, A.: The closer you get the more aware you become – a case study about psychological distance to information security incidents. In: 2017 38th International Conference on Information Systems, South Korea. Association for Information Systems (2017)

60. Bada, M., Sasse, A.M., Nurse, J.R.C.: Cyber Security Awareness Campaigns: why do they fail to change behaviour? Global Cyber Security Capacity Centre: Draft Working Paper, pp. 188–131 (2014)

61. Schroeder, J.: Advanced Persistent Training: Take Your Security Awareness Program to the Next Level. Apress, New York (2017)

62. Crossler, R., Bélanger, F.: An extended perspective on individual security behaviors: protection motivation theory and a unified security practices (USP) instrument. SIGMIS Database 45, 51–71 (2014). https://doi.org/10.1145/2691517.2691521

63. Kuo, T.-T., Kim, H.-E., Ohno-Machado, L.: Blockchain distributed ledger technologies for biomedical and health care applications. J. Am. Med. Inform. Assoc. 24, 1211–1220 (2017). https://doi.org/10.1093/jamia/ocx068

64. Dagher, G.G., Marella, P.B., Milojkovic, M., Mohler, J.: BroncoVote: Secure Voting System using Ethereum's blockchain. In: Proceedings of the 4th International Conference on Information Systems Security and Privacy, ICISSP, vol. 1, pp. 96–107. SciTePress (2018). https://doi.org/10.5220/0006609700960107

Author Index

Author Index

Printed in the United States
By Bookmasters